Debt Advice Handbook

13th edition

Mike Wolfe
Updated by Peter Madge
with John Kruse, David Malcolm, Katherine Rock and Lynsey Dalton

Child Poverty Action Group

Child Poverty Action Group works on behalf of the more than one in four children in the UK growing up in poverty. It does not have to be like this. We use our understanding of what causes poverty and the impact it has on children's lives to campaign for policies that will prevent and solve poverty – for good. We provide training, advice and information to make sure hard-up families get the financial support they need. We also carry out high-profile legal work to establish and protect families' rights. If you are not already supporting us, please consider making a donation, or ask for details of our membership schemes, training courses and publications.

Published by Child Poverty Action Group
30 Micawber Street
London N1 7TB
Tel: 020 7837 7979
staff@cpag.org.uk
www.cpag.org.uk

A CIP record for this book is available from the British Library
ISBN: 978 1 910715 56 7

Child Poverty Action Group is a charity registered in England and Wales (registration number 294841) and in Scotland (registration number SC039339), and is a company limited by guarantee, registered in England (registration number 1993854). VAT number: 690 808117

Cover design by Colorido Studios
Internal design by Devious Designs
Typeset by DLxml, a division of RefineCatch Limited, Bungay, Suffolk
Content management system by Konnectsoft
Printed in the UK by CPI Group (UK) Ltd, Croydon CR0 4YY

The authors

Peter Madge worked in the debt team at Citizens Advice Specialist Support between 1990 and 2015. The team won the Institute of Money Advisers 'Debt Team of the Year' award in 2012. Between 1992 and 2006, he was editor of the *Adviser* magazine and was a regular contributor to the magazine until it ceased publication in print in 2019, and a member of the *Adviser* editorial board between 2016 and 2019. In 2010, he was elected an Honorary Fellow of the Institute of Money Advisers. Since leaving Citizens Advice, he has worked as a freelance debt advice consultant. He currently works for Recognising Excellence as technical expert to the Money and Pensions Service's Debt Advice Peer Assessment Scheme.

John Kruse has worked as a debt adviser and trainer since the mid-1980s. He began to specialise in bailiff law in about 1988 and has since written around two dozen books on different aspects of the subject, the most significant being *Taking Control of Goods* in 2014. He was involved in the various working parties which drafted the reformed bailiff law introduced in 2014 and continues to seek improvements. John set up the Bailiff Studies Centre in 2010 as a basis for promoting best practice in enforcement law and he produces the ejournal *Bailiff Studies Bulletin*. He also trains and blogs on enforcement law.

David Malcolm is Head of Policy and Campaigns at the National Union of Students (NUS), where he has worked on student finance policy since 2003. He is author of CPAG's *Student Support and Benefits Handbook*.

Katherine Rock is the Client Experience Manager at the Money Advice Trust. She has worked for the Money Advice Trust for 15 years with the majority of that time specialising in business debt advice.

Lynsey Dalton is a trainee solicitor at CPAG.

Acknowledgements

The production of this thirteenth edition has been made possible by a number of other authors who have contributed their specialist expertise.

Katherine Rock from the Money Advice Trust has updated the chapter on business debts, Lynsey Dalton from CPAG has updated the chapter on maximising income, David Malcolm from the NUS has updated the chapter on student debts and John Kruse has revised the bailiffs chapter.

I would also like to acknowledge the efforts of the authors of previous editions of this book, most notably Mike Wolfe.

Thank you to my former colleagues at Citizens Advice Specialist Support, Marina Gallagher, Lorraine Charlton and Joe McShane, and also Debra Jones of Citizens Advice Cardiff and Vale for checking and making useful comments on the text. Thanks are also due to Mark Brough, Mark Willis and Keith Houghton for their valuable contributions. Many thanks to Shelter's Specialist Debt Advice Service for its valuable feedback.

I am most grateful to Pauline Phillips and Nicola Johnston for producing this edition. Thanks also to Anne Ketley for producing the index, and to Pauline Phillips and Kathleen Armstrong for proofreading the text.

Peter Madge

The law covered in this book was correct on 31 January 2020 and includes regulations laid up to this date.

Foreword

There have been several positive developments since I wrote the foreword to the last edition of this handbook in 2017, but many of the challenges and problems I highlighted then continue to affect the lives of people with unmanageable debt and those who advise them.

At that time, I referred to 'the recent phenomenon of deficit financial statements'. Unfortunately, advisers across the money advice sector are reporting an increase in the number of people seen with deficit budgets – with insufficient income to pay for essential household expenses, let alone make offers of payment to creditors.

Discussions at regional meetings of money advisers frequently turn to this topic, and particularly highlight the fact that many people with deficit budgets are actually in employment. Training courses, such as those developed by the Institute of Money Advisers and others, provide strategies to help advisers support their clients; however, there are many clients for whom advice cannot resolve the problems of a deficit budget and, at best, can only help them stretch insufficient income that little bit further.

Universal credit advance payments – which increased in 2018 to up to 100 per cent of the expected monthly award – may now contribute more towards living costs; however, feedback from frontline money advisers suggests that this change has done little to alleviate the hardship suffered by new claimants.

The amount of universal credit (UC) debt accrued can deter people from seeking the full advance needed to meet everyday living costs, leading many to rely on foodbanks and fall into arrears with essential expenses. This is compounded by not being permitted to have a second advance payment before the first monthly UC payment is made.

Recovery of the advance over 12 months often leads to monthly repayments substantially higher than most other creditors require. The intention to increase the repayment period to 16 months from 2021 is welcome. However, spreading a substantial debt over an extra four payments is unlikely to ease hardship in the way that adopting the single financial statement framework would do.

For the 36 per cent of UC claimants who are in work, pay cycles/delays leading to two earnings payments within one UC month, mean significantly reduced or nil UC so a claimant has to restart their claim. This causes problems for claimants attempting to budget and for money advisers attempting to help people make sustainable debt repayment arrangements.

Notwithstanding the increase in those with insufficient income to meet essential expenditure, the roll-out of the Standard Financial Statement (SFS) has been a welcome development since the last *Handbook*. Introduced by the Money Advice Service (now part of the Money and Pensions Service), it is now widely used across the sector and the SFS format has been used both in the current debt relief order application form and the pre-action protocol for debt claims.

However, there is still more to do: numerous bespoke and outdated income and expenditure forms are used by some creditors, including central and local government, making it difficult and time-consuming for clients and advisers to align financial details with the SFS. Public sector creditors also have more to do to ensure that affordable offers are accepted based on SFS criteria. To this end, the Institute of Money Advisers welcomes the work of the Cabinet Office Fairness Group and we continue to engage as a stakeholder of the group to inform its work to improve outcomes for clients with public sector debts.

I look forward to the introduction of the government's new breathing space scheme, from 2021. This 60-day period, during which charges and enforcement action from creditors will be suspended, will help those who need time to seek advice and make arrangements to deal with their debts. With an increasing number of indebted clients suffering mental ill health, especially welcome is the provision for those receiving mental health crisis treatment, who will receive the same protections until their treatment is complete.

Increasing public awareness of the availability of money advice should encourage people to get help with their debts earlier. Of course, this is likely to lead to increased demand at a time when most debt advice services are already working at full capacity. While there may be scope to work more efficiently, sufficient funding and time is also required to ensure quality of advice is not compromised and effective outcomes for clients are achieved.

For everyone committed to providing professional, high-quality debt advice, the *Debt Advice Handbook* remains an essential resource and recommended reading for students of the Certificate in Money Advice Practice, the not-for-profit sector's leading specialist qualification delivered by the Institute of Money Advisers in partnership with Staffordshire University.

Robert Wilson
Chief Executive, Institute of Money Advisers

Contents

Contents

How to use this *Handbook*

This *Handbook* is produced:

- as a guide and training aid for the new debt adviser;
- as a reference work for those who undertake debt advice alongside other sorts of advice work or other professional disciplines – eg, social workers and housing officers;
- for the specialist debt adviser as a first step in accessing primary legislation and regulations;
- for the manager or purchaser of debt advice services to help understand and evaluate debt advice.

The subjects covered within debt advice are vast and could fill many volumes. In this *Handbook*, much detail has been deliberately excluded in order to make it accessible and to make clear the structure of debt work.

Most relevant legislation and court forms are now available online from legislation.gov.uk and www.justice.gov.uk respectively and are not therefore included in the Appendices. The Civil Procedure Rules are available online at www.justice.gov.uk/courts/procedure-rules/civil and many judgments of the higher courts are available free of charge from www.bailii.org. Most debt packages used in advice agencies include standard letters and forms, and so these are also not included in the Appendices. The standard financial statement is available at sfs.moneyadviceservice.org.uk.

The *Handbook* can best be used as follows.

Training aid

The **Introduction** and **Chapters 1 to 3** are written to assist those who are interested in debt advice, and outline the processes and skills involved. These should be read by new debt advisers and those who have done some of this work and would like to think more about the structure behind their practical experience. The chapters can also be used by those who commission or manage debt advice as a means of clarifying the product with which they are dealing.

New advisers should ensure they are familiar with the rules on consumer credit (explained in **Chapter 4**) and are able to identify each type of debt (explained in **Chapter 5**) because this is fundamental to using the rest of the *Handbook*. Maximising income is a key part of the debt advice process and this is summarised in **Chapter 7**. The new adviser will also need to be familiar with the criteria to be used in prioritising debts (**Chapter 8**). S/he will find it useful to skim through the different strategies for priority and non-priority debts (**Chapters 8 and 9**). These can be examined in detail as they arise in the course of advising.

The debt adviser

If you are already familiar with the processes of debt advice, you may wish to use **Chapter 6** (minimising debts) and the strategy selection (**Chapters 8 and 9**) to help you think about the best strategy for a particular debt. This might include bankruptcy or an individual voluntary arrangement (these are discussed in **Chapter 15**). Court procedures are covered in **Chapter 10** (general information on the county court), **Chapter 11** (money-only claims), **Chapter 12** (claims for possession of goods or property) and **Chapter 13** (magistrates' court). If the client is threatened with bailiff action, refer to **Chapter 14**. Specific debts are dealt with in **Chapter 16** (business debts) and **Chapter 17** (student debts). The index will enable you to find detailed information on a particular strategy, type of debt or court process. References can be accessed via the endnotes contained at the end of each chapter if you want more in-depth information about a particular topic. Details of other useful reference material and organisations are in the Appendices.

Abbreviations

AA	attendance allowance	MP	Member of Parliament
APR	annual percentage rate	NHS	National Health Service
CA	carer's allowance	NI	national insurance
CONC	Consumer Credit Sourcebook	NISP	Networking and Information
DAPA	Debt Advice Peer Assessment		Sharing project
DRO	debt relief order	NUS	National Union of Students
CTC	child tax credit	NVQ	national vocational qualification
DLA	disability living allowance	PAYE	Pay As You Earn
DVLA	Driver and Vehicle Licensing	PC	pension credit
	Agency	PGCE	Postgraduate Certificate in
EEA	European Economic Area		Education
ESA	employment and support	PGDE	Postgraduate Diploma in
	allowance		Education
EU	European Union	PIN	personal identification number
FCA	Financial Conduct Authority	PIP	personal independence payment
GAP	guaranteed asset protection	RPI	Retail Price Index
HB	housing benefit	SAP	statutory adoption pay
HMCTS	HM Courts and Tribunals Service	SDA	severe disablement allowance
HMRC	HM Revenue and Customs	SMP	statutory maternity pay
HP	hire purchase	SPP	statutory paternity pay
IB	incapacity benefit	SSP	statutory sick pay
IS	income support	SSPP	statutory shared parental pay
IMA	Institute of Money Advisers	UC	universal credit
IVA	individual voluntary	UCAS	Universities and Colleges
	arrangement		Admissions Service
JSA	jobseeker's allowance	VAT	value added tax
MA	maternity allowance	WTC	working tax credit
MaPS	Money and Pensions Service		

Introduction

In the introduction to the first edition of this *Handbook* in 1993, its author Mike Wolfe wrote: 'Debt has always been an inevitable consequence of borrowing and is recognised by the credit industry as a necessary corollary of its lending.' This remains true, although it seems that – proportionately – clients are increasingly reporting problems relating to debts owed to government departments, local authorities and utility providers compared to problems relating to consumer debt.

While the causes of debt may not be individual, the effects are: these include the threat of action by bailiffs (also known as enforcement agents or officers) and repossession of homes. Money worries are a significant cause of relationship problems, depression, anxiety and stress, with many of those in debt receiving treatment from their GP. Many people have reported the positive impact that debt advice has had on their lives generally.

Mental health problems are both a cause and effect of debt and so it is good to see that the money advice sector and the credit industry are continuing to work together under the auspices of the Money Advice Liaison Group to produce good practice guidelines for dealing with this particular situation.

Since the last edition of this *Handbook*, the Financial Conduct Authority has issued new rules to address the problems of persistent credit card debt and excessive overdraft charges, along with new rules on creditworthiness and affordability in the consumer credit market. It has been estimated that about nine million people in the UK are affected by problem debts – that is the inability to pay debts or household bills. Advisers increasingly report that they are seeing more clients who do not have enough money coming in to meet essential household bills. Personal insolvencies are at their highest level since 2010, mainly due to the increase in individual voluntary arrangements. There has been a steady increase in total household debt since 2012 and this has now reached record levels.

The most significant change in the debt advice landscape going forward is likely to be the government's debt respite scheme, comprising both a 60-day 'breathing space' and a statutory debt repayment plan, expected to be introduced in 2021.

The number of people struggling with unmanageable debt seems likely to remain high for the foreseeable future and may even increase further, given that we have yet to feel the full impact of the UK's decision to exit the European Union.

What is debt advice?

Debt advice is defined by the Financial Conduct Authority as:[1]

> giving an opinion as a guide to action to be taken, in this case the liquidation of debts. It either explicitly or implicitly steers the customer to a particular course of action... In the Financial Conduct Authority's view, advice requires an element of opinion on the part of the adviser or something that might be taken by the debtor, expressly or by implication, to suggest or influence a course of action. Information, on the other hand, involves statements of facts or figures.

Debt advice is one component of what is now called money advice, which also comprises financial capability (the skills, knowledge and understanding to manage money). Virtually everyone has debts. But when debt becomes unmanageable, the need for debt advice arises.

Debt advice should be distinguished from 'money management' and 'financial capability'. While debt advice does include a comprehensive check of a person's entitlement to state benefits, it goes much further than welfare rights. Debt advice is, essentially, crisis management, and the other components can hopefully prevent the need for debt advice recurring or even occurring in the first place. An ideal money advice model integrates all the various components.

In the past, the words 'debt counselling' and 'money advice' have been used almost interchangeably to describe what we shall call 'debt advice'. We prefer this term to 'money advice' because of the issues discussed above. 'Debt counselling', on the other hand, can appear to suggest that debt is a problem about which individuals merely need counselling. Counselling may sometimes be important in the early stages of debt advice, but is not a substitute for the work of the debt adviser. Financial capability interventions alone cannot resolve problem debt. Debt advice is not just about making offers (token or otherwise) to the client's creditors. The processes described in this *Handbook* are not set in stone and advisers should not be afraid to step outside them in order to help their clients. Advisers should not assume that creditors and courts always get it right, but should examine their practices and their paperwork to protect their clients from inappropriate recovery and enforcement action.

And finally, adieu *Adviser* magazine. The *Adviser* first appeared in December 1986 and over the years many of its articles have featured in the footnotes of this *Handbook*. The final print version of the magazine was published in July 2019 (issue 189). The *Adviser* survives as *Adviser* online and can be accessed at: https://medium.com/adviser.

Notes

1 Financial Conduct Authority, PERG 17.5

1

Chapter 1

. . . .

Debt advice: an outline

This chapter covers:
1. Professional debt advice (below)
2. The debt advice system (p5)
3. Administration (p13)

1. Professional debt advice

- Debt advice is a set of tools and strategies used to help clients with financial difficulties. Debt advice provides help to clients by:
  - explaining the implications of non-payment of each of their debts and, on this basis, deciding which are priorities;
  - establishing whether or not they are liable for their debts, and assisting them to challenge their creditors if appropriate;
  - enabling them to maximise their disposable income;
  - assisting them to plan their budgets;
  - helping them choose a strategy (usually, but not necessarily, to reduce or stop payments) that will minimise the effects of their debt on their financial, social or personal wellbeing by giving them impartial, independent and confidential advice to enable them to make an informed choice about the options available;
  - preserving their home, essential goods and services, and liberty;
  - assisting by advice or representation with the implementation of whatever strategy is chosen.

- Debt advice is a professional activity. There is a package of attitudes, skills and strategies that are part of any debt advice service. This guarantees consistency and quality assurance.

  Debt advice can be provided by specialists or by professionals whose job primarily involves other activities – eg, housing officers. It can be provided by paid or voluntary workers. In recent years there has also been a growth in debt management companies, which charge clients a fee for setting up and handling debt repayment programmes.

Ensuring good practice

A professional debt adviser needs a mixture of skills, knowledge and attitudes, which together form the basis of good practice. For many years there was no qualification that recognised the profession of money advice or acknowledged the wide range of skills and knowledge that money advisers have. However, in 2010, the Institute of Money Advisers (IMA) (the professional association for full-time, part-time or volunteer/trainee debt advisers in England, Wales and Northern Ireland who deliver or promote free, confidential, impartial and independent debt advice services), in partnership with Staffordshire University, introduced a Certificate in Money Advice Practice. Worth 15 higher education credits and broadly equivalent to an NVQ level 4, this award is offered to IMA members with at least 12 months' full-time (or the equivalent part-time) experience in debt advice casework or a related activity. The award is gained by studying a combination of skills and knowledge based on the national occupational standards for legal advice. The course is delivered online and involves a number of modules, each ending with a formative assessment, and finally an examination, which is taken online. It is supported by a continuing professional development requirement to ensure advisers keep their skills and knowledge up to date.

In 2013, the Money Advice Service (now part of the Money and Pensions Service (MaPS)) introduced its Debt Advice Quality Framework, with the aim of raising the quality and consistency of debt advice. It comprises two parts: an organisational quality framework and an individual quality framework. The framework enables quality standards, membership codes, training and qualifications used by the money advice sector to be independently assessed and accredited the Money Advice Service. Debt advisers working in agencies holding a MaPS-accredited quality standard or membership code must be able to show that they meet the requirements of the Quality Framework for Individuals for the type of activites they undertake. Agencies must therefore review the training or qualifications undertaken by all their staff involved in delivering debt advice to ensure this is accredited. **Note:** it is the agency, rather than the individual adviser, which is accredited.

In 2018, the IMA launched its Networking and Information Sharing Project. The project (which is funded by MaPS) supports advisers by sharing information provided by partner agencies, including legal updates and Spotlight articles from Shelter's Specialist Debt Advice Service. IMA's project and Shelter provide regular training webinars, which are subsequently made available in the project's resources directory on the IMA website for advisers who could not view them in real time. The project also live streams regional Money Advice Group meetings, so advisers can join meetings remotely (or access recordings of the meetings afterwards). The directory also contains the MaPS Good Practice Toolkit, which includes sample letters and forms, templates and prompt lists, and income maximisation resources, together with guidance on when and how advisers should use these resources. Updates are made and new materials added as they become available. In the project's discussion forum advisers can share information and news, ask questions and raise social policy issues. Debt advisers can access all of the Networking and Information Sharing project resources on the IMA website, i-m-a.org.uk. Those who are not IMA members but work in the free-to-client debt advice sector can register for access.

Shelter's Specialist Debt Advice Service provides free, expert guidance on most client debt cases. The service is available to all local Citizens Advice, local authorities, housing associations, IMA members, AdviceUK members and other free sector agencies. The service is for advisers only. Advisers can submit an online enquiry at shelter.org.uk/debtadviceservice or call 0330 058 0404, 9am to 5pm, Monday to Friday.

The provision of debt advice as discussed in this *Handbook* is a regulated activity, which generally requires the adviser (or her/his employer) to be authorised by the Financial Conduct Authority (FCA). Guidance on good practice is in the FCA's *Consumer Credit Sourcebook* (generally referred to by the abbreviation CONC which is part of the *FCA Handbook* and is available at handbook.fca.org.uk/handbook) and CONC and other parts of the *FCA Handbook* are referred to in this *Handbook* where relevant.[1]

The client's best interests

In any situation where money is owed, there are two parties whose interests may conflict. As a professional debt adviser, you should know that you cannot advise both parties in such a situation, and so you must be clear that you are working only for the interests of the client. This is true even if your employment is funded by the finance industry or another creditor, such as a local authority, or if you work for an organisation that seeks to be impartial.

The FCA's *Consumer Credit Sourcebook* makes it clear that all advice given and action taken must consider the best interests of the client and must take into account:[2]

- her/his financial circumstances;
- her/his personal circumstances, including the reasons for her/his financial difficulty and whether they are temporary or long term; *and*
- any other relevant factors, including any known or reasonably foreseeable changes in the client's circumstances.

You should also take into account whether the client is a vulnerable person, the powers of the creditor and whether interest or other charges have been frozen.[3] A useful resource on treating clients in vulnerable situations fairly, *Vulnerability: a guide for advice agencies*, is available at the Money Advice Trust website, moneyadvicetrust.org.

A professional attitude

As a professional debt adviser, you should be aware of your past experiences from which you may have developed a judgemental attitude towards some clients and/ or creditors. Consciously avoid any personal bias and adopt a professional approach to the work.

You should also offer a high-quality, accessible service to all groups in society and should work towards understanding that debt can affect clients from different backgrounds in different ways.

A commitment to social policy

As a professional debt adviser, you should not allow the same recurring problems you encounter with clients to adversely affect the lives of others also, but should make known the lessons that can be learnt from your work to as wide an audience of policymakers as possible.

A sound knowledge of law and procedures

As a professional debt adviser, you should be knowledgeable and imaginative about the ways in which the law can be applied to mitigate the effects of debt. You should be able to offer and explain these to your clients.

A commitment to developing the service

As a professional debt adviser, you should take regular opportunities to enhance your skills through training, research and education, and should participate in offering this to others, so that the practice of debt advice continues to be refined and developed.

You should subscribe to periodicals (see Appendix 2), such as *Quarterly Account*, to keep up to date with developments in debt advice law and practice. Try to attend your local Money Advice Group meetings. These usually have updating and information exchange sessions, as well as presentations by creditors or representatives from other relevant organisations.

A systematic approach

As a professional debt adviser, you should apply a single systematic approach to each individual client. Also ensure that the advice you give is:
- in the best interests of that particular client;
- appropriate to her/his individual circumstances;
- realistic; *and*
- where an offer of payment is made, sustainable and based on a true and accurate assessment of the client's circumstances.

An ability to involve the client in informed choices

As a professional debt adviser, you should always try to involve the client, ensuring that s/he understands the implications of her/his situation and the steps you propose be taken. You can assist the client to make an informed choice by giving her/him all her/his available options and explaining their consequences before anything is done. Do not assume that a client is seeking a particular outcome, but establish what s/he wants and recognise that it may not necessarily be realistic or achievable.

Many advisers tend to put pressure on themselves to solve their clients' problems, and clients' expectations can add to this. Although advisers should always do the best they can for their clients, there may be times when the options are limited because matters have simply gone too far and you cannot make the problem go away. You should not feel that you have somehow 'failed' the client, as s/he is still likely to need supporting through the situation.

Many debt cases involve distressing facts, so make sure you can share and discuss these sorts of issues with colleagues and your supervisor/manager.

2. **The debt advice system**

The debt advice system is a structured set of procedures and activities that must be worked through if you are to provide the best possible service to someone with a multiple debt problem. It is designed to:
- maintain the client's home, liberty and essential goods and services;
- advise the client about her/his rights and responsibilities, and also the rights of her/his creditors;
- give the client the information s/he needs to make informed choices to deal with the debt situation;
- treat all creditors equally;
- empower the client, where possible.

A systematic approach is essential because of:
- the large amount of information and paperwork generated by most debt enquiries;
- the need to avoid overlooking a particular strategy;
- the need to keep detailed records of the agency's work – both to ensure effective advice and follow-up, but also to enable case material to be used for evaluating the service, quality of advice assessments, peer reviews and for social policy development;
- the need to train new workers in a clearly defined set of skills and knowledge;
- the need to guarantee consistency in spite of the diversity of clients using the service;

- the need to protect the adviser from the strain of having continually to 'reinvent the wheel'.

However, the system should not be seen as a straitjacket, and it does not prevent you working in a creative and flexible way in the best interests of your client. Different agencies need to develop their own systems based on demand and resources, as well as any funders' requirements.

You must undertake a wide range of tasks in order to provide effective help to clients. In practice:

- the tasks may not necessarily be carried out in the order in which they are presented;
- some tasks can be carried out simultaneously – eg, maximising income while waiting for information needed to check the client's liability for her/his debts;
- it may be appropriate for some tasks not to be carried out at all.

Note: if you are to contact third parties on the client's behalf, the client must provide a signed authority for this to happen (most agencies have a standard form for this). You must also comply with data protection legislation and obtain your clients' consent to hold sensitive personal information about them and, where relevant, to share information about their cases with third parties – eg, for monitoring or quality checking purposes.

Stages of the debt advice process

Essentially, there are three stages to the debt advice process:

- exploration;
- options;
- action.

These can, in turn, be broken down into the following steps.

- **Step one: explore the debt problem.** This includes carrying out the Money and Pensions Service's (MaPS) common initial assessment, where applicable (see p13). The extent of the client's debts, and the reasons for her/his financial difficulties and whether these are temporary or long term, must be established. This includes finding out who the client's creditors are, how much is owed to each and the action each creditor has taken to collect its debt. A creditor may have passed the debt to a firm of debt collectors or even sold the debt to a debt purchaser, in which case it is necessary to see what action the collector or purchaser has taken.[4] You should also explore whether the client has any assets as, if so, they could be at risk from creditor action (eg, bailiffs or from an insolvency option) and they might be relevant to other options (see p250). **Note:** in this *Handbook*, the term 'creditor' includes the original creditor as well as the the debt purchaser.

- **Step two: deal with urgent issues.** Emergencies, such as bailiffs' warrants, threats of disconnection of a fuel supply or loss of the client's home or liberty, are dealt with first. Where court action is involved, you can help the client to complete court forms in order to meet deadlines.
- **Step three: list the client's creditors and minimise debts.** Further information from the client, the creditor or a third party may be needed before this can be established. Specialist advice may also be required.
- **Step four: list and maximise the client's income.** Maximising income involves increasing the amount of money the client has coming in, particularly by checking that s/he is receiving all the benefits to which s/he is entitled, and also increasing the client's disposable income – eg, by reducing her/his expenditure. Although this *Handbook* treats these as two separate steps, in reality they are part of the same process. This is a potentially time-consuming step, for which it can be helpful to consult the MaPS Good Practice Toolkit (see p2). It contains materials, resources and guidance on maximising income, including signposting and referrals where appropriate.
- **Step five: list the client's expenditure.** This step should also include basic financial capability advice, including budgeting, identifying essential and non-essential expenditure and methods of money management. This also involves getting an explanation for particularly high or particularly low expenditure identified by the client.[5]
- **Step six: deal with priority debts.** These are creditors whose sanctions for non-payment include imprisonment, disconnection of essential services or loss of essential goods or the home. Usually, some form of payment is required to deal with such debts, unless a formal insolvency option is the agreed strategy and the debt can be included in that option.
- **Step seven: draw up a financial statement** showing what income a client is receiving, her/his essential expenditure and whether there is any income available to pay creditors. The financial statement is an essential tool, not only in negotiations with creditors but also in determining which options are appropriate for the client – eg, her/his eligibility for a debt relief order (see p499) or a debt management plan (see p255). There may be occasions when a client's expenditure needs to be challenged. If this is the case, discuss the reasons for this – eg, that it is unlikely to be accepted by a court or creditor.
- **Step eight: choose a strategy for non-priority debts.** Explore and discuss all available options that are suitable in the client's circumstances for resolving the debt problem, including advising on their implications. A strategy (or strategies) should then be agreed with her/him and an action plan drawn up. For each option, explain:
  – the advantages and disadvantages;
  – actual or potential consequences and implications, including the impact on credit reference files and banking services;
  – any eligibility criteria;

- the debts included in that option;
- any costs involved;
- any risks associated with that option, including the risk of costs in relation to court action.

You should also explain why these available options are considered suitable and why other available options are not considered suitable. There is no need to explain other options which are not available, unless these have been raised by the client her/himself.

Negotiate with the non-priority creditors with a view to persuading them to accept the agreed strategy. Some clients can and want to negotiate with their creditors themselves.[6] This approach enables clients to regain control of their finances and allows the advice agency to offer more support to those clients who need help with this. Such 'self-help' clients are likely to benefit from the CASHflow process discussed on p19.

- **Step nine: implement the chosen strategies.** This may involve representing the client at a court hearing, periodic reviews of the client's options or strategy, referral to another agency (eg, for a debt management plan) or arranging appropriate ongoing financial capability support for her/him. Sometimes you may have to challenge creditors on whether they are entitled to recover what they are claiming from clients – eg, if clients are not liable for their debts.

Information to clients

It is not necessary for an agency to have any written agreement with the client, but you should provide:[7]
- adequate written information about the nature of the service being offered;
- clear information about which debts will be included in any debt solution and which will be excluded, and the actual or potential advantages, disadvantages, costs, risks and conditions of each solution;
- impartial information on the range of relevant debt solutions available to the client;
- warnings:
  - that creditors may still continue to try to collect their debt and such action could incur additional costs, which will be added to the debt;
  - that the client's credit rating could be adversely affected;
  - about the importance of meeting priority commitments;
  - that correspondence from creditors should not be ignored;
  - that by entering into a repayment arrangement there is no guarantee that any current recovery or legal action will be suspended or withdrawn.

At the first interview, it is also good practice to point out:
- the agency's commitment to confidentiality;
- the steps the agency will take and the steps the client has agreed to, or is expected to, take her/himself;

- that the client should not incur any further credit commitments without discussing it first with you;
- that the client should inform you of any change in her/his financial circumstances;
- that a successful outcome cannot be guaranteed;
- details of the agency's complaints policy and of the client's right to escalate complaints to the Financial Ombudsman Service, if this has not already been explained.[8]

Monitoring creditor practices

Debt advisers should keep a record of the collection techniques and tactics used by individual creditors. This is useful in any future choice of strategy. In addition, note practices or situations that continually cause hardship to clients and monitor which creditors are responsible. The effectiveness of any pressure for change often depends on the ability of an agency to produce evidence in support of its recommendations. For this reason, case recording must be accurate and detailed, and stored in a form that allows details of particular practices and the hardship they cause to be retrieved and patterns detected.

There are frequent changes in the law and procedures that affect debt, and agencies are often in a very good position to look closely at how these are working in practice. Agencies often carry out such exercises as part of a network of local and national debt services.

Credit reference agencies

There is no right to credit and most lenders decide credit applications on the basis of 'credit scoring' – ie, a system used to assess the probability of applicants meeting their financial commitments, using information supplied on the credit application form, the lender's own records (where available) and data from credit reference agencies. Different lenders use different systems, which should not only establish the likelihood of the applicant repaying but also whether s/he can afford to do so.

There are three main credit reference agencies in the UK: Experian, Equifax and TransUnion. They provide information about clients and their credit records. They do not:

- make the decision or express any opinion about whether clients should be given credit and are unable to tell clients why they have been refused credit; *or*
- keep 'blacklists' or details of clients' credit scores.

When a creditor informs a client that it is rejecting her/his credit application, based on information from a credit reference agency, the creditor must provide details of the credit reference agency, including the name, address and telephone number.[9] Failure to do so is a criminal offence. **Note:** this requirement does not apply to agreements secured on land.

Credit reference agencies usually keep details of:
- electoral roll entries;
- county court judgments. These are held for six years from the date of judgment unless paid within one month, when any record is removed;
- bankruptcy orders, administration orders, debt relief orders and individual voluntary arrangements. These are held for six years from the date of the order or arrangement;
- credit accounts. A record is held until the account is paid off and then for a further six years;
- whether the client has defaulted on a credit agreement. A record is held for six years from the date the default was registered, normally when the account is three to six months in arrears;
- mortgage repossessions, including voluntary repossessions. These are held for six years;
- aliases, associations and linked addresses – ie, any other names the client has been known by, previous addresses or correspondence addresses, and whether s/he shares financial responsibility for an account with another person;
- a warning from Cifas – a fraud avoidance system developed to protect people whose names, addresses or other details have been used fraudulently by other people in order to apply for or obtain credit. It does not mean that the client is being accused of fraud, but any credit applications may be checked out to ensure s/he is, in fact, the applicant;
- information from the Gone Away Information Network (known as GAIN) – ie, on clients who have 'gone away' without informing their lenders of a forwarding address. This information is held for six years;
- previous credit searches by lenders in the past two years. Several searches within a short period of time may indicate attempted fraud or overcommitment.

A client's credit file should only hold information about her/him and any other person with whom s/he has a 'financial association' – ie, joint account holders or applicants, or anyone who informs the agency that they have financial ties. This allows lenders to take account of information about anyone 'linked' to the client. Although the client can ask a lender only to take account of information about her/him, this does not prevent the lender carrying out checks to make sure that this is not intended to hide a partner's poor credit rating. If there is no financial association, the client should inform the agency so the link can be removed.

Recording defaults

Guidelines from the Information Commissioner state that a client's account should not be recorded as in default unless the relationship between the creditor and the client has broken down. This means the client has been in arrears for at least three consecutive months on the contractual instalments or under an agreement to reschedule repayments. It should be recorded as in default if such payments have not been made in full for six months. Accounts which are subject to repayment arrangements or debt management plans should only be recorded as in default if the client:

- is only making token payments. However, in this situation, s/he can ask the agency to record this (known as filing a 'notice of correction') if the creditor has not done so; or
- defaults on the arrangement and the arrears are equivalent to three months' payments under the original contract; or
- is making reduced payments, but no agreed arrangement is in place.

If the lender does not agree to accept reduced payments (including token payments), although any payments the client makes are reflected in the outstanding balance recorded, arrears continue to accrue and a default may be recorded once the equivalent of three months' arrears is reached. If a creditor fails to record a default within the three- to six-month period but, for example, delays registering the default until the client misses an agreed repayment, the Financial Ombudsman Service may order the creditor to backdate the registration. A default cannot be registered in respect of an irredeemably unenforceable agreement.[10]

A zero balance on a credit reference report marked 'balance satisfied' (with or without the flag 'partially satisfied') indicates that there has been a default, but that:

- the account has been paid in full; or
- the account was included in an individual voluntary arrangement which has been satisfactorily completed, or in a bankruptcy from which the client has been discharged or in a debt relief order which was not revoked during the moratorium period; or
- the creditor has agreed to accept less than the full amount due in full and final settlement of the account.

If the information held is incorrect

A client can obtain a copy of her/his file at any time, free of charge.[11] As the different credit reference agencies hold different data from different credit providers, it is useful to get reports from the main three agencies. Request for reports can be made:

- online from:
  - Equifax (equifax.co.uk);
  - Experian (experian.co.uk);
  - TransUnion (transunion.co.uk);
- in writing. The client must provide details of her/his full name and address (including any previous names or addresses used in the past six years). See ico.org.uk/your-data-matters/credit for more information about making a written request.

If the client considers that any of the information in the file is wrong and that it is likely to cause prejudice as a result, s/he can write either to the lender or the credit reference agency. However, as the credit reference agency would have to contact the lender to ask it to investigate the complaint, it might be quicker to write to the lender and send a copy to the credit reference agency. The client should write to the lender and credit reference agency stating why the information is wrong and submitting any supporting evidence – eg, that a debt has been paid. The agency must respond in writing within 28 days, stating either that it has corrected or removed the information, or done nothing.[12] In the meantime, the information is marked 'account query' while the agency checks its accuracy. If the agency fails to remove the information or the client does not agree with the proposed amendment, s/he can ask the agency to add her/his own 'notice of correction' to the file – eg, an explanation of how the debt arose. This must be no more than 200 words long and must be sent to the agency within a further 28 days. The agency must inform the client within 28 days if it accepts the notice. If it does not, the agency must refer the case to the Information Commissioner for a ruling.

If, after writing to the lender and/or the credit reference agency, the client receives no response, s/he can complain to the Information Commissioner. A client can also complain to the Information Commissioner if s/he believes inaccurate information is being held but a 'notice of correction' is not appropriate – eg, it should be completely removed. If the information about the client's credit history is factually correct, however, it is not removed just because s/he does not want it made public.

Under the General Data Protection Regulation (GDPR), clients have the right to access the information that their creditors hold about them by making a 'subject access request' (SAR). No particular form of words is required so long as the client makes clear that s/he is asking for details of her/his own personal data held by the creditor. The creditor must respond within one month of receiving the request. The creditor cannot charge a fee for complying with the request in most circumstances. A reasonable fee can be charged to cover administration costs where requests are excessive or unfounded or if the client requests further copies of the data.

Credit repair companies that claim to be able to 'clean up' people's credit reference files (in return for a fee) should be avoided, as the information they give may be misleading or worse.

The Information Commissioner's Office (see Appendix 1) has a useful leaflet, *Credit Explained*, available at ico.org.uk. The Information Commissioner also collaborated with the credit industry on the production of a guidance document, *Principles for the Reporting of Arrears, Arrangements and Defaults at Credit Reference Agencies*, available at scoronline.co.uk/key-documents.

3. Administration

Good administrative systems and time management are essential in order to manage the debt advice process in an efficient way and to meet the client's needs appropriately.

The triage interview

Many agencies use preliminary or diagnostic interviews that do not involve providing advice, but are time-limited, fact-finding interviews designed to identify:
- what service the client needs;
- any action that needs to be taken straight away; *and*
- the next steps, which might be:
  - providing information; *or*
  - signposting or referring the client to another agency; *or*
  - arranging for the client to receive further advice, either immediately or by appointment.

A triage interview uses a specific set of questions to ensure that all relevant details have been collected. Triage is often the client's first contact with the agency. It is therefore important that it is accurate so that s/he can be dealt with appropriately. Clients who are assessed as being able to help themselves can be provided with the information to enable them to do so. A client can also be referred to other agencies if these are better placed to meet her/his needs.

The Money and Pensions Service uses a **common initial assessment** for its funded projects. This is an online triage tool. The client is asked a set of standard questions and, based on information provided by her/him, it then:
- flags up emergency situations;
- assesses the most appropriate channel for the client to access further advice, if required;
- identifies the next step for the client; *and*
- identifies potential debt remedies available to the client.

Making appropriate referrals

It is important to establish whether a case should be referred to a specialist or more experienced adviser, and whether there is a mechanism in place for referring cases, if appropriate, to other organisations.

Record key dates (eg, court hearings) and time limits so they are not missed and adequate preparation can be made. It may be appropriate to keep a record of referrals to track the outcome.

Once a case is opened, keep a record of the case and the client's name and address to ensure the file can be accessed in the future should the client return after the case is closed.

In some situations, you may do no work for the client, but instead signpost her/him to a more appropriate organisation.

Case recording

If electronic case recording and storage of documents is not available, all documents relating to a case must be kept in an adequate file. Keep all the papers in date order. Incoming letters could be stored on one side of the file and outgoing on the other. You could also use dividers to separate each different creditor, so it is easy to access each debt and monitor its progress. Alternatively, papers relating to each creditor could be kept together with a separate sheet on file to indicate the action on each debt.

You must comply with data protection legislation and obtain your clients' consent to hold sensitive personal information about them and, where relevant, to share information about their cases with third parties – eg, for monitoring or quality checking purposes.

Correspondence

Keep the client informed of each stage of the case and give her/him copies of correspondence from the creditor. Telephone conversations should be recorded in the file, including names of those spoken to and on what date. It is good practice to follow up the call with an email or letter from either you or the creditor, as appropriate, to confirm information discussed if it is relevant to the case.

Reviews

Each case should be regularly reviewed to check that replies have been received, that preparation for any court hearings has been carried out, and what the next step in the case should be. A brought-forward diary system may be useful to ensure that important dates are noted and there are regular follow-ups. There is no point keeping a file open if there is no further work to be carried out, or if the client has ceased to engage and is not responding to your attempts to make contact with her/him.

By managing the caseload, you also have a clearer idea of how many additional cases, if any, you can take on.

Cases should also be reviewed, if possible, by other advisers to check that the advice given is appropriate and correct.

Closing cases

At the outset, you should give the client an indication of how long the case will remain open. This gives you an idea of how many cases you are dealing with and when you can take on any more. As you are trying to empower the client, your aim should be that, once the work is done on the case, clients can continue with the work themselves, but with the option of possibly returning in the future should they feel unable to deal with matters themselves or if there is a change of circumstance.

A case can be closed if:
- the strategy for the client is up and running successfully; *or*
- you have lost contact with the client and s/he has not responded to your attempts to contact her/him; *or*
- the client no longer wants help from the agency or is changing advisers; *or*
- the agency is no longer able to provide a service to the client.

The Institute of Money Advisers' *Money Advice Statement of Good Practice* says that a creditor should only be informed that a case has been closed if:
- the adviser has been unable to obtain instructions from the client; *or*
- the client has informed the adviser that s/he is now dealing with the creditor in person.

This is to address the problem of a case being closed because a payment arrangement has been set up and the creditor then contacts the client directly to try to persuade her/him to increase payments. If a creditor contacts an agency again in those circumstances, it should be informed the case has been closed and it should be referred directly to the client.

If a client returns for help when creditors are asking for a review of the finances, it may be advisable to assist her/him with a new financial statement and then advise how to prepare an offer letter, with the intention that s/he acts for her/himself.

Clients should be warned that some funders have time limits on when cases can be reopened on the same issue. This can be problematic if a client fails to keep in contact, the case is closed and s/he then returns.

Notes

1. Professional debt advice

1 *FCA Handbook*, CONC 8. 'Debt advice' applies to debt counselling, debt adjusting and providing credit information services, by both profit-making and not-for-profit bodies. Local authorities and members of the legal profession are exempt from the requirement to be authorised. See also P Madge, 'Debt Advice Rules – OK?', *Adviser* 175.

2 *FCA Handbook*, CONC 8.3.2R(1) and 8.3.7R(2)

3 *FCA Handbook*, CONC 8.2.7R and 8.2.8G. See also A Chisholm, 'Consumer Vulnerability', *Adviser* 176, and G O'Malley, 'Advising Vulnerable Clients', *Quarterly Account* 41, IMA.

2. The debt advice system

4 The sale of a debt is known in law as an 'assignment' and the purchaser is known as an 'assignee'.

5 *FCA Handbook*, CONC 8.5.4R(2)

6 In one case, the Financial Ombudsman Service found that a bank had not treated a customer who had approached it for advice and assistance about her debts 'sympathetically and positively' by insisting that the income/ expenditure form she had completed had to be checked by an advice agency. See *Ombudsman News* 83, 2010 (*Adviser* 140 abstracts).

7 *FCA Handbook*, CONC 8.3

8 See *FCA Handbook*, DISP 1

9 s157 CCA 1974

10 See *Adviser* 166 abstracts and *Grace v Black Horse* (*Adviser* 167 abstracts)

11 s158 CCA 1974

12 s159 CCA 1974

Chapter 2

Key skills

This chapter covers:

1. Interviewing

There are some features of an interview with a person in debt that are important to note.

- Make it clear to the client that s/he will not be judged.
- Be aware of the ways in which your own preconceptions or attitudes affect the interview process. Recognise any negative images you may have of borrowing and debt and address them.
- Reassure the client that s/he has done the right thing in seeking advice. Being in debt can be stressful and clients may feel embarrassed at having to talk about their financial problems. It is important to build the client's trust (see p42) and to emphasise that s/he will not be judged in this process.
- Encourage the client to express her/his emotions in order to get these out of the way, so s/he can then concentrate on remembering, thinking and decision making as the interview progresses. For example, many people in debt fear imprisonment. This is not a possibility for the majority of debts, but this fear must be voiced if progress is to be made. The client may also have problems which initially do not appear to be debt related – eg, relationship issues. Clients need to be able to express whatever is important to them and their concerns so that they can then concentrate on sorting out their debts.
- Because of the numerous threats from individual creditors, many clients feel hopeless about their situation. Do not raise false expectations by dismissing these threats, but be positive and explain that it is possible to do something.

- Anticipate problems that the client may face. It is important that the client does not depart from decisions made as part of a strategy, but you are unlikely to be there when these decisions are tested. For example, you may agree with a client that, because s/he has been paying creditors who call at her/his home and not paying her/his priority creditors, the best course of action is to withhold all payments to unsecured creditors until the arrears on the client's priority debts have been cleared. This decision will not be tested until an unsecured creditor calls, perhaps late at night, making threats. The client may find it difficult to stick to her/his earlier decision unless you have already explored this possibility with her/him.

- Partners, or other people with whom the client lives, usually need to be consulted if a good decision (ie, one which is likely to be adhered to) is to be made. Many of the decisions taken involve third parties who may not be at the interview. Even if you consider that urgent action is required, this can generally be delayed long enough for the client to consult others. Occasionally, there may be compelling reasons for not doing so – eg, if there is a fear of violence.

- Tell the client about the service s/he can expect from you and the agency. Explain what is expected of the client and what you will do. This must be written down and a copy given to the client and one kept by the agency (see p8).

- Performing realistic tasks can empower the client – eg, switching fuel supplier. Modest tasks, such as asking a particular creditor about arrears, can help the client feel involved in the processes that are being carried out on her/his behalf. Although it is important to offer expertise and services, do not take over the client's life – and avoid creating dependency.

- Be impartial and do not assume that you know what is best for the client. All options which the client could access must be considered before any course of action is agreed.

2. **Negotiating**

Negotiation is a process of communication between the debt adviser or client and the creditor. It takes place over a period of time, after which an agreement is made that both sides find acceptable.

A decision must be made about whether it is appropriate for you to carry out the negotiation or whether it should be done by the client. Sometimes, it is more empowering for an adviser to support a client by providing, for example, a financial statement and some standard letters, rather than negotiating her/ himself. In the past, creditors routinely rejected offers made by clients unless and until they were made by an advice agency, even though it was the same offer and based on identical information (but see p19).

Some creditors have a policy of refusing to deal with advice agencies. If the client has authorised you to negotiate with a creditor on her/his behalf, the Financial Conduct Authority (FCA) forbids creditors to refuse to do so or to contact clients directly and bypass their appointed representatives.[1] Similarly, creditors should not refuse to deal with clients who are attempting to negotiate their own repayment arrangements. A creditor who refuses to negotiate with an adviser or a client without a justifiable reason should be challenged.

You should conduct all negotiations with the aim of resolving the debt problem and bearing in mind that the client's best interests are paramount. Ensure that s/he does not offer more than s/he can afford.[2] Do your best to enable the client to regain control of her/his financial situation as quickly as possible, as opposed to being tied into a repayment programme, which may take many years to complete (if ever).

Advisers are often in a powerful position in relation to creditors because no one in the credit industry wants to be accused (particularly publicly) of acting illegally or oppressively. If a debt adviser from a well-respected local or national agency contacts a creditor to negotiate on a client's behalf, it is likely that the creditor will want to reach a settlement. In some cases, an adviser's power is increased because debt advice is likely to lead to payment and, in others, because the creditor realises that a debt cannot profitably be pursued. This does not mean that creditors should routinely be expected to agree to every proposal that you put forward. On the other hand, if you think that the creditor is being unreasonable and/or unrealistic, consider referring the matter to a more senior person in the creditor organisation with a view to using the creditor's complaints procedure and ultimately referring the matter to the Ombudsman, if necessary.

You should support your arguments by referring to any relevant code of practice or section of the *FCA Handbook* (generally, the *Consumer Credit Sourcebook* – see p30).

CASHflow

Agencies can provide assisted 'self-help' to suitable clients by using CASHflow, a self-help toolkit. To access an updated version of this (incorporating the standard financial statement – see p56) go to moneyadvicetrust.org/advice-agencies/CASHflow.

A money adviser assists the client to draw up a financial statement which is 'locked' and so cannot be changed. The toolkit includes a suite of letters which the client can use to make offers to her/his creditors and deal with any follow up and requests for reviews.

The financial statement is produced using standard financial statement principles (see p56) and creditors have agreed to deal with offers from CASHflow-assisted self-help clients in the same way as offers from the agency itself. You should warn the client that debts may be sold on and, even though the debt

2

purchaser should be informed of any existing payment arrangements, s/he may have to come to a new arrangement with the debt purchaser.[3]

3. **Letter writing**

Much negotiation begins with a letter. While emergency applications, particularly concerning priority debts (see p237), may have to be initiated by telephone and confirmed in writing later, it is more effective to send a letter in the first instance so that full details can be enclosed. Important changes to agreements reached through negotiation should always be confirmed in writing.

It is sometimes more appropriate for you to help the client prepare a financial statement using the standard CASHflow forms and letters, which are sent from the client her/himself (see p19). The client receives the replies and must be encouraged to seek further advice, as required. In this way, the client regains control over her/his own affairs and, in the long term, may be more able to cope. In addition, your workload may be reduced.

It is essential to send letters to the right place. In many cases, local branches are unable to deal with their customers' financial difficulties and most creditors have dedicated departments instead. Wherever possible, use the address(es) provided by the creditor for dealing with communications.

Format of a letter

Letters should follow a basic format, as explained below.

Use simple language

Letters should be written in simple, clear language. 'Thank you for your letter of 11 June' is just as meaningful as 'Your communication of 11 June is gratefully acknowledged'.

Assume nothing

Letters, particularly initial letters, are generally read by a person who knows little or nothing about the client's situation. A letter should therefore contain all the background information needed to make a decision.

Holding letters

It is often necessary to write an initial letter requesting information that you need in order to advise the client and identify the available options. Such information includes:
- copies of any agreement and of any default notice (see p299) or termination letter, where relevant;
- a statement of account, showing full details of the outstanding balance and how this is calculated;
- details of any court orders or other enforcement action.

The letter should also ask the creditor to put a hold on any further collection activity and to freeze any further interest and/or charges being added to the account until the information requested has been supplied and the client has had an opportunity to put forward her/his proposals for resolving the matter. Any breaches of the Financial Conduct Authority's (FCA's) *Consumer Credit Sourcebook* (see p30) by the creditor or debt collector should also be addressed in this letter.

Use a framework

As well as standard letters or phrases, new or unusual situations require individual letters.[4] These are easier to write with a framework to follow.

- **Address.** The letter should begin with the address to which it will be sent, which must appear on your copy as well as the copy for the creditor.
- **Client and references.** Next comes the full name and address, including postcode, of the client and all references or other identifying numbers. Major creditors may have borrowers of the same name, so detailed identification is essential to avoid confusion.
- **Standard opening phrase.** This can usefully explain the agency's status. For example: 'The above has contacted us for advice about her/his financial affairs and we are now helping her/him to look at these as a whole.'
- **Outline the background.** Next, tell the story so far (although not necessarily in the holding letter as you may not have all the details at this stage). It is essential to give all the necessary background and details. Go through the story in chronological order. Keep sentences short and factual. Avoid long explanations. Do not include demands or excuses.
  The statement of facts must include those on which you are basing the strategy, in particular any unusual expenditure or special circumstances of the client or the members of her/his household. So, if you are asking for a temporary suspension of payments and interest charges, make sure you explain that there is currently no available income or capital and set out the client's future prospects.
- **Make the request.** The next stage of the letter should be the request. This needs to be clearly and simply phrased. Do not be apologetic or circumspect – link the request to the facts outlined and make it appear to be an inevitable consequence of them. Where relevant, ask the creditor to (continue to) freeze interest and/or other charges to prevent the debt from increasing further.
  The letter should continue by stating when you propose the strategy should be reviewed. You can express this either:
  - as a fixed period; *or*
  - with reference to other factors – eg, 'We will be happy to review this when Mr Parkinson gets a job.'
- **Add any special reasons.** After outlining the request, add the special reasons why this should be accepted. These may be obvious from the facts you have listed, but it is worth repeating them. If arrangements have broken down in

the past or you believe a creditor will be resistant to the suggestion, however, it is useful to list whatever special reasons you can.

- **Provide details of any offer.** If you are putting forward an offer of payment, this should be clearly described – eg, 'The first payment of £... will be made on 27 August and following payments will be made on the 27th of each month.' You should also specify the method of payment. Advise your client to begin making the payments in accordance with the offer without waiting for confirmation from the creditor, as some creditors are prepared to accept offers but do not notify their acceptance and then complain that the client has not kept to the payment arrangement.

- **Suggest an expected response.** Your letter could then suggest the kind of reply that you expect – eg, 'We would be grateful if you could confirm, in writing, that this will be acceptable.'

- **To whom should the creditor reply?** Consider whether or not it is desirable for creditors to reply to the agency or to clients directly. If there is a heavy debt advice workload, it may be advisable to ask creditors to reply directly to their customer. It may be worth explaining why this is necessary.
  You should also include your contact details and availability (or alternative contacts where appropriate), so that creditors can contact you if necessary. Some creditors and collectors contact the client directly even when asked to reply to the agency, usually in an attempt to persuade the client to increase her/his repayment offer. This is a breach of the FCA's *Consumer Credit Sourcebook* (see p30).[5]

- **Ending.** End the letter with a conventional politeness, such as 'We are very grateful for your help in this matter', followed by 'Yours sincerely/faithfully'.

---

4. **Representing clients in court**

Many debt advisers regularly represent clients at court hearings, but if your local court has not had experience of representation by lay advisers, you may need to arrange this.

The court clerk is likely to be a useful contact at the magistrates' court.

For more details about the courts, see Chapters 10, 11, 12 and 13.

Type of hearing

Chambers

The majority of hearings at which advisers represent clients are in chambers.[6] This means that the hearing is usually held in private in the district judge's office, with only the client and her/his representative, the solicitor or representative acting for the creditor, and the district judge present. The district judge does not wear a wig or gown, and everyone remains seated throughout the hearing. Before a hearing, you must give the court and creditor all the information and documents to be used at the hearing.[7]

The 'claimant' or her/his solicitor presents her/his case to the district judge. The 'claimant' is normally the creditor, except if the client has applied for something like a time order (see p366) or for a warrant to be suspended (see p382).

After this, the other side gets the opportunity to speak. As the client's representative, you have an opportunity to explain briefly the client's circumstances and make a proposal. A financial statement (see p55) is essential if making an offer of payment.

The creditor's solicitor or agent can comment on the proposal and the district judge makes an order.

It is always worth introducing yourself to the creditor's representative at the court while waiting to be called and finding out what s/he has been instructed to ask the court for. The hearing normally takes five to 10 minutes, but this can be reduced if you have successfully negotiated with the creditor or solicitor beforehand.

The court always needs to know what powers it has to make a decision. If you want the the district judge to make a particular order, make sure you can refer to the relevant place in the Civil Procedure Rules 1998 that gives her/him this power. See Chapter 10 for more information.

Open court

Some hearings (such as appeals to judges) take place in 'open court'. Courts have the discretion whether or not to allow a lay adviser to address the court on behalf of her/his client (except in the small claims procedure), but most welcome the assistance of a debt adviser. Find out the views of the judge or magistrate in advance, if possible, from an usher or clerk.

Hearings are held in public, and are more formal than hearings in chambers. A circuit judge, a district judge or magistrate hears the case. The court may be full of people waiting to have their cases heard, and solicitors or barristers waiting to represent. The creditor or a solicitor presents the case and may bring witnesses to cross-examine.

The client may be asked to speak on oath, but you may be able to present the case without the client needing to speak. It is customary to stand when addressing the judge.

Many courts do not allow lay representation, but you may be able to be a 'McKenzie friend'. This is someone who accompanies the client to the hearing, advises her/him, suggests what s/he should say and makes notes of the proceedings. If you are considering attending court as a McKenzie friend, you should read the practice guidelines available at judiciary.gov.uk/publications/mckenzie-friends.

Useful techniques

Plan well

Plan everything to be said in advance. Make sure it is logical and clear. Use notes where necessary. Rehearse presentations if possible, particularly if you are a new representative. You should inform the court if you have not had time to obtain full instructions – eg, in the case of emergency hearings or court/duty desks. It may then be in the client's best interests to request an adjournment, even if this means that the client may have increased liability for the creditor's costs.

Be brief

Local courts operate to very tight timescales (hearings are often listed for five or 10 minutes) and judges expect representations to be short and to the point. Avoid any repetition.

Summarise

The court wants to know what order it is being asked to make and the reasons why it is appropriate to make it. A written summary of the case, briefly setting out the issues, the facts and any relevant law is often helpful and can be handed out at the beginning if it has not been possible to circulate it in advance. Take copies for the judge and creditor's representative. This can then be expanded on in the presentation.

Prepare clear documents

Financial statements or other documents used to support a case should be clearly presented and photocopied for the judge and creditor's representative.

Tell the story

Explain the background to the case clearly and concisely in chronological order. Do not assume that the judge has read the papers.

Quote precedents and powers

Give clear references and explanations of any past cases cited in support of your case if it is unusual, and the legal powers on which it depends. Reference the Civil Procedure Rules (see p280) and any caselaw on which you intend to rely. Take copies for the judge and creditor's representative.

Admit ignorance

If stuck, it is better to admit this and ask for help rather than pretend otherwise. Provided your case appears reasonable, many judges are helpful if they are asked. However, this should never be used as an alternative to thorough preparation of the case. Do not pretend to be a solicitor or allow others to assume wrongly that you are one.

Use court staff

Before the hearing, tell the usher that you wish to speak on the client's behalf. S/he then informs the court clerk or the judge and tells you if there is anyone to represent the creditor.

Address the judge or magistrate

Address a district judge or magistrate as 'sir' or 'madam' and a judge as 'your honour'.

Look smart, be polite, speak clearly

Wear smart clothes (or apologise for your inability to do so – eg, if it is an emergency application). It is usually acceptable for lay representatives to dress less formally. Use standard English where possible; slang may not be understood and will almost certainly not further your case. Appear as confident as possible without being 'cocky'. Be respectful and pleasant. Use eye contact and smiles to retain the attention of the judge.

Know your own limits

Do not attempt to represent a client in court without being aware of all the possible outcomes.[8] Complex representation may require lay advisers or lawyers who are not specialists to refer to lay advocates, solicitors or barristers who are.

5. Changing policy

If a particular law, practice, structure or policy adversely affects many clients or affects vulnerable groups of clients, debt advisers should work to change the policy.

When contacting individual creditors, stress that this is a general social policy approach and not an attempt to reopen a case that has already been discussed.

Other organisations can be helpful. The ways in which creditors deal with debt may be controlled or overseen by one of a number of organisations.

You should also pass on details to umbrella organisations, such as Citizens Advice, AdviceUK or the Institute of Money Advisers.

The Financial Conduct Authority

The Financial Conduct Authority (FCA) is responsible for regulating consumer credit.

Running a consumer credit business and other credit-related activities requires authorisation by the FCA. Debt counselling, debt adjusting and providing credit information services (ie, assistance to obtain details of credit reference files or information about how to change credit reference files) are also all credit-related activities requiring authorisation.

You can check whether a firm is authorised at fca.org.uk/firms/consumer-credit-register. Firms that are not authorised can be reported to the FCA helpline (tel: 0800 111 6768). It is a criminal offence to carry out a debt-related activity without the appropriate authorisation.

Note: local trading standards departments may be able to help resolve individual cases. As the regulator, the FCA cannot provide redress in individual cases.

Ofgem, Ofcom and Ofwat

The suppliers of fuel, telecommunications and water all have regulatory bodies (see Appendix 1), which have varying powers to investigate and comment on their activities. The fuel regulatory bodies are responsible for preventing unlawful price increases or disconnections. They can also be useful in exercising pressure in other areas.

Trade associations

Many industries have trade associations. These are bodies that are regulated by their members, but impose certain agreed standards as a membership condition. A list of trade associations is in Appendix 1. Many have a code of practice or conduct, and all have some kind of complaints procedure, which can be used to resolve individual cases.

Trade associations exist primarily to protect their members. However, they can be useful in changing the behaviour of an individual company, as trade associations do not want the good name of their members to be affected by the poor behaviour of one company. The peer-group pressure they can exert, either through a complaints procedure or less formally, is probably much greater than the pressure an advice agency acting on its own could create.

Local councillors and MPs

Much debt is payable to local or national government. This includes council tax, income tax, value added tax (VAT) and rent. The statutory powers which the state has given itself to enforce these debts are considerable, so they are all priority debts. However, as government debts, they are subject to scrutiny by elected members – ie, councillors and MPs. This can provide a powerful method of ensuring that the state's powers are not used in too draconian a fashion.

Elected members are often not aware of the measures being used by their officers to collect debts. For instance, many local councillors are unaware of the extent to which their authority uses private bailiffs and, once briefed by an advice agency, can raise this as an issue and change the way these debts are collected. Under a protocol drawn up between the national bodies representing advice agencies and local government, regular liaison is encouraged at a local level on practices and policies on the collection of council tax arrears.

Ombudsmen

If the administration of debt collection by the state is poor and results in individuals experiencing hardship, a complaint can be made to an Ombudsman (see Appendix 1 for addresses). Ombudsmen are not regulators and their primary role is to help resolve individual cases. They expect the client to give the creditor the opportunity to investigate her/his complaint and resolve the matter before referring the case to them.

The Parliamentary and Health Service Ombudsman

The Parliamentary and Health Service Ombudsman investigates complaints of maladministration by any central government department. Complaints must be made via an MP. If possible, send a simple statement, with dates and supporting evidence, to the MP with a request that it be forwarded to the Ombudsman.

Local Government and Social Care Ombudsman/Public Services Ombudsman for Wales

Complaints about local government matters are made to the Local Government and Social Care Ombudsman (or the Public Services Ombudsman for Wales) and are important, even where the maladministration has been corrected in an individual case. Local government officers dislike negative adjudications by the Ombudsman and these usually lead to procedural changes to prevent a recurrence of the event complained about.

A complaint is probably best made through a local councillor, but can also be made directly by a member of the public.

The Local Government and Social Care Ombudsman/Public Services Ombudsman for Wales often investigates a particular department or function of an authority – eg, council tax collection. You should collect a few cases of maladministration and then discuss with staff at one of the Ombudsman offices whether it will investigate. A report on the work of a department is much more powerful than a single case.

The Adjudicator's Office

The Adjudicator's Office deals with complaints about the way things have been handled by HM Revenue and Customs (but not about the amount of tax or VAT the client has been asked to pay).

The Financial Ombudsman Service

The Financial Ombudsman Service handles complaints between clients and finance firms (including banks and building societies) and firms with a consumer credit licence (including debt collectors and sub-prime lenders). Since 1 April 2014 it has also dealt with complaints about debt advice providers (including not-for-profit providers and those that charge a fee). See also p284.

Ombudsman Services: Energy

For energy services, first make a complaint to the supplier and ask it to put the account on hold while it deals with the complaint. If, after 10 days, there has been either no response or an unsatisfactory response, the complaint should be escalated through the supplier's complaints procedure. Refer to its code of practice for details of how to do this. The case can be referred to the Ombudsman Services: Energy either eight weeks after the complaint was made or after the supplier has issued a 'deadlock letter' – ie, negotiations have broken down and neither party will reconsider its position. The complaint must be referred to the Ombudsman Services: Energy within either six months of the deadlock letter being issued or nine months of the complaint first being made.

Legal Ombudsman

The Legal Ombudsman considers complaints about legal services provided by lawyers (including solicitors, barristers and employees of businesses and partnerships). The complaint must relate to services provided by the lawyer to the client and, unless there are exceptional circumstances, the client must first have used the lawyer's or firm's complaints procedure. If the complaint is not resolved within eight weeks, it can be referred to the Ombudsman. The Ombudsman can consider the complaint earlier if s/he decides that delay would harm the client or if the lawyer has refused to consider it. The complaint must be made to the Ombudsman within six months of the lawyer's response and within 12 months of the matter complained of. The Ombudsman need not consider a complaint about an issue that is being dealt with by a court, unless the case is 'stayed' (ie, put on hold) either with the consent of all the parties or a court order to enable the Ombudsman to deal with it.

Monitoring local courts

Court procedures should be monitored on a local basis by debt advisers. Having collected information about the way in which a particular court operates, it is important to decide whether pressure for change needs to be exerted on the court staff, the judiciary, or both.

Neither judges nor magistrates are open to being lobbied by groups about individual decisions or types of decisions that they are required to take. However, particularly if you work for a charitable organisation with a good reputation locally, it may be possible to arrange meetings with the chair of the bench (ie, the senior magistrate, or representatives of the judges in a county court) to discuss ways in which the advice centre can assist the courts in their work or other issues of mutual concern. In practice, this means it is generally possible to discuss procedures and engage the decision makers in an analysis of the effects of their judgments.

Local liaison groups

Some public services have liaison groups (eg, a local court users' group) and you should investigate whether any such groups exist (and perhaps advocate for them if they do not). Consider becoming a member in order to gain credibility through networking, and to change policies and procedures that are unhelpful or oppressive. Some groups may have existed for a long time with a fixed membership – eg, solicitors, and members of the probation service and the police. You may have to spend time securing membership, but this may be rewarded with a direct line of communication to powerful local decision makers.

Using the media

Discussion with the various bodies outlined above can often result in useful changes that prevent continued injustice. However, it is often only when something becomes a live, public, political issue that real change can occur. It is important, therefore, to cultivate links with local and national media so that publicity can be gained for particular issues.

When considering whether to use the media, you must bear in mind general advice work issues, such as confidentiality. However, even if an individual client does not wish to have her/his case publicised, it may be acceptable for an anonymous description of the issues involved in it to be part of a media campaign. There is an almost endless demand from media organisations for examples of individuals who have suffered by being in debt. Many people do not wish to have their private affairs made public, but for others this can be an important way of regaining a sense of power after the experiences they have faced at the hands of creditors. It is certainly the way to bring an issue to public debate.

6. **Ensuring good practice**

Dealing with harassment

Many creditors harass debtors. Much of this goes unreported and unchallenged, and is expected by many clients. Section 40 of the Administration of Justice Act 1970 defines harassment as trying to coerce a person to pay a contract debt by making demands for payment that are calculated to subject a person to 'alarm, distress or humiliation, because of their frequency or publicity or manner'.

Harassment can take place in writing or orally. It can include using obviously marked vehicles, calling repeatedly at antisocial hours, or visiting neighbours or places of work. Harassment occurs if a debt collector purports to be enquiring about a person, but explains to neighbours why the enquiries are necessary. Harassment might also include posting lists of debtors in public. It includes abusive or threatening behaviour and all acts of violence. Any false representation that a type of non-payment is a criminal offence or that a person is a court official or other publicly sanctioned debt collector is also regarded as harassment.

Harassment is not a criminal offence but could give rise to civil action.[9]

Because much debt collection activity takes place verbally over the phone, at the client's home and sometimes at her/his place of work, you should always ask how demands were made and exactly what was said, and check all written communication for evidence of inappropriate behaviour.

It is important to take urgent action to protect the client from further contact. Send a letter of complaint immediately, outlining the facts as understood and warning the collector and creditor that, if not resolved to the client's satisfaction, the complaint will be taken to the next level. In cases of violence or extreme harassment, inform the police and the local trading standards department as soon as possible.

Note: feedback from creditors suggests that many advisers do not act professionally when making complaints on behalf of clients – eg, by using rude, abrupt and sarcastic language. In addition, hearsay evidence is often reported as fact instead of, for instance, 'our client informs us that…'. The complaint letter should be objective and factual, and not personalised (unless the complaint is about the actions of an identified individual).

Next, advise the client to have no further contact with the collector or creditor until the matter has been clarified. This may involve politely, but firmly, refusing her/him entry to property or not answering the telephone. Advise the client to keep a diary recording details of any further attempted collection action. If possible, take practical steps to ensure that the client's friends, neighbours or relatives know about serious harassment and are able to provide a safe haven or support to them. Some agencies give clients a sheet of their letterhead, and advise them to show this to any collectors or creditors who visit and tell them to contact the agency.

The *Consumer Credit Sourcebook*

The Office of Fair Trading's *Debt Collection Guidance* and *Irresponsible Lending Guidance* were indispensable for debt advisers, as they set out practices which the Office of Fair Trading considered to be unfair, and provided advisers with the basis for challenging unacceptable behaviour. The guidance covered anyone engaged in the recovery or enforcement of regulated consumer credit debts – ie, any credit agreement other than an exempt agreement (see p62). Much (but not all) of the guidance is now in the *FCA Handbook*, in the *Consumer Credit Sourcebook* (usually referred to by the abbreviation CONC) as rules (R) and guidance (G).

Where the source for a Financial Conduct Authority (FCA) rule or guidance is Office of Fair Trading guidance, this is cross-referenced in the *Consumer Credit Sourcebook*. Office of Fair Trading guidance ceased to have effect on 1 April 2014 and so any part not carried over into the *Consumer Credit Sourcebook* cannot be relied on as the basis for a complaint.

Chapter (or Section) 7 of the *Consumer Credit Sourcebook* applies to creditors or external debt collectors taking steps to obtain payment of a debt due under a credit agreement. It covers:
- clear, effective and appropriate arrears policies and procedures for dealing with clients who fall into arrears, including for the fair and appropriate treatment of clients who are particularly vulnerable (CONC 7.2);[10]
- the treatment of clients in default or arrears, particularly the requirement to treat clients fairly (CONC 7.3);[11]
- the requirement to provide clients with information about the amount of any arrears and the outstanding balance (CONC 7.4);
- pursuing and recovering repayments (CONC 7.5);
- exercising a continuous payment authority – ie, a mandate given by the client to, for instance, a lender, allowing it to take a series of payments from a debit or credit card without seeking express authorisation for every payment (see p124) (CONC 7.6);
- applying interest or charges (CONC 7.7);
- contact with clients (CONC 7.9);
- the treatment of clients with mental capacity limitations (CONC 7.10);
- misrepresenting the authority or the legal position with regards to the debt or the debt recovery process (CONC 7.11);
- creditors' responsibilities in relation to debt (CONC 7.12);
- data accuracy (CONC 7.13);
- settlements and disputed debts (CONC 7.14);
- statute-barred debts – ie, those that are too old to be recovered (CONC 7.15).

Specifically, the guidance states the following.
- If a creditor informs a client that it has decided not to pursue the debt, it must make her/him aware that the debt may still be sold by the creditor and the debt purchaser might decide to pursue the debt. **Note:** if the creditor has accepted a payment in full and final settlement of a debt, the creditor must formally and clearly confirm this (CONC 7.4.2R and 7.14.14R).
- A creditor must investigate if a debt is disputed on valid grounds or what may be valid grounds (eg, if the client is not the debtor, the debt does not exist or the amount being pursued is incorrect), and must provide information on the result of such investigations (CONC 7.14.3R and 7.14.5R).
- Creditors must not require someone to supply information to prove s/he is not the debtor in question (CONC 7.14.4R).
- Creditors must suspend debt collection activity if a client disputes the debt on valid grounds, or what may be valid grounds (CONC 7.14.1R).
- A creditor should not make undue, excessive or otherwise inappropriate use of statutory demands when seeking to recover a debt from a client (CONC 7.3.15G).

- Creditors must treat clients in default or in arrears difficulties with forbearance and due consideration (CONC 7.3.4R).
- If a client is in default or in arrears difficulties, a creditor must inform her/him that free and impartial debt advice is available from the free-to-client debt advice sector and refer the client to an agency. It appears that it is sufficient for a creditor to signpost a client to a debt advice agency or to the Money Advice Service by providing its name and contact details to the client (CONC 7.3.7AG).
- Creditors must not pressurise clients to pay a debt in a single lump sum or more than they can reasonably afford and must allow alternative, affordable repayment amounts if a reasonable offer is made (CONC 7.3.8G and 7.310R). Putting clients under pressure to draw a lump sum from a pension in order to pay a debt is likely to breach these requirements (CONC 7.3.10AG).
- Creditors must suspend recovery of a debt from a client for a reasonable period (ie, 30 days) if a debt adviser is assisting her/him to agree a repayment plan (CONC 7.3.11R and 7.3.12G).
- Creditors must suspend recovery of a debt from a client if notification has been given and it is reasonably believed that s/he lacks the mental capacity to make decisions about her/his debt problems, unless or until a reasonable period has been allowed for relevant evidence to be provided (CONC 7.10.1R and 7.10.2G).
- Creditors must take reasonable steps to ensure that customer data is accurate and that accurate and adequate data is passed on to third parties, such as debt collectors, debt purchasers and credit reference agencies, to avoid cases of 'mistaken identity' (where the wrong person is pursued for payment of a debt) and to ensure that clients are pursued for the correct amount of any debt (CONC 7.13).
- In relation to statute-barred debts (see p292), CONC 7.15 acknowledges that, although the debt still legally exists, a creditor must not:
  - pursue the debt if the client has heard nothing from the creditor during the relevant limitation period (but not if the creditor has been in regular contact with the client before the debt became statute-barred);
  - mislead clients about their rights and obligations – eg, by falsely claiming that the debt is still recoverable through the courts;
  - continue to press for payment after a client has stated that s/he will not be paying a debt because it is statute-barred.

Breaches of the *Consumer Credit Sourcebook* should first be raised with the creditor and debt collector concerned. If the matter is not resolved, the client should use the complaints procedure to escalate the matter to the Financial Ombudsman Service.[12] Also raise the issue with the appropriate trade body (eg, the Finance and Leasing Association or the regulator – eg, the FCA).

Codes of practice

Many creditors have their own codes of practice. For example, all gas and electricity suppliers must have a code of practice on dealing with customers in financial difficulty. Other creditors subscribe to trade associations, which have codes of practice with which members should comply – eg, the *Finance and Leasing Association Lending Code*, the *Credit Services Association Code of Practice* and the Lending Standards Board's *The Standards of Lending Practice*. Some regulators (eg, the FCA, Ofwat and Ofgem) issue guidelines on how to deal with customers in debt. There is also guidance for bailiffs in *Taking Control of Goods: national standards*.[13]

All these codes set high standards, which creditors and collectors are expected to meet in their dealings with clients. *The Standards of Lending Practice* also requires subscribers to ensure that when they sell a debt, the purchaser agrees to comply with its guidance on handling financial difficulties. The *Finance and Leasing Association Lending Code* contains equivalent provisions. Although creditors and collectors often fall short of the standards set in the relevant code of practice, they are voluntary and cannot be directly enforced in the event of non-compliance. The only remedy is a complaint, which in some cases can be referred to an independent Ombudsman (see p27).

This *Handbook* refers to codes of practice where relevant. It is often in a client's best interests to point out to a creditor or collector where there is non-compliance with a code of practice and request that it be complied with. In the case of collectors (and private bailiffs), it is also worth copying in the creditor. This does not mean that a complaint should be made in every case. The aim of a complaint should be to achieve a better outcome for the client than currently appears likely and so, if a complaint is likely to impede rather than promote negotiation, you should discuss this with the client and consider deferring it.

Clients with mental health problems

There is a clear link between debt and mental health issues. According to the Royal College of Psychiatrists, it has been estimated that one in four adults living in the UK experience a mental health problem every year. When combined with financial difficulties, mental health problems can affect not only the individuals concerned, but also the organisations with which they have relationships.

Many mental health conditions have no physical signs, and fluctuations in the severity and effects of an illness are common. In many cases, creditors are not aware that there is a mental health issue until payments have been missed and the collections process has reached an advanced stage. Even then, it may not be apparent whether the client is capable of conducting a financial transaction (see p153). Money advisers and creditors are not trained to diagnose mental health problems and often do not understand the implications. However, once a creditor is aware of the issue, it should have processes and systems in place to take account of the situation, and should respond fairly and appropriately.

Guidance on dealing with clients with mental health problems

The FCA's *Consumer Credit Sourcebook* provides information on common potential causes of limited mental capacity[14] and specific indications that should alert a lender to a client's condition.[15] Creditors should have practices and procedures for dealing with credit applications from such customers[16] and should document the steps they take to assist people to make informed borrowing decisions and to ensure they make informed and responsible lending decisions.[17] It recommends that creditors should present clear, jargon-free information to explain credit agreements and should consider presenting information in more user-friendly formats.[18]

The *Consumer Credit Sourcebook* also requires creditors to establish and implement clear, effective and appropriate policies and procedures to ensure that clients who are particularly vulnerable are treated fairly and appropriately, and it acknowledges that clients who have mental health problems or mental capacity limitations may fall into this category.[19]

However, a creditor may not be in a position to know whether a client has some form of limited mental capacity and may not be able to assess her/his level of understanding of any explanations – eg, if there is no face-to-face interaction or the internet is used for transactions.

To address this issue, the Royal College of Psychiatrists and the Money Advice Trust published *Lending, Debt Collection and Mental Health: 12 steps for treating potentially vulnerable clients fairly*.[20] This provides information to creditors on how to take a proactive approach to identify and address clients who are particularly vulnerable, including those with mental health issues. However, it recognises that not every client with a mental health problem is automatically vulnerable or unable to manage her/his money, and explains how creditors and debt collectors can take clients' mental health into account in both lending and collection situations. The briefing can be downloaded from malg.org.uk/resources/malg-mental-health-and-debt-guidelines.

In addition, the Money Advice Liaison Group has produced *Good Practice Awareness Guidelines for Helping Consumers with Mental Health Conditions and Debt*, available from malg.org.uk/resources/malg-mental-health-and-debt-guidelines.[21] Both of these publications are endorsed by the *Consumer Credit Sourcebook*[22] and include the following.

- Creditors, debt collectors and advisers should all have procedures in place to ensure that people with mental health problems are treated fairly and appropriately.
- If a mental health problem has been notified to a creditor, the creditor should allow a reasonable period for an adviser to collect the relevant evidence and

send it to the creditor. This could be extended, if necessary, if s/he has not been able to collect all the evidence by the end of one month.

- If creditors sell debts once a mental health issue has been advised, they should monitor the debt purchaser to ensure compliance with the guidelines.
- If someone in debt has a serious mental health problem, creditors should only start court action or enforce debts through the courts as a last resort and only when it is appropriate and fair for lenders to do so.
- Creditors should consider writing off unsecured debts when a client's mental health problems are long term and unlikely to improve, and if it is highly unlikely that s/he will be able to pay outstanding debts.
- Disability benefits (personal independence payment, disability living allowance and attendance allowance) should be recognised as being specifically awarded for meeting mobility and care needs. It is the client's decision whether or not to include any of these benefits as disposable income in the financial statement.

Note: these guidelines only apply to the management of debt problems and not to the stage when the debt was incurred. However, the guidelines suggest that creditors may wish to 'flag' the files of clients who have provided information, explaining the effect of a mental health problem on money management and debt issues. In addition, a client and someone holding a power of attorney for her/him could decide voluntarily to add information about her/his mental health problems to her/his credit reference file so that creditors who carry out a search as part of an application for credit are aware of the position. This can be done by a 'notice of correction' (see p12).[23]

Much of the guidelines deals with obtaining evidence to demonstrate the effect of a client's mental health on her/his ability to deal with her/his debt problems. The Money Advice Liaison Group has produced a debt and mental health evidence form (DMHEF) to assist advisers in this process (the current version in use since 1 October 2019, v.4, is briefer than earlier versions). The form, together with guidance notes for advisers and creditors (which should be read before using it) can be downloaded from moneyadvicetrust.org/creditors/Pages/ DMHEF-advisers.aspx. The guidance states that, before using the DMHEF, advisers should consider:

- whether further evidence does actually need to be collected; *and*
- if so, whether alternative evidence is available that could do the same job as the DMHEF – eg, copies of prescriptions or patient letters.

The form contains three questions to be completed by a health or social care professional who knows the client, which provide information about:

- how the client's mental health problem affects her/his ability to manage her/his money;

- how the client's ability to communicate is affected by her/his mental health problems; *and*
- anything else the professional can say which would help the client – eg, condition severity or duration, any relevant treatment being received or whether the client is in a situation of mental health crisis.

UK Finance and the Credit Services Association have advised their members to accept any suitable evidence and only ask for the DMHEF as a last resort. Where the DMHEF is used, the client must explicitly consent to a health and/or social care professional completing the form. GPs in England have agreed they will no longer charge for completing the form.

There are, however, some issues.[24]

- The form does not specifically address the question of whether or not the client was able to understand the contract s/he originally entered into. This is relevant to the enforceability of the contract and, therefore, the client's liability for the debt. This is a matter that advisers should consider first of all (see p153).
- The client must give her/his written consent to the form being used to obtain information about her/him and may lack the mental capacity to provide this. However, a third party who is authorised to act on behalf of the client can complete and sign the consent form.

7. **Budgeting advice**

Although advice on budgeting is not debt advice, you should use the procedures and skills described in other parts of this *Handbook* to assist clients to deal with their debts. Budgeting advice is now a discrete area of advice work in its own right, but it can play a useful part in the debt advice process. Discussing a person's finances can be a sensitive subject and so a good interview technique is required. Be careful not to impose your own values on a client.

It can sometimes speed up the debt advice process if the client has a session with a money or financial capability adviser. This adviser goes through the client's budget in detail and looks at ways in which s/he could cut back on expenditure. The budget can then be brought to the debt appointment.

There are particular problems when budgeting on a low income. Often, people on a low income only have access to the more expensive forms of credit. In the absence of credit, goods available are generally more expensive because it is impossible to buy enough to benefit from the lower unit prices charged for larger quantities. Similarly, a client may not have access to the cheapest sources of goods if transport is not available to the large out-of-town stores. Budgeting on a low income often requires purchasing inferior goods because money is not available to buy more expensive goods that would last longer and so be much cheaper in the long run.

If poverty exists alongside other factors, such as disability, parenthood or the breakdown of a relationship, it is likely that budgeting is constrained by the time available, which in turn is constrained by the practical and emotional demands of these other situations.

The financial statement

Very often, the process of producing a financial statement (see p55) enables a client to see the sources of her/his financial problems. When all items of expenditure have been listed, it is often clear that these cannot be met from available income. Ideally, if there is a need to cut expenditure, it will occur to the client her/himself. If this does not happen, you could suggest ways of budgeting and the likely results of such strategies to the client. Be aware of vocabulary, body language and tone of voice, to avoid giving the impression that you are judging the client. Issues such as drinking, gambling and smoking must be addressed, and you should explain to the client that these are matters which creditors are likely to raise and so have to be tackled.

On the other hand, this exercise may establish that the client is able to meet all her/his contractual liabilities together with any accruing charges as well as maintaining her/his essential expenditure, and consequently does not need debt advice or any of the strategies discussed in this *Handbook*.

'Luxury' items

There are some items of expenditure that may, in comparison to the possible loss of other goods or services, be less essential.
- Cars are generally more expensive than is realised to buy, run, maintain, tax and insure. If a car is not necessary for personal and family mobility or work requirements, the client may need to consider either selling it and getting a cheaper car, or doing without.
- In the past, telephones, particularly mobiles, have been considered a luxury. This is not always the case – eg, if someone's health might require her/him to call for assistance in an emergency or if someone has experienced racial abuse or domestic violence and this could happen again. The phone may also be an important social lifeline or a means of making emergency help available to another person outside the client's home. However, if no such factors exist, particularly if phone bills are large, the possibility of doing without or changing to incoming calls only could be considered. If a mobile phone is used, the cost (which may be less than that for a landline on some tariffs and usage patterns) and appropriateness of this should be explained. Clients who get universal credit (and have no earnings), income support, income-based jobseeker's allowance, income-related employment and support allowance or the guarantee credit of pension credit may be able to benefit from a low-cost phone package available from BT. Known as BT Basic, the line rental of £5.10 a month

includes £1.50 worth of free calls. Clients can have broadband for an additional £4.85 a month. For more details, see bt.com/btbasic.

- Cable or satellite television is expensive. If a client has an agreement that has already run for its minimum period, the adviser could discuss whether satellite TV is more important than other items on which the money could be spent. On the other hand, it may be part of a package, including the phone, where the overall cost can be justified.

The client's non-dependants

If the client is a parent and her/his adult son or daughter lives in her/his household, s/he may wish to charge her/him only a nominal amount for board. The client may want to keep the family together and the arrangement can save money – eg, by reducing childminding costs. In some cases, challenging the amount being paid by a non-dependant could lead to family disruption.

Faced with this difficult situation, a client may need information and support in order to make decisions. For example, if housing benefit or housing costs in means-tested benefits are being claimed, s/he needs to know by how much this is reduced by the non-dependant living with her/him. From the financial statement (see p55), a client can judge what might be a fair share of the total household expenditure to be attributed to the non-dependant.

Financial inclusion: the Money Advice Service

Overindebtedness and poverty often go hand in hand, particularly in deprived communities where many people are on a low income and financially excluded – ie, they lack access to basic financial products, such as bank accounts, ways of saving and affordable credit. In addition, financially excluded people can find themselves paying more for essential services, such as fuel, insurance and essential goods, because they only have access to high-cost credit provided by sub-prime lenders or loan sharks.

An important factor in financial inclusion is 'financial capability', defined by the Treasury in 2007 as:[25]

> … a broad concept encompassing people's knowledge and skills to understand their own financial circumstances, along with the motivation to take action. Financially capable consumers plan ahead, find and use information, know when to seek advice, and can understand and act on this advice, leading to greater participation in the financial services market.

Without financial capability, clients risk not getting value for money and the products they obtain not meeting their needs.

Advice on buying a specific financial product from a particular provider is a regulated activity that requires the adviser to be approved by the Financial

Conduct Authority. However, free generic financial advice is provided by the Money Advice Service. This is independent of both government and the financial services industry and aims to help people manage their money better by giving clear, unbiased money advice to help people make informed choices.

The service is available by phone or at moneyadviceservice.org.uk. The service provides free and impartial advice on budgeting, saving and borrowing, retirement planning, tax and benefits, but does not recommend specific courses of action, products or providers. It is available for everyone, but is particularly targeted at people who are financially vulnerable and those at key life stages – eg, women who are pregnant. The website contains online tools and planners, including calculators, comparison tables and a financial health check.

Credit unions

A credit union is one way of extending low-cost financial services to local communities. Credit unions are financial co-operatives owned and controlled by their members. Each credit union has a 'common bond' which determines who can become a member – eg, people living or working in a particular area. They offer savings facilities and affordable loans sourced from their members' savings. By law, a credit union cannot charge interest of more than 3 per cent a month (42.6 per cent APR), although the average is 1 per cent a month (12.7 per cent APR). Many now provide current accounts, bill-paying services through budgeting accounts, a facility to allow payment of benefits directly into a credit union account, and savings accounts.

Credit unions, together with advice agencies, offer a range of potentially complementary services which can assist in tackling financial exclusion and overindebtedness. For example, a credit union can help clients gain access to financial services and manage their finances effectively, help and encourage them to save and budget, and may even be able to provide a loan to pay off debts. However, a loan – even at a much lower rate – is not always in a client's best interests and more effective assistance can be provided by money advice.

Some credit unions have an arrangement with their local authority for housing benefit for private-rented properties to be paid directly to the credit union, which in turn forwards the money to the landlord. This ensures the client's rent is paid and avoids arrears.

There are a number of issues to consider when referring clients to a particular credit union. In order to preserve independence, you should make it clear that you are not an agent of the credit union and must not give clients unrealistic expectations of the assistance they can expect from it. Also, make it clear that a referral does not guarantee immediate access to financial services, such as a loan. Credit unions are not charities and should only lend to people who have the capacity to repay. Provided the referral is in the best interests of the client, the fact that s/he may be borrowing to pay off other debts should not be ruled out in all circumstances. Bear in mind that affordable credit is not the only financial service offered by a credit union, and that access to current and savings accounts also promote financial inclusion.

If the client defaults on a loan, the credit union becomes one of the client's non-priority creditors. Most credit unions negotiate debt repayment terms if a client has fallen into financial difficulties, but some tend to refuse low loan repayments (such as token offers) and may decide to impose membership restrictions on other products and services. If not treated as a priority, the client is likely to lose the benefits of membership.

In certain circumstances, a credit union can apply to the Department for Work and Pensions (DWP) to have loans repaid to it through deductions from certain benefits.[26] In order to do this, the credit union must agree that no interest or other charges will be added to the debt following the application. In addition, the client must:

- have failed to make payments as agreed for a period of 13 weeks and not have resumed making those payments;
- have given written permission for the credit union to provide her/his personal data to the DWP;
- not already be having deductions made to pay another eligible lender – ie, another credit union or certain other third-sector lenders;
- not already be having deductions made to repay an overpayment of benefit or a social fund loan.

Government guidance states that lenders must apply to the DWP to join the scheme and prove they meet responsible lending criteria and practice.[27] They must also have taken other reasonable steps to collect the repayments, including having written to the client on three occasions, with the final letter notifying her/him that deductions from benefit will be sought.

Notes

2. Negotiating
1 *FCA Handbook*, CONC 7.12.2R and 7.12.3G
2 *FCA Handbook*, CONC 8.2.2G(2)
3 See also C King, 'CASHflow', *Quarterly Account* 50, IMA

3. Letter writing
4 See C Wright, 'Setting the Standard', *Adviser* 180
5 *FCA Handbook*, CONC 7.2

4. Representing clients in court
6 r39.2 CPR; CPR PD 39, para 1
7 Part 1 CPR; CPR PD 23, para 9
8 For further information, see P Madge, 'Advocacy for Money Advisers', *Adviser* 44

6. Ensuring good practice
9 As in *Roberts v Bank of Scotland* (*Adviser* 160 abstracts)
10 In 2016, the British Bankers' Association published the report *Improving Outcomes for Customers in Vulnerable Circumstances,* identifying nine principles intended to improve outcomes for such customers and featuring a number of case studies. See also M Coppack, 'Are banks doing enough for vulnerable consumers?', *Adviser* 188.
11 In July 2019, the FCA published draft guidance consultation on fair treatment of vulnerable (and potentially vulnerable) customers. The consultation is now closed, and it is understood that the proposed guidance is unlikely to change before it is made final in 2020. See: fca.org.uk/publication/guidance-consultation/gc19-03.pdf.
12 *Ombudsman News 99,* 2012 contains a number of case studies involving debt collection, which are covered in *Arian* 35 caselaw update and *Adviser* 150 abstracts. See also *Ombudsman News* 114, 2013 and *Arian* 47 caselaw update. See also V Seetal, 'Debt Collection Complaints and the Financial Ombudsman Service', *Quarterly Account* 54, IMA.

13 Ministry of Justice, *Taking Control of Goods: national standards*, updated April 2014. Although not legally binding, any relevant paragraphs are useful industry guidance which can be referred to in any complaint. See also *Ali and Aslam v Channel 5 Broadcasting* [2018] EWHC 298 (Ch) at para 54.
14 *FCA Handbook*, CONC 2.10.6G
15 *FCA Handbook*, CONC 2.10.8G
16 *FCA Handbook*, CONC 2.10.11G
17 *FCA Handbook*, CONC 2.10.12G
18 *FCA Handbook*, CONC 2.10.14G
19 *FCA Handbook*, CONC 7.2.1R and 7.2.2G
20 This was originally published in April 2014 and expanded to cover vulnerability more widely to reflect the FCA's increasing attention to this issue.
21 Originally published in November 2007, the current (third) edition was published in 2015.
22 *FCA Handbook*, CONC 7.2.3G
23 A recommended form of words agreed by the credit reference agencies is at para 4.16 of the guidelines.
24 See C Trend, C Fitch and A Sharp, 'Debt and Mental Health: tools of the trade', *Adviser* 160

7. Budgeting advice
25 HM Treasury, *Financial Capability: the government's long-term approach*, 2007
26 Sch 9 para 7C SS(C&P) Regs
27 Available at gov.uk/government/publications/eligible-loan-deduction-scheme

Chapter 3

Stages of debt advice

This chapter summarises the nine stages essential to debt advice and shows how they link together as a single process. It covers:
1. Exploring the debt problem (below)
2. Dealing with urgent issues (p44)
3. Listing creditors and minimising debts (p45)
4. Listing and maximising income (p48)
5. Listing expenditure (p50)
6. Dealing with priority debts (p54)
7. Drawing up a financial statement (p55)
8. Choosing a strategy for non-priority debts (p58)
9. Implementing the chosen strategies (p58)

1. Exploring the debt problem

Debt advisers must create a trusting and safe environment in which the client can talk about her/his personal and financial affairs. This may take some time to develop, but should start at the beginning of the process, when you make it clear that any information the client provides will be treated in confidence, that you will not judge her/him and are on her/his side.

Explain the role and boundaries of the agency (eg, that it does not offer court representation), what you can and cannot do and why. Obtain as much detail as possible about the client, other members of the household, the debts and the financial situation. It is important to make the client feel as comfortable as possible so that s/he feels able to provide the detailed information needed to advise her/him properly. When collecting information, you are not intruding unnecessarily into the client's affairs, but you need that information to help her/him decide a strategy and/or negotiate with creditors. It is, therefore, important to tell the client that such information is confidential and explain how the agency's confidentiality principles operate. Often, people seek advice about a specific debt and are reluctant to discuss other debts they are managing to pay or if they feel the creditor has been particularly helpful. However, it is often impossible to deal with a particular debt in isolation. This stage can therefore include a discussion of the whole position.[1]

Advisers should gain an understanding of what has led to the client's debt situation (often a change of circumstances) and whether the situation is likely to be temporary or long term. They should also enquire about any potential future changes that may impact on the client's available debt solutions – eg, expected changes in income and/or outgoings due to the birth of a baby, retirement, redundancy or relationship breakdown.

Obtaining information from the client

Obtain as much information as possible from the client on all her/his debts at the first interview, and record this in a clear and concise manner. In practice, many clients do not bring all the required information at the outset and so much of it may have to be obtained later, possibly from other sources – eg, from a client's creditors for outstanding balances or credit reference agencies for details of the client's creditors. It is also worth checking to see whether there are any previous case notes which have been closed to ensure that a full picture of the client's situation is obtained.

If you are conducting the first interview by telephone, the client must subsequently bring or send any information to the advice agency (and a signed authority to act obtained before creditors can be contacted).

It is essential to obtain sufficient information at the earliest opportunity, as otherwise:
- income/expenditure details and, consequently, the financial statement may be inaccurate and payment offers unsustainable, leading to the client's failing to maintain the arrangement;
- you may give incorrect advice, leading the client to choose one option when another option might have been more appropriate;
- opportunities to maximise income may be lost.

Use a pro forma to record the information, which could also remind you what to ask the client in order to establish the full facts of the case. An example of a pro forma is in the Money and Pensions Service (MaPS) Good Practice Toolkit, available in the Networking and Information Sharing project resources directory on the Institute of Money Advisers website, i-m-a.org.uk. Clients often only reveal the debts they are worried about. It is therefore important that you go through all their priority commitments, whether or not they are in arrears, and then move on to the non-priority commitments. Advice could be given in each area on the consequences should the client default. Be realistic about the outcome and be honest with the client at all times.

Check that any agreements have been drawn up correctly and ensure any applicable time limits are complied with.

The first letter after the interview should confirm all the advice given, the client's options and their consequences. Outline the agreed action and the expected timescale. The MaPS Good Practice Toolkit contains examples of template confirmation of advice letters.

Keep clients informed and involved at each stage, so that they will be able to deal with the case themselves once the case is closed. Remind the client to keep you informed of any change in circumstances throughout the life of the case.

Once all the work is completed on the case, send a closure letter, detailing the work carried out and the outcome, and giving general advice on how to deal with the various creditors in the future.

2. Dealing with urgent issues

There is usually something that triggers a client in financial difficulties to seek debt advice. Often this is an emergency situation and is the first matter raised by the client with an adviser (the 'presenting issue'). After the administrative preliminaries have been carried out in accordance with the agency's policies and procedures (including the Money and Pensions Service (MaPS) common initial assessment, where appropriate – see p13), you should always check whether there is an emergency, regardless of whether or not the client has already referred to it.

An emergency is a situation that will have a detrimental effect on the client if it is not dealt with immediately. In relation to debt, this is a threat to the client's home, essential goods and services or her/his liberty. When considering whether goods or services are essential, you should always take the client's personal circumstances into account.

Examples of an emergency include the following.
- Bailiffs have either threatened to visit the client's home, or have already visited and have threatened to return and/or remove goods.
- The client is facing the imminent loss of essential goods – eg, if hire purchase goods are about to be repossessed.
- The client is about to be evicted from her/his home.
- The client is about to lose an essential service – eg, her/his fuel supply is about to be disconnected.
- A warrant has been issued for the client's arrest – eg, for non-payment of a fine.
- The client has been served with a statutory demand or creditor's petition (see p471 and p473), or other enforcement action has been taken through the courts and there is a deadline for responding.
- The client is unable to buy essential items or pay essential bills – eg, because money has been, or is about to be, taken from her/his bank account.

In many cases, immediate action is required and so there is not sufficient time to explore the client's situation in detail. If you are unable to provide the necessary assistance and/or advice to deal with the client's situation, you may need to refer her/him to another agency. In other cases, a phone call to the person dealing with the case is usually needed to ask for the matter to be put on hold while you make the necessary enquiries to enable you to give the client proper advice. For example, in the case of credit debts, creditors should allow a 30-day breathing space.[2] If possible, let the person know when you expect to be able to contact her/him again.

Sometimes creditors insist on an offer being made at this stage. Although you should try to avoid having to do so, if necessary you can prepare a 'quick and dirty' budget on which to base an offer, but should make it clear that this is subject to a full assessment of the client's financial situation. You should ensure that the client is clear on what action(s) s/he is required to take (if any) and the timescale.

For more information on how to deal with common emergency situations, see p237.

3. **Listing creditors and minimising debts**

After obtaining the client's personal and background details, including any health or disability issues, vulnerability or mental health problems, you then need the details of the debts and the creditors, including those with no arrears or creditors with whom the client has already negotiated lower payments.

A client may not have all the necessary information with her/him on the first visit to enable you to complete the creditor list. It is therefore important to agree how the missing information will be collected, by whom and when. The client's credit reference file may be a useful information-gathering tool if the client has no, or incomplete, paperwork.

The creditors

Record the following details about the client's creditors.

- **The name, address and telephone number of each creditor.** Exact company names are important, as the proliferation of credit has led to a number of creditors with very similar names.
- **Account/reference numbers.** Most creditors use reference numbers to access information about their clients, so these must be included.
- **Letter references and contact details.** If the client has received correspondence from the company, any letter reference should be noted, together with any contact details.
- **Agents' details.** Solicitors or commercial debt collectors are often used. Record details of these (and their references) separately. Record details of the person who has made most recent contact with the client. Check whether the collector has actually bought the debt (in which case s/he is now the creditor) or whether

the agent is acting on behalf of the original creditor (in which case s/he is accountable to that creditor). Creditors should inform clients when debts are either passed on to collectors or sold to third parties.

The debts

Note the following details about the client's debts.

- **Age of debt.** Find out when any credit was first granted. The length of time the agreement has run or a bill has been unpaid can be a factor in negotiation (and might even be grounds for challenging the debt). For instance, a creditor is more likely to be sympathetic if payments have been made for some time than if a new agreement is breached. The legal position on some agreements depends on when they were made. See p71 for credit agreements made before 6 April 2007. An old debt may also be 'statute-barred' – ie, unenforceable through the courts (see p292).
- **Reason for debt.** It is important to ask the reason for the debt – eg, to refute suggestions that the debt was unreasonably incurred.
- **Priority of the debt.** Note whether the debt is a priority or a non-priority. Chapter 8 explains the criteria for making this decision. If possible, check any documents or agreements to confirm this information, as clients can be unsure or may describe debts incorrectly – eg, 'hire purchase' is often used to mean 'credit sale agreement', and 'parking fine' is often used to mean 'parking charge', but they have different legal consequences (see Chapter 5).
- **The written agreement.** Check whether the debt is based on a written agreement and, if so, whether or not the client has seen it and if it has been photocopied for future reference. Ensure agreements are checked for defects that may affect their enforceability. Obtain a copy from the creditor if necessary. If there is no written agreement, it might be unenforceable. See Chapters 6 and 10 for more information.
- **Liability.** Check whether the client is responsible for the debt. Note in whose name(s) agreements were made and/or whose name(s) is/are on the bill (although this is not necessarily conclusive). This may either be the client alone, the client and a partner, or a friend or relative who acted as a guarantor. This ensures that all debts listed can be challenged where appropriate. See Chapter 6 for more information.
- **Payments.** Note:
  - the amount currently owing. State whether the figure is approximate or exact;
  - contractual payments under any original agreement and any subsequent amendment to them;
  - the existence of arrears in payments, although initially these need only be approximate;
  - the payment method.

The client may need advice about coping with doorstep collectors, changing or cancelling standing orders, direct debit arrangements or continuous payment authorities, or opening a new bank or building society account (see p54) if the current bank or building society is one of the client's creditors. However, a client should not be advised to stop or reduce contractual payments to creditors before a repayment arrangement is agreed with them, unless it is clearly in her/his best interests to do so – eg, if s/he has insufficient available income after meeting essential expenditure and/or making payments to priority creditors (see Chapter 8). When deciding what expenditure, goods and services are 'essential', you should always consider the client's personal circumstances. The date and amount of the last payment made are needed, especially for priority debts, to assess the urgency of any action.

- **Insurance cover.** Many people take out insurance (known as payment protection insurance) with a mortgage or credit agreement – eg, against sickness, death and redundancy. Sometimes, such insurance is given by the creditor as part of the contract. Always check whether a particular debt is insured and that the insurance has been correctly sold, so that this important way of minimising the debt is not overlooked (see p164).

The threats

You need to know the status of the debt – ie, what the creditor has already done to obtain repayment of the debt and what threat is posed to the client by the recovery action.

- **Warnings.** The first stage of recovery action is normally a reminder letter. Record the date of this. The exact details of further action should be noted. For example, regulated credit agreements (see p62) may require a default notice to be served before any further action is taken. Other creditors must issue different warnings – eg, a notice of a proposed disconnection of fuel or notice of an intention to seek possession of the client's home.
- **Court action.** If court action has begun, a claim form will have been issued. The date and type of claim should always be recorded. Record the court case number. Refer to the claim form to note whether a solicitor is now acting for the creditor. If so, you must deal with the solicitor, rather than the creditor, until further notice. If a date for a hearing has been set, this should be noted. In many cases, a court will already have made an order and details of the judgment, including its date, the payment or action ordered, and the time or amounts required, should be recorded. See Chapters 10, 11 and 12 for further information on court action, including what action should be taken if a judgment has been made.
- **Enforcement action.** After judgment, enforcement can mean bailiffs' action (see Chapter 14), a third-party debt order (see p332), an attachment of earnings

order (see p329) or a charging order (see p322). Note whether any of these have begun, with dates and full details.

Action to be taken

- **By the client.** Any action required of a client relating to a particular debt should be noted on the list – eg, 'get exact balance'. This section will normally be completed once the strategy has been decided.
- **By the adviser.** Record the action required on each debt. This can be crossed through when it has been carried out. If the case is complex and likely to involve a lot of work, prepare a case plan, summarising the action to be taken, who is responsible for any action and the timetable.

4. Listing and maximising income

After identifying and dealing with any emergencies and obtaining details of the client's creditors (including checking liability), the next stage is to list all possible income for the client and, if applicable, her/his family.

Whose income to include

Creditors are likely to expect the income and debts of a couple (particularly if they are married or civil partners) to be dealt with together, although there is no basis in law for this expectation (unless they are jointly liable for the debt). The overriding consideration must be the best interests of the client – the final decision rests with her/him.

A decision must eventually be made about whether to include the income of a partner or spouse or, rarely, someone else living in the client's household (although any contribution s/he makes to the household expenditure shown in the financial statement must be taken into account). This depends on several factors.

- If all the debts are in the name of one person only (or are in the joint names of the client and a previous partner) and s/he has little or no income or property against which action could be taken, the other person may be unwilling to contribute from her/his income.
- If one person has a number of debts and a partner also has a number of debts, it might be more convenient to deal with both partners' debts in one set of strategies.
- If only one person has sought advice without the knowledge of her/his partner, find out why and encourage both partners to be involved. The person who seeks advice may not know details of her/his partner's income or may not want her/his partner to know about the debts – eg, if s/he fears violence from her/him. If there is a jointly owned property, it is important to stress the possibility

of a creditor applying for a charging order and, as the court contacts the client's partner, the likelihood of her/his finding out.

- Many partners wish to pool their income and help with each other's debts, irrespective of their legal liability – eg, if they themselves could face dire consequences (eg, eviction) if they failed to do so or if all members of the household have benefited from the debt being incurred. At this stage it is, therefore, important to note the income of all household members if possible, so that a decision can be made later about which to use to implement any strategy.

What income to include

- All benefits and tax credits. **Note:** a client may decide not to use any disability benefit s/he gets (eg, personal independence payment, disability living allowance and attendance allowance) to make payments to creditors, as these benefits are intended to meet only the additional costs of disability. However, any disability benefit should be included in the list of income and in the financial statement. Usually, the disability benefit is offset by associated items of expenditure, such as mobility or care costs.

  The decision whether or not to use any unallocated disability benefit to make offers to her/his creditors is ultimately the client's, not the adviser's.

  The fact that the client is in receipt of a disability benefit should always be disclosed to creditors, as the fact that s/he is a disabled person is likely to be a relevant factor.

- Earnings – ie, net pay from full-time and part-time work.
- Self-employed earnings, net of estimated tax and national insurance contributions.
- Regular maintenance/child support payments received. Include for what and for whom they are paid.
- Investment income – eg, from savings.
- Contributions from other household members – eg, adult children living with the client.
- Occupational and other pensions.

If income has recently been unusually high or low, this should be noted and the basis on which it is assessed should be clear – eg, the average of wage slips for a representative period. Only include regular sources of income, as any offer of payment must be realistic and sustainable.

The Financial Conduct Authority (FCA) requires advisers to take reasonable steps to verify the client's income. It says that what is reasonable depends on the circumstances and the type of service the agency offers.[3] For instance, advisers working at court duty desks or providing telephone or email advice will, in practice, be unable to do this.

Verifying the client's income may also disclose that deductions are being made to pay off debts – eg, benefit or tax credit overpayments that the client has not previously disclosed, because s/he did not regard this as a 'debt'. It is usually possible to ask the creditor to reduce the rate of deductions where it can be demonstrated that these are currently unaffordable and are leaving the client unable to meet her/his essential expenditure.

Note any future changes to the client's income and/or circumstances, such as any benefits recently claimed but not yet awarded, or if a member of the household is about to start or end paid employment.

Capital

The client may have capital or potential capital in the form of realisable property or other assets that would be reasonable for her/him to use. Discuss this with her/him and make a separate note of any such items. Unless the circumstances are exceptional, creditors are unlikely to accept that a client is unable to pay her/his debts if s/he has capital, and may even refuse to accept nil or token offers of payment if they believe it would be reasonable to expect her/him to dispose of an asset.

Clients who are aged 55 or over may be entitled to take money out of their pension and may consider using some, or all, of this to either pay off their debts in full or make an offer in full and final settlement (see p119). A client considering this should be advised to obtain financial advice first – eg, from Pension Wise. S/he must consider how much s/he will receive after tax has been deducted and whether s/he will have enough money left for her/his retirement. FCA rules prohibit creditors from pressurising clients to raise funds to repay a debt, with specific reference to raising a lump sum from a pension scheme.[4]

Maximising the client's income

Follow the advice in Chapter 7 to maximise the amount of money the client has coming in. Also check whether the client is eligible for a Warm Home Discount and whether s/he would benefit from switching the supplier. Check whether the client is eligible for a grant from local or national charities or an energy company.

5. Listing expenditure

The next stage of the debt advice process is to list everything on which the client is currently spending her/his income. The client's expenditure should include the items listed on p52.

The budget sheets used with the standard financial statement (see p56) are comprehensive and useful as a checklist to ensure that nothing is missed. Most people spend money on different items in different periods of time, and it is important to standardise everything to a particular period – generally weekly or monthly. Predictable events such as Christmas, birthdays, holidays or school trips are not unreasonable items of expenditure, but they must be budgeted for.

The Financial Conduct Authority requires advisers to take reasonable steps to verify the client's expenditure and ask for explanations not only of any expenditure that is particularly high but also of any expenditure that is particularly low, but says that estimates are acceptable if precise figures are not available. Alternatively, industry-recognised standard expenditure guidelines (eg, the standard financial statement's spending guidelines (see p57)) can be used as an indicator of the client's outgoings, if appropriate. However, the client's individual circumstances must still be taken into account.[5] Although standard figures should not be used if actual figures or accurate estimates are available, they are useful as a 'benchmark' against which to test the client's level of expenditure and as a tool with which to challenge creditors who claim that the client's expenditure is too high.

By this stage, it should be clear why the debts have arisen, and how the client's circumstances have led to her/his financial difficulties. This information is essential when negotiating with creditors.

At this stage, you can also discuss overall income and expenditure with the client. Investigate examples of unusually high levels of surplus income (which may indicate that items of essential expenditure have been underestimated or possibly omitted altogether) as well as deficit budgets (which may well be due to low household income or deductions from income to pay debts, but could also indicate that income has been underestimated or possibly omitted altogether). Use Chapter 7 to increase her/his income wherever possible, and discuss which, if any, items of spending could be reduced, either permanently or temporarily. This should be done in a sensitive and non-judgemental way, and any items of high or unusual expenditure should be explained to creditors in a covering letter. Clients are not required, and should not be expected, to live on the breadline and are entitled to a reasonable standard of living. However, although it is not part of the adviser's role to dictate to clients how to spend their money, clients should be warned that excessive expenditure is likely to be challenged by creditors. If you know that creditors are likely to challenge an item of expenditure and it cannot be justified, point this out to the client and explain that, as a consequence, creditors or the court are unlikely to accept the client's offer based on it. In addition, be aware of what a court may consider reasonable for the client to spend on a particular item if it is being asked to agree to the client paying the debt at a particular rate – especially, for example, in possession proceedings where the client's home is at risk (see Chapter 12).

See Chapter 6 for information on how to minimise debts.

Items of expenditure

Housing

Costs include:

- rent/mortgage repayments;
- other secured loan repayments (there may be several);
- council tax;
- water charges;
- ground rent;
- service charges;
- an amount for household repairs and maintenance, based on a full year's expenditure if possible;
- household insurance for both buildings and contents;
- any insurance linked to a mortgage, if not already included in mortgage expenses.

Childcare

Full-time childcare may cost over £200 a week. Help with these costs may be available. See gov.uk/help-with-childcare-costs.

Fuel

Fuel costs include charges for electricity, gas and other fuels. Take an annual cost and divide it into weekly or monthly figures.

If payments to fuel suppliers include an amount for items other than fuel (eg, payment for a cooker), these should be deducted and only the fuel expenditure listed here.

Furniture and bedding

Costs should be separately itemised. This item may require research by the client or discussion with others with whom s/he lives.

Health costs

Costs include:

- prescriptions;
- dentistry;
- optical charges.

These are often high and you should check the client's entitlement to reduced or free treatment, and free prescriptions.

Transport

Costs include:

- public transport;

- the cost of owning a car or motorbike. In this case, the amount spent on tax, insurance, repairs, MOT and petrol should be included. If a car is essential (eg, for travel to work), the cost of its hire purchase (but not any credit sale) agreement should be included, with a note to explain why the item is essential.

Hire purchase
The hire purchase or conditional sale costs of any items that are essential for the individual family to own should be included, if their loss would cause serious problems – eg, a washing machine.

Fines
Instalments payable on fines should be included. See Chapter 13 for ways of reducing these.

Laundry and dry cleaning
Costs should be averaged over the previous couple of months.

Telephone, television and broadband
These costs should be converted into weekly or monthly figures.

Other household items, toiletries and food
The adviser should ensure that the individual circumstances of the client dictate the amount allowed for these items. Other household items, toiletries and food include:
- housekeeping;
- cleaning materials;
- meals outside the home, such as school lunches or canteen meals;
- expenses incurred in children going to school or being given pocket money;
- nappies and baby items.

Clothing and shoes
These are often bought seasonally and so costs must be estimated annually and divided. It is important to include all small items in this category.

Gifts, charitable donations, and religious and cultural activities
Costs include:
- donations that are an essential part of a person's membership of a religious community;
- classes for children in religious institutions (particularly mosques).

This is potentially a sensitive area. If a person is committed to such payments, they should be protected to ensure that debt does not further exclude individuals or families from community life and support.

Other costs

Other costs include:

- maintenance/child support payments;
- self-employment costs not taken into account when calculating the client's net income;
- spending for exceptional circumstances – eg, special diets or extra heating because of illness. Apparent 'luxury' items need to be explained.

Bank accounts

It may be necessary to advise the client to change the bank account into which her/his wages are paid to prevent the bank (a non-priority creditor) taking control of her/his income by exercising its 'right of set-off'.[6] If a client finds it difficult to open another account (eg, because of her/his credit reference details), s/he may find the Money Advice Service list of basic bank accounts useful. See moneyadviceservice.org.uk/en/articles/basic-bank-accounts.

If it is not possible to open a new bank account immediately, the client may have to consider exercising what is known as the 'first right of appropriation'.[7] This gives an account holder the right to earmark funds paid into the account to be used for specific purposes. This process can also be useful as a temporary measure on overdrawn accounts in order to prevent the bank from appropriating the funds to the debit balance.

The client should inform the bank in writing (before funds are paid in) specifically where they should be applied – ie, how much and to whom. The bank must honour such instructions, but it will continue to charge interest on the overdraft and may refuse to undertake further transactions.

6. Dealing with priority debts

The next stage of the debt advice process is to deal with those debts that are described as priorities. See Chapter 8 for more on this. This ensures that the threat of homelessness, the loss of goods or services or the threat of imprisonment is removed. It is essential that arrangements for dealing with these debts are negotiated at this stage so that any extra payments for priority debts can be included in the expenditure details before they become part of a financial statement (see p55).

However, a financial statement may be needed when negotiating priority debts, and this stage of the process can therefore overlap with Stage seven below.

Explain each available strategy, along with its advantages or disadvantages, to the client. S/he may need to consult with a partner or other family member, and strategy information may need to be written down. Once agreed, you can then implement the strategy by negotiation or a court application and the client must carry out her/his own agreed course of action – eg, start paying rent or set up direct debits. You must always confirm with the creditor, in writing, a strategy agreed verbally, and request an acknowledgement confirming this. Advise the client to start making any agreed payments immediately and not wait for confirmation from the creditor.

7. Drawing up a financial statement

A financial statement is an essential document. It summarises information in a standard form and allows you to present this to a creditor (or court) in a structured way. A carefully drawn-up financial statement is probably your most important negotiating tool, as it forms the justification for any repayment proposal as well as for any request for non-payment.

A financial statement should present a sufficiently clear and complete picture of the individual (or family), her/his income and expenditure, details of her/his creditors and whether there is any surplus income with which to pay those creditors. It must be based on a true and accurate assessment of the client's circumstances, and any offers made must be realistic and sustainable. Provided it is stored electronically, it is easy to amend the statement as circumstances change. It can also be a useful budgeting tool for the client as, in many cases, it may be the first time s/he has reviewed her/his income and expenditure.

A financial statement based on either the income and expenditure of a single person or the joint income and expenditure of the client and her/his partner should be fairly straightforward to prepare. More care is needed if it is based on the individual income and expenditure of a client who is a member of a couple. You may need to look at the household budget as a whole to get a clear picture of how things are arranged between the members of the household, rather than just splitting figures 50:50, or apportioning them on some other basis, as a matter of course. The financial statement should always reflect what happens in practice. For instance, if the client pays all the household bills from her/his own income and contributions from other members of the household, the financial statement should be drawn up on this basis. However, in many cases it is not possible to identify who pays what because all income is pooled. In such cases, expenditure should be apportioned proportionately to income.

The Financial Conduct Authority (FCA) recommends using the 'common financial statement' (even though it is no longer in use) or an equivalent or similar statement.[8] Many agencies now use the standard financial statement, which replaced it (see p56). If an agency does not use this, FCA guidance recommends that the format of any financial statement sent to creditors should be uniform and logically structured in a way that encourages consistent responses from creditors and reduces queries and delays.

Advisers should use all the information from the previous stages of the debt advice process outlined in this chapter when preparing the financial statement. It should include:

- the basis on which it was prepared. For example, 'This financial statement has been prepared on the basis of information submitted by:
  Mr A Client
  123 High Street
  London SW1 1ZZ';
- the members of the household whose income and outgoings are being considered together;
- a breakdown of all the income for the individual or household;
- a list of expenditure under the headings used in Stage five plus expenditure to deal with priority debts. Certain types of expenditure may be best to combine – eg, cigarettes are probably best included in 'other household items, toiletries and food' rather than on their own. No expenditure is shown for debts other than those that have been defined as priorities;
- a comparison of income and expenditure. In some cases, the financial statement may show there is more income than expenditure. Such excess income should be calculated in the statement and described as available income. If expenditure already equals or exceeds income, the available income should be stated as none. In many cases, expenditure exceeds income. This may be because amounts have been included that are not actually spent, but are what should be spent if the client were able to do so. Whatever the reason, be prepared to explain if challenged by creditors.

Explain in a covering letter any unusual items of expenditure and any special circumstances or needs – eg, whether any member of the household has a disability.

It is good practice to ask the client to check and sign the financial statement to confirm that it is accurate to the best of her/his knowledge.

The common financial statement

The common financial statement was an initiative of the Money Advice Trust and British Bankers' Association and has been replaced by the standard financial statement. The common financial statement was withdrawn on 1 April 2018.

The standard financial statement

On 1 March 2017, the standard financial statement was introduced to replace the common financial statement.[9]

The standard financial statement was developed by the Money Advice Service in conjunction with major advice providers and creditors to provide a universal income and expenditure statement and a single set of expenditure or spending guidelines. The spending guidelines are updated on the first Monday in April each year. The aim of the standard financial statement is to bring a greater degree of consistency to the debt advice process and for it to be accepted by a broader range of creditors than accepted the common financial statement – eg, the Insolvency Service. The standard financial statement consists of:

- a budget form containing a detailed list of income and expenditure;
- a two-page financial statement summarising the information obtained from the client and recorded in the income and expenditure sheets;
- standard spending guidelines for three sets of expenditure (communications and leisure; food and housekeeping; and personal costs). These are known as 'flexible costs', and the 'spending guidelines' are those which are considered reasonable for particular types of household;
- a detailed user guide, including a checklist of the types of expenditure that can be included in the flexible costs categories;
- a requirement for agencies to obtain a membership code number, which must be entered on the statement. Agencies can obtain this by completing an online application form and agreeing to the standard financial statement code of conduct.

The main differences between the common financial statement and the standard financial statement are the following.

- There are more specific fields (eg, there is a separate category for health costs), which largely replace the 'Other' category in the common financial statement and which should provide greater transparency.
- The common financial statement categories which had 'trigger figures' were 'travel', 'housekeeping', 'phone' and 'other'. The standard financial statement only has three categories with 'spending guidelines': 'housekeeping', 'personal' and 'communications and leisure'; consequently, some items of expenditure now fall into different categories.
- There is a separate 'savings' category, which allows the client to save up to 10 per cent of her/his available income (ie, the amount available to offer to creditors) up to a maximum of £20 a month (for both single people and couples). **Note:** the Insolvency Service debt relief order team has confirmed that it will not accept a savings element as an item of essential expenditure and standard financial statement guidance states that payments to priority creditors should take precedence over savings.

If the client's expenditure exceeds the guidelines, advisers are required to provide a 'meaningful' explanation to 'enable consideration of exceptional circumstances'. Creditors have committed not to challenge financial statements where expenditure falls within spending guidelines and to accept an adviser's reasonable explanations, unless they have reasonable cause to believe that the client's financial statement may be incomplete or inaccurate. *The Standards of Lending*

Practice and the *Finance and Leasing Association Lending Code* (see p33) state that if an offer of payment is made via the standard financial statement, this should be used as the basis for pro rata distribution among the client's creditors (*The Standards of Lending Practice*) or as the basis for negotiating a repayment arrangement (*Finance and Leasing Association Lending Code*).

8. **Choosing a strategy for non-priority debts**

You should know from the financial statement whether or not there is any available income or capital and of any likely changes in the client's circumstances. At this stage, you should use these factors to decide a strategy for all non-priority debts.[10] See Chapter 9 for more information.

The starting point should be what the client wants, but you must give her/him the full range of available options so that s/he can make an informed choice. All your advice should be accurate, timely, appropriate to the client's individual situation and in her/his best interests. Where the clients are members of a couple, a strategy which is suitable for one member of the couple may be unsuitable for the other member, requiring different strategies to be considered.

If the chosen strategy is to offer payments to creditors, advise the client to start making any payments offered immediately and not wait for confirmation from the creditor. If the creditor does not confirm that interest/charges have been frozen, press the creditor for a decision. If the creditor refuses to freeze interest/charges, ask for specific reasons and either urge the creditor to reconsider the decision or review the strategy with the client. If you think the creditor is not treating the client 'with forbearance and due consideration' in line with Financial Conduct Authority requirements, discuss with the client whether or not to complain.

By the end of this stage, the client will have made an informed choice of the strategy that is most likely to resolve her/his debt problem.

9. **Implementing the chosen strategies**

Although you may have done some work with the client to deal with emergencies and other issues requiring immediate action, it is only when all the information is available and decisions have been made that the major work of implementing a debt advice strategy begins. Unless the client has chosen a formal debt solution (see Chapter 15), this is done by communicating with creditors by letter, telephone, email or sometimes in person or via the courts.

If a strategy is rejected for no apparent reason, contact the creditor(s) and specifically request the reason(s). Creditors usually reject clients' proposals for the following reasons.

- Insufficient information has been provided. Provide additional information/ evidence to enable the creditor to understand the client's financial situation.
- The creditor has conflicting or different information. Clarify the position and point out that the creditor is incorrect – eg, because the client's circumstances have changed since the creditor obtained its information.
- The chosen strategy is inappropriate – eg, it is based on incorrect information. Consider the alternatives.
- The creditor's collection policies do not permit the proposal to be accepted. Either try to persuade the creditor to treat the client's situation 'with forbearance and due consideration'[11] on an individual basis or consider whether there might be a more specific challenge. For example, the Financial Conduct Authority's (FCA's) *Consumer Credit Sourcebook* requires creditors not to pressurise clients to pay a debt in a single payment or in unreasonably large amounts if this would have an adverse impact on the client's financial circumstances, or to raise money to pay the debt by selling her/his property, borrowing money or increasing existing borrowing.[12]
- The creditor's collection system cannot deal with the proposal – eg, the case cannot be transferred to its debt recovery section until there are at least three months' arrears. Deal with a more senior person who is authorised to handle the proposal or to transfer the case to someone who can.
- The client has a poor payment record or history of broken payment arrangements. Point out that previous payment arrangements were unrealistic and that the current proposals are not only realistic but sustainable.
- Items on the financial statement are disputed. Either explain or justify them, and use supporting evidence where available.
- The creditor wants more money. Ask the creditor where the additional money is to be found, given that other creditors are likely to object to having their payments reduced. Also point out that creditors should allow the client reasonable time and opportunity to repay the debt.[13]
- The creditor is determined to take court action. Point out that parties are expected to act reasonably and to avoid unnecessary court proceedings. If the matter goes to court, the judge, not the creditor, decides the rate of payment (see Chapter 11). In addition, creditors should not threaten court action in order to pressurise a client to pay more than s/he can reasonably afford.[14]
- The creditor will not deal with the agency. Point out that this is a breach of the FCA's guidelines and so could be the subject of a complaint.[15]

Some reasons for rejection could also amount to a breach of a code of practice. If appropriate, you should find out what trade association a creditor belongs to (see p26) and check with the relevant code of practice – eg, *The Standards of Lending Practice*. You should also familiarise yourself with the FCA's *Consumer Credit Sourcebook*. Complaints under a code or the FCA rules and/or guidance can be made to the Financial Ombudsman Service (see p284) or to the FCA. See Appendix 1 for details of these organisations.

If a creditor rejects a client's proposal for repayment, the client should usually make the payments regardless. If the client decides not to pay, you should be able to demonstrate there was a good reason for this and that it was in the client's best interests.[16]

Notes

1. **Exploring the debt problem**
   1 See also W McShane, 'Debt Exploration Part 1', *Adviser* 178 and 'Debt Exploration Part 2', *Adviser* 179

2. **Dealing with urgent issues**
   2 *FCA Handbook*, CONC 7.3.11R and 7.3.12G. Sections 6-8 of the Financial Guidance and Claims Act 2018 provide for a 'debt respite scheme', including a 'breathing space' to encourage people in debt to seek professional debt advice. Clients working with a debt advice agency will be protected from recovery and enforcement action by their creditors for 60 days, during which period interest will be frozen. It is understood that debts to central and local government (including council tax arrears) will be covered by the scheme, which is expected to be introduced in 2021.

4. **Listing and maximising income**
   3 *FCA Handbook*, CONC 8.5.4R and 8.5.5G
   4 *FCA Handbook*, CONC 7.3.10 and 7.3.10A

5. **Listing expenditure**
   5 *FCA Handbook*, CONC 8.5.4R and 8.5.5G
   6 See also S Edwards, 'Of Some Account?', *Adviser* 173
   7 See also J Wilson, 'First Right of Appropriation', *Adviser* 98

7. **Drawing up a financial statement**
   8 *FCA Handbook*, CONC 8.5.2G
   9 See also G Harvey, 'Standard Financial Statement', *Quarterly Account* 43, IMA

8. **Choosing a strategy for non-priority debts**
   10 See also L Oliver, 'Using Deficit Budgets', *Adviser* 180

9. **Implementing the chosen strategies**
   11 The phrase 'with forbearance and due consideration' is used in *FCA Handbook*, CONC 7.3.4R and replaces the phrase 'sympathetically and positively', which was used in various guidance codes of practice but never defined. CONC 7.3.6G contains examples of what the FCA regards as treating clients with forbearance, but note that this list is not exhaustive.
   12 *FCA Handbook*, CONC 7.3.10R
   13 *FCA Handbook*, CONC 7.3.6G
   14 *FCA Handbook*, CONC 7.3.18R
   15 *FCA Handbook*, CONC 7.12.2R
   16 *FCA Handbook*, CONC 8.6.1R

Chapter 4

Consumer credit

This chapter covers:
1. Introduction (below)
2. Authorising traders (below)
3. Regulated agreements (p62)

1. Introduction

Most clients seen by a debt adviser are likely to have at least some credit debts. Many clients only have credit debts and the majority of these are likely to be regulated by the Consumer Credit Act 1974. In addition, the Financial Services and Markets Act 2000 regulates many credit-related activities. It is, therefore, essential for a debt adviser to be familiar with this legislation.

Both Acts provide protection by:
- authorising traders (see below);
- regulating credit agreements (see p62);
- providing sanctions for non-compliance (see pp65–74);
- exercising judicial control – eg, time orders and unfair relationships (see Chapters 6, 8 and 12).

2. Authorising traders

Since 1 April 2014, all businesses must be authorised by the Financial Conduct Authority (FCA) to offer consumer credit (including credit broking) or to undertake activities in relation to debts due under a credit agreement, including debt collection and debt advice. These are all known as 'consumer credit activities'. For further information on authorisation, see fca.org.uk/publication/finalised-guidance/consumer-credit-being-regulated-guide.pdf.

You can check whether a firm is authorised at fca.org.uk/firms/financial-services-register. It is a criminal offence to carry out a debt-related activity without the appropriate authorisation. You can report firms that do not have appropriate authorisation or which are not authorised to the FCA Helpline (tel: 0800 111 6768).

An unauthorised firm or individual can become an 'appointed representative' of an authorised business as an alternative to being authorised itself/her/himself.[1] An appointed representative carries out regulated activities under the supervision of the authorised business, which must must take full responsibility for ensuring that the appointed representative complies with FCA requirements.[2]

You can find consumer credit rules and guidance in the *Consumer Credit Sourcebook*, which is part of the *FCA Handbook*, at handbook.fca.org.uk/handbook. Clients can complain to the creditor or debt collector about any contraventions, refer them to the Financial Ombudsman Service where appropriate, and report them to the FCA.

Note: since 21 March 2016, most secured loans are now covered by the rules and guidance in the *Mortgages and Home Finance: Conduct of Business Sourcebook*. This is a separate part of the *FCA Handbook* (see p114).

3. **Regulated agreements**

Most credit agreements that you will come across are regulated by the Consumer Credit Act 1974. Such agreements are known as 'regulated credit agreements'. There are, however, some important exceptions (see below).

An agreement must be made by the creditor with one or more 'individuals' or clients and the credit must be given in the course of the creditor's business. If the agreement was made on or after 6 April 2007, an 'individual' does not include partnerships comprising more than three people. If a client borrows money for a business, provided s/he is not a limited company, this is still classed as lending to an individual.

Exempt agreements

Agreements that are not regulated (and are, therefore, exempt) include:[3]
- agreements providing credit of more than £25,000 (if made before 6 April 2008) or £15,000 (if made before 1 May 1998);
- agreements made on or after 21 March 2016 for the purpose of acquiring or retaining property rights in land or in an existing or projected building, and where the borrower is a consumer – ie, acting outside her/his business, trade or profession;
- 'small agreements' not exceeding £50 – eg, vouchers;
- 'non-commercial agreements' not made in the course of business – eg, agreements between friends;
- some low interest rate credit, including loans to employees from their employers;

- agreements involving goods or services repayable in no more than four instalments in 12 months – ie, normal trade credit, for example payable in 30 days. An agreement made on or after 18 March 2015 is exempt if the number of instalments is no more than 12. For agreements made on or after 1 February 2011, the credit must be provided without interest or other significant charges, otherwise the agreement is regulated;
- mortgages taken out to buy land or property;
- secured loans for home improvements where the mortgage for the purchase of the property was provided by the same lender;
- most other secured loans taken out on or after 21 March 2016;
- accounts involving goods or services requiring payments to be made in relation to periods not exceeding three months repayable in one instalment – eg, charge cards. For agreements made on or after 1 February 2011, there must either be no, or only 'insignificant', charges payable for the credit. 'Insignificant' is not defined;
- regulated mortgage contracts (see p112) made on or after 31 October 2004, even if the amount borrowed is within the consumer credit limit;
- agreements made on or after 6 April 2008 to a 'high net worth' individual (see below);
- agreements made on or after 6 April 2008 for more than £25,000 entered into 'wholly or predominantly' for the purpose of the client's business (see below).

High net worth borrowers

The 'high net worth' exemption allows individuals to opt out of Consumer Credit Act regulation. It applies if the individual's net income is at least £150,000 a year or her/his assets (excluding her/his home and pension) are at least £500,000. Since 1 February 2011, the exemption only applies to agreements that provide credit of more than £60,260 and to agreements secured on land (but see below for agreements made on or after 21 March 2016).

The individual must sign a declaration of high net worth, supported by a statement from an accountant. The rationale for this exemption (asked for by the credit industry) is that such people have the resources to obtain their own financial and legal advice and, if such exemption were not available, might seek finance involving less formality from outside the UK.

Note: this exemption does not apply to loans made on or after 21 March 2016 if the credit is for more than £60,260 for the purpose of renovating property and the borrower is a consumer – ie, acting outside her/his business, trade or profession.[4]

Loans for business purposes

The business-related exemption applies if someone has been granted credit of more than £25,000 'wholly or predominantly' for the purpose of her/his business. If the agreement contains a declaration by the borrower that it has been entered into wholly or predominantly for business purposes, it is assumed that this is the case. However, if the agreement either contains no declaration or contains a declaration but the creditor either knows or reasonably suspects it is not true, the presumption does not apply and the issue depends on the circumstances of the case.[5]

Note: an agreement granting credit of £25,000 or less *wholly* for the purpose of the client's business is an exempt agreement if it is a 'green deal' plan for energy efficiency improvements to her/his property under the Energy Act 2011.[6]

Buy-to-let mortgages

Buy-to-let mortgages are generally considered to be a business transaction and, as such, not regulated by the Financial Conduct Authority (FCA) or subject to its rules. However, from 21 March 2016, 'consumer buy-to-let contracts' are regulated by Part 3 of the Mortgage Credit Directive Order,[7] which requires for example pre-contract illustrations, credit worthiness assessments and arrears management.

In order to be a 'buy-to-let contract', the agreement must provide that the property secured by the mortgage cannot at any time be occupied as a dwelling by either the borrower or her/his relative, but is to be occupied as a dwelling on the basis of a rental agreement. A 'consumer buy-to-let contract' is defined as: 'a buy-to-let mortgage contract which is not entered into by the borrower wholly or predominantly for the purposes of a business carried on or intended to be carried on by the borrower'. The lender may presume that the borrower is acting for the purposes of her/his business if the agreement contains a declaration by the borrower to this effect, unless the lender has reasonable cause to suspect that this it not the case. If the borrower already owns another property which has been let on a rental basis, any further buy-to-let contract is deemed to be business lending.

Secured loans

On 21 March 2016, the regulation of secured loans changed.[8] Most secured loans taken out after this date are no longer regulated by the Consumer Credit Act and are therefore not regulated credit agreements. Most secured loans taken out before this date are also no longer regulated credit agreements, even though they were regulated at the time they were taken out (the technical term for such agreements is 'consumer credit back book mortgage contracts').

The provisions that apply to regulated mortgage contracts (see p112) now apply to secured loans, provided:
- the borrower is an individual;
- the loan is secured on property; *and*
- at least 40 per cent of the property is occupied by the borrower and/or her/his family.

However, the following provisions of the Consumer Credit Act 1974 have been retained for such loans made before 21 March 2016.[9]

- The requirement for an enforcement order when:
  - a creditor breaches the rules on the disclosure of information;
  - a creditor fails to supply the client with details of the terms of an authorised overdraft agreement (see p69);
  - there is an improperly executed agreement;
  - there is an improperly executed guarantee;
  - the creditor fails to serve a copy of a default notice on a guarantor.
- A creditor can only enforce an agreement if it has complied with its duty:
  - to give information to a client or guarantor, if requested, under a fixed-sum agreement (see p157 and p145);
  - to provide annual statements to a client under a fixed-sum agreement;
  - to give information to a client or guarantor, if requested, under a running account agreement (see p157 and p145);[10]
  - to give notice of the amount in arrears;
  - to give notice of default sums;
  - to provide a client with a settlement figure, if requested (see p161);[11]
  - to provide a client with a copy of any guarantee, if requested (see p145).
- Where an agreement provides for the creditor, a broker or the supplier to be the agent of the client in pre-contract negotiations, rather than the agent of the creditor, the whole agreement is invalid.[12]
- Interest should not be increased on default.[13]
- The right to complete payments ahead of time (see p161).
- Rebates on early settlement.
- The unfair relationship provisions.[14]

Note: the transitional provision appears to have had the effect of removing the status of irredeemable enforceability from these loans, which were improperly executed prior to 6 April 2007 (see p73). Advisers dealing with a pre-6 April 2007 'consumer credit back book mortgage contract' which appears to have been improperly executed and irredeemably unenforceable should get specialist advice.

For the purpose of time orders (see p366), secured loans that are regulated mortgage contracts but which would would otherwise be regulated credit agreements are treated as if they were regulated credit agreements.[15]

The form of the agreement

The form of a regulated agreement is very important. If an agreement is not made in accordance with the Consumer Credit Act 1974, it can only be enforced with special permission of the courts. Some agreements made before 6 April 2007 are irredeemably (ie, completely) unenforceable. This means that the court does not have the power to give permission for it to be enforced.

Pre-contract information

If the agreement was signed by both parties ('executed') on or after 31 May 2005 (but see below if the agreement was made on or after 1 February 2011), the creditor must provide specified information to the client before the agreement is made.[16] This does not apply to:

- secured loans (see p129); *and*
- 'distance contracts' (see p75).

The specified information includes:

- the appropriate consumer credit heading describing the nature of the agreement;
- the names and addresses of the creditor and the client(s);
- financial and related information, such as details of any goods or services, the amount of credit, the total charge for credit, rate of interest and repayment details;
- statements of consumer protection rights and remedies.

There is no prescribed format for the information, except that it must be headed 'pre-contract information', handed to the client before the agreement is made and must be capable of being taken away to be studied. As there is no prescribed period for providing the information, the creditor can give the pre-contract information document to the client and then immediately invite her/him to sign the actual agreement.

If the creditor does not comply with the pre-contract information requirements, the agreement is improperly executed and the creditor needs the permission of the court to enforce it.

Agreements made on or after 1 February 2011

Following the implementation of the European Commission's Consumer Credit Directive 2008, there are additional pre-contract requirements for all regulated agreements,[17] except those:

- secured on land;
- for credit of more than £60,260;
- for business lending.

Pre-contract information

If the agreement was made on or after 1 February 2011, more onerous pre-contract information requirements than those described above apply instead. The pre-contract information must be provided before the agreement is made. It is the creditor's responsibility to ensure that this has been done. The information must be disclosed using the Standard European Consumer Credit Information form,[18] which must be in writing and in a format which the client can take away to consider.

The creditor must also inform the client:
- that it will tell her/him if a decision not to proceed is based on credit reference agency information;[19]
- of her/his right to request a copy of the draft agreement;[20]
- of the period of time for which the pre-contract information remains valid (where applicable).

Separate rules apply to:
- certain telephone contracts;
- non-telephone distance contracts;
- excluded pawnbroking agreements (see p122);
- overdraft agreements.

If the creditor does not disclose the required information or it does not use the proper form and format, the agreement is improperly executed and is enforceable only with the permission of the court.

These provisions are very complex and prescriptive. For guidance on the regulations, see gov.uk/government/publications/consumer-credit-regulations-guidance-on-implementing-the-consumer-credit-directive.

Explanation and advice

If the agreement was made on or after 1 February 2011, the creditor must provide the client with an explanation and advice.[21] This applies to all regulated agreements except:
- those secured on land;
- pawnbroking agreements (but see p122);
- overdrafts;
- those for credit of more than £60,260.

The client must be provided with an 'adequate explanation' of:[22]
- any features that may make the agreement unsuitable for particular types of use;
- how much the client will have to pay, periodically and in total;
- any features that could have a significant adverse effect in ways the client is unlikely to foresee;
- the main consequences if the client fails to make the payments due under the agreement;
- the effects of withdrawing from the agreement, and when and how to exercise this right.

The explanation can be verbal, in writing, or both, and should enable the client to make a reasonable assessment of whether s/he can afford the credit and the key associated risks.

In addition, if the client is taking out a payday loan, the creditor or credit broker must explain that the agreement is unsuitable to support sustained borrowing over a long period and is expensive as a means of longer term borrowing. The creditor or credit broker must enable the client to request and obtain further information and explanation about the agreement without incurring undue cost or delay.

The creditor or credit broker can require the client to acknowledge that it has provided an explanation and that s/he has received any written information. It cannot require the client to acknowledge the adequacy of this.

For further information, particularly in relation to specific categories of agreement and where agreements are marketed at a distance or by electronic means, see the *Consumer Credit Sourcebook*.[23]

There are no sanctions for non-compliance with these requirements, but the client could argue that there is an unfair relationship (see p161) or complain to the Financial Ombudsman Service (see p284).

Assessment of creditworthiness

If the agreement was made on or after 1 February 2011, the creditor must assess the client's creditworthiness. This includes the risk that the client will not make the payments due under the agreement by their due date (the credit risk), and the risk to the client of not being able to make the repayments under the agreement or of there being a significant negative effect on her/his overall financial position (the affordability risk).[24] This applies to all regulated agreements except:

- those secured on land;
- pawnbroking agreements;
- authorised overdraft agreements.

The creditor must carry out an assessment before:

- making a regulated agreement;
- significantly increasing the amount of credit under the agreement; *or*
- significantly increasing the credit limit under the agreement.

The creditor must assess the client's creditworthiness based on sufficient information of which it is aware at the time the assessment is carried out, on information obtained from the client, where appropriate, or, if necessary, from a credit reference agency. The creditor must consider the client's ability to make the repayments as they fall due over the life of the agreement. Repayments may be made out of the client's income, including income received either jointly with, or by, another person (eg, a member of the client's household), where it would be reasonable to expect such income to be available for repayments under the agreement, without the client having to borrow to make the repayments or fail to make any other payment s/he has a legal obligation to make, and without the repayments having any significant adverse effect on the client's financial situation. When considering affordability, the creditor must not take into account the existence of, or the intention to provide, or request the provision of, any guarantee or other form of security.

The creditor must take reasonable steps to determine the amount, or make a reasonable assessment, of the client's current income, including any potential reduction in the client's income during the term of the agreement which is reasonably foreseeable. The creditor may only take into account any potential increase in the client's income where there is appropriate evidence that this increase is likely to happen during the term of the agreement. The creditor must also take reasonable steps to determine the amount, or make a reasonable assessment, of the client's current 'non-discretionary expenditure'. This includes payments needed to meet priority debts and other essential expenses, together with payments the client has a legal obligation to make – eg, loan repayments or council tax. It may, therefore, be appropriate for the creditor to compare the size of the client's existing debts to her/his income as part of the assessment process. The creditor should also take into account any information it possesses which may indicate that the client is in, has recently experienced, or is likely to experience, financial difficulties or is particularly vulnerable – eg, has mental health or mental capacity issues. Where appropriate, the creditor may also take into account information obtained in the course of previous dealings with the client, but should consider whether that information remains valid, having regard to the passage of time, or whether it should be updated.

In the case of guarantor loans, as well as assessing the borrower's creditworthiness, the creditor must consider the potential for the commitments under the agreement to have a significant effect on the guarantor's financial situation.

For further information, see the *Consumer Credit Sourcebook*.[25]

There are no sanctions for non-compliance with these requirements, but the client could argue that there is an unfair relationship (see p161) or complain to the Financial Ombudsman Service (see p27).[26]

A copy of the draft agreement

If the agreement was made on or after 1 February 2011, the creditor must provide the client with a copy of the prospective agreement 'without delay' if the client requests this.[27] This applies to all regulated agreements except:

- those secured on land;
- pawnbroking agreements;
- those for credit of more than £60,260;
- those for business lending.

The creditor does not have to comply with the request if it has decided not to proceed with the transaction. Otherwise, if the creditor does not comply, it breaches its statutory duty. However, the client cannot take any action to remedy this.

Once the agreement becomes an executed agreement (signed by both parties), the creditor must provide a copy of this to the client 'without delay',[28] except if the client has been given a copy of the draft agreement and the executed agreement is identical. If this is the case, the creditor must inform the client that:

- the agreement has been executed and the date of the agreement; *and*
- s/he can request a copy before the end of the 14-day 'withdrawal period' (see p76).

In the case of authorised overdraft agreements, instead of a copy of the executed agreement, the client must be given a document containing the terms of the agreement.[29] With certain exceptions, this must be done before or at the time the agreement is made.

If the creditor does not comply, the agreement is improperly executed and enforceable only with the permission of the court.

Information that must be in the agreement

All regulated agreements (except current account overdrafts before 1 February 2011) must be made in writing, must be signed by all the borrowers and must contain the following information.[30] The agreement should also contain further terms, depending on when it was made (see pp71–74).

- The amount of credit (or the credit limit). Some creditors confuse the 'amount of credit' with the total amount of the loan. The 'amount of credit' is a technical term and is the amount borrowed less all the 'charges for credit'. An item forming part of the charges must not be treated as credit, even if time is allowed to pay it. Some creditors get this wrong, with serious consequences. For example, in the case *London North Securities v Meadows*, the clients borrowed £5,750 under a secured loan, including £750 for a premium for payment protection insurance, described in the agreement as 'optional'.[31] The county court judge found that the insurance was not optional but required by the lender and so was a 'charges for credit' item. The amount of credit was, therefore, £5,000 and the agreement was completely unenforceable. The Court of Appeal upheld this decision, with the result that the lender was unable to enforce payment of the outstanding balance of the agreement and had to remove its legal charge from the Land Registry.[32] Arguably, the agreement does not need to use the phrase 'amount of credit', but this may not be the case if the agreement is ambiguous about which figure is the amount of credit.[33]
- The rate of interest and whether it can vary (if the amount of interest is not fixed at the start).
- A notice of cancellation in the prescribed form (if the agreement is cancellable).
- A term stating how the client must discharge her/his obligations to make repayments – ie, details of payments, how many, how much and how often.

Many secured loans require the client to pay the creditor's legal fees in connection with drawing up of documents and require payment of these to be made immediately or deferred to the end of the loan period. Interest usually accrues on this amount and is compounded monthly, so by the end of the loan a substantial sum is likely to be due. Many agreements do not make clear the client's obligations in relation to such deferred fees and, as a result, the whole agreement could be irredeemably (completely) unenforceable.[34]

Note: the terms listed above are 'prescribed terms' in the Consumer Credit Act 1974. If the agreement was made before 6 April 2007 and any prescribed term is missing or stated incorrectly, or if the agreement has not been signed by all the borrowers, it is irredeemably unenforceable. This means that the court does not have the power to give permission for it to be enforced. So too is any security – eg, on a secured loan.[35]

The prescribed terms must be 'contained in' the document signed by the client. Whether 'application form' agreements (eg, for credit cards and store cards, which the client signs and returns and which then become the agreement[36]) comply with these requirements has recently been considered by the High Court.[37] It decided that it is not sufficient for a piece of paper signed by the client merely to cross-refer to the prescribed terms without a copy of those terms being supplied to the client at the point when s/he signs. However, a document can comprise more than one piece of paper, and whether several pieces of paper together constitute a single document involves looking at practical considerations rather than their form. In this particular case, the document signed by the client referred to 'the terms and conditions attached', which were fixed by a staple and were held to be one document.

Agreements made before 31 May 2005

In addition to the prescribed information listed on pp70–74, agreements made before 31 May 2005 must also contain (but see also p166):
- the appropriate consumer credit heading that describes the nature of the agreement;
- the names and addresses of the client and creditor, and a signature box;
- details of any security to be provided as part of the agreement;
- a brief description of any goods supplied under the agreement;
- the cash price(s) of any goods or services;
- the amount of any deposit or part payment;
- the total charge for credit if the amount of interest is fixed at the start. This includes not only the total interest (if any), but also other charges payable under the transaction – eg, brokers' fees and compulsory payment protection insurance. If it is a condition of the loan that any arrears owed under a different credit agreement are paid from the advance, payment of those arrears are a 'charge for credit' item if the client was unaware that the lender was going to

pay them. The arrears, however, are not a 'charge for credit' item if payment of them was part of the purpose of the loan in question, or the client agreed that they could be paid out of the loan;
- the annual percentage rate (APR);
- a statement about the client's rights – eg, termination rights and paying off the account early.

If one of the above non-prescribed terms is missing or incorrectly stated, the creditor can only enforce the agreement with the permission of the court.

Note: if the agreement was provided to the client before 31 May 2005, but was not executed before this date and became an executed agreement no later than 31 August 2005, it is covered by the rules on pre-31 May 2005 agreements. However, the creditor must have been required to provide pre-contract information to the client in the new format before the agreement was made. An agreement is 'executed' or 'made' when the last person who must sign it has done so.

Agreements made on or after 31 May 2005

In addition to the prescribed information described on pp70–74, agreements made on or after 31 May 2005 must also contain the non-prescribed terms listed below and should also set them out in a particular format in the following order:[38]
- the appropriate consumer credit heading that describes the nature of the agreement;
- the names and addresses of the creditor and the client(s);
- key financial information:
  - amount of credit or credit limit;
  - total amount payable, in the case of fixed interest rate agreements;
  - repayment details;
  - the APR;
- other financial information:
  - description of any goods or services;
  - cash price(s) of any goods or services;
  - advance payments (where appropriate);
  - total charge for credit;
  - details of interest rates and whether these are fixed or variable;
- key information:
  - description of any security provided;
  - list of default charges;
  - where applicable, a statement that the agreement is not cancellable;
  - examples of the amount required to settle the agreement early;
  - statements of consumer protection and remedies;
- a signature box;
- a cancellation box (where appropriate);

- if the client is purchasing optional insurance on credit under the agreement, a form of consent to taking out the insurance(s) to be signed by the client(s).

If any of the above provisions is not complied with, the creditor can only enforce the agreement with the permission of the court (but see p166).

Note: if the agreement was provided to the client before 31 May 2005, but was not executed before this date and became an executed agreement no later than 31 August 2005, it is covered by the rules on pre-31 May 2005 agreements (see p71). However, the creditor must have been required to provide pre-contract information to the client in the new format before the agreement was made. An agreement is 'executed' or 'made' when the last person who must sign it has done so.

Agreements made on or after 1 February 2011

The Consumer Credit (Agreements) Regulations 2010 apply to all regulated agreements (except for unauthorised overdrafts) made on or after 1 February 2011 except those:

- secured on land;
- for credit exceeding £60,260; *and*
- for business lending.

The rules outlined on p71 and p72 continue to apply in the case of these agreements, unless the creditor 'opts in' to the 2010 regulations by providing pre-contract information as outlined on p66. Creditors are likely to take advantage of these provisions so that they can use the same documentation for all their regulated agreements.

Under these regulations, which are less prescriptive than the provisions outlined on p71 and p72, agreements must contain specified information, but this does not need to be provided in any particular order or subdivided under particular headings. Information must be provided in a clear and concise manner, and be easily legible and readily distinguishable from the background. There is no box in which the client signs the agreement: the client now signs in the space provided.

If the creditor or broker does not comply, the agreement is improperly executed and enforceable only with the permission of the court.

Improperly executed agreements made on or after 6 April 2007

From 6 April 2007, the courts have discretion to allow agreements made on or after this date to be enforced even if:

- there is no agreement signed by all the borrowers; *or*
- the agreement does not contain a prescribed term or it is incorrect; *or*
- in the case of a cancellable agreement, the creditor has failed to comply with the provisions on cancellation notices.

Note: these changes are not retrospective, so the courts have no discretion to allow an improperly executed agreement made before 6 April 2007 to be enforced if the above requirements are not complied with.[39]

The court must decide whether or not to allow the agreement to be enforced and, if so, on what terms. The court can refuse to make an enforcement order if it considers it 'just' to do so (eg, if the client would not have entered into the agreement had the agreement been properly executed) or can attach certain conditions. See p318 for more information on this.

Electronic communication

Electronic communications can be used to conclude regulated agreements, and send notices and other documents. Documents may only be transmitted electronically if the client has agreed to this. Creditors can also make provision for clients to sign agreements electronically.[40]

The right to cancel: cooling-off period

A regulated agreement made before 1 February 2011 can be cancelled if it was signed somewhere other than at the trade premises of the creditor or supplier of goods and following face-to-face negotiations with the creditor or supplier (including their agents or employees). Telephone calls do not count as face to face.

If the agreement was made on or after 1 February 2011 and it is for credit of £60,260 or less, see p76.

Note: there is no right to cancel an agreement secured on land.

A copy of the agreement must be given to the client immediately s/he signs it (whether or not it is cancellable). Unless the creditor has already signed it or signs at the same time, another copy must be sent within seven days,[41] with a notice of cancellation rights. Otherwise, a separate notice of cancellation rights must be sent within seven days of the agreement being signed. The cooling-off period begins with the receipt of this second copy of the document/separate notice of cancellation rights.

An agreement must be cancelled within five days. The client must cancel in writing and, if posted, it is effective immediately even if it is not received by the creditor. The client should, therefore, obtain proof of posting or send it by 'recorded signed for'.

It is probably best to cancel an agreement initially by telephone, and then follow this up immediately by a letter, fax or email. A letter can simply state: 'I hereby give you notice that I wish to cancel the regulated credit agreement signed by me on... [date].'[42] It should be sent to the company providing the credit, with a copy to the company supplying the goods, if appropriate. Any goods already supplied under the agreement should be returned or await collection by the trader. Any deposit or advance payment for the goods must be refunded to the client.

The client can also withdraw from an agreement if, when s/he signs, it has not yet been signed by the creditor and it is not signed by the creditor on the same occasion, so that it becomes an executed agreement. The client must communicate to the creditor that s/he wishes to withdraw before the creditor signs it. Withdrawal has the same effect as a cancellation.[43] Withdrawal can be verbal (if time is short) or (preferably) in writing, including email. **Note:** if the agreement was made on or after 1 February 2011, there is an additional right to withdraw (see p76).

Distance contracts

In the case of unsecured credit agreements made on or after 1 October 2004 without face-to-face contact between the client and the creditor/intermediary, such as online, by post or on the telephone, the creditor must supply certain information to the client about her/his cancellation rights in good time before the agreement is entered into.

The creditor must also supply the same prescribed information to the client in writing in good time before the agreement is entered into. The client can waive this requirement in certain circumstances, but the prescribed information must then be supplied immediately after the agreement is made.

The client can cancel the distance agreement within 14 days:
- from the day after the agreement was made, if the written information referred to above was supplied on or before the date the agreement was made; *or*
- from the day after all the written information referred to above was supplied to the client, if this was not supplied before the agreement was made.

The client can give notice of cancellation:
- verbally, if the creditor has informed the client that notice may be given in this way; *or*
- by leaving the notice at the creditor's address. Notice is given on the day it is left; *or*
- by posting, faxing or emailing the creditor. Notice is given on the day it is posted or sent; *or*
- by sending it to an internet address or website which the creditor has indicated can be used to give notice of cancellation. Notice is given when it is sent.

Secondary contracts

If the credit agreement is a borrower-lender-supplier agreement (previously known as debtor-creditor-supplier agreements), cancellation of the credit agreement automatically cancels any secondary contract to be financed by the credit agreement,[44] except if the secondary contract has been carried out at the client's express request before s/he gave notice of cancellation – eg, if the client asked a supplier to fit double glazing, which was being financed by the credit agreement, and then gave notice of cancellation after the double glazing had been fitted.[45]

Following cancellation, the supplier must refund any sum paid by the client in relation to the contract, less a proportionate charge for any services already supplied, within 30 days.[46] No charge may be made if the supplier began to carry out the contract before the expiry of the cancellation period without the client's consent. The client must repay any money received, and return any property acquired, in relation to the contract within 30 days.

Agreements made on or after 1 February 2011

If an agreement was made on or after 1 February 2011, the client can withdraw from it within 14 days without giving any reason.[47] This applies to all regulated agreements except those:
- for credit of more than £60,260;
- secured on land.

Note: the cancellation rights described on p74 do not apply.

Notice of withdrawal must be given before the end of the 14-day period starting with the day after the 'relevant day'. This is the latest of:
- the date the agreement was made; *or*
- the date the client was informed of her/his credit limit under the agreement; *or*
- the date the client either receives her/his copy of the executed agreement or is informed that it has been executed.

The client may give notice of withdrawal either verbally or in writing using the contact details provided in the agreement.

The client must repay any credit advanced together with interest accrued up to the date of repayment, but is not liable for any other fees or charges under the agreement. The client must repay the credit and any interest without 'undue delay' and, in any event, within 30 days. If repayment has not been made within this time, the creditor can take action to recover the money, recover possession of any goods or enforce any security.

Although a client can withdraw from a credit agreement, this does not affect any contract for the supply of goods, and s/he remains liable to pay for them. Ownership of goods bought with a hire purchase or conditional sale agreement passes to the client on repayment of the credit and accrued interest.[48] The client is not entitled to return the goods to the supplier, so if s/he withdraws from the agreement, the effect is a forced cash purchase.

The former Office of Fair Trading's view of this situation was that the creditor retains the right to repossess the goods if the credit and accrued interest is not paid within the 30-day period. It is unlikely that the client is entitled to have her/his deposit or part-exchanged goods returned or to have their amount/value set off against the amount owed. This should be explained to the client as part of the creditor's required 'adequate explanation' (see p67).

Post-contract information

Annual statements

Creditors of fixed-sum credit agreements with a term of more than 12 months must provide annual statements to borrowers. If a creditor does not comply with this requirement, it cannot enforce the agreement during the period of non-compliance, and the client is not liable to pay either any interest or any default sum (see p78) accruing during that period.[49]

A creditor can still enforce a running account credit agreement (where there is already a duty to provide annual statements) during a period when it does not provide annual statements, but statements must contain warnings about the consequences of failing to make repayments or of only making the minimum repayments (which many statements already include).

Arrears notices

To avoid the situation where the client is making either reduced or contractual payments plus a payment towards the arrears and is unaware that the debt is escalating because the creditor is adding interest or charges, creditors must inform clients when their arrears reach a certain level and that interest or charges may be accruing. This applies to arrears arising after 1 October 2008 on both new and existing agreements. There are different provisions for fixed-sum and running-account agreements.

If at least two payments have fallen due under a fixed-sum credit agreement and the account has gone into arrears by the equivalent of at least two repayments, the creditor must give the client notice of the arrears in a specified form within 14 days (the 'arrears notice'), and then at six-monthly intervals until the client has cleared the arrears, any interest on the arrears and any default sum (see p78).

For running-account agreements, the notice must be given once at least two payments have fallen due and the last two payments have not been paid in full. The notice must be given no later than the end of the period when the next periodic statement is due. A further arrears notice is only triggered once the client has again failed to pay two consecutive months' payments in full.

The arrears notice must be accompanied by an information sheet about arrears produced by the FCA (see p80).

If a creditor does not comply with this requirement to give the client an arrears notice, it cannot enforce the agreement during the period of non-compliance and the client is not liable to pay any interest or any default sum accruing during this period.

Once an arrears notice is served, the client can apply for a time order (eg, if s/he wants more time to pay and/or interest or charges to be reduced or frozen in the meantime), provided s/he has given 14 days' notice to the creditor of her/his intention to do so. The client's notice must be in writing, but not in any prescribed form, and must state that s/he intends to apply for a time order and s/he wants to make a repayment proposal to the creditor. S/he must give details of that proposal. The client can also apply for a time order after a default notice has been served or during court proceedings – no 14-day notice period is required. See p366 for more information on time orders.

The duty to send an arrears notice ends once the creditor has obtained a county court judgment for the sum payable under the agreement.

Default sum notices

If money, other than interest, becomes payable under an agreement as a result of a breach of the agreement (known as a 'default sum'), the creditor must give the client a notice in a specified form. Costs ordered by a court are not payable 'under the agreement' and so do not count as a default sum.

If a creditor does not comply with this requirement, it cannot enforce the agreement during the period of non-compliance.

The creditor cannot charge any interest on the default sum until the 29th day after the notice is given. After that date, it can only charge simple interest on the default sum (although the arrears themselves continue to accrue interest at the contractual rate, provided the creditor has given the appropriate statutory notices).

Default notices

Before the creditor can terminate the agreement, demand early payment, recover possession of any goods or land (except in the case of secured loans treated as regulated mortgage contracts – see p64), or enforce any security, it must serve a 'default notice' on the client (see p299).

The notice must contain information on the client's right to terminate a hire purchase or conditional sale agreement and the procedure involved (see p104). It must also contain a statement of the creditor's right to charge interest under the credit agreement after judgment. The creditor is also required to attach a copy of the information sheet about arrears produced by the FCA (see p80).

Since 1 October 2006, default notices must give the client 14 days in which to comply, instead of the seven days previously required, regardless of whether the breach occurred before or after this date.

Home-collected credit

Home-collected credit involves the client borrowing money and the creditor's representative calling at the client's home to collect the repayments (also known as 'doorstep lending'). The FCA has been concerned about the repeated use of such credit, in particular repeat borrowing and refinancing of existing loans, thereby converting what is essentially short-term borrowing into long-term borrowing. Section 49 of the Consumer Credit Act 1949 prohibits the 'soliciting' of cash loans off trade premises unless this is in response to a signed request from the client. These provisions apply to both new and existing borrowers. The FCA does not believe that written 'permission to call', given at the time of the original loan, amounts to a 'request' under section 49 covering discussion of further loans at some future date.

New FCA guidance (which came into force on 19 December 2018) clarifies that any discussion in the client's home about new loans or refinancing must be initiated by the client either by a specific written request or, if made during a routine collection visit, an oral request.[50] Further, since 19 March 2019, home-collected credit firms must explain to clients the comparative costs of refinancing an existing loan compared to taking out a new loan to run alongside an existing loan, and this information must be provided in a durable medium.[51]

Interest after judgment

If a client defaults on an agreement, the creditor may take court action to recover the amount owed. If the judgment is made after 1 October 2008 and the creditor wants to recover any interest on the outstanding balance due under the agreement at the rate provided for in the agreement (known as post-judgment contractual interest) from the client, it must give her/him notice of its intention to do so in the prescribed form. The first notice must be given after the judgment is made and further notices must be given at six-monthly intervals. The client is not liable to pay post-judgment interest for any period for which the creditor has not served the required notice(s). As this interest is payable under the terms of the agreement – as opposed to being payable under the judgment – in addition to these notices, the creditor will also have to provide the client with annual statements showing the accrual of interest after judgment (see p312).

It is not enough that the creditor 'wants' to claim interest after judgment. The agreement must specifically allow it to be claimed (see p312).[52] The intention appears to be that if the client either refuses to pay or cannot come to an agreement with the creditor, the creditor will have to sue for it separately. The client can then defend the proceedings if s/he challenges the creditor's right to claim post-judgment interest under the contract or the amount claimed, or s/he can make an offer of payment through the court, if appropriate.

Until the judgment is made, the client only has a potential liability for post-judgment contractual interest and, even after the judgment is made, that liability is conditional on the creditor serving the appropriate notice(s). Therefore, a creditor cannot argue that such interest should have been provided for in the judgment.

If the client receives notice of the creditor's intention to claim post-judgment contractual interest, s/he should consider applying for a time order (see p366) and asking the court either to freeze, or reduce the rate of, the interest or charges.

Note: the above provisions do not apply to post-judgment *statutory* interest. This can never be claimed if the judgment is about an agreement regulated by the Consumer Credit Act 1974, regardless of the amount.

Information sheets

The FCA must prepare information sheets to accompany arrears notices and default notices.[53] From 1 October 2008, lenders must include a copy of the current information sheet with each relevant notice. The legislation says that the information sheet must be 'included' in the notice, so it is arguable that, if a notice is sent out without an information sheet, the notice is invalid.

The FCA has produced an information sheet for each notice regardless of the type of agreement involved. These are two sides of A4 in length and are available in Welsh as well as English, and can be made available in large print, audio tape and Braille. They set out some of the client's key rights, such as the right to terminate the agreement, apply for a time order or complain to the Financial Ombudsman Service. They also set out the effect of a client's failure to pay, such as the effect on credit rating, additional interest and court action by the creditor. They include a list of sources of help, such as Citizens Advice offices and National Debtline.

The information sheets (which have been in use since 27 July 2018) are available at fca.org.uk/firms/information-sheets-consumer-credit.

Notes

2. **Authorising traders**
1 s39 FSMA 2000
2 *FCA Handbook*, CONC 14

3. **Regulated agreements**
3 s8(3)(b) CCA 1974; Arts 60C-60H RAO; *FCA Handbook*, CONC App 1.3; see also PERG 2.7.19B-J
4 Sch 1 Part 2 para 4(18) MCDO
5 See *Wood v Capital Bridging Finance*, *Adviser* 170 abstracts
6 See A Pardoe, 'A Green Revolution?', *Adviser* 153 and 'Deal or No Deal?', *Adviser* 154
7 *FCA Handbook*, PERG 4.10B
8 MCDO
9 Arts 28 and 29 MCDO

10 s97(1) CCA 1974
11 s110 CCA 1974
12 s56(3) CCA 1974
13 s93 CCA 1974
14 Art 29 MCDO
15 s126(2) CCA 1974; *FCA Handbook*, PERG 4.17.2
16 s55(1) CCA 1974
17 CC(DI) Regs
18 Sch 1 CC(DI) Regs
19 s157A CCA 1974
20 s55C CCA 1974
21 s55A CCA 1974. These provisions were repealed on 1 April 2014 and are now in the *FCA Handbook*, CONC. For the position before this date, see the previous edition of this *Handbook*.

22 From 2 November 2015, see *FCA Handbook*, CONC 4.2. For the position before this date, see the previous edition of this *Handbook*.

23 *FCA Handbook*, CONC 4.2

24 *FCA Handbook*, CONC 5.2 and 5.3 were replaced by CONC 5.2A with effect from 1 November 2018.

25 *FCA Handbook*, CONC 5.2A

26 For a discussion on the Financial Ombudsman Service approach to complaints about unaffordable lending, see S McFadden, 'Unaffordable Lending: the FOS approach', *Adviser* 157

27 s55C CCA 1974

28 s61A CCA 1974

29 s61B CCA 1974

30 *FCA Handbook*, CONC 4.7 and 6.3.4R

31 *London North Securities v Meadows* [2005] EWCA Civ 956 (*Adviser* 107 and 108 abstracts)

32 *London North Securities v Meadows* [2005] EWCA Civ 956 (*Adviser* 107 and 108 abstracts)

33 See *Ocwen v Hughes and Hughes* [2004] CCLR 4 and *Central Trust v Spurway* [2005] CCLR 1

34 See *McGinn v Grangewood Securities* [2002] EWCA Civ 522 (*Adviser* 92 abstracts) and *London North Securities v Williams*, Reading County Court, 16 May 2005, unreported (*Adviser* 112 abstracts). Even if the prescribed term is present, it is unlikely that the agreement will contain the more detailed non-prescribed repayment obligations, which will make the agreement improperly executed and enforceable with leave of the court only on such terms as it thinks fit. See *Hurstanger Ltd v Wilson* [2007] EWCA Civ 299 (*Adviser* 122 consumer abstracts).

35 ss113 and 127(3) CCA 1974; Sch 6 Consumer Credit (Agreements) Regulations 1983, No.1553

36 *HSBC Bank v Brophy* [2011] EWCA Civ 67 (*Adviser* 145 abstracts)

37 *Carey and Others v HSBC and Others* [2009] EWHC 3417 (QB) (*Adviser* 139 money advice abstracts)

38 The Consumer Credit (Agreements) (Amendment) Regulations 2004, No.1482

39 For a summary of pre-6 April 2007 unenforceability arguments, see A Leakey and B Say, 'Unenforceable Agreements', *Adviser* 117, and for a discussion of the position post-6 April 2007, see G Skipwith, 'Consultancy Corner 1', *Adviser* 124

40 The Consumer Credit Act 1974 (Electronic Communications) Order 2004, No.3236. See also *Bassano v Toft and Others* [2014] EWHC 377 (QB), in which clicking the 'I accept' button that generated a document in which the words 'I accept' then appeared in the designated space on the form was held to be sufficient.

41 s63 CCA 1974

42 s69(7) CCA 1974

43 s57 CCA 1974

44 Reg 12 FS(DM) Regs. These only apply if the client is a 'consumer' – ie, the transaction must not be for the purposes of the client's business.

45 Reg 11 FS(DM) Regs. These only apply if the client is a 'consumer' – ie, the transaction must not be for the purposes of the client's business.

46 Reg 13 FS(DM) Regs. These only apply if the client is a 'consumer' – ie, the transaction must not be for the purposes of the client's business.

47 s66A CCA 1974

48 s66A(11) CCA 1974

49 For further information, see G Skipwith, 'Consultancy Corner', *Adviser* 162

50 *FCA Handbook*, CONC 3.10.3G

51 *FCA Handbook*, CONC 4.2.15R(3A)

52 Regs 34 and 35 and Sch 5 CC(IR) Regs; see P Madge, 'Interesting After Judgment', *Adviser* 131

53 s86A CCA 1974

Chapter 5

···

Types of debt

This chapter covers the sort of debts that advisers commonly encounter, whether or not they are regulated, the issues they are likely to raise, and the action advisers and clients should consider taking to deal with them.

Bank overdraft

A bank overdraft is a type of revolving credit (see p129). The bank allows a customer with a current account to overdraw on the account up to a certain amount. Repayment of the overdraft is made as money is paid into the account. Overdrafts may be 'authorised' (ie, if the client has a prior arrangement with the bank to overdraw) or 'unauthorised' – ie, if the client has no prior arrangement, but the bank nevertheless allows the account to go overdrawn.

The legal position

Bank overdrafts are regulated under the Consumer Credit Act 1974, provided the credit is for no more than £25,000 (if granted before 6 April 2008) or £15,000 (if granted before 1 May 1998). It does not matter whether the overdraft is authorised or unauthorised. No written agreement is required for an unauthorised overdraft. If the agreement for an authorised overdraft was made before 1 February 2011, no written agreement is required. If the credit is granted on or after 6 April 2008, the agreement is regulated regardless of the amount, unless it is exempt – eg, it is for business purposes and provides credit of more than £25,000 (see p62). An overdraft may be either secured or unsecured.

Special features

Interest is charged, usually on a daily basis, and repayment in full can be requested at any time. When the agreed overdraft limit is reached, cheques and transfers drawn against the account are usually stopped.

If the overdraft is not approved by the bank or the limit is exceeded, a higher rate of interest is usually charged and additional service charges may be made at the bank's discretion. Even if an overdraft is within its agreed limit, the bank may decide to apply additional charges.

When a customer has both a current account with overdraft facilities and a loan account with the same bank, it is common for banks to require payments to the personal loan account to be made from the current account. This may be done even if there are no funds in the current account, so that the higher overdraft rate of interest applies to the payments made to the personal loan account.

Similarly, if someone has her/his wages paid directly into a current account, they are always applied initially to reduce any overdraft on that account, even if debts such as mortgage arrears should be given a higher priority for repayment.

Emergency action may, therefore, be needed to ensure income is not swallowed up as it becomes available. It may be necessary to open a current account with another bank so that wages can be paid into the new account or, if this is not possible, exercise the 'first right of appropriation' and earmark the funds (see p54).

Note: banks can transfer money from a sole account to a joint account in order to pay a joint debt but not the other way round.[1] In multiple debt cases, the bank should recognise the pro rata principle when considering a payment arrangement and that priority debts should take precedence over non-priority debts, which is what the bank's debt is likely to be unless it is secured on the client's home.

It may be possible to challenge any charges added to the account (see p155).

Since 18 December 2019, banks are required by the Financial Conduct Authority (FCA) to draw up and implement policies and procedures to identify customers who are showing signs of financial strain or are in financial difficulty, and implement a strategy to reduce repeat overdraft use.

The FCA has also introduced new rules for overdraft charges, which come into effect on 6 April 2020, that will:
- prohibit banks from charging higher prices for unarranged overdrafts than for arranged overdrafts;
- abolish the right to charge fixed daily/monthly fees for overdraft use;
- require banks to price overdrafts by a simple annual interest rate and to advertise overdraft prices with an annual percentage rate (APR), to assist customers to compare overdrafts with other products.[2]

There is evidence that some banks have increased the interest rates on their overdrafts in anticipation of these rule changes.

Offsetting credits against debts

Although the bank can offset any credits received against any debt owed to it, the FCA's *Banking: Conduct of Business Sourcebook* (which has applied to retail banking since 1 November 2009) says that banks must consider the interests of their customers and must treat customers who are in financial difficulty fairly. The FCA says that if a bank is considering using set-off on a client's account, it should:[3]
- consider each case and assess how much money needs to be left in the account to meet priority debts and essential living expenses, and refrain from offsetting against that amount;

- usually provide a refund if it becomes apparent that money taken in set-off was intended for priority debts or essential living expenses (or justify why it considers it is not fair to do so);
- not use set-off on money that it knows, or should know, was received by the customer from a government department, local authority or the NHS and was intended for a specific purpose or if a third party is entitled to it.[4]

The Financial Ombudsman Service also expects banks to have given their customers a fair and sufficient opportunity to discuss the situation and repay the outstanding debt before resorting to their right to set off funds.[5]

Checklist for action

Advisers should take the following action.
- Consider whether emergency action is necessary (see Chapter 8).
- Advise the client to open a new bank account at a bank with which s/he does not have any debts.
- Check liability, including the enforceability of the agreement under the Consumer Credit Act 1974.
- If the bank has resorted to offsetting funds, check that it has complied with the guidance and codes of practice.
- Assist the client to choose a strategy from Chapter 9 as, if the debt is unsecured, it is a non-priority debt. **If it is secured, it is a priority debt**. See Chapter 8.

Bill of sale

A bill of sale is also known as a 'chattel mortgage' or even more commonly as a 'logbook loan'. It is a way of raising money by offering an item of personal property (commonly, a car) as security for a loan. The essential feature is that the mortgaged goods remain in the possession and use of the client, but ownership is transferred to the creditor, so they can be repossessed and sold if the debt is not repaid. Similar arrangements containing some, but not all, of these features are not bills of sale. For example, in the case of pawnbroking (see p122), the goods are deposited with the creditor as security, but they remain the property of the client.

Bills of sale can be used to finance the actual purchase of motor vehicles. With hire purchase/conditional sale, the dealer sells the vehicle to the creditor who then lets (hire purchase) or sells (conditional sale) it to the client. With a bill of sale, the dealer sells the car to the client who then enters into a credit agreement with the creditor (likely to be a regulated credit agreement), secured by a bill of sale. A bill of sale gives the creditor all the advantages of hire purchase/conditional sale agreements – ie:
- security for the debt;
- the right to repossess the vehicle if the client defaults;
- provided there is a term in the bill of sale, the right to forcibly enter the client's property to repossess the goods without a court order.

From the creditor's point of view, a bill of sale also removes some of the disadvantages of an hire purchase/conditional sale – ie:

- the client has no right to terminate the agreement and limit her/his liability to one-half of the total price;
- the vehicle is not protected from repossession without a court order once the client has paid one-third of the total price;
- a private individual (ie, someone who is not a motor dealer) who purchases the vehicle from the client without knowing it is subject to a bill of sale does not obtain ownership. S/he is, therefore, not protected from having the vehicle repossessed by the creditor, as would be the case if the vehicle were subject to a hire purchases/conditional sale agreement.

The legal position

Bills of sale are regulated by two pieces of nineteenth century legislation which still represent the law: the Bills of Sale Act 1878 and the Bills of Sale (1878) Amendment Act 1882.[6] The formal agreement must be set out in the way specified by these Acts. If the bill of sale secures an agreement regulated by the Consumer Credit Act 1974, there must be a separate agreement, which should comply with the Consumer Credit Act and the regulations. This requires the agreement to refer to the bill of sale. If the agreement is improperly executed, the creditor must apply for a court order to enforce its security under the bill of sale. If the agreement is completely unenforceable, the creditor cannot enforce its security.

There are a number of formalities associated with bills of sale and, if the creditor fails to comply with them, the creditor risks it being void and so unenforceable (although this does not necessarily affect the underlying credit agreement, which remains enforceable but as an unsecured debt).

Special features

In order to be valid and enforceable, a bill of sale must be registered at the High Court in London within seven days of its being made and then re-registered every five years. A copy of the registered document is forwarded to the local county court. Anyone can search, inspect, make extracts from and obtain copies of the register on payment of the prescribed fee (currently £45), by visiting the court office.

The bill of sale must also contain:

- the date of the bill of sale;
- the names and addresses of the parties;
- the amount paid by the creditor to, or on behalf of, the client, not including any item forming part of the total charge for credit in a regulated agreement secured by the bill;
- the client's acknowledgment that s/he has received the amount paid. This is obligatory, even though the money is not paid to her/him but to a third party – eg, the supplier of the goods;

- a transfer of ownership of the goods to the creditor as security for the debt;
- a description of the goods in a schedule to the bill (not in the main body of the bill);
- a monetary obligation. This can include an obligation to insure the goods or maintain the security;
- a statement of the sum secured, the rate of interest and the instalments by which repayment is to be made. Interest is an essential part of a bill and must be stated as a rate, even if it is also expressed as a lump sum. This is an area where creditors have frequently gone wrong, as it is not just a question of importing figures directly from the credit agreement. If the interest rate under a regulated agreement is not variable, there was no requirement before 31 May 2005 to include it in the agreement, as opposed to the annual percentage rate (APR). In the case of these agreements, if the bill of sale quotes the APR instead of the interest rate, it is not in the statutory form. Nor is the bill in accordance with the statutory form if the sum stated to be secured includes the interest charged under the credit agreement, because this would involve double charging of interest. Arguably, a bill of sale that refers to the credit agreement for the statement of these terms (or any of them) is not in accordance with the statutory form;[7]
- any terms that are agreed for the 'maintenance' or 'defeasance' of the security. A **'defeasance'** is a provision in a document which nullifies it if specified acts are performed. For example, when all sums due under the bill are paid, the security is void – ie, in this context, discharged. **'Maintenance of the security'** means the preservation of the whole security given by the bill of sale in as good a condition as when it was made. The following terms are included:[8]
  - to insure the goods and produce receipts for premiums;
  - to repair the goods and replace worn-out goods;
  - to allow entry to inspect the goods;
  - to allow the creditor to enter the premises in which the goods are situated in order to seize them (the bill of sale may even permit forcible entry);
- a proviso limiting the grounds of seizure. The bill of sale is void if it contains a power to seize, except in the case of:[9]
  - default in repayments or in the performance of any terms in the bill of sale necessary to maintain the security;
  - the client's bankruptcy ;
  - the fraudulent removal of the goods, or allowing them to be removed, from premises. In the case of a vehicle, this might include selling it without the lender's consent;
  - unreasonably refusing to produce the last receipt for rent, rates or taxes;
  - bailiffs taking control of goods for any debt. See Chapter 14 for more information on this;
- the client's signature. A bill need not be sealed;[10]

- an attestation clause. This is essential and must be meticulously completed. The security is unenforceable unless the client's signature is witnessed by at least one person who is not a party to the bill;[11]
- the name, address and description of the witness. The name alone without an address (which may be the business address and not necessarily a private address) and description (ie, the profession, trade or vocation of the witness) is insufficient;
- a schedule, referring to the goods included in the bill of sale. **Note:** if the bill does not have a schedule, it is void.

Clients often present themselves to advisers with either a hire purchase/conditional sale agreement or an unsecured loan. In these circumstances, if the creditor is threatening to repossess the subject of the agreement (eg, the motor vehicle), you should establish whether the debt is, in fact, secured by a bill of sale. If so, check that the credit agreement is properly executed and that the bill of sale has been validly drawn up and registered. The creditor could be asked to supply a copy of the bill of sale showing the court stamp.

If the agreement secured by the bill of sale is a regulated credit agreement, the creditor must serve a default notice before being entitled to repossess the goods on the grounds that the client has defaulted. Also, if the agreement is irredeemably unenforceable, the bill of sale cannot be enforced. If the agreement can only be enforced with a court order, the bill of sale cannot be enforced until the creditor has obtained an enforcement order.[12]

Seized goods should not be removed from the premises where they were seized until five clear days have expired.[13] During this period, the client could apply for a time order if appropriate (see p366).

If a bill of sale is believed to be invalid and unenforceable but the creditor does not accept this and threatens to go ahead with repossessing the goods, a rarely used procedure, known as applying to 'expunge' (ie, remove) the registration of the bill of sale must be used. This is, in effect, a declaration of unenforceability. As bills of sale are registered in the High Court, the application has to be made to the High Court under Part 8 of the Civil Procedure Rules, even though the bill of sale may be securing a regulated credit agreement. Specialist advice is needed.

If the creditor has already repossessed the goods under an invalid or unregistered bill of sale, the creditor should be challenged and, while the client may still owe the balance outstanding under the loan agreement, it may be possible to persuade the creditor to write off the debt. Specialist advice may be needed.

Code of practice

Following concerns about the use of bills of sale secured against vehicles, the industry now operates under a code of practice.[14] This includes the following.

• When providing pre-contract information, the client must also be provided with a copy of the Bill of Sale Borrower Information Sheet (available at ccta.co.uk/consumer/codes-of-practice).
• Clients in arrears can hand over the vehicle in full settlement of the debt and are not liable for any shortfall between the outstanding debt and the value of the vehicle.
• Consumer loans do not provide for 'balloon payments' – ie, small, initial interest-only payments, with the capital being repaid in a single, final payment.
• Charges imposed on clients in arrears must be disclosed at the pre-contract stage and must only cover the creditor's costs.
• If a client gets into difficulty, creditors must consider proposals for alternative payment arrangements and should repossess the vehicle only if attempts to arrange alternative ways of repayment fail.
• Creditors should take all reasonable steps to ensure that repossessed vehicles are sold for the highest obtainable market price.

Checklist for action
Advisers should take the following action.
• Consider whether emergency action is necessary. If repossession of essential goods is threatened, **this is likely to be a priority debt**. See Chapter 8.
• Check liability, including not only the validity of the bill of sale but also the enforceability of the agreement under the Consumer Credit Act.
• If the goods have already been repossessed, this is a non-priority debt. Assist the client to choose a strategy from Chapter 9.

Budget account

A budget account is a type of revolving credit (see p129) provided by shops. The client can spend up to an agreed credit limit and makes regular repayments.

The legal position
This type of account is a regulated credit agreement, provided the credit is for no more than £25,000 (if the agreement was made before 6 April 2008) or £15,000 (if made before 1 May 1998).[15] If the agreement was made on or after 6 April 2008, the agreement is regulated regardless of the amount, unless it is exempt (see p62).

Special features
Many large stores offer budget account facilities, which – by requiring clients to pay a monthly amount even when they have not recently purchased anything – can be a powerful incentive to continue shopping at that store. Instant credit is often available, including interest-free credit (see p110) on larger purchases.
These debts are non-priority debts (see Chapter 9).

Checklist for action

Advisers should take the following action.

- Check liability, including the enforceability of the agreement under the Consumer Credit Act 1974.
- Assist the client to choose a strategy from Chapter 9, as this is a non-priority debt.

Business debts

Many people seek advice about business debts (see Chapter 16). If a business is still trading but is facing financial difficulties, seek specialist advice from, for instance, an accountant, insolvency practitioner, local business centre or small firms advisory service on the viability of the business.

The legal position

If the business has already ceased trading, deal with debts as with any other case of multiple debt, using the same criteria to decide whether they should be treated as a priority or not (see Chapter 8).

First, establish liability for the debts. You should check whether the client was a sole trader, in a partnership or a limited company. A sole trader is personally liable for all the debts; in a partnership, all partners are 'jointly and severally' liable. In limited companies, only the directors can be held liable for any debts, and then only if they have personally guaranteed a loan or, under company law, if there has been wrongful trading or neglect of their duties as directors.

Checklist for action

Advisers should take the following action.

- Consider whether emergency action is necessary (see Chapter 8).
- Consider whether the client should be referred to a specialist agency – eg, Business Debtline (see Appendix 1).
- Otherwise, assist the client to choose a strategy from Chapter 8 for any priority debts and/or from Chapter 9 for any non-priority debts.

Charge card

A charge card (eg, American Express) is not a credit card. Purchases are made and the amount is charged to the account, but the balance must be cleared in full at the end of each charging period (usually monthly).

The legal position

Agreements for charge cards made before 1 February 2011 are exempt from the Consumer Credit Act 1974 because there is no extended credit. Agreements for charge cards made on or after 1 February 2011 are not exempt unless there are only 'insignificant' charges for the credit. There is no guidance in the legislation or in the Department for Business, Energy and Industrial Strategy guidance on what is 'significant' in this context.

Special features

In order to obtain a charge card, it is necessary to pay an annual fee and show proof of a high income.

Checklist for action

Advisers should take the following action.
- Check liability, including whether the Consumer Credit Act 1974 applies and, if so, the enforceability of the agreement.
- Assist the client to choose a strategy from Chapter 9, as this is a non-priority debt.

Child support payments

The term 'child support' is used here to describe child maintenance paid by parents under the statutory scheme run by the Child Maintenance Service. Some clients may have historic arrears from a previous scheme run by the Child Support Agency. All Child Support Agency cases have now been closed and ongoing arrangements ended. Parents needing ongoing chid support have been encouraged to make a 'family-based arrangement'. If a family-based arrangement is not possible, they must apply to the Child Maintenance Service under the '2012 scheme'.

The legal position

The statutory child support scheme is governed mainly by the Child Support Act 1991 and the Child Maintenance and Other Payments Act 2008 (as amended by the Child Support Act 1995, the Child Support, Pensions and Social Security Act 2000 and the Welfare Reform Act 2012) and subsequent regulations and amendments.

Special features

Child support payments are worked out by the Child Maintenance Service and are based on a percentage of the paying parent's gross weekly income. The percentage depends on the number of qualifying children (including any 'relevant non-resident children' – ie, a child for whom the parent is paying maintenance under another maintenance arrangement). The gross income figure used is reduced to take account of any 'relevant other children' – ie, a child for whom the paying parent or her/his partner get child benefit.

An appeal to an independent First-tier Tribunal can be made if anything relating to the child support calculation is disputed. Specialist advice should be obtained.

The Child Maintenance Service charges fees for:
- dealing with new applications (the fee can be waived for people under 19 and victims of domestic violence or abuse[16]);
- collecting payments and passing them on to the person looking after the child (the receiving parent), for which the paying parent pays 20 per cent in addition to each child support payment and 4 per cent is deducted from the payment due to the receiving parent. There are no collection fees if the parties agree arrangements for the paying parent to make payments directly to the receiving parent;
- taking enforcement action, for which fixed charges of between £50 and £300 are charged to the paying parent.

The view of the Child Maintenance Service is that enforcement of child support arrears is a priority if the paying parent is liable to pay ongoing maintenance for her/his children. There are no set rules on how quickly arrears of child support should be paid, although the Child Maintenance Service aims to clear arrears within a maximum of two years, at a rate of up to 40 per cent of the paying parent's income. However, enforcement officers have the discretion to extend this period in appropriate cases. All decisions relating to the collection and enforcement of child support are discretionary and the welfare of any child affected must be taken into account. This includes if the paying parent has a child in a new relationship. There is no right of appeal against a discretionary decision, but if necessary, a complaint can be made which might be escalated to the Independent Case Examiner or even the Parliamentary and Health Service Ombudsman.

If child support is being paid through the Child Maintenance Service's collection service, it can consider taking enforcement action as soon as a payment is missed. If child support is being paid directly to the receiving parent by the paying parent, the receiving parent should notify the Child Maintenance Service if a payment is missed. Otherwise, the Child Maintenance Service will not be aware of this. If the Child Maintenance Service then decides to take enforcement action, it will also start managing ongoing payments through its collection service (and collection fees will be charged).

The paying parent should contact the Child Maintenance Service as soon as a payment is missed to explain why and to make arrangements to pay, if s/he wishes to avoid enforcement action. The first step in enforcement is usually to make either a deduction from earnings order or, if this is not appropriate (eg, if the paying parent is not employed or is self-employed), an order to take money from a bank account. A court order is not required.

Other enforcement action requires a liability order from the magistrates' court. The court must accept that the payments specified are due from the paying parent and have not been made, but cannot question the child support calculation itself.

Note: from 12 July 2006, the six-year limitation period (see p291) on the Child Maintenance Service applying for a liability order was abolished.

If a liability order is made, it can be enforced by taking control of goods (see Chapter 14) or the county court can make a charging order (see p322) or third-party debt order (see p332). The Child Maintenance Service can also apply to the High Court for an order preventing the disposal of assets if the paying parent has disposed of, or is about to dispose of, assets with the intention of avoiding payment of child support.

If all other methods of recovering arrears have failed, the Child Maintenance Service can apply to the court to commit a person to prison for a maximum of six weeks (an option of last resort) or disqualify her/him from driving for a maximum of two years, but not both. In order to do so, the court must decide that the parent has the means to pay, but has 'wilfully refused or culpably neglected' to do so (see p407).

The Child Maintenance Service can also apply to the court to disqualify a person from holding or obtaining a passport or other UK travel authorisation for up to two years. The Child Maintenance Service has said it is only likely to use this power in exceptional circumstances and only where arrears of over £1,000 remain outstanding. The Child Maintenance Service cannot seek both disqualification from holding a passport and imprisonment.

The Child Maintenance Service can write off arrears if it considers that it would be unfair or inappropriate to enforce the liability and:

- the person with care of the child has requested that it cease taking action on the arrears; *or*
- the person with care has died; *or*
- the paying parent died before 25 January 2010 and there is no further action that can be taken to recover the arrears from her/his estate; *or*
- the arrears accrued in respect of an 'interim maintenance assessment' made between 5 April 1993 and 18 April 1995; *or*
- it has advised the paying parent that the arrears have been permanently suspended and that no further action will be taken to recover them.

If the arrears are more than £500 (or £1,000 for cases with an effective date before 1 November 2008), the parent with care is sent a notice of the intention to write off the arrears and will be given 60 days to contact the Child Maintenance Service if s/he believes that the arrears should not be written-off. The Child Maintenance Service may still decide to write off the arrears if it believes that there is no reasonable prospect of the arrears being cleared.

If the parent with care does not respond within 60 days, the arrears are automatically written off. Where the arrears are less than £500 (£1,000 for pre-1 November 2008 cases), the arrears can be written off without asking the parent with care, although s/he will still be notified. Arrears below £65 are written off and no notice sent.

The Child Maintenance Service can also consider writing off arrears that remain outstanding from the previous child support schemes run by the Child Support Agency if it considers that it will not be cost-effective to pursue the arrears.

For more information about the child support scheme, including arrears and enforcement, see CPAG's *Child Support Handbook* (see Appendix 2).

Checklist for action

Advisers should take the following action.
- Consider whether emergency action is necessary (see Chapter 8).
- Check liability.
- Assist the client to choose a strategy from Chapter 8 as **this is a priority debt.**

Civil recovery

Over the past few years, many people have been threatened with county court action by civil recovery agents for the recovery of losses allegedly incurred by retailers following allegations either of theft by employees or shoplifting by customers, in many cases involving goods of relatively low value. Although in some cases the person has been charged and prosecuted for a criminal offence, in many cases there has been no police involvement and, in most shoplifting cases, the goods have been recovered undamaged and able to be resold by the retailer.

The legal position

As well as being a criminal offence, shoplifting is a 'tort' (civil wrong).

It is a basic principle of the law of tort that a creditor can only take action if it can prove that the client's wrongful conduct caused the damage for which compensation is claimed.

Special features

Civil recovery agents typically demand damages for 'wrongful actions' and threaten to issue proceedings to recover:
- the value of goods stolen but not recovered; *and/or*
- staff and/or management time investigating and/or dealing with the incident; *and/or*
- administration costs; *and/or*
- apportioned amounts for general security and surveillance costs.

Claims for time, administration and a proportion of security costs are often based on a sliding scale of fixed costs, with the amount claimed rising in direct proportion to the value of the goods involved.

In one case, a circuit judge decided that there are recoverable amounts for:[17]
- the loss of value and/or profit of items not recovered from shoplifters;
- specific, direct costs incurred in apprehending shoplifters;

- physical damage caused by shoplifters in the course of the theft or their apprehension;
- personal injury caused by a shoplifter to a security person;
- diversion of a member of staff, such as a cashier, from her/his usual duties in order to chase and capture shoplifters.

The judge said that in order to successfully claim for staff time, the retailer must establish that the staff in question were 'significantly diverted from their usual activities' or that there was 'significant disruption to its business' or that there was loss of revenue generation. However, when observing, apprehending and dealing with shoplifters, security staff are, in fact, not diverted from their usual activities, but actively engaged in them and doing exactly what the retailer paid them to do. In these circumstances, no claim for time can be made.

The judge also said that claims for administration and apportioned security costs cannot be made unless the retailer can show that they were attributable to the activities of the shoplifter. If the amount spent by the retailer would have been the same regardless of whether the shoplifter had stayed at home or shoplifted at another retailer's premises, no claim can be made.

Checklist for action
Advisers should take the following action.
- Check liability, including the damage claimed by the retailer.
- If the retailer has taken county court action, see Chapter 11. Although these are 'small claims', representation at any hearing is advisable (see p22).
- If the client chooses not to challenge liability, assist her/him to choose a strategy from Chapter 9, as this is a non-priority debt.

Conditional sale agreement

A conditional sale agreement is a sale made on credit subject to conditions that give the client possession of the goods during the repayment period, but the goods only become the client's property when the last payment has been made. Conditional sale agreements are mostly used for motor vehicles (and are very similar to hire purchase agreements – see p104).

The legal position
Agreements are regulated credit agreements, provided the credit is for no more than £25,000 (if the agreement was made before 6 April 2008) or £15,000 (if made before 1 May 1998).[18] If the agreement was made on or after 6 April 2008, the agreement is regulated regardless of the amount, unless it is exempt (see p62).

Special features
Conditional sale has a number of special features. These are the same as those for hire purchase (see p104) and the two types of credit operate in the same way.

Checklist for action

Advisers should take the following action.

- Consider whether emergency action is necessary to prevent repossession of goods (see Chapter 8).
- Check liability, including the enforceability of the agreement under the Consumer Credit Act 1974.
- Check that the goods purchased were as described and of satisfactory quality (see p154).
- Assist the client to choose a strategy from Chapter 8, **if this is a priority debt**, or Chapter 9 if the goods are not essential.

Council tax

This is a tax administered by local authorities, comprising two equal elements – a 'property' element and a 'people' element.

For more detailed information, see CPAG's *Council Tax Handbook*.[19]

Property element

All domestic properties have been valued and placed in one of eight valuation bands in England and nine in Wales.

In England, the valuation is based on what the property would have sold for on the open market in April 1991. In Wales, properties were revalued on 1 April 2003 and the new valuations took effect from 1 April 2005. It is assumed that the property was sold freehold (or with a 99-year lease for flats), with vacant possession and in a reasonable state of repair. Under some circumstances, an appeal against this valuation can be made. Certain properties are exempt, and advisers should check to make sure that exemption has been applied for, if appropriate.

People element

The tax assumes that two adults aged 18 or over live in each household. Nothing extra is payable if there are more than two adults. One adult living on her/his own receives a 25 per cent discount. If there are no adults, there is a 50 per cent discount. If the latter applies, it may be that the property is exempt, and you should check whether this is the case.

When counting the number of adults in the household, certain people can be disregarded and this should be checked. In addition, in certain cases, there are reductions for people with disabilities whose homes have been modified or if a disabled resident uses a wheelchair in the home. **Note:** the disabled person does not have to be the person liable for the council tax.

Liability

A council tax bill is sent to each domestic property. There is a 'hierarchy' of liability, as follows:

- resident freeholder (owner);
- resident leaseholder;
- resident statutory/secure tenant (including a council tenant);
- other resident(s);
- non-resident owner (depending on the terms of her/his tenancy, a former tenant who no longer occupies the property could come into this category[20]).

If there is more than one resident who has the same interest in the property (ie, joint owners or joint tenants), they are 'jointly and severally' liable. This means that all the people concerned can be asked to pay the full charge, together or as individuals. Married couples and couples who live together are jointly liable. A single bill is sent, either in the name of one of the persons concerned, or in both names.

Students and people who are 'severely mentally impaired' are disregarded and may be exempt. They cannot be jointly and severally liable if there is someone else with the same status and legal interest in the property who is not exempt. Dwellings in which all the occupants are students and/or severely mentally impaired are exempt.[21]

Bills should be issued less any discounts, deductions and council tax reduction, and must arrive at least 14 days before the first installment falls due. The local authority usually asks for payment by 10 monthly installments but must offer the option of paying by 12 monthly installments if requested to do so. Any discount(s) can be backdated indefinitely.

There is a right to appeal to a valuation tribunal against certain decisions, including those on liability, valuations, discounts and exemptions.[22]

Local authorities have the power to reduce or remit sums of council tax, including arrears, in cases of hardship.[23]

Checklist for action

Advisers should take the following action.

- Consider whether emergency action is necessary (see Chapter 8).
- Check liability for the debt, including any associated bailiff's charges.
- Check for exemptions, discount and reductions.
- Assist the client to choose a strategy from Chapter 8, as **this is a priority debt**.

Credit card

A credit card (eg, Mastercard, Visa) is a form of revolving credit (see p129) and allows the client to buy goods or services from a trader. The trader invoices the credit card company and the client receives a monthly account showing all transactions made during that period. A minimum monthly repayment is required – often covering at least interest, fees and charges plus 1 per cent of the capital outstanding. Interest is added to balances outstanding after a specified payment date, or immediately for cash withdrawals using a credit card.

The legal position

Transactions made by credit card are linked agreements under the Consumer Credit Act 1974. Consequently, credit card companies can be held responsible for misrepresentation and for defective goods or services costing between £100 and £30,000 if the trader is unwilling to remedy the situation. This could include a claim for damages due as a consequence of the misrepresentation or other breach. The House of Lords has confirmed that overseas transactions are covered.[24]

If an additional credit card is issued to another person (usually a member of the client's family) to enable her/him to use the client's account, the client is liable for all transactions incurred by the additional cardholder, including if the client has not specifically authorised the transaction in question.

Unless the credit card agreement is a joint agreement (signed by both the client and the additional cardholder), the additional cardholder has no liability under the agreement if the client fails to pay.

If the client withdraws the additional cardholder's permission to use the credit card, the client remains liable for any transactions incurred by the additional cardholder until the client informs the creditor that the second cardholder's permission has been withdrawn in accordance with the terms and conditions of the credit card agreement. Once that has been done, the additional credit cardholder is no longer an 'authorised person' and the client has no further liability for transactions incurred by her/him.

Persistent debt

Since 19 December 2018, credit card companies have been required by the FCA to take a series of escalating steps to help clients who are deemed to be in 'persistent debt'. **'Persistent debt'** is when the amount the client has repaid towards the credit card balance over the preceding 18-month period comprises a lower amount of principal than interest and charges. The first intervention required by the credit card company is at the 18-month point, followed by subsequent interventions at 27 months and 36 months.

At the 18-month point, the credit card company must contact the client and point out the level of repayments over the previous 18 months and how increasing the level of payment would reduce both the cost and the time it would take to repay the balance. Encourage the client to contact the credit card company to discuss the her/his financial circumstances and the possibility of increasing her/his payments without an adverse effect on the her/his financial situation. Give the client details of not-for-profit debt advice providers and encourage her/ohimto contact them.

At the 27-month point, if the pattern of payments has continued so that it appears the client will remain in 'persistent debt' at the 36-month point, the credit card company must repeat the previous 18-month communication.

If, at the 36-month point, the client is still in 'persistent debt', the credit card compay must taken reasonable steps to assist the client to repay the balance more quickly and in a way that does not adversely affect her/his financial situation. The credit card company must contact the client and set out options for the client to increase payments with a view to repaying the balance within a 'reasonable period' (generally, threee to four years in the FCA's view). The credit card company must also provide the client with contact details of not-for-profit debt advice providers and encourage her/him to contact them. If the client either does not respond to the communication or confirms that one or more of the repayment options is sustainable, but that s/he will not make the payment, the credit card company must suspend or cancel the client's use of the card.

Where the client confirms the payment options are unsustainable, or the pattern of payments actually made under the repayment plan indicates that the client is unlikely to repay the balance in a reasonable period, the credit card company must treat the client with forbearance and due consideration. This might involve reducing, waiving or cancelling any interest, fees or charges and accepting token payments where the client would not otherwise be able to meet her/his priority debts or other essential living expenses.[25]

Special features

The use of a credit card is the cheapest way to obtain short-term credit (up to about six weeks) for specific items. This is because no interest is charged on most cards if the account is cleared at the first due date after a purchase is added to it. However, interest is charged immediately for cash withdrawals and there is sometimes an annual charge for cardholders.

Checklist for action

Advisers should take the following action.
- Check liability and that the goods purchased were as described and of satisfactory quality (see p154).
- Assist the client to choose a strategy from Chapter 9, as this is not a priority debt.

Credit sale agreement

Goods bought on credit sale are owned immediately by the client. Regular payments are due in accordance with the agreement. The creditor is often the supplier of the goods and this type of credit is used extensively to sell furniture and cars.

The legal position

The agreement is a regulated credit agreement provided the credit is for £25,000 or less (if made before 6 April 2008) or £15,000 (if made before 1 May 1998). If the agreement was made on or after 6 April 2008, the agreement is regulated regardless of the amount, unless it is exempt (see p62).

Special features

The creditor has no rights over the goods. The client simply takes the goods, signs the agreement, and starts to make payments. Sometimes interest-free credit (see p110) is given in the form of a credit sale agreement.

Some credit sale agreements (particularly for cars) provide that:
- the client must not sell the goods during the lifetime of the agreement; *and*
- if the client does sell the goods, s/he must pay the proceeds to the creditor.

It is arguable that this restriction on the sale of the goods is an unfair contract term, which means a client is probably not in breach of it if s/he does sell the goods. However, it is not unfair for the creditor to require payment of the proceeds, although the creditor must serve the client with a notice under section 76 of the Consumer Credit Act 1974 before being entitled to take action to enforce such a term.[26] If the client is unable to comply with such a notice, s/he is then in default. For a fuller discussion of unfair contract terms, see p155.

Checklist for action

Advisers should take the following action.
- Check liability, including the enforceability of the agreement under the Consumer Credit Act 1974.
- Check that the goods purchased were as described and of satisfactory quality (see p154).
- Assist the client to choose a strategy from Chapter 9, as this is not a priority debt.

Fines

Fines are the most common form of punishment imposed by the magistrates' or Crown Court for criminal offences.

The legal position

Magistrates' courts can impose fines for criminal offences by a wide variety of legislation. They must consider the means of the defendant 'as far as they are known to the court'.[27] Maximum amounts are laid down in regulations for each offence.

Special features

Fines should be distinguished from costs or compensation, which are often also awarded against defendants in criminal actions.

Advisers should consider emergency action if payment of a fine is difficult for a client. **This is a priority debt** (see Chapter 8). Court procedures and enforcement are explained in Chapter 13.

Checklist for action

Advisers should take the following action.

- Consider whether emergency action is necessary (see Chapter 8).
- Check liability, including for any associated bailiff's charges.
- Assist the client to choose a strategy from Chapter 8, as **this is a priority debt.**

Gas and electricity charges

Gas and electricity suppliers charge for their fuel in a number of ways. Pre-payment meters, quarterly accounts, direct debit and online schemes are common payment methods. Clients have a choice of supplier, although a supplier to whom arrears are owed can object to a transfer in certain circumstances. The industry is regulated by Ofgem. Suppliers are required to operate codes of practice on the payment of bills and disconnection, including guidance for customers who may have difficulty in paying. You should obtain copies of the codes of practice of your clients' suppliers.

Suppliers are required to take into account clients' 'ability to pay' when recovering debts.

The legal position

Electricity

A person is liable to pay an electricity bill if:

- s/he has signed a contract for the supply of electricity; *or*
- no one else was liable for the bill or her/his liability has come to an end (see below) and s/he is the owner/occupier of premises which have been supplied with electricity (known as a 'deemed contract').

A person is not liable to pay an electricity bill if:

- s/he has not a made a contract with a supplier; *and*
- someone else is liable to pay the bill and her/his liability has not come to an end (see below).

A person is no longer liable to pay an electricity bill under an actual or deemed contract if:

- s/he has terminated any contract in accordance with its terms (but s/he is still liable if s/he continues to be supplied with electricity); *or*
- s/he ceases to be the owner/occupier of the property, starting from the day s/he leaves the property, provided s/he has given at least two days' notice of leaving; *or*

- s/he did not give notice before leaving the property, on the earliest of:
  - two working days after s/he actually gave notice of ceasing to be an owner/occupier; *or*
  - when someone else begins to own/occupy the property and takes a supply of electricity to those premises.

This means that if the fuel supply is in the sole name of the client's partner who has subsequently left the home, the client is not liable for any arrears up to that date. However, s/he could be liable for the cost of any fuel supplied after this date, regardless of whether her/his partner has terminated the contract.

Advise clients to arrange for a final reading of the meter before leaving the property, if possible, and that they should, at least, read the meter themselves in order to be able to check their final bill.

Gas

A person is liable to pay a gas bill if:
- s/he has signed a contract for the supply of gas; *or*
- no one else was liable for the bill or her/his liability has come to an end, but s/he has continued to be supplied with gas (known as a 'deemed contract').

A person currently liable under an actual or deemed contract remains liable until:
- s/he terminates the contract in accordance with its terms (but if s/he still occupies the premises and continues to be supplied with gas, s/he remains liable to pay for the gas supplied); *or*
- s/he ceases to occupy the premises, provided s/he has given at least two working days' notice that s/he intended to leave; *or*
- if notice was not given before s/he left the premises, the earliest of:
  - 28 days after s/he informed the supplier that s/he has left the premises; *or*
  - the date when another person requires a supply of gas.

Advise clients to arrange for a final reading of the meter before leaving the property, if possible, and that they should, at least, read the meter themselves in order to be able to check their final bill.

Special features of gas and electricity arrears

Fuel supplies may be disconnected if there are arrears, and this is likely therefore to be a priority debt (see Chapter 8). The prioritisation of the debt depends on the client's continued need for that fuel at her/his present address.

Note: a supplier cannot transfer a debt from a previous property to a new account and then disconnect that fuel supply for the previous debt. A supply can only be disconnected at the address to which the bill relates.[28]

It may be possible to reduce charges by changing supplier. If the arrears are more than 28 days old, the old supplier can object to the transfer unless the arrears are paid. This does not apply to clients with pre-payment meters, provided the debt does not exceed £500 and the client agrees that the new supplier can collect the arrears through the meter. If the client has both gas and electricity from the same supplier, the figure is £500 per fuel. If the transfer goes ahead without objection, the arrears cannot be transferred to the new supplier.

Ten energy suppliers have signed up to the debt assignment protocol. Energy UK has produced a factsheet on this, available at energy-uk.org.uk/publication.html?task=file.download&id=5937.

A pre-payment meter can only be fitted at the address to which the bill relates (unless the client requests otherwise).

Estimated bills

Arrears of gas or electricity payments may arise as a result of high bills. While high bills may be caused by high consumption, price increases or previous underpayments, they may also be caused by estimated bills based on wrong assumptions about the amount of fuel used.

Many bills are based on estimated meter readings. Under their licence conditions, suppliers are only required to obtain actual meter readings once every two years. If the estimated reading is different to the actual reading, the client should read the meter her/himself and ask for this reading to be used in order to avoid either an overpayment or an underpayment which could lead to arrears. The name and address of the client, as well as the address to which fuel was supplied, should be noted from the bill.

If the bill is estimated and the estimated reading is higher than the actual reading, it is possible to reduce the amount owing. The bill will explain (often by means of an 'E' next to a reading) whether an estimated reading has been given. Clients can read their own meters and provide the supplier with their reading, and so should never be disconnected on the basis of an estimated bill. You should ask the client to read the meter and request an amended bill.

Backbilling

Ofgem has introduced a licence condition (applying to both electricity and gas suppliers) to protect customers from backbills. The new licence condition applies to all meter types and payment methods. With effect from May 2018, when a supplier issues a bill, it can only seek to recover charges for energy consumed in the previous 12 months unless:

- the bill was sent before the licence condition came into effect; *or*
- it has previously issued a compliant bill and is chasing previously billed charges; *or*
- the client behaves in an 'obstructive or manifestly unreasonable way'.

The new licence condition replaces the previous voluntary arrangements, which only applied to some suppliers and were not always followed in practice (see previous editions of this *Handbook*). In addition, the voluntary arrangements worked on the basis of a 'supplier at fault' principle.

Ofgem has provided a few examples of when it would consider a client's behaviour to be 'obstructive or manifestly unreasonable':

- where the client behaves unlawfully by stealing electricity or gas or not keeping her/his meter in working order (where the client is using her/his own meter); *or*
- the client prevents physical access to the meter – eg, by not allowing a meter reader into the home without good reason.

Ofgem has confirmed that it does not consider a client to be 'obstructive or manifestly unreasonable' when s/he does not supply a meter reading. If clients do not respond to requests for a meter reading, suppliers should take a meter reading themselves to avoid billing based on estimates. This means suppliers will have to put more effort into obtaining meter readings from their customers.[29]

Social tariffs

'Social tariffs' (reductions on the standard tariff) have been phased out, but clients on a low income (eg, getting pension credit) might also qualify for a £140 Warm Home Discount. See gov.uk/the-warm-home-discount-scheme for more details.

Meter faults

If a gas or electricity meter is registering fuel consumption at too high a rate, the client will receive a bill that is higher than it should be. According to the industry, meter faults are rare but, if the client believes a meter is faulty, the fuel supplier will check the accuracy of the meter if requested to do so.

See CPAG's *Fuel Rights Handbook* for more details (see Appendix 2).

Meter tampering

Tampering with a meter in order to prevent it registering or to reduce the amount it is registering is a criminal offence. Accusations of tampering usually follow a visit to the client's home by a meter reader who has noticed and reported something unusual about the meter. The supplier should write to the client informing her/him of an investigation into suspected tampering. If the meter is considered to be in a dangerous condition, it may be unusable pending the investigation. The investigation should be carried out in accordance with the code of practice and you should obtain a copy of this from the supplier.

If a client is threatened with prosecution, s/he should be referred to a solicitor.

Other assistance

Clients may be able to obtain a grant to pay off fuel debts.[30] Some energy suppliers have trust funds to help customers who are in debt, or may fund projects which provide support for the fuel poor. Grants are available for electricity and gas bills and may also be available to pay other essential household bills. Auriga Services (which works with utility companies to assist customers who are vulnerable or in financial hardship) publishes a booklet summarising the schemes, called *Help with water and energy bills*, available at aurigaservices.co.uk/wp-content/uploads/2019/10/Auriga_waterandenergy_Online.pdf.

Clients can also take steps to help save energy and reduce fuel bills. The Energy Saving Trust offers free advice on ways to reduce fuel consumption and should be aware of grants that are available locally to help cover the cost of energy efficiency measures. See energysavingtrust.org.uk or telephone 0800 444 202.

All suppliers must provide a range of free services (including quarterly meter readings) to clients who are on their Priority Services Register. This is available to clients who:

- have a disability; *or*
- are over pension age; *or*
- are chronically sick; *or*
- are visually impaired or have hearing difficulties.

See CPAG's *Fuel Rights Handbook* for more details (see Appendix 2).

Checklist for action

Advisers should take the following action.

- Consider whether emergency action is necessary (see Chapter 8).
- Check liability and whether the client is eligible for any assistance with the charges.
- Assist the client to choose a strategy from Chapter 8, as **this is a priority debt.**

Hire purchase agreement

A hire purchase agreement hires goods to the client for an agreed period. At the end of this period the client has the option to buy them (usually for a nominal amount). Hire purchase is predominantly used for motor vehicles and household goods. The creditor (who is the hirer) owns the goods, generally having bought them from the supplier who introduced the client to the hirer.

The legal position

Hire purchase agreements for £25,000 or less (if made before 6 April 2008) or £15,000 (if made before 1 May 1998) are regulated credit agreements. If the agreement was made on or after 6 April 2008, the agreement is regulated regardless of the amount, unless it is exempt (see p62).

The contract is between the client and the hirer of the goods, rather than the supplier – ie, in the case of a car, between the client and the finance company, rather than with the garage. Therefore the hirer (ie, the finance company) is liable for compensation if there has been misrepresentation (see p152) or the goods are faulty. **Note:** the Consumer Credit Act 1974 treats hire purchase and conditional sale in the same way and so what follows also applies to conditional sale agreements.

Special features

The goods belong to the hirer until the end of the agreement. The client must not sell them during this period without obtaining the hirer's permission. The client can choose to return the goods to the hirer at any time during the lifetime of the agreement. The client must first give written notice to the hirer of her/his wish to terminate the agreement. So that there is no doubt as to what the client is doing (particularly if the hirer is threatening to repossess the goods), the letter should refer to the client exercising her/his right to terminate the agreement and request instructions from the hirer on returning the goods.

The amount payable (which the client does not have to pay before either the termination of the agreement or the return of the goods) depends on the amount already paid.

- If less than half the total purchase price (as stated on the agreement) has been paid, the client must pay either half the total purchase price minus the payments already made, or any arrears of payments which have become due by the termination date, whichever is greater. In this context, the 'total purchase price' is the cash price of the goods plus the charges for credit.
- If more than half the total purchase price has already been paid, the client may return the goods and owes nothing further except any arrears on payments due.
- If the client has not taken reasonable care of the goods, s/he is liable to compensate the hirer.

When clients inform hirers that they can no longer afford the repayments and wish to end the agreement, they are often advised to surrender the vehicle voluntarily. A 'voluntary surrender' is not the same thing as a termination. A voluntary surrender has the same legal consequences as if the hirer had terminated the agreement and repossessed the goods. While hirers are under no duty to inform clients of their rights, they must not mislead them.

Hirers often put obstacles in the way of clients attempting to end their agreements – eg, by claiming that the client cannot end the agreement if it is in arrears or that the sum due on ending the agreement must be paid as a pre-condition of ending it. This is not correct; the right to end the agreement is unconditional. Default notices issued since 1 October 2008 must contain the following statement: 'You will need to pay X if you wish to end this agreement' (where X is the amount calculated as above). The former Office of Fair Trading agreed that this sum is the amount the hirer is liable to pay if s/he exercises the right to terminate and is not a condition of termination. However, the regulations have still not yet been amended to reflect this.

If the hirer challenges the client's right to end the agreement, specialist advice should be sought.

The creditor is not responsible for collecting the goods if a client terminates the agreement and, if the creditor has to collect the goods because the client refuses to return them, the client is liable for any charges incurred. On the other hand, if the creditor insists on collecting the goods, the client should challenge any collection charges the creditor seeks to impose.[31]

If the client claims to have terminated the agreement, specialist advice should be obtained if the creditor is nevertheless seeking to recover the total balance due under the agreement. The client loses the right to terminate the agreement if the hirer has already done so or called in the balance due under the agreement.

If the client defaults on payments, the hirer can repossess the goods. It must obtain a court order, unless:

- the client gives permission. This must be free and informed – ie, the client has not been misled about her/his rights; *or*
- less than one-third of the total purchase price has been paid and the goods are not on private premises.

If the hirer repossesses the goods (including in 'voluntary surrender' cases where the client returns the goods without terminating the agreement in writing), the client is liable for the outstanding balance due under the agreement, less the sale proceeds of the goods.[32]

In 2018, BrightHouse (a company that sells domestic items on hire purchase) announced while giving evidence to the Treasury Select Committee it now has a policy that:

- clients can return goods without incurring any further liability;
- the terms of loans can be extended without clients incurring any further charges;
- where clients do not pay or return the goods, the debt will be written off after 120 days if no contact can be made with the client or no payment arrangement can be made; *and*
- it no longer repossess goods.[33]

Insurance

Many hire purchase/conditional sale agreements also incorporate credit agreements for insurance sold as part of the same transaction – eg:

- payment protection insurance to cover the repayments in the event of the client's unemployment, sickness, disability or death;
- mechanical breakdown insurance;
- vehicle recovery insurance;
- accident assistance insurance;

- extended warranties or guarantees; *and*
- guaranteed asset protection, also known as shortfall insurance, which covers any shortfall if, following an accident, the write-off value of the goods is less than the balance owed to the creditor.

A credit agreement for such insurance (known as the 'subsidiary agreement') is a different, separate agreement to the hire purchase/conditional sale (known as the 'principal agreement') . However, a subsidiary agreement for such insurance (but not for any other insurance or products) can be included in the same document as the principal agreement containing only the consumer credit heading and signature box for the principal agreement.

Agreements made before 31 May 2005 should not have included credit for guaranteed asset protection in the subsidiary agreement and any such credit agreement is improperly executed and unenforceable without a court order.[34] Enforcement orders are usually granted on condition that the cost of guaranteed asset protection and its associated credit charges are removed.

The consequences of this practice are as follows.

- The client does not have the right to terminate the subsidiary agreement and so termination of the principal agreement does not affect her/his liability under the subsidiary agreement. The client must deal with this separately – eg, settle the agreement early, complain about any mis-selling of the insurance or raise any unenforceability issues.
- When calculating whether the client has paid one-third or one-half of the total price in connection with protected goods and termination rights (see above), you should take into account only the payments due or made in relation to the principal agreement. You should check the one-third and one-half figures in the agreement.
- If the client was required to take out payment protection insurance as a condition of making the hire purchase/conditional sale agreement, it may be that both agreements are irredeemably unenforceable and specialist advice should be sought.

Personal contract purchases

Personal contract purchases (also known as 'contract purchase plans') are an increasingly popular form of motor vehicle finance. A personal contract purchase is a form of hire purchase agreement, but differs in one important respect: the client does not pay the purchase price of the vehicle (together with interest). Instead, s/he pays the amount the finance company estimates the vehicle will lose in value (ie, the depreciation over the term of the agreement, typically 24 or 36 months) together with interest minus any deposit by monthly instalments. The resulting figure (ie, the purchase price less depreciation) is known as the guaranteed minimum future value. The monthly payments are usually less than under a standard hire purchase agreement. At the end of the agreement and assuming the client has made all the payments due, the client has the following options.

- Buy the vehicle. The client can pay a 'balloon payment', which is a lump sum representing the difference between the guaranteed minimum future value and the original purchase price together with a nominal fee, in order to own the vehicle. This is likely to be more expensive than taking out a standard hire purchase agreement. For more information, see moneysavingexpert.com/car-finance/personal-contract-purchase.
- Exchange the old vehicle for a new one under another personal contract purchase. Should the guaranteed minimum future value be more than the actual value of the vehicle, this 'equity' can be put towards the deposit on the new vehicle but cannot be taken in cash.
- Return the vehicle. The client has nothing further to pay except possibly:
  - any excess mileage charge. This will arise if the vehicle has done more miles than was agreed at the start of the contract. The finance company uses the estimated mileage in the calculation of the guaranteed minimum future value and so the client needs to be realistic in assessing this in order to avoid the risk of having to pay this charge;
  - the cost of any damage to the vehicle, other than normal wear and tear (as with a standard hire purchase agreement if the vehicle is returned).

As with other hire purchase agreements, the client can voluntarily terminate the agreement and return the car. The issue might then arise as to whether the finance company can recover any excess mileage charges. It is arguable that the legislation (sections 99(2), 100(1) and 100(4) Consumer Credit Act 1974) makes no provision for the recovery of such charges and, indeed, is inconsistent with the right to do so and, therefore, void under section 173. Some finance companies have argued that exceeding mileage limits falls under 'failing to take reasonable care of the goods' (section 100(4)), as the value of the vehicle will have been reduced, but 'reasonable care' in law generally means the duty to avoid causing physical damage, not pure economic loss. There has to date been no decision by any court on this issue.[35]

Checklist for action

Advisers should take the following action.

- Consider whether emergency action is necessary to prevent repossession of goods (see Chapter 8).
- Check liability, including the enforceability of the agreement under the Consumer Credit Act 1974.
- Check that the goods purchased were as described and of satisfactory quality (see p154).
- Assist the client to choose a strategy from Chapter 8, if **this is a priority debt**, or Chapter 9 if the goods are not essential.

Income tax arrears

Most income above certain fixed limits is taxable. Employees are taxed by direct deduction from their income by their employer (the pay as you earn (PAYE) scheme). PAYE taxpayers rarely owe tax on their earned income unless mistakes have been made in the amounts deducted. Self-employed people receive their earnings before tax is deducted and are responsible for paying their own tax directly to HM Revenue and Customs (HMRC). Arrears are, therefore, more likely to occur with self-employment. See Chapter 16 for more information.

The legal position

Income tax is payable under the Taxes Management Act 1970 and the Income and Corporation Taxes Act 1988 and subsequent Finance Acts and regulations.

HMRC can take control of goods for unpaid income tax without a court order and is not subject to any limitation period for taking court action to recover the unpaid income tax and any interest, but penalties are subject to a six-year limitation period (see p291). The client could even be imprisoned for non-payment. Tax debts of up to £3,000 owed by previously self-employed clients can be recovered through the PAYE system.

Special features

There are many ways of reducing liability for tax, unless it is deducted under PAYE. Self-employed people, in particular, require detailed advice on how to complete their tax returns and on any arrears that HMRC may be claiming. Self-employed people should obtain specialist help either from an accountant, Business Debtline or TaxAid if they wish to challenge the amount of any arrears claimed (see Appendix 1).

It may be possible to negotiate remission (write-off) of a tax debt if the client's circumstances are unlikely to improve – eg, if s/he is permanently unable to work because of ill health or if s/he has no hope of increasing her/his income because of her/his age.

If the business is continuing to trade, however, it is vital that the client pays any ongoing tax on time and makes arrangements to repay any tax debt, otherwise HMRC can take control of essential goods without a court order and so close down the business.

Checklist for action

Advisers should take the following action.
- Consider whether emergency action is necessary (see Chapter 8).
- Consider whether the client should be referred to a specialist agency – eg, TaxAid.
- Otherwise, assist the client to choose a strategy from Chapter 8 as **this is usually treated as a priority debt.**

Interest-free credit

This is a type of credit sale agreement in which money is loaned to buy goods without any interest being charged. It is usually offered by larger stores. Some agreements offer interest-free credit provided the total balance is paid off within a specified period and, thereafter, become ordinary credit sale agreements.

The legal position

These agreements are regulated credit agreements, provided the credit is for no more than £25,000 (if made before 6 April 2008) or £15,000 (if made before 1 May 1998), even though there is no charge for credit. If the agreement was made on or after 6 April 2008, the agreement is regulated regardless of the amount, unless it is exempt (see p62).

An agreement is exempt if it requires the credit to be repaid in no more than four instalments within 12 months of making the agreement, and in the case of agreements made on or after 1 February 2011, the credit is provided without interest or other significant charges. An agreement made on or after 18 March 2015 is exempt if the number of instalments to be paid by the borrower is no more than 12. However, if it is not exempt, it must contain all the details required by a regulated agreement (see p70) and details of the circumstances in which interest could become chargeable. Interest can be charged on late payments if the agreement contains a clause allowing it. This type of credit can be expensive if it is not repaid during the interest-free period.

Special features

Interest-free credit is offered as an inducement to buy particular goods in a particular place and, therefore, is a linked agreement (see p163).

Checklist for action

Advisers should take the following action.
- Check liability, including enforceability under the Consumer Credit Act 1974.
- Check that the goods purchased were as described and of satisfactory quality (see p154).
- Assist the client to choose a strategy from Chapter 9, as this is a non-priority debt.

Mail order catalogue

Mail order catalogues offer a way of buying goods by post and usually spread payment over a period of weeks by instalments. Payments are sometimes collected by an agent – often a friend or neighbour of the client. The arrangement is usually an ongoing one.

The legal position

Catalogue debts are regulated credit agreements whether or not there is a charge for credit, provided the credit is for no more than £25,000 (if the arrangement began before 6 April 2008) or £15,000 (if before 1 May 1998). If the arrangement began on or after 6 April 2008, the agreement is regulated regardless of the amount, unless it is exempt (see p62).

Some mail order companies provide goods on the basis that they are paid for in full on receipt. These agreements are not regulated credit agreements. If in doubt about whether a catalogue debt is regulated, obtain specialist advice.

Special features

Often clients do not receive an agreement to sign. This means that the client's liability for the debt is irredeemably unenforceable if the arrangement began before 6 April 2007 and enforceable only with a court order if the arrangement began on or after this date.[36] In these circumstances, the client is not legally obliged to settle the debt if the arrangement began before 6 April 2007, although s/he may choose to do so.

Mail order purchases can be cancelled by returning the goods within seven days of receipt.

Catalogues are often particularly important to people on low incomes as the only way of affording essential items such as bedding or clothing.

Checklist for action

Advisers should take the following action.
- Check liability by asking the creditor to supply a copy of the agreement signed by the client.
- Check that the goods were of satisfactory quality and as described (see p154).
- If the client decides not to challenge liability, assist her/him to choose a strategy from Chapter 9, as this is a non-priority debt unless the use of mail order catalogues is the only way in which s/he can buy essential goods (see p254).

Maintenance payments

Before April 1993, either the magistrates' court or county court made orders to require a parent or ex-spouse to make maintenance payments to the other partner for her/himself and/or any children.

From April 1993, child maintenance payment powers passed to the Child Support Agency (the predecessor of the Child Maintenance Service – see p90). The only new court orders made after this date are for applications not covered by the child support scheme (eg, for additional maintenance) and for spousal maintenance.

The legal position

Magistrates' courts make maintenance orders and also collect and review maintenance orders made by the county court, divorce registry and High Court.[37]

Special features

If a maintenance order is unpaid, the magistrates' court has powers similar to those for unpaid fines (see Chapter 13). Maintenance payable under a court order should be distinguished from voluntary maintenance payments, even those written as a legal agreement.

Checklist for action

Advisers should take the following action.
- Consider whether emergency action is necessary (see Chapter 8).
- Check liability.
- Assist the client to choose a strategy from Chapter 8 as **this is a priority debt**.

Mortgage

Usually, the term 'mortgage' is used to describe a loan to buy a house or flat. If repayments are not maintained, the lender can recover the money lent by repossessing the property and selling it. A 'charge' is registered on the property to safeguard the rights of the lender.

The legal position

First mortgages from building societies and the major banks are exempt from regulation by the Consumer Credit Act 1974 (see p62). Since 31 October 2004, most mortgage lending (including arranging and administering mortgages) has been regulated by the FCA (previously the Financial Services Authority).

Firms involved in mortgage-related activities must be authorised by the FCA. If they are not, they commit a criminal offence and any regulated mortgage contract cannot be enforced, unless the court is satisfied that it is 'just and equitable' to do so. To check whether a lender or intermediary is authorised, see fca.org.uk/firms/financial-services-register.

A mortgage is a regulated mortgage contract if it was taken out on or after 31 October 2004 and:
- the borrower is an individual – ie, s/he is acting as a consumer and not for business purposes;
- the loan is secured by a first mortgage on a property;
- the property is at least 40 per cent occupied by the borrower or her/his family as her/his residence.

Since 21 March 2016, secured loans which are not first mortgages are also regulated mortgage contracts if they meet the rest of the above critera and:
- the loan was made before 21 March 2016 and was a regulated credit agreement when it was made and so covered by the Consumer Credit Act 1974; *or*

- the loan was made after 21 March 2016, but would have been a regulated agreement and covered by the Consumer Credit Act 1974 if it had been made before this date.

Special features

There are a variety of different mortgages.

- **Capital repayment mortgage.** The amount borrowed ('capital') is repaid gradually over the term of the mortgage. At the beginning, repayments comprise virtually all interest, but towards the end of the term of the mortgage they are virtually all capital.
- **Endowment mortgage.** Repayments cover the interest on the capital borrowed and separate payments are made to an insurance company for the endowment premium. The capital is repaid at the end of the term of the mortgage in one lump sum from the proceeds of the insurance policy. Endowment policies aim to pay off the mortgage capital when they mature and produce extra capital for the borrower to use as s/he wishes. However, there is no guarantee that the policy will pay off even the capital, let alone provide extra money. Any client with an endowment mortgage should contact the policy provider and enquire how much the policy is expected to produce on maturity, and get independent financial advice if a shortfall is predicted.
- **Pension mortgage.** The borrower pays interest only to the lender and a separate pension premium which attracts tax relief. When it matures, the cash available from this pension pays off the capital on the mortgage and the rest funds a personal pension plan.
- **Low-start/deferred-interest mortgage.** Reduced interest is charged for the first two to three years. In some schemes, interest accrues during the first few years, but payment is spread over the remaining term of the mortgage. They are only helpful for people who expect their income to increase so that they can afford the rise in repayments after the first few years. These are sometimes known as 'discount-rate mortgages'.
- **Interest-only mortgage.** Under this type of mortgage, the client only pays interest on the loan during the term of the mortgage. This means that s/he pays lower monthly repayments to the lender during the term of the mortgage, but nothing towards the capital sum originally borrowed. So unless the client has a vehicle to repay the capital at the end of the mortgage term, such as an insurance policy, or has access to a lump sum, s/he may have to sell the property in order to repay the orginal loan. If your client is in this situation, refer to the FCA consultation on interest-only mortgages (May 2013) at fca.org.uk/publication/guidance-consultation/gc13-02.pdf.[38]
- **Fixed-rate mortgage.** The interest rate is fixed for a number of years, either at the outset or during the life of the loan. They are obviously more attractive during a period when interest rates are rising.

- **Tracker mortgage.** These mortgages guarantee to follow the Bank of England's base rate or some other rate up or down, maintaining the same differential between the rate charged and that set by the Bank of England.
- **Other types of mortgage.** These include 'capped rates', where repayments do not exceed a set level (the 'cap'), or 'collared rates', where payments do not fall below a set level (the 'collar').

See below for mortgage shortfalls after a property is repossessed.

Regulated mortage contracts

Generally, lenders and intermediaries must conduct their business with integrity, consider the interests of clients and treat them fairly. The detailed rules are set out in the FCA's *Mortgages and Home Finance: Conduct of Business Sourcebook*, available at handbook.fca.org.uk/handbook/MCOB.pdf. It is not worth downloading this document as it is amended frequently.

Following a review of the mortgage market by the FCA,[39] the following has applied since 26 April 2014.[40]

- Lenders are fully responsible for assessing whether a client can afford the loan and must verify the client's income. Although lenders can use intermediaries in this process, the lender remains responsible.
- Lenders can grant interest-only mortgages, but must have evidence that the client has a credible repayment strategy.
- When taking account of the client's income and/or assets for the purpose of an affordability assessment, lenders must obtain independent evidence and must verify the client's income and not rely on a client's (or her/his representative's) own general declaration of affordability or the client's self-certification of income.

Lenders must deal fairly with clients in arrears, and have a written arrears policy in place and follow it. This requires the lender to use reasonable efforts to reach an agreement with the client over repayment, liaise with advisers and apply for repossession only when all other reasonable attempts to resolve the situation have failed. Within 15 business days of the account falling into arrears (defined as the equivalent of two monthly payments), the lender must send the client a copy of the FCA's information sheet on mortgage arrears, together with a statement of account, including details of the arrears, charges incurred and the outstanding balance. This information must be provided at least quarterly and, even if a repayment arrangement is in place, the information must still be sent out quarterly if the account is attracting charges.

From 30 June 2010, lenders must not charge arrears fees if the client is complying with an arrangement to pay those arrears.[41] Lenders must not put pressure on clients through excessive telephone calls or letters and must not contact them at unreasonable hours ('reasonable hours' are defined as 8am–9pm).

Lenders must not use documents that look like court forms or other official documents containing unfair, unclear or misleading information designed to coerce the client into paying.

If a lender does not comply with the above rules, the client could make a complaint, or complain to the Financial Ombudsman Service if the matter cannot be resolved with the lender or intermediary.[42]

If a property is repossessed, the lender must market it as soon as possible and obtain the best price that might reasonably be paid, although the lender is entitled to take account of market conditions or other factors that might justify deferring a sale.

In October 2011, the Council of Mortgage Lenders (which has been part of UK Finance since 2017) issued industry guidance on arrears and possessions to assist lenders to comply with Part 13 of the *Mortgages and Home Finance: Conduct of Business Sourcebook* and their duty to treat customers fairly. It can be found at handbook.fca.org.uk/handbook/MCOB.

As well as guidance, this document contains examples of good practice and is an essential reference for advisers (see p354).

The FCA has introduced new rules to help clients who are up-to-date with their mortgages, but who have been unable to switch to cheaper loan deals because of changes to lending practices during and after the 2008 financial crisis and the subsequent tightening of lending standards.[43] This group of borrowers are often referred to as 'mortgage prisoners'.

Mortgage prisoners
The new rules allow mortgage lenders to provide 'more affordable mortgages' where:
- the new mortgage has a total lower expected cost and lower interest rate over the deal period (or whole term if there is no deal period) than the current mortgage; *and*
- the typical monthly payment over the new mortgage (during the deal period or if there is no deal period over the whole mortgage term) is lower than the monthly payment made in every one of the last 12 months under the current mortgage.

The new rules apply where the client:
- has a current mortgage;
- is up to date with her/his mortgage payments;
- does not want to borrow more, other than to finance any relevant intermediary, product or arrangement fee for the mortgage; *and*
- is looking to switch to a new mortgage deal on her/his current property.

The new rules also apply to interest-only mortgages. The lender can extend a mortgage term but must warn the client if this would extend borrowing into retirement.

The modified 'affordability assessment' cannot be used when the client is looking to switch to a new mortgage on a new property. The new mortgage deal does not have to be with the same lender. While the new rules may help a considerable number of clients to obtain cheaper remortgages, they will be of no assistance to those with arrears and are unlikely to help those in negative equity.

Checklist for action

Advisers should take the following action.

- Consider whether emergency action is necessary (see Chapter 8).
- Check liability. If possession proceedings have started, see Chapter 12.
- Assist the client to choose a strategy from Chapter 8 as **this is a priority debt if the debt is secured on the client's current home**. Otherwise, the arrears are a non-priority debt. Assist the client to choose a strategy from Chapter 9.

Mortgage shortfall

If a property has been repossessed by the lender and the outstanding balance due under the mortgage is more than the proceeds of sale, this is known as a 'mortgage shortfall'. A client who hands in her/his keys to the lender remains liable for any subsequent shortfall as her/his contractual liability remains.

The legal position

Provided the loan remains secured, the lender has 12 years in which to take action to recover the principal amount (ie, the capital sum borrowed) and six years to recover arrears of interest. This limitation period (see p291) starts again every time the client or her/his representative acknowledges the debt (see p293). The limitation period for the principal (but not the interest) also starts again every time the borrower, a joint borrower or agent makes a payment into the account (including payments of mortgage interest by the Department for Work and Pensions[44]). Once the limitation period has expired, it cannot be started again by further payments or acknowledgements.

In 1997, a judge in the Court of Appeal suggested that it was 'seriously arguable' that the six-year limit applied to the principal as well as to the interest.[45] After a period of considerable uncertainty, the Court of Appeal and House of Lords resolved the issue.

- The limitation period for the principal sum borrowed is 12 years from the date when the sum became payable under the terms of the mortgage deed, usually after the client has failed to pay two or three monthly instalments.[46]
- The limitation period for the interest is six years from the date when the lender had the right to receive that interest.[47]
- The fact that a mortgage deed contains an express provision under which the borrower agrees to pay any shortfall to the lender does not give the lender a fresh right of action starting on the date of sale.[48]

- The position is the same for loans that are regulated credit agreements covered by the Consumer Credit Act 1974[49] or in situations where the mortgage deed contains no covenant allowing the lender to call in the mortgage on default but it has, nevertheless, repossessed and sold the property.[50]
- The proceeds of sale are treated as appropriated first to arrears of interest and then to capital.[51]

In the majority of cases, the shortfall is made up of capital only because the interest will have been paid from the proceeds of the sale, and the whole debt is subject to a 12-year time limit. This should, however, be checked with the lender.

As a concession, lenders and insurers have agreed not to pursue the debt unless the client is contacted within six years of the date of sale of the property if:

- the lender is a member of UK Finance (or previously the Council of Mortgage Lenders) or was a subscriber to the old Mortgage Code (in practice, all the major High Street banks and building societies), or the mortgage indemnity guarantee insurer is a member of the Association of British Insurers; *and*
- no contact about the shortfall was made by the lender/insurer with the client before 11 February 2000 (see below).

'Contact' includes letters or telephone calls received but ignored by the client, but should not include letters sent to a previous address, unless these have been forwarded, and does not include failed attempts to trace the client. This concession does not apply if the client was contacted before 11 February 2000 or had entered into a payment arrangement with the lender/insurer before this date, even if the contact was made more than six years after the property was sold.

If there is a regulated mortgage contract (see p112), the lender must notify the client of its intention to recover the shortfall within six years of the date of sale of the property.[52]

Special features

A mortgage shortfall debt is, in many ways, no different from any other unsecured debt, since once the property has been sold, it is no longer a priority debt. The strategies, tactics and principles of good money advice described throughout this *Handbook* still apply. However, the debt is often disproportionately high compared with the client's usual income and expenditure and any other debts s/he owes. It can be very distressing for clients to be faced with such a huge debt.[53]

Some lenders will already have a county court judgment for money. This does not prevent the client from using any of the strategies detailed but, in addition, you may need to protect the client's interest by applying to vary or suspend the judgment. This is essential if the lender is attempting to enforce it (eg, by an attachment of earnings order) as the Limitation Act does not apply to enforcement action. Clients who have acquired assets, particularly another property, may be especially vulnerable. If possible, the client should try to resolve the shortfall debt before acquiring further assets, such as a house or flat.

It is not unusual for clients to fail to give the lender details of their new address. Some may hope they will not be found. Before entering into negotiations, always check whether the Council of Mortgage Lenders'/Association of British Insurers' concession applies (see p117). The concession is known as the 'CML agreement'. See 'What Happens if Repossession Occurs?' at cml.org.uk/consumers/payment-difficulties/what-to-do-if-repossession-occur, and then use the preceding paragraphs to check the account and, if appropriate, note any points which may be used to challenge the extent of the debt. Also check whether MCOB 13.6.4R applies (see p114).

It may be necessary to contact the lender to obtain information (taking care not to acknowledge the debt and restart the limitation period). The information required may include:

- copies of any letters written by the lender to the client, which could confirm whether or not the CML agreement applies;
- a copy of the lender's 'completion statement' following the sale of the property, which will confirm the breakdown of the shortfall;
- a full statement of account, which will confirm when the last payment was made into the account by any of the borrowers; *and*
- copies of any letter(s) received by the lender from the client, which could be acknowledgements.

Additional information may also be required, and you may need to get specialist advice if you are unsure how to proceed.

Mortgage indemnity guarantee

Most mortgage lenders have a normal lending limit of 70–80 per cent of the property's value. If someone wants to borrow a higher proportion (eg, 95–100 per cent), the lender asks the borrower to buy an insurance policy to protect it against a mortgage shortfall. This is the mortgage indemnity guarantee (or indemnity insurance or building society indemnity). The insurance premium is usually paid as a lump sum of several hundred pounds at the time of purchase. **Note:** this insurance is intended to protect the lender, not the borrower. The only value to the borrower is that, without agreeing to pay the insurance premium, s/he may be refused the amount of mortgage.

The mortgage indemnity guarantee does not pay the full shortfall. The amount paid is a proportion of the shortfall relative to the lending risk. Therefore, there will still be a shortfall owing to the lender.

However, the insurance company can pursue the client for the money paid towards the mortgage shortfall. In some cases, the client may receive a demand for money from the insurer, even though the lender has agreed not to pursue the shortfall. Alternatively, some insurers appoint the lender to collect a client's liability on their behalf. In this case, the lender contacts the client to ask for payment of the entire shortfall. Commonly, the client can expect to receive a demand from the insurer and the lender for their respective proportions of the shortfall. These cannot be ignored and must be dealt with.

Checklist for action

Advisers should take the following action.

- Check liability, including whether the debt is unenforceable because the creditor has not taken recovery action within the appropriate time limit – ie, six years for property sales where MCOB 13-6R applies (see p118) and 12 years for the capital where the Limitation Act 1980 applies (see p241).
- Assist the client to choose a strategy from the list below or one of the other strategies in Chapter 9, as this is a non-priority debt. See also Chapter 15 for insolvency options.

Consider the following strategies.

- **Write-off.** A total write-off is likely to be the most appropriate strategy if it can be demonstrated that the client has no available income or assets and that the position is unlikely to improve (see p256). In other cases, pressure should be brought (perhaps by using local politicians) to highlight the unfairness of seizing a person's home and also expecting repayment of the shortfall.
- **Bankruptcy** (see Chapter 15). Personal bankruptcy will legally and finally end the shortfall debt recovery process. It is usually appropriate when the lender/ insurer insists on pursuing the claim, bankruptcy would not adversely affect the client, and s/he needs the peace of mind and fresh start that follows.
- **Individual voluntary arrangements** (see Chapter 15). An individual voluntary arrangement is usually only appropriate if the shortfall is modest and in proportion to other unsecured debts, and the client can afford substantial repayments and/or owns a home that would be at risk in bankruptcy proceedings, or if the lender obtained a charging order (see p322).
- **Full and final settlement** (see p261). Most lenders and insurance companies will agree to accept a smaller sum than the full outstanding shortfall debt. How much is acceptable depends on to individual circumstances. Settlements in the region of 10 per cent to 50 per cent are not uncommon. You should ensure that any full and final settlement agreement includes the claims of both the lender and any insurer, and it is binding on them. **Note:** a lender who cashes a cheque sent in full and final settlement is not necessarily prevented from pursuing the balance, although cashing the cheque is strong evidence of acceptance unless there is an immediate rejection of the offer.
- **Instalment payments.** Many lenders will accept modest monthly payments towards a substantial debt, where a client's personal circumstances show this to be reasonable. The client may find it daunting to be asked to pay, for

instance, £20 a month towards a debt of £35,000 because s/he cannot see an end. On the other hand, many lenders see token payments as recognition that the client is being responsible about the shortfall. You should suggest that, provided the client keeps up the payments for, say, five years, the lender should accept this as full and final settlement and agree to write off the balance. For more information about partial write-offs, see p259. If the client has other non-priority debts and the mortgage shortfall is to be included in a pro rata payment arrangement, you should attempt to agree a total figure that the lender is prepared to accept for inclusion in the financial statement, on the basis that the balance will be written off on completion of the payment arrangement.

When preparing a strategy, bear in mind that if there was a mortgage indemnity guarantee, there may be two separate demands to negotiate – one from the lender and one from the insurer.

National insurance contributions

National insurance (NI) contributions are a compulsory tax on earnings and profits above certain levels (set annually).

The legal position

NI contributions are payable under section 2 of the Social Security Act 1975, as amended by the Social Security Contributions and Benefits Act 1992.

Special features

Employed people pay class 1 NI contributions directly from their wages and so do not build up arrears. Class 2 contributions must be paid by self-employed earners unless they have a certificate of exemption on the grounds of low income. Self-employed people have to pay class 2 NI contributions by monthly direct debit or quarterly bill. In addition, self-employed people may have to pay class 4 contributions, calculated as a percentage of their profits above a certain level (set annually). After the year end, HM Revenue and Customs (HMRC) sends out demands to self-employed people from whom it has not received the required class 2 contributions.

If a self-employed person has also employed someone else, s/he may be liable for class 1 NI contributions for the employee, as well as class 2, and perhaps 4, for her/himself.

Demands for payment should be distinguished from the notice sent to people whose contribution record is insufficient to entitle them to use it towards a retirement pension or bereavement benefits. In such cases, HMRC sends a notification giving the opportunity to make up the deficit for a particular year with voluntary (class 3) contributions. This is not a demand for payment.

It is vital that the client pays any ongoing contributions on time and makes arrangements to repay any arrears, otherwise HMRC can take control of essential goods without a court order and so close down a business. In addition, if contributions remain unpaid, the client's eventual entitlement to contributory benefits, including retirement pension, will be affected.

Checklist for action
Advisers should take the following action.
- Consider whether emergency action is necessary (see Chapter 8).
- Consider whether the client should be referred to a specialist agency – eg, TaxAid.
- Otherwise, assist the client to choose a strategy from Chapter 8 as **this is usually treated as a priority debt if the business is continuing to trade**.

Non-domestic rates

Non-domestic rates (business rates) are charged on most commercial property by local authorities. They are based on a national valuation and fixed amounts are charged across England and Wales in proportion to this.

The legal position
Non-domestic rates are payable under the Local Government Finance Act 1988.

Special features
Arrears are recovered through a liability order in the magistrates' court. If bailiffs are used by a local authority after it has obtained a liability order, there is no exemption for tools, books, vehicles or goods which are necessary for use in the client's business (as there is for council tax arrears).[54] Once a business ceases trading, it may be able to claim local discounts or reliefs from non-domestic rates and advisers should check with the local authority what is available. If the business is renting premises under a lease, it continues to be liable for the non-domestic rates for as long as the lease exists.

Local authorities can reduce or write off arrears of non-domestic rates in situations of severe hardship.[55] This is most appropriate in cases of business failure and should always be sought before considering payment.

Checklist for action
Advisers should take the following action.
- Consider whether emergency action is necessary (see Chapter 8).
- Check liability for the debt, including any associated bailiff's charges. Consider whether there are any grounds for a complaint.

- Assist the client to choose a strategy from Chapter 8 as **this is a priority debt if there is a risk of the client losing essential goods.** Otherwise, the arrears are a non-priority debt. Assist the client to choose a strategy from Chapter 9.

Pawnbroker

Money is lent against an article(s) (pawn) left with the pawnbroker as security – a pledge. The goods can only be reclaimed (redeemed) if the loan is repaid with interest. If the loan is not repaid, the pawnbroker can sell the goods.

The legal position

Pawnbrokers must be authorised by the FCA and the lending is a regulated credit agreement, provided the credit is for no more than £25,000 (if the agreement was made before 6 April 2008) or £15,000 (if made before 1 May 1998). If the agreement was made on or after 6 April 2008, the agreement is regulated regardless of the amount, unless it is exempt (see p62).

Special features

Pawnbrokers have a duty to comply with the pre-contract information requirements outlined on p66, but there some exceptions.

- Unless the client is a 'new customer' (ie, s/he has not done business with the pawnbroker in the previous three years), the pawnbroker only has to inform her/him of her/his right to receive the pre-contract information free of charge on request.
- The pawnbroker's duty to provide the client with 'adequate explanations' (see p67) only applies to:
  - the main consequences of her/his failure to make the payments due under the agreement. **Note:** the requirement to explain any features of the agreement which may make it unsuitable for particular types of use does not apply to pawnbroking agreements and so there is no requirement to explain to the client that they are a short-term product, and an expensive and unsuitable method of longer-term borrowing;
  - the effects of withdrawing from the agreement, and when and how to exercise this right. **Note:** if the client fails to repay the loan and interest within 30 days of exercising her/his right to withdraw, the pawnbroker can retain and sell the pawned goods.
- The pawnbroker does not have to assess the client's creditworthiness – ie, her/his ability to repay the loan (see p68).
- The pawnbroker does not have to supply the client with a copy of the draft credit agreement.

The pawnbroker must give the client a receipt for the goods (a 'pawn receipt') and must keep the goods for at least six months, during which time interest is charged on the money borrowed. The client retains ownership of the goods in the meantime. If the goods are not redeemed after six months:

- if the loan was for £75 or less and the goods were not subject to an earlier pledge which was renewed, ownership of the goods automatically passes to the pawnbroker and they can be sold;
- in all other cases, the pawnbroker can sell the goods, but may have to give the client notice of her/his intention to do so.

Unless the loan was for £100 or less, the pawnbroker must give the client at least 14 days' notice of her/his intention to sell the goods. The client can redeem the goods at any time before the goods are sold (except if ownership has passed to the pawnbroker) by handing in the pawn receipt, and paying off the loan and accrued interest.

It is a criminal offence for a pawnbroker to refuse to redeem a pawn unless it has reasonable cause to believe that the person handing in the pawn receipt is neither the owner of the goods nor authorised to redeem them. If the client is unable to redeem the goods, s/he must renew the pledge to prevent the goods being sold. If the goods are sold, the pawnbroker must inform the client of their sale price and provide details of the costs of sale. If the client challenges the amount for which the goods were sold and/or the costs of sale, the onus is on the pawnbroker to justify the figures.

Checklist for action

Advisers should take the following action.

- Check liability, including the enforceability of the agreement under the Consumer Credit Act 1974.
- Assist the client to choose a strategy from Chapter 9, as this is a non-priority debt (or Chapter 8 if the pawned item is essential).

Payday loan

These are small (generally between £50 and £800) loans intended to cover short-term financial difficulties such as an unexpected bill or an emergency. They are repayable in full on the client's next payday.

The legal position

Payday loans are fixed-sum credit agreements and are likely to be regulated credit agreements, as they are generally within the financial limits for regulation and are not covered by the various exemptions (see p62).

Special features

Payday loans are not appropriate for clients who are already in financial difficulties. In fact, they are likely to exacerbate any pre-existing financial problems. This is because, in such circumstances, it is extremely unlikely that the client will be able to repay the loan on the due date (typically within 31 days) and so, in addition to interest, s/he will have to pay a late payment fee (which must not exceed £15).

Since 26 May 2017, payday lenders must advertise on at least one FCA-approved price comparison website and prominently display a link to that site on their own website.[56]

From 2 January 2015:

- interest and charges must not exceed 0.8 per cent per day of the amount borrowed (the 'initial rate');
- default charges must not exceed £15 and interest on unpaid balances and default charges must not be more than the initial rate;
- clients must never have to pay back more than the amount borrowed in interest and charges.

Two of the requirements to provide the client with adequate pre-contract explanations (see p67) are of particular relevance to payday loans.

- Features of the agreement that may make it unsuitable: payday loans are a short-term product and are unsuitable for supporting borrowing over longer periods.
- Features of the agreement that may operate in an adverse manner: the effect of 'rolling over' such loans could accumulate an unmanageable level of debt. The codes of practice of the four trade associations for payday lenders issued on 24 May 2012 (known as the Good Practice Customer Charter) state that creditors should:[57]
  - not pressurise clients to roll over loans;
  - only consider rolling over a loan if a client asks; *and*
  - tell clients if there is a limit on the number of times a loan can be rolled over.

If a client is in financial difficulties and informs the creditor, the creditor should explore new arrangements for paying the debt with her/him.[58]

Continuous payment authorities

The most common method of repaying a payday loan is by debit card. Unlike standing orders and direct debits, there is confusion about whether clients can cancel a debit (or credit) card payment authority (known as a 'continuous payment authority' if it is for ongoing payment arrangements).

In the past, many banks have advised their customers that, in order to cancel a continuous payment authority, a client must approach the creditor as there is no automatic right to cancel. However, this advice appears to conflict with the provisions of the Payment Services Regulations 2009 and the correct legal position appears to be that a client has the right to cancel a continuous payment authority directly with her/his bank or card issuer by informing it that s/he has withdrawn her/his permission for the payments. The payments must then be stopped and the bank cannot insist that the client contact the payee to agree to this first.[59] The Financial Ombudsman Service also agrees with this view.[60]

Unless a continuous payment authority is cancelled as described above so that a client is not pressurised into rolling over loans and can instead try to agree an affordable payment arrangement with the lender, s/he could find her/himself with an unauthorised overdraft, subject to interest and charges, and without money to meet essential expenditure. The client may have to extend the loan, for which a fee may be charged. This means that the outstanding balance will rapidly escalate due to the high interest rate and will further exacerbate the client's existing financial difficulties.

There are restrictions on requesting part-payment under a continuous payment authority and on the number of times the creditor can request payment when previous payment requests have been refused. However, the creditor is not prevented from accepting payment (including part-payment) from a client using a means of payment other than a continuous payment authority – eg, a single payment using her/his debit card details.[61]

Checklist for action

Advisers should take the following action.

- Consider whether emergency action is necessary – eg, cancel any continuous payment authority.
- Check liability, including the enforceability under the Consumer Credit Act 1974 (although clients with payday loans made before 6 April 2007 are likely to be rare).
- If the client is in financial difficulties and the time for payment has not yet arrived, either ask the creditor not to take the payment under the continuous payment authority, or arrange to cancel the continuous payment authority if time is short or the creditor refuses to comply with the request.
- Consider whether the loan was inappropriate to the client's situation and, if there is evidence of irresponsible lending (including in dealing with the client's default and arrears), use the Financial Ombudsman Service complaints procedure (see p284).[62] If the case has already gone to court, obtain specialist support for a possible unfair relationship challenge (see p161).
- In other cases, assist the client to choose a strategy from Chapter 9, as this is a non-priority debt.

Personal loan

A personal loan is a loan offered at a fixed or variable rate of interest over a set period.

The legal position

Personal loans are regulated credit agreements, provided the credit is for no more than £25,000 (if the agreement was made before 6 April 2008) or £15,000 (if made before 1 May 1998). If the agreement was made on or after 6 April 2008, the agreement is regulated regardless of the amount, unless it is exempt (see p62).

Special features

Personal loans are widely available from banks, building societies and other financial institutions, including small moneylenders. Some personal loans have fixed interest rates and the total interest charged is set at the beginning of the period of the loan. Repayments are then made in equal instalments. Sometimes, a personal loan is part of a linked transaction (see p163). The amount to be loaned may be paid directly to the supplier rather than the borrower. With smaller moneylenders, repayments are often collected at the door by a representative.

Checklist for action

Advisers should take the following action.

- Check liability, including enforceability of the agreement, under the Consumer Credit Act 1974 (see Chapter 4).
- Assist the client to choose a strategy from Chapter 9, as personal loans are generally a non-priority debt.

Private parking charges

Many private landowners, including retail parks and supermarkets, allow customer parking on their land subject to terms and conditions, and impose charges on motorists who contravene these terms and conditions. Many landowners employ and authorise agents to manage parking and enforce terms and conditions on the land in question (known as 'car park operators'). Since 1 October 2012, it has been illegal to clamp or remove a motor vehicle without lawful authority – eg, by the police, a government agency or local authority.[63]

Note: if a client has received a penalty charge notice from the local authority, see p134.

Private landowners and car park operators cannot lawfully clamp or remove vehicles. Statutory byelaws relating to airports, ports and some railway car parks may lawfully authorise clamping and removing vehicles.

In most cases, private landowners and car park operators can only enforce parking conditions through:

- affixing a parking ticket to the vehicle containing details of the contravention, how much is due, any discount for prompt payment, how and to whom payment should be made, and details of the dispute resolution process;
- giving the ticket to the driver personally; *or*
- sending a ticket to the vehicle's registered keeper.

The legal position

Section 56 and Schedule 4 of the Protection of Freedoms Act 2012 allow the landowner or the car park operator to pursue the registered keeper of a vehicle for unpaid parking charges if s/he either refuses or is unable to identify the driver of the vehicle at the time the parking charge was incurred. However, the registered keeper cannot be held liable if s/he identifies the driver of the vehicle at the time. If the registered keeper provides evidence which is acceptable to the landowner or car park operator (or, in the event of an appeal, to the adjudicator or the court) that the vehicle concerned was a stolen vehicle at the time of the parking contravention, the registered keeper cannot be held liable.

Special features

The registered keeper of a vehicle is only liable for unpaid parking charges if the driver:

- entered into a contract to park the vehicle on private land and has contravened its terms and conditions; *or*
- trespassed by parking the vehicle on private land where there were signs showing charges for unauthorised parking.

A driver who parks in a car park with clear signage setting out the terms and conditions of the parking facility will be deemed to have accepted these conditions and entered into a contract. The terms and conditions must be sufficiently displayed throughout the car park and particularly at all entrances. The charges payable for failing to comply must be clearly stated – eg, for not displaying a valid permit. The terms and conditions must not be unfair and the penalty charges payable should be proportionate. Caselaw indicates that the courts consider charges of up to £100 reasonable.[64]

If the landowner or car park operator is a member of an accredited trade association (the British Parking Association or the International Parking Community), it can ask the Driver and Licensing Vehicle Agency (DVLA) for details of the registered keeper on the grounds it has a 'reasonable cause' to seek that information in order to enforce unpaid parking charges.[65] If a parking ticket was fixed to the vehicle at the time of the contravention or given to the driver, the landowner or car park operator must wait 28 days before seeking details of the registered keeper from the DVLA if there is no response to the parking ticket. If the contravention is detected remotely (eg, by cameras), the landowner or car park operator can apply immediately to the DVLA for the registered keeper's details.

If a request is made by a body which is not a member of either of the above trade associations, the DVLA decides whether there is a 'reasonable cause' on a case-by-case basis.

Once the landowner or car park operator has the registered keeper's details, it sends a notice to her/him for either payment or the driver's details so it can pursue the unpaid parking charge. The registered keeper has 28 days from receipt of the notice to provide the driver's details, pay the parking charge or appeal.

If the registered keeper fails to do any of these things, the landowner or car park operator may begin proceedings in the county court to recover the unpaid parking charge from her/him. If the registered keeper provides the driver's details, the landowner or car park operator must pursue the driver since the registered keeper is no longer liable.

In the case of hire vehicles, the hire company must provide details of its contract with the hirer (which invariably makes the hirer liable for any parking charges) to the landowner or car park operator within 28 days of receiving the notice in order to avoid liability.

Parking tickets issued by members of a trade association must contain details of the arrangements for the resolution of disputes or complaints. Representations must be made in the first instance to the landowner or car park operator, who may decide to cancel the ticket or reduce the charges or reject the representations. If the registered keeper is not satisfied with the response, the landowner or car park operator must offer her/him access to an adjudicator at the Independent Appeals Service. The appeal must be submitted within 28 days of the notice of rejection (this time limit can be extended in exceptional circumstances). This process is free to the registered keeper. The whole process can be conducted online (although there are facilities for appeals to be conducted on paper by post). If the registered keeper's appeal is successful, the landowner or car park operator must cancel the parking ticket.

Landowners or car park operators who are not members of an accredited trade association are not required to have an appeals process and so any disputes which cannot be resolved informally must be dealt with in the county court.

The Parking (Code of Practice) Act 2019 provides for a mandatory single code of practice for all private car park operators. The code is expected to include a new independent appeals service. At the time of writing, the code has not yet been published and there is currently no publication date. Operators who do not sign up to the code will still be able to issue parking charge notices, but will not have DVLA access, and so may have problems in enforcing them.

Checklist for action

Advisers should take the following action.

- Check to see whether the landowner or car park operator is a member of an accredited trade association and, if so, check for compliance with its code of practice.
- Check whether the client has any grounds to make representations or to appeal (see popla.co.uk).
- Otherwise, assist the client to choose a strategy from Chapter 9, as this is a non-priority debt.

Rent

Rent is payable by tenants to landlords in exchange for the use of their property. A landlord may be either a private individual or a property company, or a public sector landlord, such as a local authority or housing association.

The legal position

Rent is payable under a tenancy agreement (whether written or oral). For more details of tenancy agreements, see *Defending Possession Proceedings*, published by Legal Action Group (see Appendix 2).

Special features

After the termination of a tenancy (eg, because a notice to quit is served), a tenant can remain in possession of the home because of protection given by legislation. In these circumstances, the landlord may refer to the money due in exchange for possession of the home as 'mesne profits'. For practical purposes, this is the same as rent. Similarly, if a person is a licensee rather than a tenant, what s/he pays is not strictly rent, but a charge for use of the property. Arrears of payment due under a licence are treated in the same way as rent when giving debt advice.

Checklist for action

Advisers should take the following action.
- Consider whether emergency action is necessary (see Chapter 8).
- Check liability. If possession proceedings have started, see Chapter 12.
- Assist the client to choose a strategy from Chapter 8 as **this is a priority debt if the rent is due on the client's current home**. Otherwise, the arrears are a non-priority debt. Assist the client to choose a strategy from Chapter 9.

Revolving credit

Revolving credit is a type of personal borrowing in which the creditor agrees to a credit limit and the client can borrow up to that limit, provided s/he maintains certain agreed minimum payments. Revolving credit takes a number of different forms – eg, credit cards, budget accounts and bank overdrafts.

Secured loan

A secured loan (often known as a second mortgage) allows a homeowner to take out a (further) loan, using the property as security. The lender takes a legal charge on the property, with a similar right to repossess as the bank or building society holding the first charge on the property (in some cases, the creditor may also hold the first charge). If a property is repossessed and sold, the proceeds are distributed to meet the claims of secured lenders in the order in which loans were given.

The legal position

There are three categories of secured loans.

- **Regulated mortgage contracts**. A secured loan is a regulated mortgage contract if:
  - it was taken out by an individual (ie, someone acting as a consumer and not for business purposes);
  - it was either a regulated credit agreement when it was made or, if made on or after 21 March 2016, would otherwise have been a regulated credit agreement;
  - it is secured on residential property – ie, at least 40 per cent of the property is occupied by the client or her/his family as her/his residence.
- **Regulated credit agreements**. Unless it is exempt (see p64), the agreement is a regulated credit agreement if the loan was for £25,000 or less (if taken out before 6 April 2008) or £15,000 or less (if taken out before 1 May 1998). If the agreement was made between 6 April 2008 and 21 March 2016, the agreement is regulated regardless of the amount.
- **Unregulated agreements**, if neither of the above apply.

Note: the changes introduced by the European Commission Consumer Credit Directive to pre-contract information on p66 do not apply to secured loans.

Special features

Interest rates on secured loans with finance companies are much higher than those charged by building societies or banks for first mortgages. Loans are often repayable over a much shorter term than for first mortgages and this, together with higher interest rates, means it is an expensive form of borrowing.

Before 26 March 2016, there were special rules for entering into secured loans regulated by the Consumer Credit Act 1974. The borrower must be given a copy of the agreement, which must not be signed for seven days. S/he must then be sent a copy for signing and left for a further seven days. If the borrower does not sign, there is no agreement. The lender should not contact the prospective borrower during either of the seven-day 'thinking' periods unless asked to do so. If these rules have not been followed, the loan is not enforceable without a court order.

Checklist for action

Advisers should take the following action.
- Consider whether emergency action is necessary (see Chapter 8).
- Check whether the agreement is enforceable under the Consumer Credit Act 1974.
- Assist the client to choose a strategy from Chapter 8, as **this is a priority debt.**

Tax credit overpayments

Child tax credit and working tax credit are means-tested tax credits administered by HM Revenue and Customs (HMRC).

Overpayments of tax credits can arise, for example, if someone does not tell HMRC about a change in her/his circumstances, if s/he gives it incorrect infomation, or if her/his income falls or rises by more than £2,500 in the current year compared with the previous tax year. Some changes in circumstances must be reported immediately and are taken into account. However, changes in income do not have to be reported immediately and can be notified at the end of the tax year when the award is finalised. Clients faced with this choice may need specialist advice.

For further information about tax credits, see Chapter 7 and CPAG's *Welfare Benefits and Tax Credits Handbook*.[66]

The legal position

If there is likely to be an overpayment during a tax year, or HMRC realises during the year that an award is too high (sometimes referred to as an 'in-year' overpayment), it can revise an award and reduce payments for the remainder of the year.[67]

Overpayments that come to light when an award is finalised at the end of the year are sometimes referred to as 'end-of-year' overpayments.[68]

In the case of joint claims by couples, each partner is 'jointly and severally' liable to repay any tax credit overpaid during the year.

HMRC must issue an overpayment notice stating the amount to be repaid and the method of repayment it intends to use.[69] Recovery can be:

- by reducing an ongoing tax credits award. There are maximum amounts by which an award can be reduced to recover an end-of-year overpayment.[70] This is the method HMRC prefers; *or*
- from the person(s) overpaid, in one lump sum, or by monthly payments over 12 months, or for between three and 10 years so long as the payments are at least £10 a month. Payments of less than £10 a month should only be accepted if the overpayment can be cleared in full within three years; *or*
- by transferring the debt to the DWP to recover. This can happen if the client is no longer receiving tax credits, whether or not s/he is receiving a DWP benefit. The client must be notified that the debt has been transferred to the DWP, but this should not happen if there is an outstanding appeal or dispute about the overpayment. If this happens, the DWP can make deductions from benefit or pursue other methods of recovery without the client's consent (see p231); *or*
- from income support, jobseeker's allowance, employment and support allowance and pension credit, provided the client consents, or from universal credit without consent (if the debt is transferred to the DWP to recover, this can happen without consent); *or*

- through the PAYE system, provided the client does not object; *or*
- direct from the client's bank account, if the debt is at least £1,000; *or*
- by an attachment of earnings order (see p329).

Former partners can agree to repay different amounts, but HMRC has stated that if there is no agreement, partners will only be asked to pay a maximum of 50 per cent each, effectively treating each partner's share as a separate debt.

Interest can be added to an overpayment if HMRC considers the overpayment occurred as a result of the client's fraud or neglect.[71] The interest is recovered using the same methods as for overpayments.

Note: penalties can be imposed in some circumstances – eg, if someone makes an incorrect statement or supplies incorrect information and this is done fraudulently or negligently. Different procedures apply for the recovery of penalties.

There is right of appeal against a decision to add interest to an overpayment, and against a decision to impose a penalty.

Special features

All overpayments are recoverable, whatever the cause, although HMRC has the discretion not to recover and can decide to write off an overpayment. It has a code of practice on the recovery of tax credit overpayments, *What happens if we've paid you too much tax credits,* available at hmrc.gov.uk/government/publications/tax-credits-what-happens-if-youve-been-paid-too-much-cop26.

This states that HMRC will not pursue repayment if:

- the overpayment was caused by HMRC failing to meet its 'responsibilities'; *and*
- the claimant has met all of her/his 'responsibilities'.

Note: HMRC says that in all cases where an overpayment arose because of a change in a client's single person/couple status and a new claim has been made, it will offset the amount the claimant would have been entitled to had s/he claimed correctly.

HMRC has agreed to stop recovery action of overpayments from 2003 to 2009 either if there has been no contact for 12 months or the client cannot be traced, but it has not formally written off these overpayments.[72] However, this policy could change.

It is important to check that the client's tax credits have been calculated correctly and that s/he has, in fact, been overpaid. A client can appeal to an independent First-tier Tribunal about a matter concerning her/his tax credit entitlement. S/he must ask for a mandatory reconsideration first before s/he can appeal and must do so within the time limit.

A client cannot appeal against a decision to recover an overpayment, but the decision can be disputed. It is best practice to use the official dispute form (TC846). Recovery is not suspended while HMRC decides whether to write off any of the overpayment. If a client has requested a mandatory reconsideration or is appealing an incorrect decision, recovery is suspended pending the outcome of the mandatory reconsideration or appeal.

HMRC can remit (ie, write off) the overpayment if a client:

- has no means to repay an overpayment; *or*
- has no assets; *or*
- would experience hardship if recovery were to go ahead.

Specifically, if medical information or evidence is received that the client has a mental health problem, HMRC may agree not to pursue her/him for repayment. It refers to the Money Advice Liaison Group guidelines for guidance.

If an overpayment cannot be recovered from a deceased person's estate, it can be written off if the surviving partner was jointly and severally liable and recovery from her/him would cause hardship.

An additional means of challenging the recovery of an overpayment is to use the HMRC complaints procedure and/or to complain to the independent Adjudicator's Office (see Appendix 1). The only legal challenge to a decision to recover an overpayment is by judicial review.

If a client refuses to pay or does not keep to any payment arrangement, HMRC considers taking legal proceedings to recover the debt. There is a six-year time limit for taking court action (see p291). There is no time limit for recovery by making deductions from ongoing tax credit awards.

Checklist for action

Advisers should take the following action.

- Check liability.
- Tax credit overpayments can be a priority or a non-priority debt depending on factors including the date of the award and/or whether the client has been awarded, or migrated to, universal credit. Assist the client to choose a strategy from Chapter 8 **if it is a priority debt** or Chapter 9 for a non-priority debt.

Trading cheque or voucher

Finance companies may supply a voucher or cheque to the client to be used at specified shops in exchange for goods. Repayments, which include a charge for the credit, are then made by instalments to the finance company. The shop is paid by the credit company.

The legal position

These agreements are regulated credit agreements, provided the credit is for no more than £25,000 (if the agreement was made before 6 April 2008) or £15,000 (if made before 1 May 1998). If the agreement was made on or after 6 April 2008, the agreement is regulated regardless of the amount, unless it is exempt (see p62). If the voucher is for £50 or less, the creditor is not obliged to comply with the rules on p66.[73]

Special features

This is normally an expensive way of borrowing and limits the client to shopping in a limited number of outlets where prices may be high.

Checklist for action

Advisers should take the following action.

- Check liability, including the enforceability of the agreement under the Consumer Credit Act 1974.
- Assist the client to choose a strategy from Chapter 9, as this is usually a non-priority debt. If this is the only way the client can buy essential goods, see p253.

Traffic penalties

A number of traffic penalties, particularly parking charges and certain other fixed penalty notices such as bus lane contraventions and the London congestion charge, are recovered by local authorities using the county court under Part 75 of the Civil Procedure Rules.

Note: if the client has received a parking ticket or demand for payment from a private car park operator, see p126.

The legal position

The current legislation is the Traffic Management Act 2004, which came into force on 30 March 2008. The enforcement authority (either the local authority or Transport for London) issues a penalty charge notice which gives the registered owner 28 days in which to pay. **Note:** generally, the person or organisation registered at the DVLA as the registered keeper is responsible for paying any penalty charge, regardless of who was driving the vehicle at the time, although a prior change of ownership would be a defence so long as the DVLA confirms this. If payment is made within 14 days, the amount due is reduced by 50 per cent.

Traffic penalties (usually imposed under the Road Traffic Regulation Act 1984) registered in the magistrates' court for enforcement as fines are priority debts (see p99).

Penalty charges recoverable through the Traffic Enforcement Centre in Northampton, outlined below, are non-priority debts.[74]

Special features

The statutory provisions relating to challenging traffic penalties are complex. There is valuable information on the London Tribunals website at londontribunals.gov.uk and on the Traffic Penalty Tribunal website at trafficpenaltytribunal.gov.uk.

If payment is not made within 28 days, the enforcement authority issues a 'notice to owner' and the client has a further 28 days in which to pay the full amount or make representations on specified grounds. The enforcement authority has 56 days in which to respond. If the client's representations are rejected, s/he has a further 28 days in which to appeal. The grounds for appeal are the same as the grounds for representations. If the appeal is rejected (or any recommendation to the enforcement authority to withdraw the penalty charge notice is not accepted), the client has a further 28 days to pay. If the appeal is withdrawn before a decision is made, the time limit is 14 days.

If the amount due is not paid, the penalty is increased by 50 per cent and a charge certificate is issued. If the amount due is not paid within 14 days, the enforcement authority can register the charge certificate for enforcement in the county court. The authority can then collect the debt as if it were a county court judgment but, as it is not actually required to obtain a county court judgment in order to enforce the debt, the pre-action protocol for debt claims does **not** apply (see p281).

Once the penalty charge has been registered in the county court, it is passed to enforcement agents (private bailiffs) for collection by taking control of goods (see Chapter 14). If the bailiff is unable to collect the debt, the local authority can then use other county court enforcement methods. In practice, local authorities appear not to do so, preferring instead to leave the warrant with the bailiffs for the full 12 months.

A traffic penalty enforced through the county court does not have the sanction of imprisonment for non-payment, but the county court has no power to suspend bailiff action (see p342), nor can it make an instalment order to prevent enforcement action.

If the client claims s/he is not liable to pay the penalty on one of the specified grounds (eg, s/he was not the owner of the motor vehicle at the time), s/he should complete either the form of statutory declaration (PE3) or the witness statement (TE9) which accompanies the court order registering the charge. This must be returned to the court before the end of the 21-day period beginning with the date the order was served. The court can extend this time limit if it considers it reasonable to do so. The court will revoke the registration of the penalty charge (although the local authority can begin the process again) and any warrant of control is automatically cancelled. Any fees charged should be refunded by the local authority/bailiff.[75]

There are two potential liabilities for having no **road tax**. One is being the registered keeper of an unlicensed vehicle (criminal) and the other is late renewal of the licence (civil). Both arise under the Vehicle Excise and Registration Act 1994. The civil penalty is imposed under section 7A and the criminal offence under section 31A.

The section 31A penalty can be registered in the magistrates' court for enforcement. It is then recoverable as if payable under a conviction and is treated as a fine (see Chapter 13).

The £80 penalty under section 7A is recoverable as a debt due to the Crown – ie, by civil proceedings (see Chapters 10 and 11).

In certain circumstances, the client can complain to the Local Government and Social Care Ombudsman (in England) or the Public Services Ombudsman (in Wales) (eg, if there was a failure to consider compelling reasons for cancelling the penalty charge), but is usually expected to use the appeal procedure where appropriate, unless there are exceptional reasons not to do so.[76]

The Ombudsman can consider a complaint about the reasonableness of any action of bailiffs acting for the local authority, but does not usually consider the level of bailiffs' costs.[77]

Checklist for action

Advisers should take the following action.

- Consider whether emergency action is necessary (see Chapter 8).
- Check liability for the debt and any associated bailiff's charges. Consider whether there are any grounds for making representations and/or a complaint.
- Assist the client to choose a strategy from Chapter 9, as this is a non-priority debt.

Value added tax

Value added tax (VAT) is a tax charged by HMRC on most transactions of businesses with an annual taxable turnover of more than a certain limit, set annually. A business must be registered for VAT unless its turnover is below the limit.

The legal position

VAT is payable under the Finance Act 1972 and the Value Added Tax Act 1994, and subsequent regulations and amendments. Its scope and level are reviewed each year and changes are often made to the Act following the Budget.

Special features

VAT is a tax on the value added to goods and services as they pass through the registered business. So, although VAT is payable on purchases, this amount can be offset against the tax on the business's own sales. For example, if the total purchases in a year were £100,000 and the total sales were identical, there would be no value added and no tax payable.

A debt adviser generally encounters VAT debts after a business has ceased trading and the partner or sole trader is left responsible for VAT (see Chapter 16). Some goods are exempt and the calculation of the amount of VAT is complicated. In most cases, seek help from an accountant specialising in VAT. If VAT is overdue, a surcharge, which is a percentage of the VAT owed, is added to the debt. This amount can be appealed.

Checklist for action

Advisers should take the following action.

- Consider whether emergency action is necessary (see Chapter 8).
- Consider whether the client should be referred to a specialist agency – eg, TaxAid.
- Otherwise, assist the client to choose a strategy from Chapter 8 as **thisis usually treated as a priority debt if the business is continuing to trade.** If the business is no longer trading, the arrears are a non-priority debt. Assist the client to choose a strategy from Chapter 9.

Water charges

Water companies charge for water, sewerage and environmental services on the basis of either a meter or the old rating system, which was abolished as the basis of a local tax in April 1990 in England and Wales. Under the rating system, every dwelling was given a rateable value. Each year, water companies set a 'rate in the pound', which converts this rateable value into an annual charge. For example, a rate of 20p in the pound converts a rateable value of £300 to an amount of water rates payable of £60.

If a water meter is installed, a client pays for the actual amount of water used. Charges are per cubic metre at a rate set by the water company. A standing charge is also payable. There may also be installation and inspection charges. Separate charges are levied for sewerage and environmental services. These charges are based either on the rateable value of the property or on the amount of water used as recorded by the meter.

The legal position

Water charges are payable under the Water Industry Act 1991. Water companies may use county court action to recover arrears, as they cannot disconnect domestic properties on the ground of non-payment. Water companies may waive charges if there is an ongoing supply in accordance with their charging scheme, but tend to only do so if the property is empty, including if the occupier is in hospital or residential care.

Special features

Bills for unmetered water charges are sent out in April and payment is due in advance, unless the client takes advantage of one of the payment options offered by all the water companies. For example, payment can be made in eight to 10 instalments or weekly/monthly in cases of financial hardship. If the client defaults, the water company can take action to recover the outstanding balance for the remainder of the year.

Many of the companies' charges schemes allow them to apportion the bill if a client includes her/his water charges in a bankruptcy or a debt relief order. The company then sends a new bill to the client for the remainder of the current year. This practice should be challenged, as it clearly conflicts with the definitions of 'bankruptcy' and 'qualifying debt' in the Insolvency Act.

It is important to check that the bill refers to a property in which the client actually lives, or lived, and that the dates of occupation and name(s) shown on the bill are correct. The occupier of the property is the person liable to pay the bill. If there is more than one occupier, each is jointly and severally liable.[78]

If there is a meter, bills are issued every three or six months based on meter readings carried out by the company's staff or the client. If this is not possible, an estimated bill is issued. Bills should be checked and queried if they seem too high as there may be a hidden leak or the meter may be faulty.

Since 30 June 1999, water companies cannot disconnect for arrears of domestic water charges and this is therefore a non-priority debt (see Chapter 9), but the realistic cost of current water charges must be in the financial statement to avoid ongoing enforcement action.[79]

Ofwat guidelines, *Dealing with household customers in debt* (available at ofwat.gov.uk/publication/dealing-with-customers-in-debt-guidelines-2), sets out the following principles, which companies should include in their own codes of practice.

- Companies should be proactive in attempting to contact clients who fall into debt as early as possible and at all stages of the debt management process.
- Companies should provide clients with a reasonable range of payment frequencies and methods. The entire range of options should be properly and widely advertised to ensure that clients can select the arrangement that best suits their circumstances.
- Paperwork sent to clients should be written in plain language and in a courteous and non-threatening style, but should clearly set out the action the company will take if the client fails to make a payment or contact the company, along with the possible consequences for the client.
- When agreeing payment arrangements, the client's circumstances (including her/his ability to pay) should be taken into account wherever possible. Although payment arrangements should aim to recover the current year's charges as well as a payment towards the arrears, the guidelines recognise that the company may need to take a long-term view of the period over which the client can clear her/his debt and should accept any realistic offer of payment made by the client or a debt adviser on her/his behalf.
- Clients whose accounts have been passed to collectors should receive the same treatment as if the account had remained with the water company and the potential consequences should be no more severe than if the service were provided by the water company – ie, the collector should comply with its own industry codes of practice as well as the water company's code of practice.

Although the guidelines recognise that this may not be possible if the debt is sold (which should only be done if all other debt recovery methods have been attempted), they seem to assume that such clients will be 'won't pays' and so not entitled to the same level of 'service'.

- Some water companies use local authorities or housing associations as billing agents to bill and collect water charges from their tenants. The guidelines state that affected clients should be made aware of which organisation they are the customer and the implications of this compared with clients who are billed directly. If the water charges are collected as part of the rent, the guidelines state that where eviction for non-payment of rent (including unpaid water charges) is a possibility, alternative solutions should be found. However, it is possible that such provisions in a tenancy agreement could be challenged ounder the Consumer Rights Act 2015. In this situation, obtain specialist housing advice.

Advisers should be aware that there is a vulnerable groups scheme (known as the WaterSure scheme) available for clients on low incomes with water meters, which caps their charges. See ofwat.gov.uk/households/customer-assistance/watersure. Many water companies have set up trust funds to assist clients with paying arrears of water charges. Check your local company's website for details of any scheme operating in the area.[80]

Auriga publishes a leaflet summarising the schemes or services water (and energy) companies can provide to help customers, available at aurigaservices.co.uk or from Auriga Services, Emmanuel Court, 12–14 Mill Street, Sutton Coldfield B72 1TJ, tel: 0121 321 1324.

Checklist for action

Advisers should take the following action.

- Check liability. Consider whether the client is eligible for assistance under the water company's consumer assistance scheme(s).
- Assist the client to choose a strategy from Chapter 9, as this is a non-priority debt.

Notes

1 For a discussion on various aspects of bank transfers, see J Wilson, 'Consultancy Corner', *Adviser* 107 and 108. See also report of a complaint to the Financial Ombudsman Service (*Adviser* 107 abstracts).
2 *FCA Handbook*, CONC 5C and 5D. See also G McLean, 'FCA rein in unfair overdraft charges', *Quarterly Account* 53, IMA
3 *FCA Handbook, Banking: Conduct of Business Sourcebook* 5.1.3AG, 5.1.3BG and 5.1.4G
4 *FCA Handbook, Banking: Conduct of Business Sourcebook*, 5.1.3A and 5.1.3B
5 See Financial Ombudsman Service decision in *Ombudsman News* 84 (*Adviser* 140 abstracts)
6 See G Skipwith, 'Bills of Sale (Law Commission report)', *Adviser* 178
7 *Lee v Barnes* [1886] 17 QBD 77
8 *Re Morritt ex parte Official Receiver* [1886] 18 QBD 222
9 s7 Bills of Sale Act (1878) Amendment Act 1882
10 s1(1)(b) Law of Property (Miscellaneous Provisions) Act 1989
11 Although a party may not attest the bill, a party's agent, manager or employee may do so; *Peace v Brookes* [1895] 2 QB 451
12 s113 CCA 1974
13 s13 Bills of Sale Act (1878) Amendment Act 1882
14 For further discussion of the provisions of the code, see G Skipwith, 'Bills of Sale: codes of practice', *Adviser* 145
15 s8 CCA 1974
16 See *Guidance on Regulation 4(3) of the Child Support Fees Regulations 2014: how the Secretary of State will determine if an applicant is a victim of domestic violence or abuse*, available at gov.uk/government/publications/proposed-child-maintenance-fees-exemption-for-victims-of-domestic-violence
17 *A Retailer v Ms B and Ms K*, Oxford County Court, 9 May 2012. See also R Dunstan and G Skipwith, '(Un)civil Recovery', *Adviser* 142.

18 s8 CCA 1974
19 Council tax also applies in Scotland. For the position where a Scottish local authority is pursuing a client who lives in England or Wales for unpaid Scottish council tax, see 'Q & A with Shelter Specialist Debt Advice Service', *Quarterly Account* 52, p24.
20 *Leeds CC v Broadley* (*Adviser* 181 abstracts). See also R Curry, 'Liabilities on Leaving a Tenancy', *Quarterly Account* 49, IMA
21 For a discussion of when a resident who is disregarded can be liable for council tax, see Shelter Specialist Debt Advice Service, 'Q & A', *Quarterly Account* 52, IMA
22 See A Murdie, 'When the Ombudsman is not Enough', *Adviser* 158; *SC v East Riding of Yorkshire* (*Adviser* 164 money advice abstracts)
23 s13A LGFA 1992
24 *Office of Fair Trading v Lloyds TSB and Others* [2007] UKHL 48 (*Adviser* 125 consumer abstracts)
25 *FCA Handbook*, CONC 6.7.3A, 6.7.3B and 6.7.27-6.7.40. See also P McCarron, 'Addressing the Challenge of Persistent Credit Card Debt', *Quarterly Account* 49, IMA
26 A creditor is required to give seven days' notice of its intention to enforce a term of the agreement allowing it to demand early payment of any sum in cases where this right arises, even though the client is not in default
27 s35 MCA 1980
28 Sch 6 para 2 EA 1989; Sch 2B paras 6A and 7 GA 1986, as amended by UA 2000. Although the legislation refers to unpaid charges for the supply of gas/electricity to 'any premises', it then goes on to provide that the supplier may disconnect 'the premises'. If the legislation had intended the supplier to be able to disconnect any premises and not just the premises to which the supply relates, the legislation could have specifically said so.

29 Ofgem, *Decision: Modification of the electricity and gas supply licences to introduce rules on backbilling to improve customer outcomes*, ofgem.gov.uk/system/files/docs/2018/03/backbilling_final_decision_policy_document_-_march_5_-_website.pdf.

30 See also M Egan, 'The Good Trust Fund Guide', *Adviser* 164

31 See P Madge, 'Take it Back', *Adviser* 106

32 *First Response v Donnelly*, Durham County Court, 16 October 2006 (*Adviser* 122 consumer abstracts). For a discussion on challenging this approach to creditor termination, see C Meehan and P Madge, 'Letters', *Adviser* 125 and 127.

33 See also https://debtcamel.co.uk/brighthouse-never-never/

34 Creditors could avoid this by including two principal agreements in the same document, each containing its own consumer credit heading and signature box

35 See G Skipwith, 'Consultancy corner: PCPs', *Adviser* 185

36 s127(3) CCA 1974 (repealed from 6 April 2008, but not retrospectively, by s15 and Sch 3 para 11 CCA 2006)

37 s1 MOA 1958

38 See also C Howell, 'Interest-only Mortgages Coming to the End of Their Term', *Quarterly Account* 37, IMA

39 See L Woodall, 'Mortgage Market Review', *Quarterly Account* 33, IMA

40 *FCA Handbook*, MCOB 11.6

41 See complaint to Financial Ombudsman Service (*Adviser* 154 abstracts)

42 See P Bristow, 'One-stop Complaints Shop', *Adviser* 107, and S Quigley, 'Removing the Barriers', *Adviser* 109

43 *FCA Handbook*, MCOB 11.9 which came into effect on 28 October 2019

44 *Bradford and Bingley v Cutler* [2008] EWCA Civ 74 (*Adviser* 128 money advice abstracts)

45 *Hopkinson v Tupper*, 30 January 1997, unreported (*Adviser* 63 abstracts)

46 s20(1) LA 1980

47 s20(5) LA 1980

48 *Bristol and West plc v Bartlett*, 31 July 2002, unreported (*Adviser* 94 abstracts). For a full discussion of the issues, see P Madge, 'Out of the Blue', *Adviser* 61, and P Madge, 'About Face', *Adviser* 94.

49 *Scottish Equitable v Thompson* [2003] EWCA Civ 225 (*Adviser* 98 abstracts)

50 *West Bromwich Building Society v Wilkinson* [2005] UKHL 44 (*Adviser* 111 abstracts)

51 *West Bromwich Building Society v Crammer* [2002] EWCA 2618 (ChD) (*Adviser* 97 abstracts)

52 Under Part 13.6.4 of the *FCA Handbook*, MCOB

53 See complaint to Financial Ombudsman Service (*Adviser* 154 abstracts)

54 Reg 14(1A) Non-Domestic Rating (Collection and Enforcement) (Local Lists) Regulations 1989, No.1058

55 s49 LGFA 1988

56 *FCA Handbook*, CONC 2.5A

57 For a discussion, see H Hollingworth, 'Payday Lenders Good Practice Charter: one year on', *Quarterly Account* 31, IMA

58 See Financial Ombudsman Service decision in *Ombudsman News* 109, 2013 (*Adviser* 158 abstracts)

59 See A MacDermott, 'CPAS: the facts behind the myths', *Adviser* 150

60 See *Ombudsman News* 103

61 *FCA Handbook*, CONC 7.6.12 – 7.6.15A

62 See S McFadden, 'Payday Lending and the Financial Ombudsman Service', *Adviser* 160

63 s54 Protection of Freedoms Act 2012

64 *Parking Eye v Beavis* [2015] UKSC 67; *Vehicle Control Services v Mackie* [2017] SC DUN 24 (decision of the Scottish Sheriff Court in Dundee)

65 Reg 27(1)(e) Road Vehicles (Registration and Licensing) Regulations 2002, No.2742

66 See also M Willis, 'Tax Credits', *Quarterly Account* 42, IMA

67 s28(5) TCA 2002

68 s28(1) TCA 2002

69 s29 TCA 2002

70 Reg 12A TC(PC) Regs

71 s37 TCA 2002

72 HMRC annual report 2011/12, para 9.10

73 ss14 and 17 CCA 1974

74 Part 75 CPR

75 r70.8 CPR. See also 'Complaint against Harrow LBC' (*Adviser* 181 abstracts) and Complaint against Bury MBC, Local Government and Social Care Ombudsman, 16 00 1003

76 See P Madge, 'No Waiting', *Adviser* 68, and T Redmond, 'Parking Complaints', *Adviser* 108

77 Complaint against Redbridge London
Borough Council (*Adviser* 162 abstracts).
See also Local Government and Social
Care Ombudsman factsheet on
complaints about parking enforcement
at lgo.org.uk/make-a-complaint/fact-
sheets/transport-and-highways/
parking-enforcement.
78 In Wales, a landlord is required to
provide information to the water
company about her/his tenant(s) (the
occupiers). If the landlord fails to do so,
the landlord is jointly and severally liable
for the water charges with the tenant:
s144C Water Industry Act 1991.
79 s1 and Sch 1 Water Industry Act 1999
80 In addition, *Adviser* 105 contains a series
of articles on dealing with water debt.
See also, J Guy, 'Maximising Income:
using utility trust funds', *Quarterly
Account* 4, IMA.

Chapter 6

• •

Minimising debts

This chapter covers:
1. Introduction (below)
2. Using contract law (p144)
3. Using the Consumer Credit Act (p156)

1. Introduction

This chapter looks at the two main ways of minimising debts – using contract law and/or the Consumer Credit Act 1974 to challenge or reduce liability – eg, by checking whether or not the creditor is legally able to enforce the debt.

It is essential to accurately identify each debt before attempting to deal with it. Chapter 5 covers the most common types of credit or debt that advisers are likely to encounter. Debts fall into two groups – those covered by the Consumer Credit Act 1974 (known as regulated credit debts) and those that do not.

You should first check that the client is legally liable to pay the debts claimed by her/his creditors. In general, a debt is only owed if:
- there is a valid contract between the client and creditor. This does not necessarily have to be a written agreement (see p144); *or*
- money is owed because of particular legislation – eg, council tax or water charges; *or*
- the client has been ordered by a court to make payments to someone, or to the court itself, and there are no grounds to challenge the court order.

In addition, if the contract is a regulated credit agreement and therefore regulated by the Consumer Credit Act 1974, the creditor must comply with the Act's provisions where relevant (see Chapter 4).

Inaccurate calculations

You should check that the amount of any debt is correct and should not assume that the amount owed by a client has been accurately calculated by the creditor.

• • • •

Check the client's own records of payments and make sure that all payments have been credited to the account, and, if in doubt, request a full statement to confirm this.

Request that any recovery action be suspended while the matter is being investigated.[1] It may be necessary to contact a creditor's regional or head office if negotiations with the local branch are unsuccessful. If the creditor is not being co-operative in supplying information and the debt is a credit agreement regulated by the Consumer Credit Act 1974 (see p62), you should write to the creditor asking for a full statement of account under sections 77 and 78 of the Consumer Credit Act 1974 and enclose a payment of £1. If the creditor fails to comply with the request within 12 working days, the debt is unenforceable unless and until the information is supplied.[2] See p157 for more information.

2. **Using contract law**

A contract is an agreement between two parties that becomes binding (ie, legally enforceable) because it specifies, for example, that goods or services are to be exchanged by one party in return for a 'consideration', usually money, from the other.

The most common situation in which an amount of money claimed under a contract may not be due, or may be reduced, is when one party has not kept to her/his side of the agreement – eg, the supplier has sold defective goods. Sometimes, nothing is payable because a contract has not been made in the correct way, or any of the rules on the way in which the creditor can demand money have not been complied with. In other cases, it may be possible to reduce the amount owed because the law says that a term of the contract is 'unfair' or, in the case of credit agreements, there is an 'unfair relationship' (see p161) or there has been irresponsible lending or other grounds for complaint (see p62).

Even if you have established that a debt does exist, the client may not be liable to pay it, either because someone else is liable or because the contract is not enforceable – eg, if the creditor is outside the time limit for taking court action to recover the debt (see p291).

Joint and several liability

If more than one person enters into a credit agreement, they are each liable for the whole of the debt. This is known as 'joint and several liability'. If it is a regulated credit agreement (see p62), it must be signed by all parties in the form required by the Consumer Credit Act 1974 (including where the client is the sole borrower). If they have all not signed such an agreement and it was made before 6 April 2007, none are liable because the agreement is 'irredeemably unenforceable'.

If the agreement was made on or after 6 April 2007, the creditor cannot enforce the agreement against any of the parties without a court order (see p166).

Joint and several liability can also apply to rent arrears on joint tenancies, arrears on joint mortgages, water and sewerage charges, and to council tax on a property which is jointly owned or occupied by a couple.

Guarantors

A creditor sometimes asks for a guarantee before agreeing to lend money or provide goods or services. The guarantor agrees to make the necessary payments should the actual customer or borrower fail to do so, and is bound by the terms of the guarantee s/he has given.[3] If these terms are part of a regulated credit agreement, they are governed by the Consumer Credit Act 1974 (but not the unfair relationship provisions – see p161). If the loan agreement is unenforceable, so is the guarantee.

A guarantee must be in writing and signed by the guarantor (including guarantees entered into online where clicking on, for example, an 'I accept' button can be a signature).[4] Guarantors should be given copies of the original agreement and also any notices required to be sent to the client on default. If this is not done in relation to a guarantee of a regulated credit agreement, the guarantee is only enforceable against the guarantor with a court order. The creditor must also supply the borrower with a copy of the guarantee on request (there is a prescribed fee of £1) and the borrower can also request a copy of the credit agreement itself, again on payment of the prescribed fee (£1) (see p157).[5]

If the creditor has not properly explained to a guarantor that s/he is equally liable for the total debt, there may be a way of challenging liability if it can be shown that the guarantor has been either misled or coerced. In any case, if there is a non-commercial relationship between the debtor and the guarantor (eg, they are cohabitees), the creditor must take reasonable steps to satisfy itself that the guarantor understands the transaction and the risks s/he is taking by entering into it. The creditor can either do this itself or require the guarantor to see a solicitor. If the creditor fails to take either of these steps, but the guarantor has seen a solicitor anyway, the creditor cannot assume the solicitor has advised the guarantor appropriately when no such advice was in fact given.

If the creditor fails to take these steps and the guarantor's consent to the transaction has not been properly obtained, the creditor may not be able to enforce the guarantee.[6] The client should get specialist help.

The Financial Conduct Authority's (FCA's) *Consumer Credit Sourcebook* makes specific provisions for guarantees given for regulated credit agreements on or after 2 November 2015.
- To enable the prospective guarantor to make an informed decision as to whether to act as guarantor or not, the creditor must provide an adequate explanation of the circumstances in which the guarantee may be called in and the implications of this for the guarantor (CONC 4.2.22R).

- Rules and guidance that creditors must follow in relation to both borrowers and guarantors include (CONC 4.2.17G – 4.2.21G):
  - requiring the creditor to continue with explanations (see p67) even if the prospective guarantor states s/he does not need them (CONC 4.2.9R);
  - guidance on how creditors can provide adequate explanations online (which is how many guarantees are made), including providing a local rate number for further explanations and comprehensive FAQs.
- Where a prospective guarantor is to provide a continuous payment authority (see p124), the creditor must supply her/him with the same explanations that it is required to give to a prospective borrower, including (CONC 4.6.5R and 4.6.2R):
  - how a continuous payment authority works;
  - how the creditor will apply it;
  - how the prospective guarantor can cancel the continuous payment authority; *and*
  - the consequences of there being insufficient funds in her/his account on the due date.
- The creditor must consider sufficient information to make a reasonable assessment of the impact the guarantee might have on the guarantor's financial situation. The FCA makes it clear that the fact the credit agreement is guaranteed does not relieve the creditor of its obligation to assess the creditworthiness of the prospective borrower (CONC 5.2.5R).[7]
- Most of CONC 7 (arrears, default and recovery) applies to guarantors as well as to borrowers (CONC 7.1.4R). CONC 7.6.15A provides that, where both the borrower and the guarantor have provided continuous payment authorities and the borrower has defaulted, the creditor may only make up to two requests for payment under the borrower's continuous payment authority and, if those requests are unsuccessful, only up to two requests for payment under the guarantor's.[8]

If a guarantee has not been properly made, it can only be enforced with a court order. This includes if the guarantor has not been provided with a copy of the executed credit agreement as well as a copy of the guarantee. If a default notice has been served on the borrower by the creditor but a copy has not been served on the guarantor, the guarantee is only enforceable with a court order. The legislation does not provide for 'late' service of copies.[9] If the guarantor requests a copy of the credit agreement and/or guarantee and/or a statement of account and has paid the prescribed fee (£1), but the creditor fails to provide this within 12 working days, the guarantee is unenforceable unless and until the creditor complies with the request.[10]

The creditor must serve a default notice on the borrower before it can 'enforce any security'.[11] The FCA has provided guidance on what constitutes enforcement of the security. There is more to enforcing security than just obtaining a court judgment. Demanding payment from the guarantor or taking payment from her/ him by using a continuous payment authority or direct debit without appropriate prior notification to the guarantor is also enforcement (but not if the guarantor is given at least five days' notice before the payment is taken and is reminded that the continuous payment authority or direct debit can be cancelled). Voluntary payment by the guarantor does not count as enforcing the security nor is requesting payment, provided it made clear that this is not a demand. You can read the guidance at fca.org.uk/publication/finalised-guidance/fg17-01.pdf.

Guarantors who have debts of their own and are considering an insolvency option should bear in mind the effect of these options on their potential liability under the guarantee. In bankruptcy, that liability will be a 'contingent liability' (see p496) and, therefore, included in the bankruptcy even where the borrower has not defaulted and no demand for payment has been made by the creditor under the guarantee. Any contingent liability should, likewise, be included in an individual voluntary arrangement proposal where, by default, it will have a value of £1.[12] On the other hand, the liability under a guarantee will only be a qualifying debt for a debt relief order where that liability has crystallised following default by the borrower and service of a default notice and/or demand for payment. You should check the terms of the guarantee in order to establish whether or not the liability is a qualifying debt and, if so, the extent of the client's liability under its terms – ie, the amount of the debt.

Agents

An agent sells goods or collects money on behalf of someone else – eg, s/he may show or distribute mail order catalogues to her/his friends and neighbours, take orders and pass them on to the supplying company. S/he collects money from the customers over a number of weeks, and is liable to pay any money collected, regardless of whether or not the creditor can enforce the agreement against the customer – eg, because the customer has not signed a contract. An agent is obliged to create a separate account for each customer. If s/he does not do this, s/he can become liable for money not paid by customers for whom s/he has failed to create an account. If there is a separate account, the agent is not liable for money that customers do not pay.

An agent may lose commission with which s/he has already been credited (and so her/his own personal account may go into arrears) if someone does not keep up the payments on items bought and supplied. However, an agent is not liable for the customer's default, except in the situation discussed above.

When advising an agent about liability, it is important to check whether the amount owed includes other customers' debts. If so, provide the creditor with a clear breakdown of the accounts, and the names and addresses of customers in arrears, and ask the creditor to invoice them separately. If a client has not obtained signed agreements from her/his customers, or has received payments but not accounted for these to the creditor, s/he may be personally liable for any debt. Seek specialist advice in these circumstances.

The wrong person

A payment request may be sent to the wrong person or to the wrong address, and the person who receives the request for payment is not liable. If there is any doubt about this, check any documents relating to the debt and ask the creditor to produce original invoices, agreements and details of the money lent or the goods or services supplied. Full initials and addresses are obviously important in this process, as are reference numbers.

Using the wrong name, however, does not invalidate a debt and, if a name is shown incorrectly, particularly if it has always been inaccurate but both parties know who is intended, the debt can still be valid.

Forged signatures

If a signature on an agreement has been forged, the person whose name has been forged is not liable for any debt arising from that agreement.[13] A signature may have been forged with that person's knowledge. For example, a person who wants a loan but has reached her/his credit limit with a particular creditor may use a relative's name to obtain the loan, receive the money and make repayments. The relative knows and agrees to this. In such cases, proceed as though the signature was valid and the beneficiary of the loan should continue to maintain repayments.

A partner or close relative's signature may have been used without her/his consent – eg, if a person obtains credit by using her/his parent's name and signature without the knowledge of the credit company or the parent. If there is any accusation of fraud, the client should obtain legal advice. Fraud is a serious criminal offence and a solicitor specialising in criminal law may be required.

In some cases, the use of a more creditworthy relative's name may have been sanctioned by the credit company. If a representative of a creditor has allowed a false name to be given knowingly, that representative may be either conniving with a fraud or, if the signing occurred on her/his advice, creating a situation in which the creditor accepts that the borrower is allowed to use another name. A broker is not usually regarded as a representative of the credit company for this purpose.

You should advise the person whose name has been used that s/he does not owe the money because s/he has not signed the agreement. Be aware of the possible repercussions for the person who has signed and explain these to the client, as s/he may prefer to accept liability for the debt rather than risk, for instance, the person who has signed being prosecuted and/or a breakdown in family relationships.

Liability after a death

Although contracts come to an end on an individual's death, her/his debts do not usually die with her/him because creditors can make a claim against her/his estate – ie, her/his money, personal possessions and property. It is possible, however, that creditors will attempt to hold a partner or close relative responsible for an individual's debts, particularly if s/he lived with the person who has died, although this could involve a breach of the FCA's *Consumer Credit Sourcebook*.[14]

If someone is dealing with an estate of a person who has died, s/he has no personal liability for any debts that cannot be paid from the estate. Debts that may still have to be paid include:

- those for which someone had joint and several liability (see p144) with the person who has died. The co-debtor remains liable for the full outstanding balance owed;
- those covered by a guarantee. The guarantor remains liable for any debt covered by a guarantee if it is not paid by the estate;
- any debts if the estate has been passed to beneficiaries (including if the person handling the estate is the only beneficiary) without first paying creditors. If a client in this situation is being held personally liable by the creditors, s/he should get specialist advice;
- a mortgage remaining on a property, even if the property passes to a new owner by inheritance;
- rent arrears if someone has taken over a tenancy by succession, if these cannot be paid by the estate. A tenant by succession can lose her/his home if s/he does not pay the arrears owed;[15]
- council tax by couples with joint liability. Although a person's liability ceases at the date of death, the estate and the surviving partner remain liable for any arrears.

Note: some debts are paid off on death by insurance policies. Many mortgages and some regulated credit agreements are covered, and you should check these.

If the person who died owed money under a regulated credit agreement that was for a fixed term which had not already expired and the agreement was fully secured at the date of her/his death, the creditor cannot:

- terminate the agreement;
- demand earlier payment;
- recover possession of goods or property;
- treat any right under the agreement as terminated, restricted or deferred (other than the right to draw upon any credit); *or*
- enforce any security on the grounds that the borrower has died.

If the agreement is only partly secured or unsecured, the creditor must obtain a court order first.

If a person's debts were 'statute-barred' (see p292) at the date of her/his death, the estate can be distributed without taking that creditor's claim into account. However, if the claim has become statute-barred since the date of death, the question of whether the debt must be paid should be referred to a solicitor, as it depends on trust law.

If a client is living in the home of a person who has died and uses services (eg, fuel and water) for which the person who died was previously billed, s/he should open a new account in her/his own name as soon as possible after the death. It is important to ensure s/he does not agree to take responsibility for any debt when s/he opens the new account (although the estate of the person who died, of which the house may be part, is liable). All the occupiers of a property are jointly and severally liable for water charges.[16] However, this is a contingent liability and so does not become the client's debt until the person who was billed has failed to pay and the water company has demanded payment from the client. It is still the debt of the person who died and the estate is responsible for its payment. It is only if there is no estate or the estate is insolvent and cannot pay in full that the client can be required to pay. If the person who has died was the person who was contractually liable for any fuel bills, any arrears outstanding at the date of death were her/his responsibility and the other occupier(s) should not be required to pay those arrears if either there is no estate or the estate is insolvent and cannot pay in full.

Jointly owned property

A share in a joint bank account or jointly owned property is not part of a person's estate and passes directly to the other co-owner when s/he dies, regardless of whether s/he made a will or died intestate.[17] It is therefore not available to creditors unless, for example, a creditor has obtained a charging order on the beneficial interest in the property of one of the owners (see p326), one of the joint owners was made bankrupt or the ownership of the property was originally set up in unequal shares because, for instance, one party contributed a lump sum to the purchase.[18]

Joint owners in this situation are known as 'tenants in common'. The effect of this is that each has a potential estate against which her/his creditors (including unsecured creditors) can make a claim on her/his death. Advise joint owners to obtain legal advice on the most appropriate method of protecting themselves against potential claims on the estate by a co-owner's creditors, which could result in the loss of their home.

Even if the co-owners were not tenants in common, if a creditor with a debt of at least £5,000 presents a bankruptcy petition against the person who has died and an order is made, a court can require the surviving owner to pay the value of the deceased's share on the date of death to the trustee. The petition must be presented within five years of the death. It is advisable for a client faced with this possibility to make a payment arrangement with the creditor if s/he does not want the property to be sold. S/he should get specialist advice.

Under-18-year-olds

If a client was under 18 (a 'minor') at the time a contract was made, check whether it was for 'necessaries' (see below). If not, a court may decide the contract is not enforceable.

Necessaries

'**Necessaries**' are defined as 'goods suitable to the condition in life of a minor and her/his actual requirements at the time of sale and delivery'. Examples include fuel, clothes and possibly mobile phones. The client is expected to have paid no more than was 'reasonable' for such goods.

Note: a creditor who has given a loan to a minor to purchase 'necessaries' can recover the amount actually spent on those necessaries from her/him.[19]

Young people under 18 are often asked to provide a guarantor who is liable to pay if they cannot (see p145). If there was no guarantor and the goods were not 'necessaries', the client need not pay and the creditor is unable to use the courts to claim repayments. However, a court could order any goods to be returned if the supplier has experienced a loss.

If the client specifically informed the creditor that s/he was 18 or over on the date of the contract, although s/he may not be liable for the debt, s/he could be prosecuted for fraud if s/he attempts to challenge liability.

Contracts made under 'undue influence'

If a contract has been made under 'undue influence' (ie, if a person has taken unfair advantage of her/his influence over another person), it may not be enforceable. Undue influence may be actual – eg, if a person has been subjected to domestic abuse. Domestic abuse includes financial abuse, which is a form of controlling behaviour and includes controlling or interfering with the person's benefits, controlling her/his access to income, bank accounts or savings, and getting her/him to take out credit.

Undue influence may also be presumed – eg, if a person is persuaded to enter into a contract by someone on whom s/he relies for advice and guidance and the transaction is explainable only on the basis that undue influence was used, because it puts the person at a substantial disadvantage. This issue can often arise with guarantees (see p145). Another example is where one person takes out a loan for the benefit of another person but the loan is in the sole name of the first person.

A situation commonly arises where one partner in a couple applies for a loan for her/his own purposes (eg, to pay off debts or fund a business), which the creditor requires to be in joint names so that it can be secured on jointly owned property or so that the income of the other partner can be taken into account as part of the creditor's lending process. If it appears that the second borrower's agreement to taking out a joint loan was only given because the first borrower used 'undue influence' (eg, by saying, 'we'll lose our home if you do not sign', or by misrepresenting the effect of the transaction – see below), the second borrower may not be liable and should get specialist advice.

Although examples of creditors actually being aware that a contract has been entered into as a result of undue influence are rare, in certain situations, the law deems the creditor to have notice of the possibility of undue influence (known as 'constructive notice') and requires the creditor take certain steps to counter any undue influence to which the client may have been subject. Failure to take those steps may mean that a client who has been subjected to undue influence is able to challenge her/his liability.[20]

As well as having a potential defence to any court action taken by the creditor, the client may also be able to make a complaint which can be escalcated to the Financial Ombudsman Service which may be able to relieve the client from liability in appropriate cases. Advisers should, however, bear in mind that the outcome of a successful undue influence argument could be a pyrrhic victory in the case of a secured creditor who may still be able to enforce her/his charge against the partner's beneficial interest in the property.[21]

Misrepresentation of the terms of the contract

If a creditor misrepresents the terms of a contract to a client (ie, does not explain the transaction accurately), the transaction may be void. For example, if a creditor persuades a client to sign a legal charge by stating that a secured loan does not put her/his home at risk, the loan may not be enforceable as the client has the right to cancel the legal charge.

The client can seek compensation for any loss suffered as a consequence of a misrepresentation. As it is difficult to prove oral misrepresentation, it is important that you obtain copies of all relevant correspondence. Alternatively, if the misrepresentation can be established, the creditor may decide not to pursue the debt to avoid bad publicity.

In the case of regulated credit agreements (see p62), if the finance is arranged through the supplier or dealer, the lender is jointly liable with the supplier or dealer for any misrepresentations made by the supplier/dealer about both the goods or services supplied and the credit agreement.

Capacity to make a contract

A contract is only valid if someone has the 'capacity' to make it.[22] The Mental Capacity Act 2005 contains the following principles.

- A person lacks capacity if, at the time the contract is entered into, s/he is unable to make a decision for her/himself about it because of an impairment of, or a disturbance in the functioning of, her mind or brain. The impairment or disturbance may be permanent or temporary.
- A person is assumed to have capacity unless it is established that s/he does not.
- A person should not be treated as unable to make a decision merely because s/he makes an unwise decision.
- A person is unable to make a decision for her/himself if s/he is unable to:
  - understand the information relevant to the decision, including information about the reasonably foreseeable consequences of deciding one way or another; *or*
  - retain that information, although the fact that s/he is only able to retain the information for a short period does not prevent her/him from being able to make the decision; *or*
  - use or weigh up that information as part of the process of making the decision; *or*
  - communicate her/his decision, either in speech, sign language or some other means.

In a disappointing decision which has raised the bar for establishing that a person lacks capacity, in 2016 the High Court held that what is important is whether the person has the ability to understand the transaction and not whether s/he actually understands it.[23] Previous guidance was wrong insofar as it looked at the understanding that the person actually has. The court decided that the correct test for incapacity is whether the person has the capacity to absorb, retain, understand, process and weigh information about the key feature and effects of the transaction and the alternatives to it, if explained in broad terms and simple language. It is not necessary for the person to have the capacity to understand every aspect of the transaction. In addition, even if the person lacked capacity, the court confirmed that the transaction might not be enforceable provided the creditor either knew, or ought to have known, of the person's incapacity.

Advisers sometimes assume that, because a client has mental health or learning difficulties, any agreement s/he has entered into is automatically unenforceable. Do not assume this; medical evidence is usually needed to establish the client's lack of capacity. In many cases, the client's lack of capacity can be established, but not the creditor's knowledge or presumed knowledge. However, it is often possible to ask the creditor to write off the debt, either because there is evidence of inappropriate lending and/or the client's situation is such that setting up a debt repayment programme is not a realistic strategy.[24]

The FCA has said that creditors should take reasonable steps to ensure they have suitable business practices and procedures in place for the fair treatment of clients with limited mental capacity.[25]

Specialist advice should be obtained if the enforceability of a contract on the grounds of incapacity is being considered or if someone who appears to lack capacity is involved in court proceedings.

For further information on dealing with clients with mental health problems, see p33.

Housing disrepair

In many cases where there are rent arrears, landlords have not always fulfilled their obligations in connection with repairs. The amount of rent arrears claimed by the landlord can then be reduced by either a 'set-off' or a 'counterclaim' by the tenant. A 'set-off' is money spent by the tenant to carry out repairs required by law and is, therefore, owed to the tenant by the landlord. A 'counterclaim' is money claimed by the tenant as compensation for a failure to repair and the resultant loss.[26] Obtain specialist housing advice if this applies.

Faulty goods and services

If a client owes money on faulty goods or unsatisfactory services, s/he may be able to avoid paying all or part of the bill. A client may be able to obtain a refund on goods that are not of satisfactory quality or not as described.[27] The goods must be rejected immediately or very soon after purchase. Similarly, services should be carried out with reasonable care and skill and within a reasonable time.[28] In addition, the client may be able to claim for whatever expenses s/he has incurred as a result of the fault. Report dangerous goods to the local trading standards department.

Mistaken payments into bank accounts

A client's bank account may be mistakenly credited with money to which the client is not entitled. Although the creditor or bank has made a mistake, generally, a client is legally required to repay money which does not belong to her/him. However, a client does not have to repay money if s/he has 'changed position' through believing in good faith that the money was hers/his. Spending the money on ordinary day-to-day living expenses or repaying a debt is not a change of position, but buying something that s/he would not otherwise have bought is.

It must be unfair for the client to have to repay the money. It is *not* unfair if:

- s/he has acted in bad faith – eg, s/he was aware of the mistake; *and/or*
- full or partial repayment is possible because all or some of the money is still in her/his possession.

The bank should not pay the money back to the party that made the mistaken payment into the account without the client's permission.[29]

Default charges

Many credit agreements (as well as mortgages and secured loans) allow the creditor to add charges to the client's account in certain circumstances. These are sometimes referred to as 'arrears charges' or 'penalty charges'. Usually, the amount of the charge is fixed. Often, such charges accrue interest while they remain unpaid. Examples of situations in which charges are imposed include:

- late or missed payments;
- exceeding a credit limit; *and*
- dishonoured cheques or direct debit payments.

All these situations involve a breach of contract by the client and the charges are supposed to reflect the damages or financial loss for the creditor from this. The courts only enforce them if they are seen as a genuine attempt to estimate in advance the loss the creditor will face for the additional administration involved as a result of the client's breach of contract. The provisions are then enforceable as what is known as 'liquidated damages'.

Refused payment fees – ie, fees charged by a payment services provider (eg, a bank) for refusing to make a payment due to lack of funds – are permitted by the Payment Services Regulations 2017 so long as they are provided for in the agreement between the bank and its customer and 'reasonably correspond to the payment service provider's actual costs'.[30] FCA guidance states that payment service providers should:

- identify the actual costs that are reasonably referable to the refusal of payments; *and*
- set their charges so as to reasonably correspond to those costs over a period of time; *and*
- not derive a profit from those charges.[31]

It may be possible to challenge such default charges, arguing that they are either:

- an unfair term under the Consumer Rights Act 2015 (see below); *or*
- in the case of regulated credit agreements, under CONC 7.7 of the FCA's *Consumer Credit Sourcebook* on the grounds that they are higher than necessary to cover the creditor's reasonable costs.

What is an unfair term

A term is unfair if: 'contrary to the requirements of good faith, it causes a significant imbalance in the parties' rights and obligations arising under the contract to the detriment of the consumer',[32] provided:

- the client is a 'consumer' – ie, s/he did not make the contract in the course of business; *and*
- the agreement was made on or after 1 July 1995; *and*

- the contract is in the creditor's standard form – ie, it has not been individually negotiated.

An unfair term is not binding on the client and so cannot be enforced against her/him by the creditor. The remainder of the agreement is unaffected, provided it is capable of continuing without the unfair term.[33] Examples of unfair terms include those:[34]

- requiring clients who fail to fulfil their obligations to pay a disproportionately high sum in compensation;[35]
- that irrevocably bind clients to conditions which they had no real opportunity of becoming acquainted with before the conclusion of the contract.[36]

What action to take

If you believe a default charge is an unfair term, first check the relevant terms of the agreement and, if it allows the creditor to make the charge(s) in question, write to the creditor.

- Point out that the default charges do not reflect the creditor's actual or anticipated loss in the particular circumstances of the client's breach of contract and are, therefore, not recoverable.
- State that the default charges are also an unfair term contrary to Schedule 2, paragraph 1(e) of the Unfair Terms in Consumer Contracts Regulations 1994/1999 because they require the client to pay a disproportionately high sum in compensation for her/his failure to perform the obligations under the contract.
- Ask the creditor either to refund these charges to the client's account or else justify the level of default charges.

If the client is not satisfied with the creditor's response, s/he could take the matter through the creditor's complaints procedure to the Financial Ombudsman Service (see p284) or part defend any court action taken by the creditor (see p315).[37]

---

3. **Using the Consumer Credit Act**

The Consumer Credit Act 1974 (see p61) regulates the way in which most credit agreements can be set up. It gives the borrower certain rights. If these are denied, a court may decide that the agreement is unenforceable and, therefore, the creditor cannot require repayment.

The courts also have powers that can assist clients, specifically when the relationship between the client and the creditor is unfair to the client (see p161) and through time orders (see p366).

Requests for information

In order to check whether or not an agreement actually exists and, if so, its terms and conditions and/or whether or not the amount the creditor is claiming to be due is correct, you may need to contact the creditor for information. Creditors are required to provide certain information within 12 working days – ie, excluding weekends and bank holidays. If they fail to do so within this time limit, the agreement becomes unenforceable until they provide it.[38]

The client can request that the creditor provide:

- a copy of the executed agreement;
- a copy of any other document referred to in the agreement – eg, a bill of sale (but not a default notice);
- a statement of account containing the prescribed information (see p70), not just the amount of arrears.

The request must be in writing and must include the prescribed fee of £1 per credit agreement. It is recommended that you keep a record of postage.

When to make a request

A request for information can be made to:

- obtain information which you have been unable to get voluntarily and which is required to deal with the client's case;
- prevent enforcement action from being started while you are investigating liability (but see below);
- halt enforcement action already taking place to enable you to investigate liability (but see below).

In a number of test cases, the High Court has adopted a narrow interpretation of 'enforcement'. In this context, it means:

- repossession of any goods or land;
- termination of the agreement;
- enforcement of any security – eg, a bill of sale;
- demanding early payment;
- treating any right given to the client under the agreement as terminated, restricted or deferred;
- entering and enforcing a judgment.

If a creditor has failed to comply with an information request, it can still take the following steps, which are not treated as enforcement:[39]

- report the client's default to a credit reference agency;
- demand payment (but not early payment);
- pass the case to debt collectors;
- threaten legal action;
- issue court proceedings.

The Financial Conduct Authority's (FCA's) *Consumer Credit Sourcebook* says that creditors should not threaten court action or any other enforcement of the debt or mislead the client about the enforceability of the debt, and that any communication or request for payment should make it clear that, although the debt remains outstanding, the agreement is unenforceable.[40]

Possible responses from the creditor

- **The creditor does not reply.** Send a reminder after 14 days, pointing out that the agreement is now unenforceable unless and until the creditor complies with the request.
- **The creditor says the request must come from the client personally.** People can usually act through agents and the Consumer Credit Act 1974 does not require someone to act in person in this situation. The FCA says that, provided a proper authority is given to the creditor, the request is still 'from or on behalf of the debtor' and should, therefore, be complied with.
- **The debt has been sold and the new creditor (the 'debt purchaser') says it does not have the information and does not have to provide it because it is not the 'creditor'.** The definition of 'creditor' in section 189 of the Consumer Credit Act 1974 includes someone to whom the original creditor's rights and duties under the agreement have passed – eg, by assignment. Some debt purchasers argue that they only purchase the rights, not the duties, and so do not fit within the definition, but the High Court has held that the 'right' to enforce the agreement carries with it the 'duty' to comply with the Consumer Credit Act.[41] However, provided the client has had notice of the assignment, the debt purchaser is entitled to enforce the agreement, including by court proceedings. The right to enforce is not an absolute right because, if the client had a defence to any claim brought by the original creditor (eg, that the agreement is unenforceable), s/he also has that defence to any claim brought by the debt purchaser.
- **The creditor says it does not have to comply with the request because, for example, the loan repayment period is over or the account has been terminated.** The duty to comply with a request does not apply where no sum is, or will be or may become, payable by the client.[42] So, by implication, it does apply if a sum is, will be or may become payable by the client, which is the case if the creditor is demanding payment.
- **The creditor does not provide a photocopy but only a pro forma agreement with no client signature.** The rules say that the creditor must supply a 'true copy', which can omit any signature and so this *does* comply with the Act.[43] The fact that the creditor says it cannot locate a copy does not mean that it cannot comply with an information request. The High Court has said that the creditor can supply a reconstituted copy from any source, not just from the original agreement. If a creditor does this, it must state this when the copy is supplied. However, if the creditor is aware that there was never a signed

agreement, it cannot hide this fact by claiming that it cannot find it or by creating an untrue copy (see p73).

- **The creditor does not reply and contacts the client for payment.** Seeking payment is not enforcement, but you could point out that the agreement is unenforceable until a statement or copy of the agreement is provided and this means it cannot take any of the above action (which should be listed), but can comply by providing a 'true' copy which can be reconstituted from any source, provided it is indicated that it is reconstituted. If the agreement has been varied, the creditor must provide the original as well as the current terms and conditions. Consider complaining about any breaches of the FCA's requirements in relation to information requests or other parts of the *Consumer Credit Sourcebook*.[44]

- **The creditor complies with the request.** In order to comply, the client's address at the time of the agreement must be included and, if the agreement has been varied, the original terms and conditions must be supplied, as well as the current version. Check the agreement to see whether any other documents are referred to in it, which could help the client's case (eg, a bill of sale), and ask for copies. You should now be in a position to deal with the client's case.

If the creditor does not comply

If the creditor does not provide the information requested, this puts the client in a dilemma about whether to pay or not. If the client does not pay or does not come to a payment arrangement, s/he runs the risk of the creditor either locating the original agreement or having sufficient information to provide a reconstituted copy as well as some evidence that originally there was a properly executed agreement signed by the client. In the meantime, the debt may escalate because of the addition of default interest and charges, and the client remains liable for these. The High Court has recognised this dilemma, but has said that neither the failure to comply nor the fact that there was not a properly executed agreement mean there is an unfair relationship (see p161).[45]

However, if an agreement was made before 6 April 2007 which was not properly executed, it may be irredeemably unenforceable (see p71).

There are other arguments that can be put to creditors or debt purchasers who do not supply copies of agreements. Both the FCA's *Consumer Credit Sourcebook*[46] and the *Credit Services Association Code of Practice*[47] place obligations on creditors, debt collectors and debt purchasers to provide information, and any failure to comply could be a breach of the Consumer Protection from Unfair Trading Regulations 2008. If court action is threatened, the pre-action conduct protocols require the parties to act reasonably in exchanging information (see p281) and, if a claim is defended, the creditor (whether the original creditor or a debt purchaser) must produce any 'relevant documents'.[48]

You should note that the real issue here is not whether the creditor or debt purchaser can produce a copy of the agreement, but whether a properly executed agreement complying with the Consumer Credit Act 1974 has ever existed. If the creditor takes court proceedings, a client will only be able to defend the case on the grounds that the agreement is irredeemably unenforceable if it was made before 6 April 2007 and either it was not signed by the client or it did not contain the necessary prescribed terms (including cancellation notices where required). If the client wants to defend the case on the grounds that the agreement is irredeemably unenforceable, s/he must put forward a positive case about the circumstances in which the agreement was made and cannot just rely on the creditor's failure to produce a photocopy of the original because this does not necessarily mean that a properly executed agreement did not exist.

The client may only have a temporary defence to any county court claim by the creditor if the creditor has failed to comply with a request for information as described on p157. This is because the creditor can always comply by producing a 'true copy' and, in the meantime, the court is likely to 'stay' the case – ie, stop it from proceeding further until the creditor complies. If a client does not dispute the existence of a properly executed agreement, but you are considering defending a claim on the grounds that the original creditor/debt purchaser/collector failed to produce a copy of the agreement, get specialist advice.

You should also check that creditors have complied with sections 77A and 86B of the Consumer Credit Act 1974. Also consider using a subject access request (SAR) to obtain a copy of the personal information the creditor holds about the client (which should include a copy of any agreement and statements in the client's file). There is no fee and the creditor has a maximum of one month to comply with the request. See https://ico.org.uk/your-data-matters/. If the creditor has sent the client a letter before claim, you could also consider using the pre-action protocol for debt claims to obtain any documents you need, in order to investigate liability or the amount of the claim (see p281).

Unauthorised creditors

If a creditor enters into a regulated credit agreement (see p62), but did not have the appropriate authorisation from the FCA to undertake consumer credit activities, or a third party (eg, a credit broker) through whom the agreement was arranged did not have the appropriate authorisation, it cannot enforce the agreement. The client is entitled to recover any money or other property paid or transferred by her/him under the agreement and to claim compensation from the creditor for any loss sustained by her/him as a result of having parted with the money or property. The creditor also commits a criminal offence.[49]

The creditor can apply to the FCA to issue a notice allowing the agreement to be enforced or allowing money paid or property transferred under the agreement to be retained. The FCA can only agree to this if it is 'just and equitable' to do so. The creditor must establish that it genuinely believed that either it or the third party met the relevant criteria.[50]

If a creditor appears to be unauthorised (eg, because the company is clearly new, badly organised and unprofessional, its documentation is of a poor standard, or you have not heard of it before), check whether it has authorisation by searching the Financial Services Register online at fca.org.uk/firms/financial-services-register. Creditors who are not authorised sometimes withdraw at this point when the need for authorisation is pointed out to them. In the meantime, the client should be advised that s/he need not pay and should be informed of her/his rights concerning harassment (see p29) and under the FCA's *Consumer Credit Sourcebook* (see p30). If the creditor is a 'loan shark', see p254.

Early settlement of a credit agreement

If a regulated agreement is ended early by the client, s/he should pay less than the total amount that would have been payable if the agreement had run to its full term. If the client requests the information from the creditor, the creditor must provide her/him with a statement of the amount required to settle the agreement, together with details of how the amount is calculated.[51]

One or more partial early repayments may be made at any time during the life of the agreement.

There is a formula to ensure that creditors can recoup costs associated with setting up an agreement and, therefore, a lower percentage rebate is given for settlement during the earliest parts of a credit agreement.[52]

Unfair relationships

The Consumer Credit Act 2006 amended the Consumer Credit Act 1974 to introduce the concept of an 'unfair relationship'.[53] This enables a borrower to challenge a credit agreement on the grounds that the relationship between the creditor and the borrower in connection with the agreement (or a related agreement) is unfair to the borrower. These provisions are in addition to the Financial Ombudsman Service's jurisdiction (see p284).

The provisions attempt to address situations where the creditor has taken unfair advantage of the borrower or there has been oppressive or exploitative conduct, but not where the borrower has simply made a bad bargain. They apply to regulated and non-regulated agreements, including exempt agreements, and regardless of the amount of credit involved, except if the agreement is exempt because it is a regulated mortgage contract (see p112). **Note:** the exemption from the unfair relationship provisions does not apply to consumer credit back book contracts (see p64).

If an agreement has been paid off by a later, consolidating agreement (see p164), the earlier agreement can still be challenged, even though the relationship has ended.

The provisions also apply to completed agreements (ie, where there is no longer any sum which is or may become payable) and also where a judgment has been made.

An order may be made by a court if the client applies either as a stand-alone application or as part of court proceedings relating to the credit agreement or a related agreement. If the client alleges that the credit relationship is unfair, the onus of proof is on the creditor to show that it is *not* unfair. It is not sufficient merely to assert that the relationship is unfair; facts in support of the allegation must be set out.

Note: the unfair relationships provisions may be especially useful for clients facing court proceedings for enforcement of a debt or repossession, or where the restrictions on the Ombudsman's jurisdiction mean that a client has no option but to resort to the unfair relationship provisions in order to challenge the creditor or defend the claim. However, they should be viewed as a remedy of last resort. If you are considering taking advantage of these provisions, get specialist advice.

Relevant dates

The unfair relationships provisions have applied since 6 April 2007 to credit agreements entered into on or after this date.

From 6 April 2008, the provisions have also applied to agreements made before this date, unless the agreement was paid off in full by then.

An agreement made before 6 April 2007 consolidated (ie, paid off) by an agreement made before 6 April 2008 cannot be challenged as a 'related agreement' because this has ceased to have any effect. Such paid-off or consolidated agreements remain subject to the extortionate credit bargain provisions in the Consumer Credit Act 1974. If you are considering arguing that there is a case of extortionate credit, get specialist advice.

The court's powers to make an order under the unfair relationships provisions are not limited to matters arising after 6 April 2007. The court can also take into account matters before this date. In considering a current agreement (whenever it was made), the court can take into account a related agreement made before 6 April 2007, but cannot make an order for repayment of any sum paid under a related agreement if that agreement ceased to be in operation before 6 April 2007.[54]

What is an unfair relationship

The Consumer Credit Act 2006 does not define an unfair relationship, but it does set out, in general terms, factors that may give rise to an unfair relationship. These are:

- the terms of the credit agreement or a related agreement (see p163);
- the way in which the creditor has exercised or enforced its rights under the agreement (or a related agreement);

- anything done (or not done) by or on behalf of the creditor either before or after making the agreement (or a related agreement).

In some cases, unfair contract terms may be sufficient in themselves to give rise to an unfair relationship, but the court can also look at:
- the way agreements are introduced and negotiated;
- the way in which agreements are administered; *and*
- any other aspect of the relationship it considers relevant.

Both actions and omissions can be unfair (eg, if a creditor fails to take certain steps which, in the interests of fairness, it might reasonably be expected to take). This includes actions or omissions on behalf of the creditor – ie, by employees, associates and agents, such as brokers (but not brokers acting on behalf of the client), suppliers (who are deemed agents of the creditor) and debt collectors. These include:
- pre-contract business practices such as misleading advertisements, mis-selling products, high-pressure selling techniques, 'churning' (see p164) and irresponsible lending;
- post-contract actions, such as demanding money the borrower has not agreed to pay and aggressive debt collection practices;
- failing to provide key information in a clear and timely manner or to disclose material facts.

The court must take into account all matters it thinks relevant, including those relating to the individual client and creditor. This means that a term or practice may not be unfair in a particular case because of the client's knowledge or experience, but may be unfair in another client's case if s/he is more vulnerable or susceptible to exploitation. There is also an expectation that clients will act honestly in providing accurate and full information to enable the creditor to assess risk.

Note: the Supreme Court has held that the creditor does not need to be in breach of any rule, industry guidance or code of practice. The question is whether the creditor's relationship with the client is unfair.[55]

Related and consolidated agreements

A '**related agreement**' is:
– a credit agreement consolidated by the main agreement; *or*
– a linked transaction in relation to the main agreement (or a consolidated agreement); *or*
– a security provided in relation to the main agreement (or a consolidated agreement or a linked transaction). For example, payment protection insurance (PPI) is likely to be a linked transaction.

An agreement is *not* a related agreement if the later agreement is with a different creditor, unless the new creditor is an 'associate' or 'former associate' of the original creditor.

An agreement is **'consolidated'** by a later agreement if:
– the later agreement is entered into, in whole or in part, for purposes connected with debts owed under the earlier agreement; *and*
– at any time before the later agreement is entered into, the parties to the earlier agreement included the client under the later agreement and either the creditor or an associate or former associate.

This addresses the practice (known as **'churning'**) of creditors entering into successive agreements with a client (often before the earlier agreement has been paid off) and which usually involves not only refinancing the earlier agreement, but also providing extra finance, charging additional fees and selling further PPI, and which may, in itself, give rise to an unfair relationship.

Identifying potential unfair relationship situations

Possible examples of unfairness include:
- compounding default interest and charges, resulting in a very large debt;
- mis-selling subsidiary insurance products (such as PPI), including selling inappropriate products, aggressive selling and misleading borrowers into believing that a product is compulsory or in her/his interests, when it is not;
- failing to disclose commission paid by the insurance company to the lender and/or broker on the sale of PPI;
- misleading clients about their legal rights – eg, misrepresenting a client's right to terminate voluntarily a conditional sale or hire purchase agreement or dishonestly obtaining a client's consent for protected hire purchase goods to be repossessed without a court order;
- draconian and/or unreasonable use of enforcement rights or powers – eg, the use of orders for sale to enforce debts which were originally unsecured;
- applying unreasonable pressure on clients to sign agreements, particularly in face-to-face situations, and not giving clients sufficient time to read and consider the terms of an agreement or to take independent advice where appropriate;
- failing to assess a client's creditworthiness and irresponsible lending, including irresponsible consolidation of debts ('churning');
- replacing irredeemably unenforceable agreements with new agreements after 6 April 2007;
- obtaining payment from clients by threatening to enforce irredeemably unenforceable agreements;
- realising a secured loan by a sale of the property without obtaining an enforcement order.

Payment protection insurance

Many loans are covered by insurance against sickness and unemployment, known as payment protection insurance (PPI). If the terms of the insurance policy are met, it makes repayments towards contractual instalments. You should always check to see if repayments of a credit debt (secured or unsecured) are covered by insurance. Some policies only provide cover for a set period of time and, in the case of joint agreements, for only one of the parties, often the first person named in the agreement.

The insurance may be paid for through the monthly repayments under the credit agreement, but it is not part of the credit provided under the agreement. If the client defaults, the policy often provides for it to lapse after, say, three missed payments.

In the past, PPI was often paid for with a single premium, which was then funded as part of the credit agreement and so interest was charged on it. If the client defaulted, s/he could still claim under the policy because the premium had already been paid. Single premium PPI was invariably purchased at the same time as the credit agreement was entered into. There was considerable evidence of PPI being mis-sold and the sale of single premium payment protection policies on unsecured loans was stopped in February 2009.

If a client suggests that taking out a single premium insurance policy was a condition of being given the finance, the whole agreement may be unenforceable if it was taken out before 6 April 2007 and it was a regulated credit agreement (see p71).

In some cases, insurance companies refuse to pay – eg, if the client has an illness that started before the insurance policy began (a 'pre-existing condition') or was not employed when the policy was taken out. Some policies only provide cover for people under 65 or exclude certain situations altogether – eg, voluntary redundancy. In other cases, delays in processing claims result in creditors applying default interest/charges and/or threatening enforcement action.

Many of the unfair relationships cases that have come before the courts relate to allegations of mis-sold PPI. If the client can establish that s/he was told that the finance was conditional on the insurance being taken out, the court is likely to find that the relationship is unfair.

Sellers of PPI were usually paid a high rate of commission. The court can take into account the seller's failure to disclose this commission to the client, even though this is not a requirement of the FCA's *Insurance: Conduct of Business Sourcebook*.[56]

Following the Supreme Court's decision in *Plevin v Paragon Personal Finance* (which held that an undisclosed commission of 71.8 per cent gave rise to an unfair relationship), the FCA ruled that when a creditor assessed a complaint about an undisclosed commission, failure to disclose receipt of a commission of more than 50 per cent of the PPI premium, it should result in the client being compensated.[57] This should be the amount of commission over the 50 per cent figure plus interest already paid by the client and a further 8 per cent a year simple interest. (The courts tended to award repayment of the entire commission.[58]) Creditors should have contacted all clients whose complaints about the sale of

PPI were rejected and who were eligible to complain about undisclosed commission in the light of the *Plevin* decision.

Note: the final deadline for making new complaints about PPI was 29 August 2019.

Clients who wish to complain about the misselling of PPI may still be in time to bring an unfair relationship claim against the creditor. In *Patel v Patel,* the High Court decided that the client's cause of action was a continuing one which accrued from day to day until the relationship ended. It followed that an unfair relationship claim could be made at any time during the currency of the relationship arising under the credit agreement until the expiration of the limitation period after the relationship had ended.[59] Clients may also benefit from the more generous compensation currently being awarded by the courts – ie, the refund of the full PPI premium (as in the *Doran* case[60]) as opposed to only the excess above 50 per cent of the premium in accordance with FCA guidance.

Remedies

If the court decides that the relationship is unfair to the borrower, it can make an order:

- requiring the creditor to repay (in whole or part) any sum paid by the client;
- requiring the creditor to do, not to do, or to cease anything specified in the order;
- reducing or discharging any sum payable by the client;
- setting aside (in whole or part) any duty imposed on the client;
- altering the terms of the agreement or any related agreement.

If security is provided by a third party (eg, a guarantee) in connection with a credit agreement or linked transaction, the third party can also apply to the court under the unfair relationships provisions. In addition to the above orders, the court can order any property provided as security to be returned to her/him.

Procedural irregularities

Certain specified procedures must be followed for a regulated credit agreement to be properly executed (see pp65–74).[61] An improperly executed regulated agreement can only be enforced by a court order.[62]

Note: the court has no power to order enforcement (ie, it is 'irredeemably unenforceable') if the agreement was made before 6 April 2007, and: [63]

- it has not been signed by the client(s); *or*
- it has been signed by the client(s), but does not contain or contains inaccurate prescribed information (see p70); *or*
- in the case of a cancellable agreement, the client was not given a copy before the creditor took court action, or told of her/his cancellation rights.

If a creditor has an unenforceable agreement with a client, it should apply to the court for permission to enforce it. When making an order, the court must consider the creditor's responsibility for the improper execution and its effect on the client.[64] The court can allow enforcement on such terms as it thinks fit – eg, reduce the amount owed by the borrower, make a time order (see p366) and reduce or freeze interest/charges.[65]

If a loan is secured and if the agreement is unenforceable, so is the security.[66] The creditor should arrange to discharge the security – eg, remove any entries relating to a secured loan from the Land Registry.

A creditor may sue a client for payment of a debt without informing the court that the agreement is unenforceable. If this happens and judgment is entered against the client, s/he may be able to get the judgment 'set aside' (see p337).[67] Obtain specialist advice in these circumstances.

Notes

1. **Introduction**
   1 See also *FCA Handbook*, CONC 7.14.1R
   2 ss77-79 CCA 1974

2. **Using contract law**
   3 For a discussion on guarantees, see L Groves, 'Guarantors and Rent Arrears', *Adviser* 140, and G Skipwith, 'Guarantees, Indemnities and CCA 1974', *Adviser* 149
   4 See s7 Electronic Communications Act 2000 and *Bassano v Toft and Others* [2014] EWHC 377 (QB)
   5 ss110 and 111 CCA 1974
   6 *RBS v Etridge (No.2)* [2002] HLR 37; see also G Skipwith, 'Banks, Solicitors, Husbands and Wives', *Adviser* 95
   7 For a Financial Ombudsman Service decision relating to affordability checks made by Amigo Loans on a borrower, see ombudsman-decisions.org.uk/viewPDF.aspx?FileID=215809 and for a further decision relating to affordability checks made by Amigo Loans on a guarantor, see ombudsman-decisions.org.uk/viewPDF.aspx?FileID=215813

8 See G O'Malley, 'New FCA Rules to Protect Guarantors', *Quarterly Account* 39, IMA
9 ss105-11 CCA 1974
10 ss107-09 CCA 1974
11 s87 CCA 1974
12 r15.31(3) I(E&W)R 2016
13 Ombudsman's complaint 47/1, *Adviser* 113
14 *FCA Handbook*, CONC 7.5.2R states that creditors must not pursue an individual who they know or believe may not be the borrower under the credit agreement
15 *Sherrin v Brand* [1956] 1 QB 403
16 s144 Water Industry Act 1991
17 In *Whitlock v Moree* [2017] UKPC 44 (*Adviser* 185 abstracts), following the death of one of the two joint account holders, it was held that the standard bank form signed by the account holders which stated that all money was 'joint property with the right of survivorship' overrode the presumption that the balance in the account was the property of the deceased's estate because he had provided all the funds in the account.

18 Refer clients to gov.uk/joint-property-ownership
19 See 'Q&A', *Quarterly Account* 24, IMA
20 *RBS v Etridge (No.2)* [2002] HLR 37; see also G Skipwith, 'Banks, Solicitors, Husbands and Wives', *Adviser* 95. There is a useful summary of the position: see A Walker, 'Undue influence', *Quarterly Account* 53, IMA.
21 *Santander v Fletcher* [2018] EWHC 2778 (Ch) (*Adviser* 189 abstracts)
22 For a more detailed discussion, see C Wilkinson, 'Mental Incapacity and Debt in England and Wales', *Adviser* 138
23 *Fehily and Fehily v Atkinson and Mummery* [2016] EWHC 3069 (Ch)
24 See *Ombudsman News* 50 for details of some complaints which illustrate the approach of the Financial Ombudsman Service (*Adviser* 114 abstracts)
25 See *FCA Handbook*, CONC 2.10.10G
26 For more information, see J Luba and Others, *Defending Possession Proceedings*, Legal Action Group, 2016
27 s14 SGA 1979
28 s13 SGSA 1982
29 *Crantrave Ltd v Lloyds Bank* (*Adviser* 87 abstracts); see also P Madge, 'Consultancy Corner', *Adviser* 101. Also, for the Financial Ombudsman Service view of this issue, see *Ombudsman News* 87 (*Adviser* 142 abstracts).
30 reg 66(1)(c) Payment Services Regulations 2017
31 See fca.org.uk/firms/high-cost-credit-consumer-credit/high-cost-credit-review
32 s62(4) CRA 2015
33 s67 CRA 2015
34 Sch 2 CRA 2015
35 Sch 2 para 5 CRA 2015
36 Sch 2 para 10A CRA 2015
37 See 'Penalty Charges on Credit Cards and Current Accounts', *Quarterly Account* 78, IMA; G Skipwith, 'Penalty Shoot-out', *Adviser* 113

3. Using the Consumer Credit Act
38 ss77 and 78 CCA 1974
39 *McGuffick v RBS* [2009] EWHC 2386 (Comm) (*Adviser* 136 abstracts); *Carey and Others v HSBC and Others* [2009] EWHC 3471 (QB) (*Adviser* 139 abstracts)
40 *FCA Handbook*, CONC 13.1.6G
41 *Jones v Link Financial* [2012] EWHC 2402 (QB) (*Adviser* 154 abstracts)
42 s77(3) CCA 1974

43 Reg 3 Consumer Credit (Cancellation Notices and Copies of Documents) Regulations 1983, No.1557
44 For example, *FCA Handbook*, CONC 7.14.1R states that the creditor must suspend any steps to recover a debt if the client disputes the debt on valid (or what may be valid) grounds
45 *Carey and Others v HSBC and Others* [2009] EWHC 3471 (QB) (*Adviser* 139 abstracts)
46 For example, *FCA Handbook*, CONC 7.4.1R and 7.14.3R
47 *Credit Services Association Code of Practice*, para 2(m)
48 r31.8 CPR
49 ss19, 23 and 26-27 FSMA 2000
50 s28A FSMA 2000
51 ss94, 95 and 97 CCA 1974
52 Consumer Credit (Early Settlement) Regulations 2004, No.1483
53 ss19-22 and Sch 3 paras14-17 CCA 2006
54 *Barnes and Barnes v Black Horse* [2011] EWHC 1416 (QB) (*Adviser* 147 abstracts)
55 *Plevin v Paragon Personal Finance* [2014] UKSC 61 (*Adviser* 167 abstracts)
56 *Plevin v Paragon Personal Finance* [2014] UKSC 61 (*Adviser* 167 abstracts)
57 *Plevin v Paragon Personal Finance* [2014] UKSC 61 (*Adviser* 167 abstracts)
58 *McWilliams v Norton Finance* (*Adviser* 169 abstracts); *Nelmes v NRAM* (*Adviser* 182 abstracts)
59 [2009] EWHC 3264 (QB). *Patel* was considered in the County Court at Manchester in *Doran v Paragon Personal Finance Ltd*, 01/05/18. In that case, the claim was issued more than 13 years after the credit agreement and PPI policy were entered into but less than five years after the loan was repaid. The judge held that the claim had been brought within the six-year limitation period. The judge awarded a refund of the full amount of the PPI premium plus the interest repayments relating to that part of the loan.

60 *Doran v Paragon Personal Finance Ltd*
    (Manchester county court) 1 May 2018.
    The claim was issued more than 13 years
    after the credit agreement and PPI
    policy were entered into but less than
    five years after the loan was repaid. The
    judge held that the claim had been
    brought within the six-year limitation
    period, and awarded a refund of the full
    amount of the PPI premium plus the
    interest repayments relating to that part
    of the loan.
61 ss60-64 CCA 1974
62 s65 CCA 1974
63 s127(3) and (4) CCA 1974
64 s127(1) CCA 1974
65 See *National Mortgage Corporation v
    Wilkes* [1993] CCLR 1, *Legal Action*,
    October 1991
66 s113 CCA 1974
67 See *In the matter of London Scottish
    Finance (in administration)* [2013] EWHC
    4047 (ChD) (*Adviser* 162 abstracts)

Chapter 7

....

Maximising income

This chapter covers:
1. Introduction (below)
2. How to use this chapter (p172)
3. A–Z of benefits and tax credits (p174)
4. Calculating entitlement (p190)
5. Other help (p199)

---

1. **Introduction**

It is important to ensure that a client's income is raised where possible by checking that:
- s/he receives all the benefits and tax credits to which s/he is entitled, and that s/he is paid the correct amount;
- her/his tax liability is as low as possible;
- all possible sources of income have been explored.

Maximising income increases the amount of money coming in and minimises the expenditure going out. Checking that clients are receiving all the benefits to which they are entitled is a good starting point.[1]

If you are not a welfare rights specialist, you should consider consulting with colleagues who are, signposting the client to a website considered appropriate by your agency or referring cases to someone who is able to undertake this work.

The debt adviser's approach to income maximisation must be systematic in order to be comprehensive. You must have a working knowledge of the benefits and tax credits system and the books on income maximisation listed in Appendix 2. Materials and tools are also available on the Money Advice Service website at debtquality.org.uk. This chapter assumes general advice knowledge, but cannot explain all the ways in which income can be maximised. Instead, it describes some common ways of increasing income for people in debt.

The rules of entitlement to benefits are in detailed regulations. Many terms are not described fully here and if you are unfamiliar with them, you should consult CPAG's *Welfare Benefits and Tax Credits Handbook*, which is fully referenced to the law, including caselaw.

The criteria for entitlement are strict and must be met. In particular, these include the following.

- **Claims.** Most benefits and tax credits must be claimed, either online, on a paper form or by making a telephone claim to the Department for Work and Pensions (DWP) or HM Revenue and Customs (HMRC). Satisfying the rules of entitlement is not enough; if a claim is not made for a benefit, the client cannot receive it.

- **Time limits.** There are strict time limits for claiming all benefits. A claim must be made within the time limit, otherwise the client will lose money to which s/he would otherwise be entitled. Some benefits can be backdated, but the rules vary and some important basic benefits, like universal credit (UC) and income-based jobseeker's allowance (JSA), are difficult to backdate.

- **Appeals.** There is a right to appeal most decisions, including whether or not to award benefit. Clients must usually apply for a decision to be reconsidered before they can appeal (known as a 'mandatory reconsideration'). Appeals must be made in writing and within strict time limits, usually one month. Errors by the DWP and HMRC in awarding and calculating benefits and tax credits are common, but if the client does not appeal an incorrect decision, s/he may find s/he loses out. Decisions about whether there has been an overpayment and, in some cases, whether it can be recovered can also be appealed.

- **Residence and immigration tests.** Most benefits have residence, presence and immigration tests. A client who is a 'person subject to immigration control', sponsored, or an asylum seeker has limited access to most of the benefits in this chapter. Specialist immigration advice should always be obtained for such clients. In addition, most means-tested benefits have residence tests. These mainly affect European Union nationals.

- **Changes in circumstances.** A client must notify the authority that pays her/him benefits about any changes of circumstances that might affect her/his entitlement or the amount – eg, if s/he is claiming a benefit on the basis of being out of work and then gets a job. If s/he does not do so, she may have been overpaid and the overpayment may be recoverable.

The benefits system is complex, and there are many ways of categorising benefits. It can be helpful to think of benefits as falling into three types.

- Earnings-replacement benefits – eg, contribution-based JSA, contributory employment and support allowance (ESA) and retirement pension. Typically, these are based on national insurance contributions and are not means tested. If a client has worked or been self-employed in the past, s/he may qualify for a contribution-based earnings-replacement benefit.

- Benefits that depend on a person's circumstances – eg, personal independence payment and child benefit. These are paid because the client has certain needs or falls into a certain category – eg, s/he has a disability or a child.

- Means-tested benefits or tax credits – eg, UC, income support, income-related ESA, income-based JSA, pension credit (PC) and housing benefit. These top up a client's benefit and/or other income to a certain level, sometimes referred to as the 'safety net'. Which means-tested benefits a client can claim depends on her/his circumstances – eg, a client over pension age can claim PC and a client looking for work can claim UC or JSA.

2. How to use this chapter

The table on p173 lists common circumstances that apply to people and the benefits and tax credits that it may be possible to claim. You should check all the circumstances that could be relevant.

The A–Z of the most common benefits (see p174) outlines the main eligibility criteria for each benefit. This chapter cannot describe fully the entitlement conditions for every benefit. It is a guide to which benefits you should consider that may be appropriate for a client.

Following the A–Z is a brief explanation of how benefits are calculated, including, in particular, how the means test works. Means tests are complex and cannot be described in full in this *Handbook*. This chapter explains the basics so you can judge whether further enquiries or an application for benefit should be made. Other sources of financial help that may be available to clients are listed on pp199–205.

For more information, see CPAG's *Welfare Benefits and Tax Credits Handbook*.

Which benefits and tax credits can a client claim

The table on p173 gives an overview of the possible benefits and tax credits to which a client may be entitled depending on her/his circumstances. More than one circumstance may apply to a particular client (eg, s/he may have a child, a disability, a mortgage and work part time), in which case you should refer to each circumstance.

Some benefits and tax credits can be paid if a client does not have enough money to live on, either in addition to other benefits and tax credits, or on their own. These are:

- universal credit (UC) if s/he is in or out of paid work and her/his income is below the set minimum level required for her/his household's needs, including housing costs. **Note:** UC is replacing the current means-tested benefits for working-age people and most new claims are now for UC and not the following benefits (see p188);
- income-based jobseeker's allowance (JSA) or income support (IS) if s/he is not in full-time paid work;
- income-related employment and support allowance (ESA) if s/he has 'limited capability' for work;

- working tax credit (WTC) if s/he is in full-time paid work (what counts as full-time work varies according to the client's circumstances);
- pension credit (PC) if s/he is over the qualifying age and either in or out of full-time paid work;
- child tax credit (CTC) if s/he has children and the household income is below the set threshold;
- housing benefit (HB) if s/he is out of work or has a low income and is unable to meet her/his housing costs (restrictions apply).

Circumstance	Potential benefits and tax credits
Bereaved	Bereavement support payment
	Social fund funeral expenses payment
Carer	Carer's allowance
	UC (if under the UC system)
	IS
Responsible for a child	CTC
	Child benefit
	Guardian's allowance
	Statutory maternity pay (SMP)
	Statutory paternity pay
	Statutory shared parental pay
	Statutory adoption pay
	Maternity allowance (MA)
	Health benefits
	Healthy Start food and vitamins
	UC (if under the UC system)
Disabled	Personal independence payment
	Disability living allowance
	Attendance allowance
	Industrial injuries benefits
Has a mortgage	IS
	Income-based JSA
	Income-related ESA
	PC
	UC (if under the UC system)
Pensioner	Retirement pension
	PC
	Winter fuel payment
Pregnant	SMP
	MA
	Sure Start maternity grant
	Health benefits
	Healthy Start food and vitamins

Paying rent	Housing benefit (HB)
	UC (if under the UC system)
Sick and unable to work	ESA
	Statutory sick pay
	UC (if under the UC system)
Unemployed and seeking work	JSA
	UC (if under the UC system)
Unemployed and not seeking work	IS
	UC (if under the UC system)
Working, but on a low income	WTC
	CTC
	HB
	UC (if under the UC system)

3. **A–Z of benefits and tax credits**

Unless otherwise stated, all the benefits referred to in this section are claimed from and paid by the Department for Work and Pensions (DWP). For more information and the current rates, see CPAG's *Welfare Benefits and Tax Credits Handbook*.

Attendance allowance

Attendance allowance (AA) is a benefit for clients who are aged 65 or over when they first claim and who have care needs as a result of either a physical or mental disability. They must need:
- frequent help with personal care throughout the day; *or*
- continual supervision throughout the day to avoid danger to themselves or others; *or*
- repeated or prolonged attention at night to help with personal care or for another person to be awake for a prolonged period or at frequent intervals to avoid danger to themselves or others.

Clients must satisfy the disability conditions for at least six months. However, people who are terminally ill (ie, who have a progressive disease from which they could reasonably be expected to die within six months) should be awarded the higher rate of AA immediately.

An award of AA always makes a client better off. It is not means tested and does not count as income when calculating means-tested benefits and tax credits. Entitlement to AA may mean a client is entitled to a means-tested benefit, or a higher amount of benefit than is already being paid. In particular, an award of AA means that a client's carer could claim carer's allowance (CA – see below) for looking after her/him, or the client could qualify for an extra amount in a means-tested benefit (see p191).

AA cannot be backdated. It is not taxable.

Bereavement support payment

Bereavement support payment replaces the 'old' bereavement benefits (bereavement payment, widowed parent's allowance and bereavement allowance) for people whose spouse or civil partner dies on or after 6 April 2017. If the death was before 6 April 2017, clients may be entitled to the 'old' bereavement benefits.

In order to qualify, the client's late spouse or civil partner must either have paid sufficient national insurance (NI) contributions or been an employee and died as a result of an industrial accident or disease. In addition, the client must be under state pension age.

There are two rates of bereavement support payment:
* the standard rate, comprising an initial lump sum and a monthly amount; *and*
* the higher rate, payable to pregnant women and those with dependent children, comprising an initial lump sum and a monthly amount.

Bereavement support allowance is paid for a maximum of 18 months after the death and must be claimed within 12 months of that date. It is automatically backdated for three months.

The initial lump sum is disregarded as capital for means-tested benefits and the monthly allowance is disregarded as income for means-tested benefits and tax credits.

Carer's allowance

CA is a benefit for clients who are providing regular and substantial care (35 hours a week or more) for someone who is in receipt of AA, the middle or highest rate of disability living allowance (DLA) care component, either rate of the daily living component of personal independence payment (PIP), armed forces independence payment, or constant attendance allowance for industrial injuries disablement benefit or a war disablement pension. This includes caring for a relative or a member of the family – eg, a partner or child.

Clients who claim CA (even if it is not paid because of special rules on 'overlapping benefits') may be entitled to an extra amount, called a carer premium, in a means-tested benefit (see p190) or a carer element in universal credit (UC – see p194).

Note: a claim for CA can mean that the cared-for person receives less in means-tested benefits and so a detailed better-off calculation may be needed. Clients should be referred for specialist advice if required.

CA is not means tested, but clients cannot get it if they have earnings above a set limit. CA is taken into account in full as income for means-tested benefits and tax credits. CA is taxable.

Child benefit

Child benefit is a benefit for clients who are responsible for a child under 16 or a qualifying young person. A 'child' is someone under 16. A 'qualifying young person' is someone aged 16 to 19 (20 in some cases) who meets certain conditions, such as being enrolled on a course of full-time non-advanced education or on approved training.

To be responsible for a child or qualifying young person, the client must live with the child or contribute to the cost of supporting her/him of at least the child benefit rate.

Child benefit is not means tested, and can be paid in addition to other benefits and tax credits. Child benefit is not taxable, unless a client or her/his partner individually earns more than £50,000 a year. Child benefit is claimed from and paid by HM Revenue and Customs (HMRC).

Child tax credit

Note: child tax credit (CTC) is affected by the introduction of UC (see p188).

CTC is paid to clients who are responsible for a child or qualifying young person (see above). A client counts as responsible for a child if s/he normally lives with her/him. CTC is usually paid to the person who has been awarded child benefit for the child.

CTC is paid in addition to child benefit and can also be paid with most other benefits. People entitled to income support (IS), income-based jobseeker's allowance (JSA), income-related employment and support allowance (ESA) or pension credit (PC) automatically get maximum CTC, but it counts as income for housing benefit (HB), except for people who are at least the qualifying age for PC (see p183).

CTC is claimed from and paid by HMRC and is means tested. The means test for tax credits is different from that for benefits, and is based on annual income (see p198). CTC is not taxable.

Disability living allowance

DLA is a benefit for people who have care and/or mobility needs as a result of a physical or mental disability. Since April 2013, new claims for DLA can only be made for children aged under 16. People aged 16 to 64 who have a disability must claim PIP instead. When a child who gets DLA turns 16, s/he is normally invited to claim PIP. Many adults who already receive DLA will continue to receive it for some time until they are transferred to PIP.

DLA has two components.

To qualify for the **'care component'** the child must need:
- frequent help with personal care throughout the day; *or*
- continual supervision throughout the day to avoid danger to her/himself or others; *or*
- frequent or prolonged supervision at night to avoid danger; *or*
- prolonged or repeated attention at night.

To qualify for the **'mobility component'**, the child must:
- be unable or virtually unable to walk; *or*
- be both blind and deaf; *or*
- face danger to her/his life or health by walking; *or*
- be blind or have a severe visual impairment; *or*
- be born without feet or be a double amputee; *or*
- have a severe mental impairmant, have severe behavioural problems and be entitled to the highest rate of the care component (see below); *or*
- need supervision on unfamiliar routes.

DLA care component is paid at three different rates and the mobility component at two different rates. Children can get one or both components if they satisfy the relevant conditions. They can receive the higher rate of the mobility component from age three, the lower rate of the mobility component from age five and the care component from age three months.

The child must satisfy the disability conditions for at least three months before the start of the award and be likely to continue to satisfy them for at least the next six months. However, a child who is terminally ill (ie, who has a progressive disease from which s/he could reasonably be expected to die within six months) should be awarded the higher rate of DLA care component immediately.

An award of DLA for a child will always make a family better off. It is not means tested and does not count as income when calculating means-tested benefits and tax credits. If a client's child gets DLA, this may mean that the client is entitled to a means-tested benefit, or a higher amount of benefit that is already being paid.

DLA cannot be backdated. It is not taxable.

Employment and support allowance

Note: ESA is affected by the introduction of UC (see p188).

ESA is a benefit for clients who cannot work because of an illness or disability. Employees usually claim statutory sick pay (SSP) for the first 28 weeks of illness rather than ESA. Self-employed and unemployed people claim ESA straight away.

There are two types of ESA.
- **Contributory ESA** is paid if a client satisfies the NI contribution conditions. It is not means tested. It is only paid for 52 weeks, except if the claimant is in the 'support group' (see p178).

- **Income-related ESA** is means tested and has no NI contribution test. It is possible to receive contributory ESA, topped up with income-related ESA. It can be paid indefinitely.

A basic allowance of ESA is paid during an initial 'assessment phase' of 13 weeks. The amount of income-related ESA paid could be higher if, for example, it includes premiums (see p190) or housing costs (see p192). The client's ability for work is assessed by the DWP under a 'work capability assessment'. A small number of people are treated as having limited capability for work and do not have to undergo this – eg, people who are terminally ill, those receiving or recovering from certain types of chemotherapy and hospital patients.

After the initial assessment phase, clients who pass a medical assessment go on to the 'main phase' of ESA and may be paid an extra amount, called a 'component' (see p192), because of their inability to work. Clients are put into either:

- the 'work-related activity group' and must attend work-focused interviews and undertake work-related activity; *or*
- the 'support group' if they have a severe illness or disability.

Clients in the work-related activity group may have their benefit reduced by a sanction if they do not attend a work-focused interview or carry out work-related activity, and some clients receive multiple sanctions for repeated failures. There is a right to appeal this and it is always worth considering whether a sanction could be challenged.

Clients whose income-related ESA has been reduced by a sanction may qualify for hardship payments.

The general rule is that people cannot get ESA if they are working. Clients can do some limited work (called 'permitted work') while on ESA, but they must notify the DWP and they can lose their ESA entitlement if they earn more than a certain amount. Clients affected by these rules may need specialist advice.

Contributory ESA is not means tested, but it is affected by any income from a pension scheme/plan or an income protection insurance policy, and is subject to the 'overlapping benefit' rules (see p197).

Income-related ESA can be paid in addition to contributory ESA in some circumstances – eg, if a client has a partner. Income-related ESA is a 'passporting' benefit, which means that it can help the client to get maximum HB, free prescriptions, free school lunches for her/his children and help from the social fund. Extra amounts can be paid depending on the circumstances of the client and her/his partner – eg, premiums for carers or because of a disability (see p190).

Contributory ESA is taxable; income-related ESA is not.

Guardian's allowance

Guardian's allowance is a benefit paid to a client who is responsible for a child who is effectively an orphan. Clients can be paid it if they are entitled to child benefit for a child whose parents have died, or one has died and the whereabouts of the other is unknown, or one has died and the other has been sentenced to a term of imprisonment of two years or more or is detained in hospital by a court order.

Guardian's allowance is not means tested, does not count as income for other benefits and tax credits, and can be paid in addition to child benefit. It is claimed from and paid by HMRC.

Health benefits

Clients can qualify for the health benefits listed below if they receive:
- UC and either have no earnings or have earnings below a certain amount;
- IS;
- income-related ESA;
- income-based JSA;
- the guarantee credit of PC;
- CTC and they are not eligible for working tax credit (WTC) (eg, because they do not work enough hours to qualify), CTC *and* WTC, or WTC that includes a disability or severe disability element and they have income below an income threshold.

Clients may also qualify on the grounds of low income, and should apply directly to the NHS Business Services Authority.

The health benefits are:
- free prescriptions;
- free dental treatment;
- free sight tests;
- vouchers towards the cost of glasses or contact lenses;
- travel costs to and from hospital for treatment or services.

Each health benefit has its own rules on who is entitled – eg, prescriptions are free of charge to women who are pregnant or who have given birth in the last 12 months.

Healthy Start food and vitamins

The Healthy Start scheme provides vouchers that can be exchanged for healthy food, such as fresh fruit and vegetables, and milk. Those who qualify for vouchers can also get free vitamins. Clients qualify if they:
- are pregnant and have been for more than 10 weeks and are aged under 18;
- are 18 or over, have been pregnant for more than 10 weeks and are entitled to UC and have an income of less than a certain amount, IS, income-based JSA or income-related ESA, or to CTC (but not WTC) and have an annual taxable income below a certain amount;

- are aged 16 or over, have a child under four and get UC, IS, income-based JSA or CTC.

Housing benefit

Note: HB is affected by the introduction of UC (see p188).

HB is a means-tested benefit, claimed from and paid by local authorities to tenants to help with the cost of their rent. HB can be paid to people in and out of work.

Clients in private rented accommodation may have their HB restricted if their rent is more than a local housing allowance for their area. This is is based on the number of bedrooms a client is allowed under the rules and the local housing allowance rates set by the rent officer.

Clients in local authority or housing association accommodation may have their HB restricted if they are living in a property that has more bedrooms than they are allowed (known as the 'bedroom tax') or if their household income from benefits is above a certain amount (known as the 'benefit cap'). They may also have their amount of HB reduced by the cost of non-eligible charges, such as fuel, water or some service charges.

Clients entitled to IS, income-based JSA, income-related ESA or the guarantee credit of PC are usually entitled to have all their eligible rent met by HB, but they must make a separate claim. Clients not on a means-tested benefit can also qualify for HB if their income is sufficiently low and they have capital below a certain amount (£16,000 for most clients). There is no capital limit for clients on the guarantee credit of PC.

If a non-dependant (eg, a relative or friend) lives with the client, this can reduce the amount of HB paid. The amount of the deduction depends on the non-dependant's income. It is, therefore, vital that the correct details of the non-dependant's income are disclosed to ensure the maximum amount of HB entitlement is paid.

Claims for HB can be backdated for a maximum of one month if a client can show a continuous good cause for claiming late. Clients or their partners not in receipt of IS, income-based JSA or income-related ESA who are at least pension age can get HB backdated without needing to show a good cause for up to three months.

Clients whose HB does not cover the whole amount of their rent can apply for a discretionary housing payment to help make up the shortfall. Discretionary housing payments are paid from a cash-limited budget and are not guaranteed.

HB and discretionary housing payments are not taxable.

Income support

Note: IS is affected by the introduction of UC (see p188).

IS is a means-tested benefit that provides basic financial support for clients on a low income who are not expected to 'sign on' as available for work. To qualify, the client must:

- not be in full-time work – ie, s/he must work less than 16 hours a week. If s/he has a partner, the partner must not be in full-time work (less than 24 hours per week);
- not be a full-time student (there are some exceptions);
- pass the means test;
- have capital below £16,000;
- be in a specified group of people who can claim IS (see below).

The main groups of people who can claim IS are:

- lone parents who are responsible for a child under five;
- certain lone parents who are foster parents or who are adopting a child;
- carers – ie, people getting CA or who are 'regularly and substantially' caring for a disabled person;
- pregnant women during the 11 weeks before and 15 weeks after giving birth;
- people receiving SSP.

IS pays a basic amount for the client and her/his partner, if s/he has one. Some people who have been getting IS since before 2004 may also receive amounts for their children. IS is a 'passporting' benefit – ie, it can help the client get maximum HB, free prescriptions, free school lunches for her/his children and help from the social fund. Extra amounts can be paid depending on the circumstances of the client and her/his partner – eg, premiums for carers or because of a disability (see p190). IS includes an amount for housing costs (see p192).

IS is not taxable.

Industrial injuries benefits

The main benefit for industrial injuries is industrial injuries disablement benefit. This is for clients who:

- have a personal injury while working as an employee – eg, from an accident at work; *or*
- have a prescribed industrial disease contracted during the course of their employment – eg, asbestosis.

Clients must be assessed as having a degree of disablement resulting from a loss of faculty – eg, a reduced ability to walk because of arthritis. Clients can get industrial disablement benefit if they are still in work. It can be paid on top of contributory ESA and other non-means-tested benefits. Industrial injuries benefits are not taxable. They generally count as income for the purposes of calculating means-tested benefits, but are disregarded as income for tax credits.

Jobseeker's allowance

Note: income-based JSA is affected by the introduction of UC (see p188).

JSA provides basic financial support for people who are expected to 'sign on' as available for work and as actively seeking work. There are two types of JSA.

- **Contribution-based JSA** is paid for six months to those who have recently paid NI contributions.
- **Income-based JSA** is means tested with no requirement to have paid NI contributions.

To qualify for income-based JSA, the client must:

- not be in full-time work – ie, s/he must be working less than 16 hours a week. If s/he has a partner, the partner must not be in full-time work (less than 24 hours a week);
- not be a full-time student (there are some exceptions);
- pass the means test;
- have capital below £16,000;
- be available for and actively seeking work.

Income-based JSA pays a basic amount for the client and her/his partner, if s/he has one. Some people who have been getting income-based JSA since before 2004 may also receive amounts for their children. Income-based JSA is a 'passporting' benefit – ie, it can help the client get maximum HB, free prescriptions, free school lunches for her/his children and help from the social fund. Extra amounts can be paid depending on the client's circumstances – eg, if s/he is caring for someone or has a disability (see p190). Income-based JSA includes an amount for housing costs (see p192).

Some couples (eg, those without children) must claim what is known as 'joint-claim JSA' and both have to be available for work.

Contribution-based JSA pays a basic amount for the client and is only paid for six months. People can get both contribution-based and income-based JSA (or UC if they come under the UC system – see p188) at the same time.

Clients may have their JSA reduced by a sanction if they do not comply with certain 'jobseeking conditions' (eg, attending interviews) and for other things, such as losing a job because of misconduct, giving up work without a good reason or for not participating in specified training or employment schemes. Some clients receive multiple sanctions for repeated failures. There is a right to appeal this, and it is always worth considering whether a sanction could be challenged.

Clients can apply for hardship payments if their JSA is not paid because of a sanction and they are considered to be in a vulnerable group – eg, carers, and people who have a disability or children.

JSA is taxable.

Maternity allowance

Maternity allowance (MA) is a benefit for women who are pregnant or who have recently given birth. It is normally claimed by women who do not qualify for statutory maternity pay (SMP) – eg, self-employed women, those not currently in work or those who have not worked for the same employer for long enough to get SMP. To qualify for MA, the client must have been employed or self-employed for at least 26 of the 66 weeks before the week in which the baby is due, and have had average weekly earnings of at least £30 a week in 13 weeks of this 'test' period.

MA is not taxable.

Pension credit

PC is a benefit for people on a low income who are at least pension age. The pension age for men and women has been equalised, so the qualifying age for PC is the client's pension age – which depends on her/his date of birth. Pension age is rising to 66 (by 2020) and will eventually go up to 68.

PC is made up of a guarantee credit and a savings credit.

The guarantee credit is the basic amount paid for the client and her/his partner. It is means tested, but there is no limit on how much capital a client can have.

Extra amounts can be paid depending on the client's circumstances – eg, if she is caring for someone or has a disability (see p190). Amounts for children are not included. PC is a 'passporting' benefit – ie, it can help the client get maximum HB, free prescriptions, free school lunches for her/his children and help from the social fund. PC includes an amount for housing costs (see p192).

The savings credit is an additional amount, paid to clients who have qualifying income (eg, retirement pension) over a certain amount. However, savings credit is being phased out and is only available for people who reached pension age before 6 April 2016.

PC is not taxable.

Personal independence payment

PIP is a benefit for people of working age who have care and/or mobility needs as a result of a physical or mental disability. It has replaced DLA for new claimants aged 16 or over from 8 April 2013. Clients who get DLA are being gradually transferred to PIP.

PIP has two components – a daily living component and a mobility component. Each component has two rates – a standard rate, and an enhanced rate paid if a client's ability to carry out certain activities is severely limited by her/his physical or mental condition.

Entitlement to PIP is determined by testing the difficulty a client has performing a specified list of activities. Points are given for each activity and benefit is awarded once a specified number of points is reached. Most clients must have a medical assessment.

To qualify for PIP, a client must usually have met the disability conditions for three months and be expected to meet them for at least a further nine months. However, a client who is terminally ill (ie, who has a progressive disease from which s/he could reasonably be expected to die within six months) should be awarded the enhanced rate of the daily living component immediately.

An award of PIP always makes a household better off. It is not means tested, taxable or based on NI contributions. Entitlement to PIP may mean that a client becomes entitled to a means-tested benefit or to an increased amount of a benefit that is already being paid.

PIP cannot be backdated.

Retirement pension

Clients who reach pension age on or after 6 April 2016 can get the new state pension. Clients who reached pension age before 6 April 2016 may be entitled to an 'old' retirement pension, known as category A, category B and category D retirement pensions.

The amount of state pension a client receives depends on her/his NI contribution record. State pension is paid at a basic weekly rate, which can be increased if a client has chosen to defer the pension.

A client must claim state pension on the approved form, or by telephone or online. State pension can be backdated for a maximum of 12 months from the date s/he would have been first entitled. Any claim made after this date can be treated as an application to have the pension deferred. Clients should consider the financial implications before choosing to either have their pension backdated for 12 months or have it deferred.

State pension is not means tested, but is taken into account as income for other benefits and tax credits. It is taxable.

Social fund payments

The following payments are available from the social fund.

- **Budgeting loans.** These are for specified types of expenses, such as an item of furniture or household equipment. They are discretionary, so a loan is not guaranteed. The client must have been getting a qualifying benefit (see p185) for at least 26 weeks. The amount paid is determined by a formula based on the size of the client's family and the amount of any outstanding budgeting loan debt. Loans are repaid through weekly deductions from benefits, but are interest free. The loan must be repaid within 104 weeks. **Note:** clients getting UC cannot apply for a budgeting loan and must apply for a budgeting advance of UC instead (see p189).

- **Sure Start maternity grant.** This is a £500 lump sum payable to clients on a low income to help with the costs of a new baby. If the client is already getting a grant for another child under 16, s/he cannot get the grant. The client must be on a qualifying benefit (see below). The grant must be claimed within three months of the baby's birth (or an adoption or residence or parental order).
- **Funeral payment.** This is a lump sum to cover the basic costs of a funeral plus some other related expenses. The client must be responsible for the funeral arrangements and be on a qualifying benefit (see below). The payment may be recovered from any money or assets left by the person who died. There are also rules which exclude some people from claiming if someone else, not on benefit, could have paid for the funeral.
- **Winter fuel payment.** This is a lump-sum payment to help pay fuel bills, although it can be spent on anything the client wants. Clients must be at least pension age to qualify (see p183). It is usually paid automatically.
- **Cold weather payments** are paid to people on a qualifying benefit (see below) during recorded periods of cold weather. **Note:** there are other qualifying conditions.

Qualifying benefit

A 'qualifying benefit' for a **budgeting loan** is:
- IS;
- income-based JSA;
- income-related ESA;
- PC.

A 'qualifying benefit' for a **Sure Start maternity grant, funeral payment and cold weather payment** is:
- IS;
- income-based JSA;
- income-related ESA;
- HB (funeral payments only);
- PC;
- CTC of more than just the family element (Sure Start maternity grants and funeral payments only);
- WTC including the disabled worker or severe disability element (Sure Start maternity grants and funeral payments only);
- UC.

In some cases, a client can claim a social fund payment if her/his partner has an award of the qualifying benefit or tax credit.

Statutory adoption pay

Statutory adoption pay (SAP) is paid to clients who are (or have recently been) employees and who take adoption leave.

A client's average gross weekly earnings must be at least the NI 'lower earnings' limit. S/he must have worked continuously for her/his employer for 26 weeks by the end of the week in which s/he is notified that s/he has been matched for adoption. SAP can be paid to both women and men.

SAP is claimed from the client's employer and is paid in the same way as the client's normal pay. The employer must be given relevant notice and information within a strict time limit. SAP is paid for 39 weeks. It is not means tested, but counts as earnings for means-tested benefits. The first £100 of a client's weekly SAP is ignored for tax credits; anything above £100 is counted as employment income.

SAP is taxable.

Statutory maternity pay

SMP is paid to clients who are (or have recently been) employees and who take maternity leave.

A client's average gross weekly earnings must be at least the NI lower earnings limit. She must have worked continuously for her employer for 26 weeks up to and including the 15th week (called the 'qualifying week') before the week in which her baby is due.

SMP is paid for a maximum of 39 weeks. For the first six weeks, clients get a higher rate equal to 90 per cent of average weekly earnings and a further 33 weeks at the lower rate. These are the minimum amounts of maternity pay; the client's employer might have a more generous scheme. Clients who do not qualify for SMP may be able to claim MA. Entitlement to SMP does not depend on the client returning to work.

SMP is claimed from the client's employer and is paid in the same way as her normal pay. The employer must be given relevant notice and information within a strict time limit. SMP is not means tested, but counts as earnings for means-tested benefits. The first £100 of a client's weekly SMP is ignored for tax credits; anything above £100 is counted as employment income.

SMP is taxable.

Statutory paternity pay

Statutory paternity pay (SPP) is paid to clients who are (or have recently been) employees and are taking paternity leave because their partner has just given birth. Clients can also get SPP if they are adopting a child and their partner is claiming SAP. Clients can get more pay if their partner returns to work and they qualify for statutory shared parental pay (SSPP – see p187).

A client's average gross weekly earnings must be at least the NI lower earnings limit. S/he must have worked continuously for her/his employer for 26 weeks up to and including the 15th week (called the 'qualifying week') before the week in which the baby is due.

SPP is claimed from the client's employer and is paid in the same way as normal pay. The employer must be given relevant notice and information within a strict time limit. SPP is paid for a maximum of two consecutive weeks at either a standard rate or 90 per cent of average weekly earnings, whichever is lower.

SPP is not means tested, but counts as earnings for means-tested benefits. The first £100 of a client's weekly SPP is ignored for tax credits; anything above £100 is counted as employment income.

SPP is taxable.

Statutory shared parental pay

A client can get SSPP if s/he qualifies for either:

- SMP or SAP; *or*
- SPP and s/he has a partner who qualifies for SMP, MA or SAP.

If a client is eligible and s/he ends (or her/his partner ends) her maternity/adoption leave and pay (or MA) early, s/he can take the remainder of the 39 weeks of pay (up to a maximum of 37 weeks) as SSPP.

The client's average gross weekly earnings must be at least the NI 'lower earnings limit'. S/he must have worked continuously for her/his employer for 26 weeks up to and including the 15th week (called the 'qualifying week') before the week in which the baby is due.

SSPP is claimed from the client's employer and is paid in the same way as normal pay. The employer must be given relevant notice and information within a strict time limit. A mother must take a minimum of two weeks' maternity leave following the birth (four if she works in a factory). SSPP is paid at either a standard rate or 90 per cent of average weekly earnings, whichever is lower.

SSPP is not means tested, but counts as earnings for means-tested benefits. The first £100 of a client's weekly SSPP is ignored for tax credits; anything above £100 is counted as employment income.

SSPP is taxable.

Statutory sick pay

SSP is paid to employees who are sick and unable to work for at least four consecutive days. SSP is not paid during the first three days of illness. Clients cannot get ESA while they are entitled to SSP, but can claim IS to top up any SSP if their income and capital are sufficiently low. If a client does not qualify for SSP, s/he may be able to claim ESA or, if s/he comes under the UC system, UC, instead.

Clients must have average earnings of at least the NI lower earnings limit to qualify.

SSP is claimed from the client's employer and is paid in the same way as her/his normal pay. It is paid at a standard rate for a maximum of 28 weeks for each episode of illness. If a client is still off work sick after SSP has expired, s/he may then qualify for ESA (or UC). SSP is not means tested, but it counts as earnings for means-tested benefits and tax credits.

SSP is taxable.

Universal credit

UC is a means-tested benefit for people on a low income who are under pension age. Clients can be either in or out of work.

UC has been gradually introduced from October 2013 and is replacing the following means-tested benefits and tax credits:

- IS;
- income-based JSA;
- income-related ESA;
- HB;
- CTC;
- WTC.

UC has now been introduced nationwide for most new claimants. Current claimants of the means-tested benefits and tax credits listed above do not automatically come under the UC system, but can transfer to UC – eg, by claiming UC after a change of circumstances, or under the government's official programme. Under the official transfer process due to start in 2020, existing awards of means-tested benefits and tax credits will be brought to an end and claimants will be invited to claim UC instead.

To qualify for UC, the client must:

- meet certain residence rules and not be a 'person subject to immigration control';
- not be a student (with some exceptions);
- have a low enough income and have capital below £16,000;
- agree to meet certain work-related requirements, including attending work-focused interviews, and preparing for and looking for work.

UC (including the element for housing costs) is paid monthly in arrears. Clients can apply for an 'advance' to tide them over until their first payment. This is called a 'payment on account' and it must be repaid. Repayments are deducted from future benefit payments and the rate of repayment is difficult to reduce. It is therefore essential to have details of any repayments when drawing up the client's budget.

In exceptional circumstances, a client can request that s/he be paid more frequently (eg, every one or two weeks), or that payment be split between two partners or that rent be paid directly to her/his landlord.

Clients who need help with expenses such as buying new furniture or household equipment can apply for a budgeting advance. Budgeting advances must be repaid, usually by deductions from future payments of UC. To qualify, a client must have been getting UC for at least 26 weeks, unless the advance is needed to help her/him get work or stay in work.

Clients may have their UC reduced by a sanction if they do not comply with the work-related requirements they have agreed to in their 'claimant commitment', and some clients receive multiple sanctions for repeated failures. There is a right to appeal this, and it is always worth considering whether a sanction could be challenged.

Clients whose benefit has been reduced by a sanction may qualify for a hardship payment if they can demonstrate that their reduced level of income is causing hardship. However, hardship payments of UC must be repaid.

UC is a qualifying benefit for free school lunches (see p201), health benefits (see p179) and some social fund payments (see p184).

It is not taxable.

Working tax credit

Note: WTC is affected by the introduction of UC (see p188).

WTC is paid to a client who is, or whose partner is, in full-time paid work. The client must be:

- a lone parent with a dependent child and working at least 16 hours a week; *or*
- a member of a couple with a child, one partner who works at least 16 hours a week, and the other disabled, in hospital or in prison, or entitled to CA; *or*
- a member of a couple with a child. The couple must work 24 hours between them, with one partner working at least 16 hours a week. If only one partner works 24 hours, s/he will qualify; *or*
- disabled and work at least 16 hours a week; *or*
- aged 25 or over and work at least 30 hours a week; *or*
- aged 60 or over and work at least 16 hours a week.

WTC is claimed from and paid by HMRC. It is means tested, and counts as income for the purposes of means-tested benefits. It is claimed and assessed at the same time as CTC.

WTC is not taxable.

4. **Calculating entitlement**

This section looks at the means tests for benefits and tax credits. There are common rules for the different benefits, but tax credits are calculated differently. It also refers to other issues which affect how much money the client is actually paid.

See CPAG's *Welfare Benefits and Tax Credits Handbook* for more details.

Means-tested benefits

The basic formula for calculating means-tested benefits is as follows. See p193 for universal credit (UC). **Note:** most new claims will now be for UC.

- Work out the client's 'applicable amount' (see below).
- Calculate the client's income and capital.
- For income support (IS), income-based jobseeker's allowance (JSA), income-related employment and support allowance (ESA) and pension credit (PC), deduct the client's income from the applicable amount.
- The remainder (if any) is the amount of benefit. Housing benefit (HB) can still be awarded if income is above the applicable amount by applying a 'taper'. Sixty-five per cent of the amount of income above the applicable amount is deducted from eligible rent. Any remaining rent is met by HB.

Applicable amounts

Applicable amounts are made up of a basic allowance for the client and her/his partner, plus additional amounts (called 'premiums') to take account of their circumstances. Amounts are included in HB for children.

Check that the client's applicable amount includes all the premiums that are appropriate. Eligible housing costs for clients who are homeowners may also be included in the applicable amount of benefits other than HB.

The terms used for PC are slightly different: the applicable amount is called the 'appropriate minimum guarantee' and premiums are called 'additional amounts'. The extra amounts in ESA are called 'components'.

Carer premium and carer's additional amount

This is paid if the client is entitled to carer's allowance (CA), even if s/he is not getting it because s/he gets an 'overlapping' benefit (see p197).

Family premium

This is paid in HB if the client has a child or 'qualifying young person' in the family. Clients who have been getting amounts in their IS and income-based JSA for their children since before April 2004 should also have a family premium included in their IS and JSA. A family premium is only paid in HB claims made before 1 May 2016 and in IS and income-based JSA where claims were made before 6 April 2014.

Disabled child premium

This is paid if a child receives disability living allowance (DLA) or personal independence payment (PIP) or is blind. It is available in HB. It can be included in IS and income-based JSA if the client still gets amounts in these benefits for her/his children.

Disability premium

This is paid if the client is registered blind or receiving a 'qualifying benefit'. These include DLA, PIP, the long-term rate of incapacity benefit, and the disabled worker or severe disability element in working tax credit (WTC).

Since the introduction of ESA in October 2008, the disability premium is generally not available on grounds of incapacity for work in any new claims for IS, income-based JSA or HB. Clients who were getting it on 27 October 2008 may still do so.

There is no disability premium in PC or ESA. There is also no disability premium in HB if a client is getting ESA. Instead, either a 'work-related activity component' or a 'support component' is included in her/his applicable amount.

Severe disability premium and severe disability additional amount

This is paid if a client receives a 'qualifying benefit' (including attendance allowance (AA), the middle or highest rate of the DLA care component, or the standard or enhanced rate of the daily living component of PIP, and no one gets CA for looking after her/him). S/he must not have a non-dependant aged 18 or over normally living with her/him.

The rules for couples are more complicated. See CPAG's *Welfare Benefits and Tax Credits Handbook* for details.

Note: there is no severe disability premium under UC and claimants receiving the severe disability premium are prevented from moving on to UC in order to protect their position.

Enhanced disability premium

This is paid if the client or her/his partner is under pension age for PC and receives the highest rate of the DLA care component or the enhanced rate of the daily living component of PIP. For HB only, in certain circumstances it can also be paid for each of the client's children who receive the highest rate of the DLA care component or the enhanced rate of the PIP daily living component.

Pensioner premiums

Pensioner premiums can be paid in IS, income-based JSA and income-related ESA if the client's partner has reached pension age (see p183).

As PC is more generous, clients in these situations should claim PC instead. However, if the client is part of a couple where the other person is under pension age, s/he should seek advice before claiming PC, as s/he may be moved onto UC instead.

Employment and support allowance components

ESA has two additional components. A 'support component' is included if the client is severely ill or disabled; otherwise, a 'work-related activity component' is included. The work-related activity component has now been abolished for most new claims from 3 April 2017.

A component can only be paid once the initial assessment period is over and the client has had her/his capability for work assessed. Both components are paid at the same rate for couples as for single people.

Mortgage interest loans

From 6 April 2018, repayable loans replaced the previous benefit support for mortgage interest on certain loans secured on a client's home. Clients getting IS, income-based JSA, income-related ESA or PC can qualify for a loan. The loans can cover the interest on mortgages or other payments used to purchase a home, or on a loan to pay for specified repairs or improvements.

A client should be advised to seek independent financial and legal advice before taking out a loan for mortgage interest.

The loans attract interest, which will continue to accumulate until the loan is paid or written off.

Clients can still get an amount for housing costs included in their benefit for service charges, ground rent, co-ownership schemes, or certain types of rent.

Capital

A client cannot get means-tested benefits if her/his (and her/his partner's) capital is more than an upper limit. Capital below a specified lower limit is ignored. Any capital between the two limits is assumed to produce a certain amount of income, called 'tariff income'. This counts towards the client's income when working out how much benefit s/he gets.

There is no upper capital limit for PC (and for HB if the client is entitled to the guarantee credit of PC), but any tariff income is still taken into account.

Capital includes:

- cash;
- the balance in any bank or building society current account or savings account;
- the value of any National Savings and Investments products, including premium bonds;
- the value of any shares, gilts, bonds and unit trusts.

Some forms of capital are ignored – eg, the client's home and her/his personal possessions.

Income

Each of the means-tested benefits has different rules on what income and how much of that income is taken into account. The rules are, on the whole, more generous for PC (and for HB if the client is at least pension age) than for the other means-tested benefits. The income of couples is aggregated.

Most types of income are taken into account – eg:
- earnings from a job;
- profits from self-employment;
- retirement pension;
- other pensions;
- income from annuities;
- some benefits, such as CA and bereavement allowance;
- WTC.

Clients can be treated as still having income if it is decided that they have deliberately deprived themselves of it in order to claim benefits or increase the amount to which they are entitled (known as 'notional income'). Clients affected by this rule may need specialist advice.

There are many types of income that are disregarded, including some benefits – eg:
- AA, DLA and PIP;
- social fund payments;
- child tax credit (CTC) and child benefit. However, for IS and income-based JSA, child benefit is taken into account unless the client is getting CTC.

Some of the client's earnings can also be disregarded, depending on her/his circumstances. For HB, an amount is disregarded from earnings for childcare costs (up to £175 a week for one child or up to £300 a week for two or more children), if s/he works at least 16 hours a week, or if both partners in a couple work 16 hours or more a week. If only one partner works, they can still qualify if the other is incapacitated, or in hospital or prison.

Universal credit

UC is calculated as follows.
- Add together the various 'elements' to which a client is entitled (see p194) to arrive at a 'maximum amount'.
- Deduct any unearned income (see p196).
- Deduct 63 per cent of net earnings after disregards (see p196).
- The remainder (if any) is the amount of UC payable.

Elements

UC is made up of a standard allowance for the client and her/his partner, plus additional amounts (called 'elements') to take account of their circumstances.

Check that the client's UC includes all the elements that are appropriate.

Child element

This is an amount for each child aged under 16 or young person aged between 16 and 18 (or 19 in some cases) who is in 'non-advanced education'. From April 2017, the child element is limited to two children. This 'two-child limit' (generally) only applies to third or subsequent children born on or after 6 April 2017. There are exceptions.

Disabled child addition

An additional amount is included in a client's UC if her/his child gets either DLA or PIP. A higher amount is included if the child gets the highest rate of the DLA care component, the enhanced rate of the PIP daily living component, or who is certified as severely sight impaired or blind.

A disabled child addition can still be included even if the client does not receive a child element for the child because of the 'two-child limit' (see above).

Limited capability for work element

This element is paid if a client is assessed as having 'limited capability for work'. However, it has been abolished for most new claims from April 2017.

Note: usually a client will not be paid this element for at least three months, although there are some exceptions for those with previous claims.

Limited capability for work-related activity element

This is paid if a client is severely disabled or ill and is assessed as having 'limited capability for work-related activity'. It is paid at a higher rate than the limited capability for work element.

There is generally a 'waiting period' of at least three months before this element is paid. However, people who are considered terminally ill (ie, expected to die within six months) are awarded the element straight away. There are some further exceptions for those with previous claims.

Carer element

A carer element can be included if a client is in receipt of CA or cares for a severely disabled person for at least 35 hours a week. The disabled person must be getting AA, the middle or highest rate of the DLA care component or either rate of the PIP daily living component.

Housing costs element

A housing costs element can be included in a client's UC to cover rent and/or some service charges. **Note:** owner-occupiers may get an amount to cover certain service charges.

The amount included to cover rent depends on the size of the client's family and her/his circumstances. Most housing association and local authority tenants have their rent paid in full. However, the housing element may be reduced if the property is considered to be bigger than they need (known as the 'bedroom tax').

Tenants with private landlords have their housing costs element limited to the 'local housing allowance' for the size of property they are assessed as needing.

The housing element may also be reduced if the client has one or more 'non-dependants' living with her/him (eg, a friend or relative). The reduction is a set amount, irrespective of whether or not the client receives a contribution from her/him. No deduction is made if the non-dependant is getting either the middle or highest rate of the DLA care component or either rate of the PIP daily living component, or if s/he is aged under 21.

If the housing element does not cover the full amount of her/his rent, the client can apply for a discretionary housing payment, which is paid by the local authority.

Note: most 18–21-year-olds who are not working are not entitled to help with their rent payments (there are some exceptions).

Clients who own their own homes and are not doing any paid work can apply for a loan for mortgage interest to help with the interest on any loan secured on the property that they occupy as their home, whatever the purpose of the loan. A client should be advised to seek independent financial and legal advice before taking out a loan for mortgage interest. The loans attract interest, which will continue to accumulate until the loan is paid or written off.

Childcare costs element

Clients can get help with childcare costs in their UC if they are in paid work (or about to start paid work) and are paying for 'formal' childcare, such as a registered childminder, nursery or after-school club. The client must be:

- a lone parent;
- a member of a couple and both are working; *or*
- a member of a couple and one is working and the other has limited capability for work, is caring for a disabled person or is temporarily away from home.

The amount of the childcare element is 85 per cent of the client's actual childcare costs, up to a fixed maximum, depending on the number of children.

Income

Income is assessed on a monthly basis, with the date of the assessment period starting on the first day of entitlement to UC.

Net earnings (after tax, national insurance and occupational pension contributions) are taken into account as income. Details are provided directly to the Department for Work and Pensions (DWP) by HM Revenue and Customs (HMRC). A client's earnings are then compared to a 'work allowance'. If earnings are lower, they are ignored. If they are above the work allowance, the amount of her/his UC is is reduced by 63 per cent of the difference between the allowance and the earnings – ie, every pound of earnings reduces the client's benefit by 63 pence.

Unearned income taken into account includes JSA, ESA, CA, pensions, annuities, 'notional income' (see p193), student income, spousal maintenance and 'tariff income' from capital of between £6,000 and £16,000 (see below).

Some income, including DLA, PIP, child benefit and child maintenance, is disregarded.

Capital

Clients with capital of more than £16,000 cannot claim UC. Capital of less than £6,000 is ignored. Capital between £6,000 and £16,000 is subject to 'tariff income' – this means that benefit is reduced by one pound per week for every £250 over £6,000.

The benefit cap

The total amount of benefits that can be received by a client who is receiving HB is limited to:
* outside Greater London: £257.69 per week for single people; £384.62 for couples and lone parents;
* in Greater London: £296.35 per week for single people; £442.31 for couples and lone parents.

The total amount of benefits that can be received by a client who is receiving UC is limited to:
* outside Greater London: £257.69 per week for single people; £386.62 for couples and lone parents;
* in Greater London: £296.35 per week for single people; £442.31 for couples and lone parents.

A client's benefit income cannot therefore be maximised above this amount. There are a number of exceptions, when the benefit cap does not apply (see p197).

This benefit cap is usually administered by the DWP and local authorities and is applied by reducing the amount of UC or HB. The following benefits are included when working out whether or not the cap should be applied:
* bereavement allowance;
* child benefit;
* CTC;

- ESA (unless it includes a support component);
- HB;
- incapacity benefit (IB);
- IS;
- JSA;
- maternity allowance (MA);
- severe disablement allowance (SDA);
- widowed mother's allowance, widowed parent's allowance and widow's pension;
- UC.

Clients who are (or whose partner or child is) getting AA, WTC, PIP, ESA support component, CA, guardian's allowance, a war pension, industrial injuries disablement benefit, or UC that includes the limited capability for work-related activity component or the carer component, are exempt. If a client has worked recently, the cap is not applied for a grace period. Clients on UC who have earnings above a specified limit are also exempt.

Overlapping benefit rules

Special rules mean that sometimes a client cannot be paid more than one of the following non-means-tested benefits at the same time:
- contribution-based JSA;
- IB;
- contributory ESA;
- MA;
- retirement pension;
- widow's pension or bereavement allowance;
- widowed mother's or widowed parent's allowance;
- SDA;
- CA.

Clients entitled to more than one of the above benefits are paid the benefit that takes priority, with a top-up of any other of the benefits if appropriate.

Deductions from benefits

Clients can have deductions made from their benefit for a variety of reasons, which means the amount they are paid is less than their entitlement.

Benefit penalties for failing to take part in work-focused interviews can apply to a number of different benefits depending on the client's circumstances. Benefit sanctions can apply to UC, JSA and ESA, which mean that a client's benefit can be reduced or not paid at all.

Overpayments of benefits are usually recovered by making deductions from a client's ongoing entitlement. If a client is challenging the overpayment, s/he should ask for deductions to stop.

Deductions for budgeting loans or payments in advance can be made from UC and the rate of repayment can be very difficult to negotiate once agreed by the client.

Deductions for a wide variety of charges or debts (eg, for fuel or rent arrears) can be made from benefits – usually, the means-tested benefits: IS, income-based JSA, income-related ESA, PC and UC. For more information, see p231.

Tax credits

The basic formula for calculating tax credits is as follows.
- Work out the number of days in the client's 'relevant period'. Both CTC and WTC are awarded for the tax year, so a claim made in July runs until 5 April – the number of days in this period is the 'relevant period'.
- Work out the 'maximum amount'. Add together all the elements of CTC and WTC to which the client is entitled.
- Work out relevant income. Income is annual income and is calculated in accordance with the tax rules – basically, all taxable income is counted. There is no capital limit, but taxable income from capital counts as income.
- Compare this with a 'threshold figure'.
- Calculate entitlement. If the income figure is below the threshold, the client gets the maximum amount. If it is above, it is reduced by a taper. Forty-one per cent of the client's income above the threshold is deducted from the maximum amount. The remainder is the amount of tax credits paid.

Clients on IS, income-based JSA, income-related ESA and PC receive the maximum entitlement.

The amounts that make up CTC are:
- family element. **Note:** this is only payable if the claim includes a child born before 6 April 2017;
- child element. **Note:** a child element is not payable for a child born on or after 6 April 2017 if the client already has two or more children included in the award. There are exceptions to this general rule;
- disabled child element;
- severely disabled child element.

The amounts that make up WTC are:
- basic element;
- lone parent element;
- couple element;
- 30-hour element;
- disabled worker element;

- severe disability element;
- childcare element.

HMRC uses the previous tax year's income to make an initial award for the year (although it can use an estimate of income for the current tax year instead). At the end of the tax year, it finalises the award by comparing the client's actual income over the year of the award with that of the previous year. This could result in an underpayment, which HMRC pays back in a lump sum, or an overpayment that may have to be repaid. Decreases in income of less than £2,500 are ignored. Increases in income of less than £2,500 from one year to the next can be ignored.

Overpayments of tax credits are common and many clients have some kind of adjustment to their award. This, combined with the complexity of the system, means it is often difficult to establish whether or not a client is being paid the correct amount. Specialist advice may be needed.

Some changes of circumstances must be reported and taken into account during the year and carry a potential penalty if not reported. Other changes can be reported at the end of the year, but may result in underpayments or overpayments. Bear this in mind when giving advice about whether and when to report a change during the year.

5. **Other help**

Charities

There are thousands of charities that can provide payments to individuals in need. Some are open to everyone and others are for certain groups only, such as armed service personnel or people with specific disabilities. Many have a committee that considers applications and meets on a cyclical basis. Some of the very large charities receive very many applications a year and may place limits on people from whom they are prepared to accept applications – eg, from social workers only.

It is worthwhile investigating less well-known charities to approach, in addition to the major ones. These are either locally based or specialise in helping particular people. Some charities expect a person to have exhausted other statutory provisions before approaching them. The organisation Turn2us has a website (turn2us.org.uk) with an A–Z of all the charities that can provide financial help and, in many cases, applications for support can be made directly from the website.

The Directory for Social Change publication *The Guide to Grants for Individuals in Need* provides a list of local and national charities, advises on the most appropriate charity and gives guidance on how to make a successful application. See dsc.org.uk/publications.

Most charitable payments are ignored for means-tested benefits and tax credits if they are made regularly. Most that are made irregularly are treated as capital and so only affect the benefit if they take the client above the capital limit.

Child maintenance

Clients may be able to get child maintenance for their child(ren) if they are not living with their other parent. Child maintenance may be paid voluntarily, following a court order or following an application to the Child Maintenance Service.

Child maintenance is disregarded as income for all means-tested benefits and for tax credits.

Civil compensation for damages

Personal injury claims can be made against an individual or organisation if they have been negligent in causing damage, either by doing something or by failing to do something. Injury caused by negligence can be an issue in road traffic accidents or accidents at work, in the street or other public places. Damages for personal injury can be substantial, but can be reduced by the amount of social security benefit paid as a consequence of the injury.

If the injury occurred at work, the client should contact her/his trade union, if a member. Other clients may need to be referred to a solicitor. More information is available from:

- the Law Society on 020 7320 5797 or at lawsociety.org.uk/support-services/accreditation;
- the Association of Personal Injury Lawyers on 0115 943 5400 or at apil.org.uk;
- the Motor Accident Solicitors Society on 0117 925 9604 or at mass.org.uk.

Council tax reduction

If a client needs help paying her/his council tax, s/he may qualify for council tax reduction. Council tax reduction schemes are administered by local authorities. In England and Wales, local authorities may devise their own local schemes which must meet minimum requirements. Most schemes are means tested. See CPAG's *Council Tax Handbook* for more information.

Equal pay rules

Equality legislation provides that a woman should not be paid less than a man for work of equal value or for the same work. If a woman is in debt, it is always worth checking whether these rules might help increase her income. If a client is being paid less than others doing similar work because of her/his age, gender, disability, race, religion and belief, or sexual orientation, it could constitute unlawful discrimination. Specialist help is necessary to pursue a claim. For further details, contact the Equality Advisory and Support Service (EASS) on 0808 800 0082, or see equalityadvisoryservice.com.

Food banks

Clients who are without any means to obtain food may be able to be helped by a food bank. Most foodbanks operate on a referral basis. To find a local one, see trusselltrust.org/get-help/find-a-foodbank. Many foodbanks limit the number of times that a client can use them in a set period. Some food banks can also issue 'fuel bank' vouchers to top-up gas and electricity prepayment meters.

Free school lunches

Children are entitled to free school lunches if their family receives:
• income support, income-based jobseeker's allowance, income-related employment and support allowance or universal credit;
• child tax credit (but not if also receiving working tax credit) and their gross annual income is below a threshold;
• the guarantee credit of pension credit.

Also entitled are 16–18-year-olds who receive the above benefits and tax credits in their own right, and asylum seekers in receipt of asylum support.

In addition, in England, free school lunches are provided to all children during the first three years of primary school and, in Wales, free school breakfasts are provided to all children in local authority primary schools.

Guarantee pay

If an employer fails to provide work for an employee (ie, lays her/him off), in most cases, s/he must pay guarantee pay for five days of lay-off in any period of three months. The right to guarantee pay can be enforced through an employment tribunal. Specialist help should be obtained. A client who is dismissed for seeking to enforce this right is entitled to claim unfair dismissal to an employment tribunal, regardless of the length of her/his service.

Guarantee pay is taken into account as earnings for means-tested benefits.

For further details, see the guidance on guarantee pay at gov.uk/lay-offs-short-timeworking/guarantee-pay.

Local welfare assistance schemes

Clients who are in urgent need following an emergency or unforeseen event may qualify for help under a local welfare assistance scheme.

Schemes are administered by local authorities in England or by the Welsh government. They replaced social fund community care grants and crisis loans for living expenses in April 2013 and are intended for people who have no other source of help. Local authorities may offer goods in kind rather than cash payments. Some authorities have decided to close down schemes or restrict eligibility since April 2015, following cuts to funding.

National minimum wage

Most employees are entitled to be paid at a rate equivalent to at least the national minimum wage. A client who is entitled to the minimum wage and is being paid less than this can complain to the Acas Helpline or to an employment tribunal. For more information, contact the Helpline on 0300 123 1100 or visit gov.uk/national-minimum-wage.

Notice pay

An employee is entitled to be paid during her/his notice period if s/he works during that period or cannot work because of illness, pregnancy or childbirth, or because s/he is on adoption, parental or paternity leave or holiday, or the employer does not wish her/him to work. An employee who is dismissed without being given the correct notice is entitled to be paid her/his normal wages 'in lieu' of notice, unless the dismissal is due to gross misconduct. Notice rules are laid down in the law and these depend on length of service. Some employees may be entitled to a longer period of notice under the terms of their contract with the employer. The contract may be written or unwritten.

For further details, see gov.uk/handing-in-your-notice.

Payments for war injury

There are a number of different schemes providing benefits for those disabled, or for the dependants of those killed, in either the First World War or any conflict since 3 September 1939. Some of these schemes only cover members of the armed forces, but there are others that apply to auxiliary personnel, civil defence volunteers, merchant mariners and civilians. Who qualifies and what payments they can receive are complicated. For who may be eligible, see gov.uk/government/organisations/veterans-uk or contact the Veterans helpline on 0808 191 4218.

Private and occupational pensions

Clients who are members of an employer's (occupational) pension scheme or a private pension plan may be entitled to take benefits from these plans before the normal retirement age if, for example, they become permanently incapable of work. Benefits available from pension schemes should be closely examined and independent financial advice should be sought before making a decision to take benefits early from a private scheme.

Redundancy pay

An employee who has two years' continuous service and is not in an excluded occupation, and who loses her/his job through redundancy, might be entitled to statutory redundancy pay. If a statutory redundancy payment has not been made or is not for the correct amount, the employee can apply to an employment tribunal. There is a strict three-month time limit from the date of termination for making such an application. A client in need of advice in this situation should be referred to an employment law adviser.

Some clients may be entitled to a larger redundancy payment under the terms of their contract.

For further details about redundancy pay, see gov.uk/redundancy-your-rights.

School clothing grants

Local authorities have a discretionary power to give grants for school uniforms or other clothing needed for school – eg, for sportswear. Policies vary. Some school governing bodies or parents' associations also provide help with school clothing.

School transport

Local authorities have a duty to provide free transport for a pupil under 16 if s/he attends the 'nearest suitable school' and lives at least two miles away (if they are aged under eight) or three miles away (if they are eight or older). In addition, children must be given free transport if there is not a safe walking route, irrespective of how far from the school they live.

Social services

Local authority social services departments have statutory duties to provide a range of practical and financial help to families, children, young people, older people, people with disabilities and asylum seekers.

Special funds for sick or disabled people

A range of help is available from local authority social services departments for people with an illness or disability to assist with things like paying for care services in their own home, equipment, holidays, furniture and transport needs.

Student support

For details, see Chapter 17 of this *Handbook*, and also CPAG's *Student Support and Benefits Handbook*.

Tax allowances

The personal allowance is a basic allowance that is available to most people resident in the UK.

Clients may also be entitled to a married couple's allowance if they are married or in a civil partnership, and either they or their spouse or civil partner was born before 6 April 1935.

Those who are married or in a civil partnership and were born after 5 April 1935 may be entitled to a transferable tax allowance or 'marriage allowance'. This allows underused personal allowance up to a set limit to be transferred from one to the other partner in the marriage or civil partnership.

A client who is registered blind can claim a blind person's allowance for the whole tax year. This is in addition to the personal allowance. Any unused allowance can be transferred to her/his spouse or civil partner. If both spouses and civil partners are registered blind, they can claim an allowance each.

A backdated claim can be made for up to four years for any allowances, so check whether the client has not received an allowance to which s/he is entitled.

Tax rebate

A client who is unemployed or is laid off may be entitled to a tax rebate at the end of the tax year. However, this is reduced or may be cancelled out if s/he receives a taxable benefit. In some cases, if HM Revenue and Customs has delayed paying the tax rebate, it must pay interest on it.

Tax reliefs

Tax reliefs are amounts that are deducted from taxable income in recognition of money that is needed to be spent by the taxpayer in working. They can be claimed in addition to a personal allowance and can be backdated for up to six years. Tax reliefs for self-employed people should be calculated by a specialist adviser.

For employed people, it is possible to claim relief on any money that is spent to enable a job to be done, but which is not paid for by the employer. The expenses have to be 'wholly, exclusively and necessarily' incurred in order to do the work.

Items for which tax relief can be claimed include:
- membership of professional bodies;
- special clothing for work;
- using heating/lighting or the telephone at home for work;
- buying tools.

Another form of tax relief is the 'rent-a-room' scheme. This enables someone to let out a main room in her/his home and not pay tax on the rental income, provided the rent stays below a certain level. Even if the client cannot benefit from this scheme, there are other forms of tax relief that may be applicable if s/he lets out property. Specialist advice should be obtained.

Trade unions

Many trade unions have hardship funds for members or ex-members. Unions may also be involved in various benevolent funds and charities associated with particular industries. If a client has been a member of a union, it is worth enquiring about possible lump-sum payments or, in some cases, ongoing support.

Notes

1. **Introduction**
   1 Money and Pensions Service, *Income Maximisation Guidance,* September 2018

Chapter 8

. . . .

Dealing with priority debts

This chapter covers:
1. Deciding on priorities (below)
2. The general approach to priority debts (p210)
3. Strategies for dealing with priority debts (p214)
4. Emergency action (p237)

---

1. **Deciding on priorities**

After dealing with any emergencies, checking whether the client is liable for the debts and maximising the client's income, advisers need to identify which debts must be dealt with first – ie, which debts are priority debts. The criteria for deciding which debts are priorities are largely 'objective' – the severity of the legal remedies available to creditors determines the degree of priority. If non-payment would give the creditor the right to deprive the client of her/his home, liberty or essential goods and/or services, that debt has priority.

When considering whether goods and services are essential, you should consider the client's personal circumstances. A debt is not a priority debt merely because the creditor can prioritise itself by deducting money from the client's earnings or benefits to repay the debt without a court order, although clearly this affects the client's ability to maintain her/his essential expenditure and the income s/he has available to make payment arrangements with her/his other creditors. For a discussion of other debts which are not strictly priority debts as defined above but may, nevertheless, need to be treated as priority, see Chapter 9.

Clients often believe that priorities must be decided on the basis of the amount owed, or that any debt that is subject to a court order should be a priority. The existence of a court judgment does not automatically give priority status to a debt and there are many judgments given by courts in England and Wales each year for debts that remain unpaid. These debts only become a priority if the enforcement methods available to a creditor through the court pose a serious threat to the client's home, liberty or essential goods.

Penalties for non-payment of priority debts

Debt	Ultimate penalty
Mortgage/secured loan arrears	Eviction
Rent arrears	Eviction
Ground rent and and leasehold charges	Forfeiture of lease and repossession of property by freeholder
Council tax arrears	Imprisonment (in England only)
Unpaid fine/maintenance	Imprisonment
Child support arrears	Imprisonment
Gas/electricity arrears	Disconnection
arrears and some tax credit overpayments	Goods taken control of by bailiffs
Income tax/national insurance/VAT	Bankruptcy
Hire purchase arrears	Goods repossessed
Bills of sale	Goods repossessed

Recognising priority debts

Using the criteria outlined above, the following are priority debts.

Secured loans

Mortgages and all other loans secured against a client's home are priorities because non-payment can lead to possession action by the lender, and homelessness. One of the strategies outlined in this chapter must be adopted immediately for any secured loan in arrears. For emergency action, see p239. If the lender has already begun possession proceedings, see Chapter 12.

Rent

Rent arrears are a priority because they can lead to possession action by the landlord, and homelessness. If the landlord has already begun possession proceedings, see Chapter 12.

A client who is a tenant may find that water charges are paid as part of the rent, so s/he could be evicted for non-payment. In such cases, water charges should be considered as a priority. If a client is threatened with possession proceedings for non-payment of water charges, see Chapter 5.

For emergency action, see p239.

Ground rent and leasehold charges

A property may be bought on a long lease rather than freehold where there are communal areas – eg, in blocks of flats and housing estates with shared parking and green spaces. Long leases typically include clauses requiring occupiers to pay an annual ground rent along with service charges for upkeep of the communal areas. Some may also include provision for administration charges – eg, for consent to alter premises.

Ground rents often increase after set periods (eg, every 10 years) and increases can be substantial. Service and administration charges should be detailed in the lease and relate to the costs actually incurred by the landlord. These costs can be challenged by an appeal to an independent tribunal if they appear unreasonable.

Arrears of ground rent, service charges or administration charges are classed as priority debts as failure to pay can be viewed as a breach of the lease. They can ultimately lead to the lease being forfeited and the property being repossessed by the freeholder. There will be a court hearing if the freeholder is bringing forfeiture action.

The freeholder can only start forfeiture action for not paying ground rent if the leaseholder:

- has been in arrears for three years or more; *and*
- owes £350 or more in ground rent (or a combination of ground rent, services charges and administration charges).

A freeholder can also take action to seek a county court judgment for arrears, or ask the mortgage lender to pay as an alternative to forfeiture action, thereby adding the arrears to the mortgage.

Leaseholders can obtain free, independent advice from lease-advice.org.

Council tax

Council tax arrears are a priority because non-payment could ultimately lead to imprisonment in England. From 1 April 2019, non-payment can no longer lead to imprisonment in Wales, but it has been agreed that arrears should still be treated as a priority as councils are generally quick to take court, followed by enforcement action, that can add significant costs to the debt.

If the magistrates' court has issued a liability order (which allows the local authority to use bailiffs) or the client is facing a committal hearing or a warrant has been issued that could result in imprisonment, see p241 and p244. If the local authority has a liability order and the amount outstanding is at least £1,000, it can apply for a charging order in the county court (see p322). If the local authority has served a statutory demand on the client or issued a bankruptcy petition, see p242.

Fines, maintenance and compensation orders

Unpaid fines, maintenance and compensation orders being enforced in the magistrates' court are a priority because non-payment could lead to imprisonment. If the client is in arrears with any of these debts, even if no bailiff or other enforcement action has been taken, see Chapter 13. For emergency action, see p237.

Child support

Child support arrears are a priority debt because, in addition to being able to recover them by deductions from the client's earnings/benefits or from the client's bank account without a court order, the Child Maintenance Service can obtain a liability order which enables it to instruct bailiffs to take control of goods. Ultimately, non-payment could lead to an order disqualifying the client from driving for up to two years or even to a term of imprisonment for up to six weeks.

Utility charges

Payment for gas and electricity are priorities because suppliers can disconnect for non-payment of bills. This is also the case for other types of fuel, where the supplier can withhold delivery for non-payment. Such sanctions do not apply to arrears on non-fuel items (eg, cookers or the cost of central heating installation purchased from gas and electricity suppliers), so debts for such items are not a priority.

Help with arrears may be available from one of the energy company's trust funds. Clients on a low income (eg, getting pension credit) might qualify for a £140 Warm Home Discount. See gov.uk/the-warm-home-discount-scheme for more details.

If disconnection is threatened, make immediate contact with the supplier to challenge this and discuss ways of paying for the supply (see p238).

Water companies cannot disconnect a water supply for non-payment and so payment for water is not a priority. You should include a realistic amount for current consumption of water, but not for arrears, in the financial statement. Help with arrears may be available from one of the water industry's trust funds, or the WaterSure or WaterSure Plus schemes may be able to help with high bills (see p139). These schemes are designed to help people on low incomes in receipt of specified benefits who have a water meter and who have unavoidably high water use.

TV licence

A colour TV licence costs £157.50 a year in 2020. Payment plans are available to spread the cost (see tvlicensing.co.uk).[1] Although not a debt as such, because it is a criminal offence to use a television without a licence (for which the usual penalty is a fine), if a client either does not have a licence (but does have a television) or is behind with a payment plan, this should be treated as a priority.

Some people qualify for a concession on the cost of the TV licence – eg, clients who are aged 74, have sight impairments, or who are living in residential care. Currently, a person aged 75 or over is entitled to a free licence. However, after 31 May 2020 only people aged 75 or over in receipt of pension credit will be entitled to a free licence.

Tax and value added tax

These debts are a priority if the client is continuing to trade because HM Revenue and Customs (HMRC) can take control of goods from the client to cover unpaid tax without requiring a court order or could make the client bankrupt and put her/him out of business. If the client has ceased trading, each case must be looked at on its merits. If:

- bailiffs are involved, see Chapter 14;
- action has been started in the magistrates' court, see Chapter 13;
- action has been started in the county court, see Chapter 10;
- emergency action is required, see p237.

See also Chapter 16.

Hire purchase, conditional sale agreements and bills of sale

Some hire purchase or conditional sale agreements and loans secured by a bill of sale must be treated as priority debts if they are for goods that are essential for the client (eg, a car for work in the absence of suitable public transport), because the creditor has powers to repossess the goods if payments are not kept.

National insurance contributions

Class 4 national insurance contributions for self-employed earners are a priority because they are assessed and collected by HMRC along with unpaid income tax.

Tax credit overpayments

Where the period of the award includes 31 January 2019 or pre-dates 31 January 2019 and for some other claimants whose awards begin on or after 1 February 2019, these debts are a priority because, in addition to being able to recover an overpayment from an ongoing tax credit award or through amending the client's pay as you earn (PAYE) code, or directly from her/his bank account without a court order in some circumstances, HMRC can use bailiffs to take control of the client's goods without a court order. Although the client could even be imprisoned for non-payment, it does not appear to be HMRC policy to pursue such debts in the magistrates' courts where they would have to establish the client's non-payment was due to wilful refusal or culpable neglect before committal could be considered (see p407).[2]

2. **The general approach to priority debts**

Priority debts must be dealt with quickly and effectively. General rules about how this should be done are outlined in this section. There are also specific ways of dealing with particular types of debts (see p214–237).

Prioritise the debts

Immediate contact should be made with the creditor. If it is not possible to make a definite offer of payment immediately, ask for more time (eg, 30 days) and ask the creditor either to take no further action or to suspend any existing action during this period. If possible, the client should be advised to pay at least the current instalments in the meantime.

Generally, it is not appropriate to make offers to priority creditors on a pro rata basis (see p268) or to include priority debts in a debt management plan (see p255), and you must negotiate with them individually. It must first be decided whether to make payment:

- either as soon as possible; *or*
- over as long a period as possible.

Clients may not be in a position to make payments towards all their priority debts and so they will need to prioritise their priority debts. In this situation, it is particularly important to consider income maximisation and financial capability options (see Chapters 3 and 7). The following should be taken into account.

- If the debt is accruing interest or charges, it may be in the client's best interests to pay it off quickly.
- It might be in the client's best interests to pay off a small priority debt as soon as possible.
- The creditor's collection policies may be important – eg, a local authority's policy may be to send council tax liability orders straight to bailiffs, which increases the debt.
- The creditor may insist on arrears being cleared before the next bill is due to be delivered or payment made.
- If the client is currently earning above her/his average wage, it may be in her/his best interests to make higher payments while s/he can.
- If capital or lower cost finance is available, the debt can be cleared more quickly.
- The client's age or state of health may lead to a reduction in income. It could be in her/his best interests to make a payment before this happens.
- If the client is considering moving, it may be necessary to make a payment before doing so.
- If the client has any non-priority debts, usually s/he must make some provision for these (see Chapter 9).

You should also further prioritise the debts in the light of:

- what the client wants;
- the existence of more than one priority debt;
- the severity of the sanction available to the creditor;
- the potential consequences of using a particular strategy;
- the stage the recovery process has reached.

Consider the options

Although the decision to give one debt priority over another is to some extent a subjective one, you should always discuss with the client the range of options available and the possible consequences. Work through the following list of tasks.

- In the case of secured loans, hire purchase/conditional sale agreements and loans secured by bills of sale, check whether the client has payment protection insurance to cover the repayments in the event of sickness or incapacity, unemployment, accident or death. If the client does have insurance and her/his situation is covered by the policy, advise the client to make a claim. If the claim is refused, consider whether this can be challenged and/or also whether the policy may have been mis-sold (see p164). If the client's situation is not covered by the policy, also consider whether the policy may have been mis-sold – eg, the client's circumstances were such that s/he could never have made a claim. If the agreement is regulated by the Consumer Credit Act 1974 and the client says that taking out payment protection insurance was a condition of being granted the credit, the agreement may be unenforceable (see p164).
- In the case of secured loans, hire purchase/conditional sale agreements and loans secured by bills of sale, investigate whether the lender complied with its duty to assess the client's ability to repay in accordance with guidance produced by the appropriate regulator – eg, the *Irresponsible Lending Guidance* produced by the former Office of Fair Trading (if the loan was made before 1 April 2014), section 5 of the Financial Conduct Authority's (FCA's) *Consumer Credit Sourcebook* (if the loan was made after 1 April 2014) or sections 11 and 11A of the FCA's *Mortgages and Home Finance: Conduct of Business Sourcebook* (if the secured loan is a regulated mortgage contract made on or after 21 March 2016).
- In the case of tax, VAT or tax credit overpayments, consider what method of enforcement HM Revenue and Customs (HMRC) is using or threatening to use. Bear in mind in the case of tax credit overpayments that recovery from an ongoing award or by amending the client's pay as you earn (PAYE) code reduces the amount of surplus income the client has available to make offers to other creditors.
- Consider whether the client has any other grounds for challenging either the debt or the creditor's conduct (see Chapters 5 and 6).
- Phone the creditor as soon as possible, even if s/he does not have all the necessary information on which to base a strategy. This may help prevent further action and alert the priority creditor to the involvement of an independent agency. Invoke the 30-day 'breathing space' provisions referred to in the *Consumer Credit Sourcebook*.[3]
- If necessary, take emergency action to prevent the immediate loss of home, liberty, essential goods or services (see p237).

- Negotiate the amount, manner and time of repayments.
- Ensure the client is clear about who to pay, when to pay and how much to pay.
- Encourage the client to seek further assistance from you if s/he is facing practical difficulties with repayment arrangements.
- Monitor the initial strategy with the client. If the client's circumstances change or the original strategy is unsuccessful, you and the client must decide whether to adopt a new strategy or whether the details of the original strategy can be modified.

Consider carefully the amount of income included as 'available' to the client. The fact that a debt is priority may influence the way in which a partner's income is treated. A partner may not wish to pool her/his income and liabilities if only non-priority debts have been accrued (and there is no need to – see p48). However, if serious consequences, such as loss of home, could be experienced by the client's partner, s/he may wish to contribute towards repaying a debt for which s/he is not legally liable. This situation can also occur when a debt arose while someone was with a previous partner.[4]

Points to note

- Although many priority creditors have their own collection policies which act as guidelines for their officers, these can always be negotiated. A refusal to negotiate could give rise to a formal complaint.
- It may be necessary to contact someone in a position of authority within the relevant organisation before policies can be changed.
- Accounting periods, such as local authority financial years or other periods between quarterly bills, should not be taken as absolute dates by which current liabilities must be met.
- Lenders of secured loans often argue that arrears should be repaid in short periods. However, in an important decision, the Court of Appeal suggested that a reasonable period to clear arrears might be the whole of the remaining term of the mortgage.[5] So, if a possession action was started half way through a 30-year mortgage, it would be possible for the court to suspend an order on payment of an amount which would repay the mortgage together with the arrears over the next 15 years. On the other hand, if the secured loan is a regulated mortgage contract treated as regulated by the Consumer Credit Act 1974, the client may be able to apply for a time order (see p229 and p366). The lender should also have complied with section 13.3.2AR of the FCA's *Mortgages and Home Finance: Conduct of Business Sourcebook*. This requires the lender to make a reasonable effort to come to an agreement with the client to pay the arrears over a reasonable period (in appropriate cases, the remaining term of the mortgage) and, if no reasonable payment arrangement can be made, allow the client to remain in possession for a reasonable period to organise a sale,

and to repossess the property only if all other reasonable attempts to resolve the position have failed.

The client should be advised to:
- start making payments immediately when the strategy has been decided, as this encourages the creditor to accept the arrangements; *and*
- where possible, set up a direct debit or standing order to ensure a payment arrangement is kept.

Creditors should be asked to confirm the agreed strategy in writing. They may often require a financial statement (see p55), list of debts and written proposal before providing such confirmation. However, a delay in providing confirmation is not a reason for withholding agreed or offered payments.

---

3. **Strategies for dealing with priority debts**

Interest-only payments (for mortgages and secured loans)

A large proportion of secured borrowing is repaid by monthly payments that combine interest with a repayment of capital. In such cases, a client can reduce the payments if the creditor agrees to accept payment of only the interest without any capital repayment. Creditors need to be persuaded that a request to make interest-only payments is not just a delaying tactic or an excuse for being unable to pay anything. If a client can afford to pay the interest which is accruing on an agreement, you are not asking for anything that is either out of the ordinary or generous.

Payments towards the capital can be resumed if the client's financial circumstances improve in the future. Some creditors are prepared to wait until property is sold for the capital to be repaid. Creditors need to be satisfied either that the arrangement is a temporary one and that the client will be able to resume making the full contractual payments or that s/he will be able to repay the capital in some other way.

When applicable

Paying interest only is appropriate if the client cannot afford to pay both the interest and capital.[6] Some mortgages allow for a 'payment holiday' of a couple of months, but if this is either not applicable and/or not appropriate, the lender might consider an interest-only arrangement as an alternative. Interest-only payments cannot be used for:
- any agreement where the total interest has already been added at the beginning of the loan period and the whole amount secured against the property, because no interest is accruing on a daily basis (but see reduced payments, on p215); *or*

- an endowment mortgage, because payments are already for interest only and the capital is repaid in a lump sum at the end of the period of the loan by an endowment insurance policy (see p113).

Advantages
- It is easily accepted by priority creditors as a temporary forbearance measure.
- It prevents further action.
- It may avoid a bad credit rating.

Disadvantages
- The debt may take longer to clear than it would if full payments were maintained, or if a reduction in capital or charges could be negotiated, and so the client may pay more in the long run.
- The Administration of Justice Act 1973 requires mortgage arrears to be cleared in a 'reasonable time'.[7] Although the court could use its powers to order an adjournment or a suspended possession order to allow payments of interest only,[8] this is only possible for a short period (eg, six months), after which time an increased payment is necessary to clear the arrears in a reasonable time (see p219). Similarly, the court cannot make a time order in respect of a secured loan on this basis as it would not provide for payment of the loan (see p229 and p366).

Useful arguments
- Most mortgage and other secured lenders have policies that allow interest-only payments on a temporary basis (perhaps six months). These can often be arranged by telephone (although any arrangement must be confirmed in writing and a financial statement may be required).

Checklist for action
- Telephone or write to the creditor to propose the strategy and request written confirmation that the strategy is accepted.
- Explain the cause of the client's inability to pay – eg, because of a change of circumstances, or economic factors such as high interest rates.
- Advise the client of how much to pay and when.
- Consider advising the client to set up a direct debit or standing order to ensure payments are kept up.

Reduced payments

A creditor can be asked to renegotiate the contract that has been made so that a client can afford the payments. There are three main ways in which payments can be reduced.

- Ask the creditor to charge a lower rate of interest, either for a period of time (eg, the next year) or for the rest of the loan, even if interest has already been added to the amount payable over the whole period of the loan.
- Ask the creditor to agree to reduce the amount outstanding on a loan so that future payments (perhaps of interest only) are affordable by the client.
- Ask the creditor to allow repayments to extend over a longer period, thereby reducing the capital portion of the repayments. There must be sufficient equity to allow this – the amount of equity can be calculated by deducting the total amount of all loans secured on the property from the market value of the property.

When applicable
- The client cannot meet her/his original contractual obligations.
- If interest rates have risen significantly since the contract was taken out, or if the interest originally charged was significantly higher than available elsewhere or if, despite a general fall in interest rates, a high rate of interest continues to be charged. This is particularly true if a time order would be appropriate (see p229).
- The outstanding balance includes capitalised arrears of interest/charges, particularly if these have accrued at a high rate.
- The property against which the loan is secured is worth less than the capital outstanding, some lenders will reduce their capital outlay rather than continue to chase something which is effectively no longer a fully secured debt.
- If there is another secured loan against the same property, the first mortgagee may reduce the amount outstanding on its loan so that the client can borrow enough to be able to pay off the second mortgagee and then have one remaining loan. This might be a likely option if the second mortgagee is considering repossession and the first mortgagee wishes to continue with the business it has with its customer.
- Adverse publicity would be attracted by a repossession.
- If the property market is slow and, therefore, repossessed properties are unlikely to be saleable.

This strategy is not appropriate for endowment mortgages.

Advantages
- It reduces the amount payable and protects the client's home and essential goods.

Disadvantages
- It is difficult to gain agreement to this as a long-term strategy from creditors, particularly if the loan is more than fully secured.

- The lender may only defer interest and so the client may be faced with substantially higher payments at the end of the arrangement, which may lead to further default in the future.
- Repaying an interest-bearing debt over a longer period may result in additional interest being paid, unless the payments are sufficient to cover this or the rate of interest is reduced accordingly.
- If the capital outstanding is to be reduced, it may require changes to the legal charge that is registered on the property. The client is liable for the costs associated with this.

Useful arguments

- If a time order is possible (see p229), a creditor may prefer to negotiate changes voluntarily rather than have them imposed by the court, especially if adverse publicity is likely to be attracted by a case.
- Point out any failure by the creditor to prevent the build-up of arrears, to send the client regular statements of account or to inform the client of the need to increase payments to cover the ongoing arrears/charges.
- If the alternative for the creditor is to repossess the property, point out that, under section 13.3 of the Financial Conduct Authority's (FCA's) *Mortgages and Home Finance: Conduct of Business Sourcebook* repossession of the client's property must be a last resort, having explored all other possible options. The strategy being offered may be cheaper, as possessing and reselling a property is time-consuming and, therefore, expensive.
- In the case of regulated mortgage contracts, section 13.4.4R of the *Mortgages and Home Finance: Conduct of Business Sourcebook* requires the lender to contact the client within 15 days of her/his account falling into arrears and to provide her/him with prescribed information, including the likely charges that will be incurred should the arrears not be cleared. Any failure to comply with this could be pointed out to the lender if it has contributed to the build-up of arrears.
- In order to support arguments to reduce the amount outstanding and for reduced payments, in all cases, point out any mis-selling of any part of the loan, such as payment protection insurance, or any failure to assess the client's ability to repay. For example, if payment protection insurance has been mis-sold, it may be possible to argue that the client should have a rebate of some or all of the premium, and that the amount of interest charged should be repaid or adjusted, or that the loan agreement itself is unenforceable (see p164).
- Payments are more likely to be maintained if set at a lower level, which the client can afford.
- The sums already paid by the client have given the creditor a more than adequate return on the loan.

Checklist for action

- Telephone or write to the creditor to propose the strategy and request written confirmation of its acceptance.
- Advise the client of how much to pay and when.
- Consider a time order in Consumer Credit Act cases (see p229 and p366).

Capitalise arrears

If arrears have built up (particularly on a repayment mortgage), a creditor can be asked to add these to the capital outstanding and simply charge interest on the new capital amount. This can then be rescheduled over the remaining period of the mortgage, although it may be possible to extend the repayment period, either instead of or as well as capitalising the arrears.

When applicable

- This strategy is particularly useful when there is an improvement in the client's circumstances following a period in which arrears have built up. For example, if a client has recently become employed after a period of unemployment or returned to work after a long period of sickness, provided her/his payment record was previously satisfactory, most creditors will agree to capitalise the arrears.
- Creditors only capitalise arrears if the market value of the property is significantly greater than the amount of capital currently outstanding. They do not usually do so if it would lead to the capital outstanding being more than the value of the property.

Advantages

- It regularises the situation.
- It prevents further action.
- It can avoid a bad credit rating as the client no longer has arrears.
- The repayments are affordable.

Disadvantages

- The repayments on the loan will be increased if the loan is to be repaid within the original contractual period.
- The debt may take longer to pay off, in which case the client pays more.
- If interest charges rise, the effect is greater than when the capital was less.
- Interest is, in effect, paid on the arrears throughout the term of the mortgage.

Useful arguments

- Some creditors only consider capitalising arrears after a trial period in which a client makes regular repayments, particularly if there is little prospect of an improvement in her/his circumstances. You can, therefore, suggest that the lender review the strategy after an agreed period in which the client is able to demonstrate that s/he is able to maintain the repayments.

Checklist for action
- Telephone or write to the creditor to propose the strategy and request written confirmation that this is agreed.
- Advise the client of any change in repayments.

Scheduled payment of arrears

Secured loans

Arrears may be able to be repaid over a period of time. This may be a set amount each month, calculated to repay the arrears over a period of time acceptable to the creditor/lender and/or court. In one case, the court said that it is acceptable to repay arrears over the amount of time remaining until the end of the loan.[9]

However, you should be imaginative in your suggestions for repayment schedules. A staggered offer, in which initially a smaller amount is offered towards the arrears, followed by increased payments, is useful if it is anticipated that the client's circumstances will improve. Such an arrangement may be made directly with the creditor or may need to be ratified by the court if proceedings have already started.

If there is no spare income immediately available, so that only the normal contractual payment can be met, creditors can sometimes be persuaded to accept no payments towards the arrears for several months, particularly if there is plenty of equity (see p250) in the property. In extreme circumstances, they may be persuaded to accept no payments at all for one or two months if the client's inability to pay is clearly temporary.

Some mortgages may allow for a 'payment holiday' (usually for no more than a few months), but may require the client's payments to be up to date at the start of the period. Interest continues to accrue during any period of non-payment and is added to the outstanding balance, so that the client pays more in the long term in return for taking advantage of this concession.

Many creditors have their own internal rules about the time period over which they will spread the repayment of arrears on secured borrowing, but these periods can generally be increased by contacting regional or head offices, or formally complaining when necessary. Most lenders are subject to codes of practice which require them to treat clients 'sympathetically and positively'. The *Mortgages and Home Finance: Conduct of Business Sourcebook* requires lenders to make reasonable efforts to reach an agreement with clients over the method of paying any arrears (having regard to the desirability of agreeing an alternative to repossessing the property) and allow a reasonable time for the arrears to be repaid.[10] If you believe a creditor is allowing a policy to stand in the way of its duty to consider every case individually, s/he should consider using the complaints procedure and referring the matter to the Financial Ombudsman Service, if appropriate.

Rent, fuel and council tax

Creditors use various criteria to decide whether the repayments are acceptable, including the level of arrears, the client's previous payment record and the likelihood of the client remaining as a tenant, consumer or council tax payer in the same location.

When applicable

- After there has been an improvement in financial circumstances.
- After a debt adviser has helped the client to prioritise payments of debts.

Advantages

- Provided the income is available to repay both contractual payments and something towards the arrears, this should be readily acceptable to creditors.
- It prevents further action.

Disadvantages

- It increases the client's outgoings at a time when her/his financial difficulties may not be over.
- In the case of loans, interest accrues not only on the capital outstanding but also on the unpaid arrears so that, unless the creditor agrees to freeze interest and other charges, the repayments will continue beyond the original contractual period, sometimes, on unregulated agreements, at a penalty rate which is higher than that normally charged. Check the agreement to find out if this is the case.

Useful arguments

- Creditors need to understand why payments have not been made in the past and why they are now possible.
- Explain any changes of circumstances and the fact that the client has now reorganised her/his financial affairs to give priority to these debts.
- Explain to creditors that ability to pay needs to be the guiding factor in deciding on repayment of arrears. Point to any relevant code of practice which supports this. A carefully drawn-up financial statement is your most useful tool.
- The strategy is considered appropriate by a reputable money advice agency.
- If the creditor or court is reluctant to accept that payments will be made, the arrangement can be made subject to a review after a set period (eg, six months), so that the creditor's position is not prejudiced.

Checklist for action

- Telephone or write to the creditor to propose the strategy and request written confirmation of the repayment schedule.
- Advise the client of how much to pay and when.
- If necessary, make the appropriate application to court.

Change to a repayment mortgage

An endowment mortgage is a secured loan on which only interest is payable, accompanied by an endowment life assurance policy which is intended to pay off the capital borrowed either at the end of the agreed term or on the death of the borrower (whichever is the sooner).

For the borrower in debt, it is essential that the full amounts of both the endowment insurance payments and the interest on the loan itself are repaid on, or shortly after, the due date. The creditor relies on the insurance company to repay the capital amount lent at the end of the loan period and, if payments to the insurance company stop, the creditor is likely to call in its loan on the basis that its security is at risk, unless an acceptable proposal for repayment of the capital at the end of the loan can be made. If, on the other hand, payments to the creditor are not kept up, the amount outstanding on the loan increases and is likely to become more than the amount that will be produced by the insurance policy at its maturity. Endowment mortgages are therefore less flexible than repayment ones.

To have flexibility to capitalise arrears, extend the period of a loan or negotiate repayment of arrears over several years, an endowment mortgage needs to be changed to a repayment mortgage. The creditor does this automatically for some clients once the endowment premium is significantly in arrears.

However, to cease paying, surrender or sell an endowment policy is a major financial decision and should not be taken without specialist advice from an independent financial adviser.

When applicable

- A client is in arrears with an endowment mortgage, or is likely to go into arrears, and therefore a renegotiation on the terms of the mortgage is necessary.
- A client is unable to maintain the payments on the endowment policy.
- A client is facing a substantial period of low income and needs more flexibility.
- If the endowment policy has been running for several years, it may be beneficial to cash it in or sell it and use the lump sum to pay off arrears. Advice from a number of independent financial advisers should always be taken before surrendering an endowment policy. Some insurers charge significant fees for early surrender and, in addition, the value of the policy depends on the state of the stock market. The surrender value of a policy is frequently much less than the amount of the payments made into it to date. A sale of the policy instead usually produces a better return. However, even if a client changes to a repayment mortgage, it is better, if possible, to keep the endowment policy (without making any new payments into it) until it matures.
- The client can afford the new repayments.

Advantages
- Increased flexibility in the long term.
- Ensures that the home is not lost.
- Possible reduced monthly outgoings.

Disadvantages
- There may be an arrangement fee to convert the mortgage to a capital repayment type.
- The client must arrange separate life insurance cover.
- Some or all of the money already invested in the endowment policy may be lost (especially if it is relatively new).
- If a policy is 'assigned' to the lender, the surrender/sale value may be taken by it in full (although negotiation is possible).
- Possible increased monthly outgoings.

Useful arguments
- Creditors may be sympathetic if this is the only way of paying the mortgage, as it ensures the loan is repaid.

Checklist for action
The client should get independent advice from a specialist in this field (but not from a broker who was involved in setting up the endowment mortgage as s/he may be motivated by the knowledge that s/he will probably lose commission if an endowment policy is cancelled).

If, after taking financial advice, the client decides on this course of action, do the following.
- Telephone or write to the creditor to propose the strategy and request details of new instalments and the surrender/sale value of the endowment policy.
- Advise the client of how much to pay and when.
- If disposing of the endowment policy, ensure the full surrender value of the policy is paid to the client. Selling it rather than merely surrendering it may produce a larger sum.
- Advise the client to take advice to arrange new life assurance cover for the mortgage, if necessary.

Mortgage rescue schemes
Welsh local authorities may have funds available that they can use to prevent repossessions and the potential costs of rehousing and the resettlement of clients. The local authority decides whether to help clients with mortgage rescue and what eligibility criteria to use. Some registered social landlords in Wales also run mortgage rescue schemes. Check with the client's local authority to see whether any schemes are available in the area.

Mortgage rescue and bankruptcy

Note: mortgage rescues are no longer available in England but the risk to the property from earlier rescues in the event of bankruptcy remains.

If the a mortgage rescue has involved the sale of the client's property to a registered social landlord and the client went bankrupt in the five years following the transaction, the trustee in bankruptcy might challenge the arrangement as a transaction at an undervalue (see p495). This could put the client's home at risk if the new owner decided to sell it to pay off the trustee.

However, the Insolvency Service has said that a mortgage rescue scheme would be unlikely to give rise to a transaction at an undervalue if the client entered the scheme before bankruptcy and the registered social landlord paid the market value. However, if the client received a lump sum and used this to clear unsecured debts, the question of a preference might arise (see p495). Any shortfall would be a bankruptcy debt (although if the lender only agreed to mortgage rescue on the basis of the client entering into a new arrangement to pay the shortfall, questions of fraud arise if the client entered into the arrangement with the intention of going bankrupt and avoiding payment). The reduction in housing costs might increase the chances of an income payments agreement/order being made (see pp485–87).

Entering a mortgage rescue scheme post-bankruptcy and while undischarged would not give rise to a transaction at an undervalue, but the trustee in bankruptcy would need to be satisfied that the market value was paid for the property. Any surplus would be an asset and be claimed by the trustee. If the lender only agreed to the scheme post-bankruptcy on condition that the client entered into new arrangements to pay any shortfall, the trustee should not object, provided the client took independent advice (as should have been the case).

When applicable
- The client can no longer afford the mortgage or secured loan payments and no other strategy is available.

Advantages
- It enables the client to remain in her/his home.

Disadvantages
- The client will have less security of tenure as a tenant.

Checklist for action
- Check availability of local schemes.

Sale and rent-back schemes

These are commercial, non-government schemes that allow an owner-occupier who is unable to meet her/his mortgage repayments and who is possibly facing repossession to sell her/his home and remain in the property as a tenant. Since 1 July 2009, such schemes have been regulated by the FCA.

If a client has a complaint, this can be considered by the Financial Ombudsman Service in accordance with its normal rules (see p284).

If the proposed sale price of the property is below market value, the client should consider the implications were s/he to go bankrupt in the foreseeable future (see p465).

When applicable

- The client can no longer afford the mortgage or secured loan payments and no other strategy is available.

Advantages

- It enables the client to remain in her/his home.

Disadvantages

- The client will have less security of tenure as a tenant.

Checklist for action

- Check availability of local schemes.

Sale of the property

There are a number of circumstances in which it may be advisable to sell a home in order to repay priority creditors.

This strategy, although superficially tempting, is not generally applicable merely to repay priority debts. When other circumstances make the sale of the home inevitable or even desirable, however, debts can be cleared in this way and there may even be sufficient capital to make a full and final offer to non-priority creditors (see p261). As it is such a major decision, it is important that the client and her/his family reach it for themselves. You should ensure that the advantages and disadvantages of this strategy are understood and that the client has time to consider all the implications.

If the client is a former local authority tenant who has exercised her/his right to buy, it is worth checking whether the local authority or the housing organisation to whom its stock is now transferred operates a 'buy-back' scheme, whereby the owner sells the home back to the local authority and remains there as a tenant. Check whether the client is still within the discount repayment period. If so, a proportion of the purchase price needs to be repaid to the local authority.

If the client becomes homeless and needs to be rehoused, you or the client must explain the circumstances to the local authority in advance and gain its approval of the strategy, in writing, and its acceptance that homelessness is inevitable rather than intentional. For further details, see the *Manual of Housing Law* (see Appendix 2).

Negative equity

'Negative equity' occurs when the value of a client's property falls below the amount due under her/his mortgage or other loans secured on it. This means that, even if her/his property were sold, the client would not be free of debt and would still owe an amount (the negative equity) to the creditor. If a client wants to sell a property in negative equity, s/he needs the permission of any secured creditors who are not going to be repaid out of the sale proceeds. Section 13.3.1R of the *Mortgages and Home Finance: Conduct of Business Sourcebook* requires FCA-authorised lenders to treat clients 'fairly'. If a creditor unreasonably refuses to agree to a sale, the court can overrule it.[11] In this situation, you should obtain specialist advice.

Many lenders now offer support to clients so that they can sell their homes and so avoid repossession. These schemes are known as 'voluntary' or 'assisted voluntary' sales. The National Homelessness Advice Service has produced guidance for advisers, available at nhas.org.uk/docs/NHAS_AVS_Guide_2018.pdf.[12]

The strategies that follow in this chapter depend on the housing market. If houses cannot be sold easily, creditors may not want to repossess and a sale by the client could be undesirable or impossible. However, you should not necessarily rely on this, as lenders sometimes decide to cut their losses and repossess regardless.

If possible, it is important to reach an agreement to avoid such a situation. Section 13.3.2A(5)R of the *Mortgages and Finance: Conduct of Business Sourcebook* says that, if a payment arrangement cannot be made, the lender should consider allowing the client to remain in the property in order to sell it.

Negative equity affects whether some of the following strategies in this chapter apply. However, in most circumstances, the approach remains the same, either because a lender is prepared to ignore the negative equity or because it becomes an unsecured and non-priority debt (see Chapter 9).

Note: for what to do if there is a 'mortgage shortfall' or a claim from a mortgage indemnity insurer, see p116. These debts, although non-priority at present, must be dealt with because they represent a potential future problem if an attachment of earnings, bankruptcy or charging order were to be used at a future date.

When applicable

There are circumstances when the loss of a home may be inevitable and, indeed, the best option.
- A client has somewhere else to live as well as the property in question.
- A client has considerable equity in the home, but now the property is too large or in the wrong place for her/his current requirements and a more suitable home could be purchased at a lower price.

- Repossession is inevitable – eg, if the client's available income is too low to make an acceptable repayment proposal, a better price may be paid to an owner-occupier than to a mortgagee in possession. This can give a client equity, but her/his need for a suitable home must be paramount (see the disadvantages below).

Advantages

- It is easily accepted by priority creditors and courts. If necessary, time may be given for the sale to go through.
- It prevents further action.
- It may avoid a bad credit rating.
- It may release capital for other purposes.
- A better price is generally achieved by a voluntary sale than by a financial institution selling the property after it has repossessed it.
- It is an alternative to bankruptcy proceedings, either as part of an individual voluntary arrangement (see Chapter 15) or an informal arrangement with creditors.
- It may avoid court costs if the strategy is agreed before repossession action.
- It can be seen by the client as an opportunity for a fresh start.

Disadvantages

- The client is forced to move home. This is costly and disruptive.
- Unless the client has a buyer, it may be seen by the creditor and the court as a way of delaying possession/eviction proceedings.
- If rehousing by a local authority is required, it may be difficult to persuade it that the client has not made her/himself intentionally homeless.
- It may not be possible to find alternative suitable housing.
- The client may lose money if the housing market is depressed and s/he has only recently bought the property.

Useful arguments

- Creditors prefer to avoid repossessing and selling property and so can be persuaded of the advantages of not having to sell an empty property. A property is likely to sell more quickly if inhabited.
- The loan will be repaid in full. If the full amount will not be repaid and the creditor is unreasonably refusing to agree to a sale, the court can override the creditor's objections.[13]

Checklist for action

- Ensure that the client has suitable alternative accommodation.
- Inform the creditors of the proposed strategy.
- Advise the client to put the property on the market. If a quick sale is required, the client should explain this to the estate agent.

- Discuss with the client how much to pay, if anything, towards the mortgage until the property is sold, particularly if there is negative equity.

Refinancing

Refinancing means taking out a loan or other credit agreement to repay an existing debt.

Refinancing should be distinguished from rescheduling existing repayments, which does not involve taking on (further) credit. The FCA has recently made changes to its affordability checks to assist so-called 'mortgage prisoners' – ie, people who are unable to remortgage to a cheaper deal due to not meeting earlier affordability requirements, even though they are up-to-date on their current, more expensive payments (see p115). While clients cannot benefit if they have had arrears within the past 12 months, those paying but struggling with other debts may find the measures helpful.

When applicable

- It is common for possession of homes to be sought by second mortgagees (who may have lent money for home improvements, such as double glazing) from clients who had always managed to pay their first mortgage. The repayments on a medium-term loan from a finance company (particularly a 'non-status loan') may be greater than those on a mortgage from a high street lender. In these circumstances, the first mortgagee may be sympathetic to the client and will not want to lose her/his business simply because s/he has become unable to repay the high rate of interest charged by the second mortgagee.
- Even though possession action is not threatened, it may be obvious that a client's financial problems are caused by excessive repayment of a particular priority debt. Refinancing may, therefore, be more appropriate than asking the creditor to capitalise arrears, as this could result in higher repayments than if the loan were refinanced.
- When a cheaper form of borrowing is available to replace a priority debt. A variety of credit products can be used – eg:
  - an unsecured loan;
  - an additional advance from an existing secured lender;
  - a secured loan from a new lender;
  - a remortgage;
  - a transfer of balances to a credit card. Some credit card companies offer 0 per cent interest for a temporary period on balances transferred from other creditors.
- It should only be considered if:
  - the client's monthly outgoings will be reduced; *and*
  - the client can afford the new repayments; *and*
  - the client will also be able to meet her/his essential expenditure and any other financial commitments.

When refinancing is not applicable

Many advertisements for refinancing or debt consolidation also promote the 'feel-good factor' by suggesting that people can borrow extra spending money in addition to paying off their debts. Many people do this and, for those in financial difficulties, the effect is to exacerbate their problems. The 'churning' of loans (ie, where debts are consolidated and then consolidated again) can be very expensive because of the way the interest is apportioned; the amount of capital paid off is small and so the debt increases. The churning of loans could give rise to an unfair relationship (see p161).

Advantages

Clients can benefit from refinancing or consolidating their debts on more advantageous terms – ie:

- lower interest rates;
- lower monthly payments;
- having to deal with only one creditor.

Disadvantages

Refinancing or debt consolidation is often seen as an easy way of obtaining more credit or as a short-term solution to debt problems. The possible long-term implications may not always be understood and, without clear information on the costs involved, problems can occur – eg:

- the costs of settling existing loans (eg, early settlement charges) and finding and arranging new loans (eg, a broker's fees) can be significant;
- clients can pay more for their credit overall and have a larger debt for a longer period if the new loan is spread over a longer period of time.

Useful arguments

- If the first mortgagee is being asked to refinance a second secured loan, whenever possible emphasise the client's good payment record.
- Point out the business advantages to the creditor of refinancing the loan rather than allowing another secured lender to take possession.
- If they will not agree immediately, it is worth advising creditors to review their decision after three to six months of regular payments.

Checklist for action

- Advise the client to obtain independent financial advice and get full details of the refinancing, including new monthly instalments, arrangement fees, interest rates and the annual percentage rate.
- Inform the existing creditor of the proposed action.

Time orders

A time order is granted by the county court and sets new repayment terms and possibly lower interest rates/charges for an agreement if the court believes that the original terms should be altered. See p366 for further details.

When applicable

- A time order can only be granted for loans, credit cards, overdrafts and any other type of agreement regulated by the Consumer Credit Act 1974, including secured loans treated as regulated.[14]
- Time orders are most likely to be granted if the borrower's circumstances have changed during the period of the loan. Time orders are usually granted if the change in circumstances is expected to be temporary, but can be made for a longer period if the court accepts that it is 'just' to do so.[15]

Advantages

- The agreement of the creditor is not required if the court can be persuaded that an order should be made.
- Any possession order is suspended by the court on the terms of the time order.
- Once made, the creditor can take no further action, provided payments are maintained.
- It can reduce interest rates/charges (possibly retrospectively) and set payments at an affordable level.

Disadvantages

- Time orders are difficult to get and, because they are still rarely applied for, many judges are not familiar with the principles. Courts are required to draw a distinction between a 'deserving' and an 'undeserving' client.[16]
- The client must wait until the creditor issues an arrears notice or a default notice, or takes court action, before applying for a time order.
- Creditors' costs may be added to the debt.

Useful arguments

See Chapter 12.

Checklist for action

See Chapter 12.

Voluntary charge

Most unsecured debts are not priorities. However, very occasionally it may be advisable to offer to turn an unsecured debt into a secured one – eg, if there is a real risk of a creditor applying to make a client bankrupt. This is achieved by offering the creditor a voluntary charge secured on the client's property. Many advisers routinely dismiss creditors' requests for a voluntary charge without considering whether it would be in the client's best interests to agree.[17]

It is essential that the client obtains legal advice before signing a voluntary charge in order to safeguard her/his position should the creditor decide to enforce the charge and apply for an order for sale. As a minimum, you should ensure that the charge document is worded so that the creditor's right to do so is removed altogether (or is at least restricted), so that the property cannot be repossessed and sold against the client's wishes. In addition, almost always the client must ensure that the creditor agrees to freeze interest so that the charge is against a fixed sum that will not swallow up the equity.

Agreement also needs to be reached about whether any instalments are required by the creditor in addition to the charge.

All the above issues need to be agreed before a voluntary charge is made, and must be part of a written agreement.

If a property is jointly owned and the joint owner has no liability for the debt, her/his agreement may also be required, and s/he should be advised to get independent advice.

When applicable

Although often requested by creditors, a voluntary charge is only very rarely in the client's best interests. The only circumstances in which it may be advisable are the following.

- It is the only means to stop someone issuing undesirable bankruptcy proceedings. **Note:** although many creditors threaten bankruptcy proceedings, including issuing a statutory demand (see p471), this very rarely results in an actual petition for bankruptcy. However, a statutory demand should always be taken seriously and should never be ignored.
- It is essential to the client that no county court judgment is made – eg, because s/he would lose her/his job if this happened. **Note:** a time order may be a more appropriate way of stopping a county court judgment. A Tomlin order can also be a way of avoiding a county court judgment if it would affect a client's job. This is a form of 'consent order' where the client and the lender come to an agreement that county court proceedings will be stayed indefinitely provided agreed payments are made. If the agreement is breached, court proceedings will resume and a county court judgment will be issued.
- The creditor refuses to accept any other strategy and if the creditor obtains a county court judgment, it is likely that the court will make a charging order (see p322).
- The creditor has an automatic right to impose a charge – eg, in some circumstances, the Legal Aid Agency can register a charge on the client's home to recover her/his legal aid costs, which can be higher than a voluntary charge (currently, simple interest at 8 per cent a year is charged).

- It is known that when a person's current home is sold, s/he will not need the proceeds of sale – eg, if s/he has a terminal illness. In this situation, a voluntary charge could reduce the stress of lengthy negotiations with creditors.

Advantages
- A voluntary charge is likely to satisfy a creditor and therefore mean that no further action is taken.
- Once their capital outlay is secured by a voluntary charge, many creditors will agree to add no further interest/charges until the property is sold, and to accept the client's repayment offer or even no (or only token) payments.
- Lenders can be persuaded to agree not to enforce their charge – ie, not to force a sale but to wait for payment until the client sells the property (or remortgages).

Disadvantages
- By changing the status of a debt, a client is potentially putting her/his home at risk.
- The client may incur costs in getting legal advice to ensure a watertight agreement is drawn up.
- If the client has a partner who is a co-owner of the property, the partner needs to sign the charge document and make her/himself liable for the debt.
- The creditor may still insist on payments being made in addition to the charge.

Useful arguments
From the client's point of view, the voluntary charge is only ever the lesser of two evils. You may need to put the following arguments to the creditor.
- In practice, it is the only way the creditor will get any money.
- Making people bankrupt does not often produce money, but a voluntary charge does.
- If property prices increase, so too will the equity against which the charge is made.

Checklist for action
- Consider whether any other strategy would be more appropriate – eg, a time order.
- Advise the client to obtain full details of the terms of the charge in writing from the creditor.
- Ensure the client receives legal advice about the agreement before signing.
- Check that interest is frozen and all the other terms are acceptable.

Deductions from benefits

Certain priority arrears can be deducted from a claimant's monthly award of universal credit (UC) and paid directly to creditors.[18] Deductions can also be made from income support (IS), income-based jobseeker's allowance (JSA), income-related employment and support allowance (ESA) and pension credit (PC) at a set weekly amount.[19] Deductions can be made from contribution-based JSA, contributory ESA and some other benefits in limited circumstances. See CPAG's *Welfare Benefits and Tax Credits Handbook* for further information. Deductions from benefits are commonly used to pay off arrears of gas and electricity charges as an alternative to disconnection, or rent arrears as an alternative to eviction.

For UC, deductions for current liability can only be made for electricity, gas, water and child support maintenance and only while the claimant is in arrears for these costs. Consent for third-party deductions from UC is only required where deductions are for fuel and water liability and arrears which exceed 25 per cent of the standard allowance.

For UC, the usual deduction rate is 5 per cent of the client's UC standard allowance (the amount of this depends on whether s/he is aged under or over 25 and whether s/he is single or in a couple). Deductions for rent arrears are at a rate of at least 10 per cent and up to 20 per cent of the standard allowance. Deductions for rent arrears are only possible while the client is receiving the housing costs element in her/his UC (or lives in exempt accommodation and gets housing benefit) and s/he occupies the property to which the debt arrears apply. Deductions for court fines are at a rate of between 5 per cent of the standard allowance and a maximum of £108.35 per month. No more than three third-party deductions are allowed at one time.

In most instances, the maximum amount allowed for all the arrears listed below is 40 per cent[20] of a claimant's standard allowance, although in practice the Department for Work and Pensions (DWP) currently operates a maximum rate of 30 per cent. Deductions for rent arrears, water and fuel arrears can exceed the maximum amount if it is thought to be in the claimant's best interest.

If the deductions would be more than the maximum amount, they are paid in a set order of priority as follows:[21]

- housing costs (from April 2018, these are restricted to service charges);
- rent arrears (and related charges), if the amount of the deduction is 10 per cent of the standard allowance;
- fuel;
- council tax arrears;
- fines, if the amount of the deduction is 5 per cent of the standard allowance;
- water charges;
- child support maintenance;
- repayment of social fund payments;
- recovery of hardship payments;
- penalties instead of prosecution for benefit offences;
- recovery of overpayments of benefits or tax credits caused by fraud;
- loss of benefit for benefit offences;
- recovery of overpayments of benefits or tax credits not caused by fraud;

- repayment of integration loans;
- repayment of eligible loans;
- rent arrears (and related charges), if the amount of the deduction is more than 10 per cent of the standard allowance;
- fines, costs and compensation orders, if the amount of the deduction is more than 5 per cent of the standard allowance.

Deductions for arrears of housing costs, rent, gas and electricity and water charges cannot begin if the client (and, if relevant, her/his partner) earns more than the work allowance which applies in her/his case in the last assessment period and stops if earnings exceed the applicable work allowance in the three previous assessment periods.[22]

Note: UC deductions for priority debts are in addition to deductions for UC advance payments, so the amount of benefit a claimant is left with can be significantly reduced. In such situations, the DWP can be asked to reduce deductions, though this is discretionary.

The deduction rate from benefits other than UC is currently £3.70 a week per item (£5 a week for fines), with a maximum amount of £11.10 a week in some cases and the claimant's consent required for combinations of certain deductions above a maximum amount. If the client has more debts than can be paid from her/his benefit, they are paid in a set order of priority as follows:[23]

- housing costs – eg, service charges, including for repairs and improvements;
- rent arrears;
- fuel charges (in the case of both gas and electricity arrears, the DWP chooses which one to pay);
- water charges;
- council tax arrears;
- fines, costs and compensation orders;
- child support maintenance;
- repayment of integration loans;
- repayment of eligible loans made by certain 'not-for-profit' lenders – eg, credit unions;
- repayment of tax credit overpayments and self-assessment tax debts.

When applicable

- Deductions from IS, income-based JSA, income-related ESA, UC or PC can be made to pay for rent arrears, residential accommodation charges (not from UC), hostel payments (not from UC), fuel, water charges, council tax arrears, fines, repayments of eligible loans and child support maintenance. Deductions can also be made for the cost of home loans, loans for repairs and improvements and other housing costs, and paid to the lender.
- Direct deductions from benefit are useful if the alternative is either the disconnection of a fuel supply or an impending eviction.

- Because of the statutory maximums on the amount that can be deducted for arrears, it is often a cheaper method of paying off arrears than a repayment schedule, or than pre-payment meters that have been recalibrated to recover arrears along with current consumption. Gas and electricity suppliers often seriously overestimate current use and request an amount from the DWP far in excess of the amount actually required to cover consumption. If they do, advise the client to take daily or weekly meter readings. It is the appropriate decision maker at the DWP who decides how much to deduct for current consumption, so the client can ask for a lower deduction to be made based on her/his own readings. If refused, s/he can appeal to the First-tier Tribunal.
- Some gas and electricity suppliers insist on installing a pre-payment meter to cover current consumption and only collect arrears through deductions from benefit.

Advantages

- If the client fits the criteria for deductions from benefit, it is a simple and quick way to ensure that no further action is taken by the creditor and that arrears are paid at a relatively modest rate – particularly if money is owed to several creditors (but see below).
- Creditors are assured of payments.

Disadvantages

- Only certain debts can be paid for in this way (and council tax only at the request of the local authority, fines at the request of the magistrates' court and eligible loans at the request of the lender). If the client has more than one such debt, deductions might not be made for all of them. If this happens, there is a set order of priority.
- By reducing subsistence-level benefits, they reduce the flexibility with which a claimant can juggle her/his weekly budget. For example, for magistrates' court fines, the DWP has discretion to take the minimum amount of 5 per cent of UC, but it appears that the DWP is refusing to do this and instead is taking the maximum 30 per cent, which is leaving claimants struggling to pay for essentials. See cpag.org.uk/welfare-rights/judicial-review/judicial-review-pre-action-letters/deductions-uc for further information on challenging decisions on deductions from UC for court fines.
- Fuel suppliers may demand a large amount for current liability.
- If the client is likely to stop claiming benefit in the near future (even if only for a temporary period), direct payments must be replaced with another strategy. The client may be faced with a demand for the full amount when her/his benefit ends.

Checklist for action
- Contact the creditor to find out how much is required and, if the client can afford this amount, try to obtain the creditor's agreement to payments by deductions from benefit.
- Assist the client in her/his request for the DWP to arrange deductions.

Gas and electricity pre-payment meters

Both electricity and gas companies must provide a pre-payment meter to a customer to prevent disconnection of her/his supply, if it is safe and practicable to do so.[24] If someone has arrears on fuel bills, a pre-payment meter collects money not just for the fuel used, but also towards the arrears. For a discussion of the different types of meters available, see CPAG's *Fuel Rights Handbook*.

When applicable
- Pre-payment meters allow arrears to be collected over a period of time and are, therefore, a way of avoiding disconnection.

Advantages
- A client continues to have some access to fuel supplies and is not pressed further for the debt.
- Pre-payment meters can assist budgeting.
- Smart meters can help monitor energy use.

Disadvantages
- 'Self-disconnection' is a problem if a client cannot afford to top up a pre-payment meter and faces intermittent or extended periods of disconnection.
- In some cases, the amount of money recovered towards the arrears varies in relation to the amount of fuel used and so, in winter, not only does a client have to spend more money on fuel, s/he also has to contribute more towards her/his arrears.
- There may be costs incurred (eg, bus fares) in buying top-ups, it may be difficult for the client to get to a charging point or point of sale (eg, in the case of illness), or such places may be closed.
- A pre-payment meter is not always technically possible. This applies if gas appliances have pilot lights that could go out when the pre-payment ends and are not protected by a fail-safe device when payment is resumed.
- Pre-payment meters should not be installed if the client is at risk of leaving appliances turned on after the credit has run out, or are incapable of operating the meter or obtaining top-ups.

Useful arguments
Fuel suppliers are required to offer pre-payment facilities if this is the only means of avoiding disconnection. However, it may be necessary to argue with a supplier

about the level at which the arrears will be collected through the pre-payment meter. If a client is on UC, IS, income-based JSA, income-related ESA or PC, the amounts deducted by the DWP from benefit should be used as a maximum level of recovery (see p231).

Checklist for action

- Check exactly what type of meters are available locally.
- Contact the fuel supplier to request that a meter be installed.
- Check whether the client is eligible for the Warm Home Discount to reduce the cost of future consumption.
- Advise the client to monitor fuel consumption to check the calibration of the meter. This involves taking a meter reading each week and comparing the number of units with the amount paid.

See also Chapter 6.

Writing off debts

Both the magistrates' court (in respect of fines and council tax) and the local authority (in respect of non-domestic rates and council tax) have powers to remit (ie, write off) amounts owing in cases of hardship. HMRC can also remit taxes (although it does not formally write them off). Clients with severe financial difficulties (eg, deficit budgets) can apply for discretionary relief from council tax under section 13A of the Local Government Finance Act 1992. Councils must consider each case on its merits and should not refuse on grounds of financial impact for the council. Appeals can be made to valuation tribunals.

Note: some clients can apply for an exemption from council tax if they have a 'severe mental impairment' – ie, they have a permanent mental health issues such as dementia or severe learning disabilities. Another person living with them could then get a single person's discount. They must be eligible (but not necessarily claiming) a qualifying disability benefit – eg, personal independence allowance or UC with the limited capability for work/limited capability for work and work-related activity element included. Clients should contact the local authority to apply and ask about backdating. See CPAG's *Council Tax Handbook* for more information and other groups who are exempt – eg, certain carers, students and apprentices.

When applicable

- The client is experiencing financial hardship or is unable to meet her/his essential expenditure and the situation is unlikely to improve in the foreseeable future.

Advantages

- It reduces or removes the debt.

Disadvantages

- The client will often need to attend a means enquiry (see p392).
- The magistrates must consider whether there has been 'wilful refusal or culpable neglect' (see p407) and may therefore look at other alternatives to remittance, such as imprisonment.

Useful arguments

- **Non-domestic rates.** The closure of a business may adversely affect the amenities or employment prospects of an area.
- **Fines.** Magistrates need to see how the client's circumstances have changed since the fine was imposed or that her/his financial situation was not taken into account when the fine was originally set. Guidelines state that fines should be paid in a reasonable period, and that two to three years is exceptional.
- **Council tax.** Local authorities have complete discretion and should be encouraged to use it in all cases of hardship which fall outside the exemption, discount and council tax reduction scheme rules.[25]
- **Tax.** Remission is usually only available if the client is on a low income and has no, or insignificant, savings. HMRC must be satisfied that the client's financial circumstances are unlikely to improve sufficiently to make future recovery action worthwhile. It is unlikely to be offered to a client who is currently self-employed, although collection could be suspended in cases of serious illness.

Checklist for action

- Write to the creditor to request remittance.
- Enclose a financial statement.
- Point out any additional factors – eg, terminal illness, severe medical conditions or disability.

4. **Emergency action**

The need for debt advice very often arises as a result of a priority creditor threatening to take immediate action against someone's fuel supply, property or liberty. In such circumstances, you must always be prepared to take emergency action. In some cases, sufficient information and time are available to use one of the strategies outlined above. In other cases, neither time nor information is immediately available and, therefore, action by the creditor needs to be halted or delayed. This may be possible by making a telephone call to a creditor explaining that the client has approached the agency seeking advice and assistance, and indicating when an offer will be made.

Sections 7.3.11R and 7.3.12G of the FCA's *Consumer Credit Sourcebook* requires recovery action to be suspended for a 'reasonable period' (generally, 30 days) where the creditor has been informed that an adviser is helping a client to agree a repayment plan. However, this may not be the case when adjournments or delays have already been granted. In such situations, other emergency action must be taken.

Preventing fuel disconnection

The legislation governing the supply of gas and electricity states that supplies should not be disconnected while there is a genuine dispute about the amount due.[26] When there is any question about the amount claimed, such a dispute should immediately be registered with the relevant supplier and confirmed in writing. The supplier should be asked not to disconnect the supply until the dispute has been resolved.

Before being offered a pre-payment meter, the client should have been offered some form of repayment option to pay the arrears and cover the ongoing consumption. If this breaks down, some suppliers automatically offer a pre-payment meter as the only remaining option. You should consider explaining why the arrangement broke down (eg, it was unrealistic in the first place) and urge the supplier to enter into a new arrangement based on a financial statement.

Before disconnecting, the supplier must:
- comply with its code of practice (including providing information about reconnection);
- fit a pre-payment meter where it is safe and practical to do so;
- provide seven days' notice of the date of disconnection;
- obtain a warrant of entry if the client refuses access;
- give a further seven days' notice of its intention to use it.

A warrant of entry is granted by the magistrates' court and allows the supplier to enter the client's home (by force if necessary) in order to disconnect the supply. Although the supplier must give the client written notice that it intends to apply for a warrant, it does not have to give the client notice of the actual application. You can, however, phone the court in advance of an application, ask to speak to the magistrate who would deal with any application and make representations on behalf of the client – eg, that s/he is a vulnerable person and the supplier has unreasonably refused to agree to a repayment arrangement.

The client cannot be disconnected if:
- the bill is genuinely disputed;
- the debt is owed to a different supplier. A supplier who wants to retain the power to disconnect should object to the supply being switched;
- the debt is due from a previous occupier and the client has agreed to take over the supply;

- the debt is for something other than the supply of gas or electricity – ie, it does not relate to fuel consumption. **Note:** the supply can be disconnected for non-payment under a 'green deal plan' for energy efficiency improvements to the property made under the Energy Act 2011;
- a repayment plan has been agreed. Under its licence conditions, when arranging a repayment plan, the supplier must take into account the client's ability to pay;
- the client has agreed to have a pre-payment meter fitted and it is safe and practicable to do so. The meter should be calibrated to recover the arrears at the rate the client can afford, taking into account her/his ability to repay;
- it is between 1 October and 31 March, and the supplier either knows or has reason to believe there is someone of pension age living either alone in the property or with others over pension age or under 18;
- it is between 1 October and 31 March and someone living in the property is either severely disabled or chronically sick, unless all other reasonable steps have been taken to recover the arrears.

Clients in the last two categories are likely to be on the Priority Services Register.

Energy UK (the trade association for the UK gas and electricity industries) members have signed up to a 'safety net for vulnerable customers', under which they are committed never knowingly to disconnect a vulnerable customer at any time of year 'where for reasons of age, health, disability or severe financial insecurity that customer is unable to safeguard their personal welfare or the personal welfare of other members of the household'. For more details, see energy-uk.org.uk.

No one who is prepared to have a pre-payment meter or who is eligible for direct payments from her/his benefits or who can afford to pay for current consumption plus a payment towards the arrears should ever be disconnected. Energy trust funds or other charities may be able to help with payment of bills or to prevent self-disconnection – ie, if clients do not use gas or electricity because they cannot afford to pay for it. In the case of pre-payment meters, self-disconnection can be as a result of arrears being recovered at too high a rate. Suppliers can always be asked to confirm how arrears are being recovered, and asked to recalibrate the meter where appropriate.

If negotiations with the fuel supplier are proving unsuccessful, contact Citizens Advice or the Ombudsman Services: Energy (see Appendix 1), which have the power to intervene when disconnection is threatened. See also CPAG's *Fuel Rights Handbook* for more information.

Preventing the home being lost

When a possession order has already been granted and is followed by a warrant of possession (see p364), you may need to make an immediate application to the court on Form N244 to suspend the warrant. If the eviction is not due to take place for several days, attempt to negotiate directly with the lender (or the lender's solicitor) or the landlord, to obtain a binding agreement that the property will not be repossessed. If this is not possible or appears unlikely, or the eviction is due to take place that day or the following day, Form N244 should be submitted to the court.

Form N244 must state the grounds of the application and, if possible, include an offer of payment. The fee is court fee 2.9 – ie, £50 (and not £255 as some courts argue). See p290 for how to apply for a remission. For further information about a warrant of possession, see p364, and for how to complete Form N244, see p288.

In the case of local authority or registered social landlord tenants, there is usually an internal procedure that must be followed before a warrant is applied for, which may involve considering representations from the tenant. Check that procedure has been complied with and challenge the landlord if it has not.[27]

An application to suspend the possession warrant always stops county court bailiffs executing it (ie, carrying out its instructions) until the court has heard the application, although the court is usually very quick in arranging a hearing. The success of an application depends largely on:

- whether several arrangements have already been made but not kept to;
- your ability and the client's ability to present the case;
- how many previous warrants have been suspended;
- how long the client has been getting help from an advice agency;
- the client's ability to pay.

If it is too late to make the application to the court because the bailiffs are already on their way to carry out the eviction, phone the creditor immediately and negotiate with the bailiff, on the doorstep if necessary, for more time. Bailiffs normally have a mobile phone with them and so can be contacted right up to the point of eviction.

Preventing goods being taken control of by magistrates' court bailiffs

Bailiffs working for the magistrates' court cannot act without a warrant of control. This is a document issued by the court allowing them to take control of goods belonging to the client, which can then be sold and the money used to pay the unpaid debt.

If a warrant of control has been issued by a magistrates' court because of arrears in the payment of fines, and bailiffs are about to take control of the client's goods, it is not clear whether magistrates can hear an application to give further time to pay (see p398).

Occasionally, bailiffs agree to give a debt adviser a few days in which to produce an offer of repayment. If the client is vulnerable, try to persuade the bailiff to return the warrant to the court, citing paragraphs 70–78 of the *Taking Control of Goods: national standards* (April 2014) – see gov.uk/government/publications/bailiffs-and-enforcement-agents-national-standards. However, success to date has been limited.

See Chapter 14 for further details of bailiffs' powers.

Preventing goods being taken control of for council tax arrears

If a court grants a local authority a liability order, it can use private bailiffs (since 1 April 2014 these have also been known as 'enforcement agents') to take control of goods belonging to the client, which can then be sold and the money used to pay the council tax arrears.

Different local authorities give different instructions to their bailiffs. In some areas, a clear code of conduct exists, preventing a client's goods being taken control of if s/he is on benefit or in certain other circumstances. *Council Tax: guidance to local councils on good practice in the collection of council tax arrears* issued by the Department for Communities and Local Government in June 2013 encourages local authorities to work with debt advisers in the free-to-client sector to design protocols for enforcement action, including what might constitute a vulnerable situation and how people in these circumstances should be dealt with. This also instructs local authorities to take account of the Ministry of Justice's *Taking Control of Goods: national standards*, both in respect of their own responsibilities as creditors and the standards expected of their bailiffs, particularly if the client is a 'vulnerable person' (see p420).

Citizens Advice and the Local Government Association have produced the *Council Tax Protocol* (reissued in June 2017), which they recommend advisers and local authorities should adopt. The protocol contains practical steps to prevent clients getting into arrears but, if they do, suggests procedures to ensure bailiffs act appropriately, including a requirement that local authorities should have a process for dealing with cases where the client is indentified as vulnerable. The protocol is available at citizensadvice.org.uk/about-us/our-campaigns/all-our-current-campaigns/council-tax-protocol/.

Local authorities should actively manage their contracts with bailiffs, including having arrangements to safeguard against them entering into 'punitive' arrangements with clients, and should be prepared to deal directly with individuals at any point. The guidance reminds local authorities that: 'It is perfectly within their gift to call action back from the bailiffs at any time and where there is a case to do so they should consider such action.'

Complaints against bailiffs should be investigated properly and not just referred back to the bailiff. The guidance reminds local authorities that bailiffs are working on their behalf and they remain responsible for the bailiffs' actions.

You should know what rules (if any) the local authority uses. If an action by bailiffs breaches these, contact the local authority immediately so that its order to the bailiffs can be withdrawn. The guidance recommends the use of dedicated contacts accessible on direct lines and by electronic means so that issues can be taken up quickly.

Even if there is no clear policy, contact the local authority and ask it to consider withdrawing the warrant from the bailiffs or, if that is not possible, instructing the bailiffs to accept a lower payment offer. Bailiffs themselves may occasionally agree to delay action, but this is unlikely. There may be no need for the client to let the bailiffs into her/his home. See p420 for the rules about bailiffs' powers to enter property.

In the absence of the warrant being withdrawn, arguably, paying the debt direct to the local authority but not including payment of the bailiff's fees does not prevent the bailiff attempting to recover their fees (although if the warrant is withdrawn, it appears the bailiffs would have to look to the local authority for payment).[28]

As noted above, in appropriate cases, the local authority could be asked to write off council tax arrears.

Preventing the local authority taking bankruptcy proceedings

Many local authorities now use bankruptcy proceedings to recover council tax arrears from homeowners where the total outstanding balance due under the liability order or orders is £5,000 or more. There is no government guidance on this. However, local authorities should bear in mind the principles of proportionality and reasonableness in deciding whether to use bankruptcy proceedings, particularly the client's potential liability for substantial costs.[29] A charging order is likely to be a more proportionate recovery method, given the sums involved, and should not be rejected purely on the basis that the court might not order a sale in the event of payment not being forthcoming.

Consider making a complaint to the Local Government and Social Care Ombudsman in order to challenge a local authority's decision to resort to bankruptcy proceedings. The Local Government and Social Care Ombudsman has made the following points.[30]

- Bankruptcy should only be used as a last resort and local authorities should have a policy to this effect.
- Local authorities should record their reasons for not pursuing alternative collection methods.
- Local authorities should send letters containing clear and detailed warnings of the potential consequences of bankruptcy for the client in terms of not only the costs of the petition itself and possible loss of the home but also the far greater costs that would be incurred if a bankruptcy order were made.

- The policy should also deal with charging orders and require them to be considered as an alternative to bankruptcy. Charging orders should not be rejected on the grounds that they do not provide a practical recovery method.
- Local authorities must act proportionately and take into account the client's personal circumstances.
- Local authorities must proactively make enquiries about vulnerability.

The Ombudsman is likely to find maladministration if a local authority:[31]
- does not have a formal published debt recovery policy;
- has not gathered and considered information about the client's circumstances;
- does not include in its debt recovery policy the steps it must take before deciding on bankruptcy, committal or charging orders;
- pursues bankruptcy without clearly recording that each of these steps has been taken.

Local authorities must also take account of their duties under the Equality Act 2010, particularly if the client may have mental health issues.

You should therefore obtain the local authority's collection policy to ensure it complies with the Ombudsman's recommendations and point out any shortcomings. Use the recommendations to challenge any inappropriate use of bankruptcy proceedings by local authorities.[32]

Note: while complaining to the Local Government and Social Care Ombudsman (or the Public Services Ombudsman for Wales) is a cheap remedy, it is an after-the-event remedy and is not quick. Because of restrictions on its jurisdiction, the Ombudsman can only investigate a local authority's actions up to the issue of proceedings, although the Ombudsman retains the right to investigate in cases in which the client has unsuccessfully applied to annul a bankruptcy order.[33] Outcomes of complaints about local authority council tax collection can be viewed at lgo.org.uk/decisions. If the client is eligible for public funding and the bankruptcy petition has not yet been issued, an application for judicial review could be considered.[34] See cpag.org.uk/welfare-rights/judicial-review for help with the judicial review process.

Bear in mind that, before the local authority can take bankruptcy proceedings, it must have a liability order for the amount in question and be able to prove the existence of that liability order to the satisfaction of the court. The local authority's own computer records are not sufficient for this purpose; it must either be able to produce a sealed copy of the liability order or a statement from the magistrates' court that an order was made.[35] However, unless there was evidence that the local authority's records were incorrect, the Ombudsman would probably accept (on the balance of probability) a local authority's computer evidence that a liability order was made.

Get specialist advice if a client has received either a statutory demand or a petition from the local authority, or if a bankruptcy order has been made on the local authority's petition.

Preventing goods being taken control of by county court bailiffs

If a creditor has instructed the court to issue a warrant of control for an unpaid county court judgment, the client can make a combined application to the county court to suspend the bailiff action and to vary the judgment. This is done on Form N245. See p343 for details of how to do this and Chapter 14 for details of county court bailiffs' powers.

If the bailiff is threatening to take control of goods subject to a hire purchase or conditional sale agreement or bill of sale, specialist advice should be obtained.

Preventing goods being taken control of by High Court enforcement officers

High Court enforcement officers now enforce High Court judgments (including county court judgments transferred to the High Court for enforcement). They are private bailiffs authorised by the court to enforce debts in the High Court. See Chapter 14 for details of the powers of High Court enforcement officers.

If an enforcement officer is threatening to take control of goods, specialist advice should be obtained.

Preventing goods being taken control of by tax bailiffs

Officials from HM Revenue and Customs have the powers of bailiffs to take and sell goods to pay unpaid tax debts.[36] If they are unable to gain access to a property, they can apply for an order to force entry. Normally, a private bailiff accompanies the collector on such visits.

It is possible to negotiate with the collector directly and either suggest a repayment arrangement or submit a late return if the client does not agree with the amount of the debt and it is outside the normal time limit for appealing (see Chapter 16). If the client has no goods, the collector is likely to seek an alternative means of enforcement, such as court action or bankruptcy.

Preventing imprisonment

Magistrates' courts have the power to imprison people who refuse to pay financial penalties, maintenance, council tax or non-domestic rates. **Note:** debtors can no longer be imprisoned in Wales for arrears of council tax and non-domestic rates. See Chapter 13 for the circumstances in which they can use this power and the arguments to use against them.

Warrant with bail

When a client has failed to attend a court hearing, or sometimes just failed to keep up the payments, a warrant can be issued for her/his arrest by magistrates. In most cases, this is a warrant with bail which requires the client to surrender her/himself and be given a time and date for a court hearing.

Warrant without bail

Occasionally (usually where previous warrants have been ignored), a warrant without bail is issued. This requests the police or specially licensed bailiffs to arrest the client and hold her/him in custody until a court hearing can be arranged (within 24 hours).

If a warrant without bail has been issued, the client should report to the court at a time, depending on local circumstances, when it is likely not to be busy so that s/he will not be held in the cells for too long. This may be after lunch, if the court sits then, or first thing in the morning before other prisoners have been brought from police stations. Some courts demand that people surrender themselves to the police station rather than the courts, but there is no legal foundation for this and you should ensure that police and other court staff accept a client's surrender in court buildings.

Committal hearing

Most magistrates' courts do not imprison people until they have been given a number of opportunities to pay by instalments. Whenever someone is brought before court after the issue of an arrest warrant, s/he should be represented, if possible. S/he cannot lawfully be imprisoned if legal representation has not been made available to her/him. If a solicitor (perhaps from the duty solicitor scheme) is to provide representation, an advice agency should brief her/him first and provide a full financial statement, as it is common for unrealistic offers to be made by solicitors, which then cause the client to be brought back before the court and treated with even less sympathy because s/he has broken a previous undertaking to pay. In some courts, probation officers can obtain adjournments so that they can produce a statement of the client's means for the court. For further information about committal hearings, see p405.

After imprisonment

If magistrates have imprisoned someone for debt, it is possible that they have done so improperly, in which case an application for judicial review should be made immediately. An application for bail pending a hearing can also be made (to a High Court judge in London). The application must be made by a solicitor or barrister specialising in this field. The most likely improprieties are procedural irregularities (eg, if the court failed to consider the question of wilfulness, culpability or alternatives to imprisonment) or unreasonableness (eg, if the court expected someone on income support to pay £20 a week towards a fine), natural justice (eg, if legal representation was denied to the client) or acting *ultra vires* – eg, if the resolution setting council tax was not signed by the appropriately authorised officer of the council.

Notes

1. Deciding on priorities

1 See P Kyle, 'A simple plan', *Adviser* 185
2 See 'Q&A', *Quarterly Account* 54, IMA, pp26-27

2. The general approach to priority debts

3 *FCA Handbook*, CONC 7.3.11R and 7.3.12G
4 See P Madge, 'Till Debt Do Us Part', *Adviser* 71
5 *Cheltenham and Gloucester v Norgan* [1996] 1 All ER 449 (*Adviser* 53 abstracts)

3. Strategies for dealing with priority debts

6 In *Green v Southern Pacific Mortgages Ltd* [2018] EWCA Civ 854 (*Adviser* 186 abstracts) the court held that the lender was not required by the Equality Act 2010 to offer an interest-only mortgage to a disabled borrower as a 'reasonable adjustment'.
7 s8(2) AJA 1973
8 s36 AJA 1970
9 *Cheltenham and Gloucester v Norgan* [1996] 1 All ER 449 (*Adviser* 53 abstracts)
10 *FCA Handbook*, MCOB 13.3.2A (1) and (3)
11 s91 LPA 1925. See *Crowther v Arbuthnot Latham & Co Ltd* [2018] EWHC 504 (Comm) (*Adviser* 186 abstracts)
12 National Homelessness Advice Service, *How to exit homeownership through a voluntary or assisted voluntary sale (VAS)*, April 2018
13 *Palk v Mortgage Services Funding*, 31 July 1992 (*Adviser* 34 abstracts)
14 s129 CCA 1974 and see R Rosenberg, 'Calling Time on Time Orders', *Quarterly Account* 40, IMA; R Rosenberg, 'Mortgages and Time Orders', *Quarterly Account* 50, IMA
15 *Director General of Fair Trading v First National Bank* [2001] UKHL 52 (*Adviser* 89 abstracts)
16 See T Lett, 'Time Orders, Secure CCA Agreements and Repossessions', *Adviser* 166
17 For a further discussion, see J Wilson, 'Consultancy Corner', *Adviser* 95

18 Reg 60 and Schs 6 and 7 UC,PIP,JSA&ESA(C&P) Regs
19 Reg 35 and Sch 9 SS(C&P) Regs
20 Sch 6 para 3 UC,PIP,JSA&ESA(C&P) Regs
21 Sch 6 para 5 UC,PIP,JSA&ESA(C&P) Regs
22 Sch 6 para 3 UC,PIP,JSA&ESA(C&P) Regs
23 Note, however, that child support payments under the 2012 system are always payable, regardless of what other deductions are being made.
24 Condition 27.6 Standard Conditions of Electricity Supply Licence, OFGEM; condition 27.6 Standard Conditions of Gas Supply Licence, OFGEM
25 See A Murdie, 'Discretionary Reductions in Council Tax Cases', *Adviser* 170; in *W v Coventry CC*, the Valuation Tribunal for England allowed an appeal against the council's refusal of discretionary relief where Ms W's outgoings exceeded her income, no items of expenditure appeared 'frivolous' and it was satisfied Ms W was trying hard to address her financial situation (VTE Appeal No.4610M240354/283C) and the Vice President allowed an appeal against Folkestone and Hythe DC's refusal of discretionary relief holding that the appellant's PIP should be disregarded as income when assessing his financial hardship (VTE Appeal No.2250M213194/084C).

4. Emergency action

26 Sch 6 EA 1989; Sch 2B GA 1986
27 See B Fisher, 'Eviction Appeal Panels' and D Durden, 'A Landlord's Perspective', *Adviser* 114
28 This seems to be the effect of reg 17(1) and (2) TCG(F) Regs

29 See *Lock v Aylesbury Vale DC* [2018] EWHC 2015 (Ch) (*Adviser* 187 abstracts) in which the High Court held that, where a petition was based on unpaid council tax, there was burden on the council to show that making a bankruptcy order would achieve some useful purpose (Ms L did not work, did not own her home and did not receive any benefits).
30 Complaint against Wolverhampton City Council, 06/B/16600 (*Adviser* 128 money advice abstracts). See also Complaint against Camden London Borough Council, 07/A/12661 (*Adviser* 129 money advice abstracts), where the revenue department's failure to make internal enquiries resulted in bankruptcy proceedings against a vulnerable person. The Ombudsman said: 'The dire and punitive consequences of bankruptcy, involving a multiplication of the original debt many times over and frequently incurring the loss of the debtor's home, must be a factor to be taken into account in deciding that the "last resort" is indeed appropriate.'
31 Local Government and Social Care Ombudsman, *Can't Pay? Won't Pay? Using bankruptcy for council tax debts*, October 2011, available at lgo.org.uk/make-a-complaint/fact-sheets/benefits-and-tax/bankruptcy
32 The Local Government and Social Care Ombudsman has also issued a factsheet, available at lgo.org.uk/make-a-complaint/fact-sheets/benefits-and-tax/bankruptcy. See also A Hobley, 'Using Bankruptcy for Council Tax Debts', *Adviser* 150
33 Complaint against Newham London Borough Council, 08019113 (*Adviser* 137 abstracts)
34 See R Barnwell, 'Local Government Ombudsman and Complaints About Bankruptcy', *Adviser* 131; R Low-Beer, 'Council Tax Arrears and Bankruptcy', *Quarterly Account* 12, IMA
35 *Smolen v Tower Hamlets London Borough Council* [2006] All ER(D) 48 (*Adviser* 126 money advice abstracts)
36 s127 Finance Act 2008

Chapter 9

. . . .

Dealing with non-priority debts

This chapter covers:
1. Choosing a strategy (below)
2. The general approach to non-priority debts (p253)
3. Strategies for dealing with non-priority debts (p255)
4. Court-based strategies (p275)
5. Future schemes (p276)

---

1. **Choosing a strategy**

The majority of a client's debts are likely to be non-priority ones. They may vary from an unpaid bill of a few pounds to a loan of several thousand pounds. Non-priority debts do not usually include any of the debts listed in Chapter 8.[1] For most non-priority creditors, the remedy for non-payment is to take county court proceedings against the client and enforce the judgment through the courts if payment is not made in accordance with the court order (see Chapter 11).

When giving advice to a client on non-priority debts, take account of:
- the nature of the debt;
- the client's financial position;
- the powers of the creditor; *and*
- whether interest or charges on the debt have been frozen or reduced.

Once a sufficiently full assessment of the client's financial situation has been carried out, all options that are available to her/him, given her/his individual circumstances, must be discussed with her/him.[2] These include:
- the advantages/disadvantages;
- any eligibility criteria;
- the debts covered; *and*
- any costs and risks associated with each option.

Where the clients are members of a couple, a strategy which is suitable for one member of the couple may not be suitable for the other, requiring different strategies to be considered. The client must agree to the strategy chosen. It is not usually an appropriate option for the client to do nothing, although there are some occasions when doing nothing is in the client's best interests. For example, if a debt is about to become 'statute-barred' (ie, unenforceable because of its age), it is not in the client's best interests to acknowledge the debt by sending a holding letter to the creditor and so start time running again (see p265). Doing nothing, however, usually leaves the client uncertain as to the status of the debt.

Occasionally, a client will have not only a large amount of non-priority debt but also a high disposable income. It is not usually in her/his best interests to put such a client through the debt advice process discussed in this *Handbook*.[3] S/he may just need to be provided with some financial capability guidance on budgeting to reduce her/his monthly outgoings. It is probably not in any client's best interests for an adviser to contact creditors (except when dealing with an emergency), even by sending holding letters, until the extent of the debt problem has been investigated, as some creditors may react inappropriately – eg, by terminating facilities and registering defaults with credit reference agencies.

A number of criteria are important when deciding which strategy is the most appropriate for dealing with each of these debts.

Availability of income

Once a financial statement (see p55) has been produced, you will know whether there is any income left over for non-priority debts after payments have been arranged with priority creditors and all other essential items of expenditure have been taken into account. You should ask for explanations not only where expenditure is particulalry high but also where expenditure is particularly low. In many cases, there is not enough income, even after it has been maximised, to meet essential expenditure, but in others a significant amount may be available. Investigate examples of unusually high levels of surplus income (which may indicate that items of essential expenditure have been underestimated or possibly omitted altogether) as well as deficit budgets (which may be due to low household income or deductions from income to pay debts, but could also indicate that income has been underestimated or possibly omitted altogether).

Insurance

In the case of credit debts, check whether the client has payment protection insurance to cover the repayments in the event of sickness or incapacity, unemployment, accident or death. If the client has payment protection insurance (PPI) and her/his situation is covered by the policy, advise her/him to make a claim.

If the claim is refused, consider whether this can be challenged and a complaint made which could potentially be escalated to the Financial Ombudsman Service. If the agreement is a regulated credit agreement and the client says that taking out

PPI was a condition of being granted the credit, the agreement may be unenforceable if it was made before 6 April 2007 (see p71).

Availability of capital

It should have been established at the initial interview whether a client has any significant capital or savings available. These can include:

- bonds, savings certificates and shares;
- money put aside for specific items – eg, a holiday;
- capital that will become available in the near future – eg, a tax-free payment from a pension provider, expected redundancy pay and proceeds from the sale of a property or business;
- legacies under a relative's will.

Realisable assets

A client may have assets which are reasonable to realise. These are valuable items that could be sold to raise money – eg, antiques or works of art, cars and life assurance policies with an appreciable surrender value. Such a list should only include items of a non-essential nature. For example, a recently acquired and fairly new car that is only used for weekend trips may be a realisable asset, while one that is necessary for work is not. However, creditors must not pressurise clients to raise funds to repay the debt by selling assets (or by borrowing or increasing their existing borrowing).[4]

The client must be adequately advised about her/his options before coming to a decision about disposing of her/his assets – eg, to ensure that a car is not subject to a bill of sale or a hire purchase or conditional sale agreement, or that sale or surrender of an insurance policy is in the client's best interests. The client should be advised to obtain independent financial advice where appropriate.

Equity in the home

The equity in a person's home is the total value of the property less the amount required to pay any loans or debts secured against it, including any 'charges' (such as a mortgage, secured loan or charging order) and the costs of a sale. For example, to calculate the equity on a property on sale for £145,000:

Deduct solicitor's fee on sale	£2,000
Deduct estate agent's fee	£1,400
Deduct first mortgage (building society)	£115,000
Deduct second mortgage (after early settlement discount)	£15,000
Total deductions	£133,400
Total equity = £145,000 – £133,400 = £11,600	

If the property is jointly owned, the equity is shared in proportion to the amount each person owns (usually equally).

In many cases, there may be no equity in the property and the amount owed may exceed the value of the property, particularly if the client has defaulted on a high-interest, non-status secured loan – ie, a loan with high interest because the client has an impaired credit rating. In other cases, however, it is likely that the equity position will be favourable, particularly if the property has no outstanding mortgage.

It is important to establish whether or not there is equity at an early stage, since many creditors now seek to secure their debts (eg, by obtaining a charging order – see p322), while others seek preferential status by resorting to threats of bankruptcy (see p464). For this reason, you should stress to clients the urgency of dealing with any court papers. Although enquiries from creditors about equity do not necessarily mean that a client should sell her/his property, s/he should bear in mind that, unless the circumstances are exceptional, creditors are unlikely to agree to, for example, writing off a debt (see p256) if there are realisable assets or equity in the home. A creditor may accept, for example, a token payment (see p266) on the basis that the amount due will be repaid from the sale of the asset/property in due course.

Change of circumstances

It is important to know whether the client's current circumstances are likely to change. For example, if a client's income was until very recently quite high, but has now been reduced by a period of illness that is not expected to last very long, this must be taken into account. Similarly, if someone is about to retire or begin a new job with higher wages, these factors are vital to the strategy selected.

The amount owed

The choice of strategy is affected by the amount owing. Some strategies cost money to set up (eg, a voluntary charge – see p229) and are too expensive for a small debt. In addition, large companies often have policies to write off small amounts owed if they are not paid after a final warning. Very large debts may also be written off in appropriate cases. Do not assume that very large debts 'simply must be paid'; creditors do write off sums of several thousand pounds.

It is sometimes obvious, particularly where a small debt is concerned, that a large company has already written off an amount owed because it has not communicated with the client for several years and the client has not been contacted by a collection agent acting on behalf of the creditor. In such circumstances, it is probably best to take no action and assume that the creditor has decided not to pursue the debt. However, there has been a tendency for some creditors to sell on debts where there has been no contact for many years. This practice is in breach of the Financial Conduct Authority's *Consumer Credit Sourcebook*.[5]

Note: if there has been no contact for more than six years, the debt may be unenforceable (see p291).

Type of debt

Some debts, although not priority debts (see Chapter 8), do not fit into the usual debt advice process and so cannot be treated as straightforward non-priority debts (see p253). Separate strategies may need to be made for such debts.

Repayment period

In the case of instalment arrangements, you should always take into account the length of the repayment period – the shorter the repayment period, the more likely it is that the strategy will have a successful outcome.[6] The longer the repayment period, the more likely the client's circumstances are to change (and possibly deteriorate) and the more disheartened the client is likely to become. Although the *Consumer Credit Sourcebook* says that creditors should allow clients in financial difficulties reasonable time and opportunity to repay the debt,[7] consider whether it is in the client's best interests to propose open-ended repayment arrangements or whether to request that there should be a time limit on the repayment period.[8]

Enforcement issues

If a debt is legally unenforceable, the client is in a strong negotiating position, as s/he can decide whether or not to repay the debt, and, if so, on what terms. This may make income available for payment of other debts. On the other hand, if the creditor is in a position to take enforcement action, or has already done so, the client could be at risk of losing her/his home or essential goods. For example, a creditor may have obtained a charging order on the client's home which has substantial equity, but the client has little available income with which to make a reasonable offer. This debt may have to be treated as a priority debt as the creditor could apply for an order for sale in these circumstances (see p327).

Even if a debt is legally enforceable, it may be possible to persuade the creditor to write off some or all of it. Point out:

- any mis-selling of any part of a loan, such as payment protection insurance; *or*
- failure by a lender to assess the client's ability to repay; *or*
- 'churning' of loans (see p272).

2. **The general approach to non-priority debts**

If the suggested strategy is to be accepted by creditors, it is important that it is based on a consistent set of criteria, and that all creditors are treated alike. Treating all creditors alike does not mean that a particular creditor should not be challenged if, for instance, the debt is unenforceable, or the creditor is adopting unacceptable lending or debt collection practices. The credit industry is competitive and individuals within it are likely to reject any strategy that appears to favour another creditor. The strength of your negotiating position lies in your ability to present a strategy that is empirically based and business like. All offers to creditors must therefore be made on the same basis, using the same criteria when making choices with regard to their debts.

Where appropriate, creditors may need reminding of their obligations under the relevant industry code of practice (eg, to treat cases of financial difficulty sympathetically and positively) and under the Financial Conduct Authority's (FCA's) *Consumer Credit Sourcebook* – eg, not to pressurise clients to make payments they cannot afford, to sell property or to increase their borrowing. Also, creditors should treat clients in default or arrears fairly and with forbearance and due consideration (such as considering freezing interest or charges, deferring payment of arrears or accepting token payments for a reasonable period), and should not unreasonably require that all arrears are paid in one payment, or in unduly large amounts, and/or within an unreasonable period.[9]

When debts may need to be treated differently

If a debt which is strictly a non-priority debt has a special importance to the client, there may need to be an exception to the general principle. **Note:** if there is any possibility of the client becoming bankrupt or applying for a debt relief order in the foreseeable future, you should advise her/him about the implications of preferring such debts (see p496). Debts that *may* need to be treated differently include the following.

- **Debts created by a loan from a family or community member, or an employer.** These may, on strict legal criteria, be no different from money owed to a finance company. However, if failure to repay this debt will lead to serious financial or personal problems elsewhere in the family (eg, if a loan has been taken out to consolidate the client's non-priority debts which is secured on a family member's home) or at work (eg, dismissal), it may be necessary to give it priority over other non-priority debts. Details need to be included in the client's financial statement as expenditure and other creditors must be told of the position. However, if the client subsequently chooses an insolvency option, such as bankruptcy, there could be repercussions as such payments are likely to be regarded as 'preferences' (see p496).

- **Unsecured debts that have been guaranteed** (see p145). These may need to be given priority in order to protect the guarantor, particularly if s/he is a family member. The payments need to be dealt with in the same way as above and are subject to the same potential repercussions.
- **Debts to mail order catalogues.** These may be essential to someone on a low income as a way of budgeting for essentials such as household items and clothing, provided a low balance is maintained.
- **Bill paying services** (also known as budgeting accounts), perhaps through a credit union or a commercial lender. The client makes monthly payments to the credit union or lender, who in turn pays various agreed household bills on the client's behalf. These bills are likely to be for essential expenditure in terms of including them on the client's financial statement and, if they fall into arrears, will then be priority debts. It may, therefore, be in everyone's best interests to maintain these payments if this means there is more money available for other non-priority creditors.
- **A debt incurred through the fraud** of the client or her/his partner or a relative, where s/he could face prosecution if the debt is not paid.
- **Debts that do not fit into the usual debt advice process.** These are known as 'square peg' debts because they do not fit neatly into the priority/non-priority categories and include credit union loans (see p39), mortgage shortfalls (see p116) and traffic penalties (see p134).[10]
- **Debts to 'loan sharks'.** This expression tends to refer to illegal moneylenders who make loans at extortionate rates and enforce payment through violence or threats of violence. Once involved with a loan shark, people often find themselves permanently in debt, with late payment resulting in substantial penalties being added to the debt. As well as not being authorised by the FCA (see p61), loan sharks are often involved in other criminality and sometimes coerce their victims into committing criminal offences as a way of repaying their debts.

  Clients rarely admit to being indebted to a loan shark and often use money intended for essential expenditure in order to make their repayments. They may even claim that money is being used to repay a 'family friend'.

  If you discover that a client is a loan shark victim, it is likely the client will be reluctant to report the matter, fearing for her/his own safety or that of her/his family. As ever, the decision about the next step is the client's but it should be an informed one. You could refer the client to the Illegal Money Lending Team (tel: 0300 555 2222 in England or 0300 123 3311 in Wales). These can offer the client support and arrange to meet her/him at a safe venue (in your presence, if necessary) to discuss what remedies are available, what action can be taken and the protection that can be provided.[11]

Debt management plans

A debt management plan is an informal arrangement, under which the client agrees to repay her/his creditors. The term is usually used to describe an arrangement made on the client's behalf by a third party who also manages the plan. The arrangement normally involves an equitable distribution of the client's available income after priority payments have been made (see p268). The client makes a single regular payment (usually monthly) to the third party, who may be:

- a debt management company, which negotiates the debt management plan, collects the payments from the client and distributes them to the creditors in return for a fee paid by the client (often referred to as 'fee chargers'); *or*
- StepChange or PayPlan, both of which can arrange a debt management plan and distribute the payments to the client's creditors, but do not charge the client a fee. They are paid by the creditors through deducting a percentage of the money recovered (known as 'fair-share' arrangements). For this reason, they are part of the free money advice sector. Both have minimum criteria for setting up a plan (eg, relating to the amount of available income) and can also help clients set up individual voluntary arrangements (see p453).

If a client's agreed strategy is to make pro rata payments to her/his creditors (see p268), a debt management plan under which s/he only has to make one monthly payment, instead of a number of individual payments, may be in the client's best interests.

Note: some debt management companies do not deal with emergencies and/or priority debts. You must therefore assist the client to deal with these before s/he can be referred for a debt management plan.

The *Consumer Credit Sourcebook* requires debt management companies to signpost clients to the Money and Pensions Service's website for information about free-to-client debt advice services and to refer clients to a provider of free-to-client debt advice if the client has issues requiring urgent attention which the debt management company is either unable or unwilling to deal with.[12]

Debt management companies fall within the Financial Ombudsman Service's jurisdiction. If a client is dissatisfied with the service provided, s/he should consider making a complaint.

3. **Strategies for dealing with non-priority debts**

This section describes the available strategies for non-priority debts. They are not mutually exclusive – you may use several strategies to deal with each debt – eg, a moratorium of three months and freezing interest or charges, followed by an arrangement to make payments by equitable distribution. Alternatively, different strategies (or combinations of strategies) may be needed for individual debts – eg, some requests for write-offs, some token payments or a voluntary charge in return for a freeze of interest/charges and no payments.

Selecting a strategy is often not a single process, but may be done initially and reviewed later. The criteria described here should be equally applicable to initial or review strategies. The strategy chosen for each debt needs to be reviewed:
- if a creditor refuses to accept a particular strategy; *or*
- at the end of the time agreed by the creditor – eg, if the creditor agrees to accept no payments for six months and then to review the situation; *or*
- if the client's financial circumstances change.

Often strategies are not accepted on first application (eg, write-offs – see below) and you should always urge creditors several times to accept a realistic strategy. Second and third letters can be strengthened by details of how other creditors have come to agree to a particular strategy. If you consider a creditor is not complying with its obligations under a relevant code of practice or the Financial Conduct Authority's (FCA's) *Consumer Credit Sourcebook* (eg, it is not treating the client's individual and particular financial situation 'fairly and with forbearance and due consideration'), consider using the creditor's complaints procedure and threaten to refer the case to the Financial Ombudsman Service to resolve the matter in a fair and reasonable way.

Clients should not routinely be advised to stop payments to all their non-priority creditors while negotiations are taking place. However, in many multiple debt cases, it is appropriate for the client to reduce payments to non-priority creditors or even stop them altogether – eg, if the client does not have sufficent available income. If the client is able to make payments to non-priority creditors while still servicing her/his essential commitments, including priority debts, s/he should be advised to do so. If not, point out that the client's default will be registered with credit reference agencies and may eventually lead to court action by the creditor, but that it is still in the client's best interests not to make these payments because there is no, or very little, available income after meeting her/his essential expenditure and payments to priority creditors.

A long period without any payments at all to creditors is undesirable, unless a strategy involving non-payment has been proposed in the meantime. On the other hand, a short period during which no payments are made may be inevitable while you work out a strategy with the client.[13]

Request a write-off

A write-off should be considered if:
- there is no available income or capital and a client's circumstances are unlikely to improve in the foreseeable future (or may even worsen); *or*
- the debt is uneconomical for the creditor to collect – eg, a small amount is owed or the pro rata payment would be less than £1 a month; *or*

- there is some available income, but this will not repay the debt within a reasonable time (see also partial write-offs on p259); *or*
- the client's circumstances are exceptional and unlikely to improve – eg, s/he has a terminal illness or mental health problems that affect her/his capacity to make a contract (see p153).

A write-off means the creditor agrees not to collect any further payments and removes the account from its records. The client makes no further payments. If the debt is large, any realisable assets or equity in the client's home must be considered, as it is unlikely that creditors will agree to write off the debts of 'asset-rich, income-poor' clients unless the circumstances are exceptional. It is likely that, if the creditor took court action and the client could not make payment as ordered by the court, the creditor could either apply for a charging order against the equity in the client's home (see p322) or ask the court to make a bankruptcy order (see p470) so that goods owned by the client, or the home, could be sold.

All creditors recognise the need to write off some debts, and they make provision for this in their accounts and the interest rates they set. You may have personal anxieties about requesting a write-off, but these should not be allowed to prejudice your advice. Clients, too, may be anxious about the consequences of this strategy, so you may need to explain the reasoning behind the suggestion, and that it is being proposed to the creditor as the most economic and realistic solution available in order to financially rehabilitate the client. However, the decision whether or not to request a write-off is ultimately one for the client. A client who initially says s/he wants to pay something may change her/his mind in the light of creditors' responses to her/his financial difficulties and the realisation that her/his financial difficulties are not being resolved. The possibility of proposing this strategy to creditors should be kept under review.

Advantages
- It removes the financial and emotional stress caused by that debt.
- It enables the client to make a fresh start.
- It acknowledges that further action against the client is not appropriate.

Disadvantages
- Creditors do not agree easily to write off debts, particularly if the debt has been incurred recently.
- When creditors write off debts, they often report this to a credit reference agency. This is an agency that collects evidence, such as county court judgments or evictions, and sells details of individuals who have experienced these to creditors. If a debt is reported as written off, it may be difficult for a client to get credit in the future. For more details on credit reference agencies, see p9.

- Many creditors never formally agree to write off a debt, even when they have received a request to do so. They take no further action on it and, at some point, will write it out of their accounts. This can mean that the client is left uncertain as to whether or not the creditor has agreed to her/his request, and s/he can be vulnerable either to a change of company policy or to pursuit of a debt if her/his circumstances improve.

Useful arguments

- Outline the client's circumstances and explain that s/he has no property or goods of significant value, no income except benefits or low wages and there is no prospect of improvement in the foreseeable future. This helps creditors to see that court action is unlikely to be successful. Explain that if bankruptcy were pursued, the outcome would be the same. Medical evidence confirming, for example, the nature of any disability or that the client is unable to work may also be persuasive.
- Use the Money Advice Liaison Group's debt and mental health evidence form or other available evidence, where appropriate, to support the request (see p35).
- Inform the creditor of the total amount of debt owing to all creditors to show the hopelessness of the client's situation.
- Most creditors have a set of criteria for deciding when to abandon debt recovery, which is determined by the cost of recovering the money. Suggest that writing off a debt is likely to be the most economic solution for the creditor. For example, *The Standards of Lending Practice,* subscribed to by banks, building societies and credit card providers (see p33), suggests that creditors should take account of the client's circumstances and consider whether it would amount to a fair customer outcome to pursue or continue to pursue the debt.[14] The creditor must give reasons for refusing a request for a write-off and you should press for these to be provided, as this may help you to ask the creditor to reconsider its position.
- Creditors may be more willing to write off a debt after repeatedly withholding action on the account for three or six months (see p265).
- It is easier to get smaller debts written off.

Checklist for action

- Write to the creditor(s) proposing the strategy, enclosing any supporting evidence, and request written confirmation that the strategy is agreed.
- Advise the client to stop paying.
- A creditor may not initially accept a write-off. Ask the creditor to reconsider after, say, three to six months, and repeat the request at subsequent reviews.

Request a partial write-off

If there is some money available to meet a creditor's demands, but this will not pay off the whole debt in a realistic period of time (in line with what a court would consider reasonable), creditors can be asked to reduce the balance owing immediately or to accept agreed instalments for a set period of years, after which the balance will be written off.

Partial write-off should be seen as a means of coming to an arrangement similar to an individual voluntary arrangement and which is broadly the same as what a court would order if an income payments order in a bankruptcy application were being considered. A period of at least three to five years, but no more than seven to 10 years, should be suggested. You should also request that further interest be stopped (see p260). Partial write-off is appropriate if:

- there are no realisable assets or substantial equity that could be charged;
- the client's circumstances are such that s/he cannot repay the whole debt within a reasonable period of time;
- there is no expectation of capital or extra income becoming available soon.

Advantages

- It reduces the amount owed and gives the client a realistic target to aim for and, therefore, a framework in which s/he can regain control over her/his financial affairs.
- The client repays less money.

Disadvantages

- When creditors write off debts, they often report this to credit reference agencies and it may, therefore, be difficult for the client to get credit in the future.
- It may be difficult to get all creditors to agree to the strategy.

Useful arguments

- It can be argued that the creditor will receive more than if the client were made bankrupt, and so it is quicker, cheaper and less stressful for the client if the creditor limits its demands to that amount now.
- A partial write-off is also very similar to a composition order in an administration order (see p447) or an individual voluntary arrangement (see p453) and so creditors are only being asked to take a similar course of action to that taken in those legally binding situations, but on an informal basis. As there are no court or supervisor costs, the creditor is likely to get a higher return than in an administration order or individual voluntary arrangement.
- The creditor may be persuaded that it is better to go for something shorter term and realisable, rather than longer term but potentially expensive to collect and unlikely to be paid. Unless creditors reduce their demand to something the client can pay in the foreseeable future, the client is likely to lack the

motivation to keep up with payments. It is unrealistic for both sides to set up repayment schemes that will last more than about seven to 10 years and it is likely that such money will eventually be written off.

- If the creditor refuses to agree to this strategy initially, it is worth requesting it again after, say, 12 months of regular payments if there is still no improvement in the client's circumstances.

Checklist for action

- Agree with the client the amount of income available to creditors.
- Calculate offers and decide a payment period.
- Write to the creditor(s) proposing the strategy, with details of the offers and requesting written confirmation that this is accepted.
- Advise the client to start making payments. Consider direct debits or standing orders if the client has a current account.
- Request that interest or charges are stopped, using the arguments on below.
- Consider whether any steps need to be taken to ensure that the arrangement is legally binding on creditors (see full and final settlements on p261).

Request that interest be frozen or reduced

If a client is unable to pay the contractual payments due under an agreement, adding interest and other charges, especially if s/he is not even repaying any capital due, only increases the total balance and the debt will never be repaid. This fact has long been recognised by county courts, and statutory interest is not charged after judgment on debts which are regulated credit agreements (but see p312 for when interest can be charged after a judgment).

Whenever a repayment schedule of less than the original contractual payments is envisaged, or if no payment can be afforded at present, a request should be made to stop (or freeze) all interest and any other charges accruing on the account. This strategy should always be used in conjunction with another strategy.

The request to stop interest should be made in most cases immediately the client contacts you. However, explain to the creditor why it is considered necessary – eg, the payments the client is likely to be able to afford will not cover the ongoing interest.

The Standards of Lending Practice contains guidance to creditors on reducing or freezing interest and charges,[15] and FCA guidance on treating clients with forbearance gives as an example 'considering suspending, reducing, waiving or cancelling any further interest or charges'. Creditors often complain that advisers automatically request that they freeze interest in all cases. Requests to freeze interest should be appropriate and justified. If a creditor believes the level of the client's repayments warrants it, the creditor may refuse to freeze interest, but may instead agree to reduce it. If the loan is a regulated credit agreement, an application for a time order may be appropriate (see p229).

Advantages

- Realistic repayment schedules can be created under which debts will be repaid in a known time.
- All payments made reduce the debt. The client can see that s/he is repaying her/his debts.

Disadvantages

- Creditors may not accept the strategy, particularly if there is substantial equity in a property or the client has realisable assets which it is reasonable to expect her/him to use to pay her/his debts.
- It is not appropriate for loans where all interest is added at the beginning of the loan and there are no default interest/charges. In these cases, a partial write-off may achieve the desired result.

Useful arguments

- If a county court judgment were awarded, in practice, interest would be stopped for all regulated consumer credit agreements (see p62).
- Excessive default charges (ie, charges which are more than any actual or anticipated loss that the creditor has or may face as a result of the loss) are almost certainly unenforceable either as a penalty in common law or as an unfair contract term, and so the creditor should either reduce them or remove them altogether and should consider doing so retrospectively (see p155).
- It is a necessary incentive to the client because otherwise s/he will not be prepared to lose valuable income in pursuit of a completely hopeless goal.
- Many other creditors are being asked (or have agreed) to stop interest and, therefore, fairness demands that this creditor does too.
- Make any offer of payment conditional on interest stopping.

Checklist for action

- This strategy should always be used with another strategy.
- Write to the creditor and include a request to freeze interest and other charges, together with some justification for the request.
- Request written confirmation that this has been done.
- If the strategy is not successful initially, ask the creditor to reconsider. It may be useful to provide evidence of other creditors' agreements to freeze or reduce interest and other charges.

Offer a reduced capital sum in full and final settlement

If there is available capital or saleable assets, or if the client will have such assets in the near future (eg, because s/he intends to sell a house for reasons unrelated to the debt, or a third party, such as a friend or relative, has a lump sum s/he is willing to give to the creditor), the creditor may accept an offer of an amount less than that which is due as early settlement. This is particularly likely if there is little or no available income and the client's financial position is unlikely to improve or may even worsen. Creditors are likely to recognise that acceptance of a cash lump sum makes commercial sense. When the client's income is low and unlikely to improve, it could be an attractive alternative to waiting to see if her/his income increases over a long period. If there is more than one creditor, lump sums should usually be apportioned between them in proportion to the amount owing to each.

Ask the client if there are essentials s/he needs to purchase, or essential repairs that need to be carried out, before the lump sum is allocated to creditors.

The key to using this strategy successfully is to ensure that the lump-sum payment is not made until the creditor has agreed in writing to accept this in full and final settlement of all the money owed. Ideally, no payments should be made until all creditors have agreed and offers can – initially at least – be made on this basis. However, be prepared to adopt a flexible approach to prevent the whole strategy from failing. For example, creditors who are reluctant to accept may be persuaded by knowing that other creditors have already agreed to accept it. Other creditors may threaten the whole strategy by demanding more than their fair share, leaving insufficient funds to tempt the remaining creditors.

There is no set amount that needs to be offered and, in fact, a promise by a creditor to accept part payment is not a legally binding contract unless the client has provided what the law regards as fresh 'consideration' for the creditor's promise to forgo payment of the balance. The Financial Ombudsman Service, however, may take the view that creditors who go back on their word are not behaving 'fairly and reasonably' unless the client misrepresented her/his true financial situation.

There is a legally binding agreement if:

- an arrangement is made with all the client's unsecured creditors; *or*
- the funds are made available by a third party (eg, a relative) and the offer is made by her/him on the client's behalf; *or*
- the agreement is embodied in a formal document known as a 'deed'. The client needs to be referred to a solicitor if s/he wants a deed drawn up – eg, if there is any doubt about the trustworthiness of a particular creditor.

Advantages

- The client pays less than s/he would if repaying over a longer term.
- The client has the opportunity of a fresh start.
- It is a more immediate and convenient solution than setting up a repayment schedule over a number of years.
- Even if not all creditors accept, the client's total indebtedness is reduced and this may in turn enable another strategy to be adopted to deal with these.

Disadvantages

- The client loses the advantage of having a lump sum which could have been used for other purposes.

- Even though creditors have accepted a payment in full and final settlement, they can record this on the client's credit reference file as 'partial settlement'.
- Once aware of the existence of a lump sum, the creditor may attempt court action to obtain all the money for itself.
- If all available funds are distributed among only some of the client's creditors, the client may subsequently have little room to manoeuvre if put under pressure by other creditors.

Useful arguments

- Contact the creditor before the money is available and suggest that this is the only chance that the client will have of paying a substantial amount and that because the client wants to pay her/his debts, s/he is prepared to hand all (or if there are several debts to be treated in this way, a proportionate share) of the money over to the creditor.
- It is worth pointing out that the creditor is not going to get more by refusing the offer and taking enforcement action, and that acceptance of the offer makes more commercial sense than the client's continuing to make small payments over a long period of time. Such an arrangement may have to be made with senior staff in the creditor organisation and you should ensure you are writing or speaking to senior credit control managers.

Checklist for action

- Write to the creditor(s) with details of the offer and request acceptance in full and final settlement to be confirmed in writing.
- If the money is coming from a third party, it should be made clear that the offer is being made by her/him on behalf of the client.
- Consider specialist legal help to draw up the agreement.
- Once written confirmation is received, advise the client (or third party) to send the payment(s).
- Any covering letter sent with a cheque should explain exactly what it is for and state that it is in 'full and final settlement'. Cashing a cheque sent 'in full and final settlement' does not necessarily preclude the creditor from pursuing the balance (cashing a cheque is strong evidence of acceptance unless it is accompanied by a swift rejection of the offer).
- If money is being made available from the sale of a property, it may be necessary to obtain a solicitor's undertaking that the money will be paid to the creditor once it is sold.
- If fewer than 25 per cent in value of a client's creditors do not agree a full and final settlement, even though the remaining creditors have accepted the offer, the client could consider an individual voluntary arrangement (see p453). However, because of the costs involved, the creditors will receive less money. This could be pointed out and the creditors asked to reconsider their position.

In the unlikely event of a creditor threatening to renege on a full and final settlement if the client has made the payment, specialist advice should be sought.

Offer payment by a capital sum and instalments

When a client has capital or assets together with stable available income, but there are substantial arrears, the threat of further action can often be avoided by paying a single capital sum towards the arrears and then paying instalments towards part or all of the contractual payments. This often needs to be linked to another strategy, particularly freezing interest/charges (see p260) or a partial write-off (see p259). This is different from paying a capital sum in full and final settlement in that the payments will have to continue. It could be the fall-back position if a full and final strategy is rejected because the amount offered is insufficient to be accepted by the client's creditors and there is a reasonable amount of surplus income available.

Advantages
- The creditor is no longer pressing.
- Payments made towards the debt out of available income will be lower than otherwise.

Disadvantages
- The flexibility to use the capital sum elsewhere is lost.

Useful arguments
- If this tactic is being used to prevent imminent court action, you can argue that the creditor will obtain its money more quickly than by going to court, and more money will be available to repay the debt as there will be fewer costs. An agreement such as this must be made in writing.

Checklist for action
- Contact the creditor proposing the strategy and request acceptance in writing.
- Calculate the instalments on a pro rata basis (see p268).
- Once written confirmation is received, advise the client to send payment of the capital sum, followed by regular instalments. It may be helpful for the client to set up a direct debit or standing order for these if possible.
- Ensure that interest is stopped. If not, consider advising the client to withhold instalments until agreement is given to stop interest.
- An individual voluntary arrangment could be considered as an option if most, but not all, of the client's creditors do not accept the strategy (see p453).

Holding tactics (moratorium)

It may sometimes be important to gain time for the client when:
- there is some available income, but this is immediately required to deal with priority debts;
- there is no available income, but shortly there will be;
- available assets are being sold;
- the full situation is not yet known.

There are two types of holding tactic (also known as a 'moratorium').
- **Asking creditors to suspend collection or enforcement action.** Section 3(f) of the *Credit Services Association Code of Practice*, published in July 2017, provides a 30-day 'breathing space' if requested by an advice agency. Sections 7.3.11R and 7.3.12G of the FCA's *Consumer Credit Sourcebook* requires creditors to suspend recovery action for a 'reasonable period' (generally, 30 days) where they have been informed that an adviser is assisting a client to agree a repayment plan.
  It may be useful to request a short delay if you need to check a credit agreement or its enforceability. Some agencies write automatically to all creditors asking them to withhold action for a short period when their advice is first sought (a 'holding' letter). This is not necessary if a strategy can be formulated quickly or if you will be asking the creditor to write off the debt or to accept no payments for three months. It is wasteful of resources to employ this device automatically and can increase the stress faced by the client, as it lengthens the time before agreement with creditors about a long-term strategy is reached, and may lead to creditors routinely refusing requests.
  If a delay is needed because balances are required before a strategy can be implemented, ask the client to contact the creditors to obtain these where possible.
  If a debt is queried or disputed, the creditor (or debt collector) should investigate/provide details (as appropriate) and should cease collection activity in the meantime.[16]
  From 2021, the 'breathing space scheme' will give clients working with a debt advice agency protection from recovery and enforcement action for 60 days (see p276).
- **Asking creditors to accept no payments for a specified period.** If no money is available at present to pay non-priority debts, the creditor should be asked to accept no payments for three or six months and then to review the situation.

This is invariably a temporary strategy and so is subject to review, usually after three or six months. It is always used with another strategy – eg, asking a creditor to withhold for three months and then following this with a request for a write-off. This can be useful if it is known that the creditor is unlikely to accept a write-off immediately. If a request is made to a creditor to withhold any action and accept no payments, the creditor must always be asked, at the same time, to stop interest/charges in order to prevent the debt increasing even further.

The length of time you request no payments depends on:

- any known future changes in the client's financial position which might allow payments to begin;
- the length of time needed to repay priority debts;
- the stress faced by the client and how much breathing space s/he needs.

If the creditor agrees to withhold action and collect no payments for six months, it gives the client a substantial period of relief.

However, as this strategy can never be a permanent solution, it means that a request for a six-month delay prolongs the process of reaching one.

Advantages

- Time can give the adviser the opportunity to gather all the necessary facts and work out the best strategy.
- It removes the immediate pressure from the client, and enables payments to be made for priority debts.
- It gets creditors used to the idea that there are problems, but does not leave them in the dark.
- Almost as a matter of routine, many creditors accept a request from a debt advice agency to withhold action for a short period.

Disadvantages

- It does not actually solve anything. Some creditors refuse to stop interest and so the debt grows while no action is taken.
- It can create extra work for advisers.

Useful arguments

- Explain that considerable debts have arisen and outline the client's circumstances.
- Explain that time is required for professional debt advice.

Checklist for action

- Contact the creditor to explain the situation and request written confirmation that the account is held in abeyance. Enclose a financial statement if requesting that more than a month's payments be withheld.
- Ensure that interest/charges will be stopped.
- Advise the client not to make payments.

Offer token payments

When there is little available income, no assets or capital and the situation is unlikely to change, but it is impossible to get agreement on any other strategy, payment by instalments of a nominal or token nature may be necessary to satisfy the administrative systems of a creditor and may be the only way to prevent it from taking further action.

Clients initially seeking advice often want to make token payments rather than withholding payments or asking creditors to write off their debts, out of fear or ignorance of enforcement action, or because of previous harassment by creditors, or because they want to make some payment, however small, towards their debts. Ensure that clients do not make payments they cannot afford or which are at the expense of making payments towards their essential expenditure and any priority debts. A nominal or token payment is usually £1 a month. Even £5, £20 or more a month is regarded as a token payment by some creditors because, in reality, the debt will never be repaid at that rate.

The strategy need not be used for all creditors and should only be offered as a last resort where the creditor has refused to either write off the debt or accept no payments, or to freeze interest/charges and where court action by the creditor would be undesirable. The creditor must be asked to agree to take no further action and to stop interest in return for token payments being made. Token payments do not resolve the client's debt problems and so it is necessary to review the strategy at a later date to choose a more suitable long-term option.

If a creditor has already taken court action, but there is no available income and the court is unwilling to order no payments, the client should make a token offer to pay by instalments (eg, £1 a month) in order to prevent further enforcement action.

Token payments are essentially a short-term strategy. The FCA's *Consumer Credit Sourcebook* recommends accepting token payments for a reasonable period of time where the client has demonstrated that otherwise s/he would not be able to meet her/his priority debts or other essential living expenses.[17] This guidance reflects not only the difficulty of persuading creditors to accept no payments at all but also the belief of creditors that, firstly, people can always find some money and, secondly, that something will turn up.

All advice must be in the best interests of the client and it is not generally in the client's best interests to make payments at a higher level than s/he can afford or to make any payments at all if the client either has no surplus income or a deficit budget. However, if a creditor does not agree, for example, to a moratorium and/or to freeze interest/charges unless token payments are made, you must consider whether it is nevertheless in the client's best interests to make those payments.

Many clients whose financial circumstances mean that they are only able to afford token payments may be eligible for a debt relief order or should consider bankruptcy as a debt relief option (see Chapter 15).

Advantages

- Paying a token amount may be the only way to obtain a creditor's agreement to take no further action and stop interest/charges.

- The client feels s/he is paying something towards her/his debts and creditors can see the habit of payment being re-established.

Disadvantages
- It uses up income that is not really available.
- It encourages creditors to take an unrealistic view of people's ability to pay.
- It can be expensive for the client as it may cost as much in postage and other charges to make the payment as the payment is worth.
- The debt will never be repaid at this rate and it hangs over the client.
- Creditors can continue to apply pressure on clients to pay more.

Useful arguments
- A request for payments may be made by the creditor after you have made it clear there is no (or only a nominal amount of) available income as shown by the financial statement. Explain that, in fact, the only payment possible is a token payment because the client is cutting back on essential spending, such as food or fuel, in order to make the payment.
- If creditors are threatening court action, draw their attention to any recent low judgment amounts awarded by the county court in similar cases and suggest that even if they go to the trouble of going to court, they will get no more than a nominal amount.

Checklist for action
- Contact the creditor and wait for written confirmation of the strategy.
- Ensure that further action, and interest and other charges, are stopped.
- Advise the client to make payments. Ask for a payment book if this facilitates payments without cost.
- Review at an agreed date with the client.

Equitable distribution of available income (pro rata payments)

If there is available income, a number of debts, and no capital or realisable assets, this income should be distributed among all the non-priority creditors in a fair way. Apportioning the available income fairly is best done by a method known either as 'equitable distribution' or 'pro rata payments', where the amount of each instalment is directly proportionate to the total amount owing to that particular creditor. Clients who are using the CASHflow self-help process (see p19) are likely to be making offers on this basis and so may find the information in this section useful.

Calculate the amount due to each creditor per week or month, based on the following formula:

Amount owed to creditor ÷ total amount owed x total income available for distribution

Example

The client owes money to three creditors:

Creditor A	£1,000
Creditor B	£800
Creditor C	£250
Total amount owing	**£2,050**

(The client's total available income is £12 a month.)

Calculation:

Creditor A	1,000 ÷ 2,050 x 12 = £5.85 a month
Creditor B	800 ÷ 2,050 x 12 = £4.70 a month
Creditor C	250 ÷ 2,050 x 12 = £1.45 a month
Total repayments to creditors	**= £12.00 a month**

(Amounts may be rounded up or down for convenience, but not if this results in payments which the client cannot afford.)

If you do not use the common financial statement (see p56), standard financial statement (see p56) or some other computer-based financial statement that automatically calculates pro rata offers, this sum must be worked out for each creditor. Even if the exact balances are not known, it may be worth calculating a distribution on the basis of good estimates, as the weekly variation will probably be very small and may be acceptable to creditors.

If the calculation means there is a very low payment to a particular creditor (eg, less than £1 per month), you may wish to include in the offer letter a request that, in view of the high collection costs for such a small sum, the creditor should consider writing off the debt (see p256) or at least agreeing to a moratorium (see p265). Any payment arrangement must be sustainable and so, when calculating the amount of available income on offer to creditors, ensure some leeway in the financial statement to cope with unexpected events (eg, short periods of sickness) so that payments can still be maintained.

In the *Consumer Credit Sourcebook,* the FCA points out that clients should not usually be advised to cancel contractual payments to their creditors before a debt repayment plan has been agreed or to make payments that do not cover ongoing interest or other charges unless it is demonstrably in their best interests – eg, if someone has insufficient available income after meeting essential expenditure and/or payments to priority creditors.[18]

Unless the client has sufficient available income to be able to maintain the contractual payments on these debts, as well as servicing her/his other debts, it is in her/his best interests to offer pro rata payments, provided this is accompanied by a request for any ongoing interest and any charges to be stopped so that each payment made by the client actually reduces the debt. On the other hand, if the creditor refuses to stop interest or reduce it sufficiently, pro rata payments are almost certainly not in the client's best interests and the creditor must be urged to reconsider, or the strategy reviewed with the client.

It is usual to send to each creditor details of the amounts owed to all creditors, together with the offers made. This should not be done if the client wishes confidentiality to be maintained. However, it is helpful for the creditors to know that they have been given the whole financial position of the client as they would in an administration order or bankruptcy. If the creditor has already obtained a court order that is higher than the offer calculated, the client should consider applying to the court on Form N245 to vary the order if s/he cannot obtain the creditor's written agreement to accept the offer made and to take no further action to enforce the debt (see p341 for how to do this).

Advantages
- Equitable distribution is widely accepted by the credit industry. Many creditors think it is the only strategy that money advisers should use.
- It ensures that all non-priority debts are dealt with together.
- It is based on court practices. This is how money is distributed to creditors when an administration order is granted (see p445).
- Many creditors automatically freeze interest/charges once an offer is accepted.

Disadvantages
- A client may be left with little financial flexibility and money only for basics.
- Unless coupled with a partial write-off (see p259), many debts may take years to clear.
- If the payments do not cover ongoing interest/charges, the debt will never be repaid.

Useful arguments
- The strongest argument in favour of this strategy is its fairness. It can be presented as a business-like response to a difficult situation, ensuring that every creditor is treated in a way which gives them the maximum possible amount.
- Sections 7.3.8G and 7.3.10R(1)–(2) of the FCA's *Consumer Credit Sourcebook* states that creditors should allow for 'alternative, affordable payment amounts to repay the debt in full where the client or an adviser makes a reasonable proposal to repay the debt', and must not pressurise a client 'to pay a debt in one single or very few repayments or in unreasonably large amounts and/or within an unreasonably short period of time'.

- It is exactly what would happen if a court were to grant an administration order or in bankruptcy, and is the kind of order which a court should make every time it makes an instalment order. The creditor cannot expect to do better.
- This strategy has often been used successfully where it can be shown that the person is starting to pay her/his creditors and wants to treat them all fairly. In addition, consideration should be given to asking for a partial write-off where offers will be paid for two or three years only (see p259 for details).
- Creditors who subscribe to the common financial statement (see p56) or the standard financial statement (see p56) generally accept that a pro rata offer should be accepted (but not necessarily that interest/charges will be frozen). Non-acceptance suggests that the creditor has other information about the client, which it should be asked to disclose.
- Many creditors now have strict criteria for automatically accepting repayment offers based either on a minimum payment or percentage of the debt or repayment over a maximum period in exchange for concessions on interest/ charges.

Checklist for action
- Agree with the client the amount of income available for creditors.
- Calculate offers to creditors. Consider a partial write-off where the suggested repayment period will not clear the debts within a reasonable time (see p259).
- Write to the creditors with offers. Suggest a write-off if offers are low.
- Ensure that interest and other charges are stopped.
- Advise the client to make payments – consider direct debit or standing order if the client has a current bank account. Ask for a payment book if this allows payment without cost. The client should not wait until all the creditors have accepted before starting to make payments.
- Consider whether a referral to a non-fee-charging debt management company might be in the client's best interests – ie, s/he would have to make one monthly payment for distribution among her/his creditors (see p255).

Consolidate the debts

Debt consolidation involves the client either taking out a new loan or increasing existing borrowing in order to pay off multiple debts. Debts can be consolidated by:
- an unsecured loan. These are likely to be small and so of limited potential;
- a further advance from an existing mortgage or secured lender, also secured on the client's property;
- a secured loan from a lender other than the existing mortgage provider, in addition to the existing mortgage;
- a remortgage with a new lender to replace any existing mortgage or secured loan;
- the transfer of balances to a credit card.

For many people in financial difficulties, this is likely to make the situation worse.

The *Consumer Credit Sourcebook* states that creditors must not pressurise a client into 'raising funds to repay the debt by selling their property, borrowing money or increasing existing borrowing'.[19]

Clients who are not in arrears and can meet their monthly commitments have the option of either carrying on with their existing agreements or refinancing them individually on more advantageous terms. However, for the average client struggling to meet her/his commitments, the other options discussed in this *Handbook* are likely to be more suitable. If considering this option, the client should always be advised to obtain independent financial advice.

Advantages

- Multiple agreements are replaced by a single agreement. The client only has to deal with one creditor.
- The consolidation loan is likely to be on better terms than the agreements it replaces, such as lower interest rates and monthly repayments.
- If the balance transfer is on the basis of a low or zero interest rate and the client can settle the balance before any balance transfer offer expires, the flexibility of a credit card enables consolidation to take place without incurring any additional costs.
- The client's credit rating can be improved or the creditors prevented from registering defaults by the debts being repaid.

Disadvantages

- Debt consolidation often involves replacing unsecured non-priority debts with a secured priority debt, with the client's property at risk if s/he defaults.
- Loans to clients with impaired credit ratings (non-status loans) are likely to be at higher rates of interest than those available to people with a clean credit record (status loans).
- There are usually costs associated with switching debts – eg, brokers' fees and early settlement charges.
- Although debt consolidation tends to involve lower monthly payments, it is often over an extended period, increasing the total amount payable by the client.
- Many debt consolidation loans are refinanced before running their full term (a process known as **'churning'**), which means that the client often has to borrow more as most of the repayments on the original loan will be interest rather than capital and there are early settlement charges. There may also be further costs (eg, a broker's fee), which are often added to the new loan.

Equity release loans

An equity release or lifetime mortgage enables a property-owning client to release equity from her/his home. It is secured on the client's property and is a way of raising capital to repay debts. The term of the loan is the client's lifetime, at the end of which all the capital becomes due. The interest is rolled up and the client is not required to pay anything while s/he is alive. These loans are only available to clients over 60 and the older the client is the more s/he can borrow (depending on the amount of equity in the property). The interest rate is usually fixed. If at the time of death there is a shortfall because there is no longer equity, the lender must write off the outstanding balance and cannot pursue it from other funds the client may have in her/his estate.

This type of loan may involve the conversion of unsecured borrowing into secured borrowing and is only appropriate if there is plenty of equity in the property. It is most useful if the client is finding it particularly stressful owing money to a number of different creditors, or if creditors are proving difficult to negotiate with. Clients must always be advised to obtain independent financial advice.

Advantages
- The loan prevents further action by the creditors.
- It may be a means of releasing equity from the property to use for other purposes, such as insulation or heating, which in turn can reduce living costs.

Disadvantages
- The equity in the home is reduced by the value of the loan and will be steadily eroded by the accruing interest.
- On the client's death, the property will have to be sold to repay the loan, which may result in dependants who lived with the client being left homeless.

Checklist for action
- Advise the client to obtain independent financial advice.
- Ensure the client obtains full details about the terms and conditions and the cost of the loan before signing any agreements.
- Inform creditors of the proposal and ask them to take no further action to enable the loan to be set up.

Selling the home

When there is no available income, capital or realisable assets other than a home, sale may be considered. It should not be considered if the financial situation is likely to improve or if the sale of the home would result in homelessness. It is only appropriate as a way of dealing with non-priority debts if there is sufficient equity to satisfy most creditors' demands and to cover the costs of selling and moving, and when the stress of debts is creating unacceptable problems for the household.

The sale of a property is often recommended to people who are in debt as an easy way out of the situation, but it should be remembered that courts rarely order a property to be sold to satisfy unsecured borrowing and only after a charging order (see p322) has been made and an order for sale subsequently applied for (see p327), or a bankruptcy order made. If, however, an expensive house can be sold and a more modest one, which would nonetheless satisfy the client's needs, can be bought, this can be an acceptable way of coping with a debt problem and perhaps also having money left over for other purposes.

A client may have been advised (sometimes by family or friends) that s/he has no alternative other than to sell her/his property and s/he may, therefore, approach you at a stage where this process has already begun. By examining the other strategies outlined in this chapter, it may be possible to demonstrate that selling the home in these circumstances is not the only option. The state of the housing market may also mean that this strategy is not easily achievable.

If a local authority or housing association rehouses people following a sale of their home, it usually only does so if it is clear that the sale is the only means to prevent eviction. Some local authorities still consider that the sale of a property makes someone intentionally homeless and, therefore, not eligible for rehousing under homelessness legislation. However, the code of guidance for local authorities states that a person should not be treated as intentionally homeless if her/his house was sold because of financial difficulties, and you should draw attention to this if necessary.[20]

In Wales, a successful mortgage rescue (see p222) may mean that funds are raised for non-priority creditors.

Advantages
- It can clear the debts.
- It may raise capital for other purposes.
- The client may see it as providing the opportunity for a fresh start.

Disadvantages
- It releases equity held in the property to satisfy unsecured creditors in a way a court may not order.
- It may not be possible to find alternative suitable housing.
- Moving house is a major disruption and costs a lot of money.
- The client may lose money if the housing market is depressed.
- The sale may take a long time or, in the midst of a recession, prove impossible, and the benefits of choosing this strategy may be lost.

Useful arguments
- Creditors receive a lump sum, either paying the debt in full or partially in full and final settlement (see p261).

Checklist for action
- Discuss the pros and cons of selling a property with the client.
- Telephone or write to creditors to inform them of the strategy and obtain written confirmation that they will take no further action.

- Advise the client to put the property on the market with a reliable estate agent.
- Check that suitable alternative accommodation is available.
- Once it has been decided to put the property on the market, write and inform the creditors of this and ask them to withhold interest charges or any other action until sale prices are available. Creditors may require a letter from an estate agent and, if a confirmation of a request to sell a property is available, this can be photocopied and sent. They may also want a letter from the client's solicitor confirming her/his share of the proceeds of sale to be forwarded directly to them.

Voluntary charge

Occasionally, but only as the 'lesser of two evils', it is advisable to turn an unsecured loan into a secured one in order to prevent any further action being taken. This is a very high-risk strategy and should not be undertaken lightly. It is described in detail on p229.

4. **Court-based strategies**

General stay

If a court order has been made, or is about to be made, and there is no available income, capital or assets, the county court can make an order for a general stay of judgment or enforcement. This means that the court will order that there is no enforcement of the judgment either until something happens (eg, there is another court order following a change in the client's circumstances) or for a fixed period, possibly with a review at the end. See p342 for an explanation of the court's power to make such an order and how you can help the client make an application.

Administration order

If a client already has at least one county court (or High Court) judgment against her/him and her/his total debts do not exceed £5,000, s/he can apply for an administration order. The client makes one monthly payment to the court, which 'administers' it and divides it equitably among all creditors. See p445 for details.

Bankruptcy and debt relief orders

Bankruptcy is a legal procedure in which the inability of a client to pay her/his debts is acknowledged and the majority of unsecured creditors can no longer pursue their debts, which are eventually written off. A third party (known as the 'trustee in bankruptcy') takes over the handling of the client's financial affairs for the benefit of her/his creditors and distributes a proportion of any available income and/or capital resources to them.

Bankruptcy may be a suitable strategy for a client if:

- debts have arisen which creditors will not write off;
- s/he does not own a home or has little or negative equity;
- s/he does not have any available assets or capital;
- s/he has a low available income compared with the amount of debt, which means it would take many years to repay her/his creditors.

Although not strictly a court-based option, a debt relief order operates in a similar way to bankruptcy and may be an appropriate option for clients who have:

- total debts of £20,000 or less;
- available income of £50 a month or less;
- gross assets worth £1,000 or less (the client can also own a motor vehicle worth less than £1,000).

See Chapter 15 for further details, including the advantages, disadvantages and consequences.

Individual voluntary arrangement

An individual voluntary arrangement is a means whereby a client can protect her/himself from further action from creditors by entering into a legally binding arrangement with them, supervised by an insolvency practitioner. It is often described as informal bankruptcy and should be considered before bankruptcy itself. See Chapter 15 for further details.

Time order

An application for a time order may be appropriate either to prevent a creditor under a regulated credit agreement from obtaining a judgment or to freeze interest or other charges. See p366 for further details.

5. **Future schemes**

Breathing space scheme

From early 2021, a 'breathing space' scheme will be introduced under the Financial Guidance and Claims Act 2018. It will give those with problem debts the right to legal protections from creditor action while they receive debt advice to find appropriate debt solutions. The scheme will be administered by the Insolvency Service.

To access a breathing space, clients will be required to seek FCA authorised debt advice either face-to-face, by telephone or online. Clients must be assessed as being in problem debt and advisers must consider that a breathing space is the best option and that there is a realistic chance of entering a debt solution within the period of the breathing space.

The breathing space can last for 60 days, during which interest and default charges should be suspended and 'most enforcement action' paused. Attachments of earnings would not be stopped (as it was deemed too costly for the courts).

Only one breathing space will be permitted in any 12-month period, unless the client is undergoing a mental health crisis. In this situation, the protections will continue throughout the full mental health treatment period.

If a client leaves a breathing space without entering a debt solution, interest, default fees and other charges will restart but cannot be charged retrospectively.

Debt advice agencies will be expected to carry out a 30-day check to ensure the client remains eligible. However, they will be required to remove clients who fail to pay their ongoing liabilities despite having the means to do so. Where a client fails to pay due to having insufficient means, debt advice agencies will have the discretion to remove clients from the scheme.

Debts excluded from bankruptcy will also be excluded from the breathing space.

Check gov.uk for further information.

Statutory debt repayment plans

Statutory debt repayment plans will be introduced under the Financial Guidance and Claims Act 2018. At the time of writing, the details of the scheme have not been finalised. The scheme is not expected to be available to clients when the breathing space is introduced in early 2021 but will instead be developed over a longer time frame. The aim of the statutory debt repayment plan is to enable clients with problem debt to enter into formal agreements with their creditors to repay their debts in full over an extended period. Clients will benefit from the following protections.

- No further interest, default charges or fees can be charged during the plan and creditors will not be permitted to make such charges retrospectively if a client leaves the plan early.
- All collections and recovery action on debts included in a plan will stop when the plan commences. Unlike with the breathing space, existing attachments of earnings will stop.
- Creditors will not be permitted to contact clients for debt payments, although they will still be able to make contact in regard to business as usual or where required by legislation – eg, for the provision of statements, arrears notices and notices of default sums.
- Creditors will be prevented from starting any new court action and proceedings already underway will be suspended.
- Creditors will not be permitted to take any further enforcement action, including deductions from benefits and wages or bailiff action.

- Supply disconnections and new instalment of pre-payment meters will be prevented, provided the plan is adhered to and ongoing bills are paid.
- Evictions for unpaid rent under section 8 of the Housing Act 1988 will be prevented, although landlords will still be able to evict tenants under the 'no fault' provisions of section 21.

To be eligible, it is expected that clients must:
- be able to repay their debts over a 'reasonable timeframe' – expected to be an average of seven years and not more than 10 years. This will be assessed using the standard financial statement; *and*
- access debt advice; *and*
- either have agreement from their creditors on the terms of the plan or the Insolvency Service must rule that the proposed plan is 'fair and reasonable', in which case creditors are obliged to comply with it.

The debts excluded from a statutory debt repayment plan will mirror those excluded from bankruptcy – ie, fraudulent debts, criminal fines, confiscation orders, child maintenance payments and debts arising from orders made in family proceedings, social fund loans, student loans and personal injury liabilities.

Debt advice agencies will be required to complete annual reviews with clients.

Clients will be able to enter a month-long payment break once in every 12 months, in order to be able to deal with short-term shocks in income.

Check gov.uk for further information.

Notes

1. Choosing a strategy

1 Where a client with a tax credit overpayment has migrated to UC and HMRC transfers recovery to the DWP, the debt will be recovered as if it were a benefit overpayment and so strictly can be considered a non-priority debt as it will continue to be recovered as if it were a benefit overpayment, even where no benefit is in payment.

2 *FCA Handbook*, CONC 8.3.2R, 8.3.3G, 8.3.4R and 8.3.7(5)

3 See J Phipps, 'It's Debt Jim, But Not As We Know It', *Adviser* 88

4 *FCA Handbook*, CONC 7.3.10R(3) and 7.3.10AG. See also P Connearn, 'The ABC of Money Advice – Pension Freedom and Paying Debts – Parts 1 and 2', *Quarterly Account* 53 and 54, IMA

5 *FCA Handbook*, CONC 7.15.9R

6 *FCA Handbook*, CONC 8.2.2G(2)

7 *FCA Handbook*, CONC 7.3.5G

8 See also J Kruse, 'The Death of Pro Rata?', *Adviser* 115

2. **The general approach to non-priority debts**
   9 *FCA Handbook,* CONC 7.3.2G, 7.3.10R(3), 7.3.4R and 7.3.10R(1)-(2)
   10 See C Wright, 'Square Peg Debts', *Adviser* 172
   11 See also P Richardson, 'Help Us Stop Loan Sharks Now', *Adviser* 141
   12 *FCA Handbook,* CONC 8.2.4R and 8.3.7(3)

3. **Strategies for dealing with non-priority debts**
   13 *FCA Handbook,* CONC 8.6
   14 Lending Standards Board, *The Standards of Lending Practice,* p9, para 11
   15 Lending Standards Board, *The Standards of Lending Practice,* p9 para 9
   16 *FCA Handbook,* CONC 7.14.1R and 7.14.3R. *The Credit Services Association Code of Practice* 2017 contains similar provisions in s2(t).
   17 *FCA Handbook,* CONC 7.3.5G(3). See also *The Credit Services Association Code of Practice* 2017, s3(g)
   18 *FCA Handbook,* CONC 8.6.1R, 8.6.3R and 8.6.4G
   19 *FCA Handbook,* CONC 7.3.10R(3) and 7.3.10AG
   20 Ministry of Housing, Communities and Local Government, Department *Homelessness Code of Guidance for Local Authorities,* April 2019, s11.18. There is similar guidance in Wales.

Chapter 10

Action in the county court: general

This chapter covers:

1. Introduction

The majority of cases involving debt are dealt with by a single county court in one of a network of 173 hearing centres throughout England and Wales. Cases are heard by district judges and circuit judges, assisted by part-time judges, with some decisions being delegated to court staff. Judges are experienced barristers and solicitors.

Procedures in the county court are laid out in the Civil Procedure Rules 1998, available online at justice.gov.uk/courts/procedure-rules/civil/rules. The Ministry of Justice and HM Courts and Tribunals Service (HMCTS) are responsible for the courts. HMCTS publishes various leaflets and guides on court procedure, available free of charge from court offices and gov.uk/government/collections/court-and-tribunal-forms. Leaflet EX343 sets out how court users can complain: *Unhappy with our Service: what can you do?* (the complaint form is Form EX343A, available from gov.uk/government/publications/form-ex343a-complaint-form). All forms of discrimination should be challenged and taken up with the court as part of debt advisers' social policy work.

The court manager and her/his staff are responsible for carrying out the court's administrative functions – eg, processing applications and fixing hearing dates. It is a good idea to establish a working relationship with your local court. Many courts have users' groups and/or court desks for unrepresented parties. Debt advisers cannot represent their clients in court, except at hearings allocated to the small claims track (see p316), but judges have increasingly recognised the value of such representation and rarely refuse to allow advisers to speak on clients' behalf. However, only legal representatives can sign court forms on behalf of clients.[1]

2. Before starting court action

Pre-action protocols

The Civil Procedure Rules contain codes of practice that both parties are expected to follow before any court action is started. These pre-action protocols and a pre-action conduct practice direction are are published in *The Civil Court Practice*[2] (available at justice.gov.uk/courts/procedure-rules/civil).

There have been protocols for possession claims for rent and mortgage arrears for some years and a protocol for debt claims was introduced on 1 October 2017. This can be accessed at justice.gov.uk/courts/procedure-rules/civil/pdf/protocols/debt-pap.pdf.

Regardless of whether there is a protocol for the specific type of case, the practice direction expects the parties to act 'reasonably and proportionately' in exchanging sufficient information to enable them to understand each other's position, make informed decisions and to attempt to resolve the matter without starting court proceedings, including considering alternative dispute resolution (see p284).[3] This should usually include:

- the creditor writing to give details of the claim; *and*
- the client:
  - providing a detailed written response within a reasonable period (14 days is suggested in the case of undisputed debts); *or*
  - acknowledging the letter within 14 days if s/he cannot provide a detailed response within that period and then providing a full response within 30 days if third-party involvement is required (or possibly longer if specialist advice is required).

If the practice direction is not complied with, the court can 'stay' (ie, suspend) the proceedings until the required steps have been taken, or make an order not to allow costs or to pay costs to the other party (see p315). The court is not concerned with minor or technical infringements and looks at the overall effect of the non-compliance on the other party when deciding whether to impose sanctions.

Pre-action protocol for debt claims

The protocol applies to all debt claims where:

- the creditor is a business (including sole traders and public bodies);
- the client is an individual (including sole traders); *and*
- no other specialised protocol applies – eg, for rent or mortgage arrears.

The protocol states that its aim is to:
- encourage early engagement, communication and exchange of information between the parties;
- enable parties to resolve debt claims without court proceedings, including by agreeing reasonable repayment plans or alternative dispute resolution – eg, the Financial Ombudsman Service (see p284);
- encourage parties to act reasonably and proportionately with one another – eg, not running up costs which do not bear a reasonable relationship to the amount of the debt; *and*
- support the efficient management of proceedings that cannot be avoided.

Before starting proceedings, the creditor should send a 'letter of claim' to the client, which should contain the following information:
- the amount of the debt, and whether interest and charges are continuing;
- if there was a verbal agreement, who made the agreement, what was agreed (as far as possible, what words were used) and where and when it was agreed;
- if there was a written agreement, the date of the agreement, the parties to it and the fact that a copy of the agreement can be requested from the creditor;
- if the debt has been sold, the details of the original debt and creditor, when it was sold and to whom;
- if regular instalments are currently being offered by or on behalf of the client or are being paid, an explanation of why the offer is not acceptable and why a court claim is still being considered;
- details of how the debt can be paid – eg, the method of and address for payment and details of how to proceed if the client wants to discuss payment options;
- the address to which the completed reply form annexed to the protocol and accompanying the letter should be sent.

It should also include:
- a statement of account detailing any interest and charges applied; *or*
- the most recent available statement of account with details of any interest and charges applied since that statement; *or*
- where no statements are provided, details of any interest and charges applied to the debt since it was incurred; *and*
- a copy of the information sheet, reply form and standard financial statement, all of which are annexed to the protocol.

The letter of claim should be clearly dated near the top of the letter and posted to the client on the day it is dated or, if this is not reasonably possible, the following day. If the client does not respond within 30 days, the creditor can start proceedings for the debt (subject to any other obligations the creditor has to the client – eg, under the Financial Conduct Authority's *Consumer Credit Sourcebook*). The reply form gives the client the following options:

- admitting all, or part, of the debt and to pay or propose payment terms for the amount admitted;
- confirming s/he is seeking debt advice;
- disputing all or part of the debt; *or*
- requesting documentation from the creditor to enable her/him to understand the debt.

If the client requests documentation, the creditor has 30 days in which to either provide it or provide a written explanation of why not. The creditor cannot start proceedings less than 30 days after the documentation and/or explanation have been provided and must also give the client 14 days' notice of its intention to start the claim.

If seeking debt advice, the client must indicate on the reply form whether obtaining this will take longer than 30 days and, if so, provide details. In such cases, the creditor should allow a reasonable amount of time for this advice to be obtained. The creditor cannot start proceedings less than 30 days after the reply form has been received and must give the client 14 days' notice of its intention to do so.

If the client does not fully complete the reply form, the creditor should attempt to contact her/him and obtain any additional information it requires to understand the client's position. The creditor cannot start proceedings less than 30 days after the reply form has been received and must give the client 14 days' notice of its intention to do so.

If the client indicates that s/he is disputing all or part of the debt, the parties should take appropriate steps to try to resolve the dispute without starting proceedings and consider alternative dispute resolution – ie, negotiation, referring the matter to a formal compaints process, such as the Financial Ombudsman Service and mediation.

If the client has proposed a payment arrangement and this is not accepted, the creditor should inform the client in writing and give reasons for refusing the proposal. If the proposal is accepted, the creditor should not start proceedings while the arrangement is in force. If client defaults on the arrangement, the creditor must send an updated letter of claim and comply with the protocol again. It need not send any further documents which have already been supplied to the client within the preceeding six months.

If the client responds but no agreement is reached, the creditor must give the client 14 days' notice of its intention to start proceedings, unless there are exceptional circumstances – eg, if the limitation period is about to expire (see p291).[4]

Note: some housing advisers have suggested that, because landlords routinely apply for money judgments in possession claims on the ground of rent arrears, the protocol for debt claims applies to that part of the claim. Although this is arguable, it has not yet been tested, but it might be a useful negotiating tactic in appropriate cases.

Alternative dispute resolution

Using the Financial Ombudsman Service

The Financial Ombudsman Service is a form of alternative dispute resolution. If a complaint has been (or could be) referred to the Financial Ombudsman Service, the court may agree to stay the proceedings.[5] The Financial Ombudsman Service considers requests to prioritise cases where the client might clearly be disadvantaged by having to wait – eg, through financial hardship. It may, therefore, be worth asking for a case to be prioritised where this can be demonstrated.

The Financial Ombudsman Service has been able to consider complaints against banks and building societies since December 2001 and against all other holders of consumer credit licences in relation to regulated consumer credit debts since 6 April 2007 (although not in relation to events that occurred before this date – see p65). From 1 April 2014, it has been able to consider complaints against any firms carrying out regulated activities, including 'debt-related activities'.[6] This means it can consider a complaint about:

- the original creditor, a debt purchaser or a debt collector in relation to a regulated credit debt if the events occurred before 1 April 2014;
- a debt collector in relation to an exempt credit debt, even if the events occurred before 1 April 2014;
- the original creditor or a debt purchaser in relation to an exempt credit debt if the events occurred on or after 1 April 2014.

The Financial Ombudsman Service is not a regulator. Its role is to resolve individual disputes between clients and businesses. It does not consider complaints about the way businesses reach their commercial decisions.

In regulated consumer credit cases, although the Financial Ombudsman Service cannot consider a complaint about events that occurred before 6 April 2007, it can 'take account' of them. This means that if the complaint is about, for example, excessive charges added to an account before 6 April 2007 which the client did not find out about until after this date, it cannot adjudicate on whether or not those charges are excessive. On the other hand, if the complaint relates to excessive charges added to an account on or after 6 April 2007, in adjudicating on the complaint, the Financial Ombudsman Service can look at the agreement to see what it says, even if it was made before 6 April 2007.

The Financial Ombudsman Service does not determine whether or not a relationship is unfair (see p161). It resolves disputes on the basis of what is 'fair and reasonable'. The Financial Ombudsman Service looks at the relevant legislation, regulations, any official guidance, relevant codes of practice and standards, and good industry practice at the time of the conduct complained about. This means it can take into account the same issues that a court would consider, but can come to a different conclusion. The Financial Ombudsman Service has an inquisitorial remit and so conducts its own enquiries, rather than just relying on what the parties tell it.[7]

Businesses that fall within the Financial Ombudsman Service's jurisdiction must have a written complaints procedure, and must publicise and operate it. The Financial Ombudsman Service cannot consider a complaint unless the business has had an opportunity to deal with it first. The client should therefore initially complain in writing to the company concerned. On receipt of a complaint, the creditor should:

- acknowledge the complaint promptly; *and*
- keep the client informed of progress; *and*
- send a 'final response' in writing within eight weeks.

A 'final response' is one which:

- either accepts the complaint and offers redress; *or*
- does not accept the complaint, but offers redress anyway; *or*
- rejects the complaint and gives reasons for this; *and*
- informs the client that if s/he remains dissatisfied, s/he has a right to refer the matter to the Financial Ombudsman Service within six months, and encloses a consumer leaflet.

If no final response has been received after eight weeks, the client can complain to the Financial Ombudsman Service, provided the complaint is within its jurisdiction. Provided a letter is clearly the business's last word on the matter, the Financial Ombudsman Service accepts the complaint, even if fewer than eight weeks have elapsed and even if it does not contain information on the client's referral rights.

Unless the circumstances are exceptional or the business does not object, a complaint to the Financial Ombudsman Service must be made within:

- six months of the date of the final response. This time limit must have been made clear in the final response, otherwise it does not apply; *and*
- six years of the matter complained of taking place; *or*
- if later, within three years of the client's reasonably becoming aware s/he might have grounds for complaining.[8]

A complaint to the Financial Ombudsman Service should contain the following information:

- the client's details;
- details of the business complained about;
- reference/account numbers;

- copies of the final response (if any) and of any other relevant documents – eg, the agreement and correspondence;
- a summary of the complaint. This should set out the 'story' in the client's own words, if possible, rather than take the form of a legal-type submission (this can be done later in the process, if necessary);
- how the client wants the business to address the issue. The Financial Ombudsman Service does not grant a remedy just because a business has broken rules – this is the job of a regulator. There must be some consumer detriment, not necessarily financial, such as distress, inconvenience, injury or damage to reputation;
- a letter of authorisation if the adviser is submitting the complaint on behalf of the client.

The complaints form is available at financial-ombudsman.org.uk/consumers/how-to-complain. There is an online form and a form which can be downloaded and posted, or you can phone 0800 023 4567. If the Financial Ombudsman Service accepts the complaint, it attempts to resolve the dispute through mediation – ie, assisting the parties to come to an agreement. If not, an adjudicator forms a preliminary view, which is circulated to the parties. If they accept this, the dispute is settled. If they do not, the case is referred to the Ombudsman for determination. If the Ombudsman upholds the complaint, the business can be ordered to:

- pay compensation for financial loss up to a limit of £350,000 for complaints about actions taken on or after 1 April 2019 and £160,000 for complaints about actions taken before that date but not made to the Ombudsman until after that date; *and/or*
- pay compensation for non-financial loss (this tends to be a few hundred pounds maximum); *and/or*
- take appropriate action to remedy the issue complained about – eg, remove excessive charges from an account.

Financial Ombudsman Service decisions are binding on the business, but not on the client, who can still take the matter to court if s/he remains dissatisfied. A Financial Ombudsman Service decision cannot be appealed. If the business fails to comply with the decision, it can be enforced through the courts. You should seek specialist advice if this becomes necessary.

More information can be found on the Financial Ombudsman Service website (financial-ombudsman.org.uk). Details of the monthly newsletter, *Ombudsman News*, which often contains features and case studies of interest and relevance to money advisers, are available on the Financial Ombudsman Service website. Informal guidance on practice and procedure is available from 020 7964 1400 or technical.desk@financial-ombudsman.org.uk.

In addition, the Financial Ombudsman Service now publishes the final decisions ('determinations') made by an Ombudsman (but not the recommendations made by adjudicators which have been accepted by the parties). These are at financial-ombudsman.org.uk/data-insight/ombudsman-decisions. Decisions can be searched for based on a particular creditor or a specific issue.

There is an increasing emphasis on the use of alternative dispute resolution, with some courts offering the services of local court-based mediation schemes. The parties are encouraged to use some form of alternative resolution and, even after a county court claim has been issued, the court can 'stay' (ie, suspend) the proceedings to enable them to settle their dispute by mediation or other means. Although the courts have no power to compel parties to do so, when deciding the amount of any costs to be awarded, they can take into account the efforts made before and during the proceedings to resolve the dispute in some other way (see p315).

Defended claims that are normally allocated to the small claims track (see p317) are referred to HMCTS's free mediation service, provided all the parties indicate in their directions questionnaire (see p316) that they agree to mediation.[9]

3. **Taking court action**

The person or organisation bringing court action is called the 'claimant'. The person or organisation against whom court action is brought is called the 'defendant'.

Most forms used in court proceedings are prescribed and can be identified by their number and title in the bottom left-hand corner. It is important that debt advisers familiarise themselves with these. The forms advisers most commonly encounter are available at gov.uk/government/collections/court-and-tribunal-forms.

Types of claim

Court action may involve the following.
- Money-only claims – eg, for repayment of an amount due under a loan, overdraft or credit card agreement. See Chapter 11 for more information.
- Claims relating to agreements regulated by the Consumer Credit Act that are not for money only – eg, for possession of goods supplied under a hire purchase agreement. See Chapter 12 for more information.
- Claims relating to land – eg, for possession of a house by a mortgage lender or landlord. See Chapter 12 for more information.
- All other claims – eg, a claim for the return of goods supplied under an agreement not regulated by the Consumer Credit Act. These differ from money-only claims in that, if the client does not respond to the claim, the

creditor must make a formal application to the court for judgment and submit supporting evidence. You should obtain specialist help if you come across these claims.

Applications: Form N244

Applications are usually made on Form N244 – eg, an application to set aside a judgment or to suspend a High Court writ of control or to stay (ie, put a hold on) enforcement of a judgment debt.[10] Guidance notes to help complete the form are in leaflet N244 available from gov.uk/government/collections/court-and-tribunal-forms.

An application can also be made verbally at a hearing that has already been fixed and can be made without using Form N244, but the creditor and the court should be informed (if possible in writing) as soon as possible.[11]

The various sections of Form N244 should be completed as follows.

- **Header.** The court name is likely to be 'In the County Court Business Centre', but otherwise will be the name of the court which last contacted the client – eg, 'In the county court at Northampton'. 'Fee account' is a fee payment system available for businesses who regularly use the courts. The 'Help with fees – Ref no.' box should be completed with the reference number provided by the court if the client has successfully applied online for full or partial remission of the court fee (see p290).
- **Section 1** should be completed with details of the client's name, unless s/he has a legal representative (eg, a solicitor) acting for her/him.
- **Section 2** should usually indicate that the client is the defendant (unless s/he has a legal representative acting for her/him or, exceptionally, if s/he is the claimant).
- **Section 3** asks what order the client is seeking and why. This information must be supplied.[12] The following are suggested wordings for some common applications.
  - **Redetermination/reconsideration:** 'The judgment be paid by instalments of £x per month because I cannot afford to pay at the rate determined.'
  - **Variation:** 'Payment of the judgment debt be varied to £x per month because my circumstances have changed and I can no longer afford to pay at the rate ordered.'
  - **Suspension:** 'Payment of the judgment debt be suspended under s71(2) of the County Courts Act 1984 on the ground that I am no longer able to pay it because…'
  - **Stay of enforcement:** 'Any enforcement proceedings against me be stayed until a further order is made (Rule 3.1(2)(f) of the Civil Procedure Rules).'
- **Section 4** asks whether a draft of the order being applied for has been attached. This is not usually required unless the application is being made by consent.
- **Sections 5 and 6** ask for information about the application. The client must indicate whether or not s/he wants the court to deal with the application at a

hearing or at a telephone hearing. If a hearing is requested, the court fixes a time and date, and notifies the parties at the same time as it serves Form N244. You should use your experience to estimate hearing times, but can just leave the box(es) blank. If no hearing is requested, the application is referred to a district judge to decide whether it is suitable for consideration without a hearing. If no hearing is requested, the district judge may disagree and order a hearing anyway and the other party can apply to set aside or vary any order made without a hearing.[13] You should only ask the court to deal with an application without a hearing if it will not automatically be transferred to the client's local court, and should also ask the court to use its discretion to transfer the case to the client's local court if it decides that a hearing should take place.[14] If it is not possible (or it will be extremely difficult) for the client to attend a hearing in person, s/he can ask the court to arrange a telephone hearing on Form N244. If it is the creditor's or lender's application, the client can request a telephone hearing in writing.[15]

- **Section 7** should contain details of any hearing date already allocated for the case.
- **Section 8** should usually specify a district judge for the hearing.
- **Section 9** should usually specify the other party/ies as the persons to be served with the application.
- **Section 10** should indicate whether the client is relying on a separate witness statement, her/his statement of the case or the evidence set out in the box on Form N244 in support of her/his application. The amount of text that can be fitted into the box is limited to 840 characters and so, in many cases, a separate witness statement may be needed. Evidence is required in certain cases (eg, set-aside applications) and the court can ask for evidence in support of an application. The client will not usually have served a defence and so any facts that s/he wants the court to consider should be set out in the box and any written evidence referred to and attached – eg, a financial statement. The client should sign the statement of truth at the foot of the box. There is no need for a financial statement to contain a statement of truth.
- **Section 11** should be signed and dated, and the details of the client's address completed.

Clients with mental health problems

A client who 'lacks capacity' for the purposes of the Mental Capacity Act 2005 (see p153) is a 'protected party' in any county court proceedings and can only take part in them through another person, known as a 'litigation friend'.

A creditor can issue a claim and it can be served on a client who is a protected party even if s/he does not have a litigation friend, but any further steps taken before a litigation friend has been appointed (eg, entering default judgment (see p311) or taking enforcement action – see p318) is of no effect unless the court subsequently ratifies it.[16]

4. **Court fees**

Most steps taken in court proceedings have a fee to cover administrative costs, which must be paid to the court before the particular step can be taken. The fees are set annually by statutory instrument and details can be obtained from any court office, the HM Courts and Tribunals Service (HMCTS) website or leaflet EX50 (see gov.uk/government/collections/court-and-tribunal-forms).

Joint litigants are jointly liable to pay the fees. If one qualifies for full or partial remission (see below), the other must pay the full fee, unless s/he also qualifies for full or partial remission. If neither qualify for remission, they must either agree between them which one will pay the fee or come to an arrangement to pay the fee between them.

If the client has no money with her/him to pay the fee and does not apply for remission, the court may nevertheless process the court action in an emergency if the interests of justice would be compromised if a delay occurs – eg, to suspend an eviction the following day. The decision is made by a court officer and her/his decision is final. The client must undertake to apply for fee remission within five days and to pay the fee if this application fails. If the client fails to do so, the matter is referred to the district judge who may revoke any order made in the court action.

Remission of fees

A client who is not being funded by the Legal Aid Agency for the proceedings may be eligible for full or partial remission of the fees if the amount of her/his capital and her/his income are below certain limits.[17]

If the client is aged 61 or over, a capital threshold of £16,000 applies, irrespective of the level of fee. If her/his capital is worth £16,000 or more, s/he does not qualify for remission. If s/he is under 61, a sliding scale of fee bands with different capital thresholds applies – eg, for a fee of up to £1,000, the capital threshold is £3,000.

The 'disposable capital' of the client's household is taken into account – ie, the client's own capital and any capital belonging to her/his partner, such as savings, investments and second homes, including jointly held capital. Some capital is disregarded – eg, the family home and the household's furniture and effects.

In addition to having capital below a certain amount, a client is exempt from paying all or part of a fee if her/his (and/or her/his partner's) gross monthly income (excluding certain benefits and payments and tax credits) is below a certain amount. This figure depends on whether the client's household includes children. If her/his gross monthly income is more than the threshold, s/he must pay £5 towards the fee for every £10 excess income above the threshold.

If the client's gross monthly income is more than £5,085 (if single) or £5,245 (if a member of a couple) plus £245 for each dependent child, s/he is not eligible for any fee remission.

If the client is getting universal credit (with gross annual earnings of less than £6,000), income support, income-based jobseeker's allowance, income-related employment and support allowance or the guarantee credit of pension credit, s/he gets full fee remission, provided the amount of her/his capital is low enough.

In addition, the court has discretion to allow full or partial remission of a fee if there are exceptional circumstances. Guidance suggests that the client may not have to pay a fee if there has been an unexpected event that has seriously affected her/his ability to pay the fee and that this circumstance is exceptional – eg, s/he has received a letter or notice threatening action due to non-payment of bills. The decision is made by the court officer and is a final decision which cannot be appealed.

An application for fee remission should be made on Form EX160 or completed online at gov.uk/get-help-with-court-fees (this generates a reference number which must be included on the court application). HMCTS publishes an accompanying leaflet (EX160A) (also available from the website). Clients do not need to provide proof of their income unless the court requests it. In the case of someone getting benefits, the court will contact the Department for Work and Pensions if necessary.

If the application for remission is not made at the same time as the court action is taken, any fee can be refunded retrospectively, provided an application is made within three months of the fee being paid. This time limit can be extended if there is a good reason.

A refusal of full or partial remission can be appealed to the court delivery manager in writing within 14 days. The letter should state why the client believes the decision is wrong and can include further information and evidence. The court manager should notify her/him of the decision on the appeal within 10 days. There is a further right of appeal to the operational manager, again within 14 days. There is no further appeal.

5. **Time limits**

Court action to recover debts must be taken within certain time limits. These are mainly contained in the Limitation Act 1980, although some debts have their own time limit – eg, council tax. These time limits are known as '**limitation periods**'.

Most limitation periods run from the date the 'cause of action accrued'.[18]

The date the cause of action accrued is ignored. For example, if a client defaulted on 30 November 2000, a six-year limitation period would have ended on 30 November 2006.

Note: if a debt (eg, an overdraft) is repayable 'on demand', until the demand is made there is no cause of action and the time limit does not begin to run.[19]

If the only thing preventing a creditor from taking court action is the need to comply with a procedural requirement, the time limit accrues regardless.[20] However, a default notice – which is needed before a creditor under a regulated credit agreement can take certain specified steps (see p299) – is not regarded as a procedural requirement. The service and expiry of a default notice (where required) which has not been remedied by the client is, therefore, necessary to begin the limitation period in such cases. This, in theory, allows the creditor to defer the start of the limitation period indefinitely, allowing court proceedings to be started a significant time after the date the client last made a payment under the agreement – ie, the date of actual default.[21] **Note:** service of a default notice is not required to recover sums which have already accrued due under a consumer credit agreement – eg, a claim for arrears only when the limitation period would run from the date the missed payment(s) should have been made under the terms of the agreement.

Common limitation periods

Unsecured regulated credit agreement: six years from the date of expiry of a default notice (where required) which has not been remedied. See below for cases where, under the terms of the agreement, a further notice is required to terminate the agreement before the creditor can take action to recover the outstanding balance.

Other unsecured borrowing: six years from default unless repayable 'on demand' when the time period does not start until the date of the demand or unless, under the terms of the agreement, termination of the agreement by the creditor is a pre-condition of court action to recover the outstanding balance. In this case, the period starts from when the agreement is terminated.[22]

Interest: six years from default in payment. Each amount of interest charged to an account has its own six-year limitation period. Once the capital is statute barred, so is any claim for interest, even if that interest was added to the account less than six years ago.

Fuel debt: six years from the date of the bill.

Telephone charges: six years from the date of the bill.

Water charges: six years from the date of the bill.

Council tax: six years from the date of the bill (demand notice).

Rent arrears: six years from the date the rent became due. Each amount of rent due has its own six-year limitation period.

Possession of land: 12 years from default in payment.

Mortgage shortfall: six years for arrears of interest from the date the interest became due; 12 years for the outstanding capital from the date the right to receive the money accrued (usually after default in payment of one or more contractual instalments). See p116.

Once the relevant limitation period has expired, a debt is said to be '**statute-barred**'.[23] The effect of a debt being statute-barred is that it prevents court action. However, the debt still legally exists and can be recovered by any other lawful method.[24] The *Consumer Credit Sourcebook* states that a creditor must not attempt to recover a statute-barred debt if it has not been in contact with the client during the limitation period nor after the client has stated that s/he will not be paying the debt because it is statute-barred. Pursuing a complaint could be considered in appropriate cases.[25]

Limitation periods are only relevant to when the creditor must take the initial court proceedings. The time limit ceases to run once court proceedings are issued. If the creditor obtains a judgment, the limitation period does not apply to the enforcement of that judgment.

A limitation period that has already started can be repeatedly restarted by an 'acknowledgement' or 'part payment'.

If a client receives a claim form for a debt which is statute-barred or partly statute-barred (eg, in the case of rent or interest), and s/he wishes to avoid a judgment being made against her/him, s/he must defend the claim on the ground that the debt is statute-barred.[26] Once s/he has done so, the onus switches to the creditor to prove that the claim is not statute-barred. Where relevant, you should advise clients who are considering raising limitation defences in relation to regulated credit agreements who cannot recall if, and/or when, they received a default notice and/or are unable to provide you with a copy, but have received a 'letter before claim', to query when the default notice was served when responding to the 'letter of claim' and also ask for a copy.

A bankruptcy order or a debt relief order do not prevent the limitation period from running (in the event that the debt remains recoverable after the client's discharge or at the end of the moratorium period) but the limitation period is suspended for the duration of an individual voluntary arrangement so that, if this fails, creditors whose debts might otherwise have become statute-barred may still be able to take court action to recover them.[27]

Acknowledgements

An acknowledgement means that the client has, in effect, admitted liability for what is being claimed. No amount need be specified. An acknowledgement must be in writing and signed by the client (or her/his agent – eg, a debt adviser).

The debt must be acknowledged either to the creditor or its agent. This means the client cannot acknowledge a debt on the telephone and letters from the creditor to the client cannot restart the limitation period. On the other hand, you could inadvertently acknowledge a debt when writing to a creditor on behalf of the client.

An admission of part of a debt together with a denial of liability for the balance is not an acknowledgement of the disputed balance. The phrases 'outstanding amount' and 'outstanding balance' have been held to be acknowledgements as has a letter expressing concern about the amount of the claim, but not about the fact of a claim being made.[28] An acknowledgement by one co-debtor only restarts the limitation period against that debtor and not any co-debtors. Once a debt becomes statute-barred, the limitation period cannot be restarted by any subsequent acknowledgement.

Part payments

In order to restart the limitation period, a payment must be made by the client (or a co-debtor) or agent, to the creditor or agent and must be in respect of the particular debt in question. For this purpose, the Department for Work and Pensions is treated as the client's agent when making payments of mortgage interest to lenders.[29] If part of the debt is disputed and a payment is made, the client must make clear that the payment relates to the undisputed part of the debt and ask the creditor to appropriate the payment to that part of the debt.[30]

A payment of interest restarts the limitation period for the capital, but not the interest. In practice, payments are usually allocated first to interest and then to capital. **Note:** once the capital is statute-barred, so is any claim for interest, even if that interest was added to the account less than six years ago. Similarly, a payment of rent arrears does not restart the limitation period for any other rent outstanding. Writing off part of a debt does not count as a payment. Once a debt has become statute-barred, the limitation period cannot be restarted by any subsequent payment. However, the client cannot recover any payment(s) made, as the effect of a debt being statute-barred is only to prevent court action. The debt still legally exists and can be recovered by any other lawful method.[31]

---

6. **Appeals and adjournments**

Appealing to a judge

If a client disagrees with a judgment or order made by a district judge, s/he must appeal if s/he wishes to challenge the judge's decision.

The client can appeal to a circuit judge against any decision made in a county court by a district judge (unless it was made by consent) on the grounds that the decision was:[32]

- wrong – eg, the district judge wrongly decided a legal issue or wrongly exercised her/his discretion by reaching a decision which no reasonable judge could have made; *or*
- unjust – ie, there was a serious procedural or other irregularity in the proceedings.

An appeal must be made on a point of law, not on things like a change in the client's circumstances. If new evidence becomes available, this may be a ground for appeal if the court considers it would be in the interests of justice to have a rehearing.[33]

The client must obtain permission to appeal:
- verbally from the district judge at the end of the hearing; *or*
- if permission was refused or not applied for, from the circuit judge in the notice of appeal.

Permission is only given if:
- the court considers that the appeal has a real prospect of success; *or*
- there is a compelling reason why the appeal should be heard. The Civil Procedure Rules contain no guidance on when this might apply.

The district judge must give written reasons for granting or refusing the client permission to appeal on Form N460.

The client must appeal:[34]
- within the time specified by the district judge when granting permission verbally; *or*
- within 21 days of the date of the decision being appealed.

An appeal must be made on a Form N161 (N164 in small claims cases). A fee of £140 (£120 for small claims) is payable. See p290 for details about applying for remission. If the claim is on the small claims track, the restrictions on cost orders also apply to appeals.[35]

If the client has possible grounds for appeal, specialist advice and assistance will be required, and usually the client must be referred to a solicitor.

Adjournments

An adjournment is a court order to delay a hearing, either for a specified amount of time or indefinitely. The county court can either adjourn or bring forward the date of a hearing at any time. It can decide to do this itself or because one or both of the parties have applied.[36]

As one of the main aims of the Civil Procedure Rules is to avoid delays in hearing cases, it is important, if possible, to attend court to apply for an adjournment in case it is not granted.

An application for an adjournment on the grounds of illness should be accepted, provided it is supported by a sick note, unless there is evidence that the illness or medical evidence is not genuine. Similarly, if an important witness cannot be present, a district judge should adjourn a hearing.

It is reasonable to grant an adjournment if there would otherwise be a miscarriage of justice. For example, if a client comes to a court desk in a county court hearing centre at 10am to ask for representation at a possession hearing a quarter of an hour later, it should be argued that there are (or may be) legal points which the court must hear and which cannot be adequately presented without further preparation. However, there must be some explanation of why the client has left it until the last minute to obtain advice or representation.

It is not a sufficient reason to adjourn a hearing simply because one (or even both) of the parties is not yet ready. Judges are often impatient or suspicious of applications to adjourn which they believe are merely means to prolong an action in which they believe the creditor should succeed. On the other hand, if the need for the adjournment arises because the creditor (or its representative) has failed to supply information or documents reasonably required by the client in connection with her/his defence, the judge is more likely to grant the adjournment.

A district judge should consider the merits of an adjournment, whether or not one or both parties are requesting one. However, it is clearly much easier to get an adjournment if the creditor agrees, and it is always worth contacting the creditor or its representative before applying for one.

Notes

1. Introduction
1 Barristers, solicitors and their employees, and people authorised by the Lord Chancellor to conduct litigation under s11 CLSA 1990

2. Before starting court action
2 This is an expensive two-volume publication (plus a separate volume containing prescribed forms), published by LexisNexis. It is known as the *Green Book* and is published annually with supplements. In addition to the rules, the *Green Book* contains annotations and commentary, tables summarising various common procedures, details of court costs and fees, the pre-action protocols and excerpts from relevant legislation.
3 CPR PD, para 3
4 For further details, see T Lett, 'Pre-action Protocol for Debt Claims', *Quarterly Account* 46, IMA
5 In *Derbyshire Home Loans v Keaney* (*Adviser* 124 abstracts), Bristol County Court stayed possession proceedings for two months to enable the borrower to pursue a possible complaint in view of the lender's failure to respond to his proposals.

6 *FCA Handbook, Dispute Resolution: complaints*, DISP 2.3, handbook.fca.org.uk/handbook/disp/2/3.html, which contains links to the definitions of 'regulated activities' and 'credit-related regulated activities'.
7 *R (on the application of Williams) v FOS* [2008] EWHC 2142 (Admin)
8 *FCA Handbook*, DISP 2.8R. See also R Rosenberg, 'Legal Round-up', *Quarterly Account* 50, IMA for a discussion of two FOS decisions on the time limit for unaffordable loan complaints made more than six years after the loans were taken out.
9 r26.4A CPR

3. Taking court action
10 CPR PD 23
11 CPR PD 23, paras 2.10 and 3(5)
12 r23.6 CPR
13 CPR PD 23, para 2.4
14 Quoting r30.2(1) CPR
15 CPR PD 23A, para 6
16 r21.3(4) CPR. See also C Bradley, 'The MCA 2005 and Litigation Issues', *Adviser* 127

4. Court fees
17 For further discussion, see J Phipps and E Wilkinson, 'Fee Remissions', *Adviser* 161

5. Time limits

18 *Reeves v Butcher* [1891] 2 QB 509. See C
Wilkinson, 'Consultancy Corner: default
dates for debt limitation purposes',
Adviser 173

19 *Goldsmith v Chittell* (*Adviser* 179
abstracts)

20 *Swansea County Council v Glass* [1992] 2
All ER 680

21 *Doyle v PRA Group* [2019] EWCA Civ 12
(*Adviser* 188 abstracts). See also R
Rosenberg, 'Legal Round-up', *Quarterly
Account* 52, IMA and C Bott, 'Limitations
after Doyle', *Quarterly Account* 54, IMA

22 For example, as in *BMW Financial
Services v Hart* [2012] EWCA Civ 1959
(*Arian* 43, caselaw update)

23 For a discussion of tactics when dealing
with statute-barred debts, see C
Wilkinson, 'Consultancy Corner', *Adviser*
109, including a suggested response
letter to a demand for payment.

24 But note *FCA Handbook*, CONC 7.15.4
and 7.15.8, which restrict a creditor's
right to attempt recovery of statute-
barred debts.

25 CONC 7.15.4R and 7.15.8R

26 CPR PD 16, para 13.1

27 *O'Brien v Osborne* [1852] 10 Hare 92

28 *Bradford and Bingley v Rashid* [2006]
UKHL 37 (*Adviser* 117 abstracts); *Phillips
and Co v Bath Housing Co-operative*
[2012] EWCA Civ 1591 (*Arian* 41,
caselaw update)

29 *Bradford and Bingley v Cutler* [2008]
EWCA Civ 74 (*Adviser* 128, money
advice abstracts)

30 *Ashcroft v Bradford and Bingley* [2010]
EWCA Civ 223 (*Adviser* 140, abstracts)

31 But note *FCA Handbook*, CONC 7.15.4
and 7.15.8, which restrict a creditor's
right to attempt recovery of statute-
barred debts.

6. Appeals and adjournments

32 r52.11(3) CPR

33 r52.11(1)(b) CPR

34 r52.4 CPR

35 *Akhtar v Boland* [2014] EWCA Civ 943
(*Adviser* 165, abstracts). See also
Dammermann v Lanyon Bowdler [2017]
EWCA Civ 269 (*Adviser* 185 abstracts)

36 r3.1(2)(b) CPR

Chapter 11

Action in the county court: money claims

This chapter covers
1. Starting a money claim (below)
2. Admitting a money claim (p303)
3. The judgment (p306)
4. Defending a money claim (p315)
5. Enforcing a judgment (p318)
6. Preventing enforcement (p337)

This chapter deals with court action by creditors who are claiming only money from the client. If the creditor is taking action to recover property or goods as well as, or instead of, money from the client, see Chapter 12.

Note: before starting proceedings, most creditors must first comly with the pre-action protocol (see p281), which aims to resolve the matter without court action.

1. Starting a money claim

Court proceedings start when the county court issues a 'claim form' at the request of the creditor (known as the 'claimant').

A claim form cannot be issued in the High Court unless the creditor expects to recover more than £100,000 and can justify the matter being dealt with by a High Court judge.[1] This is rarely possible in ordinary debt cases, and so there should be no reason for creditors to issue proceedings in the High Court. However, some creditors may be able to issue a claim in the county court, obtain a county court judgment and transfer the case to the High Court for enforcement (see p321).

Debts regulated by the Consumer Credit Act 1974

The High Court cannot deal with claims related to secured or unsecured agreements regulated by the Consumer Credit Act 1974 (see p62), or actions linked to such agreements, regardless of the amount of the claim. If you encounter such cases being dealt with in the High Court, get specialist advice.

Default notice

A 'default notice' must be issued by a creditor for all debts regulated by the Consumer Credit Act 1974 before court action can start for early payment of money due under an agreement. A default notice is usually required in debt cases where arrears are claimed along with the money which would become due if the agreement ran its course. It is not required if the time allotted to an agreement is already over but an outstanding balance remains, or if only arrears are claimed.

The default notice must contain details of:
- the type of agreement, including the name and address of the creditor and client;
- the terms of the agreement which have been broken;
- for fixed-sum credit, the early settlement figure;
- the action needed by the client – eg, to pay arrears in full by a certain date;
- the action the creditor intends to take if the client is unable to comply with the default notice – eg, refer to debt collection or start court action.

A default notice served on or after 1 October 2008 must contain the following further information.
- If the notice relates to a hire purchase or conditional sale agreement, information on the client's right to terminate the agreement, including the amount of her/his liability if s/he exercises this right (see p104).
- Where applicable, a statement that the client may have to pay contractual interest in the event of the creditor obtaining a judgment (see p79).
- A copy of the current Financial Conduct Authority information sheet on default.

The client must be given at least 14 days to carry out the required action. If the default notice requests payment, it must contain a statement about time orders and about seeking advice from a local Citizens Advice office, solicitor or trading standards department.

If a default notice is not complied with, a creditor can:
- terminate the agreement; *and*
- demand earlier payment of money due under an agreement.

If a default notice is not completed correctly (eg, it does not give the client sufficient time to respond or the arrears figure is incorrectly stated), it is invalid and the creditor must issue a fresh notice before taking action.[2]

Creditors do not always automatically initiate court action if a default notice is not complied with and so, even if the time limit has expired, it is always worth trying to negotiate with a creditor in order to prevent court action. Clients often claim not to have received default notices and so bear in mind that a default notice is treated as served for this purpose if it is sent by post to the client's last known address.[3]

Which court deals with the claim

Claims to recover a sum of money are started by creditors in the County Court Money Claims Centre in Salford, but the claim is issued in the name of the County Court Business Centre in Northampton. Such claims are known as 'money claims'. Large creditors that issue county court claims in bulk and prepare claims on computer can start their claims in the County Court Business Centre which charges a lower court fee. The County Court Money Claims Centre and the County Court Business Centre deal with the matter either by post or electronically unless it is transferred to another court.

Automatic transfers

The case is automatically sent (transferred) to the client's 'home court' (ie, the county court hearing centre that serves the address where the client lives) if:[4]

- the client defends the action (see p315); *or*
- there is a request for a redetermination of a decision by the court (see p310); *or*
- the district judge decides that a request for an instalment order should be dealt with at a hearing; *or*
- there is an application to set aside a default judgment (see p337); *or*
- the creditor applies to increase the amount payable under a judgment (see p341); *or*
- there is a request for a reconsideration of a decision by the court relating to a client's application to vary the amount payable under a judgment (see p341); *or*
- the creditor applies for an information order (see p319), a third-party debt order (see p332) or an attachment of earnings order (see p329). A request for a warrant of control (see p321) is made to the Money Claims Centre or the Business Centre, unless the case has already been sent to another county court hearing centre.

In Money Claims Centre cases, if the client's defence is that s/he paid the debt before the claim was issued, this is checked with the creditor before the case is transferred. This also happens if the client admits part of the debt but disputes the balance. In Business Centre cases, all defences are checked with the creditor before the case is transferred.

Automatic transfers are only available if the defendant is an individual.

If automatic transfer does not apply, the court has the discretion to transfer a case if:

- it would be more convenient or fair for a hearing to be held in another court; *and/or*
- the facilities available at the court where the case is currently being dealt with are inadequate because a party or witness has a disability.

The claim form

The claim form (Form N1) must contain a concise statement of the nature of the claim and a 'statement of value'. This states the amount the creditor is claiming and whether s/he expects to recover:

- not more than £10,000; *or*
- more than £10,000, but not more than £100,000; *or*
- more than £100,000.

The amount claimed includes the court fee paid by the creditor to issue the proceedings and, if a solicitor has been instructed, an amount for the solicitor's costs. The court fee and solicitor's costs vary with the amount claimed. The claim form must state the amount of any interest claimed.

Details of the court of issue (usually, the County Court Business Centre) and the unique reference number allocated to the case appear in the top right corner of the claim form.

The claim form must be served on the client within four months of issue. This is usually done by the court by first-class post. The claim form is usually deemed to have been received on the second business day after it was posted – ie, if posted on Monday, it is deemed to have been received on Wednesday (Saturdays, Sundays, Bank Holidays, Christmas Day and Good Friday are not counted).[5] In Business Centre cases, the claim form is deemed to have been served five days after issue.

See p338 if the client states that s/he did not receive the claim form before judgment was entered or any enforcement action taken by the creditor.

The particulars of claim

The claim form must be accompanied by the 'particulars of claim', or these must be sent to ('served on') the client by the creditor within 14 days of the claim form being served. The particulars of claim must include a concise statement of the facts relied on by the creditor (including the details of any contract) and must be verified by a 'statement of truth' – ie, that the creditor believes the stated facts are true. A copy of any written agreement should (but not must) be attached (this is not required if the claim form and particulars of claim are issued by the Business Centre).[6]

If the claim form includes the particulars of claim, it must be accompanied by:

- a response pack, including an acknowledgement of service (Form N9);
- a form for admitting the claim (Form N9A);
- a form of defence and counterclaim to be used if the client disputes the claim (Form N9B);
- notes for the client on replying to the claim form (Form N1C).

If the particulars of claim are served separately from the claim form, the forms must be served with the particulars of claim. This may be important as the client's time for responding to the claim runs from the deemed date of service of the particulars of claim.

Responding to the claim form

The client must respond to the claim form/particulars of claim within 14 days of service (ie, the response must be received on or before the 14th day after the date s/he is deemed to have received the claim form/particulars of claim, regardless of when s/he actually received it), or within 19 days of issue if issued by the Business Centre. **Note:** all days count when calculating the 14- and 19-day period, not just 'business days'.

The client can:

- send ('file') a defence or counterclaim to the court (see p315); *or*
- file an acknowledgement of service at the court within the 14- or 19-day period if s/he is unable to file a defence in time or wishes to dispute the court's jurisdiction – eg, if a creditor has issued proceedings for an amount due under a regulated consumer credit agreement in the High Court rather than, as required, in the county court. Once an acknowledgement of service has been filed, the client must file the defence within 28 days of the date of service of the claim form/particulars of claim; *or*
- send ('serve') an admission to the creditor, admitting the whole of the claim (see p303); *or*
- still send the admission to the creditor outside the 14- or 19-day period, provided the creditor has not requested a default judgment (see p311); *or*
- file an admission and defence at the court, admitting part of the claim but disputing the balance or making a counterclaim (see p315).

Filing and serving documents

Documents are normally served by post. However, parties can file documents at court by fax.[7] A document is not treated as filed until it is delivered by the court office's fax machine, so it is good practice to telephone the court and check it has been received. A fax delivered after 4pm is treated as filed the following day. Fax should not be used for routine or non-urgent documents nor, unless it is unavoidable, to deliver documents which attract a fee and those relating to a hearing that is less than two hours ahead.[8]

If a court or court office has published an email address for filing documents on the HM Courts and Tribunals Service website, the parties can send a document listed on the website to the court by email. This is not possible if a fee is payable for the particular step in the proceedings. Documents that can be filed by email include the acknowledgement of service, partial admission, defence and the directions questionnaire.[9]

If a claim has been issued electronically, a client can file an acknowledgement of service, part admission and defence electronically online. The claim form contains a password to enable her/him to access the case. A document is not filed until the transmission is received by the court. The time of receipt is recorded electronically. If a transmission is received after 4pm, the document is treated as filed on the next day the court office is open.

All parties to a claim can be served with documents, including the claim form, electronically if they have given their prior written consent to accept electronic service and a fax number or email address to which they should be sent. A fax number or email address included on a letterhead, claim form or statement of case is sufficient.[10]

2. Admitting a money claim

The admission and statement of means form

The admission form (Form N9A) provides the creditor and the court with information about the client's financial circumstances, and allows the client to admit the amount owing and make an offer to pay the debt. See p315 if the client only agrees that part of the amount claimed is due.

The statement of means accompanying any admission is a vital document. It may be all the creditor knows about the client's ability to pay. Apart from any information provided by the creditor, it is the sole basis for the court's decision about the rate of payment if the creditor does not accept the offer made by the client (see p307).

Completing Form N9A

Note: this section is also relevant to completing Form N245 (application to suspend a warrant of control or reduce an instalment order) and Form N56 (reply to attachment of earnings application). See p342 and p329.

Form N9A does not always fit the circumstances of the particular client. Be prepared to amend it as necessary in order to give the creditor and the court as complete and accurate a picture as possible of the client's situation. In addition, the headings in the income and expenditure sections do not always reflect the headings on a financial statement. Also, if a couple pool their income, it may not be possible to say who is paying for what. In such a case, the amount of the partner's income which is contributed to the expenditure listed should be shown as 'other income', unless the offer is being made on the basis of a joint financial statement, in which case the partner's income should be shown.

When Form N9A has been completed, it should be photocopied and sent by 'recorded delivery' to the address shown on the back of the claim form (Form N1). The copy should be kept on file.

- **Personal details.** This section should show the name, address and date of birth of the client. If there are joint defendants, separate forms should be completed and it should be made clear whether the offer made in Box 11 is a joint one as, otherwise, it is assumed that the offers are separate even though they are for identical amounts. Alternatively, if the income and expenditure are joint, each N9A form could offer half of the available income and cross-refer to the other form.

- **Dependants**. This information is needed to explain the level of expenditure. A partner should be included on the form as a dependant, even if s/he has an independent source of income. If a partner does not wish to be considered as a dependant, this fact should be noted either in the box or in an accompanying letter. S/he must, however, be included on the form because s/he is a member of the household and her/his presence may affect the level of instalment payments.
- **Employment**. Every employment status of the client should be shown (s/he may have more than one). If the client believes the standard boxes do not accurately describe her/his status, an additional description can be inserted. Take-home pay is entered in the income section. Courts do not take account of information provided by self-employed clients in Section 3 when determining a rate of payment and so the question about annual turnover for self-employed people appears unnecessary. However, the information may influence the decision the creditor makes on whether or not to accept the offer of payment. However, if the information is not easily available, it is sufficient to indicate employment status only.

    Details of any tax or national insurance arrears should be included in Sections 8 or 9. Other business debts should be included in Sections 8, 9 or 10, although Form N9A is not suitable for including income and expenditure details of a business that is still trading. If the client is a sole trader, s/he must make sure that her/his business and private expenses are not mixed. It might be appropriate for such a client to include the 'net profit' of the business as her/his income (ie, the income from the business less the expenses of the business) with provision for tax and national insurance (which is the client's personal liability) either in the expenditure section along with the household expenditure or as a debt if there are arrears. Guidance to court officers suggests that, if a client is still trading, unless the creditor is prepared to accept her/his payment offer, the papers should be referred to the district judge.
- **Bank accounts and savings**. Court officers are instructed to see whether an amount is available to pay either a large lump sum or a regular amount towards a debt. They should ignore any amounts that are less than one-and-a-half times a client's monthly income or seven times her/his weekly income.

    If the amount shown is more than the ignored amount and some, or all, of the money in an account is needed to pay a priority creditor, it is important that the money is not shown as being available for a non-priority debt. So, if the amount is intended to meet the expenses detailed in Section 7, this should be made clear, otherwise the court officer assumes it is available to pay the debt.

If the client has a joint bank account, only her/his share of any savings need be declared.

- **Property**. This section provides background information to the creditor and may indicate whether the debt could ever be enforced by a charging order in the event of default on the judgment (see p322). The client could fit into more than one category (eg, rented and council property), so could tick either or both boxes.

- **Income**. This section requires details of the client's income from all sources (including any disability or incapacity benefits, and benefits for children). See p48 for how to treat clients who are couples to help decide whether to show joint income and expenses on the form (see notes to Section 7).

  The decision is further complicated by the instruction at the top of Section 7. If, for example, a partner (or any other member of the household) pays all fuel bills, those items should not be included as an expense unless that person's contribution is included in 'Others living in my home give me'. Court officers are instructed to convert all figures to either weekly or monthly amounts for consistency, and so the form should be completed in the same way.

- **Expenses**. Unless joint income and expenditure figures are being used, only include items of expenditure actually paid for by the client out of her/his income, plus any contribution from, for example, a partner, disclosed in Section 6 (see notes for Section 6).[11] A major problem with this section is the absence of many categories of essential expenditure. These can be added in the space marked 'Others' and need not be limited to the three lines given – eg, TV packages, internet, telephone or mobile phone bills, insurance premiums and childcare costs. Always explain what 'other' expenditure is and use a covering letter to explain its importance, if necessary. The expenses figure at the end of Section 7 should be accurate and the items a court may consider 'non-essential' should be included, where possible, in one of the named categories listed on the form. If disability/incapacity benefits, or benefits for children cannot be fully accounted for in Section 7, a note should be added to explain that these payments are intended to meet the costs associated with disability, incapacity or bringing up children and are not intended to be used to pay unrelated debts. This should only be done with the client's agreement following discussion. It is not an adviser's role to decide how clients spend their money.

  Travelling expenses cover either fares or vehicle running costs plus petrol. Mail order catalogues are often used to budget for clothing, bedding and small household items, and so expenditure for these items can be listed in that section if the client pays for these items this way.

  Section 7 should include details of payments to meet the regular costs of ongoing services provided by priority creditors, including water charges (but any arrears of water charges should appear in Section 10, regardless of the instruction in Section 8).

Expenditure figures need to reflect accurately the actual spending as far as possible.

- **Priority debts.** This section requires information about offers which have already been accepted to prevent action by priority creditors in pursuit of arrears. Therefore, before submitting Form N9A it is desirable that arrangements with priority creditors have been made. If an arrangement has not yet been made with one or more priority creditors, state the total arrears outstanding to that creditor and amend the form by adding, for instance, 'payment to be arranged' or 'offering £x a month'. Otherwise, if the total arrears figures are given, court officers are advised to assume that arrears will be repaid in three months, except for hire purchase and mortgage arrears which might be spread over one to two years. If offers have been made, but a reply is awaited, they should be included on the form. Include priority business debts, such as VAT or income tax, here.

  Clients may be uncertain about what proportion of payments to priority creditors are to cover arrears. In this case, to save time, total payments, including arrears, could be entered in Section 7 under 'Expenses' and a note written in Box 8 to indicate this.

- **Court orders.** Only existing court orders should be listed, except the one subject to the present action. Use a separate sheet or financial statement if there is not enough room on the form.

- **Credit debts.** This section requires details of payments already arranged with other non-priority creditors who have not obtained a court order. The three spaces provided for such debts may not be adequate and another sheet may be needed. Only the amounts currently being paid, if any, should be included, but an accompanying financial statement is useful information to indicate the level of indebtedness and offers made to other creditors, as well as indicating how the offer on Form N9A has been calculated.

- **Offer of payment.** If the client wants to avoid a judgment for immediate payment, s/he must make an offer of payment in Box 11 – however small – in order to trigger the next step in the procedure. If there is available income, an offer should normally be made on a pro rata basis, but some kind of offer should always be made, even if it is only a nominal figure – eg, 50p or £1 a month.

3. **The judgment**

'Judgment' is the formal term for the court's decision in a case. Before judgment, the creditor is trying to establish that the client owes the money. After judgment, liability cannot be denied unless the client appeals (see p294) or applies to set the judgment aside (see p337). Sometimes the Civil Procedure Rules uses the phrase 'judgment or order'. This refers to the court document that establishes that the client is liable for the debt. A 'judgment debt' is a sum of money ordered to be paid by the judgment or by a court order in civil (ie, non-criminal) proceedings.

The court can order the client to pay the creditor:

- by monthly instalments; *or*
- in one instalment – eg, within 14 or 28 days; *or*
- immediately ('forthwith'). This means the client is inevitably unable to comply with the order and is automatically in arrears with the judgment.

If a client is unable to pay at the rate ordered by the court, s/he can take action to change the terms of the judgment (see p337).

If the creditor does not apply for judgment within six months of the expiry of the client's time for responding to the claim, the action is 'stayed' and the creditor must apply to the court for permission to proceed with it.[12]

After judgment, if the amount required is not paid within a month, details are entered in the Register of Judgments, Orders and Fines. This information is publicly available and is used by many credit reference agencies. Entries are cancelled six years after the date of judgment.

The creditor's response

When the creditor receives Form N9A (see p303), it decides whether to accept or reject the client's offer of payment. If the creditor accepts, it requests the court to enter judgment on Form N205A/225 for the sum claimed to be paid as offered and the court sends the client a copy (N30(1): judgment for claimant (acceptance of offer)). The creditor is not required to send a copy of Form N9A to the court when accepting the offer and so the court has no information on the client's ability to pay the judgment.

If the client fails to comply with the terms of the judgment, the creditor can decide whether to use one or more means of enforcement in order to obtain payment (see p318). Some creditors request orders for immediate payment ('forthwith') as a matter of course so they can take enforcement action immediately because the client will not have paid the debt, although in the case of charging orders, default in payment is no longer necessarily required (see p322).

If the client does not 'request time to pay', the creditor may specify the terms of the judgment (including immediate payment) and the court enters judgment accordingly. If the creditor does not specify any terms of payment, the court enters judgment for immediate payment.[13] A 'request for time to pay' is defined as a 'proposal about the date of payment or a proposal to pay by instalments at the times and rate specified in the request'.[14] So, if the client wants to avoid a judgment for immediate payment, s/he must make an offer of payment on Form N9A – however small – in order to trigger the next step in the procedure.

If the creditor rejects the offer, s/he must inform the court and supply reasons for the refusal and a copy of Form N9A. The court then enters judgment for the amount admitted and determines the rate of payment.

How courts calculate instalment orders

The amount is not more than £50,000

If the amount involved is not more than £50,000 (including costs), the rate of payment may be determined by a court officer.

Court officers carry out a determination without a hearing. HM Courts and Tribunals Service provides guidance on how to do this.[15] The following is a summary. The references are to the box numbers on Form N9A. The total income (Box 6) is the starting point. To this may be added any savings (Box 4). From this total income, the following are deducted:

- expenses (Box 7);
- priority debts (Box 8);
- court debts (Box 9);
- credit debt repayments (Box 10).

Court officers are instructed to use common sense when assessing essential items of expenditure and to allow a reasonable amount for items not listed in Box 7, but which are essential to the client's household – eg, payments for a vehicle or childminder to enable the client to work, or the cost of travelling to and from work. Although court officers are not expected to assess whether any of the amounts are too high, 'frivolous' and 'non-essential' items are disregarded. These are specified as:

- children's pocket money;
- money for gambling, alcohol or cigarettes;
- money for newspapers or magazines (unless essential for the client's work);
- holiday money.

However, the guidance gives the court officer discretion to allow £15 a week for 'sundries' (presumably per household).

The guidance also reminds court officers that creditors must state reasons for rejecting offers. Rejecting an offer because of the amount of the debt or the length of time it has been outstanding or because the offer is 'too low' is not sufficient unless the creditor can demonstrate inaccuracies in the information provided by the client.

The client should be allowed sufficient resources and time to pay priority debts, although court staff are instructed to make certain assumptions about what is a reasonable period for clearing such arrears. Although court officers are instructed to take a common-sense approach to credit debts, the guidance also states that 'there is no logical reason why these debts should take precedence over a county court judgment'.

The resulting figures are then transferred to a 'determination of means calculator' contained in the determination of means guidelines and the court officer works out the rate of payment based on the amount of 'disposable (available) income'. In some courts, the creditor is expected to complete the calculator electronically, but this does not mean the creditor decides which figures to allow or disallow, or what order is made. The guidance states that if the disposable income is:

- higher than the offer but lower than the figure the creditor is prepared to accept, the instalment order should be for the amount of disposable income;
- higher than the figure the creditor is prepared to accept, the instalment order should be for the amount the creditor is prepared to accept;
- lower than the offer, the instalment order should be for the amount the client has offered unless this is 'unrealistically high';
- nil or a negative figure, either the instalment order should be for the amount the client has offered (unless unrealistically high) or the matter should be referred to the district judge for advice or a decision.

When the court has decided on the rate of payment, it notifies both the creditor and client of the order made (on Form N30(2)). Either party can apply to the court for a reconsideration of this decision (known as 'redetermination' – see p310).

The guidance recognises that Form N9A is designed for individual, rather than business, debts and that, unless a business has provided information about its financial position, it is difficult for court officers to make a decision on the rate of payment. If the creditor has indicated the terms on which s/he will accept payment by instalments, the court officer can enter judgment accordingly. Otherwise, s/he is instructed to refer the matter to the district judge.

If the amount is more than £50,000

If the amount involved is more than £50,000, the rate of payment must be determined by a district judge.

A district judge may carry out a determination with or without a hearing (although hearings are very rare). In some courts, claims for less than £50,000 are also referred to the district judge for a determination.

The district judge must take into account:[16]

- the client's statement of means;
- the creditor's objections;
- any other relevant factors. Increasingly, this includes the fact that the client is a homeowner but the instalment offer is so low that it will not pay off the judgment within a reasonable period.

The district judge is not required to follow the guidelines issued to court staff. If the district judge decides to hold a hearing, the case is automatically sent to the client's home court (see p300).

When the court has decided on the rate of payment, it notifies both the creditor and client of the order made (on Form N30(2)). Either party can apply to the court for a reconsideration of this decision (known as 'redetermination' – see below).

Redetermination by a district judge

Note: if the decision on the rate of payment was made by the court without a hearing and the client is unable to afford the rate of payment, the following procedure (and not the procedure for varying payments on p341) should be used. If judgment was entered, either in default or on acceptance of the client's offer of payment, the following does *not* apply and the client should instead use the procedure for varying the rate of payment on p341.

If the court has decided the rate of payment without a hearing (a determination), either the creditor or the client can ask for the amount to be reconsidered (redetermined) by a district judge within 14 days of the order being served. No court fee is payable.[17] The client can request a redetermination regardless of whether the original determination was made by a court officer or the district judge (provided there was no hearing).

District judges are not bound by the determination of means guidelines and can make whatever order they think fit. If there is available income, Form N9A should be carefully completed so that a decision can be made from the form alone, and the decision is more likely to be upheld by a district judge if the creditor asks for a redetermination. This is particularly important where large amounts are owed or a creditor is particularly aggrieved for some other reason – eg, the creditor runs a local business which has provided goods or services to the client but no payments have so far been made under their agreement.

Most forms of enforcement of a judgment require the client to have defaulted on the terms of payment. However, the trend is for district judges to reject low or nominal offers of payment and make an order for immediate payment to enable the creditor to enforce the judgment. Such offers may be seen as unrealistic and the creditor may not be regarded as being unreasonable in refusing to accept an offer of payment which will take many years to pay off the judgment, if ever. If the client has property, assets or savings, these may be put at risk if no affordable instalment order is in place. On the other hand, if the client's financial difficulties are temporary, it is worth pointing this out to the court as, in these circumstances, the district judge may be more willing to make an instalment order at a low rate on the basis that it will be reviewed. However, in a decision made in 2018, the Court of Appeal decided that, for the court to make an instalment order, there must be a realistic expectation that the creditor would receive payment within a reasonable period of time.[18] In a case where a client could not really afford to pay anything, the court considered 'it could not interfere with the judgment creditor's right to seek enforcement of the judgment by whatever means are available to them'. What was a reasonable period would depend on the facts of the case. On the one hand, there would be cases where the creditor had its own cashflow requirements to consider and, on the other hand, there would be cases where allowing a period of time for full payment would not cause any significant prejudice to the creditor.

A client whose position is unusual may benefit from the wider discretion of a district judge if, for instance, payment could be made from money which s/he expects to receive in time or if s/he is seriously ill and likely to gain sympathy. All such arguments should be made clearly, and the application should be made by letter giving reasons why the matter should be reconsidered. The court arranges for the case to be sent to the client's home court.

If the original determination was made by a court officer, the redetermination may take place without a hearing unless one is requested. If the original determination was made by a district judge, the redetermination must be made at a hearing unless the parties agree otherwise. There is usually no indication on the judgment as to who carried out the original determination. Although you can establish this by a phone call to the court office, it is usually better to ask for a hearing so that the client's case can be put to the district judge in person. The decision is one for the client, not the adviser.

The request should always refer to redetermination under rule 14.13 of the Civil Procedure Rules, specify whether or not a hearing is required and set out why the original determination should be reconsidered – eg, the client cannot afford to pay the judgment at the rate ordered by the court but can pay at the rate of £x a month in accordance with the attached financial statement. If the client asks for the matter to be dealt with without a hearing, the request could be accompanied by a witness statement from the client setting out her/his case.[19]

If the determination was made by a district judge at a hearing, there is no right to request a redetermination. If circumstances change, either party can apply for a variation in the rate of payment ordered (see p341).

Default judgment

If the client fails to reply to the claim form (this includes a 'nil' or no offer of payment), the creditor can request that the court enters judgment in default on Form N205A/225. Default judgment cannot be entered if the client has, within the specified time limits:[20]

- filed a defence; *or*
- filed an acknowledgement of service; *or*
- filed or served an admission together with a request for time to pay (even if this is outside the time limit, provided judgment has not already been entered[21]).

The creditor must specify the date by when the whole of the debt is to be paid (which may be immediately) or the rate at which it is to be paid by instalments. If none is specified, the judgment is for immediate payment.[22]

If you think that default judgment has been entered, or is about to be, check with the court. If it has not been entered and the client files a defence, it appears that the creditor cannot request a default judgment on the basis that a defence filed outside the time limit specified in the Civil Procedure Rules is not a valid defence unless:

- an extension of time has been granted by the court under rule 3.1(2)(a) of the Civil Procedure Rules; *or*
- the creditor has agreed to an extension of time under rule 15.5 of the Civil Procedure Rules.[23]

However, if judgment has already been entered, the client should apply either to vary it (see p341) or set it aside (if appropriate, see p337).

Interest charges after judgment

In some cases dealt with by debt advisers, no interest is chargeable after a county court judgment is made. This is important, not only because it means that any payments the client is able to make reduces the amount outstanding, but also because, if the creditor knows that interest charges will have to stop once the matter is taken to court, s/he may be persuaded to stop charging interest once a client begins to experience difficulties in repaying.

The court can include simple interest in any judgment, at such a rate as it thinks fit, from the date the debt fell due to:[24]

- the date of payment, in the case of a debt paid before judgment; *or*
- the date of judgment ('discretionary interest'), in the case of debt for which judgment is entered.

Statutory interest

Some judgments carry simple interest from the date of judgment to the date of payment at the rate specified from time to time (currently 8 per cent a year since 1 April 1993; 15 per cent before this date). This is known as 'statutory interest'.[25]

Since 1 July 1991, county court judgments for £5,000 or more have carried statutory interest unless:

- under the terms of the judgment, payment is either deferred to a specified date or is to be made by instalments. Interest does not accrue until either the specified date or the date the instalment falls due; *or*
- the judgment arises out of a consumer credit agreement regulated by the Consumer Credit Act 1974;[26] *or*
- a suspended possession order is made; *or*
- an administration order or attachment of earnings order is in force.[27]

Since 27 May 2019, county courts have more flexibility over awarding interest and may order that statutory interest shall begin to run from a date before the relevant judgment was given.

Interest ceases to be due when enforcement proceedings (other than charging orders) are started in a county court, but if these do not recover any money, interest accrues as if the enforcement proceedings had never started.

It seems that if the client defaults under the terms of the original judgment and then obtains a variation or suspension of the judgment, interest does not accrue.

For the position where county court judgments are enforced in the High Court by Writ of Control, see p414.

Discretionary interest

Discretionary interest must be claimed specifically by the creditor in the particulars of claim and included in the 'amount claimed' figure on the claim form (Form N1). It cannot be claimed in addition to any other interest being charged at the same time, nor can it be awarded to run after the date of judgment. Provided the creditor restricts its claim to the rate of interest payable on judgment debts (currently 8 per cent a year – see p312), the claim for interest can be included in a default judgment or judgment on admission. Such a claim is not subject to the Limitation Act 1980 (see p291), but the client can ask the court to reduce the amount of interest included in the judgment if there has been a long delay in starting the proceedings with no satisfactory explanation for that delay.[28]

If a client wants to challenge a claim for discretionary interest, s/he must file a defence (see p315).

Contractual interest

Some credit agreements contain provisions for lenders to charge interest on the amount borrowed and additional interest in the event of default by the client ('contractual interest'). The general rule is that, once the lender obtains judgment, the right to any further contractual interest ceases. However, an agreement may contain a clause stating that the creditor can continue to charge contractual interest after a judgment is made. The House of Lords has ruled that such a clause is 'fair'.[29] Following the judgment in *Forward Trust v Whymark*,[30] which allowed lenders to obtain judgment for the outstanding balance of a loan without giving credit for any early settlement rebate, many lenders issue proceedings for the full sum owed (including interest pre-calculated to the end of the agreement). Other lenders (where the interest rate is variable) limit the claim and the judgment to the principal amount outstanding plus accrued interest to the date of judgment, while reserving the right to issue separate proceedings for the ongoing interest.

Clients who are paying off the judgment can be confused and alarmed to receive statements showing the debt increasing and demands from the creditor for additional payments. The judgment is satisfied once the amount sued for (plus costs) has been paid. Creditors who claim to be able to 'add' contractual interest to the judgment should be challenged, as should creditors who claim that a charging order enables them to recover post-judgment contractual interest, regardless of the position under the judgment.[31]

Before 1 October 2008 (or subsequently if the judgment does not relate to an agreement regulated by the Consumer Credit Act 1974), if creditors wished to include ongoing contractual interest in a judgment, they should have sought a judgment for the amount of interest to be decided by the court.[32] Although the House of Lords in *Director General of Fair Trading v First National Bank* declared that judgments should take account of accruing contractual interest so that courts could consider making time orders (see p366), it declined to decide whether the rules then in force actually allowed such judgments to be made.[33]

If a judgment is made on or after 1 October 2008 in relation to a regulated consumer credit agreement and the creditor wishes to pursue a claim for post-judgment contractual interest, it must serve a notice on the client stating its intention to charge interest after judgment and informing her/him of her/his right to apply for a time order (known as the 'first required notice'). This notice cannot be given until after the judgment has been made.

Subsequently, the creditor must serve further notices, containing details of the interest charged, at six-monthly intervals as well as annual statements (see p79 and p77). The creditor cannot charge post-judgment contractual interest for any period before the service of the first required notice or during any period when the creditor has failed to serve a subsequent notice.

In the case of fixed-sum regulated consumer credit agreements, advisers should also check that the creditor has served the statements required under section 77A of the Consumer Credit Act 1974 and that any statements are compliant (see p77).

Although these provisions only apply to judgments made on or after 1 October 2008, they apply to regulated agreements whenever made (provided the agreement contains a provision specifically allowing the creditor to charge interest after judgment).[34] If the agreement does not include such a provision, the creditor cannot charge contractual interest after judgment. Default notices served on or after 1 October 2008 (see p299) must contain a statement of the creditor's right to claim post-judgment contractual interest.

Once the judgment is paid off, the creditor must issue fresh proceedings to recover any post-judgment contractual interest to which it claims to be entitled. To avoid this, the client could apply for a time order in Box 11 of Form N9A as follows: 'I ask the court (1) to make a time order in the terms of my offer and (2) to amend the loan agreement in consequence so that no further contractual interest accrues after the date of judgment.'

Alternatively, the client can wait until the first required notice is served and then apply for a time order as above.

If a creditor threatens to pursue additional interest by taking further proceedings, you should obtain specialist advice.[35]

4. **Defending a money claim**

The defence and counterclaim form

Form N9B provides the client with an opportunity to explain the circumstances and facts of any dispute, which should be stated clearly and in sufficient detail. A defence should be submitted where there is one – eg, if the debt has already been paid. If the client cannot afford to pay the debt, this is not a defence, and the client should follow the admission procedure described on pp303–306.

A counterclaim can be made if the client has lost money because the creditor has failed to carry out her/his legal obligations, although a court fee is payable (unless the client is able to obtain remission – see p290).

Form N9B should be returned to court within 14 days of service of the particulars of claim. If the particulars of claim are served with the claim form (as is usually the case), the date of service is the date the claim form is deemed to have been served (see p302). If a defence cannot be prepared within this time, the client should return the acknowledgement of service (Form N9) to the court. S/he automatically then has a further 14 days in which to file a defence – ie, 28 days from the date of service of the claim form/particulars of claim. The client may need to obtain specialist consumer or legal advice before completing Form N9B.

If some of the claim is admitted and time is required to pay that amount, but some is disputed, both Forms N9A and N9B should be completed and returned to court. **Note:** these should not be sent to the creditor.

Challenging the creditor's costs

The pre-action conduct practice direction (see p281) imposes a general obligation on creditors to act reasonably in negotiations and avoid unnecessary court action. If this has not been complied with, the creditor's costs can be challenged.[36] The client must show that:
- s/he has made reasonable attempts to avoid court action; *and*
- issuing proceedings was not a proportionate response by the creditor to the client's attempt to settle the matter.

Examples of when this might be successfully argued include if:
- the client has made a payment arrangement with the creditor before proceedings were started and has complied strictly with it;
- the client has made what you regard as a reasonable payment offer but the creditor has unreasonably demanded higher payments – eg, other creditors have accepted offers made on the same basis and the creditor is unable to demonstrate where any additional payments are to come from;
- the creditor has not warned the client (as required by the pre-action protocol) that it intends to take court action by sending her/him a 'letter of claim' (also called a 'letter before action'), setting out details of the debt and warning the

client that, unless payment is made within a stated period (eg, 30 days), court action will be taken without further notice;[37]
- the creditor has acted unreasonably – eg, refused to negotiate or breached a code of conduct.

The court is required to take account of the conduct of both parties and also to assess the reasonableness of any offer made.

Beware of substituting what you consider to be reasonable for what a district judge is likely to consider reasonable, as the client must pay any additional costs incurred. As a general rule, district judges do not consider it unreasonable for a creditor to seek a judgment which the client appears unable to pay. On the other hand, the district judge may consider it unreasonable for a creditor to refuse an offer of payment, issue proceedings and then accept the same offer made on Form N9A.

Just because the creditor has failed to comply with the letter of the pre-action protocol, the court may not necessarily deprive the creditor of its costs. The protocol says that the court 'will consider whether all parties have complied in substance with the terms of the protocol and is not likely to be concerned with minor or technical infringements, expecially when the matter is urgent'. If the court decides the default has made no difference to the client's position, it is unlikely to deprive the creditor of its costs.

Allocating the case to the appropriate track

Defended cases in the county court are allocated to a 'track' (see p317). This determines the way the case in managed by the court. If the client disputes the debt on grounds other than that it was paid before the claim was issued and the claim is a 'money claim', a court officer sends both parties a notice of proposed allocation on Form N149A (small claims track), N149B (fast track) or N149C (multi-track).[38]

The notice of proposed allocation also requires the parties to complete a 'directions questionnaire' on Form N180 (small claims) or Form N181 (fast track and multi-track). Unrepresented parties are served with the appropriate directions questionnaire by the court. Other parties must download the appropriate form from http://hmctsformfinder.justice.gov.uk.

The completed questionnaire must be returned to the court within 14 days (small claims) or 28 days (fast track and multi-track). No fee is payable. It is very important that the client returns the completed directions questionnaire to the court within the time specified. If either party to a money-only claim fails to return the completed directions questionnaire on time, the court serves her/him with a further notice, giving her/him seven days within which to comply. If s/he again fails to do so, her/his claim or defence is struck out (ie, deleted), allowing the other party to ask for judgment unopposed.[39]

On receipt of the completed questionnaire, the case is automatically sent to the client's home court. This court:

- allocates the case to a track (see below); *or*
- sets a hearing date to consider allocation; *or*
- makes an order on the future conduct of the case ('case management directions'); *or*
- summarily disposes of the case (see p318); *or*
- if requested on the questionnaire by both parties, suspends further action for up to one month to enable the parties to try to settle the matter.

The tracks

The **'small claims track'** is the normal track for cases with a financial value of not more than £10,000.[40] On allocating the case, the court gives standard directions for its future conduct and fixes a hearing date at least 21 days ahead. The case is normally heard in private by a district judge. Debt advisers can represent clients at the hearing. Even if the value of the claim is more than £10,000, the court can still allocate the case to the small claims track.[41] The court does not usually allow more than a day for the hearing and so cases that are likely to last longer may not be considered suitable for this track by the court.

Even if the creditor wins the case, the client cannot be ordered to pay the creditor's costs (including the costs of any appeal) except:[42]

- the fixed solicitor's costs of issuing the claim;
- any court fees paid by the creditor;
- witness travel expenses or loss of earnings (not more than £95 a day);
- experts' fees, if any, not exceeding £750;
- 'costs to be paid by a party who has behaved unreasonably' (see below).

The Court of Appeal has approved the following definition of 'unreasonable behaviour':[43]

> Conduct cannot be described as unreasonable simply because it leads in the event to an unsuccessful result or because other more cautious legal representatives [or litigants in person] would have acted differently. The acid test is whether the conduct permits of a reasonable explanation. If so, the course adopted may be regarded as optimistic and as reflecting on a practitioner's [or litigant in person's] judgement, but it is not unreasonable.

If the case is to be allocated to the small claims track, provided the parties agree to mediation in their directions questionnaire, the case is referred to the free HM Courts and Tribunals Service mediation service.

The case is not sent to the client's home court until four weeks after the last directions questionnaire was filed, unless the court has been informed in the meantime that the case has been settled (in which case the claim is either stayed (ie, halted), discontinued (ie, withdrawn) or dismissed (ie, cancelled).

The '**fast track**' is the normal track for cases with a financial value of no more than £25,000, which the court estimates can be heard in a day.[44] On allocating the case, the court gives case management directions and sets a timetable in which those steps are to be taken. At the same time, the court also fixes either a hearing date or a period within which the hearing is to take place. The hearing of the case should take place within 30 weeks.

The '**multi-track**' is the normal track for all other cases – ie, cases with a higher financial value that cannot be heard in a day, or more complex cases requiring individual directions.[45] On allocating the case, the court either gives case management directions with a timetable in which those steps are to be taken (although no trial date or period is fixed) or fixes a hearing to consider the issues in the case and the directions that are required.

Summary disposal

In certain circumstances, the court can deal with a defended case without holding a full hearing. This is known as 'summary disposal'.

The court can 'strike out' (literally, delete) the particulars of a claim or defence if:

- no reasonable grounds are disclosed (eg, 'the money owed is £1,000' or 'I do not owe the money') for either bringing or defending the claim; *or*
- it is an abuse of the court's process – eg, if it raises issues which should have been dealt with in a previous case involving the same parties; *or*
- it is satisfied that a case either has no real prospects of success or is bound to succeed or fail on a point of law and there is no other compelling reason for the matter to go to trial. To have a 'realistic prospect of success' the case must be a convincing one and not be merely arguable.[46]

If there are significant factual issues between the parties, none of the above are appropriate.

The court can take this step either on its own initiative or if one of the parties applies. Courts are now more proactive in this area than in the past and you should therefore exercise great care when preparing defences and counterclaims. Defences which lack detail are likely to be struck out – ie, the defence must set out the relevant facts and reasons for disputing the claim.

If either the particulars of claim or defence are struck out, this means that it cannot be relied on and the party is unable to proceed. The court can then enter 'summary judgment' for the other party.[47]

---

5. **Enforcing a judgment**

Once judgment has been given, it is the creditor's responsibility (not the court's) to collect payment of the amount ordered by the court. It is, therefore, important

for the client to record all payments made and obtain receipts. If the client does not pay in accordance with the judgment, the creditor can attempt to enforce payment through the court by obtaining:
- a warrant of control (see p321);
- a charging order (see p322);
- an attachment of earnings order (see p329);
- a third-party debt order (see p332).

Explain to a client that, provided s/he keeps to the terms of the judgment, the creditor cannot take enforcement action, however unhappy it may be with the terms of the judgment (except to apply for a charging order if the judgment or order was made on or after 1 October 2012 – see p322). Emphasise that, if the judgment states that a certain payment should be made each month, it is important this amount is paid every single month by the date stated in the judgment. If payments are made in advance in a lump sum to cover future months and no payments made in the following months, the client has defaulted on the terms of the judgment and the creditor can take enforcement action against her/ him. For example, if a judgment states that payment must be made at the rate of £2 a month, but the client pays £6 to cover three months. If no payment is made in the second month, the client has defaulted.

The creditor can use any available method of enforcement, and can use more than one method, either at the same time or one after the other.[48] However, while an attachment of earnings order is in force, the creditor cannot take any other type of enforcement action against the client unless the court gives permission.[49]

See p337 for how to prevent enforcement.

Information order

An information order is an order for the client to attend the court, in person, to be interviewed by a court official about her/his means or any other matter about which information is needed to enforce a judgment. An information order is commonly known as an 'oral examination'.

An information order is not a way of enforcing a judgment, but an information-gathering process. A creditor can apply for an order at any time to obtain information, even where enforcement of the judgment has been stayed or the client has not defaulted or missed payments.[50]

A creditor who has obtained a judgment against someone can apply to court on Form N316 for an information order requiring that person to attend a hearing at the county court hearing centre serving the address where the client lives before either a district judge (if there are 'compelling reasons') or, more usually, a senior court official.

The information order is on Form N39 and must be served personally on the client at least 14 days before the hearing. Within seven days of service, the client can require the creditor to pay her/his reasonable travel expenses to and from the court. These are likely to be added to the judgment and so ultimately paid by the client, but it is always worth the client requesting travel expenses from the creditor because if they are not paid, s/he cannot be committed to prison for non-attendance at the hearing. Form N39 contains a list of documents that the client is required to bring to court – eg, pay slips, rent book, credit agreements and outstanding bills. The creditor can ask the court to add further documents to the list.

At the hearing, the court officer asks the client a set of standard questions contained on Form EX140 (available from http://hmctsformfinder.justice. gov.uk). This is a 12-page questionnaire designed to find out what money, goods, property or other resources the client has to satisfy the judgment, in order for the creditor to decide what action to take next. The creditor can ask additional questions. The client must answer on oath. The client must attend the hearing. If s/he does not appear, refuses to take the oath or to answer any questions, or possibly if s/he fails to bring any documents listed on Form N39 to the hearing, the court can make a suspended order committing her/him to prison unless s/he attends a further hearing and complies with the other terms of the original order – ie, produces documents and takes the oath. If s/he again fails to comply, s/he will be arrested and brought before the judge to decide whether or not s/he should be committed to prison. In practice, the client will not be sent to prison provided s/he co-operates in the process, and cannot be committed if s/he requested travel expenses for the first hearing and these were not paid by the creditor.

You can help a client who has been served with an information order by providing a financial statement and a list of other debts and capital resources (including any equity in a house) in accordance with the information required by Form N39, together with a letter explaining why the client is unable to obtain any of the required information. You can also help by going through the questions on Form N39 with the client before the hearing.

An information order is usually followed by further action, if any is possible – eg, the creditor may apply for an attachment of earnings order or a charging order. It is therefore important to pre-empt this, if possible, by submitting the above information to the creditor, implementing the most appropriate strategy for all the debts, and agreeing this with the creditor who has requested the information order before the hearing, which may then no longer need to take place. If this cannot be agreed, it may still be appropriate to offer the strategy to all the other creditors, and this fact (along with any responses available) can be reported at the hearing. If the client has defaulted on payments, an application for variation of the judgment should be made to prevent enforcement. The court can also treat the hearing as an application for an administration order (see p445).[51]

Warrant of control

A warrant of control is a document that allows the county court bailiff (or 'enforcement agent') to take and sell goods belonging to the client to pay a judgment debt plus any court fees and costs. If the client does not keep to the payments ordered by the court, the creditor can ask the court to issue a warrant of control once a payment is missed, provided it remains unpaid when the warrant is issued.[52] The warrant can be for the whole amount of the judgment outstanding or just the arrears, which must be at least £50 or the amount of one monthly instalment (or four weekly instalments), whichever is greater.

Following an application, the warrant is issued to one of the 12 Warrant of Control Support Centres in England and Wales which will initially manage the warrant by:

- attempting to contact the client to check that s/he is aware of the judgment, inform her/him that the warrant has been issued and provide information about the next steps, available options and signpost to debt advice;
- identifying potentially vulnerable clients, informing the creditor and and asking them how they wish to proceed;
- engaging with the client to try and resolve payment of the warrant through:
  - encouraging the client to engage and make an arrangement to pay directly with the creditor; *or*
  - discussing the possibility of agreeing a longer term payment plan by completing a statement of means form and suspending the warrant with the creditor's agreement; *or*
  - agreeing an informal payment plan (maximum of three months following an initial payment) which will be managed by the centre.

If the centre is unable to contact the client or the client does not engage or defaults on an agreed repayment plan, the warrant is passed back to the court for the bailiff to be instructed to visit the client.

Goods can be taken unless the amount shown on the warrant plus costs are paid. Certain goods are exempt from being taken (see p426).

The client can apply for the warrant to be suspended (see p343).

A creditor who wishes to issue a warrant more than six years after the date of the judgment must obtain the prior permission of the court. Ordinarily, the delay itself means the court will refuse permission, unless the creditor can explain the delay and show that there are exceptional circumstances.[53] If the creditor does not get permission, the client can apply to discharge the warrant on Form 244 (see p288).

A county court judgment may be transferred to the High Court for enforcement by taking control of the client's goods if the judgment is between £600 and £5,000. It must be transferred if it is for more than £5,000. Judgments relating to agreements regulated by the Consumer Credit Act 1974 cannot be transferred to the High Court, regardless of the amount of the judgment.[54] If you come across a judgment relating to a regulated consumer credit agreement which has been transferred to the High Court for enforcement, get specialist advice.

The transfer to the High Court takes place using the 'fast track procedure' under CPR 83.19. This involves requesting the county court for a certificate of judgment combined with a request for a writ of control on form N293A. The grant of the certificate operates as an order to transfer the proceedings to the High Court which then issues the writ. This procedure is only available for enforcement of judgments by writ of control.

It is the general practice of High Court enforcement officers to charge statutory interest on debts between £600 and £5,000 from the date of the certificate – on the basis that the judgment is now treated as a High Court judgment – and to continue to charge statutory interest on judgments for £5,000 or more. It is arguable that judgments for less than £5,000 should not attract statutory interest even when being enforced in the High Court because under the County Court (Interest on Judgment Debts) Order 1991 statutory interest is only applied to 'relevant judgments' defined in the Order as: 'a judgment or order of a county court for the payment of a sum of money of not less than £5,000'. However, this argument has not been tested in court and it is by no means certain that a judge would accept it.[55]

See Chapter 14 for more information about bailiffs.

Charging order

A charging order is a court order that secures the amount owed under the judgment usually against the client's interest in a property, and this is then entered on the Land Registry.

When the property is sold, the judgment debt, together with court fees/costs and any statutory interest (but not contractual interest),[56] must be repaid out of the balance of the proceeds of sale after any prior mortgages or charges are paid.

A charging order can only be made if judgment has been entered and, if the judgment was made before 1 October 2012, the client has defaulted on its terms. If the judgment was made before 1 October 2012 under which the client was required to pay a sum of money by instalments, it is arguable that a charging order cannot be made unless the client defaults on the instalment order. At the very least, if the client has not defaulted, this is a matter which the court must take into account in the exercise of its discretion whether or not to make a charging order. **Note:** although the client can apply for a variation at any time (see p341), if, in the meantime, the creditor applies for a charging order and obtains an interim order (see p323), the variation may not prevent the charging order being made.[57]

If the judgment was made on or after 1 October 2012, a charging order can be made even though the client has not defaulted in payment of the instalment order.[58] However, when deciding whether or not to make a charging order, the court must take into consideration the fact that the client has not defaulted.

The effect of a charging order is to turn an unsecured debt into a secured one. Some district judges regard this as reasonable, even if the client has not defaulted on the instalment order, especially in cases of nominal offers, or if it appears that the client's offer of payment will not clear the debt for many years. You should follow the process outlined on pp303–11 as far as redetermination, if necessary, in order to obtain an instalment order that will prevent any further enforcement action (except by way of a charging order), provided the client does not default.

Although charging orders are normally made against a person's home (including a part share in a home – see p326) or business premises, they can also be made against shares or the client's interest under a trust.

Charging orders are frequently sought by creditors and this trend is likely to continue.

Interim charging order

Applications for charging orders are made to the County Court Money Claims Centre. The creditor must first apply for an interim charging order on Form N379.[59]

The application must include details of the outstanding balance due and the amount of any arrears of instalment payments due under the judgment. The creditor must also provide details of the client's interest in the property to be charged, and details and addresses of all other creditors if this information is known to the creditor – eg, if you have previously sent the creditor a financial statement containing details of the client's other debts.[60]

The application is dealt with by a court officer (without a hearing) unless the application concerns a judgment where an instalment order was made before 1 October 2012 or the court officer considers that the application should be dealt with by a district judge. Unless the district judge transfers the application for the final charging order to the client's home court for a hearing, a copy of Form N379 and the interim charging order must be served by the creditor on:

- the client;
- any joint owner;
- the client's spouse or civil partner, if known; *and*
- any other creditors identified on Form N379,

within 21 days of the interim order, so they have the opportunity to object.

The creditor must also file a certificate of service at the County Court Money Claims Centre in relation to each person served, together with a statement of the amount due under the judgment, within 28 days of the date of the interim order.[61]

Any party may request that a decision by a court officer be reconsidered by a district judge within 14 days of being served with the interim order. Reconsideration will take place without a hearing.[62]

The creditor applies to the Land Registry to register a 'notice' or 'restriction' on the property. This is a warning that an application is about to be made for a final charging order and means that if the client attempts to dispose of the property or her/his interest in it, the creditor is informed and can object to the transaction. The Land Registry sends a copy of the registration to the client as soon as it is received. This effectively 'blocks' any transfer or sale of the property made with the intention of avoiding the charge.

Final charging order

The second stage in the charging order process is for the creditor to obtain a final charging order. A district judge decides whether to make the interim charging order final, or to discharge it. S/he should take into account both the personal circumstances of the client and whether any creditors would 'be likely to be unduly prejudiced by the making of the order'. If the judgment was made on or after 1 October 2012, is payable by instalments and the client has not defaulted, the court must take this into account (but may still make the final charging order).[63]

After a charging order has been made, the creditor can wait until the property is sold, in which case it is paid out of the proceeds of sale. Alternatively, it can apply to the court for an order for sale (see p327).

Note: some creditors argue that a charging order allows them to enforce payment of accrued contractual interest even though it forms no part of the judgment. If a creditor tries to argue this, get specialist advice.[64]

Objecting to the order

If the client or any other person served with the interim order wishes to object to the final order being made, s/he must file at the County Court Money Claims Centre and serve on the creditor written evidence stating the grounds for this.[65] S/he must do so no later than 28 days after the interim order was served. Any relevant documents should be attached.

The County Court Money Claims Centre must then transfer the application for the final charging order for a hearing at the county court hearing centre for the district in which the client lives. This court must serve notice of the hearing on the client and all the other people served with the interim order.

Unless the application for the final charging order has been transferred in this way, the application is considered by a district judge without a hearing once the period allowed for objecting to the making of the order has expired.[66]

If the client wants to defend the charging order, the following arguments could be used.

- Some creditors believe they can apply for a charging order at any time, so check whether any of the instalment payments due under a judgment have been missed and, if so, whether they have now been brought up to date. If no instalments have been missed or they have been brought up to date, the court cannot grant a charging order, unless the judgment was made on or after 1 October 2012 (see p322).[67]

- Check whether an application to vary the judgment was submitted and the variation order granted before the interim order was made. If it was, provided the new payments have been maintained, the application for a charging order should fail, unless the judgment was made on or after 1 October 2012 (see p322). However, a variation order made after the date of the interim order does not prevent a final order being made regardless of the date of the judgment.[68]

- Check whether other creditors have been notified of the charging order application, as the charging order could unduly prejudice their rights and, therefore, should not be made final. If the court was not given details in the charging order application of other creditors of which the creditor in question was aware (eg, because they had been included on a financial statement), it can be argued that the creditor has not complied with the rules and the client has been denied a fair hearing, as the court must take into account prejudice to creditors.[69] Alternatively (and more usually), the district judge may adjourn the case while other creditors are notified. If none of the creditors lodges an objection, this 'prejudice to other creditors' argument may fail.

- The client is technically insolvent and so a charge in favour of one creditor prejudices the rest. This will be the case if there was insufficient equity in the property to cover all the debts in full and:
  - there is, or is about to be, an arrangement to distribute the proceeds of sale on a pro rata basis among the client's creditors; *or*
  - an individual voluntary arrangement proposal is being made; *or*
  - the client is petitioning for bankruptcy or another creditor is doing so.

  However, a final charging order made after a bankruptcy petition has been presented against the client is not necessarily set aside once a bankruptcy order is made, unless the court was expressly made aware of the existence of the petition before the final charging order hearing.[70]

Note: a client cannot object to a charging order on the grounds that the application was made more than six years after the date of judgment or that the property is in negative equity.[71]

Conditions attached to a charging order

A charging order can be made either with or without conditions.[72]

A client could apply for a condition to be imposed to prevent the charging order being used as a basis for an order for sale in certain circumstances – eg, after the youngest child of the family ceases to be in full-time education. The court should be asked to consider the possibility of enforcement by the creditor and should either attach conditions or, if there is no instalment order in place or the current order is unaffordable, suspend it on terms (see p326).

If the client intends to ask the district judge to attach conditions to the final order or to suspend it on terms, s/he should submit written evidence in the form of a witness statement together with a financial statement. If a final order has already been made, it is still possible to apply to the court to vary or discharge the order if it seems that the court did not consider the client's circumstances at the time the order was made or her/his circumstances have since changed. A co-owner or a joint occupier who is a spouse or civil partner can also apply.[73]

Suspending a charging order

If the judgment was made on or after 1 October 2012 and an instalment order is already in place, see p322.

Enforcement of a final charging order may be suspended on payment of instalments.[74] The client can apply for these payments to be varied if her/his circumstances change. Some district judges say that they cannot suspend the charging order or they cannot consider the application as part of the process for making an interim or final charging order. However, because the court should attempt to deal with as many aspects of the case as it can at the same time, it should be asked to deal with the application at the same time.[75]

Because a charging order is an indirect method of enforcement (ie, it only secures payment but does not actually produce any money at the time), a creditor may decide to use one or more other method(s) of enforcement as well. It is, therefore, good practice to apply for a variation of the judgment if either there is currently no instalment order in place or the instalment order is unaffordable (see p341), as well as a suspension of, or the attachment of conditions to, the charging order (see p342).[76] In practice, applying at the final charging order hearing for an order suspending enforcement of the charging order and all other enforcement action achieves the same result, provided the client pays instalments as ordered.

Joint ownership of property

A charging order can be made against a client's share in a property. If a client owns only part of a property, a charging order can still be made, but it only applies to her/his share.

If a charging order is made, the creditor becomes a party with an interest in the property and can apply for an order to sell the property[77] so that the creditor's interest can be realised.[78]

The court must take into account:[79]

- the intentions of the owners at the time of the original purchase – ie, the purpose for which the property was bought. For example, it may be that a court should not order the sale of an asset that was bought for a specific purpose, until the need for it has ceased to exist. If this is a correct interpretation, a family home should not be sold until all members of the family have ceased to need it;

- the welfare of any child who occupies the property as her/his home;
- the interests of any secured creditor.[80] In one case, the Court of Appeal ordered the sale of a property where there was sufficient equity to pay only part of the debt and the client was apparently unable to make any offer of payment.[81]

All the circumstances should be considered, including the size of the judgment debt and the value of the property. The personal circumstances of the client and other occupiers should be explained to the court in detail. Point out:

- that it is not equitable (or fair) for a whole family or group of occupants to be evicted for the debt of one of their members;
- any special factors – eg, age, disability, illness, need for stability at work or school, availability of alternative housing, and the effect on children;
- the history of the loan.

If an application for an order for sale is made (see below), a claim form is sent to all co-owners of the property. This may include someone who does not owe money to the creditor who has obtained the charging order. However, because that person owns part of the property against which the debt is secured, the court must treat her/him as a joint defendant in the case. This means s/he is entitled to be heard at the hearing of the application and to put forward her/his own case, if necessary.

If a divorce petition (or application to dissolve a civil partnership) has been served, any application for a charging order (or order for sale) should normally be considered along with the finances and property of the couple.[82] In these circumstances, an application for an adjournment should be made to enable the matter to be considered by the family court.

One important side effect of a charging order on a jointly owned property is that it 'severs' any joint tenancy. This means that if either of the joint owners dies, her/his share no longer passes automatically to the survivor but, instead, is dealt with as part of her/his estate (see p149). One of the consequences of this is that any creditors have an estate against which to claim.

Order for sale of property

Note: if the judgment was made on or after 1 October 2012 and there is an instalment order in place, the creditor cannot apply for an order for sale unless the client has defaulted on the instalment order and no order for sale can be made if any arrears due under the instalment order have been paid by the date of the hearing for the order for sale.[83]

Note also: an application for an order for sale is both serious and legally complex. Specialist advice should always be obtained.

An order for sale is a court order to sell a property that is the subject of a charging order so that the debt can be paid out of the proceeds. It is only possible after a charging order has been made final and if any conditions or terms attached to the order have not been met.

An order for sale cannot be made in relation to an agreement regulated by the Consumer Credit Act 1974 where the amount owed is less than £1,000.[84]

A district judge must use her/his discretion to decide whether to order a sale.[85] It is an extreme sanction and is a draconian step to satisfy a simple debt. It is therefore only likely to be used if a client's failure to pay has been intentional or where a sale is the only realistic way in which the debt will be paid. Human rights issues have, so far, not had much effect on applications for orders for sale. It is arguable that a court faced with an application for an order for sale should always consider whether it is proportionate to deprive the client of her/his home in order to satisfy a modest debt. In assessing proportionality, the court should also consider whether the creditor seeking the order has bought the debt and how much it is out of pocket.[86] In the past, applications for orders for sale have been very rare.

The creditor must apply using the procedure under Part 8 of the Civil Procedure Rules. This requires a hearing in all cases. The application is made to the court that made the charging order. The client should complete and return the acknowledgement of service not more than 14 days after the service of the claim form, together with a request for transfer to the client's local court (where appropriate) and any written evidence, indicating that s/he intends to oppose the order for sale and her/his reasons for doing so.

It is vital that clients attend and are represented at this hearing.

If possible, any instalments in arrears should be paid by the hearing date. If the judgment was made on or after 1 October 2012, this prevents an order for sale being made and may well prevent it in other cases. Even if a sale is ordered, the court can suspend the order on terms (eg, payment by instalments) or postpone the order for sale until a future date – eg, when the youngest child of the family reaches 18. Discuss with the client a way of ensuring that the charging order creditor is paid, and this debt must now be treated as a priority (see Chapter 8). A full financial statement should be completed and an offer of payment made if possible. If not, consider whether there are any exceptional circumstances that could be used to prevent an order being made. Always recheck that the client's income is maximised (see Chapter 7).

If the court accepts the client's offer of instalments, ask it to adjourn the application for an order for sale on condition that the client makes the payments. If an order for sale is made and not suspended, the client is normally given 28 days to pay the debt or leave the property. If this does not happen, the creditor can apply for a warrant of possession (see p364).

Attachment of earnings order

An attachment of earnings order requires an employer who is paying wages, statutory sick pay or an occupational pension to a client to deduct some of it and make payments to the court to meet the debt. It prevents the creditor from enforcing the debt by a warrant of control, a charging order (and, arguably, an order for sale) or third-party debt order without first obtaining the permission of the county court.[87]

Note: the courts cannot make an attachment of earnings order against the pay or allowances of a member of the armed forces, but arrangements can be made through the Defence Council for compulsory deductions to be made from the client's pay, even if the client is stationed outside the UK.

Attachment of earnings orders cannot be used to deduct amounts from state benefits or tax credits.

They can be made by the magistrates' and the county courts. See p395 for information on attachment of earnings orders made for magistrates' court fines or attachment of earnings orders made under liability orders.

The county court can make an attachment of earnings order to cover a default on any judgment debt (including High Court judgments, which must be transferred to the county court for enforcement[88]).

A creditor can request an attachment of earnings order for any unpaid judgment debt over £50. If the creditor is applying to enforce a judgment made in the Business Centre in respect of a money-only claim and the case has subsequently been transferred to a different hearing centre, the application must be made to that hearing centre. Otherwise, if the judgment was made in the Money Claims Centre or the Business Centre, the application must be made to the county court hearing centre that serves the address where the client lives (the client's 'home court').

The client receives a notice of the application (Form N55), together with Form N56 to complete, showing a statement of her/his means. Form N56 is similar to Form N9A (see p303), except there is provision to include a partner's income. **Note:** the time limit for returning Form N56 is only eight days. If the client does not return Form N56, the court can order her/him to complete a statement of means and the client's employer can be ordered to supply a statement of earnings. This must always be completed and returned to the court, as failure to do so can lead to a summons for a personal appearance. Failure to comply can lead to imprisonment.

Requesting a suspension

There is space on Form N56 to request that a suspended attachment of earnings order be made. This allows the client to agree to make regular payments. A request for a suspended order should always be granted, unless an attachment of earnings order is already in force. A client may decide to make a request if an attachment of earnings order could lead to her/his dismissal by her/his employer.

How the order is made

A court officer uses the information supplied on Form N56, together with a formula contained in the protected earnings calculator contained in the determinations of means guidelines, to make an attachment of earnings order and set a 'protected earnings rate' (see p308). This is an amount that the court considers is the minimum the client, and any dependants, need to live on. The income support or income-based jobseeker's allowance level is considered the minimum amount required plus housing costs, essential work-related expenses and other court orders. If, after taking into account any partner's income or other sources of income, the client has less than this amount (the protected earnings rate), an order is not made.

The guidance instructs court officers to disregard disability living allowance, attendance allowance and personal independence payment when calculating income. It suggests that deductions from earnings (the 'normal deduction rate') are set at between 50 per cent and 66 per cent of the client's 'disposable income' – ie, the difference between the client's net earnings and the protected earnings rate.

If the client does not give sufficient information on Form N56, the court officer refers the matter to the district judge to make an order.

Both the client and the creditor have 14 days in which to give notice to the court that they object to the terms of the attachment of earnings order. If either objects, a hearing is arranged in the client's home court, at which the district judge can make any order s/he thinks appropriate. An objection can be made by letter stating the grounds – eg, if the protected earnings rate or the normal deduction rate does not leave the client with sufficient income for her/his essential expenditure.

A court can decide to make an administration order (see p445) when considering an attachment of earnings order if the total indebtedness is below the administration order limit.[89] The court should always consider this if there are other debts. If attachment of earnings is to be accepted by the client, converting it to an attached administration order can simplify repayments.

The effect of an attachment of earnings order

An attachment of earnings order reduces a client's flexibility to manage her/his own affairs and it may endanger her/his employment because it notifies the employer of debts. Some employers (eg, security firms or those where money is handled) may have a policy of dismissing anyone against whom a judgment is made. If this happens, the client should get specialist employment advice.

An attachment of earnings order tells the employer the total amount due under the judgment(s) concerned, and gives the normal rate to be deducted each week or month and states the protected earnings rate. The employer can only make deductions from any earnings in excess of the protected earnings rate. If the client's earnings are insufficient to enable the full, or any, deduction to be made, any resulting shortfall cannot be carried forward to the next payday.

Even if the principle of an attachment is accepted, you could argue against the normal deduction figure suggested. An offer could be made in Box 10 of Form N56 on a pro rata basis if the client has more than one non-priority debt. A good financial statement is the basis of this argument, showing how repayment of priority creditors represents essential expenditure and that amounts to cover these should be included in the protected earnings rate.

If an attachment of earnings order is made, a fee (currently £1) can be added to each deduction by the employer to cover administrative costs. If a client leaves a job, s/he must notify the court within seven days of any new employment and income. Failure to do so is an offence that could be punishable by a fine. If the client becomes unemployed or self-employed, s/he should write to the court immediately.

A county court attachment of earnings order does not take priority over an attachment of earnings order made to recover fines, maintenance or local taxes or a deduction from earnings order made to recover child support arrears, even if made earlier, but does take priority over a direct earnings attachment made by the Department for Work and Pensions to recover benefit or tax credit overpayments or social fund loans, provided the county court attachment of earnings order was made earlier.[90]

The combined effect may be to reduce the client's resources to a very basic level. In such a case, the client should be advised to apply to vary the attachment of earnings order on Form N244, quoting section 9(1) of the Attachment of Earnings Act 1971 (see p341).

Consolidated attachment of earnings order

If:[91]

- there are two or more attachment of earnings orders for debt; *or*
- one attachment of earnings order is in force and a second one is applied for; *or*
- one attachment of earnings order is in force and the client has at least one other county court judgment,

the client can ask the court to consolidate these two debts and all other debts on which there is a judgment. The court can also make such an order on its own initiative.

No procedure is specified, but the client should provide the court with details of the other judgments and a financial statement. There is no limit on the number of judgments or the amount owed. The advantage of this procedure is that there is only one protected earnings rate and one deduction figure. Some clients welcome this opportunity to avoid making several payments each month themselves.

Third-party debt order

A third-party debt order instructs someone (the 'third party') who owes money to the client (eg, a bank holding her/his savings) to pay the money to the creditor instead. Third-party debt orders were previously known as 'garnishee orders'.

A third-party debt order may only be given to a creditor who has already obtained a judgment that is not being complied with.[92]

The order is made in two stages. Firstly, the creditor must apply for an interim third-party order on Form N349. If the creditor is applying to enforce a judgment made in the Business Centre in respect of a money-only claim and the case has subsequently been transferred to a different hearing centre, the application must be made to that hearing centre. Otherwise, if the judgment was made in the Money Claims Centre or the Business Centre, the application must be made to the county court hearing centre which serves the address where the client lives (the client's 'home court').

An interim order temporarily prohibits the third party from making any payment which reduces the amount s/he owes the client to less than the amount specified in the order – ie, the balance of the debt plus the costs of the application. **Note:** any funds paid into the account following the interim order being served are not affected.

The interim order is followed by a final order after a hearing in front of a district judge. This must be at least 28 days after the interim order is made. If the client wants to object to the final order being made, s/he can apply to have the hearing transferred to her/his local court if necessary. At least three days before the hearing, the client (and also the third party) must file at court and serve on the creditor any written evidence in the form of a witness statement, setting out the grounds of objection.

When making a final order, the district judge has full discretion and should consider the position of both the client and any other creditors (if known).[93] If, for instance, the application relates to an account into which all the client's monthly income is paid, you should argue this would be unreasonable and would cause hardship to the client and her/his family, as well as preventing payments to other (possibly priority) creditors.

If the third party is a bank or building society, on receipt of the interim order it must search for all accounts held in the client's name, freeze them and give details to both the court and the creditor within seven days. The bank or building society can deduct £55 from the client's account balance towards the costs and expenses of responding to the order, regardless of the amount in the account. Similarly, the bank or building society must inform the court within seven days if the client has no account. If the bank or building society claims to be entitled to any of the money in the account, it must inform the court within seven days and state its grounds.

The court cannot make a third-party debt order in relation to a joint account if the other account holder is not liable for the debt under the judgment.[94]

Note: although the Department for Work and Pensions cannot itself be subject to a third-party debt order in relation to benefit payments, once the payment is in the client's bank or building society account, the bank or building society can be the subject of a third-party debt order in relation to the funds in that account.

An order cannot be made in respect of a joint debt if the judgment is against the client alone. However, a third-party debt order could be used if, for example, a client had told a creditor that an amount of capital would shortly be due from an endowment insurance policy in her/his sole name. The creditor could obtain a third-party debt order against the insurance company after the amount became due but before it had been paid out. For this reason, it is important not to reveal details of future money available to a client if it is required to pay priority creditors or to be shared among a number of creditors.

Note: in 2012, the High Court decided that a third-party debt order could be made against a tax-free lump sum that the debtor was entitled to draw from his pension fund, but which he had elected to defer.[95] The court made an order under section 37 of the Senior Courts Act 1981 requiring the debtor to authorise the creditor's solicitor to exercise his right to elect to withdraw the lump sum. Once made, the lump sum was due for payment and a third-party debt order could be made at that point.

Hardship payment order

If, because of an interim third-party debt order, a client finds her/his bank account frozen and s/he or her/his family is experiencing 'hardship in meeting ordinary living expenses' as a result of not being able to withdraw money from the account, s/he can apply to her/his local county court for a hardship payment order. The client must produce written evidence to prove both her/his financial position and the need for payment. Applications are made on Form N244 (see p288). The fee is £255 (full or partial remission can be applied for). Two days' notice of the hearing must be given to the creditor, but the court can dispense with this in cases of 'exceptional urgency' (when the court fee is £100). The court can permit the bank or building society to make one or more payments out of the account either to the client or some other specified person.[96]

Enforcing foreign judgments

Clients may find themselves incurring debts to creditors in other countries. For example, a client may have lived overseas and taken out a loan or a credit card with a local bank and is now in arrears, or may have gone on holiday and incurred charges for healthcare which were not covered by her/his insurance. If the creditor wrote to the client to demand payment and the client did not respond, it may have started proceedings in that country and obtained a judgment against the client which it now wants to enforce in the UK. (**Note:** the fact that the debt was incurred abroad does not prevent the creditor bringing proceedings against the client in the UK). The law on the recognition and enforcement of foreign judgments in the UK derives from: European treaty law; UK statute law; and common law (ie, derived from caselaw rather than legislation). Following the UK's exit from the European Union on 31 January 2020, there is a transitional period for implementing the European Union (EU) withdrawal agreement which is due to end on 31 December 2020. The position below will, therefore, continue to apply for the time being, but may change after that date so far as European treaty law is concerned.

- **Judgments obtained in EU member states in proceedings that started on or after 10 January 2015.**[97] These are automatically recognised and there is little formal procedure to be followed. The creditor must obtain a standard certificate of enforceability of the judgment from the relevant EU court. Copies of both the certificate and the judgment must be served on the client before any enforcement proceedings are taken. It can then be be enforced in England and Wales in the same way as any other judgment by the methods outlined on pp318–33. There is no limitation period as such, provided the judgment is still enforceable in the EU country. The client can challenge the recognition of a judgment if it was a default judgment and s/he was not given sufficient notice of the proceedings. This does not apply if the client had the opportunity to challenge the default judgment but failed to do so. If the client wants to challenge the creditor's right to enforce its judgment, s/he must apply for an order refusing to recognise or enforce the judgment.

- **Judgments obtained in EU member states in proceedings that started before 10 January 2015.**[98] It is relatively straightforward for a creditor to obtain recognition and move to enforce these judgments. The creditor must make an application to the High Court for the judgment to be registered. This application is made without the client being given notice. The application must include an authenticated copy of the judgment, written evidence in support of the application and a standard certificate of enforceability from the relevant EU court. There are limited grounds on which the High Court can refuse to recognise and enforce the judgment. Once the judgment has been registered, the creditor must serve a copy of the registration order on the client. It can then be be enforced in England and Wales in the same way as any other judgment by the methods outlined on pp318–33. There is no limitation period as such, provided the judgment is still enforceable in the EU country. Recognition can be refused if the judgment was a default judgment and the client was not given sufficient notice of the proceedings. This does not apply if the client had the opportunity to challenge the default judgment but failed to do so. If the client wants to challenge the creditor's right to enforce its judgment, s/he must appeal against the granting of the registration order.

- **Judgments obtained in Iceland, Norway or Switzerland.**[99] It is relatively straightforward for a creditor to obtain recognition and move to enforce these judgments. The creditor must make an application to the High Court for the judgment to be registered. This application is made without the client being given notice. The application must include an authenticated copy of the judgment, written evidence in support of the application and a standard certificate of enforceability from the Icelandic, Norwegian or Swiss court. There are limited grounds on which the High Court can refuse to recognise and enforce the judgment. Once the judgment has been registered, the creditor must serve a copy of the registration order on the client. It can then be be enforced in England and Wales in the same way as any other judgment by the methods outlined on pp318–33. There is no limitation period as such, provided the the judgment is still enforceable in Iceland/Norway/Switzerland. Recognition can be refused if the judgment was a default judgment and the client was not given sufficient notice of the proceedings. This does not apply if the client had the opportunity to challenge the default judgment but failed to do so. If the client wants to challenge the creditor's right to enforce its judgment, s/he must appeal against the granting of the registration order.

- **Judgments obtained in certain dependent territories of EU member states.**[100] It is relatively straightforward for the creditor to obtain recognition and move to enforce these judgments. The creditor must make an application to the High Court for the judgment to be registered. This application is made without giving the client notice. The application must include an authenticated copy of the judgment, written evidence in support of the application and a standard certificate of enforceability from the foreign court. There are limited grounds on which the High Court can refuse to recognise and enforce the judgment. Once the judgment has been registered, the creditor must serve a copy of the registration order on the client. It can then be be enforced in England and Wales in the same way as any other judgment by the methods outlined on pp318–33. There is no limitation period as such, provided the judgment is still enforceable in the foreign country. Recognition can be refused if the judgment was a default judgment and the client was not given sufficient notice of the proceedings. This does not apply if the client had the opportunity to challenge the default judgment but failed to do so. If the client wants to challenge the creditor's right to enforce its judgment, s/he must appeal against the granting of the registration order.

- **Judgments obtained in various Commonwealth countries and British overseas territories.**[101] It is relatively straightforward for a creditor to obtain recognition and move to enforce these judgments. The creditor must make an application to the High Court for the judgment to be registered. This application is made without giving the client notice. The application must include an authenticated copy of the judgment and written evidence in support of the application, but such judgments are only recognised and registered if the original court had jurisdiction over the client. Once the judgment has been registered, the creditor must serve a copy of the registration order on the client. It can then be enforced in England and Wales in the same way as any other judgment by the methods outlined on pp318–33. The creditor must apply for registration of the foreign judgment within 12 months of the date of the judgment. Recognition can be refused if the client was not duly served and did not receive sufficient notice of the proceedings. Enforcement of judgments for taxes, fines or penalties is not allowed. Recognition can also be refused if the judgment was obtained by fraud or if the foreign court did not have jurisdiction over the client. The High Court will accept that the foreign court had jurisdiction if the client was ordinarily resident or had her/his place of business within the court's jurisdiction, or accepted the foreign court's jurisdiction by voluntarily taking part in the proceedings. If the client wants to challenge the creditor's right to enforce its judgment, s/he must apply for the registration order to be set aside.

- **Judgments obtained in Australia, Canada, India, Pakistan, Jersey, Guernsey, the Isle of Man, Israel, Suriname and Tonga.**[102] It is relatively straightforward for a creditor to obtain recognition and move to enforce these judgments. The creditor must make an application to the High Court for the judgment to be registered. This application is made without giving notice to the client. The application must include an authenticated copy of the judgment and written evidence in support of the application. Once the judgment has been registered, it can then be enforced in England and Wales in the same way as any other judgment by the methods outlined on pp318–33. The limitation period is six years from the date of the judgment. Recognition can be refused if the client was not duly served and did not receive sufficient notice of the proceedings. Enforcement of judgments for taxes, fines or penalties is not allowed. Recognition can also be refused if the judgment was obtained by fraud or if the foreign court did not have jurisdiction over the client. The High Court will accept that the foreign court had jurisdiction if the client was ordinarily resident or had her/his place of business within the court's jurisdiction, or accepted the foreign court's jurisdiction by voluntarily taking part in the proceedings, or if the proceedings concerned land situated in the foreign country. If the client wants to challenge the creditor's right to enforce its judgment, s/he must apply for the registration order to be set aside.

- **Judgments obtained in any other jurisdiction, including the United States, Russia and China.**[103] Such judgments can only be enforced by the creditor starting fresh proceedings in England and Wales to enforce the foreign judgment as a debt. Summary judgment can usually be obtained against the client on the basis that s/he has no real prospect of successfully defending the claim (see p318).[104] Once a judgment has been obtained in England and Wales, it can then be enforced in the same way as any other judgment by the methods outlined on pp318–33. The limitation period for starting the fresh proceedings is six years from the date of the foreign judgment. A judgment can be refused if the client was not duly served and did not receive proper notice of the foreign proceedings or the opportunity to defend her/himself. Enforcement of foreign judgments for taxes, fines or penalties is not allowed. A judgment can also be refused if the foreign judgment was obtained by fraud or if the foreign court did not have jurisdiction over the client. The High Court will accept that the foreign court had jurisdiction if the client was ordinarily resident or had her/his place of business within the foreign court's jurisdiction or accepted the foreign court's jurisdiction by voluntarily taking part in the proceedings. In addition, the foreign court will be presumed to have had jurisdiction if the client was present in the foreign country when the proceedings were commenced. If the client wants to dispute the creditor's right to enforce its judgment, s/he must raise any challenge to the enforcement of the foreign judgment as a defence to the claim.

Cases on the recognition and enforcement of foreign judgments in England and Wales are usually heard in the High Court.[105] In general, the High Court does not recognise or enforce foreign judgments which are subject to an appeal in the foreign country. If a client has a a foreign judgment debt which the creditor is trying to enforce and which the client wants to challenge, you should get specialist advice.[106]

Scotland and Northern Ireland

If a creditor wants to enforce a judgment made in Scotland or Northern Ireland in England and Wales (or vice versa), it must obtain a standard certificate from the original court and make an application to the High Court for this to be registered. It must apply within six months of the certificate being issued. Once the certificate has been registered, a copy of the registration order must be served on the client.

6. **Preventing enforcement**

There are a number of steps clients can take to prevent enforcement, or further enforcement, action.

Setting aside a judgment

If a judgment is 'set aside', its effect is cancelled and the client and creditor are put back into the position they were in before judgment was obtained. This includes the creditor cancelling any enforcement action.[107]

The court *must* set aside a default judgment if:[108]

- judgment was entered before the client's time for filing an acknowledgement of service or a defence had expired (see p302); *or*
- the client served an admission on the creditor, together with a request for time to pay before the judgment was entered (see p303); *or*

- the client paid the whole of the claim (including any interest or costs due) before judgment was entered. If the client paid the whole of the claim before the claim form was issued, s/he should have filed a defence (see p315).

The court also has the discretion to set aside a judgment if:[109]
- the client has a real prospect of success in the claim; *or*
- the court is satisfied that there is some other good reason why the judgment should be set aside/varied or the client allowed to defend the claim; *or*
- there has been an error of procedure, such as a failure to comply with a rule or practice direction.

Serving the claim form

Provided the creditor's claim form is served in accordance with the Civil Procedure Rules, the fact that the proceedings only came to the client's attention after judgment was entered is not a ground, in itself, for it to be set aside, even if the client alleges s/he did not receive the claim form.

The claim form is treated as having been served in accordance with the Civil Procedure Rules even if it is returned undelivered to the court, provided it was sent to the client's 'relevant address'. This is the client's usual or last known address unless:
- the creditor has reason to believe it is no longer the client's current address; *and*
- the creditor is able to establish the client's current address; *or*
- the creditor is unable to establish the client's current address, but considers there is an alternative place or method of service.

A claim form must be served no more than four months after its date of issue (although the creditor can apply to the court to extend this period). The High Court has held that a claim form was validly served when it was posted in accordance with the rules during its four-month period of validity but its deemed date of service was out of time.[110]

If the creditor has reason to believe that the client's usual or last known address is not her/his current address (eg, because letters have been returned marked 'gone away'), the creditor must take reasonable steps to find out her/his current address. If the creditor can establish the client's current address, the claim form must be served at that address. Provided this is the client's current address, the claim form is treated as having been served, even if the client does not actually receive it or it is returned to the court.[111]

In *Moloney v Lombard North Central plc*, L sent a pre-claim letter to M at 16 Minet Avenue but it was returned by the Post Office as undelivered. Enquiry agents visited Minet Avenue but were unable to establish whether M lived there. They did, however, find out that he was the owner of a property at 222A Chapter Road. On that basis, L issued and served proceedings at that address. There was no response and so L entered judgment in default and began enforcement action. Eventually, M found out about the claim and applied to set aside the judgment, claiming that he had always lived at Minet Avenue apart from a period when he was in Ireland. The Court of Appeal held that, on the evidence, because the claim had been served at Chapter Road this was not good service and ordered that the judgment be set aside. Although L had identified a connection between M and Chapter Road, L had not taken 'reasonable steps' to establish that this address was the address for service. Since L had not taken sufficient steps to establish M's correct address, the claim should have been served at his last known address, Minet Avenue.[112]

The claim form is treated as having been served by the alternative method or at the alternative place, even if it does not reach the client or is returned to the court. If the creditor is both unable to establish the client's current address and there is no suitable alternative place or method of service, the client's usual or last known address is still the relevant address (even though it is unlikely that the claim form will come to the client's attention) and a claim form sent to that address is treated as having been served, even if it does not reach the client or is returned to the court.

If the claim form is treated as having been served under the above rules, unless one of the mandatory grounds for setting aside applies (see p337), if the client wants to apply for a set-aside, one of the discretionary grounds must be relied on (see p338).

On the other hand, if the claim form has not been properly served, the client can apply to have the judgment and any enforcement action set aside. In the usual case, the court can only refuse a set-aside either if there has been no prejudice to the client or possibly if the client has been guilty of 'inexcusable delay', in making the application.[113]

Applications

If an application to have a judgment set aside is made on a discretionary ground, the court must take into account whether or not the client acted promptly in making the application – ie, with all reasonable speed once s/he found out about the existence of the judgment. When applying for a judgment to be set aside, the client should always try to find an argument based on the facts or law of the case (eg, 'I do not owe the money because the goods supplied under a linked agreement were of unsatisfactory quality'), rather than personal circumstances – eg, 'I did not know how to reply to the claim form'. Although not strictly required by the Civil Procedure Rules, the client should explain why s/he failed to respond to the claim form – eg, although failure to receive the claim form may not be a set-aside ground in itself, it could be a valid explanation for failing to respond. The onus is on the client to show the defence is a 'convincing' one as opposed to merely 'arguable'.

Unless the client wants to defend the claim or the creditor has already taken enforcement action (which would also be cancelled), it may be preferable for the client to apply to vary or suspend the terms of payment of the judgment (see below) or to vary the amount for which the judgment was entered where the only dispute is the amount for which the client was liable. Applying to set aside a judgment does not automatically prevent or delay any enforcement action by the creditor.

The application to set aside should also contain an application for a stay of enforcement pending the hearing, quoting rule 3.1(2)(f) of the Civil Procedure Rules. The application is made on Form N244 and must be supported by a statement from the client in Section 10. A fee of £255 is payable (see p290 for applying for full or partial fee remission). The case is sent to the county court hearing centre serving the address where the client lives (the client's 'home court').

If the client wants to set aside a county court judgment transferred to the High Court for enforcement, it seems that the application must still be made to the county court.[114] However, if you are faced with this situation, get specialist advice.

If the client has admitted the debt and judgment was entered on the basis of Form N9A, s/he should apply for permission to withdraw the admission[115] and defend the claim.[116] Form N244 must also contain a request for a transfer to the county court hearing centre serving the address where the client lives (the client's 'home' court), where appropriate, plus a request for a stay of enforcement.

If there has been a hearing in the county court, the client can apply to have the order set aside and the matter reheard if s/he did not attend the hearing and an order was made in her/his absence. S/he should apply to the court where the hearing took place on Form N244. The fee is £255 (see p290 for applying for full or partial remission).

The court will want to know why the client did not attend and whether there has been a miscarriage of justice. The court is unlikely to order a rehearing if the client deliberately failed to attend or if the court is satisfied that there is no real prospect of the original order being changed. The court will not allow an application for a rehearing purely on the grounds that the client did not receive notice of the hearing date without enquiring as to why s/he did not receive it. On the other hand, the court should not refuse an application for a rehearing just because s/he failed to provide the creditor or lender with a forwarding address. In general: [117]

- if the client is unaware that proceedings are imminent or have been served, s/he has a good reason for not attending any hearing;
- if the client knows of the existence of proceedings but does not have a system in place for receiving communications about the case, s/he is unlikely to have a good reason for not attending any hearing.

Suspending a charging order

If a final charging order has been made but no application was made to suspend its enforcement by an order for sale on payment of instalments, the client can still make this application, if necessary, on Form N244 (see p288). Alternatively, if the judgment was made on or after 1 October 2012, the client could apply for a variation (see below), which has the same effect as a suspension. A fee of £50 is payable (see p290 for applying for full or partial fee remission).

You could also contact the creditor and ask whether it intends to apply for an order for sale and to confirm its position in writing. In many cases, the creditor has no intention of applying for an order for sale and so, provided an instalment arrangement can be agreed, in most cases, the creditor will be prepared to confirm this.

If an instalment order is in place, it is unlikely that the court will make an order for sale if there has been no default, although (strictly) if the judgment was made before 1 October 2012, not defaulting on an instalment order does not prevent an application for an order for sale from being made. If the judgment or order under which the client is required to pay a sum of money by instalments is made on or after 1 October 2012, the court cannot make an order for sale unless the client has defaulted on the instalment order *and* any arrears of instalments remain unpaid.[118]

Varying payments due under an order

If the decision on the rate of payment was made by the court without a hearing and the client is unable to afford it, s/he should request a a redetermination (see p310). However, if judgment was either entered in default or on acceptance of the client's offer of payment, the following procedures apply instead.

If the creditor believes s/he can persuade the district judge that the client can afford to increase her/his payments, it can apply for the rate of instalments to be increased. An application is made on Form N244 (see p288) and the case is automatically transferred to the county court hearing centre which serves the address where the client lives (the client's 'home court') for a hearing.

Once an order for payment has been made, either in default or on acceptance of the client's offer of payment, the client can apply to the court that made it to have it varied at any time.[119] S/he does not need a particular reason for making this application, although it will normally be because s/he can no longer afford the original instalment order because of a change in circumstances or because the original order was made in ignorance of a material fact. In the case of default judgments for immediate payment, a successful application for a variation prevents the creditor from taking subsequent enforcement action, provided the client complies with the terms of the variation order.

The variation can include changes to either the amount of instalments or their frequency and is made on Form N245, which is very similar to Form N9A (see p303 on how to complete this). Form N245 should be sent to the court that made the judgment. If it is also being used to apply to suspend a warrant of control, it should be sent to the enforcing court instead (see p343). If Form N245 is being used to apply to suspend a warrant of control, an application for a variation should be made at the same time by ticking both boxes. A fee of £50 is payable to cover both applications. See p290 for details about full or partial remission.

When helping a client to apply for a variation order, it is helpful to send a letter to accompany Form N245, with a copy to the creditor, outlining the reasons for the application, especially if this is the first contact you have had with the creditor.

The court sends a copy of Form N245 to the creditor and if s/he does not respond within 14 days, the variation *must* be granted in the terms applied for.[120] If the creditor objects within 14 days, a court officer uses the determination of means guidelines to decide what the order should be.

Once the variation order has been made, either the creditor or client has 14 days to apply to the court for a reconsideration if they do not agree with the terms (see p310). The case is automatically sent to the county court hearing centre serving the address where the client lives (the client's 'home court') and a hearing arranged. At the hearing, the district judge can make whatever order s/he thinks just.

Advisers should keep a copy of Form N245. Clients may wish to ask the court for a receipt or, if the form is to be posted, send it by special delivery or obtain a certificate of posting. Follow up any application which is not dealt with within 21 days of Form N245 being posted to, or filed at, the court.

If the order for payment was made by a court officer or the district judge without a hearing and the client is out of time to apply for a redetermination, or it was made by the district judge at a hearing, the client can only apply to vary the order on the grounds of a change of circumstances (including information not previously before the court). The application is made on Form N244 (see p288).[121] A fee of £50 is payable. See p290 for applying for full or partial fee remission. The case is not automatically sent to the client's home court and so an application for this should be included on Form N244, quoting rule 30.2(1) of the Civil Procedure Rules.

If the order for payment of the judgment was made in the High Court either in default or on acceptance of the client's offer of payment, you should get specialist advice on how to apply for a stay of execution by writ of control and a variation of the judgment.

Suspensions and stays

An application for a variation on Form N245 must include an offer of payment. If even a nominal sum cannot be found, the client can apply for the judgment to be suspended or 'stayed' (see also p303 on Form N9A).

A 'suspension' is usually on terms (eg, provided payments are made) and a 'stay' is usually until an event occurs – eg, until a particular date. Applications should be on Form N244 (see p288) and are more likely to be accepted if there are compelling reasons – eg, if the client has serious mental or physical ill health or is in prison. A fee of £50 is payable on the basis that the application is 'to vary a judgment or suspend enforcement'. See p290 for details about full or partial fee remission. The case is not automatically sent to the county court hearing centre serving the address where the client lives (the client's 'home court') and so an application for this must be made on Form N244, quoting rule 30.2(1) of the Civil Procedure Rules.

Suspension of a warrant of control

If payments ordered under a judgment are missed and the creditor applies to the county court for bailiffs to enforce the debt, the client receives an enforcement notice from the court warning that a warrant to take control of the client's goods has been issued and giving a date after which the goods will be taken control of. Bailiffs may call at the client's home to try to take goods to sell. See Chapter 14 for details of the powers of county court bailiffs.

Form N245 should be completed in order to suspend the warrant. The client should tick the box requesting a 'suspension of the warrant' and also the box requesting 'a reduction in the instalment order' (even if the current terms of the judgment are for immediate payment). **Note:** the bailiffs can continue to attempt to take control of goods until the application has been heard and a decision given. Form N245 should be sent to the county court hearing centre which serves the address where the client lives (the client's 'home court'). A fee of £50 is payable, which covers both applications. See p290 for details about applying for full or partial fee remission.

The client could apply to have the matter 'stayed' (see p342). However, in order to prevent her/his goods being taken into control, an offer of payment must be made on Form N245, but this could be a token amount (eg, £1 a month) if the client is realistically unable to afford payments. Write to the creditor and explain the client's circumstances. If payments cannot be afforded, explain why such enforcement is not appropriate.

An offer of payment may not be appropriate if the client has no goods that could be taken into control (see p426 for excluded items) and there are no other methods of enforcement open to the creditor – ie, a charging order, third-party debt order or attachment of earnings order. In these circumstances, ask the creditor to consider writing off the debt (see p256).

Once the court receives Form N245, a copy is sent to the creditor, which has 14 days to agree to the client's proposal or not. If the creditor agrees, the warrant is suspended and the client is ordered to pay the amount offered. If the creditor does not agree to a suspension on any terms, a hearing is arranged at the client's home court, where the district judge decides whether or not to suspend the warrant and on what terms. If the creditor agrees with a suspension but not the proposed terms, the procedure described on p341 for varying an order is followed.[122]

Note: in some cases, county court judgments are enforced in the High Court. Once you are aware that High Court bailiffs (known as enforcement agents) have been instructed, get specialist advice.

Insolvency options

If the client has a judgment (either a county court or High Court judgment) and her/his total debts are not more than £5,000, s/he should consider applying for an administration order (see p445). Otherwise, the client could consider an individual voluntary arrangement, bankruptcy or a debt relief order. See Chapter 15 for further details on all these options.

Notes

1. Starting a money claim

1 CPR PD 7A, para 2
2 *Brandon v American Express* [2011] EWCA Civ 1187 (*Adviser* 149 abstracts)
3 s176(2) and (3) CCA 1974; *Lombard North Central v Power-Hines* [1995] CCLR 24
4 r2.3(1) CPR
5 r6.14 CPR; *Anderton v Clwyd County Council* (*Adviser* 93 abstracts)
6 CPR PD 7C, para 1.4, and PD 16, para 7.3
7 r5.5 CPR; CPR PD 5A, para 5.3
8 CPR PD 5A
9 CPR PD 5B. For further information, see justice.gov.uk/courts/procedure-rules
10 rr6.3(d) and 6.20(1)(d) CPR and CPR PD 6A, para 4

2. Admitting a money claim

11 For a discussion on drafting separate financial statements, see P Madge, 'Till Debt Do Us Part', *Adviser* 71

3. The judgment

12 r15.11 CPR
13 r14.4(6) CPR
14 r14.9(2) CPR
15 Lord Chancellor's Department, *Determination of Means: guidelines for court staff*, revised April 2011
16 CPR PD 14, para 5.1

17 Advisers should refer court staff who query this to 'What Happens Next?' in Lord Chancellor's Department, *Determination of Means: guidelines for court staff*, April 2011, item 3.4.5
18 *Loson v Stack* [2018] EWCA Civ 803 (Adviser 185 abstracts)
19 For more information about the use of witness statements and how to draft them, see G Smith, 'Keep Your DJ Happy', *Adviser* 109
20 r12.3 CPR
21 r14.2(3) CPR. There are two conflicting High Court decisions on whether a creditor is entitled to enter judgment in default if the client files their acknowledgement of service or defence out of time but before judgment has been entered. In *McDonald v D & F Contracts Ltd* [2018] EWHC 1600 (TCC) it was held that the creditor was entitled to enter judgment in default in such circumstances but in the later case of *Cunico Resources v Daskalakis* [2018] EWHC 3382 (Comm) it was held the creditor was not so entitled. In accordance with the decision in *Colchester Estates (Cardiff) v Carlton Industries* [1984] 2 All ER 601, until such time as the CPR are amended, the later decision is to be preferred and followed – ie, *Cunico Resources*.

22 r12.5 CPR
23 See footnote 21
24 s69 CCA 1984; s35a SCA 1981
25 s17 JA 1838
26 Many district judges seem to be
unaware that statutory interest cannot
be charged on county court judgments
arising out of agreements regulated by
the Consumer Credit Act 1974, even if
the judgment is for £5,000 or more.
They can find confirmation in Art 2(3)(a)
County Courts (Interest on Judgment
Debts) Order 1991 No.1184 (the text of
which is in the commentary to s74 CCA
1984 in *The Civil Court Practice* (the
Green Book), vol 2.
27 CC(IJD)O 1991
28 *Adamson v Halifax plc* [2002] EWCA Civ
1134 (*Adviser* 115 abstracts); *Socimer
International Bank v Standard Bank*
[2006] EWHC 2896 (Comm) (*Adviser*
121 abstracts)
29 *Director General of Fair Trading v First
National Bank* [2001] UKHL 52, 25
October 2001, unreported (*Adviser* 89
abstracts)
30 *Forward Trust v Whymark* [1989] 3 All ER
915
31 In *Chubb and Bruce v Dean* [2013] EWHC
1282 (Ch) (*Adviser* 159 abstracts), the
High Court held that the enforcing court
had no power to add post-judgment
contractual interest to the amount
recoverable. See also *Parr v Tiuta
International Ltd* [2016] EWHC 2 (QB)
(*Adviser* 174 abstracts)
32 rr12.6, 12.7 and 14.14 CPR. In the *First
National Bank* case, the House of Lords
assumed the creditor could take further
court action, but the point was not
argued and so the issue remains unclear,
at least so far as pre-1 October 2008
judgments are concerned.
33 *Director General of Fair Trading v First
National Bank* [2001] UKHL 52, 25
October 2001, unreported (*Adviser* 89
abstracts)
34 s130A CCA 1974, as inserted by s17
CCA 2006

35 For further discussion of these issues, see
P Madge, 'Interest After Judgment
Under Regulated Consumer Credit
Agreements', *Legal Action*, December
1990; P Madge, 'A Point of Interest',
Adviser 59; P Madge, 'No Further
Interest', *Adviser* 79; P Madge, 'Full
Circle', *Adviser* 89; R Rosenberg, 'Interest
After Judgment: is it the end of the
road?', *Quarterly Account* 62, IMA

4. Defending a money claim
36 See also r1 CPR (the 'overriding
objective'); P Madge, 'Using the
Overriding Objective', *Adviser* 96
37 *Phoenix Finance Ltd v Federation
Internationale de l'Automobile, The Times*,
27 June 2002
38 CPR PD 7C, para 5.3 sets out a different
procedure for claims issued by the
Business Centre: all defences are
referred by the court to the creditor,
which has 28 days to confirm whether
or not it wishes to proceed. If so, the
case is automatically sent to the client's
home court. If there is no response, the
claim is stayed.
39 rr26.2A – 26.5 CPR
40 CPR PD 27
41 CPR PD 26, para 8.1(2)
42 r27.14 CPR
43 *Dammermann v Lanyon Bowdler* [2017]
EWCA Civ 269
44 CPR PD 28
45 CPR PD 29
46 *ED and F Man Liquid Products Ltd v Patel*
[2003] EWCA Civ 472 (*Adviser* 101
abstracts)
47 CPR PD 3 and 24

5. Enforcing a judgment
48 r70.2(2) CPR
49 s8 AEA 1971
50 *Sucden Financial v Garcia* [2009] EWHC
3555 (QB) (*Adviser* 139 money advice
abstracts)
51 Order 39, r2, Sch 2 CCR
52 s86(3) CCA 1984
53 r83.2 CPR; Sch 2 CPR; *Patel v Singh*
[2002] EWCA Civ 1938 (*Adviser* 105
abstracts)
54 Order 8(1A) HCCCJO, as amended
55 See *Spotlight*, November 2019, Shelter
Specialist Debt Advice Service
56 See also P Madge, 'Charging Interest',
Adviser 76 and *Chubb and Bruce v Dean*
[2013] EWHC 1282 (Ch) (*Adviser* 159
abstracts)

57 *Ropaigealach v Allied Irish Bank* [2001] EWCA Civ 1790 (*Adviser* 90 abstracts). In *Mercantile Credit v Huxtable* (CA) (*The Independent,* 17 March 1987; *The Times,* 1 April 1987), the court held that where a charging order nisi (now interim order) was obtained after the judgment debt was set to be paid by instalments, there was no jurisdiction to make a charging order as long as the instalments were being regularly paid by the debtor. *Huxtable* is quoted with approval in *Ropaigealach* at paras 8 and 9. Although that decision was made under s86(1) CCA 1984 (which prior to 6 April 2014 prevented any 'execution' of an order where instalments were up to date but since that date only refers to warrants of control), the legal position expressed in these cases is, arguably, still good law for judgments made prior to 166 April 2014 subject to the amendment made to the Charging Orders Act in relation to judgments made on or after 1 October 2012. See also Spotlight, May 2019, Shelter Specialist Debt Advice Service.

58 s93 TCEA 2007
59 r73.3(2) CPR
60 CPR PD 73, para 1.2
61 r73.7 CPR
62 r73.5 CPR
63 s1(5)-(8) COA 1979
64 See also *Chubb and Bruce v Dean* [2013] EWHC 1282 (Ch) (*Adviser* 159 abstracts)
65 r73.10 CPR. 'Written evidence' is a person's evidence set down in writing and signed to the effect that the maker of the statement believes the facts stated are true. See CPR PD 32 for the formalities of witness statements. Unless specifically required, an affidavit should not be used in preference to a statement.
66 r73.10(6) CPR
67 *Mercantile Credit Co Ltd v Ellis, The Times,* 1 April 1987, confirmed in *Ropaigealach v Allied Irish Bank* [2001] EWCA Civ 1790 (*Adviser* 90 abstracts)
68 *Ropaigealach v Allied Irish Bank* [2001] EWCA Civ 1790 (*Adviser* 90 abstracts). For a further discussion of the position after 1 October 2012 in relation to judgments made both before and on or after that date, see: P Madge 'Still Charging On', *Adviser* 156
69 COA 1979

70 *Rainbow v Moorgate Properties* [1975] 2 All ER 821; see also *Nationwide BS v Wright* [2009] EWCA Civ 811 (*Adviser* 136 money advice abstracts)
71 *Fraenkl-Rietti v Cheltenham and Gloucester* [2011] EWCA Civ 524 (*Adviser* 146 abstracts)
72 s3(1) COA 1979
73 s3(5) COA 1979; r73.9 CPR
74 s71(2) CCA 1984 gives the county court power to suspend or stay any judgment or order on such terms as the court thinks fit.
75 r1.4(2)(i) CPR. Also, if a date has already been fixed for a hearing, any other applications should be dealt with at that hearing; CPR PD 23, paras 2.8 and 2.10
76 Alternatively, an additional term or condition could be requested in the witness statement submitted for the final charging order hearing that all other enforcement action be stayed, provided the client pays instalments as ordered.
77 Under s14 TLATA 1996
78 For a discussion of charging orders and orders for sale, see R Dakin, 'The ABC of Money Advice', *Quarterly Account* 29 and 30, IMA
79 s15 TLATA 1996. These provisions do not apply if the client is the sole owner of the property, even if it is the family home; *Wells v Pickering* [2000] EWHC 2540 (Ch) (*Adviser* 96 abstracts)
80 s15 TLATA 1996. These provisions do not apply if the client is the sole owner of the property, even if it is the family home; *Wells v Pickering* [2000] EWHC 2540 (Ch) (*Adviser* 96 abstracts)
81 *Bank of Ireland v Bell* [2001] 2 FLR 809
82 *Harman v Glencross* [1986] 1 All ER 545
83 s3(4C) and (4E) COA 1979
84 s3(4C) and (4E) COA 1979
85 s3(4) COA 1979
86 See M Robinson, 'Home Page', *Adviser* 146
87 s8(2) AEA 1971
88 r70.3 CPR
89 s4(2) AEA 1971
90 See J McShane and M Gallagher, 'Benefit Overpayments and Direct Earnings Attachments', *Adviser* 166
91 rr89.18-89.22 CPR
92 *Mercantile Credit Co Ltd v Ellis, The Times,* 1 April 1987
93 *Rainbow v Moorgate Properties* [1975] 2 All ER 821
94 *Hirschhorn v Evans* [1938] 3 All ER 491

95 *Blight and Others v Brewster* [2012] EWHC 185 (Ch) (*Adviser* 152 abstracts)
96 r72.7 CPR
97 EU Regulation 1215/2012
98 EU Regulation 44/2001
99 Lugano Convention 2007
100 Brussels Convention 1968
101 Administration of Justice Act 1920
102 Foreign Judgments (Reciprocal Enforcement) Act 1933
103 Common law: *Adams v Cape Industries* [1990] Ch 433
104 r24 CPR
105 The procedure is contained in Part 74 CPR; CPR PD 74A
106 For more detailed information, see G O'Malley, 'Enforcement of Foreign Debt in England and Wales', *Quarterly Account* 38, IMA

6. **Preventing enforcement**
107 r70.6 CPR
108 r13.2 CPR
109 r13.3 CPR
110 *Jones v Chichester Harbour Conservancy* [2017] EWHC 2270 (QB), (*Adviser* 183 abstracts)
111 rr6.9, 6.15 and 6.18 CPR; CPR PD 6, paras 9.1-9.3. The rules allow the creditor to take steps to effect service at an alternative place or by an alternative method and ask the court to validate it retrospectively. Provided the court makes the order, the claim form is treated as served.
112 *Moloney v Lombard North Central plc* [2016] EWCA Civ 1347
113 *Nelson v Clearsprings (Management) Ltd* [2006] EWCA Civ 1252 (*Adviser* 119 abstracts)
114 s42(6) CCA 1984, which says that the county court's powers to set aside a judgment continue to apply
115 Under r14.1(5) CPR
116 Under r3.1(2)(m) CPR
117 *Estate Acquisition and Development v Wiltshire* [2006] EWCA Civ 533 (*Adviser* 118 abstracts)
118 s93(3) TCEA 2007. Rules of court can provide otherwise, but at the time of writing, no such rules had been made.
119 r40.9A(8)-(15) CPR
120 r40.9A(11) CPR
121 CPR PD 14, paras 6.1-6.2
122 r83.7 CPR

Chapter 12

· ·

Action in the county court: possession of goods and property

This chapter covers:

1. Recovering goods on hire purchase or conditional sale (p349)
2. Recovering property (p351)
3. Recovering owner-occupied property (p353)
4. Recovering rented property (p372)
5. Preventing enforcement (p381)

This chapter deals with court action by creditors when they wish to recover goods or property from a client. See Chapter 11 if the creditor is claiming money only.

Note: in some cases, in addition to making an order for payment of money, the court can order a client to give up possession of goods or property to the creditor. However, it can usually suspend the order if the client makes payments to the creditor as ordered by the court. See p350, p362 and p376 for more details.

Debts regulated by the Consumer Credit Act 1974

If the court action concerns a regulated credit agreement (except secured loans treated as regulated mortgage contracts – see p64), the creditor must first send the client a default notice before it can take action to repossess goods or property (see p299).

The High Court cannot deal with claims related to secured or unsecured regulated credit agreements, or actions linked to such agreements, regardless of the amount of the claim.

If the client's case involves a regulated credit agreement (or any other case) being dealt with in the High Court, you should get specialist advice.

Chapter 12: Action in the county court: possession of goods and property
1. Recovering goods on hire purchase or conditional sale

12

1. **Recovering goods on hire purchase or conditional sale**

A creditor requires a court order to repossess goods on hire purchase or conditional sale if at least one-third of the total cost has been paid (see p94 or p104) or if the client has paid less but has refused to allow the creditor to enter private property in order to take back the goods.

The creditor must first serve a default notice and include in the section on what action may be taken that goods can be repossessed. See p299 for further information about default notices. In these cases, the 'Consumer Credit Act procedure' applies.

- The claim must be started in the county court hearing centre for the district in which the client either lives or carries out her/his business (or did when s/he made her/his last payment).
- The court fixes a hearing date when it issues the claim form (Form N1 – see p301), and notice of the hearing date is given when the claim form is served.
- The particulars of claim (containing the prescribed information – see p301) must be served with the claim form.
- The claim form and particulars of claim are accompanied by Forms N1(FD) (note for defendants), N9C (admission unspecified amount and non-money claims) and N9D (defence/counterclaim). There is no acknowledgement of service.

Unless the client is merely disputing the amount s/he has already paid, you should obtain specialist advice on any other potential defences. If the client disputes the claim, the court will either:

- deal with the case at the hearing; *or*
- allocate the case to a track (see p316) and make directions; *or*
- give directions to enable it to make a decision on allocation.

The client's response

The client is not required to file either an admission or a defence, but s/he should do so as the court can take account of a failure to do so when deciding on its order for costs in the case – eg, if an unnecessary hearing has to take place as a result. The creditor cannot request a default judgment. If the client fails to respond, the hearing must still go ahead.

The client can admit the claim on Form N9C and make an offer. The court can then make an order for the return of the goods, which is suspended provided the client makes payments in accordance with her/his offer (a 'time order').[1]

The statement of means is similar to that on Form N9A (see p303).

The client should complete Form N9C by:

- indicating whether or not s/he still has the goods in her/his possession;

12

Chapter 12: Action in the county court: possession of goods and property
1. Recovering goods on hire purchase or conditional sale

- admitting liability for the claim; *and*
- offering to pay the unpaid balance of the total price. This figure is contained in the particulars of claim.

The admission should be returned to the court, not sent to the creditor. A copy is sent by the court to the creditor. If the creditor accepts the amount admitted and the offer of payment, it informs the court, which enters judgment and sends a copy to the client (Form N32(2) HP/CCA). No one need attend the hearing. If nothing is heard from the court, the client should attend the hearing. If the creditor does not accept the amount admitted or offer of payment, or the client does not respond, the hearing proceeds.

Negotiating before the hearing

Always try to negotiate with the creditor before the court hearing. Most creditors prefer to receive payments rather than repossess secondhand goods. Resuming the contractual payments is often enough to persuade the creditor to withdraw or adjourn the court action. If no agreement can be reached, a hearing takes place and the client should attend, with a financial statement indicating her/his ability to pay. A court is unlikely to accept a long-term substantial reduction in payments (eg, £20 a month when the contractual agreement is for £120), but may accept a short-term reduction – eg, £20 a month for three months, then £120 a month. Unless an application for a time order is made (including completing Form N9C – see p349) or the hearing is adjourned, the court appears to have no power to make an order for payment of less than the contractual instalments.

Decisions the court can make

The court has a general power to adjourn for a short period if required, but only does so if there are compelling reasons (see p295).

If the client offers to pay the outstanding balance and the court accepts the offer, it orders the return of the goods but suspends the order, provided the payments are maintained.[2] If there is no acceptable payment offer, the court orders that the goods be returned without giving the client the option of paying for them. The judgment is on Form N32(1) and gives the delivery date for the client to return the goods. If the goods are no longer in the client's possession, the court cannot order their return.[3] The creditor must then obtain a judgment for the outstanding balance due under the agreement, or the client could apply for a time order once the default or arrears notice has been issued (see p366). **Note:** selling or disposing of goods is an offence. In such circumstances, rather than returning Form N9C (which requires the client to state that s/he has the goods), the client may prefer to make an offer of payment by email or letter supported by a financial statement.

If the client does not make payments or fails to return the goods as ordered, it is arguable that the creditor cannot just repossess the goods if they are 'protected'. The creditor should instead ask the court to issue a warrant of delivery.

Note: returning the goods to the creditor is not the end of the matter. The creditor sells the goods and sets the proceeds of the sale against the remaining balance due. There may well be a shortfall that the client is liable to pay. The creditor must apply to the court for a further hearing date to obtain an order for payment of the money.[4]

If the client's circumstances change, s/he can apply to vary the order.

Warrant of delivery

A warrant of delivery is a document that allows a county court enforcement agent (a bailiff) to remove goods that are the subject of a hire purchase or conditional sale agreement if the court has ordered that the goods be returned to the creditor. It is issued by the court following a request from the creditor that the client has not returned the goods as ordered by the court or is in breach of a suspended return of goods order. The warrant may allow the client to pay the value of the goods as an alternative to allowing them to be taken by the bailiffs. The client can apply for the warrant to be suspended and for delivery of the goods to be postponed (see p381). It is always worth approaching the creditor to negotiate an agreement before applying back to the court.

2. **Recovering property**

Note: this chapter only covers the action taken when there are unpaid payments due under a mortgage (or other secured loan) or unpaid rent due under a tenancy. It does not cover the details of all the law in these areas and you should therefore refer to specialist books and to a housing specialist where necessary.[5]

A landlord or a mortgage lender can start action in the county court for possession of a tenant's or owner-occupier's home by completing a claim form (Form N5) and particulars of the claim (Form N119 for tenants and N120 for mortgages). The creditor cannot request a default judgment (see p311) or apply for summary judgment (see p318) in this type of action. If the client does not respond, the hearing must still go ahead.

There must be a hearing to consider the merits of the claim. The procedure is contained in Part 55 of the Civil Procedure Rules. Possession claims are normally brought in the county court hearing centre for the area in which the property is situated. A claim may only be brought in the High Court in 'exceptional circumstances'. If you encounter a possession claim or order made in the High Court, you should obtain specialist advice.

Note: a client cannot be forced to leave her/his home against her/his will unless a court order and warrant have been obtained.

Negotiating before the hearing

You should always try to negotiate with a creditor and reach a satisfactory agreement before going to court. This is preferable to relying on the decision of a district judge and avoids the possibility of things 'going wrong' at the hearing. In addition, the following apply.

- If an order is made for possession of the property and/or payment of rent arrears, the court usually orders the client to pay the landlord's costs.
- Most mortgages allow the creditor to charge all her/his costs to the client in connection with default and repossession without needing a specific order for costs made by the court.
- It is important to avoid unnecessary court hearings or delays.
- Ideally, both parties should apply for the matter to be adjourned generally (ie, without a future hearing date) on the agreed terms (see below).

Often landlords and lenders insist on a suspended possession order (see p362) being made rather than agreeing to the case being adjourned on the basis of the agreed terms. This puts the client's home at risk, but it may result in a better order for her/him than if the matter had been left to the discretion of the district judge. If the creditor agrees to a suspended possession order, check that any solicitor representing the landlord or lender has been informed and obtain written confirmation of the terms of the proposed suspended order so this can be produced at the hearing if there is any dispute. See Chapter 8 for possible strategies.

If the agreement to clear the arrears was made before the landlord or lender issued court proceedings and the client has not defaulted under the agreement, ask the court to adjourn the matter and not allow the landlord's or lender's costs. This is because the Civil Procedure Rules and paragraph 6 of the pre-action conduct practice direction (see p281) require people to act reasonably in trying to avoid the need for court proceedings (see p281).

In addition, a lender that issued proceedings in these circumstances would be in breach of the spirit of the mortgage arrears pre-action protocol (see p355). In the case of social landlords, if the payment agreement is made before the issue of proceedings, under paragraph 10 of the rent arrears pre-action protocol, the landlord should agree to postpone proceedings, provided the client keeps to the agreement. If the payment arrangement was made after proceedings were issued, the landlord should agree to an adjournment (see p384 and p295).

3. **Recovering owner-occupied property**

If the loan is a regulated credit agreement under the Consumer Credit Act 1974 (see p62), a default notice (see p299) must first be issued. The lender must obtain a court order before it can take possession (including where the secured loan is a regulated mortgage contract), but the client could give her/his informed consent to the lender taking 'peaceable possession'.[6]

In the case of other mortgages, the lender can take peaceable possession if the client has abandoned the property and left it empty. If the client returns the keys to the lender, this is known as a 'voluntary surrender' and the lender takes peaceable possession by accepting the keys.

Guidance to lenders

If the mortgage was made on or after 31 October 2004 (or on or after 21 March 2016 in the case of secured loans), it may be regulated by the Financial Conduct Authority (see p112). If so, the lender is required by the *Mortgages and Home Finance: Conduct of Business Sourcebook* to deal 'fairly' with borrowers in arrears and have a written arrears policy and procedures.[7] This should include:

* providing clients with details of missed payments, the total amount of arrears, the outstanding balance due under the mortgage, any charges incurred to date, an indication of possible future charges and a copy of the current Money Advice Service's information sheet *Problems Paying Your Mortgage* (available from moneyadviceservice.org.uk);
* making reasonable efforts to come to an agreement with the client about repaying the arrears;[8]
* liaising with an adviser or agency if the client arranges this;
* allowing a reasonable time for repayment, bearing in mind the need to establish, where feasible, a practical repayment plan in the client's circumstances (in appropriate cases, arranging repayments over the remaining term of the mortgage);
* granting the client's request for a change to the payment date or method of payment (unless the lender has a good reason for not agreeing to this);
* if no reasonable repayment arrangement can be made, allowing the client to remain in possession of the property to enable it to be sold;
* repossessing the property only where all other reasonable attempts to resolve the situation have failed.

The lender must take into account the client's circumstances and consider whether it is appropriate to agree to:

* extend the term of the mortgage;
* change the type of mortgage – eg, repayment mortgage to interest-only mortgage;

- defer interest payments;
- capitalise the arrears;
- make use of any government mortgage rescue initiatives (see p222).

If arrears have been capitalised and rescheduled over the remaining term of the mortgage, they are no longer arrears and so cannot be relied on as the basis for a repossession claim. If a client does not pay the full monthly contractual instalment, the lender must allocate the payment in a way that minimises the arrears (which should have the effect of minimising the default interest and charges).

The lender should also have given the client certain prescribed information (see p114). In addition, many mortgage lenders do not seek possession until payments of mortgage interest are three, or even six, months in arrears.

In October 2011, the Council of Mortgage Lenders (which is now part of UK Finance) issued industry guidance on arrears and possession to assist lenders to comply with their duty to treat customers fairly. It can be found at cml.org.uk/policy/guidance/all/industry-guidance-on-arrears-and-possession-to-help-firms. This includes examples of good practice for lenders, including:

- encouraging clients at the earliest opportunity to contact independent free money advice providers, and providing a dedicated contact point within the arrears handling department for money advisers;
- when agreeing repayment arrangements, assessing income and expenditure including using financial statements prepared by money advisers, ensuring staff have the flexibility to agree repayment periods suitable for individual circumstances and taking into account repayment levels ordered by the courts and other priority debts;
- if no reasonable repayment can be made, informing clients that they can stay in the property to sell it, explaining how this will work and considering:
  - ways of helping clients to end their home ownership, including through an assisted voluntary sales scheme; *and*
  - when they will allow sales at shortfall to proceed – ie, if the client is in negative equity;
- applying for a possession order only when:
  - all attempts to contact or liaise with the client have failed; *or*
  - it has not proved possible to agree an affordable repayment arrangement; *or*
  - the client has not been able to maintain the agreed repayments;
- not applying for a possession order:
  - when a reasonable negotiated settlement is possible; *or*
  - to discipline clients into maintaining payment arrangements; *or*
  - if an arrangement is in place to which the client is adhering; *or*
  - if an arrangement to pay is entered into after the proceedings have started, and consider agreeing to the hearing being adjourned instead;

- checking that the mortgage arrears pre-action protocol has been complied with, including completing the compliance checklist before the hearing.

If a lender does not treat a client fairly, a complaint could be made to the Financial Ombudsman Service (see p284).

Pre-action protocol

The mortgage arrears pre-action protocol (which is part of the Civil Procedure Rules) aims to encourage lenders and borrowers to reach an agreement without the need for proceedings. It makes it clear that starting a possession claim should 'normally' be the last resort and should not 'normally' be started unless all other reasonable attempts to resolve the situation have failed. The parties (or their advisers) should take all reasonable steps to discuss with each other the reasons for the arrears, the client's financial circumstances, whether the client's financial difficulties are temporary or long term and the client's proposals to clear the arrears 'in a reasonable time'. There is no guidance in the protocol on what this might be (unlike for rent arrears – see p372).

Lenders must consider postponing possession action if:
- the client has made a claim:
  - to the Department for Work and Pensions (DWP) for a benefit that includes an amount for housing costs – eg, income support; *or*
  - under a payment protection insurance policy; *or*
  - to a local authority under the mortgage rescue scheme or other means of homelessness prevention support.

  S/he must have supplied all the information necessary to process a claim and have a reasonable expectation that it will be successful; *or*
- the client can demonstrate that s/he has taken (or will be taking) reasonable steps to sell the property at an 'appropriate price' (presumably one which will clear the mortgage and any other loans secured on it) and that s/he continues to actively market the property; *or*
- the client has made a 'genuine complaint' to the Financial Ombudsman Service about the possession claim. As a complaint has to be made first to the lender and is only referred to the Financial Ombudsman Service if the lender either fails to issue a final response or rejects the complaint, it is unlikely that lenders will accept that complaints are genuine unless the Ombudsman agrees to investigate.

If the lender decides not to postpone issuing possession proceedings, it must inform the client at least five business days before doing so.

The lender must be able to explain to the court what actions it has taken to comply with the protocol, and have two copies of Form N123 available at the hearing. This is a checklist verified by a statement of truth in which the lender confirms that it has taken various steps. These include checking whether a tenant of the client is occupying the property, whether the tenant was authorised by the lender and what order the lender is seeking in the light of the information obtained. Failure to produce Form N123 would give the court grounds to strike out a possession claim for failure to comply with a rule,[9] although it might prefer to adjourn the hearing to enable the lender to comply.

If the lender does not comply with the protocol

If a lender does not comply with the mortgage arrears pre-action protocol, the court does not have grounds to refuse to make a possession order. However, if the court believes that the lender has not complied with the substance of the relevant principles and requirements (as opposed to minor or technical shortcomings which have had no overall effect on the situation), it can:

- 'stay' (ie, suspend) the proceedings until the steps which ought to have been taken have been taken; *and/or*
- make an order not to allow costs, or pay costs, to the other party.

If the lender appears not to have complied, you should point this out and argue that no further action should be taken, provided the client complies with her/his obligations under the protocol, such as by making payments or actively pursuing a claim for payment protection insurance, benefits or a proposed sale of the property. Also point this out on Form N11M (see p359) and put the arguments to the district judge at the hearing for any dismissal, or (more likely) for the possession claim to be adjourned, or in relation to costs.

Note: if the client has not complied with the protocol, the court takes this into account.[10]

The claim form

The possession claim form (Form N5) includes the date and time of the hearing. It must be accompanied by a particulars of claim (Form N120). The lender can use its own particulars of claim, provided it contains details of:[11]

- the identity of the property to be recovered;
- whether the claim relates to residential property;
- the ground(s) on which possession is claimed;
- the mortgage or charge;
- every person in possession of the property (to the best of the lender's knowledge);
- whether any charges or notices have been registered under the Family Law Act 1996 or Matrimonial Homes Acts 1967–1983;
- the date of any tenancy entered into between the borrower and a tenant, whether or not the tenancy was authorised by the lender and, if so, what steps the lender intends taking in respect of the tenancy;
- the state of the account between the client and lender, including:

- the amount of the advance, any periodic payments and any repayment of interest required to be made;
- the amount which would have to be paid, taking into account any allowance for early settlement, to redeem the mortgage at a stated date not later than 14 days after the start of proceedings, including solicitors' costs and administrative charges;
- if it is a regulated consumer credit agreement, the total amount outstanding under the terms of the mortgage;
- the rate of interest payable originally, immediately before any arrears accrued and at the start of proceedings;
- a schedule of arrears, showing all amounts due and payments made together with dates and a running total of the arrears either for the previous two years or from the date of default, if later;
- details of any other payments required to be made as a term of the mortgage (such as insurance premiums, legal costs, default interest, penalties, and administrative and other charges), whether any of these payments are in arrears and whether or not they are included in the periodic payment;

- whether or not the loan is a regulated consumer credit agreement and the date(s) on which the appropriate notices under the Consumer Credit Act 1974 have been served;
- information that the lender knows about the client's circumstances and, in particular, whether s/he is in receipt of benefits and whether direct mortgage interest payments are being received from the DWP;
- any previous steps taken by the lender to recover either the money secured under the mortgage or the property itself, including dates of any court proceedings and the terms of any orders made;
- the history of arrears (if longer than two years). This should be stated in the particulars and a schedule of the arrears should be exhibited to a witness statement and served separately, at least two days before the hearing.

All the above requirements are covered in paragraphs 1 to 9 on Form N120. The lender may also include a money-only claim arising out of an unsecured loan agreement. Although the lender can obtain a money judgment in respect of such a debt, it cannot be enforced as part of any possession order.[12] The lender does not normally seek an order for costs, as the mortgage normally allows for these to be added to the outstanding balance automatically.

The particulars of the claim must be verified by a statement of truth.

'Possession claim online'

Certain specified county courts can now operate a scheme known as 'possession claim online', which enables lenders to issue claims for possession electronically at possessionclaim.gov.uk/pcol.

The particulars must contain the same information referred to above with one exception. If the lender has already provided the client with a schedule of arrears showing all amounts due and payments made, together with dates and a running total of the arrears either for the previous two years or from the date of default if later, the particulars of claim may contain a summary of the arrears stating:

- the amount of the arrears on the date of the lender's pre-action letter;
- the dates and amounts of the last three payments (or, if less than three payments have been made, the dates and amounts of those payments); *and*
- the arrears on the date possession proceedings are issued.

However, if the lender only includes the summary information listed above in the particulars of claim, it must serve a full arrears history on the client within seven days after the issue of the claim, but at least two days before the hearing, and verify this by a witness statement or verbally at the hearing.

Proceedings are issued according to the property's postcode supplied by the lender. If this is not the client's local county court hearing centre, s/he can ask the court to transfer the case.[13]

After the claim form is issued

The hearing (which takes place in private) is normally set for between 28 days and eight weeks after Form N5 is issued. The claim form and particulars of claim must be served on the client at least 21 days before the hearing. Within five days of notification of the hearing date, the lender must send a notice to the property addressed to 'the occupiers' containing details of the claim. The purpose of this is to alert anyone living there who is not the borrower but who may want to oppose the claim for possession. The lender must also send a notice to any creditor registered at HM Land Registry as having a mortgage or secured loan on the property.

The lender must also write to the local authority for the area in which the property is situated and inform it about the hearing. The lender must be able to confirm at the hearing that these steps have been taken (a witness statement is sufficient). The Ministry of Housing, Communities and Local Government has provided guidance to local authorities on what to do with this information to enable them to include it within their overall strategy on preventing homelessness.[14]

Written evidence may be given at the hearing and should be filed at court and served on the other side at least two days before the hearing date. Evidence of the arrears, including interest, should be up to the date of the hearing and refer to a daily rate, if necessary. If the claim cannot be dealt with on the hearing date because there appears to be a substantial dispute, the district judge should give directions and allocate the case to a track (see p316).

Responding to the claim

There is a 'defence' form (Form N11M) which is supposed to be completed and filed at court within 14 days of Form N5 being served, but which may be filed at any time before the hearing. The questions are straightforward, although they are not cross-referenced to the numbered paragraphs in the particulars of claim. It is not a defence as such, but a reply to the claim. It is not essential to respond, but it is advisable to do so, as any delay caused by the client's failure to file the defence may mean further liability for costs. Although there will be a hearing, it is helpful if the district judge has been prepared for the client's circumstances and arguments by submitting a well-completed reply form.[15] A copy of the form is also sent by the court to the lender.

The online claim form contains details of the user name and password to access the website where the client can complete and file the form online. The website contains a user guide, although most of the information is only relevant to lenders and there is no guidance on how to complete Form N11M.

Completing Form N11M

Form N11M should be completed as follows.

- **Question 1** requests details of the client's personal circumstances, including her/his date of birth.
- **Question 2** relates to paragraphs 2 to 4 on Form N120, which should be confirmed as correct, or details of any disagreement given.
- **Question 3.** Check the level of arrears as carefully as possible. The court may not make an order if it is unsure that the arrears figure is correct.
- **Question 4** needs completing only in cases where possession is sought (perhaps partly) on grounds other than arrears.
- **Questions 5 and 6** are primarily addressed to borrowers whose loans are regulated credit agreements.

  Question 5 asks whether the client wants the court to consider whether the terms of the loan agreement are 'fair'. This appears to apply to the unfair relationship provisions of the Consumer Credit Act 1974 (which do not apply to regulated mortgage contracts), as well as to unfairness under the Consumer Rights Act 2015 (which apply to all agreements, not just Consumer Credit Act-regulated agreements). Although one of the main principles of Financial Conduct Authority regulation is that lenders must treat their customers fairly, it is not clear to what extent a court could consider a breach of its rules as a defence to possession proceedings.[16]

  Question 6 asks whether the client intends to apply for a time order (see p366). An application may be made either on this form (which does not have a fee) or by notice of application (Form N244) (which has a fee, but full or partial remission may be possible – see p290).[17] As there is only room to tick a box on the N11M, any applications should be supported by written evidence in the form of a witness statement, setting out the grounds.

- **Question 7**. If the arrears have been paid in full by the date of the hearing, the case should be adjourned.[18]
- **Question 8**. If an agreement has been reached, details should be included. In this case, the reply should ideally be accompanied by a letter requesting a general adjournment. If the lender agrees, it should also write to the court indicating its agreement to a general adjournment. If the agreement has been running since before the action started, the client may argue there was no need to take court action, and ask for the matter to be adjourned generally and challenge any costs the lender seeks to charge.[19] S/he should send proof of payments, or include a written request from the lender that an order be made and suspended on payment of whatever sum has been agreed.
- **Question 9**. A client should answer 'yes' if agreement has not been reached. **Note:** clients who fail to ask the court to consider instalments might later find this used against them if a local authority is considering the question of the intentionality of their homelessness.
- **Question 10** asks for the amount, in addition to the contractual payments, being offered. This question may not be relevant as it is not always necessary for the client to be able to afford the contractual payments for the court to make a suspended possession order. For the position if the client is applying for a time order, see p366; for other cases, see p361.
- **Questions 11–13** relate to income support, income-based jobseeker's allowance, income-related employment and support allowance and pension credit. It is important to check with the DWP what payments have been made before attending court, so that any misunderstandings with the lender can be resolved. Remember to convert weekly benefit amounts to calendar monthly amounts to compare with monthly mortgage payments. **Note:** the form has not been updated to include universal credit. Until it is, amend the form by hand to provide the information relevant to the client.
- **Questions 14–25** relate to dependants (and non-dependants), bank accounts and savings, income and expenditure, priority debts, court orders and credit debts similar to those required on Form N9A (see p303) and should be filled in similarly.
- **Question 26**. The client should not answer 'yes' to Question 26 ('If an order is made will you have somewhere to live?'), unless the accommodation is absolutely certain. The date given, even in such cases, should always be realistic.
- **Question 27** is important because it gives the client the opportunity to explain:
  - any breaches of the FCA rules, especially the principle of treating clients fairly and any breaches of the *Mortgages and Home Finance: Conduct of Business Sourcebook* which although not a defence to the possession claim as such, may be relevant in whether the court uses its discretion;[20]
  - the circumstances in which the loan was made, if relevant – eg, to refinance unsecured borrowing in response to high-pressure selling;

 – why the arrears arose;
 – what circumstances were beyond her/his control;
 – why it would cause particular hardship if eviction was ordered.

Powers of the court to deal with possession action

If a court is considering an action for the possession of a private house, it has wide-ranging powers in relation to the protection it can potentially give a client with a mortgage or a secured loan not regulated by the Consumer Credit Act 1974.[21] These include:

- adjourning the proceedings (see below); *or*
- suspending a possession order (see p362); *or*
- postponing the date of the possession (see p363).

If an agreement is regulated by the Consumer Credit Act 1974 (see p62), the court should consider making a time order. This can be specifically requested by the client. See p366.

Adjournments

The court has a general power to adjourn any proceedings for a short period.[22] For example, if the client needs more time to obtain money advice or the lender is required to clarify the arrears, the court may adjourn the matter, usually for 28 days. The court may attach terms to the adjournment – eg, that basic instalments are paid or that no further interest is added to the loan. The court can also adjourn the proceedings for a short time to enable the client to pay off the mortgage in full – eg, by selling the property, or otherwise satisfying the lender.[23]

The court sends out a written notice giving the date and time of the next hearing. If the property is about to be sold or the arrears cleared in full in some other way, the court may adjourn with 'liberty to restore'. This means that there will not be another hearing, provided the expected action happens. However, if the expected action fails, the lender can ask for a hearing to be restored.

You may wish to argue that the matter should be adjourned, rather than have a suspended possession order granted. An adjournment is preferable because no further action, including enforcement, can be taken without a further court hearing. For clients who are vulnerable because of age or disability, this can be a valuable tactic. The court could:

- **adjourn with liberty to restore** – eg, because the arrears have been, or are about to be, paid in full, or the property is in the process of being sold or an agreement to pay the arrears has already been agreed;
- **adjourn for a fixed period** (eg, 28 days) for the client to get further advice or for the lender to produce correct particulars of claim;
- **adjourn generally** because there is a repayment plan agreed and working.

Suspended possession orders

The court can suspend a possession order on such 'conditions with regard to payment by the mortgagor [the borrower] of any sum secured by the mortgage or the remedying of any default as the court thinks fit', provided the client can pay both the arrears and the future contractual payments within a 'reasonable period'.[24]

The terms of the order will usually be for basic instalments plus £x towards the arrears. However, a number of court cases show this is not always necessary. In one case, an order was made for payment of £250 for one month and £500 for two months, with a review thereafter on the basis that the client had good prospects of obtaining employment within that period.[25] In another case, the client offered £150 a month until mortgage interest became payable by the DWP, which would cover the current payments.[26] Although the arrears would increase in the meantime, they would be cleared within three-and-a-half years. The court made an order accordingly.

In each case, the court held that the test was not whether the client could currently pay the contractual payments, but whether s/he would be able to clear the arrears and pay the contractual instalments within a reasonable period.

In *Cheltenham and Gloucester v Norgan*, the Court of Appeal said that a starting point for 'reasonable period' should be the remaining period of the mortgage.[27] This valuable precedent strengthens the money advice case for setting repayments at a level the client can afford. In exceptional cases, a 'reasonable period' could be longer than the remaining mortgage.[28] The decision also guides the court on points it should take into consideration, including the means of the client and the value of the lender's security.

When a client defaults, the terms of her/his mortgage may mean that s/he has to pay default interest on the arrears and also various fees. In 1992, a district judge suggested that such additional interest/charges should not be taken into account when calculating the arrears for the purpose of establishing whether a client can pay off the arrears and future payments within a reasonable period. This view was confirmed in a case in Northern Ireland, which, although not binding in England and Wales, is persuasive.[29] The court held that the arrears comprised only the missed monthly payments, and that any interest or charges should be added to the capital and included in the regular monthly instalment.

On the whole, courts appear satisfied that, for a long-term agreement, such as a mortgage, the security is safe. A clear financial statement is an essential tool. Identify the basic mortgage instalment separately from the payment towards the arrears to demonstrate to the court that the client is able to afford the contractual mortgage payments as well as being able to pay off the arrears within the period requested.

Tactically, you should still look for an affordable sum rather than spreading the arrears over as long a period as possible, just in case further difficulties arise in the future. Do not be intimidated by creditors and solicitors who say they want the arrears cleared in a shorter fixed period – eg, three years. The court will make its own decision and it should be familiar with the *Norgan* case.

If the arrears cannot be paid by instalments and the mortgage can only be repaid out of the proceeds of sale of the property, the *Norgan* decision does not apply. In *Bristol and West Building Society v Ellis,* however, the Court of Appeal held that the 'reasonable period' for a suspended order could be the time it would take to organise the sale of the property.[30]

What is a reasonable period depends on the circumstances of each case. Factors the court could take into account are:

- the extent to which the balance of the mortgage, as well as the arrears, is secured;
- whether there is little equity and the value of the security is at risk, in which case a short period of suspension might be appropriate;
- whether there has already been delay and/or there is negative equity or insufficient evidence of the property's value, in which case an immediate possession order might be appropriate.

Note: check the wording of a suspended (or postponed) possession order carefully to see whether it provides for the order to cease to have effect once the client has paid the arrears in accordance with its terms. If the client then falls into arrears again, the lender must obtain a further order and cannot just issue a warrant of possession. If no mention is made that the possession order ceases to have effect once its terms have been complied with, it continues to have effect unless or until the client applies to discharge it under section 36(4) of the Administration of Justice Act 1970. If the client does not do so and falls into arrears again, the lender can apply for a warrant of possession and the client must apply to suspend it. If you are involved at the possession order stage, you can request the district judge to word the suspended possession order so that it is discharged once the arrears are cleared.[31]

The lender must apply to the court for permission to enforce the order if more than six years have elapsed since the date of the original possession order.[32]

Postponing possession

A court should grant either a deferred or suspended possession order if the proceeds of the sale will fully cover the mortgage, so that a client can remain in her/his home while it is sold.[33]

Creditors have challenged suspended orders made to allow time for properties in negative equity to be sold. The Court of Appeal has held that if the mortgage cannot be cleared from the proceeds of the sale, the court has no jurisdiction to suspend the order,[34] but the court may adjourn the proceedings for procedural reasons.[35] However, in the case of *Cheltenham and Gloucester v Booker*, the Court of Appeal confirmed the court's jurisdiction to postpone, giving possession to the lender for a short period to enable the client to sell the property.[36] In addition, the

Financial Conduct Authority's *Mortgages and Home Finance: Conduct of Business Sourcebook* requires lenders to allow people to remain in possession of the property for a reasonable period to organise a sale in cases where no payment arrangement can be made.[37]

Produce written evidence from, for instance, an estate agent that the property is on the market and of the sale price, details of any offers received and, if an offer has been accepted, evidence about how far the conveyancing process has reached, including any proposed completion date from the client's solicitor.

The warrant of possession

If there is no real chance of clearing the arrears or the mortgage, the court makes a possession order, which is usually effective in 28 days. If the client has special reasons (eg, ill health or a new home is not yet available), the court may extend this to 56 days. At the end of the specified period, the lender can apply back to the court for bailiffs to execute a 'warrant of possession' (also known as a 'warrant of eviction' – see p378). The order states that if the client does not leave the property, the lender can ask the court to instruct the bailiff to evict her/him without a further hearing. It also states that the client can apply to the court to postpone the eviction.

A warrant of possession allows a county court enforcement agent (a bailiff) to evict the occupants from their home. The client receives notification that a possession warrant has been obtained on Form N54. It states the exact date and time when the bailiffs will carry out the eviction. The bailiffs can physically remove the occupants from their home, if necessary, and hand over possession of the property to the mortgage company. This is usually followed by the lender's agent changing the locks to prevent the client moving back in. Form N54 informs the client that:

- a possession warrant gives the bailiff authority to remove anyone still in the property when the eviction takes place;
- s/he should act immediately to get advice about the eviction or rehousing from an advice agency, solicitor or local housing department;
- s/he can apply on Form N244 (see p288) for the court to suspend the warrant and postpone the date for eviction;
- s/he must attend the hearing of the application or it may simply be dismissed, incurring further costs;
- if s/he can pay off any arrears, s/he should contact the lender or the lender's solicitor immediately.

Form N54 must also contain details of the bailiff and the client or her/his solicitor.

When dealing with a warrant of possession, you should either negotiate directly with the lender or help the client make an application to the court to suspend the warrant (see p382). County court bailiffs acting for a mortgage company which has issued an eviction warrant can change the locks and evict the client if no application has been made to suspend it. They can use necessary reasonable force to carry out the eviction.

A judgment or order for the possession of mortgaged property may also be enforced in the High Court by writ of possession. The bailiff does not need to give any advance warning of her/his intention to evict the client, and so clients with outright possession orders or who are in breach of the terms of a suspended or postponed possession order should be advised to apply to vary the terms of the possession order, as they may not get the opportunity to apply to the court to suspend the writ (see p382).

Granting a possession order should not, however, be seen as the end of the line. Even when this has occurred, lenders still do not want to repossess homes unnecessarily and it may be possible to negotiate terms directly with the creditor that are more acceptable than those imposed by the court. Such variations should at least be agreed in writing and the court asked to vary the relevant order, with the consent of the other party if possible (see p382).

Arguing against a possession order

In some cases, the situation when the loan was made is relevant. In particular, if a client was badly advised to take out a new secured loan by a financial adviser or the lender itself, this should be pointed out to the court – eg, if there has been irresponsible lending. The early history of the loan can be vital in obtaining the sympathy of the court.

If mortgage interest should have been paid by the DWP but has not been or if a claim is pending, this should be brought to the court's attention. Similarly, if penalties have followed slow payments from the DWP, these should be challenged (and compensation sought from the DWP with the help of an MP if necessary).

If the loan is a regulated credit agreement and covered by the Consumer Credit Act, check whether the agreement has been drawn up correctly and, if not, whether this makes it irredeemably unenforceable or enforceable only if the court gives permission (see p166).[38]

If the mortgage agreement was made after 1 July 1995 and its terms include 'arrears charges', 'fines' and interest penalties on early settlement, it might be possible to challenge it under the Consumer Rights Act 2015 to reduce the amount payable by the client. It may also be possible to challenge the lender's charges on the grounds that they were unreasonably incurred and/or unreasonable in amount.

Debt advisers sometimes agree to a suspended possession order on the grounds that this is a technicality and does no more than safeguard the lender's position. This is a very dangerous view and means that any future default in payment or the accruing of further mortgage arrears puts the client at serious risk of losing her/his home. If a suspended order is going to be made, the amount of instalments towards arrears should be set at a level that provides some leeway for the client faced with an unexpected and essential item of expenditure.

It is unnecessary to argue against a possession order if a time order is made. If this is the case, the order for possession should be suspended, provided the time order is complied with. A time order should, therefore, always be considered (see below) in cases of regulated credit agreements.

Time orders

A 'time order' is an order which allows a court to reschedule the payments under a credit agreement regulated by the Consumer Credit Act 1974 (or, in the case of regulated mortgage contracts, treated as regulated by the Act). If a time order is made, a client can pay any sum owed under a regulated credit agreement by instalments, payable at whatever frequency the court thinks is 'just', having regard to the client's means and any surety.[39] In the case of possession action, the 'sum owed' is the outstanding balance of the loan.

If the only reason an agreement secured on property (eg, a 'consumer credit back book mortgage contract' – see p64) is not regulated by the Consumer Credit Act is because it is a regulated mortgage contract (see p112), it can be argued that it should be treated as if it were a regulated agreement for the purposes of time orders.[40] You should get specialist advice if you are considering using this argument. However, the time order provisions do not apply if the agreement is exempt from regulation for any other reason.[41]

Note: if the time order provisions apply,[42] you should challenge district judges who will only consider making orders for payment of contractual instalments plus arrears.

Time orders are unpopular with the credit industry. Some lenders prefer to negotiate out of court rather than have a time order, so the threat of an application can be part of the client's negotiating tactics.

Creditors often argue that courts can only make time orders in cases of 'temporary financial difficulty', but this does not appear to be the case. The House of Lords suggested in the *First National Bank* case that the fact that a borrower's difficulties are not temporary is not necessarily an obstacle to making a time order: '... the broad language of s129 should be so construed as to permit the county court to make such an order as appears to it just in all the circumstances' (including any amendment to the loan agreement – eg, freezing or reducing interest as it considers just to both parties).[43]

Although time orders extending over a long period are generally regarded as undesirable, in the same case, the House of Lords confirmed that the court has the discretion to make whatever order it considers 'just' in the circumstances of the case.[44]

The Consumer Credit Act 1974 gives the court discretion to make a time order in all possession cases, involving regulated credit agreements 'if it appears to the court just to do so'.[45] To use this discretion properly, the court must consider the justice of an order in each case. The circumstances and terms of the loan, the reasons for default and the client's payment record are relevant circumstances.

Some creditors argue that, once judgment has been entered, the court no longer has the power to make a time order as there is no longer any 'sum owed' under a regulated agreement – ie, the debt is now owed under the judgment. However, section 129(2)(c) of the Consumer Credit Act 1974 says that a time order can be made 'in an action … to enforce a regulated agreement' and section 130(1) specifically allows the court to make a time order where a client has made an instalment offer in response to a county court claim. Finally, none of the House of Lords' judgments in the *First National Bank* case suggest that the court cannot make a time order in relation to a judgment debt.

If you come across a case in which the creditor denies that the court has the power to make a time order, get specialist advice.

If a time order is granted, the client's full liability to the creditor is discharged when s/he has made all the payments ordered. If a hearing is required, the court should transfer the hearing to the client's local court on its own initiative.[46]

When a time order is appropriate

A client can apply for a time order if money is owed under a regulated agreement and:[47]

- the creditor has served:
  - a default notice; *or*
  - a notice of intention to recover goods or land; *or*
  - a notice requiring early payment because of default; *or*
  - a notice seeking to terminate an agreement; *or*
- enforcement action has been taken by the creditor (including an application for an enforcement order); *or*
- the creditor has served an arrears notice, and the client has given the creditor 14 days' notice of her/his intention to apply for a time order and has made a repayment proposal.

An application for a time order is generally appropriate in the following circumstances.

- Current circumstances make payments impossible, but the client's income is likely to increase – eg, if s/he is currently on short-time working or experiencing a period of unemployment or benefit disqualification. A time order can still be considered, however, if there is no foreseeable improvement in circumstances.
- The original agreement was harsh on the client (eg, s/he was disadvantaged in negotiations or ignorant of its implications) or there is evidence of irresponsible lending. In these circumstances, the court may be sympathetic to using a time order in the interests of justice.

- An application might persuade the creditor to negotiate realistically and reduce the payments due under a regulated agreement.

Time order applications can be made for both secured and unsecured debts, although they are mainly applied for in relation to secured debts.

In *Director General of Fair Trading v First National Bank*, the House of Lords recommended that a time order application could be made where a creditor was continuing to charge contractual interest after judgment. This can be done by adding in Box 11 of Form N9A: 'I ask the court to (1) make a time order in the terms of my offer and (2) amend the loan agreement in consequence so that no further contractual interest accrues after the date of judgment.'

Applications

An application can be made by the client after receiving a relevant notice using Form N440.[48] A fee of £280 is payable. See p290 for details about full or partial fee remission. The borrower is the claimant and the lender is the defendant.

An application can be useful when a lender is demanding very high payments towards the arrears, or in other ways pressurising the client, but does not start court action itself and refuses to negotiate. It is much more common for an application for a time order to be in response to a claim for possession.

If the lender has already issued proceedings against the client, an application for a time order can be made in the client's defence (Question 6 on Form N11M) or on Form N244. After the court order has been made, an application to vary that order to a time order can be made. Any application should be supported by a witness statement.

The application must show that a time order is just to both the creditor and the client and indicate the terms that are required. Include:

- the circumstances of the client at the time s/he took out the loan, the situation now and her/his likely prospects for the future;
- the purpose of the loan;
- the client's payment history;
- the amount of the loan, the interest rate charged and any default charges;
- the value of the security;
- the payments that can be made now, and if and when these can be increased in the future, including a financial statement;
- the implications the time order will have on any changes required to the original agreement, particularly the extra time required and the reduction in interest rate required.

The court must be just to both parties and it therefore considers the client's position, including whether s/he was able to afford the agreement when s/he entered into it (and, if not, whether there is evidence of irresponsible lending), whether the cause of the arrears is temporary and whether s/he will be able to afford to resume at least contractual payments at a foreseeable future date.

The court also considers whether there is adequate security for the lender and how the interest rate charged compares with that of other lenders.

Example

A couple took a secured loan at 28 per cent APR to pay for double glazing and maintained payments for 18 months. The wage earner then had a serious accident and was unable to work. She should be fully recovered in about nine months when he will resume employment and the contractual payments. The loan is secured against the couple's home, which has adequate equity. On these facts, a court should grant a time order.

The amount due

A time order can be made for 'the sum owed'. This phrase has been the subject of much dispute, but has now been clarified by the Court of Appeal. It means 'every sum which is due and owing under the agreement'. If possession proceedings have been brought, this is the total indebtedness, and this was confirmed in the *Barnes* case (see below). In the case of unsecured regulated loans, it is usually the total amount due.

The amount due (and subject to a time order) is therefore the sum of:
- the amount borrowed; *and*
- the total charge for credit (early settlement rebates should not be applied to this); *and*
- any default interest properly charged up to the hearing date; *less*
- all payments made to date.

The lender should make clear to the court the total sum owed and the present arrears as well as the contractual instalments. Check these calculations, if possible. The lender should also be asked to confirm in writing:
- if the client makes the contractual payments plus £x towards the arrears, how much s/he will still owe at the end of the loan repayment period; *and*
- the monthly payment the client needs to make to repay the loan by the end of the contractual period.

How much to offer

The offer of payment should be according to the client's ability to repay and her/his personal circumstances. In *Southern and District Finance v Barnes*, an order was made for £25 a month for six months, then nearly £100 a month for the remaining 174 months.[49]

Varying other terms

Having decided the instalments and their timing, the court can also amend either the rate of interest or the length of the loan, provided it is 'just to both parties and a consequence of the term of the order'.[50] It is, therefore, important to demonstrate that a reduction in interest is a necessary consequence of a reduction in payments in order to prevent a loan running for too long. This may simply be a reduction in interest on the arrears, or a reduction in interest on the arrears and principal during the period of reduced payments, or a longer term reduction.

The court does not have the facilities to calculate interest charges. You could consider approaching your local trading standards office for help with this or asking the court to require the lender to make the necessary calculations.

Reviews

A time order can be varied or revoked by the court on the application of a creditor or client.[51] This power to review should be sufficient to persuade district judges who resist time orders that one can safely be granted because it can later be reviewed.

After property has been repossessed

A warrant of possession is executed on the date and time stated in the warrant. A bailiff comes to the property accompanied by a locksmith and a representative from the lender. The bailiff may use force to enter the property and evict all the occupants. If opposition is expected, the bailiff may be accompanied by a police officer to prevent a breach of the peace (not to enforce the eviction). The locksmith changes the locks. Any of the client's property left in the home will therefore be locked inside. The client can ask the lender for access to the home to remove her/his property within a reasonable period, usually two weeks.

Once a warrant has been executed, the court cannot suspend the possession unless:

- the original possession order itself is set aside; *or*
- the warrant has been obtained by fraud; *or*
- there has been oppression or abuse of process in its execution. Court staff providing misleading information could amount to 'oppression', but unless there has been 'fault' on the part of the lender or the court, there is no abuse of process.[52]

The property is then sold by the lender (called the 'mortgagee in possession'), which has the following responsibilities.

- The lender must take proper care of the property. This includes making essential or emergency repairs (eg, mending a leaking pipe) and may include simple maintenance (eg, mowing the lawn, painting the windows), but not include improvements – eg, refitting the kitchen.
- The lender must sell the property at the best price reasonably possible. If it does not do so, the client can complain to the Financial Ombudsman Service.[53] Most lenders get at least two valuations to ensure the price is fair and sell

through an estate agent in the usual way. Sale by auction is usually considered to achieve a fair market price, although a reserve price is set.

- The lender should sell the property as soon as possible. The lender is not under an obligation to delay the sale in the hope of obtaining a better price. The lender must balance the need to prevent the debt increasing with market factors.
- The lender must account to the client for money received and charged in respect of the property (see below).[54]

After the sale of the property, the lender balances the payments and proceeds of the sale against the outstanding mortgage (the 'account'). The sale proceeds are applied first to any arrears of interest and are usually sufficient to cover these, so that any shortfall is likely to consist of the capital borrowed.

If the mortgage is less than the payments and proceeds of sale, the balance should be paid to the client as soon as reasonably possible. If the mortgage is more than the payments and proceeds, the client should be informed as soon as possible and asked to make up the difference, usually referred to as a 'mortgage shortfall' debt.[55] In order to recover any debt, the lender must produce an account to show all payments made and proceeds of the sale versus the amount of the mortgage and its other costs to show the balance outstanding.

The client is legally obliged to repay the mortgage and all the costs associated with recovering the debt. Once the property has been sold, the shortfall debt is unsecured. Although the lender should inform the client of the amount of the shortfall as soon as possible after the sale, inevitably the client will have moved and, in the absence of a forwarding address, it may take some time to trace her/him. It is not unusual for people to remain unaware of the shortfall debt for several years.

To lose a home is not necessarily the end of the line for a client. Many lenders do not take any action immediately following a forced sale because they recognise the client is likely to have financial problems that caused the arrears and therefore could not afford to pay anything anyway. However, many lenders keep records of repossessed borrowers and are likely to attempt to recover any shortfall at a later date when either her/his situation is known to have improved or the general economic situation is better. It is also possible that such lenders could sell these debts at a later date to companies whose standards of collection are more draconian than those of the original mortgage lender. If the lender decides to recover the shortfall from the client, it must inform her/him of this decision within six years of the date of sale.

It is, therefore, vital to advise a client whose home is sold by a secured lender that there may be future attempts by the lender to recover this money.

For more details on dealing with mortgage shortfall debts, see p116.

4. **Recovering rented property**

Before a landlord can take court action to repossess the client's home, it must serve a formal notice on the client which contains the date after which court action can be started (usually four weeks). In the case of rent arrears, the client should try to come to an arrangement with her/his landlord before court action begins to pay the arrears in addition to the on-going rent.

Guidance to social landlords

Social landlords (ie, local authorities and housing associations) must follow certain steps before issuing claims for possession based on rent arrears alone.

The Pre-Action Protocol for Possession requires the following claims by Social Landlords.

- The landlord should contact the client as soon as reasonably possible to discuss the reason for the arrears, the client's financial circumstances (including any entitlement to benefits) and repayment of the arrears by affordable amounts based on her/his ability to repay. The landlord should also advise the client to seek advice from the free money advice sector.
- If appropriate, the landlord should apply for the arrears to be paid by the Department for Work and Pensions by deductions from the client's benefit.
- The landlord must provide rent statements on a quarterly basis.
- If the landlord is aware that the client is under 18 or particularly vulnerable (eg, has mental health issues), it should take steps to ensure the client's rights are protected – eg, consider a community care assessment.
- If there is an outstanding housing benefit (HB) or universal credit housing element claim, the landlord should work with the client to resolve any problems and, in most circumstances, should not issue possession proceedings (see p380).
- After serving the statutory notice seeking possession, the landlord should continue to try to contact the client to discuss the matter and, if an arrangement is made for payment of the current rent and an amount towards the arrears, should agree to postpone the issue of proceedings provided the client complies with the agreement.
- At least 10 days before the possession hearing, the landlord must provide an up-to-date rent statement, confirm the details of the court hearing and of the order the landlord is seeking, and advise the client to attend the hearing.
- If, after the issue of proceedings, an arrangement is made for the payment of the current rent and an amount towards the arrears, the landlord should agree to adjourn the hearing, provided the client complies with the agreement.
- If the client fails to comply with any payment arrangement, the landlord should warn her/him of its intention to start, or continue with, possession proceedings and give the client a clear time limit within which to bring her/his payments up to date.

Courts should take into account the conduct of both landlord and client when considering whether the protocol has been followed and what orders to make. If the landlord has unreasonably failed to comply, the court may:

- order the landlord to pay the client's costs; *and/or*
- adjourn, strike out or dismiss the claim (unless it is a mandatory ground).

If a client has unreasonably failed to comply, the court may take this into account when considering whether it is reasonable to make a possession order.

Be prepared to bring the terms of the protocol to the attention of landlords and district judges and point out that it is not a voluntary code of practice, but part of the Civil Procedure Rules. Advisers can download a copy from justice.gov.uk.

Note: some housing advisers have suggested that, because landlords routinely apply for money judgments in possession claims on the ground of rent arrears, the protocol for debt claims applies to that part of the claim. Although this is arguable, it has not yet been tested but it might be a useful negotiating tactic.

The claim form

The particulars of claim, on Form N119, in a possession action for rented property must include:[56]

- what property is to be recovered;
- whether the claim relates to a dwelling house;
- full details of the tenancy agreement;
- the grounds on which possession is claimed;
- details of every person living in the property;
- the amount due at the start of proceedings;
- a schedule ('rent statement') showing all amounts of rent due and payments made over the previous two years, or from the date of first default if within the two-year period;
- the daily rate of rent and any interest;
- any previous steps the landlord has taken to recover the arrears;
- the date notice to quit or other notice was given to the tenant, specifying the type of notice;
- any relevant information known about the tenant's circumstances, including whether s/he is in receipt of benefits and whether any deductions from benefit are being paid directly to the landlord.

If the landlord uses the 'possession claim online' process (see p357), the particulars must contain the same information as above with one exception. If, before proceedings are issued, the landlord has provided the client with a schedule of arrears showing all amounts due and payments made, together with dates and a running total of the arrears, either for the previous two years or from the date of default (if later), the particulars of claim may contain a summary of the arrears stating:

- the amount of the arrears on the date of the landlord's notice of seeking possession;
- the dates and amounts of the last three payments or, if fewer than three payments have been made, the dates and amounts of those payments; *and*
- the arrears at the date of issue of the possession proceedings.

As a notice of seeking possession is a statutory requirement for secure and assured tenancies, most landlords should be able to take advantage of the provision allowing the arrears to be summarised. However, if the landlord only includes the summary information in the particulars of claim, it must serve a full arrears history on the client within seven days after the issue of the claim and verify this by a witness statement or verbally at the hearing.

Responding to the claim

The client should reply to the claim on Form N11R.

- **Question 1** requests details of the client's personal circumstances, including date of birth.
- **Question 2** relates to paragraphs 2 and 3 of Form N119 and should either be confirmed as correct or details given of any disagreement.
- **Question 3** asks about the service of the 'notice seeking possession' or equivalent. Check that this has been done in the prescribed manner.
- **Question 4** asks the client to check the rent arrears as stated by the landlord. This should be done carefully.
- **Question 5** only needs completing if possession is being sought on grounds other than rent arrears – eg, for nuisance.
- **Question 6** asks for any counterclaims that the client may have. There are a series of counterclaims or 'set-offs' that can be made by a tenant when a landlord claims possession.
  - Under a tenancy created before 15 January 1989, a landlord may be charging more than the fair rent set by the rent officer. In such cases, not only is the excess over the fair rent not recoverable or counted as arrears for the purposes of seeking possession of the property, but the client can also claim back all the overpaid money for up to two years.[57]
  - A counterclaim can be made for disrepair if a landlord has failed to keep her/his statutory obligations to repair the exterior or main structure of the property or facilities for the supply of water, gas, electricity or removal of sewage. The client can claim the rent arrears should be reduced by an amount to compensate her/him for this loss, which can be done by

completing the defence part of the reply to the possession claim form. However, in order to safeguard her/his rights, a client should either pay the rent or open an account into which to pay it. In one case, a county court judge still made an order for possession because of rent arrears despite awarding an amount for damages for disrepair that was greater than the actual arrears. The decision to order possession was subsequently overturned by the Court of Appeal.[58]

Consider obtaining the advice of a specialist housing adviser if a landlord has failed in some contractual obligation – eg, has not provided furniture as agreed or redecorated a property as regularly as promised. In such cases, it may be necessary to refer the matter to a solicitor before proceeding.

- **Question 7** asks for details of payments made since the claim form was issued.
- **Question 8**. If an agreement has been reached, details should be included and the reply should ideally be accompanied by a letter requesting a general adjournment. The landlord should be asked to write separately, if it can be persuaded to agree to this course of action rather than to an order suspended on payment of whatever sum has been agreed. If an unrealistic offer was previously made (perhaps under pressure) and broken, this should be made clear. If the landlord is a social landlord, refer to the rent arrears pre-action protocol to check whether it has complied with it (see p372).
- **Question 9**. The client should answer 'yes' if agreement has not been reached. Note that clients who fail to ask the court to consider instalments might later find this used against them if a local authority is considering the question of the intentionality of their homelessness.
- **Question 10** asks for the amount in addition to the rent that is being offered. If money is not yet available for the arrears, the court can be asked (probably on a separate sheet) to make an order suspended on payments of £x extra each week or month, with the first payment on a specified date in the foreseeable future. Alternatively, a token offer could be suggested for the first months' payments, followed by something more realistic.
- **Questions 11–15** relate to income support or HB (if the client gets universal credit, see p360). It is important to know the up-to-date position with regards to any HB (or discretionary housing payment) claims (particularly if rent is paid directly to a landlord or if non-dependant deductions vary with the movement of non-dependants). If the landlord is a social landlord and is aware that an HB claim is pending, refer to the rent arrears pre-action protocol.
- **Questions 16–27** relate to dependants (and non-dependants), bank accounts and savings, income and expenditure, priority debts, court orders and credit debts similar to those required on Form N9A (see p303) and should be completed in the same way.
- **Question 28**. The client should not answer 'yes' to this question ('If an order is made will you have somewhere to live?') unless the new accommodation is absolutely certain. The date given should always allow for 'slippage'.

- **Question 29** is important because it gives the client the opportunity to explain:
  - why the arrears arose;
  - what circumstances were beyond her/his control;
  - why it would cause particular hardship if eviction were ordered;
  - why an expensive property was rented (if applicable).

  If the landlord is a social landlord, any breaches of the rent arrears pre-action protocol can be pointed out here (see p372).

What counts as rent arrears

In many cases, particularly when the local authority is the landlord, some of what is claimed as rent arrears may not, in fact, be so. For example, amounts of overpaid HB that an authority wishes to recover may be added to a client's rent account as though they were arrears. In fact, even where such an amount has properly become payable (and the client has been given the right of appeal), such amounts do not constitute unpaid rent. They can be included in a rent account, provided they are clearly distinguished from rent that is owed to the local authority, but should not appear on a claim form as rent arrears.

However, in non-local authority tenancy cases, if HB has been paid directly to the landlord and the local authority has exercised its right to recover any HB overpayment directly from the landlord, the amount recovered can be treated as rent arrears.[59]

In some cases, a client may also have amounts of water charges, rent arrears from a previous tenancy or other non-rent charges included in her/his rent arrears. These amounts should not appear on a claim form, unless they are specifically included in the rent for the client's home. If the tenancy agreement provides for water charges to be collected by the landlord and for them to be treated as rent, it may be possible to argue that this is an unfair term under the Consumer Rights Act 2015 (see p155) because it creates the possibility of the client being evicted on the basis of arrears of water charges. As an unfair term is unenforceable, this is a defence to the possession proceedings, depending on whether the arrears also include any 'true' rent.

Powers of the court to deal with possession action

There are a number of grounds on which possession may be sought when rent is unpaid, and these differ slightly according to whether the client has a private or social landlord and whether her/his tenancy began before or after 15 January 1989. **Note:** you must be certain about the status of the client's occupancy before giving advice about a possession claim.

A client may receive a possession claim form on grounds that are not connected to a debt. This *Handbook* does not cover these matters. For a detailed explanation of all the grounds upon which possession might be sought, see *Defending*

Possession Proceedings (see Appendix 2), or consult Legal Action Group or a specialist housing advice service, such as Shelter.

The court's role in every case of arrears, except those of some assured tenants who are more than 13 weeks in arrears (see below), is to decide whether or not it is 'reasonable' to make an order for possession and whether or not to suspend this on particular terms (usually payment of the normal rent plus an amount towards the arrears). This means that, as long as the client keeps to the payment ordered by the court, the landlord cannot regain possession of the property. If a client is in receipt of a means-tested benefit, an amount equivalent to the rate of direct deductions from benefits (see p233) may be accepted by the court. If the client does not attend the hearing or there is no request for time to pay the arrears from her/him, the order may be made for possession to be given up in a certain period of time – for a minimum of 14 days or a maximum of 42 days, but usually for 28 days.

Courts can award fixed costs in all cases where a possession order is made.

Assured tenants

The court must make a possession order to a landlord if the client is an assured tenant and, at the date of the hearing, at least eight weeks' or two months' rent (three months' if paid quarterly) is unpaid (ground 8).[60] The landlord must prove there was two months' rent in arrears (or three months' if paid quarterly) both at the time when the notice of seeking possession was served and at the date of the hearing, which need be only two weeks later.

There are two other grounds for possession for rent arrears: grounds 10 (if there is any amount of rent arrears) and 11 (if the client is regularly late paying the rent).

The court does not have to consider reasonableness if ground 8 is being used, so even if delays in the payment of HB caused the arrears (see p380), this could still lead to a possession order being granted. The court has no power to adjourn, except for procedural reasons or in exceptional circumstances.[61] You should pressure the local authority to make an emergency payment before the hearing and, if it fails to do so, local politicians and the Local Government and Social Care Ombudsman or Public Services Ombudsman for Wales should be informed.

The court will not grant a possession order if, by the date of the hearing, the arrears are reduced to even a nominal amount (eg, £1) below two or three months' rent. It may sometimes be worthwhile for a client to borrow money, particularly from family or friends, to ensure s/he does not become subject to this mandatory ground. See also Chapter 7 for ways of maximising income.

In practice, social landlords rarely used ground 8 but tend to use grounds 10 and 11. You should always check which ground(s) the landlord is using. Landlords tend to use ground 8 and accelerated possession proceedings for assured shorthold tenancies.

The warrant of possession

A warrant of possession gives county court bailiffs the power to evict the occupiers and change the locks. The court issues a warrant following a request from the landlord if the client has not voluntarily left the property by the date ordered by the court at a possession hearing or has not kept to the terms of a suspended order for possession. In order to prevent eviction, an application must be made for the warrant to be suspended (see p382). The notice of eviction (Form N54) informs the client about this.

If the landlord wishes to use High Court bailiffs to execute a writ of possession, s/he must first obtain the permission of the court. The court can only grant permission if it is satisfied that the occupant(s) received sufficient notice of the possession proceedings and so had the opportunity to apply to the court – eg, to suspend the possession order.[62]

Note: you should check the wording of any suspended (Form N28) or postponed (Form N28A) possession order carefully to see whether it provides for the order to cease to have effect once the client has paid the arrears in accordance with its terms. If the client then falls into arrears again, the landlord must obtain a further order and cannot just issue a warrant of possession.

Generally, a warrant of possession cannot be issued without the court's permission if a tenant has breached the terms of a suspended possession order. However, since 1 October 2018, a landlord does not need the permission of the court to issue a warrant of possession where the breach of the suspended possession order is the failure to pay rent or rent arrears.[63]

Form N325A (request for a warrant of possession following suspended possession order) and Form N445 (request for reissue of warrant) require the landlord to certify that:[64]

- the whole or part of any instalments due under the judgment or order have not been paid and the balance now due is as shown; *and*
- the land which is the subject of the judgment or order has not been vacated.

Tenants of properties with mortgage arrears

A client may pay rent to someone who is buying a property with a mortgage. If the client became a tenant after the date the mortgage started but the lender's permission was not sought or granted in accordance with the terms of the mortgage, she is known as an 'unauthorised' tenant of a mortgage borrower and is unlikely to be able to defend a possession claim brought against her/his landlord.

However, an affected client can apply to the court to 'stay' or suspend the execution of a possession order for up to two months to allow her/him sufficient time to obtain suitable alternative accommodation.[65] The client can apply at the hearing of the possession claim or subsequently. S/he must have first approached the lender for a written undertaking not to enforce the order for two months and the lender must have refused to give this. It is arguable that a failure to respond, even after reminders, counts as a refusal as there is no time limit within which the lender is required to respond. Such a request could be made verbally or in writing. The client's application should be made on Form N244 (see p288). The fee is £50. See p290 for details on applying for full or partial fee remission.

The court can only postpone the execution of the order once. The court must take account of the client's circumstances, including any breaches of the tenancy agreement. The court can order the client to make payments to the lender.

In the case of buy-to-let lending, the terms and conditions of the loan usually incorporate consent to tenancies being created. Provided the terms and conditions have been complied with, guidance from the Council of Mortgage Lenders issued in June 2009 on buy-to-let arrears and possessions advises lenders that the tenancy is binding and the lender will take possession of the property, subject to the terms and conditions of the tenancy. The lender can only evict the tenant in accordance with landlord and tenant law. The position is the same for other tenancies created after the loan was entered into to which the lender has specifically consented.

Arguing against a possession order

It may be possible to argue that it is 'unreasonable' to make a possession order. Courts take into account the view that a landlord is entitled to the increase in capital value of her/his property and to revenue from rent. Argue that the existence of an agreement to clear the arrears or even a reasonable offer coupled with an ability to pay the ongoing rent makes a possession order unnecessary and, therefore, unreasonable.

Arguments can be based on the client's circumstances (eg, s/he has children, or is sick or disabled) or her/his finances – eg, s/he has been dependent on benefits for some time. If an improvement in circumstances can be shown (eg, s/he is about to get a job), this will probably help convince the court that it is unreasonable to make a possession order. Other arguments could be based on the position of the landlord – eg, the landlord's identity was unknown or s/he had failed to collect rent or arrange for an agent to do so.

Note: an outright possession order is not necessarily a breach of a client's human rights under Article 8 of the European Convention on Human Rights (respect for family and private life).[66]

Any defence the client offers may be helped if s/he has begun to pay the contractual rent and something towards the arrears by the time the hearing takes place. Such payments should have been recorded by the landlord or, if the landlord has refused to accept payments before the court hearing, the money should have been paid into a separate account. Proof of payment made should be taken to the hearing.

Arrears because of non-payment of housing benefit

If a client's rent arrears are due to the fact that she has not been paid her/his HB, or they have arisen while s/he was waiting for a decision on her/his claim for HB or a discretionary housing payment (to cover the shortfall between the HB s/he gets and the actual rent, possibly as a result of the 'bedroom tax'), this can be a powerful argument for saying it is unreasonable for the court to make an order, particularly if it is a social landlord. In addition, the rent arrears pre-action protocol (see p372) says that the landlord should make every effort to establish effective ongoing liaison with the HB department and should also offer to assist the client with her/his HB claim, in particular, if s/he has:

- provided the local authority with all the evidence required to process her/his HB claim;
- a reasonable expectation of eligibility for HB; *and*
- paid any other sums due to the landlord that are not covered by the HB claim (or has applied for a discretionary housing payment to cover the shortfall).

The landlord should not issue possession proceedings on the grounds of rent arrears but should (with the client's consent) make direct contact with the local authority HB department.

If the landlord is not a local authority, the client can ask the court to consider making a third-party costs order against the local authority – ie, for the local authority to pay the landlord's costs. This can only be done if the local authority is:[67]

- made a party to the proceedings for the purposes of costs only; *and*
- given a reasonable opportunity of attending the hearing for the court to consider the question.

This requires action to be taken before the possession hearing itself and you should consider obtaining specialist housing advice. A threat to seek an order for costs may prompt the local authority to expedite the HB claim and clear the arrears. Otherwise, if possible, the client should obtain a letter from the local authority explaining when HB will be paid and take this to the hearing.

Postponing possession

The standard form for a 'suspended' possession order in rent arrears cases is Form N28A. This is, in fact, a postponed possession order. It does not set a date for possession, but allows the landlord to apply to the court to fix a possession date in the event of the client defaulting on the order. However, the landlord must first give the client 14 days' notice of its intention to apply and invite her/him to bring the arrears up to date or provide an explanation for her/his non-payment. The landlord's application can be dealt with without a hearing, although the court could list it for a hearing. If the court grants the application, a date for possession is fixed (usually the next working day). The landlord still needs to issue a warrant of possession if the client does not leave the property voluntarily and the client can still apply to suspend the warrant (see p382).[68]

Note: before 1 July 2009, the prescribed form was Form N28. This suspended possession order is still a prescribed form. Check the practice in your local county court and encourage any courts still using Form N28 to stop doing so.

5. **Preventing enforcement**

Setting aside a judgment

If there has been a hearing in the county court, the client can apply to have the order 'set aside' (see p337) and the matter reheard if s/he did not attend the hearing and an order was made in her/his absence. The court must consider whether the client:

- acted 'promptly' – ie, with all reasonable speed once s/he found out that the court had made an order against her/him;
- had a good reason for not attending the hearing; *and*
- has a reasonable prospect of success at any rehearing.

The court is unlikely to order a rehearing if the client deliberately failed to attend or if the court is satisfied that there is no real prospect of the original order being changed.[69]

The court will not allow an application for a rehearing purely on the grounds that the client did not receive notice of the hearing date without enquiring why s/he did not receive it. On the other hand, the court should not refuse an application for a rehearing just because s/he failed to provide the creditor or lender with a forwarding address. In general:[70]

- if the client is unaware that proceedings are imminent or have been served, s/he has a good reason for not attending any hearing;
- if the client knows of the existence of proceedings but does not have a system in place for receiving communication about the case, s/he is unlikely to have a good reason for not attending any hearing.

Suspending a warrant of delivery

If the client wants to keep goods that are the subject of a hire purchase or conditional sale agreement, s/he can apply on Form N244 (see p288) to suspend the warrant of delivery. A financial statement should be supplied. Form N244 should be sent to the enforcing court. A fee of £50 is payable. See p290 for details about full or partial fee remission. An offer of payment must be made that will realistically repay the agreement and arrears. A court is unlikely to agree to very small payments compared with the original contractual sum. If this is not possible, try to renegotiate with the creditor the payments due under the agreement, or consider a time order (see p366).

Varying the terms of a suspended or postponed possession order

If the repayments under a suspended order, or any other terms of an order, require a change, the client can apply back to the court for the order to be changed or varied. Application is on Form N244 (see p288) and a fee of £50 is payable. See p290 for details on applying for full or partial fee remission. It is always better to apply to vary an order if circumstances have changed, rather than be served with a warrant and have to apply to suspend it. For example, if the client is on maternity leave and therefore has a reduced income for a period, she could apply for a reduction in payments, or if a client unexpectedly finds employment, s/he can apply for a possession order to be suspended because s/he can now make payments.

Suspending a warrant of possession

Following the issue of a warrant, a notice of eviction on Form N54 is sent or delivered from the court, stating a date and time when the bailiffs will evict the client from her/his property. The client can apply for a warrant of possession to be suspended at any time before the date and time specified on the warrant, although it is preferable to apply as early as possible.[71]

Form N244 should be completed (see p288), showing:

- how the client's circumstances have changed since the possession order was made;
- that the equity or rental revenue of the creditor is not threatened by a suspension;
- a well-supported offer of payment and a lump sum (or first payment), if possible;
- if the client does not wish to remain in the property, that arrangements are in hand for sale of the property or rehousing, but that this will take time.

Form N244 should be accompanied by a financial statement. **Note:** a fee of £50 is payable.[72] See p290 for details on applying for full or partial fee remission. If possible, take the form to the court rather than posting it as there will be little time available.

If the lender or landlord issued the possession action using the 'possession claim online' process and the client wants to make her/his application online, any court fee must be paid either by debit card or credit card. The possession claim online website contains a list of organisations through which the client can claim full or partial fee remission online. Otherwise, Form N244 must be filed, and any application for fee remission must be made, in person.

A hearing is granted almost immediately and the client must attend. You should always try to negotiate directly with the creditor before the hearing and ensure that if an agreement has been reached, the details are communicated to the solicitor or agent who will be representing the creditor at the hearing. If possible, arrange for confirmation in writing so the client can take this to the hearing in case there is any dispute. If no agreement can be reached, the matter must be presented clearly before the district judge, using similar arguments to those covered on p294. At the same time, it may be necessary to ask for the payment order to be varied (reduced) to a level the client can afford.

In theory, there is no limit to the number of applications that can be made to suspend a warrant, but if the client persistently applies and then fails to make payments, the application may be refused and s/he may be told that s/he cannot make any further applications without leave of the court. In this case, assuming that the application is realistic, the client must ask for leave of the court to apply, on Form N244, before continuing on the same application to explain the reasons. The court usually considers granting leave to apply first. If granted, it then considers the application for suspension in the same hearing.

If the application is refused, the eviction usually takes place on the date and time on the warrant. The client may ask for a short suspension (eg, two weeks) to find alternative accommodation. Alternatively, in mortgage cases, if repossession is granted, the client could ask to stay in the property while the lender sells it.[73] After the execution of the warrant of possession (ie, the eviction), no order for its suspension can be made unless:

- the possession order itself is set aside; *or*
- the warrant was obtained fraudulently; *or*
- there had been an abuse of the process or oppression in the execution of the warrant.[74] It appears that 'oppression' is not limited to conduct by the creditor but can extend to conduct by the court – eg, misleading information from court staff on the procedure for suspending a warrant.[75]

Appealing to a judge

If a client disagrees with a judgment or order made by a district judge and none of the options discussed on pp381–82 are applicable, s/he must appeal if s/he wishes to challenge the judge's decision.

If the judgment or order with which the client disagrees was made in her/his absence, s/he should consider applying to set aside the order and for a rehearing, as described on p294. An appeal might be appropriate if, for instance, the client did not act 'promptly' or did not have a good reason for not attending the hearing but not, for example, if her/his case has no reasonable prospect of success.[77]

Adjournment

An adjournment is a court order to delay a hearing either for a specified amount of time or indefinitely. The county court can, at any time, either adjourn or bring forward the date of a hearing. It can decide to do this itself or because one or both of the parties have applied.

If a client unsuccessfully applies for an adjournment and the case is dealt with in her/his absence, s/he should normally apply to set aside the judgment or order and apply for a rehearing on the grounds discussed above rather than appeal. However, the client could appeal a refusal to set aside the judgment or order, provided there are grounds.

See p295 for more information.

Notes

1. Recovering goods on hire purchase or conditional sale
1 s130(1) CCA 1974
2 s135 CCA 1974
3 s135(2) CCA 1974
4 CPR PD 7B, para 3.3

2. Recovering property
5 For a summary of recent developments in mortgage arrears cases, see M Robinson, 'Mortgage Possession Update', *Adviser* 147

3. Recovering owner-occupied property
6 ss126 and 173(3) CCA 1974
7 See *FCA Handbook*, MCOB 13 at handbook.fca.org.uk/handbook/mcob/13
8 Under *FCA Handbook*, MCOB 12.4, if the client has a payment shortfall, any payments received must be allocated first to paying off the balance of the shortfall (excluding interest and charges). If the client has a payment arrangement for the arrears and is keeping to it, the lender should not impose any arrears charges.
9 r3.4(2)(c) CPR
10 See C Howell, 'Preventing Mortgage Repossessions', *Quarterly Account* 33, IMA

11 CPR PD 55, paras 2.1-2.7
12 CPR PD 55, para 1.7
13 r30.2(1) CPR
14 Available at gov.uk/government/publications/lender-notification-of-repossession-proceedings-to-local-authorities-non-statutory-guidance
15 For a general discussion of the court's powers, see M Robinson, 'Mortgage Possession in the County Court', *Adviser* 123
16 s151(2) FSMA 2000. In *Thakker v Northern Rock (Asset Management) plc* [2014] EWHC 2107 (QB), the High Court dismissed the borrower's appeal against a possession order and held that the lender's breach of the MCOB was not a defence to the possession claim.
17 CPR PD 55A, para 7.1
18 *Halifax Building Society v Taffs* [1999] CLY 4385 (CA) (*Adviser* 81 abstracts)
19 See C Evans, 'The New Rules are Working!', *Adviser* 79
20 For a discussion on how this might be applied in mortgage possession proceedings, see N Clayton, 'Mortgage Conduct of Business Rules and Mortgage Repossessions', *Quarterly Account* 8, IMA
21 s36 AJA 1970 and s8 AJA 1973
22 r3.1(2)(b) CPR

23 See *Birmingham Citizens Permanent Building Society v Caunt* [1962] 1 All ER 163

24 Under s36 of the AJA 1970 and s8 of the AJA 1973. See *Zinda v Bank of Scotland* [2011] EWCA Civ 706 (*Adviser* 147 abstracts). These powers are unlikely to apply to 'all monies charges' securing a debt repayable on demand (eg, a bank overdraft), since the client must pay the whole outstanding balance within a 'reasonable period'; see *Habib Bank v Taylor* [1982] 1 WLR 1218.

25 *Royal Bank of Scotland v Elmes*, Clerkenwell County Court (*Legal Action*, April 1998, p11)

26 *Halifax plc v Salt and Bell*, Derby County Court, 29 December 2007 (*Adviser* 127 abstracts)

27 *Cheltenham and Gloucester v Norgan* [1996] 1 All ER 449 (*Adviser* 53 abstracts)

28 See for example, *Abbey National v Padfield*, Bristol County Court, 26 July 2002 (*Adviser* 96 abstracts)

29 *Santander (UK) plc v McAtamney and Others* [2013] NIMaster 15 (*Adviser* 160 abstracts)

30 *Bristol and West Building Society v Ellis* [1996] 29 HLR 282

31 See *Zinda v Bank of Scotland* [2011] EWCA Civ 706 (*Adviser* 147 abstracts)

32 r82.2(3) CPR. See also *Zinda v Bank of Scotland* [2011] EWCA Civ 706 (*Adviser* 147 abstracts)

33 *Target Home Loans v Clothier* [1993] 25 HLR 48

34 *Cheltenham and Gloucester Building Society v Krausz* [1996] 29 HLR 597

35 *State Bank of New South Wales v Harrison* [2002] EWCA Civ 363 (*Adviser* 95 abstracts)

36 *Cheltenham and Gloucester v Booker* [1996] 29 HLR 634

37 *FCA Handbook*, MCOB 13.3.2AR(5)

38 Enforcing a possession order in relation to an unenforceable agreement without obtaining the permission of the court could give rise to an unfair relationship: see *In the matter of London Scottish Finance* [2013] EWHC 4047 (Ch) (*Adviser* 162 abstracts)

39 s129(2)(a) CCA 1974

40 s126(2) CCA 1974

41 *FCA Hndbook*, PERG 4.17.2(G). For further discussion of the implications of these provisions following the implementation of the Mortgage Credit Directive on 21 March 2016, see R Rosenberg 'Mortgages and Time Orders', *Quarterly Account* 50, IMA

42 s38a AJA 1970

43 See P Madge, 'Full Circle', *Adviser* 89 for a full discussion of the implications of the *First National Bank* decision. For a summary of the development of time orders, see P Madge, 'Time Goes By', *Adviser* 148.

44 *Director General of Fair Trading v First National Bank* [2001] UKHL 52 (*Adviser* 89 abstracts)

45 s129(1) CCA 1974

46 r3.1(2)(m) CPR

47 s129(1) CCA 1974, as amended by s16 CCA 2006

48 For practical guidance on making a time order application, see S Coles, 'Time Orders: what's all the fuss?', *Quarterly Account* 11, Institute of Money Advisers

49 *Southern and District Finance v Barnes* [1995] CCLR 62, CA (*Adviser* 50 abstracts)

50 s136 CCA 1974

51 s130(6) CCA 1974

52 *Cheltenham and Gloucester Building Society v Obi* [1996] 28 HLR 22 (*Adviser* 65 abstracts). Where the lender executed a warrant of possession after the borrower had telephoned it and paid off the arrears as arranged, the court set aside the warrant as an abuse of process: *Blemain Finance v Ridley*, Darlington County Court, 2012, unreported (*Adviser* 155 abstracts).

53 See for example, 'Complaint Relating to Possession of a Property – and its Subsequent Sale Below Market Value', *Ombudsman News* 103/11, June/July 2012

54 See A Walker, 'Movin' On – the mortgagee in possession', *Quarterly Account* 50, IMA

55 For a full discussion of this issue, see D McConnell, 'No Equity?', *Adviser* 53

4. Recovering rented property

56 CPR PD 55, para 2

57 ss44 and 57 RA 1977

58 *Trevantos v McCullough* [1991] 19 EG 18

59 Reg 93(2) HB Regs

60 Sch 2 Housing Act 1988

61 *North British Housing Association v Matthews* [2004] EWCA Civ 1736 (*Adviser* 109 abstracts)
62 r83.13(8) CPR
63 r83.2(3)(e) CPR
64 *Cardiff City Council v Lee (Flowers)* [2016] EWCA Civ 1034 (*Adviser* 181 abstracts)
65 Mortgage Repossessions (Protection of Tenants etc) Act 2010
66 *Lambeth London Borough Council v Howard,* [2001] 33 HLR 636, [2001] EWCA Civ 468 (*Adviser* 88 abstracts)
67 r48.2 CPR; Part 19 contains the procedure for adding parties.
68 CPR PD 55, paras 10.1-10.10

5. Preventing enforcement
69 The application is made 'in the interests of justice' under r3.1(2)(m) and (7) CPR; *Hackney London Borough Council v Findlay* [2011] EWCA Civ 8 (*Adviser* 145 money advice abstracts)
70 *Estate Acquisition and Development v Wiltshire* [2006] EWCA Civ 533 (*Adviser* 118 abstracts)
71 For issues to consider when dealing with warrants of possession for rent arrears, see M Robinson, 'Hard Times', *Adviser* 149; see also J Luba and D Malone, 'Staying, Suspending and Setting Aside Possession Warrants', *Legal Action,* June 2012
72 Sch Civil Proceedings Fees (Amendment) Order 2014, No.874, Fee 2.7. This fee is payable on an application 'to vary a judgment or suspend enforcement, including suspending a warrant of possession'.
73 *Cheltenham and Gloucester Building Society v Booker* [1996] 29 HLR 634
74 *Hammersmith and Fulham London Borough Council v Hill, The Times,* 25 April 1994; see also *Cheltenham and Gloucester Building Society v Obi* [1994] 28 HLR 22
75 *Hammersmith and Fulham London Borough Council v Lemeh* [2001] 33 HLR 23 (*Adviser* 83 abstracts); *Lambeth London Borough Council v Hughes* [2000] All ER(D) 622 (*Adviser* 84 abstracts)
76 *Bank of Scotland v Pereira* [2011] EWCA Civ 241

Chapter 13

· ·

The magistrates' court

This chapter looks at how the magistrates' court operates as both a creditor and a collector of debts. It covers:

1. The magistrates' court (below)
2. Financial penalties (p388)
3. Enforcing a financial penalty (p394)
4. Council tax (p402)
5. Wilful refusal and culpable neglect (p407)

---

1. **The magistrates' court**

The magistrates' court is best known as the first tier of the criminal justice system. There are about 300 magistrates' courts in England and Wales, which deal with over 90 per cent of all criminal cases. The administration of magistrates' courts in England and Wales is the responsibility of HM Courts and Tribunals Service (HMCTS), which is part of the Ministry of Justice.

Magistrates have traditionally been lay volunteers (ie, unpaid and not legally qualified), although it is increasingly common for them to be full time and paid, particularly in London and urban areas. Paid magistrates are called district judges and are either barristers or solicitors.

Lay magistrates depend on their legally qualified clerks (known as justices' clerks) for much of their decision making. A **justices' clerk** is a civil servant and usually a qualified barrister or solicitor. S/he is present at all hearings to direct the way the hearing proceeds and to advise the magistrates on the law and procedure, and on the penalties available and any guidance on their use, but should not otherwise take any part in the proceedings. The justices' clerk may delegate these tasks to appropriately qualified assistant justices' clerks (or 'legal advisers'). All justices' clerks must discuss matters of law (including practices and procedures) in order to ensure that the advice given to the magistrates is consistent.

The justices' clerk also has administrative functions in relation to the magistrates and the individual court. This includes allocating responsibilities to assistant justices' clerks and other court staff – eg, issuing summonses, timetabling hearings, collecting payments, such as fines, and conducting means enquiries.

· · · ·

Fines officers are court staff with the power to enforce fines. Since the implementation of the Courts Act 2003, many decisions on fines enforcement that used to require court hearings (such as applications for further time to pay and deciding the enforcement action in cases of default) are now dealt with by fines officers.

In September 2016, HMCTS set up a historic debt team to recover financial penalties which had remained unpaid for up to 10 years. In 2017, the team's activities were extended to recovering outstanding financial penalties over 10 years old. Collection of other financial penalties may be handled by the National Compliance and Enforcement Centre rather than individual courts. These penalties do not become statute-barred (see p291).

The role of the adviser

Your main role as debt adviser is to prepare a financial statement and list of debts for the client to take to court hearings and perhaps a letter explaining her/his circumstances.

You may also represent the client or act as a 'McKenzie friend' (see p23). Check local practice to see whether you are allowed to represent clients. The justices' clerk is likely to be a useful contact at the magistrates' court. Sometimes, you will need to liaise with probation staff or solicitors, particularly in respect of unpaid fines. It is helpful to establish links between the advice agency and the probation service so that once you have produced the financial statement and details of debts, the client can be put in touch with the probation service for assistance and support at the court hearing. Probation officers and assistants are normally based at the court. Some advice agencies now staff help desks at their local magistrates' courts.

If a committal warrant has been issued for the client to be imprisoned, it is usually advisable to obtain good legal representation for her/him. Free legal representation is available for committal hearings.

2. **Financial penalties**

A fine is the most common penalty imposed by magistrates' courts in criminal cases. Magistrates can also impose 'victim surcharges', and make costs orders and compensation orders (see p389). These are all known as 'financial penalties'.

When setting financial penalties, the court must take the seriousness of the offence and the offender's financial circumstances into account.[1] The penalty is reduced if the client pleads guilty.

For offences committed on or after 13 April 2015, the client may have been ordered to pay a charge in respect of the court's costs (known as the 'criminal courts charge'). This is enforceable in the same way as a financial penalty. In the magistrates' court, this charge could range from £100 to £1,000. The criminal courts charge was abolished from 24 December 2015, but clients on whom the charge was imposed before that date remain liable to pay it. For details of the different treatment of the criminal courts charge in bankruptcy and debt relief orders, see p497 and p500.

The client may be required to complete a means enquiry form (available from the court office), although many clients who plead guilty and ask the court to deal with the matter in their absence do not provide information about their means. HM Courts and Tribunals Service has its own statement of means form (Form MC100), which can be downloaded from gov.uk/government/collections/court-and-tribunal-forms.

Costs are at the discretion of the court, but are usually ordered and fixed at the time.

If a client cannot afford to pay both a fine and compensation, the magistrates should order the client to pay compensation rather than impose a fine as well.

If the offence was committed after 1 April 2007 and the client is ordered to pay a fine, or a fine and compensation (in either case with or without costs), s/he may also be ordered to pay a 'victim surcharge', currently set within a range of £32 to £181. This is used to fund services for victims and witnesses. If the client does not have the means to pay both the compensation and the surcharge, priority is given to compensation and the surcharge can be reduced to nil, if necessary. If the client does not have the means to pay both a fine and the surcharge, the fine should be reduced to enable the surcharge to be paid.

Compensation orders

A magistrates' court can impose a compensation order alongside a fine or other sentence and must give reasons for not making an order in cases in which it is empowered to do so.[2] A compensation order is intended to be a simple way for the injured party in a criminal case to get compensation without having to sue in the county court. Compensation orders are often made in cases involving criminal damage or petty theft. They are collected by the court and paid to the victim.

The powers to remit a fine (see p391) do not apply to compensation orders. The only circumstances in which a compensation order could be changed are if:[3]

- a client appeals against either the conviction or the compensation order. A solicitor is needed for this and there are strict time limits; or
- subsequent civil proceedings demonstrate that the loss in respect of which the order was made was less than that stated in the order; or
- a compensation order is made for stolen goods which are later recovered; or
- the client has experienced a substantial reduction in her/his means, which was unexpected at the time the order was made, and they seem unlikely to increase for a considerable period.

Compensation orders are difficult to change. If a client is appearing in a criminal court on a charge that might result in a compensation order, you should advise her/him to take a clear statement of means with her/him. A representative should also be prepared to argue that, in view of the client's other debts, s/he should not have a compensation order awarded against her/him. The court must consider a client's financial statement and debts when making a decision.[4]

Costs awarded with a fine or compensation order are treated in exactly the same way as the compensation order – ie, they cannot be remitted by the court.

Payments

When imposing a financial penalty, the court can order:

- immediate payment; *or*
- payment within a fixed time; *or*
- payment by instalments.

Magistrates' courts are discouraged from inviting applications for time to pay and usually ask the client how much can be paid immediately. The court can search the client for any money that could be used to meet the financial penalty, but this power is rarely used.

Financial penalties should generally be capable of being paid within 12 months. This is not a fixed rule, but the period should not exceed two to three years.[5] If the client is unable to do this, this might be because there has been a change of circumstances since the penalty was imposed or that it was fixed without adequate financial information. In either case, consider asking for all or part of the financial penalty to be remitted – ie, totally or partially written off at a means enquiry (see p391).

However, when applying for further time to pay or a remission, bear in mind that financial penalties are a priority debt and that they were imposed as a punishment, and this affects the court's attitude to their recovery. Non-payment of a fine can be viewed as an attempt to avoid punishment.

The current fines enforcement scheme attempts to remove the need for hearings by giving fines officers the power to decide on the level of instalments and the enforcement step(s) to be taken. Once the fine has been imposed, therefore, a hearing before the magistrates is only likely to take place if the client appeals against the fines officer's decision or if the fines officer refers the matter to the magistrates following a number of unsuccessful attempts to enforce the fine.

Payments are applied by the court in the following order:

- compensation orders;
- costs;
- fines.

If the client defaults on payment, this affects any term of imprisonment s/he is also ordered to serve. However, if the magistrates' court is collecting a Crown

Court fine, the Crown Court will already have fixed the term of imprisonment the client must serve for defaulting on the payment of the fine, but not of any costs or compensation. Although the sentence can be reduced proportionately by part payment or remission, the magistrates have no power to vary the actual sentence.

Problems can arise if a client has more than one fine or compensation order. Courts do not always make it clear to clients how their payments will be applied, which can lead to enforcement action being taken on one matter, even though regular payments are being made in respect of another. Financial penalties can be paid either:

- consecutively, with the client allowed to clear the oldest first with no enforcement action taken on later ones; *or*
- concurrently, with payments credited to each outstanding financial penalty.

The client should be advised to request whichever method is in her/his best interests.

Debt advisers are likely to be concerned with the client's difficulty in paying financial penalties after they have been imposed, rather than with the conditions attached on the day of sentence. You may, therefore, have to negotiate with HMCTS staff or bailiffs (enforcement agents) about unpaid financial penalties.

Fines (except parking or other fixed penalty offences) can be paid online using a debit or credit card. The client must have the letter giving notice of the fine to pay in this way, as it contains the relevant references.

Transfer of fines

If a client moves to a different magistrates' court's area but still has a financial penalty to pay at the magistrates' court in the area where s/he used to live, it may be advisable to apply to the original court for a fine transfer order to the new local court.[6] This should make payments easier to arrange.

Remitting fines

If the client's circumstances have changed since the fine was imposed, the court can remit (ie, cancel) all or part of the fine.[7] There must be a means enquiry (see p392). The court can also remit a fine that was imposed in the absence of information about the client's means and, as a result, was set too high.

You should always argue for full remission of a fine if a person is on benefit or in serious debt (although the court may take into account the client's financial position at the time the financial penalty was imposed and any other resources available to her/him). The magistrates should be urged to consider full or partial remission if the guidelines on the time for payment of a financial penalty have not been observed (see p390).

The magistrates do not have the power to remit costs or a victim's surcharge (see p389) and can only remit compensation orders or the criminal courts charge in limited circumstances.

Lodging fines

If a client is serving a prison sentence, s/he can apply to the magistrates' court to 'lodge' (link) any outstanding fines to the prison sentence (including where the client is serving a sentence for non-payment of a magistrates' court fine). This has the effect of writing off the fine so that the client is no longer required to pay it following her/his release. Prison staff can provide clients with the necessary forms.

If the client has not dealt with the fine while serving her/his sentence, following her/his release s/he can attend a 'fines clinic' at the magistrates' court and apply for the fine to be remitted (s/he will need to provide details of the fine and her/his release papers).

Means enquiry

Before the court can remit a fine or take certain types of enforcement action (see p394), there must be a hearing (a 'means enquiry') at which the client is present and which looks at the client's ability to pay the financial penalty and reason for her/his default. The client can be questioned by the magistrates' clerk or magistrates.[8]

Magistrates may have little knowledge of the benefits system and of many items of ordinary expenditure, and you should ensure that a full financial statement is prepared and given to the magistrates, even if this means adding considerably to the court's own form. This should include an explanation of any essential expenditure that you believe may be questioned by the court. In addition, magistrates may not take into account items of expenditure that the client has prioritised over payment of the financial penalty, but which the magistrates regard as non-essential. Magistrates usually take account of expenditure on housing (including fuel), clothing and food for the client and her/his dependants, water charges and council tax. However, there is no consistent approach and you should establish local practice.

Information should also be made available about the reason for any non-payment, the client's financial position at the time of the previous order and her/his future prospects, as appropriate.

Fixing a return date

Following a means enquiry, magistrates may order payment of the amount due by a certain date or fix an amount to be paid periodically and give a date when the client must return if s/he has not paid either the amount due or all the instalments. If the client fails to appear, a warrant of arrest can be issued. You should try to ensure that the order is one with which the client can realistically comply with or, if s/he defaults, that s/he can show this was not due to her/his 'wilful refusal' or 'culpable neglect' (see 407).

Varying and setting aside a financial penalty

A magistrates' court may vary, or even rescind, a sentence or other order it has made (but not a sentence or order made by the Crown Court) if it appears to be in the interests of justice to do so.[9] Although this is a discretionary power, it could be a quick and effective way of cancelling or reducing a financial penalty that has been wrongly imposed or is demonstrably too high. There is no time limit on making the application and the client does not have to show any change of circumstances since the financial penalty was imposed. **Note:** this provision cannot be used as a way of asking the court to take back a warrant of control from bailiffs (enforcement agents).

In addition, if the case was dealt with in the client's absence and s/he had no knowledge of the summons or the proceedings, s/he can make a statutory declaration to this effect. Since 7 October 2019, a declaration can be made before an assistant justices' clerk or other nominated officer and the client does not need to be sent off to a solicitor. This results in the conviction being rendered void and the financial penalty being set aside. There is a new hearing and so this option needs to be carefully considered.[10] The statutory declaration must be delivered to the magistrates' court within 21 days of the proceedings first coming to the client's knowledge. There is discretion to extend the time limit if the court decides it was not reasonable to expect the client to comply with it.[11]

If either of these options is being considered, the client should be referred to a solicitor. If neither of the above applies and the client maintains her/his innocence of the offence(s), s/he should be referred to a solicitor for a possible appeal or application for judicial review. There are short time limits.

Registration of the financial penalty

The financial penalty is registered in the Register of Judgments, Orders and Fines. This means that if the client defaults, information about this is available to credit reference agencies and may affect her/his ability to obtain credit. The entry must be cancelled if:
- the financial penalty is paid within a month of its being registered;
- the client's conviction is set aside or reversed;
- the financial penalty has been remitted in full;
- five years have elapsed since the date of the client's conviction.

3. **Enforcing a financial penalty**

Collection order

A magistrates' court that is either imposing a new financial penalty or enforcing payment of an unpaid financial penalty must make a collection order. The collection order sets out:

- a breakdown of the sum due – ie, the amount of the fine and/or compensation order and/or costs;
- whether the client is an 'existing defaulter' – ie, whether s/he has already defaulted on payment of another financial penalty and, if so, whether that default can be disregarded;
- whether an attachment of earnings order or an application for deductions from benefits has been made and, if so, the repayment terms that apply if the order or application fails (known as 'reserve terms'). If not, the payment terms;
- which fines office will deal with the case; *and*
- the consequences of default.

If the client is an existing defaulter

If the client has defaulted on a previous penalty and s/he has failed to show the court there was an adequate reason for the default, the court must:

- make an attachment of earnings order (see p395) if the client is in employment, provided it is not impracticable or inappropriate to do so (see below); *or*
- apply to the Department for Work and Pensions (DWP) to make deductions from benefits (see p396) if the client is in receipt of income support (IS), income-based jobseeker's allowance (JSA), income-related employment and support allowance (ESA), universal credit (UC) or pension credit (PC), provided it is not impracticable or inappropriate to do so.

If a fixed penalty has been registered in the magistrates' court for enforcement, the client is deemed to have no adequate reason for default, and so can be treated as an existing defaulter.

Impracticable or inappropriate

There is no guidance on the meaning of **'impracticable or inappropriate'**. It could include a situation where the court has no information about the client's financial circumstances or where, for example, there is an existing council tax attachment of earnings order and the client would be left with insufficient income to meet essential expenses if another order was made. It could also include a situation where deductions are already being made from the client's benefit for debts with a higher priority.

If the court is satisfied that the client has shown an adequate reason for her/his default, an attachment of earnings order or an application for deductions from benefits can still be made, but only if the client consents, unless the financial penalty consists solely of, or includes, a compensation order. If so, the court must make an attachment of earnings order or apply for deductions from benefits, unless it is impracticable or inappropriate to do so.

If a client does not want an attachment of earnings order or deductions made from her/his benefit, check before the court hearing whether s/he has any outstanding financial penalties. If so, the client should be advised either to bring her/his payments up to date or to provide the court with an explanation of the default and of the possible adverse financial consequences of any attachment of earnings order or deductions from benefits.

If the client is not an existing defaulter

If the client is not an existing defaulter, the collection order sets out the terms on how the financial penalty must be paid. An attachment of earnings order or a request for deductions from benefits can only be made if the client consents, unless the financial penalty consists solely of, or includes, a compensation order. If it does, the court must make either an attachment of earnings order or apply for deductions to be made from the client's benefits, provided it is not impracticable or inappropriate to do so (see p394).[12] Where appropriate, clients should be advised to resist any pressure to agree to such a course of action in favour of voluntary payments.

Attachment of earnings orders

Attachment of earnings orders made in the magistrates' courts are not made in the same way as those made in the county court (see p329). Instead, fixed deductions are made from the client's net earnings using the percentage deductions in the table below.

Net earnings

Monthly	Weekly	Daily	Deduction rate
Up to £220	Up to £55	Up to £8	0%
£220.01 to £400	£55.01 to £100	£8.01 to £15	3%
£400.01 to £540	£100.01 to £135	£15.01 to £20	5%
£540.01 to £660	£135.01 to £165	£20.01 to £24	7%
£660.01 to £1,040	£165.01 to £260	£24.01 to £38	12%
£1,040.01 to £1,480	£260.01 to £370	£38.01 to £53	17%
£1,480.01 and over	£370.01 and over	£53.01 and over	17% of this threshold and 50% of the remainder

Attachment of earnings orders for fines take priority over existing attachment of earnings orders for payment of judgment debts, administration orders and attachment of earnings orders made by the DWP (except those to recover child support) and have equal priority with other attachment of earnings orders – eg, for council tax arrears.

Employers must deal with such orders in date order. The client's net earnings are calculated after making the deductions due under previous orders.

Deductions from benefits

The court can apply to the DWP to deduct payments towards a financial penalty from the client's UC, IS, income-based JSA, income-related ESA or PC.

The maximum amount that can be deducted is £5 a week or, if the deductions are being made from UC, 5 per cent of the client's standard allowance for the relevant assessment period up to a maximum of £108.35. If the client is in receipt of contribution-based JSA or contributory ESA, the maximum deduction is 40 per cent of the amount of JSA or ESA for a person her/his age.

Fines have low priority, however, and deductions can only be made in respect of one application at a time.

If the client is likely to experience hardship as a result of deductions being made, write to the DWP explaining this and ask it not to enforce the court's application.

For more information on deductions from benefits, see p231.

Varying the terms of a collection order

The client is sent a copy of the collection order. If there has been a change in her/his circumstances since the order was made (or last varied), s/he can ask the fines officer to vary the order (or the reserve terms – see p397). The application must be made in writing. S/he need not have defaulted. However, if the client has defaulted on the payment terms, any enforcement action can continue while her/his application to vary the order is being dealt with. S/he can also ask for the order to be varied if s/he is making further information available about her/his circumstances – eg, if her/his circumstances have not changed, but s/he did not provide full information about them on a previous occasion. The fines officer can require her/him to provide a statement of her/his financial circumstances and it is an offence not to comply. There is no limit to the number of times a client can ask for a variation, but s/he needs to be aware that the fines officer can vary the payment terms in a way which is less favourable to the client than the current terms. A client can appeal against the fines officer's decision to the magistrates' court within 10 working days (see p397).

If the attachment of earnings order or deductions from benefits fails

If the attachment of earnings order or an application for deductions from benefits fails (eg, if the client leaves her/his employment or the DWP is unable to comply

with the request because of other, higher priority deductions), the fines officer must send the client a 'payment notice' informing her/him:
- the order (or request) has failed;
- the 'reserve terms' in the collection order now apply;
- what s/he must do to comply with the reserve terms;
- of her/his right to apply to vary the reserve terms.

The client can ask the fines officer to vary the order on the grounds that there has been a change in her/his circumstances since the reserve terms were set (or last varied).

If the client defaults on the collection order

The client is in default if s/he does not comply with the payment terms (or, if they have taken effect, the reserve terms) of the collection order. The fines officer may refer the case back to the magistrates' court or decide to enforce payment her/himself. Provided there is no outstanding request to vary the reserve terms or no outstanding appeal to the magistrates about a previous decision not to vary the reserve terms, the fines officer can send a 'further steps notice', setting out what steps s/he intends to take. S/he can:
- make an attachment of earnings order or request deductions from benefits;
- issue a warrant of control (see p398);
- register the financial penalty in the Register of Judgments, Orders and Fines;
- apply to have the financial penalty enforced in the High Court or the county court (see p402).

If the fines officer wants to take a step or steps which was not specified in the further steps notice, s/he can issue a replacement notice, specifying the step or steps. The client can appeal to the magistrates' court against the replacement notice within 10 working days (see below).

Note: contact the fines officer immediately if there are arrears on an order as it may be possible to agree a new payment arrangement, particularly if the financial penalty can still be paid within the original period allowed by the court.

Appeals and referrals

The client can appeal to the magistrates' court by letter within 10 working days (ie, excluding Saturdays and Sundays, Christmas Day, Good Friday and bank holidays) against a fines officer's decision:
- to vary the terms of a collection order;
- to vary reserve terms;
- to issue a further steps notice.

On an appeal, the magistrates' court may:
- confirm or vary the payment terms (or any reserve terms);

- confirm, quash or vary a further steps notice;
- discharge the collection order and exercise any of its standard powers (see below).

On a referral to the magistrates' court by the fines officer, the magistrates can:
- confirm or vary the payment terms (or any reserve terms);
- discharge the collection order;
- exercise any of the powers referred to in this chapter.

If the court discharges the collection order, it retains control of the collection and enforcement process itself, rather than delegating it to the fines officer. The 'standard powers' given to the magistrates are much wider than the powers given to fines officers, although some can be exercised by both.

If a fines officer refers the case to the magistrates' court either instead of issuing a further steps notice or after taking any of the steps listed in it, the magistrates may increase the fine (but not any other part of the financial penalty) by 50 per cent, provided they are satisfied that the client's default on the collection order is due to her/his 'wilful refusal or culpable neglect' (see p407). The increase is enforced as if it were part of the fine.

To ensure the client attends a referral hearing, the fines officer may issue a summons directing her/him to attend the magistrates' court at a specified time and place. If the client fails to attend, the court issues a warrant for her/his arrest by a civil enforcement officer. The warrant is either with or without bail – ie, the client is either bailed to attend court, or is arrested and brought before the court. Before executing the warrant, the enforcement officer tries to obtain full payment. If you discover that a client is subject to a warrant without bail, advise her/him to surrender her/himself to the court on a day when the court is sitting to deal with fine defaulters, and prepare a financial statement for her/him to take with her/him.

Warrant of control

The court can issue a warrant of control if a client fails to pay a financial penalty as ordered by the court.[13] This means bailiffs are instructed to take control of the client's goods and the proceeds of their sale are paid to the court. Although there is now more emphasis on using attachments of earnings and deductions from benefits, warrants of control are frequently the first enforcement method used. This is because many financial penalties are imposed in the client's absence, with the court having no information about her/his means.

No hearing is required before a warrant of control is issued, although the court can postpone issuing one if it wishes.[14] There does not need to be a means enquiry before issuing a warrant of control,[15] but if there is evidence that the client has sufficient assets to pay the debt, the magistrates should take control of her/his goods rather than commit her/him to prison.[16]

The magistrates' court can only withdraw a warrant after it has been issued in limited circumstances.[17] If the fines officer has issued a warrant of control under a further steps notice or a replacement notice, s/he may withdraw the warrant if s/he is satisfied that it was issued by mistake – eg, if the client was believed to be in default under her/his instalment arrangement, but the payments were, in fact, up to date.[18]

If the fines officer refers a case to the magistrates' court while a warrant of control remains outstanding, the magistrates may 'discharge' it – ie, withdraw the warrant if they would have had the power to do so under section 142 of the Magistrates' Court Act.[19] These provisions are intended to allow magistrates to withdraw a warrant issued by the fines officer in order to rectify a mistake.

The court can withdraw a warrant if there is evidence that the client is vulnerable and enforcement would either not be in the interests of justice or might bring the process into disrepute.

The use of bailiffs (enforcement agents)

HM Courts and Tribunals Service (HMCTS) has national contracts with private bailiffs firms to execute warrants of control. If there is a conflict between the terms of the contract and the legislation which governs bailiffs' powers,[20] the legislation prevails. For more information about bailiffs, see Chapter 14.

Bailiffs collecting financial penalties (but not most other debts) can use reasonable force, if necessary, to enter and search any premises if it is reasonably required.[21] This power, however, is rarely used and should only be exercised in accordance with the bailiff firm's own procedures and HMCTS instructions and as a last resort.

Bailiffs must not enter, re-enter or remain on premises where the only person present is a child (ie, under 16) or a 'vulnerable person'.

There is no definition of a 'vulnerable person' in the legislation. However, the guidance *Taking Control of Goods: national standards* (available at gov.uk/government/publications/bailiffs-and-enforcement-agents-national-standards) contains a section on vulnerable situations and includes lone parents and unemployed people in its list of potentially vulnerable people.

Regulations contain a detailed list of goods that bailiffs cannot seize (see p426).[22]

Bailiffs must give at least seven days' notice of their intention to visit the client to take control of goods (known as an 'enforcement notice'). A warrant must be executed within 12 months from the date of the enforcement notice. This 12-month period can be extended by the court. It is also extended if the client and the bailiff agree a payment arrangement before any goods are taken into control.

The bailiff must sell the client's goods within 12 months from the date they are taken into control. This 12-month period can be extended by written agreement between the client and the bailiff.

There are no restrictions on the days bailiffs can take control of goods. They can do so between 6am and 9pm, unless they are visiting business premises, are part way through taking control of goods or the court orders otherwise. However, the contract states that visits should begin at a reasonable time and at least one attempt must be made outside 'normal' working hours – ie, 8am to 6pm, Monday to Friday. Visits should not be made on Sundays, Good Friday, Christmas Day, bank holidays or at a time that is likely to be inappropriate to the client's religious beliefs (if these are known).

Money payments supervision order

The court can make a money payments supervision order, appointing someone to 'advise and befriend the defendant with a view to inducing him to pay the sum adjudged to be paid' – ie, supervise the client during the payment of the financial penalty.[23] This is normally a probation officer or a fines officer. **Note:** the court is not required to hold a means enquiry (see p392) before making an order, nor is the client's consent required, but since the client's co-operation is essential to the working of the order, it is normally required. As a matter of good practice, the money payments supervision order should specify the terms of payment.

Imprisonment

If a client falls into arrears with payment of a financial penalty, the court may order her/his imprisonment.[24] There is a similar power to detain under-21-year-olds in a young offenders' institution, but there are additional restrictions.[25] The minimum term of imprisonment is five days and the maximum term that can be imposed by a magistrates' court is 12 months.

Note: once a warrant of control has been issued, imprisonment cannot be considered unless the warrant is returned stating that there were no goods.[26] You should consider asking solicitors to argue that, if a warrant has been returned because the bailiffs were unable to gain access to the client's property, imprisonment is not an option open to the court, but this argument has not been tested in the higher courts.

There must first be a means enquiry, at which the court must be satisfied:[27]

- if the original offence was punishable by imprisonment, that the client appears to have sufficient means to pay the sum immediately; *or*
- that the default is due to the client's 'wilful refusal' or 'culpable neglect' (see p407) and that all other methods of obtaining payment have been considered or tried, but have been either inappropriate or unsuccessful, including a money payments supervision order (see above), if available.

Imprisonment should only be considered if the client's default is due to her/his 'wilful refusal' or 'culpable neglect'. In practice, the court often assumes that, if a person has paid nothing, this is deliberate. You should encourage solicitors and other representatives to argue strongly that it is impossible to find money from a client's low income, even for priorities like financial penalties. However, even if the court is satisfied that the client had the means to pay, it must still demonstrate that it has considered all the non-custodial alternatives. Over the past few years there has been considerable publicity about the number of wrongful committals. This has generally been due to inadequate means enquiries and/or failure to follow the above rules.

Any term of imprisonment must be proportional to the size of the financial penalty. The period is determined by a statutory scale and depends on the amount of the financial penalty outstanding. A stay in prison can be avoided by immediately paying the outstanding balance. Any costs of unsuccessful bailiff action can be added to the amount the client must pay to obtain her/his release. The length of any period of detention (whether actual or suspended) can be reduced by paying a proportion of the outstanding balance.[28] For information about 'lodging' (ie, linking) outstanding financial penalties to a prison sentence, see p392.

If the court decides to impose a period of imprisonment, it can be postponed in certain situations – eg, if the client keeps to a payment arrangement.[29] This is known as a 'suspended committal'. The conditions can be varied if, for example, the client's circumstances change and s/he can no longer comply with its terms.

A suspended committal order cannot be combined with any other enforcement order.

If the client fails to comply with the postponement conditions, another hearing must be held before s/he can be sent to prison. S/he must be given the opportunity to attend the hearing in order to make representations on why the committal warrant should not be issued. This involves persuading the magistrates that circumstances have changed since the previous hearing (including new facts). The court can still consider remission at this stage.

Although the rules state that notice of the hearing is deemed to be served if it is sent by 'special' or ''ecorded signed for' delivery to the client's last known address, the High Court quashed a sentence of imprisonment where a notice had been returned to the court as undelivered.[30] The High Court said that the magistrates should have adjourned the hearing until the client had been served with notice of the hearing.

Short local detention

After a means enquiry, instead of imposing imprisonment, the magistrates can order the client to be detained for the remainder of the day, either in the court building or at a police station up until 8pm. S/he must be released in time for her/him to get home on the same day. The magistrates can also order the client to be detained overnight at a police station until 8am the next morning.[31] This is not imprisonment and so the restrictions on imprisoning clients do not apply, but (as with imprisonment) the financial penalty is wiped out.

It might be appropriate to ask the magistrates to consider this option if they have ordered the financial penalty to be paid immediately, the client is unable to do so and the magistrates are not prepared to allow her/him time to pay.

Attendance centre order

Following a means enquiry, if the court has an attendance centre available to it and the client is under 25 years old, the magistrates can order her/him to attend the centre for between 12 and 36 hours.[32] Attendance can be required for two to three hours at a time, usually on Saturday afternoons.

High Court and county court orders

The fines officer may apply to the High Court or a county court for an order that is only available in these courts – eg, a third-party debt order or charging order.[33] An application is unlikely to be made unless the fines officer believes that none of the other available collection methods is likely to be successful, but a High Court or county court remedy is.

For more information on these enforcement methods, see Chapter 11.

4. Council tax

Magistrates' courts have two distinct roles in relation to the collection of council tax. These are to decide whether to:
- issue a liability order (see below); *or*
- commit someone to prison (see p405).

Liability orders

Issuing an order

The local authority can request that the court issue a liability order against a client. This states that an amount of tax is due from the client, that s/he has not paid it and that s/he is therefore liable.

Note: a local authority cannot apply for a liability order after a period of six years has elapsed, beginning with the date on which the tax became due.

The client's duty to pay council tax does not arise until the demand notice (ie, the bill) is served.[34] Demand notices should be served 'as soon as practicable' after the date on which the local authority first sets the amount of council tax for the year in question. However, if a bill is sent late, this does not automatically invalidate it – the client must establish that s/he has experienced substantial 'prejudice' as a result.[35]

The client is summonsed to attend a hearing. The summons must be served at least 14 days before the hearing date. The summons is properly served by:

- delivering it to the client; *or*
- leaving it at the client's usual or last known place of abode; *or*
- posting it to the client's usual or last known address; *or*
- leaving it at, or posting it to, an address given by the client as an address at which service of the summons will be accepted.

This means that the client does not necessarily have to actually receive the summons.[36]

Failure by the local authority to follow the rules on billing and reminder notices can be raised as a defence at the hearing, as can the fact that the bill has been paid. However, issues concerning the client's liability for, or exemption from, council tax cannot be raised at the hearing, but must be dealt with through the appropriate appeals procedure, although the court usually adjourns the hearing if an appeal is pending.[37]

If the client is disputing liability, consider appealing to a valuation tribunal. This hears appeals about banding, liability, entitlement to a discount, a reduction or exemption, and how the amount of council tax due has been calculated. The valuation tribunal cannot consider wider issues, such as whether the local authority sent the council tax bill at the correct time.[38]

If the client has claimed council tax reduction and her/his claim has not yet been decided, or an appeal is pending, the magistrates can adjourn the matter.[39] However, the Local Government and Social Care Ombudsman has repeatedly found local authorities guilty of maladministration where council tax arrears wholly or mainly arose as a result of their failure to determine council tax benefit (the predecessor to council tax reduction) claims and where the client had provided the information requested or a reasonable excuse for any delay, and can be expected to follow the same line where council tax reduction is concerned.[40]

If payment is made after the liability order has been applied for, the local authority can ask for an order for payment of its reasonable costs. In England, there is no cap on these costs; in Wales, the costs cannot exceed £70. **Note:** the issue is not whether the costs themselves are reasonable but whether the local authority has reasonably incurred those costs in the process of the recovery action taken to date. The client is entitled to be informed what costs are included in the sum claimed and how it was calculated.[41] The magistrates cannot be asked to allow time to pay at this stage.

After the liability order is made

A liability order allows the local authority to pursue collection of the debt by any of the following:

- a payment arrangement;
- a warrant of control (see p398 and Chapter 14);
- an attachment of earnings order (see p395);

- deductions from the client's universal credit (UC), income support (IS), income-based jobseeker's allowance (JSA), income-related employment and support allowance (ESA) or pension credit (PC) (see p396);
- a charging order in the county court, provided there is at least £1,000 outstanding under one or more liability orders (see p322);
- bankruptcy (provided at least £5,000 is outstanding) (see Chapter 15).

The local authority can also request that information about the client's means be supplied.

Enforcement of a liability order is done by the local authority, unless it chooses to return to the magistrates' court to seek the imprisonment of the client.[42]

Local authorities can only use one of the above enforcement methods at a time for each liability order they are enforcing. If the local authority is using deductions from benefit to recover one liability order, it cannot use any other method of enforcement to recover any other liability order. The Department for Work and Pensions does not make deductions for a later liability order until an earlier one has been paid off.[43]

In theory, once the local authority has obtained a liability order, there is no time limit on enforcement.[44]

Setting aside a liability order

Local authorities can apply to the magistrates' court to quash ('set aside') the liability order on the grounds that it should not have been made.[45] If the magistrates' court is satisfied that the liability order should not have been made, it must quash the order.

If the magistrates' court is satisfied that the local authority is entitled to a liability order, but for a lesser amount, it must make a liability order for:

- that lesser amount; *plus*
- any sum included in the quashed order for the costs reasonably incurred by the local authority in obtaining that order.

The local authority should apply for the liability order to be set aside in writing, requesting that the magistrates' court relist the local authority's application for the liability order and setting out why the original liability order should not have been made.

Magistrates' courts must consider the following before setting aside a liability order.[46]

- There must be a genuine and arguable dispute about the client's liability to pay.
- The liability order must have been made as a result of some substantial procedural error, defect or mishap.
- The set-aside application must have been made promptly once the client had notice of its existence.

If the summons for the liability order was not properly served (see p402), the Administrative Court has recommended a procedure for setting aside the liability order to avoid expensive litigation.[47]

- On discovering the existence of the liability order, the client should promptly inform both the local authority and the magistrates' court that the summons was not properly served.
- The local authority should then satisfy itself as to whether or not the client's assertion is correct.
- If this is established, the client and the local authority should co-operate in making a joint application to the magistrates' court to have the liability order set aside.

If the local authority accepts that the order should not have been made, but refuses to apply to set it aside, the client can consider making a complaint to the Local Government and Social Care Ombudsman or Public Services Ombudsman for Wales, particularly if s/he is out of time to apply her/himself.

Committal to prison

Since 1 April 2019, it has not been possible for local authorities in Wales to start proceedings for the committal of clients for non-payment of council tax. In England, if an application to commit someone to prison is made, the court must arrange a hearing and hold a means enquiry (see p392).[48] These proceedings can only begin once a warrant of control has been issued and returned because insufficient or no goods belonging to the client could be found for whatever reason, including if it was because the bailiffs could not gain entry.

Do not rely on the court to produce paperwork. You should prepare a full statement of income, expenditure and debts, as well as a clear explanation of any particular difficulties facing the client.

The court must decide whether the client has shown 'wilful refusal' or 'culpable neglect' in failing to pay (see p407). The magistrates should consider the issue for the whole period up to the date of the committal hearing. In all cases, they must also consider the client's ability to pay at the date of the hearing. Courts often equate failure to pay with refusal or neglect to pay regardless of the client's financial situation. For this reason, make sure you produce evidence about the client's income and spending and other priority debts. Free legal representation is available to assist clients at these hearings as well as at committal hearings concerning financial penalties.

Note: many magistrates' courts do not allow lay representatives in committal hearings. If the magistrates do not accept you as a representative, you can act as a 'McKenzie friend' (see p23).

The High Court has held that magistrates must enquire about means and consider whether the failure to pay was a result of wilful refusal or culpable neglect and a committal order can only be made if one of those is the case. In order to determine whether the client has been guilty of culpable neglect, the means enquiry must consider the period of time over which the debt was owed and should also consider the client's current position to see whether s/he is in a position to pay the debt and should then go on to see which enforcement options are available.[49] The High Court has repeatedly advised magistrates that the purpose of committal in such cases is to obtain payment and not to punish the client.[50] Therefore, although there is no statutory obligation to do so, local authorities, as well as magistrates, should consider alternative viable methods of enforcement and not refuse reasonable offers of payment.[51] However, a suspended committal order is regarded as a method of enforcement in its own right.[52] Orders should not be suspended for more than two to three years and partial remission should be considered in order to reduce the sum in respect of which the order is being made.[53] The magistrates must take account of the principle of proportionality, with the maximum term being reserved for the most serious cases. The magistrates should use the tables of sentences provided for fines as a guide to the appropriate level of sentences. See *Anthony and Berryman's Magistrates' Court Guide* for more information.

The increasing reluctance of magistrates' courts to make committal orders has led to many local authorities resorting to bankruptcy proceedings as an enforcement method if the client is a homeowner – in many cases, for debts that are only just above the £5,000 bankruptcy limit. For more details, see p242.[54]

Outcome of the committal hearing

If the court decides there has not been either 'wilful refusal' or 'culpable neglect' (see p407), it can either remit (write off) all or some of the arrears,[55] or make no order at all. **Note:** local authorities can write off council tax arrears themselves (see p236).

Although there is no time limit in which a local authority must enforce a liability order, the High Court has said that magistrates should consider remitting the debt on their own initiative where more than six years have elapsed between the date of the original default under the liability order and the committal hearing.[56]

If the magistrates decide there has been 'wilful refusal' or 'culpable neglect', they can issue a warrant committing the client to prison for up to three months. They can (and usually do initially) suspend this warrant on payment of regular instalments. This means that, so long as the agreed payments are kept, the client will not be imprisoned. However, unlike financial penalties, the court no longer has the option to remit the debt. If the client fails to comply with the terms of the suspended order, the magistrates must satisfy themselves that s/he had the ability to pay before they can activate the committal order by arranging a further means enquiry.[57]

If the arrears and costs to date are paid in full after the local authority applies for committal, no further recovery action can take place. If the client has been imprisoned, s/he must be released. If partial payment is made, the period of imprisonment is reduced proportionally. If the part payment is made after the term of imprisonment has been fixed but before the client begins to serve the sentence, the period to be served is also reduced proportionally.

The maximum fee for committal is £315 and this is added to the arrears and other costs, imposing an even greater burden of debt on clients, particularly those on a low income.

If a client is sent to prison, no further enforcement action can be taken for any arrears and costs that remain unpaid. They are still owed, but cease to be priority debts.

---

5. **Wilful refusal and culpable neglect**

There are a number of situations in which magistrates acting as debt collectors must decide whether a client's non-payment is due to her/his 'wilful refusal' or 'culpable neglect'.

Although magistrates' courts have been making decisions based on their interpretation of this important phrase for many years, the two phrases are not defined in the legislation. There is little guidance on what factors should be taken into account when making a decision, but the client's conduct must be 'blameworthy' in some way.

The client should only be found guilty of '**wilful refusal**' if s/he has made a deliberate decision not to pay the amount due, even though s/he is able to do so – eg, on a point of principle. However, a finding of 'wilful refusal' does not automatically justify a sentence of imprisonment; the two questions must be considered separately.

'**Culpable neglect**' is more difficult. It means a reckless disregard of the court order and usually involves a situation where the client spends any available income on non-essential items rather than on paying the financial penalty. It is not sufficient for the magistrates to find that the client had available income and did not pay; they must also find out why it has not been paid.[58] If a couple are in receipt of benefits intended for both of them, the non-claimant client can be found guilty of 'culpable neglect' if there has been a 'household' decision not to pay.[59]

To prove 'culpable neglect', it must be shown that:
- money was available, but it was not paid to the court or local authority; *and*
- this was due to a failure which demonstrates an avoidable choice to use the money for other purposes.

Evidence in the form of a financial statement should demonstrate to the court that the client's 'choices' were impossible and that a failure to pay was not 'culpable'.

Most courts assume that, if a person has ignored reminders or suspended committals, s/he has culpably neglected payment. This assumption should be challenged. Argue that a client:
- did not have any money available after paying for essential items; or
- was too stressed to be culpable; or
- did not understand the need to pay; or
- was not skilful enough to balance a very difficult budget; or
- was wrongly advised not to pay.

When representing a client, it is helpful to begin by presenting a financial statement and evidence about her/his debts and social circumstances before asking the court to make a specific decision on the question of wilfulness or culpability. After the court has decided this, you can argue about an affordable instalment arrangement, if necessary.

It is useful to obtain the court's agreement to conduct proceedings in this format because it encourages the court to think about wilfulness and because it allows you to rescue something if the initial decision is unfavourable.

Notes

2. **Financial penalties**
1 If no information is available, the court is entitled to assume a weekly income of £400. The court can remit all, or part, of the fine if the client subsequently provides evidence of her/his means: ss164 and 165 Criminal Justice Act 2003. If the client is on a low income (including benefits), s/he is currently deemed to have a weekly income of £110.
2 ss1(1) and 35(1) PCCA 1973
3 s37 PCCA 1973
4 s35(1)(a) PCCA 1973
5 *R v Olliver and Olliver* [1989] 11 Cr App R (Sentencing) 10
6 s89 MCA 1980
7 s85 MCA 1980

8 *R v Corby Metropolitan Council ex parte Mort, The Times*, 12 March 1998
9 s142 MCA 1980, as amended by CAA 1995
10 s14 MCA 1980
11 See G Skipwith, 'Consultancy Corner', *Adviser* 148

3. **Enforcing a financial penalty**
12 Art 11 Collection of Fines (Final Scheme) Order 2006, No.1737
13 s76 MCA 1980
14 s77(1) MCA 1980
15 *R v Hereford Magistrates ex parte MacRae, The Times*, 31 December 1998
16 *R v Birmingham Justices ex parte Bennett* [1983] 1 WLR 114

17 *Crossland v Crossland* [1992] 2 FLR 45, confirmed in *R v Hereford Magistrates' Court ex parte MacRae, The Times,* 31 December 1998
18 s88 Legal Aid, Sentencing and Punishment of Offenders Act 2012
19 s88 Legal Aid, Sentencing and Punishment of Offenders Act 2012
20 Part 3 and Sch 12 TCEA 2007
21 Sch 12, para 18 TCEA 2007
22 TCG Regs
23 ss56(2) and 88 MCA 1980
24 s76 MCA 1980, restricted by s82
25 s88(5) MCA 1980 and ss1(5) and 5A CJA 1982
26 s76(2) MCA 1980
27 s82 MCA 1980
28 s79 MCA 1980
29 s77 MCA 1980
30 *R v Doncaster Justices ex parte Harrison* [1998] 163 JP 182
31 ss135 and 136 MCA 1980
32 s60 Powers of Criminal Courts (Sentencing) Act 2000
33 s87(1) MCA 1980

4. Council tax
34 Reg 34(3) CT(AE) Regs; *Regentford Ltd v Thanet District Council* [2004] EWHC 246 (Admin) (*Adviser* 103 abstracts)
35 Reg 19(1) CT(AE) Regs; *Regentford Ltd v Thanet District Council* [2004] EWHC 246 (Admin) (*Adviser* 103 abstracts); *North Somerset District Council v Honda Motors and Others* [2010] EWHC 1505 (QBD) (*Adviser* 148 abstracts)
36 Reg 35(2) and (2A) CT(AE) Regs, as amended
37 *R v Bristol Justices ex parte Wilsman and Young* [1991] 156 JP 409
38 *Hardy v Sefton Metropolitan Borough Council* [2006] EWHC 1928 (Admin) (*Adviser* 125 abstracts)
39 *SC v East Riding of Yorkshire Council*; *CW v East Riding of Yorkshire Council,* Valuation Tribunal for England 27.05.15 (*Adviser* 164 abstracts; *Arian* 49 caselaw update) confirms that the valuation tribunal can consider the merits of a refusal of discretionary reduction and not just the procedural aspects of the decision-making process.
40 For a more detailed discussion of the role of the Local Government and Social Care Ombudsman, see A Hobley, 'Local Taxation and Bailiffs', *Adviser* 129

41 Reg 34(5)(b) and (8) CT(AE) Regs; *R (on the application of Rev Paul Nicolson) v Tottenham Magistrates and Haringey LBC* (*Adviser* 170 abstracts)
42 Local Authorities are permitted to contract out enforcement of council tax and non-domestic rates and authorise, for example, a firm of bailiffs, to exercise its functions under the Local Authorities (Contracting Out etc) Order 1996 No.1880.
43 Reg 52(2)(b) CT(AE) Regs
44 *Bolsover District Council v Ashfield Nominees Ltd* [2010] EWCA Civ 1129
45 Reg 36A CT(AE) Regs, as inserted by reg 5 CT(AE)(A) Regs
46 *R (on the application of Newham London Borough Council) v Stratford Metropolitan Council* [2008] EWHC 125 (Admin); see A Murdie, 'A Low Key Anniversary', *Adviser* 130, p56
47 *R (on the application of Tull) v (1) Camberwell Green Magistrates' Court (2) Lambeth London Borough Council* [2004] EWHC 2780 (Admin) (*Adviser* 113 abstracts). If the magistrates refuse the application, the court pointed out that they will have acted unreasonably and could have a costs order made against them if an application for judicial review were necessary.
48 Reg 41(2) CC(AE) Regs; reg 44(2) CT(AE) Regs
49 *R (Woolcock and Bridgend Magistrates' Court) v Cardiff Magistrates' Court and Bridgend County Council* [2017] EWHC 34 (Admin), *Quarterly Account* 43, IMA
50 Re-emphasised in *R (Woolcock and Bridgend Magistrates' Court) v Cardiff Magistrates' Court and Bridgend County Council* [2017] EWHC 34 (Admin), *Quarterly Account* 43, IMA
51 *R v Sandwell Justices ex parte Lynn,* 5 March 1993, unreported; *R v Alfreton Justices ex parte Gratton, The Times,* 17 December 1993
52 *R v Preston Justices ex parte McCosh, The Times,* 30 January 1995
53 *R v Newcastle upon Tyne Justices ex parte Devine,* 23 April 1998 (QBD); *R v Doncaster Justices ex parte Jack and Christison, The Times,* 26 May 1999
54 See also A Murdie, 'End of the Debtor's Prison in Sight? – Challenging Committal to Prison for Council Tax', *Quarterly Account* 51, IMA
55 Reg 42(2) CC(AE) Regs; reg 48(2) CT(AE) Regs

56 *R v Warrington Borough Council ex parte Barrett*, 18 November 1999, unreported; *R v Gloucestershire Justices ex parte Daldry*, 12 January 2000, unreported

57 *R v Felixstowe Justices ex parte Herridge* [1993] Rating Appeals 83

5. **Wilful refusal and culpable neglect**

58 *R v Watford Justices ex parte Hudson*, 21 April 1999, unreported

59 *R v Ramsgate Magistrates ex parte Haddow* [1992] 157 JP 545

Chapter 14

Bailiffs

This chapter covers:

1. Introduction

A bailiff is someone who acts on behalf of creditors or courts to collect debts, repossess homes or goods and to execute certain arrest warrants. This chapter looks at the role of bailiffs in taking control of goods to recover debts. The government prefers to refer to bailiffs as 'enforcement agents'.

There are several different types of enforcement agent operating in England and Wales. Some are civil servants, employed by government departments, such as HM Revenue and Customs and HM Courts and Tribunals Service. Most are private agents: either High Court enforcement officers enforcing judgments of the High Court, and county court, or 'certificated' bailiffs, recovering all other debts that are enforceable by taking control of goods. They all enforce liabilities by the statutory procedure of taking control of goods.

Note: bailiffs can only take goods to recover an outstanding liability in the circumstances described in this chapter. Some bailiff firms also undertake debt collection work. If a firm of bailiffs is collecting an unsecured consumer debt or a benefits overpayment, it does not have any special legal powers, despite the fact that the firm may describe itself as 'bailiffs' in its letterhead.

The role of bailiffs is changing. In the past, their primary role was to seize goods. Since April 2014, when the law on enforcement was reformed, the emphasis is as much on 'compliance' and agreeing instalments as on enforcement. Arranging affordable instalments for clients in multiple debt may still be difficult, but it may be easier than in the past. For commercial reasons, many firms may be prepared to agree payment plans through call centres, rather than by sending out agents to visit. Even so, the timescale offered may not be long.

2. **When bailiffs are used**

Civil court judgments and orders

An adviser may encounter three different types of order being enforced by taking control of goods:
- High Court judgments (see below);
- county court judgments (see below);
- road traffic penalties (see below).

High Court judgments

The High Court uses bailiffs (**High Court enforcement officers**) to enforce the following judgments by taking control of and selling goods:
- High Court judgments of any amount;
- county court judgments over £5,000 for debts that have not arisen from an agreement regulated by the Consumer Credit Act 1974 (see p62);
- county court judgments between £600 and £5,000 for debts that have not arisen from an agreement regulated by the Consumer Credit Act 1974 if the creditor chooses to transfer them to the High Court for enforcement.

High Court enforcement officers are private bailiffs. They have similar powers to county court bailiffs, but are preferred by some creditors because, being private bailiffs, they are considered more effective. They are authorised by the Lord Chancellor, rather than holding a county court certificate like other private enforcement agents. However, their staff are probably also certificated bailiffs.

County court judgments

HM Courts and Tribunals Service employs bailiffs in each county court hearing centre (**county court bailiffs**), responsible for enforcing all warrants in that court's area. The bailiff may enforce the following judgments by taking control of and selling goods:
- all judgments based on agreements regulated by the Consumer Credit Act 1974;
- all judgments under £600;
- any other judgment up to £5,000, unless the creditor chooses to transfer it to the High Court for enforcement.

Road traffic penalties

Local authorities may use **private bailiffs** to enforce unpaid orders for road traffic penalties – eg, parking charges, congestion charges and traffic violations. Any sum payable is recoverable by a warrant of control as if it were payable under a county court order and is also regulated by the Civil Procedure Rules.[1]

Commercial rent arrears

Private landlords cannot use bailiffs to take control of goods for rent arrears in residential properties. They must use repossession proceedings (see Chapter 12).

If there are rent arrears for *commercial* premises (eg, shops, offices and factories), landlords can initiate taking control of goods without preliminary court action. This process is called 'commercial rent arrears recovery'.

The following principles apply.

- The exact nature of the business tenancy is not important. However, the lease between the landlord and tenant must be in writing.
- Only commercial premises are covered. If any residential accommodation is attached, such as a flat over a shop, the commercial rent arrears recovery process cannot be used and other remedies must be sought.
- Only rent in the narrow sense of the term may be recovered in this way. If the lease also makes provision for payment of service charges, insurance and other costs and these fall into arrears, these must be enforced by other means, such as forfeiture proceedings.
- The commercial rent arrears recovery process only applies to current tenancies. If the lease has been terminated, the procedure is not available.
- A minimum amount of arrears, equivalent to seven days' rent, must be due before a landlord can instruct bailiffs. However, as most commercial leases are payable quarterly or perhaps monthly, this restriction is unlikely to be relevant.
- A client can set off against her/his rent arrears any amounts owed by the landlord for breach of the lease (such as disrepair) that have been the subject of a successful claim for damages. If this is the case, s/he can apply to a court to cancel, or delay, commercial rent arrears recovery.

Provided the above conditions are met, the landlord can issue a 'warrant of control' (see p398 and p415) to a bailiff. Thereafter, the process is identical to all the other debts described in this chapter.

Other debts

Many public bodies have a statutory power to take control of goods if money is owed to them.

Local taxes

Both council tax and business rates are enforceable by taking control of and selling goods. **Local authority officers** or **private bailiffs** are used, provided they are certificated.

Debts to HM Revenue and Customs

HM Revenue and Customs can take control of goods to collect any unpaid taxes (both income tax and indirect taxes such as VAT), class 1 and 4 national insurance (NI) contributions and overpayments of tax credits. A **private bailiff** may attend, but only to assist and advise.

Magistrates' court orders

Taking control of goods may be used by magistrates' courts as a way of enforcing orders for unpaid civil debts (ie, tax and NI contributions) and damages, as well as compensation orders, costs and fines, including those from the Crown Court, Court of Appeal and Supreme Court. Many courts restrict the use of warrants of control to fines and fixed penalty offences (eg, for driving offences) or to sums under £100 to £150.

Magistrates' courts use either their own **civilian enforcement officers** or firms of **private bailiffs** to collect unpaid fines. These bailiffs are appointed by HM Courts and Tribunals Service.

Child support maintenance

The Secretary of State for Work and Pensions can take control of goods to collect arrears of child maintenance due to the Child Support Agency or Child Maintenance Service under a magistrates' court liability order. **Private bailiffs** are used.

The enforcement of child support arrears in this way was challenged by a non-resident parent on two grounds.[2] He argued that use of bailiffs could prejudice the welfare of the children in his household and that it was a violation of Article 8 of the European Convention on Human Rights (protection of home and family life). The Court of Appeal rejected both his arguments and confirmed that the arrears were an unpaid debt and it was reasonable to seek to enforce its recovery. There was already a charging order against his home and the court decided it was preferable for the family to face the loss of non-essential household items than to face the loss of their home.

---

3. **How bailiffs are instructed**

Whatever the type of bailiff or debt involved, the process of taking control of goods is started by issuing an instruction (a liability order, writ or warrant) to the bailiff for the specific sum due from the client. How these are issued (and how they can be stopped) depends on the type of order, writ or warrant.

High Court writ of control

If a High Court judgment (and county court judgments transferred to the High Court for enforcement – see p412) is unpaid, it may be enforced by issuing a 'writ of control'. This instructs the High Court enforcement officers to take control of sufficient goods to cover the full amount of the judgment debt, plus interest and costs. Unlike in the county court (see below), no part warrants are possible: the writ is issued for the whole judgment.

If the client has a judgment debt, s/he should apply immediately on Form N244 for a 'stay' of the High Court execution in order to suspend the writ, and then for a variation of the terms of payment of the county court judgment. See p288 for how to do this.

County court warrant of control

A creditor can apply to the county court for a warrant of control when a client has defaulted on the terms of payment of a judgment debt (see p321). A warrant may be issued for the whole of the balance due under the judgment, or for just a portion of the arrears (known as a part warrant). If the judgment was payable by instalments, the bailiff may be asked to take action for one-monthly instalments (or four-weekly instalments, as appropriate) or for not less than £50, whichever is the greater.

Some lenders often prefer to apply for part warrants, as these are considered more likely to be effective. As a result, creditors may repeatedly use the threat of taking control of a client's goods following her/his default on an instalment order.

At any time after the issue of the warrant, the court can suspend or 'stay' its execution. The client can also apply to the court to vary the judgment. An application for both can be made on Form N245 (see p341).

Road traffic penalties

If a penalty imposed by a parking attendant or traffic camera is not paid, the relevant local authority can obtain an order from the Traffic Enforcement Centre, based at the county court in Northampton, confirming liability. The local authority can enforce this by issuing a warrant of control to private certificated bailiffs with whom it has a contract.

It can often be difficult to negotiate instalment repayments with the bailiffs, as they are usually instructed to collect the whole debt and not to accept instalments. Although the order is made by the county court, it cannot intervene to suspend the warrant. Normally, the only way of challenging the warrant is to challenge the original charge or order, initially through the Traffic Enforcement Centre, and then through the Traffic Penalty Tribunal or London Tribunals.

The Civil Procedure Rules, which set out the procedures in the county court and High Court, specify that, if the order is cancelled, the bailiffs' warrant 'shall cease to have effect'.[3] Further enforcement is, therefore, not permitted. However, it is not clear whether costs incurred previously are also rendered null and void. In the past, local authorities and bailiffs took the position that fees already charged had been added to a warrant in good faith and were therefore lawfully due. However, since 2016, the Local Government and Social Care Ombudsman has ruled in at least half a dozen cases that cancelling a court order revokes all fees added to the penalty.[4] These must be refunded if the debtor has paid them. Threatening to issue a claim for a refund may persuade the bailiffs to reimburse the client.

Commercial rent arrears

A landlord of commercial premises can instruct bailiffs to act on her/his behalf as soon as the minimum level of arrears has been accrued by a tenant. This is an amount equal to seven days' rent (not including any interest or VAT that may be charged). The landlord, or her/his managing agent, issues a warrant of control containing the prescribed information to her/his chosen bailiffs.

Income tax

The issue of a warrant of control for income tax arrears does not have to be sanctioned by a court. Initially, demands for payment are made from computer collection centres and then by the local collector. If the client is still seen to be 'neglecting or refusing' to pay, a warrant is issued internally by a senior HM Revenue and Customs (HMRC) officer.

If you are dealing with the threat of bailiffs for unpaid tax, you should contact the relevant tax office. If the client's offer is accompanied by a financial statement, the collector will probably accept a reasonable proposal to clear the debt (though possibly only over a period of between six and 12 months) and 'stay' (suspend) the warrant. The collector may also be persuaded to take no action if a debt is clearly unrecoverable.

VAT

HMRC may take control of goods to recover arrears of indirect taxes, such as VAT, or to close down a business in order to prevent the problem reoccurring. Little warning is given once the final demand for payment has been ignored, and it is often difficult to negotiate anything but the severest terms of repayment.

The enforcement process is started when a VAT return is made by a trader without enclosing full payment of the VAT due or, if a return has not been made, s/he has been assessed as owing over a minimum prescribed figure of £200. At this stage, the HMRC officer collecting VAT arrears often tries to negotiate directly with the client. If this fails, a final demand notice is issued. If the client still neglects, or refuses, to pay and at least £200 is still due, a warrant is issued. In either case, the adviser may be able to agree that enforcement is 'stayed' (suspended) while instalment payments are made, although the timescale allowed to negotiate may be short.

Local taxes

If the client has defaulted on paying her/his council tax or business rates, the magistrates' court issues a liability order (see p402) to enable the local authority to use a variety of enforcement measures, including taking control of goods. If the client is liable for the tax, the court has no power to intervene in the enforcement, either at this stage or later, nor can it set terms of payment.

The local authority instructs the bailiffs with whom it has a contract to collect the amount due. You can either come to an agreement directly with the bailiffs or try to persuade the local authority to withdraw its liability order. Many local authorities want to come to reasonable arrangements with clients if these are likely to result in regular payments. Bear in mind the local authority's own code of practice on council tax enforcement when negotiating on these debts, especially when seeking to have the instruction withdrawn. Most authorities have some sort of statement of guidance or service-level agreement. These often give more favourable payment terms to those on means-tested benefits. You should also consult the Department for Communities and Local Government guidance, *Council Tax: guidance to local councils on good practice in the collection of council tax arrears.*[5]

Magistrates' court order

If a client defaults on a magistrates' court order for payment, the whole sum ordered to be paid falls due and may be enforced by taking control of goods. The bailiffs are normally instructed to collect the whole debt immediately and not to agree instalment payments.

Decisions about how and when to enforce a fine are taken by the fines officer at each magistrates' court. A 'further steps notice' is issued after a client defaults in making payments and this determines how the fine is then pursued.

If the court allowed time to pay or set instalments, or if the client was absent at the hearing, a warrant cannot be issued until the court serves written notice on her/him stating the total balance due, the instalments ordered and the date when payment begins. Once these conditions have been satisfied, a warrant may be issued on default.

If there is a hearing before a warrant is issued, either because a review date has been set by the court or because the client is required to be present (eg, if the hearing involves maintenance), the client may have a chance to prevent her/his goods being taken. S/he can apply to have the warrant postponed by the magistrates' court at the hearing – eg, by agreeing revised payment terms. It is, however, almost impossible for the court to suspend or withdraw a warrant once it is with the bailiffs. Although they have no legal power to intervene with the bailiffs, some fines officers may agree to do so.

Note: if the procedure before the warrant of control is issued is unlawful, the warrant itself is also unlawful. For instance, in one case, it was decided that a distress warrant had been illegally issued because the preceding further steps notice was invalid.[6]

See also Chapter 13 for more information.

4. **Bailiffs' powers**

The powers of bailiffs are set out in legislation.[7] In addition, the Ministry of Justice publishes *Taking Control of Goods: national standards* for enforcement agents. This provides minimum standards of business management and best practice in enforcement work, and reinforces and supplements the law. It is an essential tool and reference source for advisers. Copies can be downloaded from gov.uk/ government/publications/bailiffs-and-enforcement-agents-national-standards. The standards were updated in April 2014 to reflect the changes made by new legislation, and a more substantial revision has been promised.

Although the standards do not include a mechanism for monitoring or enforcing how they are applied, you could raise a failure to comply with them in any complaint (see p436).

Some creditors (especially local authorities) may also impose additional restrictions on their enforcement agents and have their own local specific codes of practice that they should follow.

Courts and the enforcement process

Courts now have a more significant role in directing and supervising the conduct of enforcement than in the past. This applies to all forms of taking control of goods, not just the actions of bailiffs enforcing court orders. The High Court oversees enforcement of writs of control, and magistrates' courts supervise aspects of their warrants of control – ie, extending time limits, entry rights and details of sale. Otherwise, the county court regulates the enforcement of all other warrants of control and liability orders – eg, in the case of council tax enforcement.

Throughout the process of taking control of goods, bailiffs must serve notices stating what they have done and what it has cost the client. This is designed to ensure greater clarity and openness for clients, and to facilitate payment arrangements by encouraging them to engage more (and sooner) with enforcement agencies.

Documents must be provided at each stage, from the initial enforcement notice to the ultimate stage of removing and selling the goods. The form of many of these notices is prescribed in regulations and bailiffs must ensure that the correct document is issued at the correct time and in the correct form.

The enforcement notice

A bailiff must first serve an enforcement notice on the client, warning that a warrant of control has been issued against her/him. The notice must be in a prescribed form and must contain specified information. The notice usually gives the client seven clear days' notice of the intended bailiff's visit.

The notice period of seven 'clear' days does not include the day of service and also excludes any intervening Sundays, bank holidays and public holidays during the period when enforcement action may be taken. However, in certain cases, it is possible for the bailiff to apply to a court to reduce the notice period if assets might be vulnerable, but such applications are likely to be rare.

The notice can be served by several means, including by post, fax, email, delivery to the client's premises or by hand. The bailiff must protect the debtor's confidentiality when serving notices. They should be placed in sealed envelopes and marked 'private and confidential' when left at shared properties to prevent the disclosure of an individual's financial affairs to third parties.[8] In cases of road traffic enforcement, if the bailiffs discover that the debtor's address has changed, they must notify the local authority who must apply to the court for the warrant of control to be reissued with the correct address.[9] Notices served at incorrect addresses are likely to be invalid, unless the debtor has been deliberately misleading about her/his address.[10]

The bailiff has 12 months from the date of the enforcement notice to take control of goods. At this initial stage, the client can attempt to negotiate repayments with the bailiff, and the legislation encourages bailiffs to come to agreements. If an instalment arrangement is agreed, the 12-month period is renewed every time the client makes a payment and only begins to run from the date of any default. If a bailiff fails to take control of goods within the initial year, it is possible to apply to court for a further 12 months' extension, although this is likely to be rare.

In cases of commercial rent arrears recovery, a client can apply to court to 'set aside' or postpone the enforcement notice – eg, because of a dispute over the amount demanded as rent or because of allegations that the landlord has not carried out repairs.

Binding the client's goods

The enforcement notice (or the court warrant or writ issued to the bailiffs) has the effect of 'binding' all the client's property. This includes all the client's goods, except those that are exempt (see p426) or protected (see p483).[11]

When goods are 'bound' in this way, they cannot be given or transferred to someone else. If goods are sold when subject to the binding power, the new owner is treated as a co-owner of the goods by the bailiff. If goods are transferred or given to someone else, the operation of the warrant is not affected and they can still be taken into control, unless a transfer was made in good faith to someone unaware of the bailiff's pending visit.

Note: binding is not the same as taking control of goods. To take control, the bailiff must still attend the premises, enter and go through the full process of identifying, listing and securing the goods. The effect of binding is simply to prevent a client wrongfully dispersing her/his goods after receiving warning of a bailiff's visit.

Entering premises

As a general rule, bailiffs acting on lawful instructions can enter premises to take goods. This right of entry also applies to their assistants and to any necessary removal or lifting equipment they bring with them. However, there are rules on how this right should be applied.

Note: the rules on entering premises also apply when bailiffs need to re-enter premises – eg, to remove goods or to check that goods are still present.

A bailiff *cannot* enter premises, and must not remain on premises, if:[12]

- the debtor is a child under 16 years of age; *or*
- the only people present on the premises are either a child or a 'vulnerable person' (including if there are more than one of each or a combination of both). The legislation does not define who a vulnerable person might be. However, *Taking Control of Goods: national standards* provides some detailed guidance on this, identifying disabled people and people recently bereaved as being among those likely to be vulnerable.[13] The bailiff must assess the situation s/he finds at the premises and must make a decision on whether or not to proceed. Many creditors and bailiffs' companies will have guidance and procedures on identifying and responding to potential vulnerability. These must, of course, be observed during the enforcement process, meaning that, if the debtor or a representative flags up a potentially vulnerable debtor, the creditor must take time to respond, probably putting enforcement on hold and asking for more evidence.[14]

See p439 for how to refuse a bailiff access.

Time

A bailiff can enter premises to search for and take control of goods on any day of the week. In general, an entry should only take place between the hours of 6am and 9pm. However, these time limits do not apply in the following situations.[15]

- If the goods to be taken into control are on premises that are used (whether wholly or partly) for business purposes and these are only open for business between 9pm and 6am, the bailiff may enter and remain on the premises during the business's opening hours.
- Following a specific application from a bailiff, the court can make an order authorising an entry to take place outside the permitted hours – eg, if there is a risk that goods may be removed if the bailiff's visit were to be delayed.
- If a bailiff entered within the permitted hours or in either of the above situations and needs to conclude the process, s/he can remain on the premises during the prohibited hours if it is 'reasonably necessary' to continue to search

for, take control of, inspect or remove goods, and provided s/he does not remain on the premises for an unreasonable time in order to accomplish this.

Place

The premises that bailiffs are entitled to enter are defined as either 'relevant' or 'specified' in the new law. The difference between the two is very important because it determines whether or not a court warrant to enter is required in advance.

A bailiff can treat premises as 'relevant' and can enter them if s/he reasonably believes that they are the place (or one of the places) where the client usually lives, or carries out a trade or business. 'Premises' are defined as 'any place' and so include vehicles, vessels, aircraft, hovercraft and tents or other movable structures. See p424 for taking control of goods on highways. Bailiffs can only enforce the recovery of commercial rent arrears at the premises in respect of which rent arrears are outstanding.

In some circumstances, other premises can be entered in order to search for an indebted client's goods – eg, a garage rented by the client or a property belonging to someone else. However, to do this, the bailiff must first apply to the court for a warrant authorising entry. The application will identify a particular address for which the bailiff seeks permission to enter; these are the 'specified premises' to which the warrant will apply. Before issuing a warrant, the court must be satisfied that there is reason to believe that there are goods worth taking into control on the premises and that it is reasonable to issue the warrant, taking all the circumstances into account.[16] However, if a bailiff enters or takes control on third-party premises without having the necessary warrant, the actions will be illegal.[17] The same will be the case if a warrant has been issued in respect of certain specified premises, but the bailiff then uses it to enter another location.[18] Damages and compensation may be awarded where the wrong premises have been entered.[19] Given the costs and delay of such applications, however, it is unlikely that many will be made.

Note: there is no automatic right to take control of goods found on private land – eg, car parks or at third parties' properties. This can only be done with a prior court order. This means that clamping cars, other than on the highway or on a client's own drive, is unlawful.

Method of entry

Bailiffs can only enter premises by:[20]
- a door or another usual means of entry – eg, a loading bay at business premises; *or*
- any usual means of entry to premises that are not buildings – ie, the normal access route to an aircraft, ship, hovercraft, tent or other moveable structure.

Note: bailiffs are prohibited from entering premises by climbing over gates, fences, hedges or walls. Entering through a window or skylight is also illegal.

Entry should generally be 'peaceable'. Unlawful force includes the use of locksmiths, pushing a person out of the way and preventing a door being closed – eg, by placing a foot across the threshold. It is also unlawful for a bailiff to enter against a person's will or to refuse to leave a property once clearly asked to do so by the occupier.[21] Bailiffs can only 'force' entry in three limited situations. These are:

- in order to enforce magistrates' court fines. However, in practice, HM Courts and Tribunals Service prefers to supervise closely the use of force by the bailiffs it uses and generally expects to sanction any use of force (which seldom happens);
- to enter business premises to enforce High Court or county court judgments; *or*
- with a specific warrant permitting forced entry issued by a court. Such a 'break-open' warrant is only issued in a small number of restricted situations – either if the bailiff is attempting to recover a tax debt enforceable under section 127 of the Finance Act 2008 *or* the premises are those to which the goods have been deliberately removed in order to avoid their being taken into control.[22] In *both* cases:
  - the goods must be (or are likely to be) on the premises, must belong to the debtor and must be ones which can be taken into control; *and*
  - the bailiff must have explained to the court the likely means of entry, the type and amount of force required and how s/he proposes to leave the premises in a secure state; *and*
  - the court must take into account all the circumstances, including the sum outstanding and the nature of the debt.

If a bailiff is taking control of goods on a highway, a court may issue a warrant allowing the use of forced entry only if:[23]

- s/he is attempting to collect taxes due under section 127 of the Finance Act 2008, or to recover a debt enforceable by one of the writs or warrants listed below; *and*
- s/he has explained to the court the type and amount of force required to take control of the goods; *and*
- the court has taken into account all the circumstances, including the sum outstanding and the nature of the debt.

Relevant writs and warrants

The writs and warrants that justify a warrant being granted to allow forced entry on a highway are:

– High Court writs of control enforcing sums of money;

– county court warrants of control enforcing sums of money, but not those issued by the Traffic Enforcement Centre to recover a traffic contravention debt;

– a magistrates' court warrant of control issued for a fine under section 76 of the Magistrates' Courts Act 1980;
– High Court writs and county court warrants of delivery and of possession which also confer a power to take control of goods and sell them to recover a sum of money.

Warrants issued by a court to allow forced entry, whether to premises or on a highway, may require the police to assist the bailiff. At the time of writing, it is not yet known how the police will react to these new powers.

Identification

A bailiff must show the client, and any person who appears to be in charge of the premises, evidence of her/his identity and authority to enter the premises (ie, the bailiff's certificate and the warrant, writ or liability order), if s/he is requested to do so. The agent must supply the documents, but they need not be in physical form: electronic copies on a laptop or tablet are sufficient.[24] A request may be made before the bailiff enters the premises or at any later time while s/he is still there.[25]

Taking control of goods

The powers of bailiffs to take control of goods (ie, to secure sufficient assets to cover the debt and any outstanding costs) are in the Tribunals, Courts and Enforcement Act 2007 and in the Taking Control of Goods Regulations 2013. This is a statutory procedure that bailiffs must follow exactly.

Time and place

The rules on the time and place for taking control of goods mirror those for entering premises (see p420 and p421). Goods must be taken into control within 12 months of the date the enforcement notice is served, unless a court allows longer or payments have been agreed with the client. A bailiff can take control of goods on any day of the week and, generally, between 6am and 9pm. However, these restrictions do not apply if:[26]

- the goods to be taken into control are located on premises which are used (whether wholly or partly) to carry out a business and the premises are open for business during the 'prohibited hours' of 9pm to 6am;
- there is a court order allowing goods to be taken into control outside the permitted hours because there is a risk of assets being taken away; *or*
- the bailiff began the process of taking goods into control within the permitted hours (or at a time allowed by either of the above bullet points) and it is necessary to complete that process during prohibited hours, provided the bailiff does not remain on the premises for an unreasonable time to do this.

Goods may usually only be taken into control on the highway, or at the client's home or place of business.

Ways of taking control of goods

To take control of goods , a bailiff must do one of the following:[27]
- secure the goods on the premises where s/he finds them (see below); *or*
- secure the goods on a highway where they are found or within a reasonable distance of that place (see below); *or*
- remove the goods and secure them elsewhere (see p425); *or*
- make a controlled goods agreement (see p425).

Note: one of the above means of taking control must be used and the detailed rules in the regulations must be followed. In practice, many bailiffs do not follow the correct procedures. If a bailiff does not take control of goods by one of the above ways, the goods will not have been taken into control. Always check what has been done and challenge if it is incorrect. If the bailiff has not followed the prescribed procedure, the client may be able to claim damages. Also, remember that goods must not be taken into control if there is only a child and/or a vulnerable person on the premises (see p420).[28]

Securing goods on the premises

In general, goods may be secured:[29]
- in a cupboard, room, garage or outbuilding; *or*
- by fitting an immobilisation device. In such cases, a notice in the prescribed form must be fixed in a prominent position to warn the client that clamping has taken place; *or*
- on premises used solely for business purposes by leaving a bailiff to guard the goods taken into control; *or*
- by locking up the whole of any business premises, or that part of any premises used for business where there is mixed business and residential use – eg, if the premises comprise a shop and flat above, the shop can be secured. Access to essential facilities should be preserved. Taking control of goods by locking up the entire premises should be the last resort when no other options are feasible.

Securing goods on a highway

It may be possible to take control of livestock, or perhaps business stock and materials, on a highway, but in the vast majority of cases these provisions relate to cars, vans and lorries.

A vehicle must be secured by an immobilisation device supplied by the bailiff, unless the client voluntarily surrenders the keys to the vehicle to the bailiff. This is the only way that bailiffs can obtain the keys of a car. They cannot be taken from debtors against their will so as to immobilise a car – a clamp must be used instead. At the time of immobilising the vehicle, the bailiff must provide a written warning that clamping has taken place to the client. The clamped vehicle must remain immobilised where it was found for at least two hours, unless the sum outstanding is paid or an agreement to release the vehicle, on part payment of the liability, is made between the bailiff and the client. After this minimum period has expired, the bailiff may remove the vehicle to storage, ensuring that it is then properly cared for.[30] After removal, the vehicle is secured as described below.

Removing the goods

Immediately removing goods is lawful and may still be used. However, because of the costs of removal and storage, it is only likely to be used for valuable and mobile assets. Unless there are exceptional circumstances, the goods must be removed to a secure location within a 'reasonable distance' of the place where they were initially taken into control. The premises chosen should be safe and secure.[31]

Controlled goods agreements

A 'controlled goods agreement' is an agreement whereby a client retains custody of the goods, but acknowledges that the bailiff has taken control of them. The client agrees not to remove or dispose of the goods, nor to permit anyone else to do so, before the debt is paid.

A controlled goods agreement can only be made by:
- a debtor aged 16 years or over;
- a person aged 18 or over who has been authorised by a debtor to enter into an agreement on her/his behalf. There is currently no guidance on the form of authorisation that bailiffs should accept and so this provision may cause problems for bailiffs and clients – clear written authority is ideal; express verbal authority may be acceptable.
- a person who is found to be in 'apparent authority' on premises used (wholly or partly) for trade or business purposes. Employees left in charge of running a shop or cafe in an owner's absence are likely to qualify to sign agreements.

In all cases, an agreement must not be made with a person who appears not to understand the effect of the agreement and would not be capable of entering into it. This may be because of language difficulties, mental disability or mental illness, and should be apparent to a bailiff after even a relatively brief discussion with someone. As with decisions on whether someone is 'vulnerable' (see p420), this will initially be a matter for the bailiff to determine.

An agreement must be in writing and signed by both the bailiff and the person entitled to sign. It must set out the details of the parties and the amount owed, and *must* include the terms of the repayment arrangement, which must be made with the client at the same time. The controlled goods agreement must also incorporate a list of the goods taken into control. Sufficient details of the goods must be provided to enable the owner to identify them. This list can be omitted if one is also included in any notice of entry or taking control of goods, or if a stand-alone inventory has been provided (see p429).

A copy of the signed agreement must be provided to the signatory and, if that person is not the debtor, to her/him personally as well. This can be done by leaving the copy in a conspicuous place on the premises where the goods were taken into control. If the debtor is known to share the premises with other occupiers, the copy should be delivered in a sealed and addressed envelope.[32]

Note: in practice, because of the strict conditions attached to controlled goods agreements, many bailiffs may do without them and just agree an unsecured repayment plan with a debtor.

Which goods can be taken

A bailiff can only take control of goods if they are the sole or joint property of a debtor.[33] If goods are jointly owned, the bailiff must obtain full details of the co-owner and record them on the inventory, as the co-owner must be included in subsequent proceedings, receive copies of all notices and be paid her/his share of the proceeds of any sale.

A bailiff cannot take control of goods with a total value of more than the outstanding amount plus an amount for future costs. In other words, taking control of goods must be reasonable and not excessive. However, a bailiff can take control of goods of higher value if there are insufficient goods of a lower value in the premises.[34] *Taking Control of Goods: national standards* reminds bailiffs that if the value of the goods available is disproportionately low compared with the debt and the costs, proceeding with enforcement is not justifiable.[35] Challenge cases where you think the bailiff has taken too much (or the goods were worth too little to justify the costs). So, for example, taking a car worth £52,000 for a parking penalty of £392 is very likely to be excessive.[36] Goods which are the sole property of any third party are wholly exempt from being taken. If they are taken, this can be challenged (see p428). This includes children's goods, as well as goods that are the sole property of spouses, partners, relatives and hire companies. *Taking Control of Goods: national standards* also protects items exclusively used by children, even if they are the debtor's property.[37]

Exempt goods

Some items are exempt and cannot be taken into control.[38] These are:

* the client's only or principal home. This can include a tent, caravan and mobile home;
* items of equipment (eg, tools, books, vehicles, telephones and computer equipment) that are needed personally by the client for her/his employment, business, trade, vocation, study or education. The total value of the items or equipment must not be more than £1,350. Even if the goods are assessed at their resale value at auction, this is a very low ceiling and may not provide significant protection to many businesses. **Note:** recent court cases have

clarified what is *not* a 'tool of the trade' – eg, a college lecturer could not claim that his motobike used to get to work was exempt and an artist could not claim a tugboat as a tool. However, a car used as a private hire taxi is exempt if its value is under the specified figure;[39]

- clothing, bedding, furniture, household equipment and provisions that are reasonably required to satisfy the basic domestic needs of the client and members of her/his household. These include, but are not limited to:
  - either a cooker or a microwave, but not both;
  - a refrigerator;
  - a washing machine;
  - a dining table large enough, and sufficient dining chairs, to seat the client and the members of her/his household;
  - beds and bedding sufficient for the client and the members of her/his household;
  - one landline telephone or, if there is no landline telephone at the premises, a mobile or internet telephone which may be used by the client or a member of her/his household;
  - any item or equipment reasonably required for the medical care of the client or any member of her/his household, or for safety or security – eg, an alarm system;
  - sufficient lamps, stoves or other appliances to satisfy the basic heating and lighting needs of the client's household;
  - any item or equipment reasonably required for the care of a person under the age of 18, a disabled person or an older person;
- assistance dogs (including guide dogs, hearing dogs and dogs for disabled people), sheep dogs, guard dogs and domestic pets (it is not clear whether this means just domestic dogs or other species too);
- a vehicle:
  - on which a valid disabled person's badge is displayed because it is used for (or there are reasonable grounds for believing it is used for) a disabled person;
  - used for (or there are reasonable grounds for believing that it is used for) police, fire or ambulance purposes;
  - displaying a valid British Medical Association badge or other health emergency badge because it is being used for (or there are reasonable grounds for believing that it is used for) health emergency purposes;
- items being used at the time the bailiff attempts to take control if it is likely that taking them will give rise to a breach of the peace – eg, a power tool 'in use' means that the item is in a person's hands or is being operated by her/him. The tool or machine in question must be the client's property, but it does not have to be operated by her/him personally to be exempt – eg, it could be being used by an employee or subcontractor.

If a client's goods are taken into control and s/he wants to dispute this on the grounds that the items are exempt, s/he should write to the bailiff company, stating her/his reasons. The bailiffs must copy this to the creditor, who must then decide the matter within seven days. If the creditor accepts that the goods are exempt, they are released from control and can be recovered. If the creditor does not accept that the goods are exempt, the bailiff is informed and notifies the client of the creditor's response.[40]

If the client is still not satisfied, s/he can apply to the relevant court on Form N244 (see p288), claiming that the goods taken into control should be exempt. The court gives directions on the conduct of the hearing of the matter and, ultimately, it goes to a trial.[41] The unsuccessful party should expect to pay the other side's legal expenses, so clients should consider carefully whether it is advisable to initiate litigation.[42]

Goods belonging to other people

Other than jointly owned and partnership property, goods of other third parties cannot be taken into control.[43] As with all goods, bailiffs should only take them into control where they are satisfied that there is good evidence they are owned by the debtor. If there are indications that assets might be third-party property, the bailiff should investigate and should have good reasons for then deciding to take control.[44]

If possible, the claim to third-party ownership should be made at the time of the bailiff's attendance, and while the goods are being taken into control, either by the debtor or by the third-party owner. The bailiff is under an obligation to consider and investigate any claim, considering any evidence as to ownership that may be available. At the same time, a bailiff has to apply her/his common sense: in a case considered by the Local Government Ombudsman (LGO) in 2019, the debtor had moved back into his mother's house after an eviction in which he had lost most of his possessions. His mother had lived in her house for 30 years. Faced with this situation, the LGO felt that the bailiff's strict approach – threatening to take everything into control unless documentary proof was provided – was unreasonable. The LGO said: 'In cases such as this, the bailiff should consider all the circumstances and evidence they have regarding ownership, rather than insist on proof.'[45]

A special procedure exists for third parties to follow to make a formal claim for the release or return of their goods if they have been taken into control. Bailiffs and creditors ought to supply details of this procedure when necessary.[46]

If someone believes that her/his goods have been wrongfully taken into control, s/he should write to the bailiff company, stating the grounds for claiming ownership and providing evidence, if possible. The bailiff must copy this claim to the creditor within three days, who must then decide on the matter within seven days. If the creditor accepts that the goods were wrongfully taken, they are released from control and can be recovered by the owner. If the creditor does not accept that the goods were wrongfully taken, the bailiff is informed and notifies the third party of the creditor's response.

If the third party is not satisfied, s/he can apply to the relevant court, claiming that the goods taken into control belong to her/him, not the debtor. This is done on Form N244 (see p288). After receiving notice of the application, the bailiff must not sell the goods, unless directed to do so by the court – eg, because they are perishable.

The court may direct the bailiff to sell or dispose of the goods if the third party fails to make the required payments to court. These are an amount equal to the value of the goods (or a proportion of it as directed by the court), along with an amount for the bailiff's storage costs. The court determines the amount of the bailiff's costs and when the sum should be paid. In cases of financial hardship, the court may allow someone to pay less than the full value of the goods.

If the bailiff disputes the court's valuation of the goods, any underpayment is determined by a valuation by a qualified independent valuer. The sum underpaid should then be paid by the claimant within 14 days of the copy of the valuation being provided. Even though a third party may make the payment(s) required, the court may still direct the bailiff to sell or dispose of the goods before it determines her/his claim, if it considers it appropriate. The bailiff must pay the proceeds of sale or disposal to the court.

Once all the necessary payments have been made, the court gives directions on the hearing of the matter and, ultimately, it goes to a trial. The unsuccessful party should expect to pay the other side's legal expenses.

Inventories

In addition to a notice confirming that goods have been taken into control, a bailiff must provide the client with an inventory of the goods involved.[47]

The inventory must include:

- the names and addresses of the parties;
- the name and address of any co-owner of the goods. The rights of co-owners are explicitly protected and they must receive copies of all subsequent notices and must be paid their share of the value of the goods as a first call on the proceeds of any sale;
- confirmation that the goods listed on the inventory have been taken into control; *and*
- a list of the goods taken into control, giving sufficient details to enable the client or co-owner to identify them – eg, the model, make, serial or registration number, colour, usage or other identifying feature.

The inventory may be combined with a controlled goods agreement or with any other notice given, as long as a sufficient list is provided at the same time as the agreement or notice and the goods taken into control are the same as those listed.

Bailiffs require a good deal of information to complete inventories in the manner required and detailed enquiries are needed to establish ownership, usage and the need for items to be listed. This should mean an end to sloppy and vague lists of goods, and prevent goods being taken into control of which clients are unaware. However, in practice, many vague and generalised inventories are produced. These should be challenged as being in breach of the law. It is arguable that without a valid inventory, goods have not been taken into control.

Selling goods

The purpose of taking control of goods is to provide valuable security that can be realised if the client fails to pay. However, given the emphasis on 'compliance' and payment arrangements, selling assets has been rare in the past and may be even rarer in the future.

Removing goods for sale

If goods have been secured on the premises, they must be removed before they can be sold. Forced entry may be necessary to enable this. **Note:** the general rules on the rights of entry to premises (see p420) also apply when bailiffs need to re-enter premises to remove goods.

Bailiffs collecting fines and tax debts or enforcing judgments may simply force re-entry without any warning. If a client defaults on the terms of repayment included in a controlled goods agreement (see p425), s/he must be given a notice of a bailiff's intention to force re-entry to remove the listed goods (see below). In other cases, a court order is required to permit a forcible re-entry.

The notice of re-entry given after a breach of a controlled goods agreement should give at least two clear days' notice (not counting the day of the notice, the day of removal and any intervening Sundays or bank holidays). If a bailiff applies to a court, however, the court can order that a shorter period of notice be given if it is satisfied that, if the order were not made, the goods would be likely to be moved from the premises in order to prevent them being taken.

The notice must be dated and provide details of the parties, the debt and the means by which payment may be made to prevent the goods being removed and sold. It must be be served by fax or other means of electronic communication, hand delivery, or in person. Postal service cannot be used. The bailiff is responsible for ensuring that the notice is given and must keep a record of when it is served.

After the goods have been removed for sale, the bailiff must provide a written and signed notice of removal to the client. This:

- confirms that a removal has taken place;
- provides a list of items that have been removed if these are different to those items listed after taking control, otherwise the inventory supplied previously is sufficient (this is to allow for the fact that the debt has reduced by payments made since the goods were initially taken into control); *and*

- confirms the procedure for making payment so that the sale of goods can be prevented.

If any of this information is not immediately available to the bailiff at the time of removal, it should be provided to the client as soon as reasonably practicable.

Having re-entered the premises, the bailiff is required to leave them as effectively secured as s/he finds them.

The bailiff must take reasonable care of the goods removed from the premises. Goods should be kept in the same condition as they were found. If the bailiff acts negligently, the client can claim damages.

The sale

Bailiffs have a general duty to sell or dispose of the goods for the best price that can reasonably be obtained.

At least seven clear days from the day of removal must elapse before a sale can take place. However, perishable goods can be sold on the day after removal. 'Perishable' items are those which would be unsellable or would lose their sale value or have it substantially reduced if they were sold after the seven-day waiting period. They include items of declining value (eg, seasonal goods), as well as food.

A bailiff must make or obtain a valuation of the goods that have been removed for sale and must give the client, and any co-owner, an opportunity to obtain an independent valuation. The bailiff must do this within seven days of the removal. The valuation must be in writing. Where appropriate, a separate value for each item taken into control should be stated. The client and any co-owner should both be provided with copies. If the bailiff does not conduct the valuation, a qualified independent valuer should be used. If the valuation notice is not issued by the bailiff, it may invalidate any sale that follows.[48]

The bailiff must then give written notice of the date, time and place of the sale to the client and any co-owner. If the sale notice is not provided, the debtor loses a chance to recover her/his goods and this can render the sale unlawful. The individual might then be entitled to recover the value of the items sold and other damages.[49] The minimum period of notice is seven clear days before the date of sale – the date of sale must be within 12 months of the day on which the bailiff took control of the goods. This period may be extended (repeatedly if necessary) by agreement in writing between the creditor and client before the end of the period. This provision gives a client an opportunity to make instalment payment arrangements to discharge the debt and is likely to have the effect of postponing the deadline for sale. A controlled goods agreement must incorporate terms of repayment (see p425). Such an arrangement will presumably have the effect of postponing the sale deadline.

The goods must be sold by public auction (including online), unless a court permits otherwise following an application by the bailiff. A qualified auctioneer (or an independent and reputable provider in the case of an online auction) must be employed.

There are detailed rules on how the sale must be conducted and ownership of the goods transferred. In particular, a sale cannot be fully completed if a third-party claim to ownership is outstanding (see p428).

Final accounts

Immediately after the goods have been sold or disposed of, the bailiff must provide the client and any co-owner with a statement detailing:

- the items sold or otherwise disposed of;
- the sum received for each item;
- the proceeds of the sale;
- how the proceeds of the sale were applied to the costs and the debt;
- any recoverable expenses incurred (see p434).

The bailiff must also provide a copy of all receipts for expenses incurred by the auctioneer, whether at an auction house or at the client's premises. This duty does not apply if the goods were sold by an online auction or by other means of disposal.

If the client pays the outstanding amount at any time after the bailiff has incurred expenses, but before the sale or disposal of the goods, the bailiff must provide her/him with:[50]

- a statement of recoverable expenses (see p434);
- any receipts for expenses, unless they relate to a sale by an online auction or any other sale other than a public auction; *and*
- a statement of any fixed and percentage fees that have been charged.

Fees and expenses

Bailiffs can recover money from debtors to cover the cost of their actions. In the past, this was a major source of contention between clients and enforcement agents, but the current rules on fees have substantially reduced the number of disputes. There are special rules on charging fees to vulnerable debtors (see p436).

Fees

Bailiffs can charge fixed fees for three stages of the enforcement process (see below). They can also charge additional fees if the debt is above a certain amount. In addition, they can claim for certain limited expenses (see p434), most of which only arise at the very last stage of the enforcement process.

Fixed fees can be charged for the following activities.

- **Compliance.** This covers initial activities, such as receiving instructions from creditors and preparing and setting up accounts, confirming the personal details of the client, sending out the enforcement notice, the initial contact and negotiations with the client, processing payments received, general office administration, handling complaints and managing instalment plans.

- **Enforcement**. This covers initial visits and all aspects of taking control of goods through to the decision to remove the goods. This stage is split in two for High Court enforcement (see p434).
- **Sale or disposal**. This covers all aspects of the concluding parts of the process, from attending to remove goods to the place at which the sale will take place or starting to prepare for the sale if it is held on the premises, carrying out the sale, dealing with the proceeds, to returning unsold goods and final reports. **Note:** removing goods for sale and removing goods in order to take control of them (see p425) are distinct stages of the process. Goods have only been removed for sale if a written valuation has been provided within the seven-day time limit (see p431).

As soon as one of the above stages has started, the fee is chargeable, even though all the activities covered by the stage may not have been carried out or completed. The fees and expenses allowed are recovered from the 'proceeds' of the enforcement process – ie, the money received from the sale or disposal of goods and any money received in payment from the client.

The Ministry of Justice and HM Revenue and Customs have issued guidance to bailiffs, which states that a client should not have to pay VAT on enforcement fees. This is because VAT is a tax charged on services provided by businesses to customers. As the creditor is the bailiff's customer, any VAT invoices should be sent to the creditor. However, High Court enforcement officers continue to charge VAT to judgment debtors, not to creditors.

If the bailiff's instruction is withdrawn for some reason, any fees incurred up to that point do not have to be paid by the client.[51]

Standard fees

For all debts, except those enforced by the High Court, the following fees may be charged. This is referred to as the 'standard' scale.

Standard fees	
Compliance	£75
Enforcement	£235
Sale or disposal	£110

If the debt is more than £1,500, the enforcement and sale fees may be increased by an additional 7.5 per cent of the amount by which the debt exceeds £1,500 (fees are not included when calculating this total).

High Court fees

There are higher fees for debts enforced by the High Court.

High Court fees	
Compliance	£75
First enforcement	£190
Second enforcement	£495
Sale or disposal	£525

There are two stages of High Court Court enforcement.

- **First stage.** This applies when the High Court enforcement officer and the client enter into a controlled goods agreement. It covers all activities relating to enforcement from first attending the premises until the agreement is completed or breached.
- **Second stage.** This applies when the High Court enforcement officer and the client do not enter into a controlled goods agreement. It covers all activities relating to enforcement from first attending at the premises until the commencement of the sale or disposal. If the enforcement officer and the client entered into a controlled goods agreement, but the client later breaches it, this second enforcement fee also applies and covers all subsequent activities relating to the enforcement of the writ from the time at which the client breaches the agreement to the commencement of the sale or disposal stage. There is some evidence that High Court enforcement officers are avoiding controlled goods agreements so as to be able to charge this higher fee. The fee is also charged when immediate payment of the debt is made to the High Court enforcement officer or where the High Court enforcement officer was unable to contact the debtor – possibly not what was envisaged by Parliament when making these rules.

If a judgment debt is more than £1,000, the first enforcement and sale fees may be increased by an additional 7.5 per cent of the amount by which the debt exceeds £1,000 (fees are not included when calculating this total).

Expenses

Limited expenses may be recouped from clients by bailiffs. These must be 'reasonably and actually' incurred and cover:

- the cost of storing goods that have been taken into control and removed from the premises or highway;
- the cost of hiring a locksmith to use reasonable force to enter premises and to secure premises following forcible entry;
- court fees for any successful applications made by the bailiff.

Bailiffs must provide copies of receipts for all expenses they claim. No other costs may be passed on to the client.[52]

Costs of selling the goods

In addition to charging a prescribed fee, bailiffs can recover the costs incurred in selling (or otherwise disposing of) the goods. The bailiff may recover from the client:

- the auctioneer's commission. If the sale is held on premises provided by the auctioneer, this must not exceed 15 per cent of the amount realised by the sale of the goods. If the sale is held on other premises, the auctioneer's commission is limited to 7.5 per cent of the amount realised by the sale;
- the auctioneer's expenses; *and*
- reasonable expenses incurred in advertising the sale.

If the goods are sold through an online auction site or in some other way, the bailiff may recover 7.5 per cent of the sum realised by the sale of the goods. These sale costs may only be recovered from the proceeds of the enforcement process. No other expenses relating to sale can be recovered.[53]

Exceptional costs

In very limited circumstances, in addition to the fees and expenses outlined above, bailiffs can recover other expenses from the client. Provided the creditor's consent has been obtained, a bailiff can apply for a court order allowing her/him to recover exceptional expenses. The court must be satisfied that the expenses were necessary in order to enforce effectively the sum to be recovered, and must take all the circumstances into account, including the amount to be recovered, and the nature and value of the goods being taken into control.[54]

Multiple warrants

If a bailiff is enforcing more than one warrant or liability order against a client at the same time, there are special rules limiting the fees that can be charged. Although the bailiff can charge a compliance stage fee for each instruction received, s/he must (unless it is impracticable to do so) take control of goods under all the instructions at the same time and sell or dispose of all the goods taken into control on the same occasion. In such cases:

- there is just one fixed fee for each stage, regardless of the number of instructions being enforced; *and*
- the percentage fee due for each stage, if any, is calculated on the basis of the total amount to be recovered under all the warrants.

For example, instructions should be consolidated and enforced together if they are received within a few of weeks of each other.[55]

As far as possible, bailiffs must minimise their expenses that can be recovered from clients by dealing with the all the goods to which the instructions relate together and on as few occasions as possible.[56]

Vulnerable clients

If the client is a 'vulnerable person', a bailiff cannot charge fees for the enforcement stage(s) or recover any related expenses unless the client has been given adequate opportunity to get assistance and advice on the enforcement process before proceeding to remove goods that have been taken into control.[57] 'Vulnerability' is not defined in the regulations and no guidance is given to enable bailiffs to assess what an 'adequate opportunity' to get advice might be.

If a client disputes the fees

If a client disagrees with the fees charged, s/he can apply to the High Court or county court for it to assess the bailiff's bill.[58] Form N244 should be used (see p288). The court can only assess whether the fees should have been applied and whether they were calculated correctly or whether the expenses were permissible. If the client wants to argue that the amounts charged were unlawful, s/he cannot apply in this way and must use another remedy – eg, paying under protest to release the goods and then issuing a claim to recover the amount paid.

---

5. **Complaints about bailiffs**

If a client is unhappy about the conduct of a bailiff, s/he can threaten or take court action, or make a complaint. **Note:** many bailiffs now have body-worn video cameras that record all visits to premises. Ask the bailiff company to check the footage and request a copy to view yourself. This may resolve a dispute without any further action being necessary.

Taking court action

In the past, if a warrant was invalid or there had been a procedural error, threatening county court action could help a client negotiate or have the enforcement process withdrawn. However, it is no longer possible to initiate a small claim on the basis that the bailiff's misconduct constituted a trespass and so invalidates the entire enforcement process and associated costs. Instead, a client can apply on Form N244 to the appropriate court for an order awarding damages or the return of goods.[59] Given that the application is not heard under the small claims procedure, you should be aware that clients are at risk of having to pay costs if their application is unsuccessful.

You should always check whether any goods taken into control are exempt or belong to a third party (see p426 and p428).

Complaining to the bailiff

If there is a problem, always first complain to the bailiff company itself. Find out who the complaints manager is and write to her/him directly. Contacting the individual bailiff is rarely useful, other than to agree a 'stay' on recovery.

Bailiff firms have a duty to deal with complaints promptly under their trade body complaints procedures and under *Taking Control of Goods: national standards*. In addition, if they are acting for a public authority, such as a local authority or government department, the bailiffs should also be treated as 'public authorities', with all the duties this implies. For example, they should give reasons for their decisions, so that if they refuse to treat a person as vulnerable, they should explain why.

Complaining to creditors

Bailiffs are generally called 'enforcement agents' now; this term emphasises the legal fact that they act as an 'agent' for a creditor, exercising the creditor's enforcement powers on their behalf. Creditors, such as local authorities, are therefore responsible for what their agents do and should investigate complaints against them seriously. The fact that a case has been passed to bailiffs for enforcement does not divest the creditor of overall responsibility for the case. They are liable for the enforcement agents' actions and they are also still expected to monitor cases and to deal with representations made directly to them rather than to the bailiff.[60] Although it is always worthwhile contacting the bailiffs to complain about their actions, it may be unproductive if the point at issue is whether they should have been instructed at all or if the terms of repayment set by the contract with the creditor are impossible for the client to meet. For instance, council tax contracts often require the bailiff to collect within three months. In such cases, the bailiffs are bound by their contract with the creditor to enforce the warrant issued to them, and other than asking them to 'stay' the action while negotiations are carried out, little else may be possible.

Taking Control of Goods: national standards requires creditors to act proportionately when using bailiffs. This includes their decision to use taking control of goods as an enforcement measure and what terms of repayment they consider to be acceptable. The guidance emphasises that bailiffs act as creditors' agents and that a creditor is legally liable for them. Creditors are also required to operate clear controls and complaints procedures. They should therefore always be notified about wrongful acts by their agents, as this may help bring pressure to bear in individual cases and may lead to improved monitoring more generally. Direct contact with a creditor is particularly important if the personal circumstances of the client are at issue. A complaint may be made about either the incorrect use of legal powers or a failure to follow a code of practice.

Complaining to a professional organisation

If a complaint to a firm of bailiffs is not dealt with satisfactorily, a complaint could be made to the bailiffs' professional or trade organisation – the High Court Enforcement Officers Association and the Civil Enforcement Association (see Appendix 1). This can be particularly effective in cases of poor administration and customer care by bailiffs' firms. However, when making a complaint, remember that these bodies exist to promote their members' interests and are not entirely independent or impartial.

The complaints procedures can be found on the associations' websites.

Both organisations also have disciplinary codes.

Serious breaches of professional ethics or of procedure may lead to an investigation and a penalty being imposed on the bailiff, such as being excluded from membership and, as a result, from the profession (although this is rare).

A complaint could also result in at least an apology and perhaps compensation, such as a refund of fees.

The Civil Enforcement Association also has a code of practice regulating members' business practices, which may be of some assistance.

Complaining to the Ombudsman

Most creditors for whom bailiffs act are public sector bodies and are subject to supervision by an Ombudsman. If a creditor's own complaints procedure fails to produce a satisfactory outcome for the client, a complaint can be made to the Local Government and Social Care Ombudsman (or Public Services Ombudsman for Wales), the Parliamentary and Health Service Ombudsman or to the Adjudicator's Office (about HM Revenue and Customs).

In the case of local authorities, before a complaint is made to the Ombudsman, the case can be taken up by the local authority's monitoring officer. This person is usually the chief legal officer and it is her/his duty to consider whether there has been maladministration or whether the local authority has acted unlawfully. It can sometimes be helpful to refer a case to the monitoring officer if the department in question is unwilling to intervene or negotiate, but you believe its bailiffs have acted unlawfully.

Court proceedings

If a complaint has been unsuccessful, court proceedings can be initiated against the bailiffs in order to recover a client's goods or obtain financial compensation. Because of the risk of costs linked to these claims, the most appropriate form of court action for many clients may be to complain against the bailiff's county court certificate. This can be done if the bailiff's conduct has indicated that s/he is not a 'fit and proper person' to hold a certificate or does not have an adequate knowledge of the law.[61] The client should apply to to the court on a simple complaint form (Form EAC2). There is no fee and the client is not liable for any costs, unless the judge thinks that her/his grievance was unfounded and an 'abuse of court process'.[62]

Note: although High Court enforcement officer staff may hold county court certificates, the High Court enforcement officers in charge of the company does not. They are authorised by the Lord Chancellor and there is no independent judicial oversight of the conduct of officers comparable to that in certification.

6. **Emergency action**

People often only seek advice when the 'crunch' comes, such as a visit from a bailiff. In order to gain time so that a client's finances can be investigated and an overall repayment strategy devised, you may need to consider one or more of the following emergency measures.

Refuse the bailiff access

It is common for a debt adviser to be first consulted when a client hears from bailiffs. If this is the case, the best advice to protect a client's goods from being taken into control is to ensure that the bailiffs are not given access to the property and for the client to remove any goods that are outside the home (especially cars) to a place where they will not be seen.

Although it is not wholly clear from the legislation,[63] a 2019 decision of the Local Government Ombudsman confirmed that it is still the lawful right of someone in debt to refuse to open a door to a bailiff or to allow her/him across the threshold.[64] A very small number of debts allow bailiffs to force entry (see p421), but these powers are seldom used.

Note: there is a very slight risk that these actions may constitute the offence of 'obstructing' an enforcement agent, and some bailiffs might argue this.[65] However, *Taking Control of Goods: national standards* advises that if an enforcement agent implies or states that refusing entry is an offence, this is a misrepresentation of the bailiff's powers.[66]

Bailiffs try to visit more than once to gain access (and they have 12 months in which to do so), so clients should be advised to be vigilant, and keep doors locked. If the client lives in a block of flats or a house in multiple occupation, a bailiff may be discouraged from making repeat visits if it appears that gaining access may be difficult. If bailiffs are unable to enter, they will eventually return the instruction to the creditor indicating whether or not there are sufficient goods to satisfy the debt. They rely on what they can see through windows to decide this.

If the bailiff fails to raise the amount of money due, however, this is not the end of the recovery process; other means are tried. Debts for fines and local taxes often go back to the court for it to consider committal to prison (see p400 and p405). A client can be given a prison sentence for 'wilful refusal' or 'culpable neglect' to pay (see p407) and a bailiff may threaten that failure to give access will be construed by the court as wilful refusal. However, there are no reported instances of anyone being committed to prison on this ground.

Note: if bailiffs have already gained access or taken control of goods, they might subsequently force their way in to remove goods for the same debt (see p430). In addition, certain bailiffs can force initial entry (see p422).

Get the warrant withdrawn from the bailiff

In all cases, you should aim to remove the matter from the hands of the bailiff and place it back for consideration by the creditor.

In the civil courts, the client should apply immediately to suspend the warrant. For county court action, this is done on Form N245 (see p343). For High Court action, an application for a variation of the judgment and a stay of execution should be made on Form N244. Magistrates' courts do not have such a power, but it may be worthwhile speaking to the court's fines officer to see what scope s/he has to intervene. It may be possible for the fines officer to refer the case back to the magistrates for a further hearing.

In situations where there is no power to suspend a warrant through the courts and the client cannot afford to pay a lump sum, the only option may be to persuade the creditor that the warrant should be withdrawn because of the client's personal or financial circumstances. This may be because s/he should be treated as vulnerable or because s/he comes into one of the categories of people who are exempt from this method of enforcement under the creditor's code of practice. In many cases, payment terms must be negotiated at the same time, and often these will be for instalments of sums much lower than it would have been economic for the bailiff to collect.

Raise a lump sum to clear the debt

If the tactics in this section have been unsuccessful, or if the goods have already been taken into control, the client may need to pay the debt in full to avoid her/his goods being sold. This may violate certain basic principles of money advice, but is often the only option that a client is prepared to consider. It may also make financial sense, as the replacement cost of the items in question may be much more than the total required by the bailiffs. See Chapter 7 for ways of maximising income.

Notes

2. When bailiffs are used
1 Part 75 CPR
2 *Brookes v Secretary of State for Work and Pensions and Child Maintenance and Enforcement Commission* [2010] EWCA Civ 420

3. How bailiffs are instructed
3 Part 75 CPR
4 See, for example, LB Harrow (15 010 743) and LB Hackney (16 001 711)
5 Available at gov.uk/government/publications/council-tax
6 *R (Guest) v Woking Metropolitan Council* [2008] EWHC 2649 (Admin)

4. Bailiffs' powers
7 In particular, Part 3 and Sch 12 TCEA 2007 and TCG Regs
8 Tamworth Borough Council (19 002 774)
9 Part 75.7 CPR
10 *Miller v CES* (2016)
11 Sch 12 paras 4-6 TCEA 2007
12 Reg 23 TCG Regs
13 Ministry of Justice, *Taking Control of Goods: national standards*, April 2014, paras 74, 76 and 77
14 See these LGO decisions: Westminster City Council (15 008 786), Peterborough City Council (17 004 860), Birmingham City Council (17 007 152), Malvern Hills District Council (17 015 143) and Mendip District Council (18 003 107)
15 Reg 22 TCG Regs
16 Sch 12 paras 14-15 TCEA 2007
17 *Rooftops South West v Ash Interiors* [2018] EWHC 2798
18 *Midtown Acquisitions LP v Essar Global Fund Ltd* (2016)
19 Middlesbrough Borough Council (17 012 520); Wrexham County Borough Council (201504498, 2016)
20 Ministry of Justice, *Taking Control of Goods: national standards*, April 2014, paras 57-61
21 Bristol City Council (18 005 149)
22 Reg 28 TCG Regs
23 Reg 29 TCG Regs

24 Preston City Council (17 000 407)
25 Sch 12 para 26 TCEA 2007
26 Regs 9, 12 and 13 TCG Regs
27 Sch 12 para 13 TCEA 2007
28 Reg 10 TCG Regs
29 Reg 16 TCG Regs
30 Regs 17-18 TCG Regs
31 Reg 19 TCG Regs
32 Regs 14-15 TCG Regs
33 Sch 12 para 10 TCEA 2007
34 Sch 12 para 12 TCEA 2007
35 Ministry of Justice, *Taking Control of Goods: national standards*, April 2014, para 68
36 Manchester City Council (15 015 253)
37 Ministry of Justice, *Taking Control of Goods: national standards*, April 2014, para 64
38 Reg 4 TCG Regs
39 *Fouda v LB Southwark & Newlyn plc* [2015] EWHC 1128
40 r85.8 CPR
41 r85.9 CPR
42 r85.12 CPR
43 Sch 12 para 10 TCEA 2007; Ministry of Justice, *Taking Control of Goods: national standards*, April 2014, para 67. These also stress the bailiff's duties to avoid securing or removing the goods of third parties and to inform third parties of their rights.
44 *Rooftops South West v Ash Interiors* [2018] EWHC 2798
45 Harborough District Council (18 012 739)
46 LB Ealing (15 016 609)
47 Sch 12 para 34 TCEA 2007
48 LGO decision, LB Merton 18 019 888
49 LGO decision, LB Merton 18 019 888
50 Reg 14 TCG(F) Regs
51 Reg 17 TCG(F) Regs; Ministry of Justice, *Taking Control of Goods: national standards*, para 3.1
52 Reg 8 TCG(F) Regs
53 Reg 9 TCG(F) Regs
54 Reg 10 TCG(F) Regs; r84.14 CPR
55 LB Hounslow (16 012 800); Powys County Council (201502998, 2016)
56 Reg 11 TCG(F) Regs
57 Reg 12 TCG(F) Regs

58 Reg 16 TCG(F) Regs

5. **Complaints about bailiffs**
59 Sch 12 para 66 TCEA 2007
60 Plymouth City Council (18 013 949);
    Liverpool City Council (18 010 221)
61 The Certification of Enforcement Agents
    Regulations 2014, No.421
62 r84.20 CPR

6. **Emergency action**
63 Sch 12 para 14 TCEA 2007
64 Bristol City Council (18 005 149)
65 Sch 12 para 68 TCEA 2007
66 Ministry of Justice, *Taking Control of
    Goods: national standards*, April 2014,
    para 20

Chapter 15

. . . .

Personal insolvency

This chapter covers the formal debt relief options available to clients who are unable to pay their debts:

1. Insolvency options: summary (below)
2. Administration orders (p445)
3. When to use bankruptcy and individual voluntary arrangements (p449)
4. Individual voluntary arrangements (p453)
5. Bankruptcy (p464)
6. Debt relief orders (p499)

---

1. Insolvency options: summary

Someone is said to be 'insolvent' if s/he is unable to pay her/his debts as they fall due. In many cases, people are able to resolve their financial problems by coming to the informal arrangements with their creditors discussed earlier in this *Handbook*. There are also currently four ways in which a client can reach a formal arrangement with her/his creditors.

- **Administration order** (see p445). This is a county court order that prevents individual creditors taking enforcement action without permission from the court and which requires that all the debts of a person be dealt with together.[1] Once the administration order is completed, any outstanding balance is no longer payable. However, this is currently not a viable option for someone whose total unsecured debts exceed £5,000.
- **Individual voluntary arrangement (IVA)** (see p453). This is a formal arrangement made between the client and her/his creditors that creates a legally binding agreement between them. The arrangement allows the client to defer payment of her/his debts and/or the creditors to accept less than 100 per cent of their debts. Provided a certain percentage of the creditors agree to accept the arrangement, on its completion the balance of the debts is written off. In the meantime, the creditors agree not to take recovery action. However,

secured creditors cannot be included in an IVA unless they agree. Student loans and child support cannot be included at all.

- **Bankruptcy** (see p464). An official receiver or an insolvency practitioner is appointed to handle the client's financial affairs for the benefit of her/his creditors. This person is known as the 'trustee in bankruptcy'. Bankruptcy can be requested by the client, by one or more creditors or by the supervisor of a failed IVA. Bankruptcy generally lasts for 12 months, after which time the client is discharged and released from all her/his unsecured debts other than those specified in the legislation.

- **Debt relief order (DRO)** (see p499). This gives the client a 12-month moratorium, during which time creditors cannot force the client to pay the debts included in the DRO. Following the moratorium, the client is discharged from all the debts included in the order (other than those incurred fraudulently). DROs are suitable for clients:
  - who do not own their own homes; *and*
  - whose total debts (other than some specifically excluded debts) are £20,000 or less; *and*
  - whose available income does not exceed £50 a month; *and*
  - whose total assets (apart from some motor vehicles and other basic assets) are worth no more than £1,000; *and*
  - who are not currently subject to a bankruptcy order, a bankruptcy restrictions order/undertaking, a debt relief restrictions order/undertaking, or an IVA; *and*
  - who have not had a DRO within the previous six years.

The legislation governing insolvency is contained in the Insolvency Act 1986 as amended, particularly by section 71 and Schedules 18 and 19 of the Enterprise and Regulatory Reform Act 2013 and the Insolvency (England and Wales) Rules 2016. (There is a destination table which identifies where provisions in the previous (1986) rules can be found in the new rules at gov.uk/government/news/table-of-destinations-for-insolvency-rules-now-available.) The government agency which deals with insolvency-related matters is the Insolvency Service. Its website provides links to tools and information for debt advisers, including portals for making applications for bankruptcy and DROs on behalf of clients, the DRO intermediary guidance notes, the Insolvency Service's *Technical Manual* and useful forms, including a template to appeal against the adjudicator's decision to refuse to make a bankruptcy order (available at gov.uk/guidance/debt-advisor-tools-and-information). **Note**: the *Technical Manual* is no longer updated and may even be removed from the website. Advisers should consider making freedom of information requests[2] to the Insolvency Service to ensure they have up-to-date versions of commonly referred to sections.

2. **Administration orders**

An administration order is a county court order that prevents individual creditors taking enforcement action without permission from the court and which requires that all the debts of a person be dealt with together.[3] An administration order can include a composition under which the client is required to pay less than 10 pence in the pound in satisfaction of her/his debts (see p447).

The client must have at least two debts, including one judgment against her/him in either the county court or High Court. Although debts registered in the county court for enforcement as if they were payable under a court order, such as traffic penalties registered for enforcement in the Traffic Enforcement Centre, are defined as 'judgments or orders' for the purposes of some parts of the Civil Procedure Rules, and some courts have accepted them as a 'judgment' for the purposes of the client meeting the qualifying conditions for an administration order application, strictly, they are registered for enforcement 'as if' they were a county court order. If this practice was challenged, it might be difficult to satisfy a judge that the debt met the definition of 'judgment' for this purpose. Debts registered for enforcement in the county court can, however, be included in an administration order.

The client makes a single monthly payment to the court, which then distributes it equitably among the creditors.

The client must apply for an administration order on Form N92 which can be obtained from the client's local county court office. There is no fee, but costs are added to the sum the client repays, at 10 pence per pound repaid. Clients can make payments towards an administration order by cheque/postal order made payable to HM Courts and Tribunals Service, in cash at the court counter, or by credit/debt card in person at the counter or by telephoning the court.

The court can also arrange for the issue of an Allpay card which can be used to make payments at local shops or post offices with a PayPoint facility.

Once the administration order is completed, any outstanding balance of any debt is no longer payable.

An attachment of earnings order is usually made if the client is employed, unless s/he asks the court not to make one on Form N92, setting out her/his reasons – eg, if her/his employment will be affected once her/his employer finds out about the administration order. See p329 for more on the advantages and disadvantages of attachment of earnings orders.

Once an administration order is granted, it is unlawful for any creditor to approach the client for payment of any debt included in it without the court's permission (including resorting to 'self-help' remedies such as deductions from benefits). Interest and charges are effectively frozen on all debts included in the order. The court charges a percentage administration fee (currently 10 per cent) for all the money collected and distributes this quarterly. Provided the client makes all the payments required by the administration order, s/he is discharged from all the debts in it, including any debts subject to a judgment.

Administration orders are registered at the Registry Trust and will probably affect a client's ability to get credit.

Completing the application form

Form N92 requires a list of all the client's debts. These must not exceed £5,000. Administration orders can only be given to individuals, but debts that are jointly owed must be included. If a person is jointly and severally liable, s/he should include the whole value of the debt. Even if finances are shared, couples cannot apply together and should make individual applications if both want to deal with their debts in this way.

Guidance (Form N270) on completing Form N92 states that the client should list all her/his debts in Part B (list of creditors) and appears to require arrears of priority debts to be included in Part A (statement of means) as part of the client's expenditure, even when it is intended that the debt should be included in the administration order. It is suggested that such debts should not be listed in both Parts A and Part B. They should be listed in Part A only if the client is asking the court not to include the debt(s) in the administration order, and should be listed in Part B if the client is asking the court to include the debt(s) in the administration order. Proof of the debts is needed, along with Form N92.

Some courts have queried the inclusion of debts such as council tax arrears and debts that would not be covered by bankruptcy, such as fines, but these can all be included.[4] Some local authorities object to the inclusion of council tax arrears in an administration order on the grounds that they have an attachment of earnings order and that this continues regardless. This is incorrect and should be challenged.[5]

Social fund loans and benefit overpayments can be included in an administration order even if the client is in receipt of a benefit from which deductions can be made, since deductions cannot be made while the administration order is in force unless the court gives permission (which, in practice, never seems to be asked for).

The proposed order

Some administration orders are decided by court officers without a hearing. A notice of the application and a calculation (the 'proposed order') is sent to creditors, explaining what they can expect to receive. A district judge is only involved if the amount offered by the client is insufficient to repay the debts in a 'reasonable time'. Guidance to court staff suggests this is three years.

If court staff cannot make an order, a district judge decides the matter. S/he can either propose a longer repayment period or make a composition order (see p447). S/he can do this with or without a hearing. **Note:** a district judge can make an order without a hearing, but cannot dismiss an application for an administration order or exclude any debts from the order without a hearing.[6]

If a court hearing is required, the client and all the creditors are sent notice, details of the debts and the proposed terms of the order. The creditors must send a corrected balance to the court, if required. See p448 for details about the hearing.

If the court staff prepare the order, a copy is sent to the client and all the creditors, who then have 14 days in which to object to the administration order being granted. This is an opportunity for the client to object to the level of instalments, as well as for the creditors to object to their being included. If no objections are received, a 'final order' is made. If objections are received, a hearing must be arranged to consider them.

Composition orders

A district judge can order that a client pays only a proportion of her/his debts. This is known as a 'composition order'. This should be considered if the debts cannot be cleared in a reasonable time (see above for what this means). **Note:** an application for a composition order can only be decided by a district judge and cannot be rejected without a hearing.

You should help the client work out the monthly amount available to offer creditors. If this amount will not clear the debts plus the 10 per cent charge made by the court in three years, suggest that a composition order be made in the box in Section C of Form N92.

The percentage of each debt offered is calculated by establishing the total time available for payments (ie, 36 – the number of months in three years) multiplied by the monthly payment offered, deducting 10 per cent from this total, and then dividing the resulting figure by the total of the debts owed, and finally showing this as a percentage.

Example

Sean has £75 a month available income and owes a total of £4,500. A suggested composition would be to offer:

36 x £75 = £2,700 total amount to be paid

Less 10% administration (£270) = £2,430

2,430 ÷ 4,500 = 0.54 (the proportion to be paid)

0.54 = 54% (the percentage to be paid)

In this case, the following wording can be inserted in the box: 'I ask that the court consider making a composition order at the rate of 54 pence in the pound.' The client should also use this box to explain her/his reasons for not wanting an attachment of earnings order, where applicable.

In many cases, the actual order is not opposed, but a composition may be. However, provided you are prepared with facts and figures to justify the financial necessity of what you argue, such orders are increasingly acceptable to courts.

The court hearing

There will be a court hearing if a district judge thinks one is necessary – eg, if s/he refuses the application, or either the client or a creditor objects to the terms of the proposed order. Creditors may attend the hearing (but rarely do), at which a district judge decides whether or not to grant the order. The court normally grants an administration order unless the information given is incorrect or it appears that the order would unreasonably deny a creditor another type of remedy. If creditors object merely because they want to take action in pursuit of their debt, you should argue that this would result in other creditors being treated less fairly.

Reviewing an administration order

An administration order can be reviewed at any time by the court. The client, any creditor included in the order or the court itself can request a review. Some orders contain a provision for periodic reviews. If the client wants to apply for a review, s/he should write to the court explaining why the review is being requested (usually because of a change in circumstances) and enclose a financial statement. The court then arranges a hearing.

On review, the court may:[7]

- reduce the payments;
- suspend all payments for a specified period of time;
- add or vary a composition order, including theoretically varying it to 0 pence in the pound;
- reinstate a revoked order (but see below);
- make an attachment of earnings order to secure payments due under the order;
- revoke the administration order.

Although creditors can apply to be added to an administration order, there is no specific provision allowing clients to add a creditor. New creditors can sometimes be included by a review on the basis that there has been a change of circumstances, although some courts apply the rules strictly and only allow the creditors to apply.

Revoking an administration order

Once made, an administration order is not invalidated if the debts are found to exceed the £5,000 limit, but the court can revoke the order. The court might take this step if it thought the client had 'abused' the administration order by obtaining further credit.[8]

If a client misses two consecutive payments or persistently fails to pay on time, the court should send a notice requiring either:

- payment;
- an explanation;
- an application for a variation;
- a proposal for payment of arrears.

If the client fails to do one of the above, the administration order is revoked in 14 days. If the client replies, the matter is referred to the district judge, who may either order a hearing or revoke, suspend or vary the order. If the order is revoked, suspended or varied without a hearing, creditors or the client can object within 14 days and a hearing must be held.

At a hearing, the district judge considers all the circumstances of the case and makes one of the decisions listed above.

If the district judge decides to revoke the order, the court no longer collects and distributes payments. The creditors are informed that they are free to pursue their debts individually. In practice, only a small proportion of creditors contact clients following the revocation of an administration order. In theory, when an administration order is revoked on the ground of failure to make the payments required under the order, the court may impose the same restrictions on the client as would apply to an undischarged bankrupt for a period of one year (see p479), but, in practice, these powers do not seem to be used.[9]

3. **When to use bankruptcy and individual voluntary arrangements**

Bankruptcy and individual voluntary arrangements (IVAs) are both options available to an insolvent client, who, therefore, needs to be advised on which is the most appropriate option for her/him.

Bankruptcy is only likely to be the preferred option for a client if s/he has a number of unaffordable debts, no assets (or little or no equity in her/his home), low available income to pay creditors so that s/he could not clear her/his debts within three years, and it is unlikely that her/his situation will change in the foreseeable future. S/he must also have no need for credit in the medium term.

An IVA is likely to be the preferred option if a client has a number of debts plus a particular reason for wanting to avoid bankruptcy (eg, to avoid losing the family home), and is able to make a substantial offer, but s/he is either unable to persuade her/his creditors to accept an informal arrangement or the only informal arrangement they will accept is open ended and likely to take many years to complete. However, IVAs do not end in automatic discharge, as bankruptcy does (usually after 12 months – see p497). If the client fails to keep to the arrangement, s/he could still face bankruptcy if s/he is unable to reach agreement with her/his creditors to vary it.

You should take the following factors into account.

Risk to current assets

Some property solely owned by a client is put directly at risk in bankruptcy. In practice, many things which a person uses may be owned by someone else – eg, a partner. Jointly owned property or property in which the client has a beneficial interest, particularly the family home, is indirectly at risk because the trustee may be able to sell it in order to realise the bankrupt client's share (see p488).

There is more flexibility with an IVA, as creditors are usually offered regular payments. Although most IVAs require clients who are homeowners to obtain a valuation of the family home towards the end of the arrangement, with a view to raising a lump sum by borrowing against the equity in the property (see p455), clients are not expected to sell their homes unless they choose this as part of the arrangement. However, other assets are at risk if the creditors do not agree to exclude them from the IVA. Assets that would be disregarded in bankruptcy are excluded from an IVA.

Risk to future assets

When considering either bankruptcy or an IVA, the client should bear in mind the potential risk to any future assets, particularly if s/he expects to inherit property in the near future or already owns assets, which may have no or little value now, but which are likely to have a realisable value within the next few years.

IVAs usually contain 'windfall' clauses – eg, stating that any assets with a value of more than £500 the client acquires during the term of the arrangement can be claimed for it. It is, however, possible to make arrangements with potential donors – eg, by asking them to change their wills. (**Note:** this is not regarded as disposing of property as a will only takes effect when the person dies rather than when s/he made it.)

Bankruptcy lasts for only 12 months and income payment agreements/orders for three years, whereas IVAs tend to last for around five years.

Effect on future credit

Both bankruptcy and IVAs are a matter of public record. The Individual Insolvency Register contains details of bankruptcies, IVAs (including post-bankruptcy IVAs), bankruptcy restrictions orders and bankruptcy restrictions undertakings. Bankruptcy records remain on the register for three months after the date of the client's discharge. IVA records remain until the arrangement ends (plus a further three months if an insolvency practitioner agrees to act as a nominee in respect of a proposal made on or after 6 April 2010). Records of bankruptcy restrictions orders (which last for between two and 15 years) remain on the register until they come to an end. Credit reference agencies keep details on file for six years.

Although lenders can give credit to a bankrupt person, it is likely to be more expensive to obtain credit both before and after discharge. In addition, it is an offence for either an undischarged bankrupt, or a person who has been discharged from bankruptcy but is subject to a bankruptcy restrictions order or undertaking, to obtain credit of £500 or more (including ordering goods on credit) without disclosing her/his status.[10] This declaration may make it impossible for a person to run her/his own business because s/he is unlikely to be given further credit.

Although there are no legal restrictions on a client with an IVA obtaining credit, most arrangements state that the client cannot obtain credit of more than £500 without the supervisor's permission. If s/he does, it is a breach of the arrangement and it might be terminated by the supervisor as a result.

Effect on employment or office

Being an undischarged bankrupt prohibits someone from:
- engaging in business in a name other than that in which s/he was bankrupt without disclosing it to people with whom s/he has business dealings;[11] *and*
- acting as a director of, or directly or indirectly promoting, forming or managing, a limited company without the court's permission;[12] *and*
- acting as an insolvency practitioner.[13]

These restrictions end on discharge, unless a bankruptcy restrictions order or undertaking is made (see p479). A bankruptcy restrictions order or undertaking may also affect her/his ability to belong to a professional body. This should always be checked before proceeding with bankruptcy. If it appears there is a risk that post-bankruptcy restrictions may be imposed, a client should be advised to consider whether any of these restrictions would affect her/him.

The professional rules of solicitors and accountants make it virtually impossible for people who have been made bankrupt to work in these professions. Other employers may be unwilling to employ a bankrupt person, especially if s/he is responsible for handling money. Charity law limits the ability of people who have been made bankrupt and subject to bankruptcy restrictions orders and undertakings to serve on management committees. The bankruptcy of a sole trader does not necessarily mean the business will close, but it will be difficult for it to continue in view of the above restrictions and the following factors.
- If there are items of business equipment used by the person's employees rather than by her/him personally in the business, s/he cannot claim exemption for them (see p483) and the trustee may insist on a sale. Stock in trade is not exempt from sale by the trustee.
- The bankruptcy (and any subsequent restrictions order or undertaking) may be advertised and publicised locally, and this may damage the reputation of

15

Chapter 15: Personal insolvency
3. When to use bankruptcy and individual voluntary arrangements
. . . .

the business as well as of its proprietor. All bankruptcy orders are advertised in the *London Gazette* (but see p476).

- The person will find it extremely difficult to operate a bank account, not only because of the credit restrictions, but also because of the possibility of the trustee making a claim against any balance in the account.

These restrictions do not apply to someone with an IVA.

Effect on housing

Bankruptcy may result in the loss of the family home (see p488). Many tenancy agreements contain provisions allowing the landlord to end the tenancy and repossess the property in the event of a tenant's bankruptcy. If the client has rent arrears, the landlord can still apply for a possession order even though the rent arrears are a bankruptcy debt (see p372).

In the case of a bankrupt homeowner, if there is sufficient equity, the trustee can usually force a sale unless the family can raise a sufficient amount to buy out the trustee's interest (see p490).

In the case of an IVA, although creditors expect the value of the person's interest in the family home to be taken into account, there is little likelihood of the property having to be sold. The IVA protocol (see p454) says that clients should not be required to sell their property instead of releasing equity. If the client cannot release equity, protocol-compliant IVAs are extended for a further 12 months.

Effect on reputation and stress

Bankruptcy can be a humiliating experience for many people. There is a possibility of a public examination of the client's conduct and financial affairs in open court, although this is very rare. There may be an advertisement in the local paper. If the client's conduct is considered blameworthy, s/he may be made the subject of a bankruptcy restrictions order or undertaking, with the possibility of local publicity. Bankruptcy has the potential to add considerably to a person's stress. On the other hand, there is a certainty about bankruptcy, which can reduce stress – most creditors are forced to accept the situation and can no longer pursue the client for payment.

IVAs do not carry stigma, but can be time consuming to draw up and gain agreement for, which could add to stress. In addition, the situation is not finally resolved until the last payment is actually made, and they can fail if there is an adverse change of circumstances which in turn could lead to the client's bankruptcy.

Costs

If a client wants to apply for her/his own bankruptcy, s/he must pay a deposit (currently £550) in addition to an adjudicator's fee (currently £130). Lack of resources sometimes prevents someone from obtaining a bankruptcy order, although if the client is unable to raise the adjudicator's fee/deposit, a charity or trust fund may help. See, for example, turn2us.org.uk.

There should be no need for a client to pay any fees for an IVA in advance, as a free initial interview may be available and most insolvency practitioners collect their fees out of the ongoing payments made into the arrangement. A person may pay more for the 'privilege' of avoiding bankruptcy: the fee for arranging and supervising an IVA is likely to be in the region of £3,000 to £4,000, with a typical arrangement fee being £1,500 and 15 per cent of realisations during the period of the IVA (plus VAT). Some IVA providers argue that the client does not actually pay the fees because they come out of the total 'pot' paid into the IVA. In practice, however, only part of the money paid into an arrangement actually goes to creditors. However, creditors – particularly banks – have increasingly expressed their dissatisfaction with the level of fees, which in turn has led to downward pressure on fees, which must be voted on and agreed by the creditors. Fees are generally based on the amount paid into the IVA rather than on an hourly rate for any work done.

4. **Individual voluntary arrangements**

When an individual voluntary arrangement is appropriate

Only an individual can enter into an individual voluntary arrangement (IVA), including someone who is currently bankrupt and for whom an IVA is a more attractive option (see p498).

An IVA can be explored if the client wishes to avoid bankruptcy and has at least £50 a month available income and/or a lump sum or non-essential asset available to pay her/his creditors.

An IVA lasts for a fixed period. This is usually not more than five or six years, unless a single-payment IVA is agreed involving a lump sum, and so an IVA should be considered if an informal payment arrangement is likely to last longer. If a client has no assets that are at risk in bankruptcy, s/he may want to consider bankruptcy, rather than an IVA, because if payments have to be made, they will only last for a maximum of three years (see p485).

There is no maximum or minimum level of debt for an IVA, but, in view of the costs involved, it is unlikely to be appropriate unless the client has two or more debts totalling at least £8,000. An IVA is unlikely to be appropriate if the client:

- is not insolvent; *and*
- has no surplus income; *and*
- can pay debts in full within six years.

A client faced with being made bankrupt by a creditor (see p470) should always consider an IVA as an alternative option if s/he does not want to become bankrupt and is not in a position to challenge the creditor.

Straightforward consumer individual voluntary arrangements

The individual voluntary arrangements protocol

The IVA protocol provides a standard framework for straightforward consumer IVAs and includes standard documentation and terms. The protocol has been updated and the current version applies to all protocol-compliant IVAs entered into since 1 June 2016 (a 2020 version of the protocol is expected, but details were not available at the time of writing). Details can be found at gov.uk/government/publications/individual-voluntary-arrangement-iva-protocol.

The protocol sets out a standard approach to:
- ensuring the client has received full and appropriate advice;
- the content of the proposal to the client's creditors;
- assessing and verifying the client's income and expenditure;
- dealing with the equity in the client's home; *and*
- the terms and conditions to be included in the IVA.

Creditors are expected to accept a protocol-compliant IVA and not propose any unnecessary modifications. If they vote against it, they are expected to disclose their reasons to the IVA provider.

A client is likely to be suitable for a protocol-compliant IVA if s/he has:
- a regular sustainable income – eg, from employment or from a regular pension; *and*
- several lines of credit; *and*
- uncomplicated assets.

A reasonably steady income stream is necessary in order for the client to be suitable to be dealt with under the protocol. Self-employed clients are suitable if that self-employment produces a regular income. If income is uneven or unpredictable, this should be highlighted in the proposal. Clients with more than 20 per cent of their income from bonuses or commission or who are unemployed may not be suitable. Clients with debts below £5,000 or who meet the criteria for a debt relief order are not suitable for an IVA.

The client should not have any disputed debts. In order to give creditors confidence that the proposed IVA is the most appropriate solution to the client's debt problems, IVA providers carry out a 'due diligence' process. This means the client is given appropriate advice, including information on the advantages and disadvantages of the various options available for resolving her/his particular debt problem. Previous attempts to resolve the client's financial difficulties must be included in the proposal, together with an explanation of their failure and details of any payments made to an advice provider. The protocol also reassures creditors that the IVA provider has verified the information contained in the proposal. Creditors generally accept financial statements drawn up in accordance with the standard financial statement (see p56) guidelines. **Note:** if the client is under 55, only minimum pension contributions should be allowed as essential expenditure – the IVA protocol imposes some restrictions on the pension contributions made by clients aged 55 or above.

The client's home

The protocol applies whether or not the client is a homeowner. If the client is a homeowner, the IVA must deal with the equity in the home. The position under the current version of the protocol (which, it is understood, is likely to change significantly under the 2020 version) is as follows.

Six months before the end of the IVA, the client is expected to remortgage or take out a secured loan to release any equity above £5,000 up to a maximum of 85 per cent of the 'loan-to-value' – ie, 85 per cent of the valuation less any outstanding mortgage, provided the increased remortgage or secured loan payments are not more than 50 per cent of the monthly payment into the IVA and that the remortgage or secured loan term does not extend beyond the date of the client's state retirement age or the existing mortgage term. The remortgage or secured loan repayments are deducted from the client's contribution to the IVA. If, as a result, the client's payments into the IVA fall below £50 a month, the IVA is concluded. If the client is unable to remortgage in this way, the IVA is extended for up to 12 months.

Standard terms and conditions

In addition to the protocol, there are standard terms and conditions.

The supervisor (see p461) carries out a review of the client's income and expenditure every 12 months and the client is expected to increase her/his contributions to the IVA by 50 per cent of any net surplus. Overtime, bonus and commission payments in excess of 10 per cent of the client's normal take-home pay must be disclosed and 50 per cent of the excess paid to the supervisor. If the client is made redundant during the IVA, s/he must pay any amount in excess of six months' take-home pay into the IVA.

The supervisor can also reduce the dividend payable by up to 15 per cent without referring back to creditors to reflect changes in the client's income and expenditure.

The client is allowed one payment break of up to six months and the IVA is then extended accordingly. In addition, the client may be allowed a 'payment holiday' of up to nine months if, because of an emergency item of expenditure or other unforeseen reduction in income, s/he is unable to make her/his full contributions or anything at all. The IVA is extended accordingly.

The supervisor can extend the IVA for up to six months without the agreement of creditors if the client has failed to disclose income.

Many IVAs provide that, if the client defaults, the arrangement automatically comes to an end and/or the supervisor may make the client bankrupt. The standard terms state that, if the client's contributions fall more than three months in arrears (unless this has been agreed) or s/he has failed to comply with any of her/his other obligations under the IVA, the supervisor should give the client up to three months to remedy or explain any default. If the client fails to do this, the supervisor must either issue a certificate of termination bringing the arrangement to an end or refer the matter to the creditors within 28 days to:

- vary the terms of the IVA; *or*
- bring the arrangement to an end by issuing a certificate of termination; *or*
- make the client bankrupt.

Advantages and disadvantages

Advantages
- The client avoids the stigma or publicity that is attached to bankruptcy.
- Debts included in the IVA are partially written off, no further interest or charges are added and any enforcement action by those creditors ceases.
- The client is not forced to sell her/his home.
- IVAs are flexible and can be drawn up to meet the client's situation. For instance, clients can propose stepped repayment arrangements, and assets are not automatically lost if the creditors agree – eg, because, overall, they will be better off than in bankruptcy.
- Creditors should receive higher payments than they would in a bankruptcy.
- Unsecured creditors who vote against the IVA are still bound by it.
- The client is not subject to the restrictions imposed in bankruptcy and so can still be a company director without the court's permission, and may find it easier to obtain credit for a business than s/he would following bankruptcy.
- The client could be in a profession that means s/he could lose her/his job in the event of bankruptcy – eg, accountancy or the legal professions.
- An IVA is time limited and does not involve any investigation of the client's affairs (although the client does have to confirm that s/he has not entered into any 'antecedent transactions' – see p495).

Disadvantages
- The client must have two or more unsecured creditors and unsecured debts of at least £8,000 for an IVA to be a viable option.
- If the IVA fails, the debts plus any interest or charges which have accrued become payable in full.
- The client is generally required to make higher payments over a longer period than in a bankruptcy.
- The costs of an IVA are relatively high and may have to be paid in advance (although it should be possible to find an insolvency practitioner who does not require upfront fees).
- A significant proportion of the instalments paid into an IVA goes to pay the insolvency practitioner's fees and, if the IVA fails, the client may find that s/he

has made substantial payments but has made little or no repayment to creditors.

- Assets are at risk if the creditors do not agree to exclude them.
- The client may still be made bankrupt if the IVA fails and the costs of the unsuccessful IVA are added to the debts.
- The client is closely monitored by the supervisor during the period of the IVA and must report any changes of circumstances.
- The client's proposal must be realistic and sustainable over the term of the IVA because, if her/his circumstances change, the IVA may fail if the supervisor cannot persuade the creditors to agree to a new arrangement.
- IVAs are a matter of public record and future applications for credit could be affected.

Applying for an individual voluntary arrangement

The first step is to find an insolvency practitioner prepared to act for the client. Many advice agencies have referral arrangements with insolvency practitioners and can arrange an initial free consultation. If you have no contacts, use gov.uk/find-an-insolvency-practitioner to find an insolvency practitioner in your area. Avoid companies which say they can refer clients to an insolvency practitioner in return for a fee.

Insolvency practitioners are required by their regulators to make sure that the client is given an explanation of all the options available, the advantages and disadvantages of each and the likely costs of each so that the debt solution best suited to her/his circumstances can be identified. This explanation should be confirmed to the client in writing.[14]

The insolvency practitioner's fees are agreed as part of the IVA. Most insolvency practitioners do not charge upfront fees, but are paid on an ongoing basis from the payments made into the IVA and before the creditors are paid.

The client should take as much information on her/his financial affairs as possible to the insolvency practitioner, including details of debts, assets, income and expenditure.

The proposal

The insolvency practitioner draws up a 'proposal' for the client's creditors. S/he has a duty to ensure a fair balance between the interests of the client and the creditors. In the proposal, the client makes a repayment offer to the creditors.

The proposal must be accepted by creditors owed 75 per cent or more of the total amount of the client's debts. However, only the debts of the creditors who actually vote are counted (see p460). For example, if the client has total debts to creditors of £20,000, but only £10,000 worth of creditors vote, the proposal can be approved, provided at least £7,500 worth of creditors vote in favour.

To gain acceptance, a proposal should contain a more attractive financial offer than the creditors could expect to receive in a bankruptcy. This means paying a higher dividend to creditors, and the proposal sets out how the client intends to achieve this. It is an offence for a client to make any false representations or to act (or fail to act) in a fraudulent manner with the intention of having an IVA proposal approved.[15]

If both members of a couple want to enter into IVAs covering debts in their sole and joint names, they cannot make a joint proposal. They could make separate proposals that involve a joint repayment arrangement, containing sole and joint debts based on one financial statement and involving only one set of fees (which is therefore cheaper than two unrelated IVAs). However, in order to obtain approval of their IVAs, each proposal must be considered separately and each member of the couple must obtain the required majority of her/his own creditors in favour.

What the proposal must include

The proposal must include:

- details of the proposed arrangements, including why an IVA is the appropriate solution and likely to be accepted by creditors. IVAs do not usually provide for the client's debts in full. They normally provide for her/his available income and the proceeds of the sale of any assets to be distributed to creditors on a pro rata basis, with the balances being written off – ie, a composition;
- the anticipated level of the client's income during the period of the IVA;
- details of all assets (and their estimated value) and of any assets available from third parties, such as relatives or friends;
- details of any charges on property in favour of creditors and of any assets that the client proposes to exclude from the IVA. It is usual to make some arrangement for realising the client's share in any equity in the family home and, if this provision is included in the IVA, the client should be aware of its significance;
- details of the client's debts and of any guarantees given for them by third parties. **Note:** the approval of an IVA does not prevent creditors from recovering their debt from any guarantor(s) and a guarantor can only claim a dividend in the IVA once the debt has been paid off in full;
- the proposed duration of the IVA and the arrangements for paying creditors, including the estimated amounts of payments and frequency. IVAs do not normally last longer than five or six years;
- details of the supervisor, and of the fees to be paid to the nominee and the supervisor;
- whether the client has previously made any IVA proposal in the previous 24 months and, if so, whether:
  - that proposal was approved and the IVA has been completed; *or*
  - that proposal was rejected or the IVA was terminated and, if so, how that proposal differs from the present one.

Note: student loans cannot be included in an IVA. Similarly, a student loan cannot be included as part of the client's income for the purposes of an IVA.[16] Child support arrears cannot be included in an IVA.[17]

It is usual for IVAs to contain provisions for any 'windfall' payments (eg, assets received by the client during the term of the IVA) to be taken into account. Protocol-compliant IVAs (see p454) also make specific provisions to deal with receipt of redundancy payments. It is also usual to include specific proposals about any beneficial interest the client may have in the family home.

In the case of a protocol-compliant IVA, the proposal should also contain details of any other previous attempts to deal with the client's financial problems and the reasons why these were unsuccessful. The IVA provider should give the client advice and information on the advantages and disadvantages of all available debt solutions (including bankruptcy). The proposal may contain details of any recommendations made to the client and the reasons s/he has decided to propose an IVA.

Note: an experienced insolvency practitioner will be aware of the proposals that are likely to be acceptable to creditors and the court, and will ensure that the proposal complies with the requirements of the Insolvency Act. The insolvency practitioner is required to endorse the notice of the proposal to indicate that s/he is prepared to act and will not do so unless s/he is satisfied that the proposal is viable.

After the proposal is made

Once the insolvency practitioner has signed the proposal, s/he becomes the client's 'nominee'.

Once the proposal is made, the client must prepare a statement of affairs, containing details of the matters contained in the proposal.

Within 14 days, the nominee must submit a report to the client's creditors stating in her/his opinion:

- whether the proposed IVA has a reasonable prospect of being approved and implemented;
- whether a meeting of the client's creditors should be held to consider the proposal.

At the same time, the nominee should also submit:[18]

- her/his comments on the client's proposal;
- a copy of the proposal;
- a copy of the statement of affairs;
- a copy of the endorsed notice of proposal of the nominee's agreement to act;
- where applicable, a statement that no application is to be made for an interim order (see p460).

Interim orders

Until the IVA is approved, the client is vulnerable to enforcement action by creditors. To avoid this, once the insolvency practitioner has become the nominee, the client can apply to the court for an 'interim order'.[19] If an interim order is granted:[20]

- a creditor cannot attempt to make the client bankrupt;
- a landlord cannot repossess the client's property without permission of the court;
- court proceedings or other enforcement action (including taking control of goods) cannot start or continue against the client or her/his property without the court's permission.

The application is made to the court for the insolvency district in which the client resides.[21] It must be accompanied by a witness statement and a copy of the notice of the proposal endorsed with the nominee's consent to act. A court fee of £280 is payable. Remission may be available (see p290).

It is no longer compulsory for a client to apply for an interim order and so s/he can put forward her/his proposal for an IVA without applying for one. However, the client is vulnerable to any enforcement action by a creditor until the IVA is agreed – eg, if a creditor has applied for a charging order, the client will need to apply for the consideration of the final order to be adjourned so that the debt can be included in the IVA.

Applications for interim orders are rare.

Note: see p461 if the client or a member of her/his family is at risk of violence and does not want details of her/his address to be entered on the Individual Insolvency Register.

The creditors' decision

Since April 2017, a meeting of all the client's creditors is not required.[22] However, there will be a meeting if one is requested by:

- 10 per cent in value of the creditors; *or*
- 10 per cent of the total number of creditors; *or*
- 10 individual creditors.

Creditors are asked to make decisions by a variety of means, including by correspondence, electronic voting and virtual meetings. The creditors consider the proposal and vote on it. The proposal can be amended by the creditors, but the client must consent to any modifications.

The proposal must be approved by 75 per cent or more of the creditors (in value of debts owed to them) who vote on it. Some smaller creditors do not vote. Certain creditors, such as banks, always vote and, as they also tend to be the largest creditors, any proposal is unlikely to be approved unless these creditors agree. The practice of some banks of referring all proposals they receive to a voting house (which recommends an acceptance or refusal) means that they can influence the content of the proposal and its eventual outcome, even if as individual creditors they would not be in a position to block the IVA.

The nominee may discuss the proposal with creditors beforehand to obtain agreement.

The creditors cannot approve a proposal that would affect the rights of a preferential creditor in bankruptcy (such as arrears of wages owed to employees of the client) or the rights of secured creditors (such as a mortgage lender) without their consent.[23] Unless the IVA specifically excludes a secured lender's right to enforce its security, it may still be able to do so even if it has agreed to being included in the IVA.[24]

If the proposal is approved, it takes effect immediately and is binding on every creditor entitled to vote. Creditors who did not receive notice of the meeting are still entitled to be paid in accordance with the terms of the IVA and the client must make payments to them as well as to the creditors who were notified.[25]

Usually, the creditors also approve the nominee's appointment and s/he becomes the 'supervisor' of the IVA.

After the meeting

The outcome of the meeting, virtual or otherwise, must be reported to the creditors within four business days or, if an interim order is made, as soon as possible after the report is filed in court.

Within 14 days of the date of the meeting, the supervisor must send details of the IVA and of the client to the Secretary of State to enter on the Bankruptcy and Insolvency Register. The register comprises two parts: the Individual Insolvency Register, containing details of bankruptcies, IVAs and debt relief orders, and the Bankruptcy and Debt Relief Restrictions Register, which contains details of restriction orders and undertakings.

Clients at risk of violence

If disclosure of the client's current address could lead to violence against her/him or a member of her/his family who normally lives with her/him, a court may order that:[26]

- details of the client's address be withheld from any court file;
- the client's details entered on the Individual Insolvency Register must not include details of her/his current address;
- if a post-bankruptcy IVA is made which results in the bankruptcy order being annulled (see p498), any notice permitting this must not include details of the client's address.

An application to withhold an address if someone is at risk of violence can be made by the client, the nominee/supervisor, the official receiver or the Secretary of State, but in practice, is likely to be made by the client. The application can be made as soon as the nominee agrees to act in relation to an IVA proposal which may be preferable for the client as s/he then has certainty that her/his address will not be advertised.[27] The application can also be made after the IVA is approved.[28] Form 1AA should be completed and must be accompanied by a witness statement containing sufficient evidence to support the application. The nominee/ supervisor must be named as the respondent to the application and the client should obtain her/his written consent to the application and attach it to Form 1AA. The court fee is £50 (£160 if the court decides there needs to be a hearing). Remission of the fee is available although advisers report that some courts are not charging the fee even where the client does not strictly qualify for remission because of the nature of the application (see p290).

Challenging an individual voluntary arrangement

The client, or any creditor, can appeal to the court against the IVA within 28 days of the creditors' meeting on the grounds that:
- there were irregularities in the way the meeting was held – eg, the proposal contained misleading or inaccurate information; *or*
- the arrangement unfairly prejudiced the rights of a creditor – eg, if the meeting approved a proposal to include a debt which is not provable in bankruptcy, such as a magistrates' court fine, thus preventing the creditor from taking action to recover full payment.

Because an IVA is an agreement between the client and her/his creditors, in theory any debt can be included (apart from secured creditors who can only be included if they specifically agree, child support arrears and student loans). However, in the case of other debts which cannot be proved in bankruptcy and/or are still payable by the client after discharge from bankruptcy (see p497), it may be necessary to replicate their treatment in bankruptcy in order to avoid creditors successfully challenging the approval of an IVA in which they find themselves unwilling participants. This can be done either by agreeing to exclude them altogether and leaving them to be paid outside the IVA or by including them with their agreement.

If a creditor challenges an IVA and the court considers the challenge is justified, it may:[29]
- revoke (or suspend) the IVA; *or*
- direct that a fresh creditors' meeting be held to consider a new agreement or reconsider the existing agreement (and renew any interim order).

Completing the individual voluntary arrangement

The insolvency practitioner's role as supervisor of the IVA is to implement it and ensure the client carries out her/his side of the arrangement as agreed, seeking guidance from the court, if necessary.

The supervisor arranges the sale of any assets that need to be sold, and collects the payments due from the client and distributes them to the creditors.

Most IVAs contain 'windfall' clauses, which require the client to account to the supervisor for any lump sums such as an inheritance to which s/he becomes entitled during the IVA. **Note:** payment protection insurance refunds are treated as an asset in the IVA rather than a windfall and so are regarded as having always been part of the IVA. Protocol-compliant IVAs are drawn up in such a way that the supervisor can claim any refund received by the client, including after the IVA has been completed. If the windfall or payment protection insurance refund is sufficient to enable the debts and fees to be paid in full, the arrangement may allow for statutory interest to be payable (currently 8 per cent). **Note:** creditors may be willing to forego statutory interest and a variation can be requested for this.

If the client's circumstances change, s/he should be advised to contact the supervisor immediately, as it may be possible for the original agreement to be varied. This depends on the terms of the IVA: any well drawn-up IVA will contain such a power, and it is a standard term of a protocol-compliant IVA.

The supervisor may be able to extend the period of the IVA to enable the client to complete the payments. IVAs often make provision for such eventualities, either by giving the supervisor a degree of discretion and/or by making specific provision for variation or extension of the IVA. Protocol-compliant IVAs provide for both. If the IVA contains no such provisions, even though a 75 per cent majority was needed for its original approval, it is likely that all the creditors included in the IVA would have to agree to any variation.

Provided the client complies with the IVA, s/he is discharged from her/his liability to all creditors covered by it at the end of the period. The legislation makes no provision for the client to be given any formal confirmation that s/he has successfully completed the IVA – eg, a certificate. However, it is a standard term of a protocol-compliant IVA that the supervisor issues the client with a 'completion certificate' once the client has complied with the terms of the IVA. The Court of Appeal has confirmed that the effect of the completion certificate is to discharge the client from any further liability, but that the debts scheduled to the IVA are not written off. This means that, for example, where the right to claim a payment protection insurance refund is an asset of the arrangement and a refund is made after the completion of the IVA, it is payable to the creditors, not the client.[30]

Completion of the IVA does not automatically discharge any co-debtor, including the client's spouse or partner, and provision for this must be specifically included and agreed. However, unless the joint income is used to fund the IVA (or the partner/spouse has no income), creditors may challenge the IVA.

If the terms of the IVA are not complied with, the supervisor is usually able to petition for the client's bankruptcy, but under a protocol-compliant IVA (see p454) need not do so. If the supervisor decides it is not worth doing this (eg, because there are insufficient funds paid into the IVA), individual creditors may decide to do so instead. The client must then negotiate with them separately if s/he wants to avoid bankruptcy.

Complaints against insolvency practitioners and individual voluntary arrangement providers

Sometimes, a client is dissatisfied with a decision made by the insolvency practitioner or some other aspect of the IVA process – eg, if an IVA was not an appropriate solution for her/him. If the client is unhappy with the advice given by a debt management company which recommended the IVA, a complaint can be made and, if necessary, escalated to the Financial Ombudsman Service. If the client is unhappy with the actions of the insolvency practitioner, s/he should complain directly to the insolvency practitioner in the first instance. If the client is unable to resolve the complaint directly with the insolvency practitioner, s/he can make a complaint to the Insolvency Service using the online form at gov.uk/complain-about-insolvency-practitioner.

5. Bankruptcy

Who can become bankrupt

A client may become bankrupt if:
- s/he is unable to pay her/his debts and applies for her/his own bankruptcy (see p467); *or*
- a creditor is owed at least £5,000, or two or more creditors are owed a total of at least £5,000 between them, and applies to have the client made bankrupt (see p470); *or*
- s/he has defaulted on an individual voluntary arrangement (IVA) and the supervisor or a creditor included in the IVA applies for her/his bankruptcy (see p475).

A court (in the case of a creditor's petition) or the adjudicator (in the case of a client's bankruptcy application) only has jurisdiction to make a bankruptcy order if:
- the centre of the client's main interests (see p468) is in England and Wales; *or*
- the centre of the client's main interests is not in a European Union (EU) member state and the client is domiciled in England and Wales, or at any time in the previous three years s/he has been ordinarily resident or has had a place of residence in England and Wales or has carried on business in England and Wales.[31]

Note: this remains the position during the transitional period following the UK's exit from the European Union on 31 January 2020 but may change after 31 December 2020, the current date for the termination of the transitional period. See p468 for more information.

Advantages and disadvantages

Advantages

- Bankruptcy can remove the uncertainty and anxiety caused by negotiating with a large number of creditors simultaneously.
- There can be a sense of relief for the client.
- The client usually pays less than the amount owed. In cases where payments are required, there is one payment to the trustee rather than individual payments to creditors. Payments usually last for three years.
- It can be a fresh start; the process is intended to rehabilitate the client.
- Creditors must accept the situation and contact with the client should stop. Most creditors are unable to take further action against the client (see p496).
- The process is certain.
- After discharge, most types of debt are written off and can no longer be pursued by creditors (see p497).

Disadvantages

- The client will almost certainly lose any assets of value that can be sold, unless they are exempt (although even then the client may have to accept a replacement of lower value).
- If the client acquires any asset between the dates of the bankrutcy order and her/his discharge, s/he must notify the official receiver who may claim the asset (unless it is exempt).
- If there is equity in the family home (ie, it is worth more than the mortgage and any other debts secured on it), the trustee will want to realise the client's share of this. This may lead to the home being sold. However, this cannot happen if the value of the client's share (after-sale costs) does not exceed £1,000.
- If the client owns a business and employs people, or the business has a value, the employees may have to be dismissed and the business sold.
- If the client has mortgage or rent arrears, the home could be at risk because the trustee in bankruptcy may not allow payments towards the arrears to be taken into account when assessing the client's available income. Bankruptcy does not prevent a secured lender from taking possession proceedings. A landlord can also take possession proceedings on the grounds of rent arrears even though those arrears are covered by the bankruptcy. In addition, the landlord may be able to enforce a suspended possession order if further arrears accrue post-bankruptcy or even if the arrears included in the bankruptcy are not paid,

or there are grounds other than rent arrears to start possession proceedings – eg, persistent delay in paying rent. In addition, the client's tenancy agreement may contain a so-called 'insolvency clause' enabling the landlord to seek possession of the property in the event of the client's bankruptcy (or DRO). The client's tenancy agreement should always be checked for such a clause as part of advising on bankruptcy (or a DRO).

- If a client is an undischarged bankrupt or subject to a bankruptcy restrictions order or bankruptcy restrictions undertaking, s/he cannot obtain credit of £500 or more without disclosing her/his status and s/he may find it more difficult to open a bank account, even a basic one (see p483).

- The process can be expensive. A client who has been made bankrupt by a creditor or following a failed IVA and who wishes to pay off the debts in order to preserve an asset (eg, the family home) must also pay post-bankruptcy costs and these could be substantial.

- The client must allow her/his financial affairs to be scrutinised by officials who may take criminal action if irregularities are found. S/he may also become subject to a bankruptcy restrictions order or bankruptcy restrictions undertaking (see p479). However, apart from the restriction on obtaining credit, this may have no effect on her/him.

- The client may be barred from certain public offices or may be unable to practise certain professions – eg, as an accountant or solicitor.

- The client's credit rating continues to be adversely affected after discharge and this will probably make running a business or buying a home in future very difficult because the cost of credit may be higher, assuming s/he can obtain it.

- The client may feel judged and humiliated. Some clients may feel there is a stigma attached to bankruptcy and this could be reinforced in cases where a bankruptcy restrictions order or bankruptcy restrictions undertaking is made.

- The client's immigration status may be affected and so specialist immigration advice should be obtained. Sources of immigration advice available locally can be searched for at http://find-legal-advice.justice.gov.uk.

- While undischarged or subject to a bankruptcy restrictions order or bankruptcy restrictions undertaking, the client cannot be a company director without permission of the court (which may be granted on condition that the client makes payments from her/his income for the benefit of creditors). Also, s/he cannot trade under any name other than the one used at the date of the bankruptcy order without disclosing the name under which s/he went bankrupt to everyone with whom s/he does business.

- The names of people who are made bankrupt are published in the *London Gazette*, the Individual Insolvency Register (which is a public register) and may also be published in the local press. Bankruptcy restrictions orders and bankruptcy restrictions undertakings may also attract local publicity, and friends and neighbours may find out about the client's financial difficulties

and, if a bankruptcy restrictions order is made, that s/he has been found to have acted irresponsibly in relation to her/his financial affairs.
- Not all debts are written off at the end of bankruptcy – eg, social fund loans, student loans, fines, compensation orders, compensation for personal injury or death, maintenance and child support and debts incurred through fraud.
- Secured creditors are not affected by bankruptcy and can still enforce their security.
- Joint debts are not written off, as creditors can still pursue the non-bankrupt co-client. If s/he is the client's partner, the family will still be in financial difficulties unless s/he has taken separate action to resolve her/his debt problems.

If a client wants to make her/himself bankrupt

The debtor's bankruptcy application

If a client wants to make her/himself bankrupt, s/he must apply to an official of the Insolvency Service called the 'adjudicator' on the grounds that s/he is 'unable to pay her/his debts' (although it is possible to become bankrupt for only one debt which the client is unable to pay).[32] This involves completing an online application form, called the 'debtor's bankruptcy application', including details of the client's income and expenses in the format of the standard financial statement (see p56). This can be downloaded from gov.uk/guidance/debt-advisor-tools-and-information, which also includes guidance notes *Guidance for Debt Advisers*. The client can download this her/himself from https://apply-for-bankruptcy.service.gov.uk. Once the application has been created, there is no time limit within which it must be completed and submitted.

An adjudicator's fee of £130 is payable together with a deposit of £550. The total fee of £680 can be paid either online by debit, third-party credit or pre-paid cards (Insolvency Service guidance states that clients should not use their own credit cards) by logging into her/his application and quoting her/his payment reference number, or in cash at any Royal Bank of Scotland branch.[33] Payment by instalments is available for clients paying online. The minimum instalment is £5 and there is no time limit within which full payment can be made. Cash payment must be of the full amount. Cheques are not accepted. Fees being paid by charities should be paid in cash or through the Insolvency Service website at https://apply-for-bankruptcy.service.gov.uk/third-party-payment, quoting the client's payment reference number. Neither the adjudicator fee nor the deposit can be remitted.

Note: see p476 if the client or a member of her/his family is at risk of violence and does not want details of her/his address to be entered on the Individual Insolvency Register.

The centre of the client's main interests

The adjudicator can only make a bankruptcy order if:

- the centre of the client's main interests is in England and Wales; *or*
- the centre of the client's main interests is not in a EU member state and the client is domiciled in England and Wales, or at any time in the previous three years s/he has been ordinarily resident or has had a place of residence in England and Wales *or* has carried on business in England and Wales.

This remains the position during the transitional period following the UK's exit from the European Union on 31 January 2020 but may change after 31 December 2020, the current date for the termination of the transitional period.

A person's 'centre of main interests' is the address from where s/he administers her/his affairs on a regular basis (eg, her/his professional address) and where contact with her/him can be made.

The centre of main interests of a client who operates a business or carries out a professional activity is presumed to be in England and Wales if her/his main place of business is situated in England and Wales, unless s/he has moved her/his place of business to England and Wales within the three months prior to applying for bankruptcy. In the case of other clients, their centre of main interests is presumed to be in England and Wales if their usual residence is in England and Wales, unless they have moved to England and Wales within the six months prior applying for bankruptcy. If the client administers her/his financial affairs on a regular basis in a EU state (other than Denmark), s/he must usually apply for bankruptcy there.[34]

A client who has an 'establishment' in England or Wales, but whose centre of main interests is in a EU state (other than Denmark) cannot apply for her/his own bankruptcy in England or Wales unless under the rules of that other state s/he would be unable to apply for a bankruptcy order in that state. An 'establishment' is the place where the client carries out, or has carried out, her/his business in the three months before applying for the bankruptcy order. Business carried out on an occasional basis does not count, nor does merely having a property, such as a holiday home, in England or Wales.[35]

If a client has previously lived abroad, s/he may not be able to apply for a bankruptcy order in England and Wales. Specialist advice should be obtained.

The adjudication process

Once the client's application has been created and s/he has her/his reference number, there is no time limit within which the application must be completed and submitted to the adjudicator. There are nine sections to the application.

- **Section 1** asks for personal details, including details of the client's household and whether s/he is a homeowner or a tenant.
- **Section 2** requests details of the client's current and recent employment history over the previous 12 months, including any self-employment within

the previous three years and whether the client has been a director of a limited company within the previous 12 months.

- **Section 3** asks for details of the client's bank account(s) including details of any joint account holder and the current balance(s). Any bank or building society accounts which the client has may be frozen and so any money needed to cover everyday living expenses should be withdrawn before the application for a bankruptcy order is made.

- **Section 4** asks for details of assets and their valuation, specifically vehicles, pensions and insurance policies and cash. This section also asks for details of any assets sold, transferred or given away in the previous five years and details of any solicitor, accountant, bookkeeper or financial adviser who has acted for the client in the previous five years.

- **Section 6** asks for details of the client's income and expenditure. This section follows the structure and terminology of the standard financial statement, including the savings element (see p56).

- **Section 7** asks for details of any current legal claims in which the client is involved, including whether the client has been legally separated, divorced or had a civil partnership dissolved in the last five years. Any current magistrates' court proceedings should also be included.

- **Section 8** asks for information about the client's debt history, including reasons for being unable to pay her/his debts, previous insolvency options used and also details of any preferences made by the client in the last two years (see p496).

- **Section 9** is the submission page and asks the client to confirm various matters, including whether the debts listed have been included in another bankruptcy application, whether the client has received debt advice, whether the client has applied for a person at risk of violence order (see p476) and whether the client is aware of anyone else petitioning to make her/him bankrupt.

Once the application has been completed and the application fee paid in full, it can be submitted directly to the adjudicator. A copy should be printed and given to the client. Once submitted, the application cannot be withdrawn. The adjudicator carries out certain verification checks, including of the electoral register, the Individual Insolvency Register and the client's Equifax credit file, and may ask the client to supply further information in support of the application.

The adjudicator has 28 days in which to determine the application, although the majority are determined within 48 hours. The adjudicator must determine whether the following requirments are met:

- the adjudicator has jurisdiction to determine the application;[36]
- the client is unable to pay her/his debts. When determining this, the adjudicator takes into account any undrawn pension pot which the client could access. If a client could clear all her/his debts using this, s/he should get specialist advice;

- no bankruptcy petition is pending against the client; *and*
- no bankruptcy order has been made in respect of any of the debts included in the application.

If s/he is satisfied that the above requirements are met, the adjudicator *must* make a bankruptcy order. If s/he is not satisfied that the above requirements are met, s/he must refuse to make a bankruptcy order. The adjudicator cannot adjourn an application or refer the client for debt advice or for an IVA or a DRO.

If the application is refused, the client is informed of the reason(s) and that s/he can ask for a review by email within 14 days. If a request is received, the adjudicator reconsiders the application within 21 days but may not consider any new information. Following the review, the adjudicator either makes a bankruptcy order or confirms the decision to refuse the client's application.

If the application is again refused, the client is informed of the reason(s). S/he can appeal within 28 days to the the the court for the insolvency district where the client resides. A template form of appeal is available at gov.uk/guidance/debt-advisor-tools-and-information.[37] The court fee is £95. Remission may be available (see p290). Unlike the adjudicator, the court can consider new information.[38]

If a bankruptcy order is made, the adjudicator uploads a copy of the order to the client's online account and allocates the case to an official receiver on a rota basis who may not be based in the client's local Insolvency Service office. However, should the official receiver require to interview the client in person, the case will be transferred to the client's local office.

If a creditor wants to make a client bankrupt

Creditors who are considering making a client bankrupt must bear in mind that the process is intended to benefit all creditors, not just themselves. They could bear all the costs of obtaining a bankruptcy order only to find that other creditors receive more, and they could even end up with nothing at all if the client has no income or assets.

A creditor can apply for someone to be made bankrupt if it is owed at least £5,000, which the person 'appears' unable to pay. Two or more creditors who are owed a total of at least £5,000 between them can petition together. The creditor must satisfy the court that the client is unable to pay by either:[39]

- serving a 'statutory demand' on the client with which s/he fails to comply (see p471); *or*
- unsuccessfully attempting to enforce a court judgment against the client. Where the creditor has used enforcement agents (bailiffs), they must have made serious attempts to enter the client's home and take control of goods. It is not enough that the bailiff has merely visited the client's home and been unable to gain access.[40]

If the enforcement method chosen by the creditor produces no or insufficient money, the creditor can petition for bankruptcy.[41] However, it seems that councils issuing bankruptcy petitions for unpaid council tax not only have to show that the debt is due and unpaid, but also that the client's bankrupt will serve some useful purpose.[42]

Serving a statutory demand

Serving a statutory demand is the most common method used by creditors to satisfy the court of the client's inability to pay. A statutory demand is a document demanding that the client either pays the debt in full or 'compounds for the debt' – ie, comes to an agreement with the creditor, usually by an acceptable offer of payment by instalments, or offers security for the debt which is acceptable to the creditor.

There is no prescribed form, although HM Courts and Tribunals Service (HMCTS) has produced a number of templates which can be found at gov.uk/government/collections/court-and-tribunal-forms.

The statutory demand does not have to be issued by the court or even seen by it at this stage. The creditor cannot claim the costs of issuing the statutory demand unless and until the court actually awards them.[43]

A creditor does not need a judgment in order to be able to serve a statutory demand for the debt. However, without a judgment, the creditor might find that the client is able to challenge the existence of the debt. A creditor who has a judgment is not required to attempt to enforce it; the creditor can serve a statutory demand instead.

If the client does not comply with the statutory demand within 21 days, the creditor can ask the court to issue a creditor's petition and ask the court to make a bankruptcy order.

Challenging a statutory demand

Some creditors use statutory demands as a method of debt collection. The courts have said that this is only an abuse of process if the creditor is aware the debt is reasonably disputed.[44] The Financial Conduct Authority's predecessor, the Office of Fair Trading, discouraged the use of statutory demands unless:

- it was commercially viable; *and*
- its use was considered reasonable; *and*
- there was a realistic prospect of bankruptcy proceedings being taken.

Circumstances in which the use of a statutory demand might not be considered reasonable, therefore, include if:

- the debt is known to be 'statute-barred' (see p292); *or*
- a valid dispute remains unresolved; *or*
- the client has provided adequate proof that s/he is unemployed and has no assets; *or*

- the client has demonstrated that there is no (or minimal) equity in her/his home, that s/he has no other assets and has made a reasonable payment offer; *or*
- bankruptcy would result in the client losing her/his job and s/he has provided a financial statement and made a reasonable offer of payment.

Responding to a statutory demand

Although the creditor may have no intention of making the client bankrupt, statutory demands should never be ignored. On receipt of a statutory demand, the client should be advised about the consequences of bankruptcy. If s/he does not want to become bankrupt, s/he should consider:

- applying for an administration order or proposing an IVA as an alternative to bankruptcy;
- making payment(s) in a lump sum or by instalments either to clear the debt in full or reduce it below the £5,000 bankruptcy limit so that the creditor cannot ask the court to issue a bankruptcy petition;
- offering a payment in full and final settlement of the debt. This could either be in a lump sum or by instalments. The client should be prepared to demonstrate either that s/he has no assets (including if the home has no or only minimal equity) or that it would not be reasonable to expect her/him to realise them. If the debt is subject to a judgment, as well as trying to negotiate with the creditor, the client should apply to the court to vary this to enable payment by instalments, with a view to arranging this before the creditor can obtain a bankruptcy order;
- applying for a time order if the debt is regulated by the Consumer Credit Act 1974 (see p366);
- offering a voluntary charge over her/his property as security for the debt (see p229);
- applying to set aside the statutory demand within 18 days of service (see below).[45]

Setting aside a statutory demand

If the statutory demand has been 'set aside' (ie, cancelled), the creditor cannot apply for a bankruptcy order. The client can apply for the demand to be set aside:

- on the grounds that there is dispute about the money said to be owed. If the creditor has obtained a judgment, at this stage, the court does not enquire into the validity of the debt. If this is an issue, the client should be advised to consider applying to set aside (see p337) or appeal the judgment (see p294), although the client can still raise any dispute at the hearing of the petition (see p473);[46]
- on the grounds that the client has a counterclaim against the creditor, which equals or exceeds the amount of the debt (if this merely reduces the debt below the bankruptcy level of £5,000, the statutory demand cannot be set aside);[47]

- on the grounds that the creditor holds security, which equals or exceeds the amount of the debt;
- on 'other grounds' – eg, the debt is 'statute-barred' (see p292) or the demand has not been signed.[48] A statutory demand based on a judgment debt is not statute-barred even if the judgment was made more than six years ago.[49]

The application is made on Form IAA which is available at gov.uk/government/collections/court-and-tribunal-forms. It must be supported by a witness statement to which a copy of the statutory demand must be attached (if the client has it in her/his possession). If the application is made more than 18 days after the date of service of the statutory demand, the application must include a request for an extension of time with evidence explaining the delay.[50] The application is made to the court for the insolvency district where the client resides.[51] Three copies of each form must be filed. There is no court fee. If the judge considers there are no grounds for the application, s/he can dismiss it without a hearing. Otherwise, a hearing is arranged at which the district judge considers the application.

The court does not set aside a statutory demand on the grounds that the creditor has unreasonably refused an offer of payment or security, or even on the grounds that the creditor has refused to consider such an offer. However, this ground *can* be used at the hearing of the petition. Nor does the court set aside a demand on the grounds that it is for an excessive amount. In such a case, the client is supposed to pay the amount admitted to be due and only apply to set aside the amount in dispute. The court will not 'do a deal' with the client to set the statutory demand aside on condition that s/he makes a payment. The court can set aside a statutory demand for a disputed debt, provided it is satisfied there are reasonable grounds of success.

If the application to set aside the statutory demand is dismissed, the creditor is given leave to present her/his bankruptcy petition.

The creditor's petition

A creditor must present a bankruptcy petition if it wants to continue with the bankruptcy process, but this can only be done if the debt is at least £5,000. The petition must contain certain prescribed information.[52] HMCTS has produced a template, available at gov.uk/government/collections/court-and-tribunal-forms. There are different templates depending on whether the creditor is an unsatisfied judgment creditor or has served a statutory demand. The creditor must file the petition at the court, together with:

- a witness statement that the facts stated in the petition are true; *and*
- a court fee of £280; *and*
- the deposit of £990.

Responding to the petition

The petition must be served personally on the client. It is still not too late to prevent a bankruptcy order being made, but the client must give at least five business days' notice to the court and to the creditor of her/his intention to oppose the making of a bankruptcy order. The client can still raise any 'genuine triable issue' even if s/he did not apply to set aside the statutory demand, but s/he cannot put forward any matter on which the court has already ruled against her/him unless there has been a relevant change of circumstances.

Where personal service is not practicable, evidence that the following steps have been taken will usually be sufficient to justify the court making an order for an alternative method of service ('substituted service'):[53]

- a personal call at the client's residence/place of business;
- a letter referring to the call, its purposes and the date of a further call;
- an attempt to arrange an appointment for personal service through the client's solicitor, if any.

The bankruptcy hearing

The hearing is before a district judge. At the hearing, the creditor must prove that s/he has delivered the petition to the client (and, if relevant, that the statutory demand has been brought to the client's attention) and file a certificate that the debt is still outstanding.

If the client has paid the debt (excluding any creditor's costs) in full before the hearing date, it is dismissed, but the district judge may still order the client to pay the creditor's costs.[54] If not paid, these will have to be the subject of fresh enforcement proceedings, which could be bankruptcy proceedings if the order is for £5,000 or more. Some creditors claim that, unless the client has paid their costs before the date of the bankruptcy hearing, a bankruptcy order will still be made. This is not correct and should be challenged. The court cannot make a bankruptcy order unless it is satisfied that 'the debt in respect of which the petition has been presented' has neither been paid, nor secured, nor compounded for.[55] Because the creditor's costs are not a 'debt in respect of which the petition was presented', the client cannot be made bankrupt on this petition for those costs.[56]

If the client has reduced the debt (excluding any creditor's costs) to less than £5,000 in between the issue of the petition and the hearing date, the court has the discretion to make a bankruptcy order, taking into account the client's previous conduct.[57] Even if the petition is dismissed, the client could be ordered to pay the creditor's costs.

The court has discretion to refuse to make a bankruptcy order in certain circumstances, including if execution on a judgment has been stayed (including an instalment order for payment), or that an appeal is pending against the judgment or order, or if the creditor has unreasonably refused to accept an offer to pay the debt by instalments, a reduced sum in full and final settlement, or an offer to secure the debt.[58] The High Court has pointed out that a creditor can take into account any history of default, partial payments and broken promises on the part of the client and to consider its own interests, and that 'acting reasonably' is not the same as 'acting justly, fairly or kindly'.[59]

A client can be referred to an approved intermediary (see p512) for a DRO to be made instead of a bankruptcy order but *only* with the consent of the creditor who issued the bankruptcy petition. As the effect of a DRO is that no further payments are made to creditors, it is unlikely a creditor would agree to one unless it was satisfied that the client had no assets and no income and would never be in a position to make payments towards the debt.

It is not unusual for the parties to reach an agreement about payment of the debt, and the hearing of the petition can be adjourned, but repeated adjournments should not be allowed unless there is a reasonable prospect of payment within a reasonable time.[60] If an agreement is reached and the creditor does not want to proceed with the bankruptcy, the petition can be dismissed with the permission of the court. The client may, however, find her/himself being ordered to pay the creditor's costs if the court decides that it was reasonable for the creditor to resort to bankruptcy to recover the debt.

If a supervisor of an individual voluntary arrangement wants to make a client bankrupt

If the client is subject to an IVA, the supervisor can petition for a bankruptcy order on the grounds that:[61]

- the arrangement was based on false or misleading information supplied by the client; *or*
- the client has failed to comply with the terms of the IVA.

In the case of protocol-compliant IVAs (see p454), the supervisor must obtain the creditors' approval before taking this step.

After a bankruptcy order is made

The role of the official receiver

When a bankruptcy order is made (either because the client has applied for her/his own bankruptcy or a creditor or supervisor has successfully petitioned), the court notifies the official receiver who automatically becomes the client's trustee in bankruptcy ('the trustee'). The official receiver contacts the client soon after the bankruptcy order is made, which could be on the same day.

The official receiver's main role (as official receiver as opposed to trustee) is to:

- investigate the client's conduct and financial affairs, and report to the court; *and*
- obtain control of the client's property and any relevant documents.

The client may be asked to complete a questionnaire and it will be helpful for the client to have a copy of her/his bankruptcy application to refer to.

A client is usually offered a telephone interview with an examiner (a member of the official receiver's staff). The examiner checks the client's answers and asks questions to obtain any additional information. In other cases, the client must attend an interview at the official receiver's office.

The client is required to co-operate with the official receiver. S/he must give up possession of her/his assets (with some exceptions) and hand over any papers that are reasonably required.[62] Failure to do so could result in her/his discharge being delayed. The official receiver can arrange for her/him to be examined in public by the court about her/his financial affairs and the causes of her/his bankruptcy, although this rarely happens if the client has co-operated fully with the official receiver. The official receiver can arrange for her/his mail to be redirected, if appropriate.[63] In appropriate cases, the official receiver can apply to the court to impound the client's passport to prevent her/him from leaving the country.

It is an offence for the client to do anything that intentionally conceals information or property from the official receiver or trustee, or to deliberately mislead the official receiver or trustee about property which s/he had either before or after the bankruptcy. Criminal charges can be brought against a client, leading to a fine and/or imprisonment. However, if the client can show that there was no intention to mislead or defraud, this counts as a valid defence.

It is also an offence for the client to leave (or attempt to leave) with assets of £1,000 or more which should have been given up to the official receiver.[64]

The official receiver has a duty to investigate every bankruptcy unless s/he considers such investigation unnecessary.[65] Any criminal offences revealed must be reported to the authorities. S/he usually visits any business premises, and may also visit the client's home, but this is rare. If the official receiver does visit, s/he may remove any items of value which are not exempt (see p483).

Clients at risk of violence

The official receiver registers the bankruptcy at the Land Registry, advertises it in the *London Gazette,* inserts details in the Individual Insolvency Register (see p461) and may advertise it in one local paper.[66]

If the disclosure of the client's current address or whereabouts could lead to violence against her/him or other members of the family who live with her/him, the court may order that:[67]

- details of the client's address be removed from any court file;
- the client's details entered in the bankruptcy order must not include details of her/his current address;
- the details of the client's current address given to the Land Registry be removed. This is important if the client still owns an interest in a previous address through which s/he might be traced;
- any gazetted or advertised notice must not include details of the client's current address;

- the details entered on the Individual Insolvency Register must not include details of the client's current address (or that such details must be removed).

The application not to have details disclosed can be made by either the client, the official receiver, the trustee in bankruptcy or the Secretary of State, but is most likely to be made by the client. The application is made to the court for the insolvency district in which the client resides.[68] The Insolvency Service has produced a number of template application forms, available from gov.uk/government/collections/insolvency-service-forms-england-and-wales.

The application can be made either after the bankruptcy order is made or before the bankruptcy order is applied for, which may be preferable for the client as the client then has certainty that her/his address will not be advertised. The official receiver must be named as respondent to the application on the form if the application is made after the date of the bankruptcy order. The application must be accompanied by a witness statement containing sufficient evidence to support the application. The client must also either produce a copy of the official receiver's consent to the application (if relevant) or, if this is not available, the witness statement must indicate whether consent has been refused.[69] **Note:** the legislation does not give the adjudicator any role in this process if the application is made before the date of the bakruptcy order.

The court fee is £280. Remission may be available (see p290) although advisers report that some courts are not charging the fee even where the client does not strictly qualify for remission because of the nature of the application.

The application should comply with paragraph 16 of the *Practice Direction – Insolvency Proceedings* available at justice.gov.uk/courts/procedure-rules/civil/rules/insolvency_p6.

The application is referred to the district judge, who considers whether s/he can deal with it without a hearing. A hearing should be ordered if:[70]

- the court is considering refusing the application; *or*
- the respondent's consent is not attached to the application; *or*
- the district judge considers that a hearing is appropriate for some other reason.

The role of the trustee

The trustee is responsible for handling the client's affairs and getting as much money as possible for her/his creditors. The trustee gathers and sells all the property previously owned by the client and distributes the proceeds among her/his creditors.

On the making of the bankruptcy order, the official receiver automatically becomes the trustee (although in appropriate cases, the official receiver can decide to appoint an insolvency practitioner as trustee), and the client's estate 'vests' in the official receiver as trustee – ie, ownership of all her/his property (except certain items – see p483) passes automatically to the trustee. The client cannot sell anything, but if arrangements have already been made to sell something (eg, the home), the trustee almost certainly approves this, provided it is a proper commercial transaction. The proceeds are then used towards satisfying the expenses of the bankruptcy and the creditors.

Property that vests in the trustee includes property in countries outside England and Wales, although there may be practical issues for a trustee in taking control of and realising this.

The client may have property which cannot be disposed of and/or is subject to obligations which would involve expenditure to the detriment of the estate, and hence the creditors – eg, a business lease. The trustee can dispose of such 'onerous property'.[71]

If the client attempts to give away or sell her/his property after the bankruptcy petition is issued but before the property passes to the trustee, this transfer is void. The court can confirm a sale but, in the absence of this, the property still forms part of the client's estate and can be recovered and sold by the trustee.

The sale of jointly owned property requires the consent of the co-owner or a court order. If a client acquires any property before discharge, s/he must inform the trustee within 21 days. The trustee then has 42 days (during which the client must not dispose of the property) in which to claim the property for the estate.[72]

How money is paid

The trustee contacts the client's creditors and invites them to 'prove' their debts – ie, submit claims (creditors owed less than £1,000 do not need to do this). Creditors must, therefore, contact the trustee and demonstrate that they are owed the money.[73] The court can prevent any creditor who is entitled to submit a claim from attempting to recover the debt in any other way.[74]

The only debts that cannot be proved are:[75]
- fines;
- maintenance orders (other than orders for payment of a lump sum or costs) and child support;
- debts from certain orders of the criminal courts, including confiscation orders and the criminal courts charge;
- student loans; *and*
- social fund loans (if the bankruptcy petition was presented on or after 19 March 2012).

Note: secured loans do not need to be proved because the rights of a secured creditor are not affected by bankruptcy. Secured creditors can, theoretically, remove their security and ask to be included in the list of creditors. If they force a sale of the home, they can be included as creditors for any unsecured balance due.

The trustee works out the value of the debts and any assets. S/he lists the following, which are priorities to be paid first:[76]

- bankruptcy expenses (including amounts due to the trustee, the court or the Insolvency Service, which charges for the official receiver's services). This often leaves creditors with nothing;
- expenses of, for instance, estate agents to realise assets;
- contributions owed by the client to occupational pension schemes;
- arrears of wages to employees for four months before the bankruptcy (up to a maximum of £800 each);
- from 6 April 2020, payments due to HM Revenue and Customs (HMRC) collected by the client on her/his behalf – ie, VAT, PAYE and national insurance contributions;
- other ('ordinary') creditors. These creditors receive nothing until the other 'preferential' creditors have been paid in full. If paid at all, these creditors generally receive only a percentage of the value of their debt;
- deferred debts – eg, debts due to the client's spouse;
- interest on any of the above from the date of the bankruptcy order.

Any surplus is returned to the client.

Restrictions during bankruptcy

Pre-discharge restrictions

A client who is an undischarged bankrupt cannot:

- obtain credit of £500 or more from a creditor without disclosing her/his status as an undischarged bankrupt;
- engage in business in a name other than the one under which s/he was made bankrupt without disclosing that name to people with whom s/he has business dealings;
- act as a director of, or directly or indirectly promote, form or manage a limited company without permission from the court;
- act as an insolvency practitioner or an intermediary for DROs (see p512);
- act as a charity trustee (unless s/he is a director of the charity and has obtained permission from the court).

A breach of any of the above is a criminal offence, but the restrictions usually end on discharge (see p497).

Post-discharge restrictions: bankruptcy restrictions orders and undertakings

People who are regarded as 'culpable' because they have acted recklessly, irresponsibly or dishonestly may be subject to an extended period of restrictions through a bankruptcy restrictions order or a bankruptcy restrictions undertaking.

Bankruptcy restrictions orders and undertakings are most commonly made because the client has:

- contributed to the bankruptcy by neglecting her/his business affairs (usually, tax affairs);
- entered into transactions either to prefer friends or relatives ahead of other creditors or at an undervalue;
- incurred debts with no reasonable prospect of being able to repay them.

If a court makes an order or the client agrees to an undertaking, the above restrictions on obtaining credit, engaging in business, involvement in a limited company and acting as an insolvency practitioner continue for a minimum of two years and a maximum of 15 years from the date the order or undertaking was made.[77]

In addition, being subject to a bankruptcy restrictions order or bankruptcy restrictions undertaking may affect a client's employment or her/his ability to hold certain offices – eg, s/he cannot serve as an MP, local councillor, a member of the Welsh government or Northern Ireland Assembly, or sit in the House of Lords, or act as a school governor.[78]

According to the Insolvency Service, the vast majority of bankruptcy restrictions orders or undertakings are for two to five years. Most are bankruptcy restrictions undertakings given by clients (see p482).

Example

A 61-year-old man was declared bankrupt in June 2015 on a petition presented by HMRC. Shortly after HMRC started the bankruptcy proceedings against him, he withdrew his entire pension of more than £30,000. When interviewed by the official receiver, he said he had £10,500 remaining which he said was being 'looked after' by a family member. He was instructed to pay the money to the official receiver, but he failed to do so and instead instructed his family member to keep the money on his behalf. After court proceedings, only £4,500 was recovered. In September 2016, a 10-year bankruptcy restrictions order was made.

A breach of a bankruptcy restrictions order or bankruptcy restrictions undertaking is punishable as a bankruptcy offence.[79]

A register of bankruptcy restrictions orders, interim restrictions orders and bankruptcy restrictions undertakings can be inspected at no charge in the Individual Insolvency Register at gov.uk/search-bankruptcy-insolvency-register. It may also be in the client's local press. The client can apply to the court to order that details of her/his current address be withheld on the grounds that there is a reasonable risk that disclosure could lead to violence towards her/him or a member of her/his family who lives with her/him (see p476).

Bankruptcy restrictions orders

When considering an application for a bankruptcy restrictions order, the court can take any behaviour of the client into account, but must specifically take into account whether s/he has:[80]

- failed to keep records which account for a loss of property by her/him, or by a business carried out by her/him. The loss must have occurred in the period beginning two years before the petition and ending with the date of the application;
- failed to produce records of this kind on demand by the official receiver or the trustee;
- entered into a transaction at an 'undervalue' (see p495);
- made an excessive pension contribution;
- failed to supply goods or services which were wholly or partly paid for and which gave rise to a provable claim in the bankruptcy;
- traded before the start of the bankruptcy when s/he knew, or ought to have known, that s/he would be unable to pay her/his debts;
- incurred before the start of the bankruptcy a debt which s/he did not reasonably expect to be able to pay (this appears to include increasing the amount of debt on a credit card);
- failed to account satisfactorily for a loss of property or for an insufficiency of property to meet bankruptcy debts;
- carried on any gambling, 'rash and hazardous speculation' or 'unreasonable extravagance', which may have contributed to or increased the extent of the bankruptcy or which took place between the presentation of the petition and the start of the bankruptcy;
- neglected her/his business affairs, which may have contributed to or increased the extent of the bankruptcy;
- been fraudulent;
- failed to co-operate with the official receiver or the trustee.

Note: only conduct on or after 1 April 2004 can be taken into account.[81]

The conduct that the court is required to take into account addresses behaviour by consumers as well as by traders, and behaviour both before and after the bankruptcy order. If no period is specified, it is likely that the more serious the misconduct, the longer the period over which it is taken into account.

The court must also consider whether the client was an undischarged bankrupt at some time during the six years ending with the date of the bankruptcy to which the application relates. However, it is understood that the existence of two bankruptcies is not considered to be misconduct in itself, but it allows the court to put misconduct in context.

An application for a bankruptcy restrictions order must be made by the Insolvency Service or by the official receiver and within one year from the date of the bankruptcy order. It must be supported by a report and evidence.

The hearing date must be fixed for no earlier than eight weeks from when the court decides on the venue. Since the application is made as part of the bankruptcy proceedings, rather than in separate proceedings, the hearing takes place in the client's local bankruptcy court. The hearing is in public.

The application must be served on the client not more than 14 days after the application was filed at court, together with:

- at least six weeks' notice of the hearing;
- a copy of the report;
- any further evidence in support of the application in the form of a witness statement; *and*
- an acknowledgement of service.

The client must:

- return the acknowledgement of service to the court, indicating whether or not s/he intends to contest the application, not more than 14 days after the application is served. Otherwise, s/he may attend the hearing, but cannot take part unless the court agrees;
- file at court any evidence opposing the application which s/he wishes the court to consider, within 28 days of being served with the application and supporting evidence;
- serve copies on the Insolvency Service/official receiver within a further three business days.

Within 14 days, the Insolvency Service/official receiver must file at court any further evidence and serve a copy on the client as soon as reasonably practicable.

The court may make a bankruptcy restrictions order regardless of whether or not the client attends the hearing or submitted any evidence.[82]

In order to avoid the need for court proceedings, the Insolvency Service/official receiver may instead accept the client's offer of a **bankruptcy restrictions undertaking** – ie, the client agrees to accept the bankruptcy restrictions. An undertaking has the same effect (including the consequences of a breach) as an order from the court from the date it is accepted.

The official receiver informs the client of the period s/he thinks the court will make the bankruptcy restrictions order for and the client must decide:

- whether or not s/he accepts there is a case for a restrictions order; *and*
- whether or not s/he wants to avoid going to court and risk a longer period.

Interim bankruptcy restrictions orders

Because the client must be given at least six weeks' notice of an application for a bankruptcy restrictions order and an application must be made within 12 months of the bankruptcy order (unless the court gives leave to apply later), there may be a gap of several months between the date of discharge and the date of hearing when the client is not subject to any restrictions. In this situation, the Insolvency Service/official receiver can apply to the court to make an interim order.

An interim bankruptcy restrictions order has the same effect as a full order and lasts from when it is made until:[83]

- the application for the bankruptcy restrictions order is determined; *or*
- the Insolvency Service/official receiver accepts a bankruptcy undertaking; *or*
- it is revoked.

Only two business days' notice of the application is required and the hearing is in public. The Insolvency Service/official receiver must file a report and evidence.[84]

How bankruptcy can affect a client

Protected goods

Some goods do not pass to the trustee and cannot be taken. These include:[85]

- tools of the trade, including a vehicle, which are necessary and used personally by the client in her/his 'employment, business or vocation'.[86] Stock is not protected, which usually means that the business must close down if it depends on stock;[87]
- household equipment necessary to the basic domestic needs of the client and her/his family. This should include all clothing, bedding, furniture and household equipment and provisions, except perhaps particularly valuable items (eg, antiques and works of art) or luxury goods with a high resale value – eg, expensive TVs.

If the value of any protected goods exceeds the cost of a 'reasonable replacement', the trustee can require them to be sold for the benefit of the creditors. In practice, this rarely happens but, if it does, the trustee must provide the funds to enable the client to replace the goods.

The trustee can visit a bankrupted person and remove goods or close a business. In practice, however, this is mainly done in cases of businesses or domestic properties in which there may be valuable goods. If the client acquires any asset which is not protected in the period between the bankruptcy order and her/his discharge, the trustee may claim it within 42 days of becoming aware of it.[88]

Bank accounts

The client's bank account may be frozen.

There is no legal reason why a client cannot have a bank account. All the major banks and building societies offer fee-free basic bank accounts to undischarged bankrupts, as these are considered suitable because they involve no credit facilities. Post Office card accounts are not suitable for all clients. There is, however, the possibility of being able to open a credit union current account, although not all credit unions offer these.

If the client's bank honours a cheque after the date of the bankruptcy order, the transaction is not void if either:[89]

- the bank did not have notice of the bankruptcy order before honouring the cheque; *or*
- it is not reasonably practicable to recover the payment from the person to whom it was made.

Utility companies

Although utility companies cannot insist on payment of pre-bankruptcy arrears as a condition of continuing to supply services, they may require a security deposit or insist on installing a pre-payment meter. It may, therefore, be necessary to transfer the accounts to a non-bankrupt member of the family. The policies of a client's utility suppliers should be checked before petitioning for bankruptcy so that the client knows what to expect.

Motor vehicles

The trustee must deal with any motor vehicle owned by, or in the possession of, the client as a matter of urgency, as it is a potential source of liability for the trustee.

If the client claims the vehicle is exempt, s/he must communicate this either during the interview with the official receiver or in correspondence, setting out the reasons(s).[90]

If a car is essential for her/his employment (eg, if there is no reasonable alternative transport to and from work), the client may be allowed to keep it, although if it is particularly valuable the trustee may order it to be sold to allow a cheaper replacement to be bought. If a car is accepted as exempt and is worth less than £2,000, it will not be sold. A maximum of £1,000 is usually allowed for a replacement vehicle, but could be more depending on the circumstances.

Insolvency Service guidance on the definition of 'employment, business or vocation' includes bankrupt clients who are informal, full-time carers of a disabled friend or relative (including a child) who use a vehicle in connection with that role. Although receipt by the client of carer's allowance is not essential, the Insolvency Service regards this as indicative that the client is pursuing a 'vocation' as a carer.

Previous Insolvency Service guidance said that a motor vehicle could never be regarded as an item of 'household equipment'. Current guidance now allows the official receiver to consider claims from bankrupt clients that a motor vehicle is necessary to meet basic domestic needs. 'Necessary' in this context means that no reasonably practical alternative exists to meet a genuine need. The test of necessity is not satisfied just because using a motor vehicle is more convenient than the alternatives, unless these are likely to be more expensive.

According to the Insolvency Service, the people most likely to come within the guidance are clients who are disabled and need a vehicle for mobility. The vehicle must be used personally by the client. If s/he requires assistance to travel in the vehicle, it does not fall within the guidance.

Clients who live in urban areas with reasonable public transport are unlikely to be able to benefit from the 'domestic needs' guidance (other than because of disability). However, even in an urban area, it might be possible to claim exemption on the grounds that a vehicle is necessary to transport children to school if there is no public transport alternative or if children attend different schools and it is not possible to get all children to school on time without use of a car or the distance to travel would make walking or cycling an impractical alternative. Although using a taxi rather than owning a vehicle might be considered reasonable for undertaking a weekly shop, the cost of daily or frequent journeys by taxi might be considered excessive when set against the costs of maintaining and running a car.

If a motor vehicle is not exempt, a member of the client's family or a friend may be able to negotiate to buy the vehicle to enable the client to retain it.

If the vehicle is subject to a hire purchase or conditional sale agreement, the finance company may be able to terminate the agreement and repossess the vehicle if the client becomes bankrupt. The trustee always contacts the finance company and so the finance company may seek to repossess it. In other cases where there is insufficient equity to make it worth the trustee's while selling the vehicle her/himself, s/he may invite the finance company to repossess the vehicle.

A mobile home that is not parked on a protected site (ie, a site registered by the local authority), but under an informal arrangement, is more likely to be regarded as a 'motor vehicle' than a 'house' even if it is the client's permanent residence. The question of whether it is exempt under the 'domestic needs' category therefore arises. A mobile home parked on a registered site with a degree of immobility may be regarded as a 'house'. A caravan used as a permanent residence with a degree of site permanence and immobility is also likely to be regarded as a house.

Income payments orders

If the client has at least £20 a month available income, the trustee may suggest a weekly or monthly payment to the trustee from her/his earnings via an income payments agreement. If payment is not agreed, s/he can apply to the court for an income payments order. This must be applied for before the client is discharged and the order must specify the period for which it is to last. This must be no longer than three years from the date of the order. These payments are ordered to be paid to the trustee and can be required of either the client or employer under an attachment of earnings order.[91] Either the client or the trustee can apply to vary the order (both before and after discharge).

The court must leave sufficient money for the reasonable domestic needs of the client and her/his family. An income payments order should not be sought if the client's only source of income is state benefits (which includes all forms of income supplement and support provided by central or local government, including war disability pensions) but, where the client has benefit and non-benefit income, the trustee can consider an income payments agreement or order. However, this will only be up to the amount of the non-benefit income even if the client has more than this amount in surplus income. Arrears of benefit paid to the client after the date of the bankruptcy order should not be claimed where the client's only income is state benefits.

If the client has an income payments agreement (see p487) and there is a change of circumstances, the trustee can still apply to the court for an income payments order rather than vary the agreement.[92]

Calculating the order

The trustee should calculate the client's available income by deducting from her/his actual income the household outgoings, less contributions from other members of the household towards these (either actual or assumed). For the treatment of pensions, both those in payment and those which the client could choose to access, see p487.

Note: the official receiver calculates the client's surplus income using the standard financial statement. Although the official receiver also uses the standard financial statement spending guidelines when assessing a client's reasonable domestic needs (see p56), the client's expenditure can still be queried even if it is within the spending guidelines as these are viewed as a benchmark and are not treated as an allowance. If a standard financial statement has been completed by the client with a debt adviser within the six months prior to the date of the bankruptcy order, the official receiver may use that standard financial statement to establish the client's surplus income and so a copy of that standard financial statement should be sent to the official receiver.

Bankruptcy does not affect a landlord's right to recover her/his property from a defaulting tenant and a bankruptcy order can still be made and suspended post-bankruptcy order, but not on payment of rent arrears.[93] Any suspended possession order in force at the date of the bankruptcy order could be the subject of an application to vary the suspended possession order. Guidance states the official receiver should not make a client homeless and and should not take any steps to interfere with the payments being made.

Generally, no allowance should be made for payments relating to bankruptcy debts, but where the rent plus arrears is considered reasonable for rent, an allowance should be made. Where the payments appear excessive, the client should be asked to attempt to vary the arrangement with the landlord, which is something you could assist the client to do.

Any surplus is available income and, provided this is at least £20 a month, the order is assessed at the full amount of the surplus income. If the client has both benefit and non-benefit income, the amount of the order should not exceed the non-benefit income figure – ie, payment should not come out of the client's benefit income.

The client may apply to the court to vary an income payments order or for it to cease before its specified date.[94]

Income payments agreements

The client can come to an agreement with the trustee about a payment arrangement and incorporate it into a written income payments agreement without applying to the court. An income payments agreement is enforceable as a court order just like an income payments order and can be varied by either:[95]

- a further written agreement; *or*
- the court, on the application of either the client or the trustee.

In the first instance, clients are offered an income payments agreement. If the client thinks that the household expenditure claimed is reasonable but the trustee does not agree, the client does not have to sign an agreement, but can leave the decision to be made by the court. Provided the client has not acted unreasonably, it is unlikely that the court will order the client to pay any costs of the application even if the court ultimately agrees with the trustee.

Pensions

If the bankruptcy order was made on a petition presented to the court before 29 May 2000, personal pensions are part of the bankrupt client's estate and must be paid to the trustee by the pension company. This is the case whether the payments fall due during or after the bankruptcy.[96]

Trustees may argue that occupational pensions pass to them as a matter of course, and so the position should be checked with the pension company. However, although an occupational pension cannot normally be claimed directly by the trustee, the income could be made the subject of an income payments order (see p485).[97]

If the bankruptcy order was made on a petition presented on or after 29 May 2000, all pension rights under 'approved pensions', including personal pension plans, are excluded from the client's estate (ie, they do not vest in the trustee). However, if the client becomes entitled to the pension (including a lump sum) during the period of the bankruptcy, it could be made the subject of an income payments order.[98]

'Approved pensions' are any occupational or personal pension schemes registered with, and approved by, HMRC for tax purposes. They include retirement annuity contracts and stakeholder schemes. It can be assumed a pension is approved if one or more of the following applies:

- the pension is an occupational pension scheme with nationally based organisations;

- the policy is operated by a major pension provder/insurer – eg, Scottish Widows and Legal and General;
- the annual pension statement received by the client states that the scheme or policy is registered for tax purposes under section 153 of the Finance Act 2004.

If none of the above establishes whether or not the pension is approved, the client should be advised to contact her/his pension provider to confirm if the pension is registered with for tax purposes under section 153 of the Finance Act 2004.

The Court of Appeal has held that, if a client is entitled to receive payments (usually a tax-free lump sum and/or monthly pension payments) from a scheme and can do so merely by asking for it, the pension does not fall within the definition of 'income' for the purposes of an income payments agreement or income payments order, unless the client had elected to draw that pension.[99]

Note: if a client has a pension fund from which s/he could draw on, this may affect whether s/he is considered to be unable to pay her/his debts for the purposes of an application for a bankruptcy order or a DRO. If the client can access her/his pension pot and this would clear her/his debts in full, specialist advice should be sought.

Insurance policies

Ordinary term life assurance policies or endowment policies are not exempt and usually pass to the trustee in the normal way. If a third party is named as beneficiary under the policy, the policy does not normally vest in the trustee. However, if a client was originally the beneficiary under the policy but transferred the right to receive the proceeds to a third party as a gift or without getting the cash value of the policy in return from the beneficiary, this is a transaction at an undervalue (see p495) and the trustee may be able to seek to overturn it and claim the benefit of the policy.

Student loans

Student loans made by the Student Loans Company or Student Finance Wales, whether made before or after the bankruptcy order, are not part of the client's estate and so cannot be included in an income payments order or agreement.

The Student Loans Company or Student Finance Wales does not carry out credit checks as part of its loan application process. Any clients who are considering bankruptcy and intend to become students can be reassured that their bankruptcy will not affect any student loan application.

Owner-occupied homes

If the client has a beneficial interest in her/his home, that interest automatically becomes the property of the trustee in bankruptcy on her/his appointment. The trustee protects her/his interest by registering either a notice or a restriction at the Land Registry.

If the home is solely owned by the client, the legal title vests in the trustee and the client's interest, which passes to the trustee, is the whole value of the property. If it is jointly owned, only the client's share vests in the trustee, but this does not prevent the trustee from taking action to realise that share. The trustee can realise the value of that interest (eg, by selling it to a joint owner or forcing a sale of the property) and this does not have to be done before the client's discharge from the bankruptcy. There is also the possibility that the client may have a beneficial interest in another property (eg, a former home – see p492) which the trustee might seek to realise.

The trustee has a three-year 'use it or lose it' period from the date of the bankruptcy order to deal with the client's interest in a property which, at the date of the bankruptcy order, is her/his sole or principal residence, or that of her/his spouse/civil partner or former spouse/civil partner. Otherwise, the interest no longer forms part of the client's estate and transfers back to her/him. It is, therefore, no longer available to pay the client's bankruptcy debts. However, this does not happen if, during the three-year period, the trustee:[100]

- realises the interest – eg, by selling her/his interest to the client's partner or some other third party. The full sale price must be paid to the trustee before the end of the three-year period; *or*
- applies for an order for sale or possession; *or*
- applies for a charging order in respect of the client's interest; *or*
- comes to an agreement with the client about payment for her/his interest.

If the case has reached the two years and three months point and the client's interest in the property is worth at least £5,000 and it is not possible to attract an insolvency practitioner to act as trustee (generally, the value of the client's interest is less than £25,000) or sell the client's interest to a willing purchaser, the official receiver should consider applying for a charging order. If the trustee decides to take this option, the charging order is for the value of the client's interest in the property at the date of the charging order (including a deduction for the estimated costs of sale from the value of the property – currently 3 per cent) plus simple interest at the prescribed rate (currently 8 per cent a year) plus the costs of the application. However, where the value of the client's interest is more than the total amount owed to the client's unsecured creditors, the charging order is limited to the amount owed to unsecured creditors at the date of the application plus other amounts payable out of the client's estate such as the bankruptcy expenses and statutory interest plus simple interest at 8 per cent a year and the costs of the application as above. Therefore, the client retains the benefit of any subsequent increase in the value of the property.

Note: the three-year period can be extended by the court for such longer period as it thinks just and reasonable, taking into account all the circumstances of the case.[101]

Low-value exemption

If the value of the client's interest is less than the prescribed amount (£1,000), the court *must* dismiss any application by the trustee in bankruptcy for:[102]
- an order for the sale or possession of the property; *or*
- a charging order on the client's interest in the property.

In valuing the client's interest in the property, the court must disregard:[103]
- any loans secured by mortgage or other charge against the property;
- any other third-party interest – eg, a joint owner's share of equity;
- the reasonable costs of sale, currently estimated at 3 per cent of the gross value of the property.

Realising a client's interest in the property

If another person shares ownership of the home and there is sufficient equity, the trustee tries to sell the client's share to that person. S/he must obtain an up-to-date valuation at her/his own expense, plus details of any outstanding mortgages or secured loans, and pay her/his own legal costs (£211 under the low-costs conveyancing scheme).

If the property is jointly owned, the trustee requires the value of the client's share (usually, 50 per cent of the equity) plus her/his legal costs, but allows some discount to take account of the savings made from not having to take possession of the property and conduct the sale. Any increase in the value of the property as a result of expenditure by either party after the date of bankruptcy should also be taken into account.

If the property is solely owned by the client, s/he may be able to buy back her/his interest from the trustee. If there is equity, the purchase money will have to come from a third party – eg, a friend or relative. Mortgage lenders are reluctant to agree to people buying an interest in property, unless they take some responsibility for the mortgage. In the case of jointly owned properties, the co-owner(s) is already responsible for the mortgage. In the case of solely owned properties, however, before agreeing to transfer her/his interest to a partner or third party, the trustee must ensure that arrangements have been made between the proposed transferee and the mortgage lender(s) for future payment of the mortgage.

The trustee usually seeks a court order for the sale of a jointly owned property if the non-bankrupt owner will not or cannot purchase the beneficial interest and there is sufficient equity. If there is a spouse or civil partner and/or children, their interests should be considered, but after a year these are overridden by the interests of the creditors unless the circumstances of the case are exceptional (see p492). This means that, in practice, homes are not sold for at least a year after the bankruptcy.

In deciding whether to order the sale of a house, the court must consider:[104]
- the creditors' interests;

- whether the spouse/civil partner contributed to the bankruptcy;
- the needs and resources of the children and spouse/civil partner;
- other relevant circumstances (but not the client's needs).

If at the date of the of the bankruptcy order there is negative, or the equity is less than £1,000, the case is reviewed as soon as possible.
- If the property is in negative equity and the official receiver considers there is no reasonable prospect of a surplus becoming available from the property within the three-year period, s/he should consider taking steps to transfer her/his interest back to the client (known as early revesting).
- If the client's share in the property is valued at less than £1,000 and the official receiver considers there is no reasonable prospect of a surplus in excess of £5,000 being available within the three-year period, s/he should consider early revesting.
- If the value of the client's share in the property is worth more than £1,000, the trustee invites the client or a third party, such as a co-owner or family member, to buy back the client's share.
- If it is not possible to sell the client's share in this way and there is not sufficient equity to attract an insolvency practitioner to act as trustee, the official receiver as trustee should transfer the property to the Long Term Asset Distribution Team (LTADT). LTADT will review the position at the two year and three month stage. Where the value of the client's interest is greater than £25,000 and there is no willing purchaser, the official receiver should seek the appointment of an insolvency practitioner to act as trustee.

If a charging order is obtained on the client's share in the property, the trustee is not subject to any limitation period for seeking an order for its sale – ie, s/he can apply to the court for an order for sale at any time in the future.[105]

If a property is sold, the trustee sends any money due to the co-owner or other person with an interest in the property on completion. It is important that people who share a home with a bankrupt person are independently advised by a solicitor, particularly if they have made direct contributions to the purchase price, because they may have an equitable or beneficial interest in the property for which they should be paid, even if they are not an 'owner' on the deeds.

Endowment policies
If there is an endowment policy in place to pay a mortgage, it may vest in the trustee who can arrange for it to be sold. The policy is treated as an asset and taken into account when valuing the client's interest in the property if:[106]
- it has been formally assigned to the mortgage lender;
- the policy document is held by the mortgage lender;
- the mortgage lender's interest in the policy for repayment of the mortgage has been noted with the insurance company; *or*

- there has been a specific agreement between the mortgage lender and the client that the policy will be used to pay the mortgage.

This may result in there being sufficient equity for the trustee to realise the property.

Exceptional circumstances

If an application is made for the sale of a property which is, or has been, the home of the client or the client's spouse or civil partner or former spouse or civil partner, and it is more than one year after the date the client's estate vested in the trustee, the court must assume that the interests of the bankrupt's creditors outweigh all other considerations, unless the circumstances of the case are exceptional. Family hardship caused by the bankruptcy is not considered an exceptional circumstance.[107]

Exceptional circumstances

Before the Human Rights Act came into force on 2 October 2000, caselaw established that circumstances could only be exceptional if they were unusual. However, the decision in *Pickard and another v Constable* contains a useful summary of the current interpretation of the test.[108]

1. Even if there are exceptional circumstances, the court can still make an order for sale.

2. Exceptional circumstances relate to the personal circumstances of one of the joint owners and/or their children, such as a physical or mental health condition but not those of the bankrupt client.

3. Exceptional circumstances cannot be categorised or defined. The court must make a judgment after considering all the circumstances.

4. To be exceptional, the circumstances must be 'outside the normal melancholy consequences of debt and improvidence' or 'compelling reasons not found in the ordinary run of cases'.

5. It is not an exceptional circumstance that the spouse and children are faced with eviction because there are insufficient funds to provide them with a comparable home.

6. Creditors have an interest in an order for sale being made even if the whole of the net proceeds go towards the expenses of the bankruptcy and they receive nothing. This situation is not an exceptional circumstance.

The court can postpone the sale of the property to a future date which it considers 'fair and reasonable' – eg, until the ill/disabled person has either died or chosen to leave the property or for a set period of time. 'Exceptional circumstances' should be supported by verifiable evidence.[109]

Beneficial interest

If the property is in the sole name of the bankrupt client, her/his (non-bankrupt) partner may be able to argue that s/he has a beneficial interest in the property – ie, s/he is entitled to a share of the proceeds of sale. If this can be established, the trustee cannot claim against the partner's share of the property. So, if the property is sold, the partner is entitled to be paid the value of her/his share and does not have to make any payments to the trustee.[110]

On the other hand, if the property is in the sole name of a non-bankrupt partner, the trustee may try to establish that the client has a beneficial interest. The trustee also investigates whether the property was put into the partner's sole name in circumstances that could amount to a transaction at an undervalue (see p495).

Beneficial interest is generally assumed to be the same as the legal interest and so, unless the legal documentation of the property states otherwise, the starting position is that the client has a 50 per cent beneficial interest in jointly owned property (if there is one joint owner). If the property is solely owned by the client, it is assumed that s/he has a 100 per cent beneficial interest.

If a family home has been bought in the joint names of a cohabiting couple who are both responsible for any mortgage but there is no express declaration of their beneficial interests, they are both equally entitled to the beneficial interest unless there is evidence that they had a different intention at the time they acquired the home or they later intended that their respective shares would change.

The onus of proving that the parties intended their beneficial interests to be different from their legal interests is on the party seeking to establish this.

If the property is in the sole name of one of the partners, joint beneficial ownership is not presumed. The trustee looks at whether it was intended for the non-owner party to have any beneficial interest in the property and, if so, what it is. There must have been a common intention for one of them (the legal owner) to hold the property on behalf of the both of them. If there is no evidence of discussions leading to an actual written or verbal agreement, arrangement or understanding between the parties, a common intention to share the property can be inferred from their conduct.

The other partner may have acquired a beneficial interest either by:
- a court order; *or*
- an agreement, either at the time the property was acquired, or subsequently, that s/he should have a beneficial interest – eg, by making substantial contributions to the household expenditure; *or*
- a common intention to hold the beneficial interests in the property in shares other than in the same proportion as the legal title and by materially altering their position – ie, acting to her/his detriment; *or*
- making a direct financial contribution to the purchase of the property – eg, by:
  - paying some or all of the deposit; *or*
  - making contributions to the mortgage repayments; *or*
  - paying for substantial improvements to the property.

Living in someone else's house (even as a partner, civil partner or spouse), sharing household expenses and fulfilling ordinary domestic duties, such as looking after the property and bringing up children, do not of themselves entitle someone to a beneficial interest unless these can be seen as making an indirect contribution towards the mortgage repayments.

If the other partner has a beneficial interest, the value of her/his share depends on the value of her/his contributions, any agreement between the parties and any inferences that can be drawn from their conduct.[111]

Even if the trustee is dealing with a jointly owned property, there may be a question about whether one of the parties has more than a 50 per cent share in it. If the property is held in joint names as joint tenants, this is considered to be conclusive evidence of an intention to hold the property in equal shares, unless one of the parties can demonstrate fraud or that there has been a mistake in the conveyance, or that there has been undue influence (see p151) or a declaration of the beneficial interests. If Land Registry Form TR1 has been used (compulsory for all transfers since 1 April 2008), there is a specific declaration of trust tick box. The House of Lords has said that, if there is no declaration of trust, the presumption should be that properties in joint names are owned in equal shares rather than in proportion to the parties' financial contributions to its purchase.[112] If a party seeks to argue otherwise, the onus is on her/him, and unequal contributions to the purchase are not sufficient on their own.

Specialist advice should always be sought if you have grounds for believing that either the client or someone else may have a beneficial interest in a property which could be the subject of a claim by the trustee.[113]

Rented accommodation

Assured, protected and secure tenancies do not automatically vest in the trustee, but can be claimed within the 42-day period, if they have a value, but this is relatively rare.

Pre-bankruptcy rent arrears are a 'bankruptcy debt', which cannot be excluded from the bankruptcy and are provable like any other bankruptcy debt.

The landlord has no 'remedy' in respect of that debt.[114]

However, the Court of Appeal has ruled that:[115]

- a landlord can take possession action based on rent arrears which are a bankruptcy debt and any possession proceedings pending at the date of the bankruptcy order should not be put on hold ('stayed');
- at the hearing, the court can make an outright possession order or suspend the possession order, but cannot suspend the order on condition the client pays the arrears; nor can the court give judgment for those arrears;
- any suspended possession order should be made on condition that the client pays the current rent (plus any costs awarded after the date of the bankruptcy order).

In the case of assured and secure tenancies, the landlord can use some other breach of the tenancy not involving rent arrears as a ground for possession. For example, if the tenancy contains a forfeiture clause on bankruptcy, the landlord could obtain a possession order on that ground.[116] Before the client petitions for bankruptcy, the tenancy agreement should be checked for such a clause and enquiries made about the landlord's policy on enforcing it.

If there is a suspended possession order already in force when the client goes bankrupt, the landlord could still apply for a warrant if the order was not complied with.

The safest course of action for a tenant with rent arrears or subject to a possession order who is considering bankruptcy is to make enquiries about the policies and practice of the landlord and the local district judge. If rent arrears have accrued after the date of the bankruptcy order, whether or not there are pre-bankruptcy rent arrears, there are no restrictions on the landlord taking proceedings.[117]

Transactions at an undervalue and preferences

Transactions at an undervalue

A transaction is said to be made at an 'undervalue' if it involves an exchange of property for less than its market value. This may be innocent, with everyone acting in good faith, but if a trustee considers that such a transaction has reduced the assets available to creditors, s/he can apply to the court, which can set the transaction aside (see below).[118]

Examples of transactions at an undervalue include:
- gifts (including money);
- working or selling goods for nothing or for an amount significantly less than the value of the labour or goods;
- giving security over assets for no benefit in return;
- transferring an interest in property to a former partner (but not under a court order on divorce unless there are exceptional circumstances, such as fraud[119]).

The trustee can apply to the court to have a transaction at an undervalue set aside if:[120]
- it was carried out in the five years before the date of the bankruptcy order; *and*
- the client was insolvent at the time or the transaction led to her/his insolvency; *or*
- the transaction was carried out within two years of the date of the bankruptcy order, regardless of whether or not the client was insolvent.

If the transaction was with an 'associate' (eg, partner, relative, partner's relative, business partner or employer), it is assumed that the client was insolvent at the time of the transaction, unless it can be shown otherwise.

Note: there are different rules on transactions at an undervalue for DROs (see p504).

Preferences

If the client has done something before the bankruptcy which has put a creditor or a guarantor of one of her/his debts into a better position than they would have been in the event of the client's bankruptcy (eg, giving a voluntary charge or paying them in full), this may be a 'preference' if other creditors have not been similarly treated. In addition:

- the client must have intended putting them in a better position; *and*
- the client must have been insolvent at the time or the action must have led to her/his insolvency;[121] *and*
- the payment must have been made in the six months before the date of the bankruptcy order (or in the two years before if the preference was to an 'associate' – eg, spouse, partner or other relative, business partner or employer/ employee).[122]

If the preference was to an 'associate', it is assumed that the client intended putting her/him in a better position, unless it can be shown otherwise. An exception to this is if the person is only an associate because s/he is an employee. Paragraph 31.4A.37 of the *Technical Manual* gives some examples of the types of transactions which may be viewed as preferences by the official receiver.

Note: there are different rules on preferences for DROs (see p504).

Action the trustee can take

In the case of either transactions at an undervalue or preferences, the court can restore the position of the parties by, for example, requiring any property or money to be returned to the trustee, ordering the release of any security, or ordering that the trustee be paid for goods or services. Protection is given to third parties who act in good faith without notice of the circumstances.[123] Previously, the trustee did not take court action for less than £5,000, but there is no longer any minimum amount.

Enforcement action by creditors

Once a bankruptcy petition has been presented to the court or a bankruptcy order has been made, the court can order any existing court or enforcement action being taken by creditors to be discontinued in order to preserve the client's property for the benefit of all of her/his creditors. Once the bankruptcy order has been made, anyone who is a creditor of the client with a debt provable in the bankruptcy (see p478):[124]

- is prohibited from exercising any remedy against the property or person of the client in order to enforce payment of the debt; *and*
- is not allowed to start any new court action against the client before her/his discharge without the permission of the court – eg, for a post-bankruptcy debt.[125]

If the client has a benefit overpayment, the Department for Work and Pensions (DWP) cannot carry on making deductions from benefit to recover it. It must 'prove' for the debt in the usual way (see p478).[126] **Note:** whether or not an overpayment is a bankruptcy debt depends on when it occurred, not on when the decision to recover was made.[127]

For the position on rent arrears, see p494, and on secured creditors, see below.

Discharge

Clients made bankrupt on or after 1 October 2013 are discharged after 12 months, unless the official receiver or the trustee in bankruptcy applies to the court and the court is satisfied that the client is failing, or has failed, to comply with her/his obligations under the Insolvency Act 1986 – eg, she has not co-operated with the official receiver/trustee. In this case, the court may order the suspension of the 12-month period either for a set time or until a specified condition is fulfilled.[128]

Effect of discharge

After discharge, the court issues a certificate to the client on request. There is a £70 fee. The client is automatically released from all her/his debts, including 'contingent debts or liabilities' (see p498) except:[129]

- to secured creditors. If the home was sold, but insufficient equity raised to pay the secured lender, this debt is no longer secured, but the unsecured part remains unenforceable provided the mortgage or secured loan was taken out before the bankruptcy, even if the home was not sold until after discharge. Any jointly liable person remains liable for the whole debt;
- student loans;[130]
- fines, including the criminal courts charge, victim surcharge and compensation orders (but the client is released from parking and other charges enforced through the Traffic Enforcement Centre);[131]
- maintenance orders and other family court orders, child support and debts from personal injury claims (although the court does have the power to release liability for these in full or in part);
- debts incurred through fraud, including benefit and tax credit overpayments;
- social fund loans if the bankruptcy petition was presented on or after 19 March 2012;
- debt arising from certain other orders of the criminal courts, including confiscation orders.

Occasionally, the trustee is still working on something (eg, the sale of a home) when discharge is granted. In this case, that asset can still be realised and distributed after discharge despite the fact that the recipients of the funds could not otherwise pursue payment.

The duties to co-operate with, and to provide information to, the official receiver and/or trustee continue after discharge for as long as it is reasonably required.[132] The Insolvency Service has set up regional trustee and liquidator units in order to deal with long-term matters.

Credit reference agencies record bankruptcies, but it is not necessarily impossible to obtain credit again after discharge.

Contingent debts and liabilities

A contingent debt or liability is 'any debt or liability to which [the client] may become subject after the commencement of the bankruptcy (including after [her/his] discharge from bankruptcy) by reason of any obligation incurred before the commencement of the bankruptcy'.[133]

Contingent debts are bankruptcy debts, even though they did not exist at the date of the bankruptcy. A common example of such a debt is a mortgage shortfall, where the obligation under the mortgage (or secured loan) existed before the date of the bankruptcy order, but the property was not sold until after the date of the bankruptcy order or even after the client's discharge, leaving a shortfall debt.

Before a Supreme Court decision on 24 July 2013, the phrase 'any obligation' was narrowly defined by the courts and the following debts had been held not to be contingent liabilities and, therefore, not bankruptcy debts:

- the outstanding balance of a client's current year's council tax liability where the local authority was not in a position to apply for a liability order because the client had failed to comply with a reminder or final notice;
- benefit or tax credit overpayments made before the date of the bankruptcy order, but where the decision to recover was not made until after the date of the bankruptcy order;
- court costs awarded after the date of the bankruptcy order in relation to proceedings that had commenced before the date of the bankruptcy order.

The above debts are now all bankruptcy debts. The DWP accepts that a benefit overpayment where the period began before the date of the bankruptcy order but ended after the date of the bankruptcy order is also a bankruptcy debt. HMRC and local authorities should also accept this for tax credits and benefits respectively.

Annulment

A bankruptcy order can be annulled (cancelled) at any time by the court if the client has either repaid the debts and bankruptcy expenses in full,[134] or has provided full security for them, or if there were insufficient grounds for making the order in the first place.[135] The client then becomes liable once again for all the bankruptcy debts. A bankruptcy order can also be annulled if a creditors' meeting has approved a proposal for an IVA (see p453).[136]

In cases involving petitions presented on or after 6 April 2010, if the bankruptcy is to be annulled on the grounds of full payment of the debts and expenses (including the trustee's remuneration and expenses), the client can apply to the court for a ruling that the trustee's remuneration charged and/or expenses incurred are excessive and should not be allowed.[137] Such an application must be made no later than five business days before the hearing of the application for annulment.

When deciding whether the debts have been paid or secured, the court can take into account a solicitor's undertaking to pay them out of funds due to be paid to the client.

The court has power to rescind a bankruptcy order if there has been a change of circumstances since the order was made and this may again benefit creditors.[138]

6. Debt relief orders

A debt relief order (DRO) gives the client a 12-month moratorium, during which time the creditors specified on the order cannot force the client to pay those debts.[139] Following the moratorium, the client is discharged from all the debts included in the order (other than those incurred fraudulently).

Although it is more than 10 years since the DRO solution was introduced, practice is continually evolving. The *DRO Toolkit* is an essential resource for both advisers and approved intermediaries and is available on AdviserNet (for Citizens Advice advisers and intermediaries) and on the Institute of Money Advisers (IMA) and Wiseradviser websites[140] (for other advisers and intermediaries). The monthly bulletins and quarterly updates published by the Shelter Specialist Debt Advice Service regularly provide information and advice about DROs and can be found in the Resources Directory of the Networking and Information Sharing Project section of the IMA website (i-m-a.org.uk). In 2019, the Insolvency Service published the *DRO A–Z Guidance* which sets out technical matters and will, hopefully, be updated regularly. The Insolvency Service also publishes *Intermediary Guidance Notes* which contains information about the roles of the Insolvency Service and approved intermediaries as well as guiidance on completing the DRO application form (at the time of writing, version 17.0 is due to be published). These can be obtained from your agency's competent authority.

Debt relief orders and bankruptcy

DROs have a lot in common with bankruptcy, but there are significant differences.
- The cost to the client of applying for a DRO is considerably less than the cost of applying for a bankruptcy order.
- The client can apply for a bankruptcy order on her/his own, but needs the assistance of an intermediary in order to apply for a DRO.
- Creditors can object to a DRO being made, but cannot object to a bankruptcy order being made on a debtor's bankruptcy application.
- There is no maximum debt level for a bankruptcy order and no preconditions on income or assets.

- If the client has entered into a transaction at an undervalue or given a preference within the prescribed period, this may be set aside by the trustee in bankruptcy, but could prevent the client from obtaining a DRO. On the other hand, there is no provision for the official receiver to set aside such a transaction if a DRO has been made.
- There is no provision for revoking a bankruptcy order on the grounds that the client's financial circumstances have improved prior to discharge.
- Assets do not vest in the official receiver, and so a DRO does not involve any realisation of assets or require clients to make any payments to their creditors.
- Contingent liabilities cannot be included in a DRO.
- A DRO only releases the client from the debts included in the application. Bankruptcy releases the client from her/his 'bankruptcy debts' (see p497), whether or not they are listed in the statement of affairs.

Who can apply for a debt relief order

A client who is unable to pay her/his debts and who meets the eligibility conditions (see p503) can apply for an order in respect of her/his 'qualifying debts'.

Qualifying debts

Any secured debt is not a qualifying debt. Otherwise, any debt for an identifiable sum which is not excluded qualifies for a DRO. **'Excluded debts'** are:

- fines (including compensation, but not the criminal courts charge nor, according to the Insolvency Service DRO Team, costs orders) and confiscation orders. This does not include costs of enforcement – eg, bailiffs' charges;
- child support assessments and maintenance orders;
- student loans;
- damages for personal injury or death arising out of negligence, nuisance or breach of contractual, statutory or other duty;
- social fund loans.

Issues with particular types of debt

Business debts

Business debts are 'qualifying debts' for the purposes of a DRO, provided the client is personally jointly or severally liable for them.[141]

Contingent liabilities

Unlike in bankruptcy, contingent liabilities are not qualifying debts because they do not fit the definition of a qualifying debt as being 'a liquidated sum payable either immediately or at some certain future time'.[142]

Credit union debts

Credit union debts are considered as secured debts to the extent of the value of the client's shares. If the debt exceeds their value, the excess is a should be included in the DRO as an unsecured debt and the balance as a secured debt. The value of the client's shares should not be included as assets if these have been assigned to the credit union. The full amount of the debt counts towards the debt limit (see p504).

Foreign debts

Debts owed to overseas creditors should be included. Although the client is protected from enforcement action by the creditor in England and Wales, the DRO may not be recognised in other countries, including European Union states and Scotland (which has its own legal system). The client may therefore face enforcement action in countries outside England and Wales, even after s/he has been released from liability for the debt in England and Wales.

Fraudulent debts

Unless otherwise specifically excluded (see p500), debts incurred through fraud are qualifying debts which count towards the DRO debt limit (see p504) and which must, therefore, be included in the application. The client is protected from enforcement action from her/his creditors during the moratorium period (see p499), but is not released from liability for such debts at the end of this period (see p497). This means that benefit providers cannot make any deductions from benefit during the moratorium period even if the overpayment is fraudulent.

Guarantors

If a client has a DRO, this does not release any guarantor (or any other person liable for the debt, such as a co-debtor) from her/his liability.

If the client is guarantor for someone else's debt, her/his possible future liability under the guarantee is not a qualifying debt. There must be an actual liability to pay an amount, either immediately or at some certain time in the future. This means that, until the borrower defaults, the client has no liability. If the borrower has defaulted, check the terms of the guarantee to see at what point the guarantor becomes liable and whether s/he is liable for the outstanding balance owed to the creditor or just the missed payments.

Hire purchase agreements

If the agreement is in arrears, the amount due and unpaid must be included in the DRO. This includes the outstanding balance if this is due and payable under the terms of the agreement – eg, if it has been called in by the finance company.

If the agreement is in arrears but the outstanding balance is not due and payable, the arrears must be included in the DRO. The client can decide not to include the outstanding balance, if it is not due and payable (see above), but, it will still count towards the £20,000 total debt limit (see p504). Check the terms of the agreement and any notices the client has received from the finance company to see whether the agreement contains any terms under which it could be terminated if the client enters into any formal insolvency procedure.

If there are no arrears, the client can choose not to include the debt in the application and s/he remains liable for the remaining payments. The outstanding balance does not count towards the £20,000 total debt limit (see p504) provided:

- the agreement is not in arrears; *and*
- the repayments are made by a third party where these are more than £50 a month.

Motor Insurers' Bureau claims

The official receiver says that any third-party claim which has either been settled by the Motor Insurers' Bureau or is the subject of a judgment against the client is a liquidated sum. Any compensation for personal injury or death included in the claim is an excluded debt (see p500). Any other types of claim (eg, for loss of earnings) are qualifying debts and should be included in the DRO (subject to the £20,000 total debt limit – see p504).

Advance payments of universal credit

Advance payments of universal credit (UC) are not loans. Before making an advance payment, the client is given notice of her/his liability to repay it, usually by deductions from subsequent payments of benefit. The Insolvency Service has confirmed that any advance payment which has not been fully recovered at the date of the application for a DRO is a qualifying debt.

If deductions from benefit incorrectly continue after the date the DRO is made and these are subsequently repaid to the client, the official receiver does not regard these repayments as an increase in income or property for the purposes of revoking the order (see p510).

Penalty charges

There are numerous penalty charge notices. Some of these are qualifying debts, some are excluded debts and others may be the subject of prosecution and a fine in the magistrates' court as the potential consequences of non-payment. It is impossible to produce a comprehensive list of all the different penalty charges, but if the client discloses that s/he has an unpaid penalty charge, you should apply the following rules.[143]

- If the consequence of non-payment is that the penalty charge is recoverable as a civil debt or can be registered for enforcement as if it were payable under a county court judgment, the penalty charge is a qualifying debt and should be included in the DRO.

- If the consequence of non-payment is that the penalty charge can be registered in the magistrates' court for enforcement as if it were payable under a conviction, the penalty charge is a fine and is an excluded debt.
- If the consequence of non-payment is that the client *may* be summonsed to the magistrates' court and prosecuted for an offence, the penalty charge is a qualifying debt and so should be included in the DRO. Any subsequent prosecution is not regarded as a 'remedy in respect of the debt' and a conviction could lead to a fine which would be an excluded debt.[144]

Unenforceable debts

In principle, all unpaid qualifying debts should be included in a DRO application and, unless the client owes money to a 'loan shark' (see below), this is only an issue if the inclusion of the debt would take the client over the £20,000 total debt limit (see p504).

The official receiver says that if an adviser has satisfied her/himself that a qualifying debt is unenforceable (eg, because it is 'statute-barred' – see p292) or is irredeemably unenforceable under the Consumer Credit Act 1974 (see p71) *and* there is evidence that the debt is unenforceable (eg, a court order or letter from the creditor acknowledging this), the client can choose not to include the debt in the DRO and it does not count towards the £20,000 total debt limit.

Note: if the official receiver subsequently finds out that a debt was not statute-barred or unenforceable and, as a result, the debts exceeded the £20,000 limit, the DRO is revoked.

Debts owed to loan sharks (see p254) can be included in a DRO. However, the official receiver has said that if the client fears for her/his safety, s/he can choose to leave the debt out and it does not count towards the £20,000 limit.

Water charges

If the client has an unmetered account, her/his water charges to the 31 March following the date of the DRO application are a qualifying debt and so must be included in the DRO. Most water companies have 'insolvency clauses' in their charges schemes whereby, in the event of the customer entering a formal insolvency procedure (such as bankruptcy or a DRO), her/his water charges are apportioned up to the date of the DRO/bankruptcy order and the customer is then issued with a new bill for the remainder of the charging year to 31 March.

Although the client can choose to pay the new bill, the water company's view can be challenged, both as an attempt to exercise a remedy in respect of the debt and to contract out of the statutory insolvency scheme.[145] Specialist advice should be obtained in such cases.

Qualifying conditions

In order to obtain a DRO, the client must be unable to pay her/his debts and must either be domiciled in England and Wales at the date of the application or have been ordinarily resident or carried out business in England and Wales during the previous three years.[146] In addition, on the date the official receiver determines the application (the 'determination date') s/he must not:

- be an undischarged bankrupt, or subject to an individual voluntary arrangement (IVA), a bankruptcy restrictions order, a bankruptcy restrictions undertaking, a debt relief restrictions order or debt relief restrictions undertaking;
- have had a DRO made within the previous six years;
- have a bankruptcy petition pending against her/him, unless the court has referred her/him for a DRO;
- have qualifying debts above the prescribed limit of £20,000;
- have surplus monthly income above the prescribed limit of £50;
- have property (assets) valued at above the prescribed limit of £1,000 (but see below where the client owns a single domestic motor vehicle).

Transactions at an undervalue and preferences

The official receiver can refuse to make a DRO if the client has entered into a transaction at an undervalue (see p495) or given a preference to anyone (see p496) at any time during the two years before the application is made or during the period between the application date and the determination date. **Note:** these are different time limits to those for bankruptcy. **Note also:** the client need not have intended to give a preference (although the official receiver considers this when exercising discretion).

Payments made directly to the client's creditors by third parties using their own funds are not considered to be preferences for the purpose of a DRO order, neither are payments made by clients out of their surplus income to priority creditors. However, lump sum payments to priority creditors *do* need to be reported as preferences (including the source of the funds and why the payment was made) so that the DRO Team can make the decision, even if this is unlikely to be a decline.[147] Payments in respect of a fixed-penalty notice where the consequences of non-payment are potentially a prosecution and fine in the magistrates' court are not considered to be preferences. Contractual payments made to creditors and payment of instalments under a county court (or High Court) judgment are not considered to be preferences. Repayment of loans to friends and family are likely to be considered preferential and could lead to the DRO being declined.

Calculating the value of property and amount of surplus income

When calculating the value of property and the amount of surplus income, the following property is disregarded:

- tools, books and other items of equipment (but not motor vehicles) that are necessary for the client's personal use in her/his employment, business or vocation;

- clothing, bedding, furniture, household equipment and the necessary provisions for satisfying the client's basic domestic needs and those of her/his family;
- a single domestic motor vehicle belonging to the client and worth less than the prescribed amount (currently £1,000); *or*
- a single domestic motor vehicle belonging to the client which has been specially adapted for the client's use because of her/his disability.

Property is valued at its gross, rather than net, realisable (and not replacement) value and so clients who are homeowners do not qualify even if their property has negative equity.

When calculating the client's surplus (or available) income, the official receiver must take into account any contribution made by any member of the client's family to the amount necessary for the reasonable domestic needs of the client and her/his family. In practice, the client's financial statement must be completed using standard financial statement principles (see p56). A DRO is an individual remedy and so, if the client is a member of a couple, the financial statement must show the client's available income and not that of the couple.[148]

If the client has an attachment of earnings order, a direct earnings attachment or is having deductions from benefits made which will cease once the DRO is made (because creditors must cease exercising any remedy in respect of qualifying debts during the moratorium period), prepare the client's financial statement on the basis of her/his earnings before the deductions are made. Include any essential expenditure that is needed for the client's reasonable domestic needs, even if it is now unaffordable. Provided the client's surplus income is still £50 a month or less, the application for a DRO can proceed. However, you should explain to the official receiver on the application form or in a separate email that the client is subject to an attachment or earnings order or deductions from benefits and that her/his budget has been prepared on the basis of including essential expenditure which is currently unaffordable, but will be affordable once the order or deductions stop.

Issues with particular types of expenditure

No payments can be included in the client's essential expenditure for any debt included in the DRO.

Rent arrears and payments under controlled agreements

Rent arrears and payments under controlled agreements are not an allowable expense, whether the rent arrears are payable under a suspended possession order or under an agreement made with the landlord. However, rent arrears and payments under controlled agreements can be paid after a DRO is made, either from the client's surplus income or by a third party.

Hire purchase payments

Ongoing hire purchase payments are only an allowable expense if:
- the client chooses to omit the outstanding balance from the DRO (see p501); *and*
- the goods would be disregarded goods if they belonged to the client – ie, if they are a single domestic motor vehicle worth less than £1,000 or one that has been specially adapted because the client has a disability or where the goods are necessary to meet the client's basic domestic needs; *or*
- where the expenditure is necessary to meet the client's reasonable domestic needs.[149]

Issues with particular types of property[150]

Cash

Cash in hand or in a bank account can be disregarded if it is intended to be used to pay for the essential expenditure listed in the income/expenditure section of the application. Regardless of its original source, cash is property unless it represents arrears of disability benefits (ie, attendance allowance, disability living allowance and personal independence payment) or equivalent benefits paid to armed forces personnel.

Money owed

If the client is owed money, it is regarded as property unless s/he has unsuccessfully attempted to recover it and these attempts are documented. Arrears of child support and compensation owed to the client through the magistrates' court are not property for this purpose.

Pensions

Any undrawn 'approved' pension entitlement should not be taken into account when assessing the value of the client's property. However, if the value of the pension fund (net of any income tax payable and charges on withdrawal) exceeds the client's total debts, the official receiver says that consideration should be given to whether the client is 'unable to pay' her/his debts and that advisers should contact the official receiver to discuss whether a DRO is likely to be made in these circumstances.

Right to claim compensation

The client's right to claim compensation from another person or organisation is potentially property, but not if the claim is purely personal to the client – eg, for personal injuries. However, if the claim includes a claim for a 'pecuniary loss' (eg, lost wages), only that part of the claim is regarded as property.[151] Claims for compensation to the Criminal Injuries Compensation Authority are not regarded as property, even if pecuniary losses are included.

If the client is pursuing a claim, her/his solicitor should be contacted to confirm whether or not the other party has accepted liability and how much compensation the client is likely to receive, and then specialist advice should be sought about whether the client's right counts as property for DRO purposes.

Note: if a client becomes entitled to receive compensation during the 12-month moratorium period (see p499) or even afterwards, this could lead to any DRO being revoked. This also applies to rights to action that are not regarded as property at the pre-order stage. It might be in a client's best interests to resolve any potential or pending compensation claims before deciding whether or not a DRO is the most appropriate option.

This advice also applies to clients who have outstanding claims for refunds of premiums for mis-sold payment protection insurance in connection with any credit agreements (see p164). The official receiver says:

- refunds are not property until the creditor or insurance company accepts the claim and the amount of any refund has been agreed;
- creditors can exercise any contractual right to set off the refund against any debt owed by the client. If this is done before the DRO application is made, it is not regarded as a preference. If it is done during the 12-month moratorium, it is not regarded as a remedy in respect of the debt;
- any refund paid to the client during the moratorium period could result in the DRO being revoked.

Any funds received before the DRO application can be paid pro rata to qualifying creditors without involving any issue of preference.

Making the application

The application is made to the official receiver online through an approved intermediary.[152] It must be made on a prescribed form and contain prescribed information. A fee is payable (currently £90) and there is no remission. The fee can be paid by instalments through Payzone or a post office. There is no time limit for payment of the fee, but clients who are close to the maximum debt ceiling should be aware that accruing interest and charges may take them over the limit if they take too long to pay the fee.

In order to reduce the costs and speed up the process, the official receiver makes certain assumptions when determining an application, unless s/he has reason to believe otherwise, that:

- the client is unable to pay her/his debts; *and*
- the specified debts are qualifying debts; *and*
- the client satisfies the conditions for a DRO (see p503).

On receipt of an application and confirmation that the fee has been paid, the official receiver may:

- defer consideration of the application to enable her/him to make enquiries; *or*

- refuse the application on the grounds that:
  - the client does not meet the criteria; *or*
  - the client has given false information in connection with the application; *or*
  - the application is not on the prescribed form or does not contain the prescribed information; *or*
  - the client has not answered questions to the official receiver's satisfaction; *or*
- make a DRO containing details of the client's qualifying debts.

The official receiver also carries out verification checks. The Individual Insolvency Register is checked to see if the client is currently an undischarged bankrupt, subject to an IVA, a bankruptcy restrictions order or undertaking, or a debt relief restrictions order or undertaking. The official receiver also carries out a credit reference check through Experian to check the client's identity, residence and total debts.

Common reasons for DROs being declined are because:
- the client's total debts are found to exceed £20,000;
- the client has had a previous DRO in the last six years.

It is good practice for advisers to carry out these checks themselves and to address any issues disclosed before applying for a DRO – eg, if the credit report incorrectly shows that the client's total debts are over £20,000. If it is not possible to get the Experian report amended before submitting the DRO application, the evidence demonstrating the inaccuracy of the report should be submitted to the official receiver by email or fax before the application itself, with a request that the evidence be taken into account when considering eligibility for the DRO. If this is not done, the order is declined. The official receiver tends not to reconsider such decisions, but the client can resubmit the application provided either the report has been amended or the evidence is submitted. This costs the client a further £90 fee.

Note: see p509 and p476 if the client or a member of her/his family is at risk of violence and does not want details of her/his address to be entered on the Individual Insolvency Register.

After the application is made

Once the application is made, the client must co-operate with the official receiver. This includes providing any information that the official receiver may require.

If the official receiver declines to make the order, s/he must give her/his reasons to the client. The fee is not refunded. The client can apply to the court and ask it to overrule this decision. In practice, the official receiver is prepared to reconsider decisions and should be asked to do so before any court application is made.

If an order is made, details are registered in the Individual Insolvency Register (see p461) (and on the client's credit reference file). If the client has reasonable grounds for believing that s/he or any member of her/his family who normally resides with her/him would be at risk of violence if her/his current address or whereabouts was disclosed, this can be flagged up on the application form. Where applicable, the official receiver does not enter details of the client's current address on the register pending an application to the court for an order confirming that her/his details should not include her/his address. The application (known as a 'person at risk of violence' (PARV) order) is made to the court for the insolvency district in which the client resides.[153] There is no prescribed form, but the Insolvency Service has produced a number of template forms which are available at gov.uk/government/collections/insolvency-service-forms-england-and-wales ('Debtor application for an order for non-disclosure of current address'). The application can be made either after the DRO is made or before the DRO application is submitted, which may be preferable for the client as s/he will then have certainty that her/his address will not be advertised. The court fee is £280. Remission can be applied for, although advisers report that some courts are not charging the fee even where the client does not strictly qualify for remission because of the nature of the application.

Where a client needs a PARV order, the DRO Team says this should be obtained *prior* to the submission of the DRO application and a copy emailed to the DRO Team when the application is submitted. Where an application indicates a PARV order is required to withhold the client's address, but this has not yet been obtained, the DRO Team says that it proposes not to process the application until a PARV order is obtained. At the time of writing, it was not clear how long the DRO Team would be prepared to hold on to an application and whether it would be declined once any deadline had passed with the loss of the client's £90 or returned for resubmission when a PARV order had been obtained. Depending on the length of any delay, an intermediary would need to check the client was still eligible and update the application as necessary.[154]

Any creditor listed in the DRO may object in writing to the order being made or to the inclusion of details of their debt(s) on the prescribed grounds (ie, that the client is not eligible for the DRO; it is not a valid ground that the creditor does not want to be included) within the prescribed period – 28 days after the creditor has been notified of the order.

The official receiver must consider every objection and may conduct an investigation if s/he considers it appropriate. If the official receiver decides to revoke the DRO, s/he must give the client details of the objection and the grounds and give the client 21 days in which to respond, stating why the order should not be revoked. If the official receiver decides to revoke the DRO, s/he can do so with immediate effect or at a future date, no more than three months later in order to give the client time to make payment arrangements with her/his creditors. The client can apply to the court to overrule this decision.

Reporting changes in circumstances

Once a DRO is made, the client must inform the official receiver as soon as reasonably practicable of any increase in her/his income during the moratorium period, or of any property s/he acquires. The purpose of this is to ensure that s/he remains eligible for the order. If not, the DRO could be revoked. When reporting an increase in income, an up-to-date financial statement should also be provided, amending any items of expenditure that have changed since the date of the application. If the client's surplus income is found to exceed £50 a month, the client's DRO could be revoked.

The annual uprating of benefits is not a change that must be reported. Receipt of winter fuel payments or a maternity grant must be reported and do not lead to revocation of the DRO. Attendance allowance, disability living allowance, personal independence payment and 'equivalent benefits' are disregarded, including the enhanced and severe disability premiums of employment and support allowance and back-dated arrears of these benefits, but their receipt must be reported. Arrears and on-going payments of employment and support allowance itself are not disregarded and neither are the limited capability for work/limited capability for work and work-related activty elements of universal credit.[155]

Unless accompanied by an increase in income which takes the client's surplus income over £50 a month, provided the client reports the acquisition of any property (including lump sums of income) to the official receiver within 14 days and the value of the property does not exceed 50 per cent of the client's qualifying debts, the official receiver treats any property acquired by the client during the moratorium period as follows.

- If the value of the property is £1,000 or less, the official receiver does not revoke the DRO.
- If the value of the property is between £1,000 and £1,990, the official receiver considers all cases on their merits.
- If the value of the property exceeds £1,990, the DRO is usually revoked unless there are exceptional circumstances.

The only situation in which a DRO must be revoked is if the client dies. In all other cases, the decision to revoke is discretionary and the official receiver should take the individual circumstances of the case into account before making a decision.[156]

The effect of a debt relief order

Once the DRO is entered on the Individual Insolvency Register, a moratorium takes effect in respect of the specified debts, and the creditors specified in the order have no remedy in respect of their debts. This means they cannot force the client to pay the debts included in the DRO. They are also prohibited from issuing proceedings to enforce their debts or from presenting a bankruptcy petition without permission of the court. Any pending court proceedings may be stayed. The moratorium period is one year. During the moratorium, the client is subject to the same restrictions as in bankruptcy – eg, on obtaining credit (see p479).

The making of a DRO revokes an enduring power of attorney and also a lasting power of attorney so far it relates to the donor's property or affairs.[157]

Unless the moratorium period is terminated early, at the end of the moratorium the client is discharged from her/his qualifying debts listed in the order (but not from any debts incurred through fraud[158]).

Payments to creditors

With a few exceptions, clients cannot make payments to any creditor included in the DRO but, in appropriate cases, a third party can make the payments from her/his own income on the client's behalf (see below). The rights of secured creditors (including if a bailiff has a controlled goods agreement) are unaffected and the client may continue to make payments from her/his surplus income in order to protect the goods. Alternatively, a family member or friend could continue to make the payments.

The client can pay any rent arrears included in the DRO out of her/his surplus income if s/he is at risk of repossession or if, for example, her/his landlord will not agree to a transfer request unless the arrears are paid. Alternatively, a family member or friend could continue to make the payments.

Although the client could apply to vary an existing suspended possession order to provide for payment of her/his current rent only or ask the court to suspend any post-DRO possession order on payment of current rent, there is no guarantee that the court will make such an order and specialist housing advice should be obtained before an application is made.

If a hire purchase debt is included in a DRO, a third party can either make the payments from her/his own income on the client's behalf in order to protect the goods from repossession by the creditor or arrange to transfer the agreement into her/his own name with the consent of the creditor and the client.

Overpayments of benefits or tax credits can only be included in a DRO if the recovery decision has been made before the date of the DRO application. Such overpayments cannot be recovered by deductions from ongoing benefits or tax credits either during or after the moratorium period (unless the debt was incurred through fraud when recovery by deductions can be resorted to after the end of the moratorium period[159]). The DWP says that where the overpayment period is either entirely before the date of the DRO or spans the date of the order, its policy is to to suspend recovery until the end of the moratorium period when the debt will be written off it if was included in the DRO, but normal recovery action will recommence in the case of fraudulent overpayments. If the overpayment decision was not made until after the DRO was approved (so that it could not be included), it is DWP policy to suspend recovery of that overpayment until the end of the moratorium period. The DWP applies the same policy to social fund loans even though they are excluded debts.[160] The DWP should be challenged if it fails to comply with this policy and continues with deductions regardless of the DRO, although if the overpayment has been included in the order, the DWP could be challenged for exercising a remedy in respect of the debt.

The role of intermediaries

In order to obtain a DRO, a client must apply through an approved intermediary. Intermediaries are authorised by competent authorities (such as Citizens Advice and the Institute of Money Advisers) and cannot charge fees in connection with an application. The responsibilities of intermediaries include:
- assisting clients to make applications;
- checking that applications have been properly completed;
- sending applications to the official receiver.

Intermediaries must:
- inform the client that the official receiver carries out verification checks (see p508);
- assist the client to complete the online application if, after having the various debt options explained to her/him, s/he wishes to apply for a DRO. An intermediary must submit an application to the official receiver if instructed to do so by the client, even if the client has been advised that there are other available options, and/or that the application will be rejected and s/he will consequently lose the £90 application fee;
- draw the client's attention to all the qualifying conditions, the effects of a DRO (including the duties and restrictions on the client as well as the moratorium period and discharge from the scheduled debts); *and*
- explain the possible consequences of providing false information or omitting information from a DRO application – eg, the possibility that the order could be revoked and the consequences of that in relation to her/his creditors, plus possible criminal and/or civil penalties such as a debt relief restrictions order (see p514).

An intermediary may also assist the client to:
- identify what information is required to complete an application;
- establish whether or not her/his total debts, income and assets exceed the prescribed amounts; *and*
- ensure the application is fully completed.

Intermediaries are advised to write 'confirmation of advice' letters covering these areas and, if the advice is that the client is not eligible for a DRO, to get the client to sign the letter if s/he insists on going ahead. The use of a standard post-DRO letter reminding clients of their responsibilities and what happens next is also recommended.

The Insolvency Service expects intermediaries to satisfy themselves that applications are accurate and, where possible, to verify the information supplied by clients. If the client insists on submitting the application against the intermediary's advice, because it is clear s/he does not qualify (eg, the client's debts exceed the £20,000 limit), then the application can indicate this.

To assist intermediaries, the Insolvency Service has provided *Intermediary Guidance Notes* on completing the application and the *DRO A–Z* containing technical information, which are updated from time to time, together with a regular newsletter. These are available from competent authorities and the *Intermediary Guidance Notes* can also be obtained from gov.uk/guidance/debt-advisor-tools-and-information.[161] It is essential that intermediaries familiarise themselves with, and use, these documents when advising clients and preparing applications. At the time of writing, version 17 of the *Intermediary Guidance Notes* was expected imminently.

A DRO toolkit is also available, which can be accessed either in AdviserNet, the IMA's website (i-m-a.org.uk) or at Wiseradviser (wiseradviser.org).

The role of the official receiver

The official receiver can amend the DRO during the moratorium period to correct errors or omissions. However, s/he cannot add any debt(s) not specified in the application. This means that, unlike in bankruptcy (where provable debts are covered by the order even if they are not included in the application), if any debt which would have been a qualifying debt for DRO purposes is omitted from the application, it cannot be added at a later date. Ultimately, it is the client's responsibility to inform the intermediary of all her/his debts. It is advisable for the client to obtain a copy of her/his credit reference reports (and essential to obtain a report from Experian) before an application is completed to ensure, as far as possible, that all qualifying debts are included.

In addition to being under a duty to report to the official receiver certain changes of circumstances, including if s/he moves to a new address, and to co-operate with requests for information from the official receiver, if the client becomes aware after the order is made of any error or omission in the information supplied in support of the application, s/he must inform the official receiver as soon as possible.

The DRO notification letter sent to creditors also invites them to inform the official receiver of any conduct or behaviour by the client that may be relevant.

The official receiver may revoke the order (but is not required to do so) if:

- information provided by the client is incomplete, inaccurate or misleading;
- the client has failed to co-operate with the official receiver or provide the required information;

- a bankruptcy order has been made against the client or s/he has proposed an IVA to her/his creditors;
- the official receiver should not have been satisfied that the client met the conditions for making it (see p503);
- at any time after the client applies for an order, s/he no longer meets the conditions on the monthly surplus income and/or assets;
- the client dies (in which case, the order *must* be revoked).

Common reasons for revocation are:
- the value of the client's property (assets) is found to be in excess of £1,000;
- the total of the client's debts is found to be in excess of £20,000;
- the client has died.

The official receiver can revoke the DRO either with immediate effect or at a specified date no more than three months ahead. S/he must consider whether the client should be given the opportunity to make arrangements with her/his creditors for payment of her/his debts.

A creditor or client who is dissatisfied with the official receiver's decision can apply to the court to overrule this decision. In practice, the official receiver reconsiders any decision if asked to do so.[162]

Offences and restrictions

As with bankruptcy, it is a criminal offence for the client to:
- make false representations or omissions in connection with a DRO application;
- fail intentionally to co-operate with the official receiver or knowingly or recklessly make false representations or omissions in relation to information supplied in connection with a DRO application or after a DRO is made;
- conceal or falsify documents;
- dispose of property fraudulently;
- deal fraudulently with property obtained on credit.

During the moratorium (or while a debt relief restrictions order or undertaking is in force), the client cannot:
- obtain credit of £500 or more without revealing her/his status to the lender;
- trade in a name that is different from that in which the DRO was made without revealing the name in which the order was made to everyone with whom s/he has business dealings;
- be a director of a limited company without the permission of the court.

A breach of any of these requirements is a criminal offence.

If, during the course of any enquiries, the official receiver believes that the client has been dishonest or irresponsible (either before or during the period of the DRO), s/he can apply for a debt relief restrictions order, or obtain an undertaking from the client, on the same grounds as a restrictions order or undertaking can be applied for in bankruptcy and for the same two- to 15-year period (see p479). The effect of a debt relief restrictions order or undertaking is to extend the restrictions that applied during the moratorium. Unless the court orders otherwise, the revocation of the DRO does not affect any debt relief restrictions order or undertaking.

Notes

1. Insolvency options: summary
1   s112 CCA 1984
2   Email FOI@insolvency.gov.uk.

2. Administration orders
3   s112 CCA 1984
4   *Preston Borough Council v Riley, The Times*, 19 April 1995; see also *Various v Walker*, Walsall County Court, 3 January 1997 (*Legal Action*, May 1997); *Various v MM, HW and CE*, Birmingham County Court, 23 October 1997 (*Legal Action*, January 1998)
5   *Various v MM, HW and CE*, Birmingham County Court, 23 October 1997 (*Legal Action*, January 1998); *A v Fenland District Council*, Kings Lynn County Court, August 1997 (*Adviser* 64 abstracts). The decision to the contrary in *Lane v Liverpool City Council*, Liverpool County Court, 19 May 1997 (*Adviser* 69 abstracts) appears wrongly decided in light of the decision in *Re: Green* [1979] 1 All ER 832 that an attachment of earnings order is not an assignment of the debt. See also *Nolan v Stoke on Trent City Council* (*Adviser* 118 abstracts), in which the court held that continuing to receive money under an attachment of earnings order was a 'remedy' and ordered the local authority to refund the sums deducted since making the administration order.
6   r5(6) and (8) CCR 39
7   r14 CCR 39
8   s112(5) CCA 1984
9   s429 IA 1986

3. When to use bankruptcy and individual voluntary arrangements
10 s360 IA 1986
11 s360 IA 1986
12 s1 Company Directors Disqualification Act 1986
13 s390 IA 1986

4. Individual voluntary arrangements
14 Insolvency Practitioners Association, *Statement of Insolvency Practice 3.1*, available at insolvency-practitioners.org.uk/regulation-and-guidance/sips
15 s262A IA 1986
16 Reg 8(b) Education (Student Loans) (Repayment) (Amendment) Regulations 2010, No.661
17 *CMEC v Beesley* [2010] EWCA Civ 1344 (*Adviser* 141 abstracts)
18 s256A IA 1986; r8.19 I(E&W) Rules 2016
19 s253 IA 1986
20 s252 IA 1986
21 r10.48 I(E&W) Rules 2016
22 I(E&W) Rules 2016
23 s258 IA 1986
24 *Rey v FNCB* [2006] EWHC 1386 (ChD) (*Adviser* 117 abstracts)
25 s260 IA 1986
26 rr20.1-20.3 I(E&W) Rules 2016; see also M Gallagher, 'Bankruptcy etc: address withheld orders', *Adviser* 142
27 r20.2 I(E&W) Rules 2016
28 r20.3 I(E&W) Rules 2016
29 s262 IA 1986
30 *Green v Wright* [2017] EWCA Civ 111 (*Adviser* 181 abstracts)

5. Bankruptcy

31 s265 IA 1986; EU Regulation 2015/848
32 *Re: Hancock* [1904] 1 KB 585
33 If the client has an overdraft, s/he should be advised that there could be an issue with using a debit card to pay the adjudicator's fee as it could be said that the client had increased the overdraft with no reasonable expectation of it being repaid.
34 See P Madge, 'Centre of Interest', *Adviser* 93; EU Regulation 2015/848
35 EU Regulation 2015/848
36 See *Budniok v Adjudicator*, Insolvency Service (*Adviser* 182 abstracts) – a successful appeal against the Adjudicator's decision that the debtor's centre of main interest was not in England and Wales.
37 r10.48 I(E&W) Rules 2016
38 For further information, see M Gallagher, 'Bankruptcy Goes On-line', *Adviser* 174
39 s268 IA 1986
40 *Re: a Debtor, The Times*, 6 March 1995
41 *Skarzynski v Chalford Property Co* [2001] BPIR 673 (ChD)
42 *Lock v Aylesbury Vale DC* [2018] EWHC 2015 (Ch) (*Adviser* 187 abstracts)
43 *Howell v Lerwick Commercial Mortgage Corporation* [2015] EWHC 1177 (Ch)
44 *Griffin v Wakefield Metropolitan Borough Council*, 24 March 2000 (*Adviser* 116 abstracts)
45 The creditor must do all that is reasonable to bring the statutory demand to the client's attention: paras 11.2 and 12.7 IP-PD – IP.
46 IP-PD – IP, para 11.4.4.
47 *Howell v Lerwick Commercial Mortgage Corporation* [2015] EWHC 1177 (Ch)
48 r6.5 I(E&W) Rules 2016
49 *Re: Ridgeway Motors* [2005] EWCA Civ 92 (*Adviser* 109 abstracts); *Munshi v Architectural Association*, High Court, 2015, unreported (typographical error did not render statutory demand unclear)
50 para 11.4.2 IP-PD
51 r10.48 I(E&W) Rules 2016
52 rr10.7-10.9 I(E&W) Rules 2016
53 para 12.7 IP-PD
54 See *Reliance Wholesale Ltd v AM2PM Feltham Ltd* [2019] EWHC 1079 (Ch)
55 s271(1)(a) IA 1986
56 *Lilley v American Express* [2000] BPIR 70 (ChD), p74 letter E and p77 letters E-G
57 *Lilley v American Express* [2000] BPIR 70 (ChD)
58 s271 IA 1986. See also r10.24 I(E&W) Rules 2016 and *Barker v Baxendale-Walker* [2018] EWHC 1681 (Ch) where an application to stay the petition was dismissed on the ground that a request for permission to appeal was not the equivalent of a pending appeal.
59 *Ross and Holmes v HMRC* [2010] EWHC 13 (ChD)
60 r10.23 I(E&W) Rules 2016; *Edgington v Sekhon* [2015] EWCA Civ 816 (*Adviser* 173 abstracts) - where the application at the hearing was refused on the ground that it was made too late and there was no specific proposal nor evidence of ability to pay; see also *Day v Refulgent* [2016] EWHC 7 (Ch) (*Adviser* 174 abstracts). In *Barker v Baxendale-Walker* [2018] EWHC 1681 (Ch), the judge held: 'The court, of course, has power to adjourn the petition but the practice is to do so only if there is credible evidence that there is a reasonable prospect that the petition debt will be paid within a reasonable time.'
61 s276 IA 1986
62 s291 IA 1986
63 s371 IA 1986
64 s358 IA 1986
65 s289 IA 1986
66 r10.32 I(E&W) Rules 2016, which enables the court to suspend registration until further order.
67 See M Gallagher, 'Persons at Risk of Violence Orders', *Adviser* 177
68 r10.48 I(E&W) Rules 2016
69 CPR Insolvency Proceedings PD, para 18
70 CPR Insolvency Proceedings PD, para 18(2)
71 s315 IA 1986
72 s307 IA 1986
73 r15.28 I(E&W) Rules 2016
74 s285 IA 1986
75 r14.2 I(E&W) Rules 2016
76 Sch 6 IA 1986
77 Sch 4A para 4 IA 1986
78 Guidance on the main statutory consequences flowing from a bankruptcy restrictions order or undertaking can be found on the Insolvency Service website.
79 Sch 21 EA 2002 and s389 IA 1986
80 Sch 4A para 2 IA 1986

81 Art 7 Enterprise Act 2002 (Commencement No.4 and Transitional Provisions and Savings) Order 2003, No.2093
82 rr11.2-11.5 I(E&W) Rules 2016
83 Sch 4A para 5 IA 1986
84 r11.6 I(E&W) Rules 2016
85 s283(2) IA 1986
86 In *Birdi v Price* [2018] EWHC 2943 (Ch) (*Adviser* 188 abstracts), the judge held that equipment used by the debtor's employees but not physically used by the debtor were not 'used personally', although this did no mean that exclusive use was necessarily required. The Court considered the earlier decision of *Wood v Lowe* [2015] EWHC 2634 (Ch) (*Adviser* 173 abstracts), where the judge held that the exemption did not cease to apply because the debtor was unable to use the tools for a time due to ill health. L's tools were, therefore, exempt (on the basis that it was not unlikely that L would ever work again). The judge also suggested (without hearing argument) that the exemption did not require the bankrupt to physically use the tools: 'A bankrupt may for example set up a small business... in which the tools may be used by another. They still provide the bankrupt with the facility to earn, which is the rationale of the exemption.' In relation to the part of the *Wood* decision relating to the use of tools by the debtor's employees, until such time as the Court of Appeal considers the issue, the later decision in *Birdi* is to be preferred.
87 In *Mikki v Duncan* [2016] EWCA Civ 1312 (*Adviser* 181 abstracts), the court held that only physical assets owned by the client could be exempt as a tool of the trade; a vehicle subject to a hire purchase agreement could not be a tool of the trade.
88 ss308 and 309 IA 1986
89 s284 IA 1986
90 See M Gallagher, 'Bankruptcy: keeping the car', *Adviser* 122
91 s310 IA 1986
92 *Re: Edmondson* [2014] EWHC 1494 (ChD) (*Adviser* 165 abstracts)
93 Chapter 31.7.82 TM; *Sharples v Places for People Homes* [2011] EWCA Civ 813 (*Adviser* 147 abstracts)
94 Sch 19 para 7 EA 2002
95 s310A IA 1986

96 *Re: Landau (a bankrupt), The Times*, 1 January 1997
97 *Kilvert v Flackett, The Times*, 3 August 1998
98 s11 and Sch 2 Welfare Reform and Pensions Act 1999
99 *Horton (Trustee in Bankruptcy) v Henry* [2016] EWCA Civ 989 (*Adviser* 179 abstracts)
100 s283A IA 1986
101 s283A(6) IA 1986 and r10.170 I(E&W) Rules 2016
102 s313A IA 1986
103 Art 3 Insolvency Proceedings (Monetary Limits) (Amendment) Order 2004, No.547
104 s335A IA 1986, as inserted by TLATA 1996
105 *Doodes v Gotham* [2006] EWCA Civ 1080
106 See para 31.35M TM at http://tinyurl.com/987z25k
107 s335A IA 1986
108 *Pickard and another v Constable* [2017] EWHC 2475 (Ch) (*Adviser* 184 abstracts)
109 See, for example, *Martin-Sklan v White* [2006] EWHC 3313 (ChD), *Nicholls v Lan* [2006] EWHC 1255 (ChD) (*Adviser* 122 abstracts) and *Brittain v Haghighat* [2009] EWHC 90 (ChD) (*Adviser* 132 abstracts). In *Grant v Baker* [2016] EWHC 1782 (Ch) (*Adviser* 177 abstracts), although the High Court agreed that the circumstances were exceptional, it allowed an appeal against an order for indefinite postponement on the basis that the underlying purpose of the bankruptcy legislation is to enable a bankrupt's interest in a property to be realised and made available for distribution among her/his creditors. The court substituted the order for indefinite postponement by a postponement for 12 months.
110 If the non-bankrupt partner makes payments after the date of the bankruptcy order, any payments of capital increases her/his share, but not any payments of interest or interest only: see *Byford v Butler* [2003] EWHC 1267 (ChD) (*Adviser* 104 abstracts).
111 *Stack v Dowden* [2007] UKHL 17 (*Adviser* 123 abstracts); *Jones v Kernott* [2011] UKSC 53 (*Adviser* 149 housing abstracts)
112 *Stack v Dowden* [2007] UKHL 17 (*Adviser* 123 abstracts)

113 For a discussion on this issue, see M Allen, 'Whose House is it Anyway', *Quarterly Account* 8, IMA
114 s285(3)(a) IA 1986
115 *Sharples v Places for People Homes; Godfrey v A2 Dominion Homes* [2011] EWCA Civ 813 (*Adviser* 147 abstracts)
116 See for example, *Cadogan Estates v McMahon* [2001] 1 AC 378
117 *Sharples v Places for People Homes; Godfrey v A2 Dominion Homes* [2011] EWCA Civ 813
118 s342 IA 1986
119 *Hill v Haines* [2007] EWCA Civ 1284
120 ss339 and 341(1) IA 1986
121 s340 IA 1986
122 s341 IA 1986
123 s342 IA 1986
124 s285 IA 1986
125 See P Madge, 'Debt Remedies in Insolvency, *Adviser* 154
126 *SSWP v Payne and Cooper* [2011] UKSC 60 (*Adviser* 149 abstracts)
127 See Shelter's Specialist Debt Advice Team, 'Bankruptcy and benefits', Enquiry of the month, October 2019 in the Resources Directory of the NISP section at i-m-a.org.uk.
128 s279 IA 1986
129 s281 IA 1986
130 Reg 80(2)(b) Education (Student Loans) (Repayments) Regs 2009
131 Even though the criminal courts charge has been abolished, in cases where it has been imposed, a client who has gone bankrupt after it was imposed will still not be released from it on discharge.
132 ss291(5) and 333(3) IA 1986
133 s382(1)(b) IA 1986
134 See D Pomeroy, 'Bankruptcy Annulment', *Adviser* 113 and *Halabi v Camden LBC* [2008] WLR(D) 46, in which the court held that the practice of annulling bankruptcy orders on the basis of a solicitor's undertaking to make the required payments was not legal and the annulment order should provide for it not to take effect until the trustee confirmed that all the required payments had actually been made.
135 s282 IA 1986
136 s261(1) IA 1986
137 rr10.143 and 18.35 I(E&W) Rules 2016

138 *Fitch v Official Receiver* [1996] 1 WLR 242. Setting aside orders on the basis of which a bankruptcy order was made are grounds for rescission not annulment: *Yang v Official Receiver* [2017] EWCA Civ 1465 (*Adviser* 132 abstracts). In *Amin v Redbridge LBC* 2018] EWHC 3100 (Ch), Mr Amin found himself held liable for the costs of the official receiver and the council of the petition (but not of the rescission application) when the bankruptcy order was rescinded following the setting aside of the liability orders. See also A Shafiq, 'Made Bankrupt for Council Tax? To annul or rescind? That is the question...'

6. Debt relief orders

139 For an overview, see M Gallagher, 'Debt Relief Orders', *Adviser* 132
140 wiseradviser.org
141 For a full discussion of issues relating to self-employed clients, see L Charlton, 'Debt Relief Orders and the Self-employed', *Adviser* 155
142 s251A(2)(a) IA 1986
143 See L Charlton, 'DROs and Penalties', *Adviser* online, 13 August 2019
144 See L Charlton, 'Q&A with the Shelter Specialist Advice Service', *Quarterly Account* 49, IMA, pp26-27
145 See P Madge, 'Deep Water', *Adviser* 143 and 'Deep Water 2', *Adviser* 177
146 Clients who are not British citizens and who are considering applying for a DRO should be advised to consult an immigration solicitor first, as it may affect their immigration status and any application for British citizenship.
147 See L Charlton, 'Q&A with the Shelter Specialist Debt Advice Service', *Quarterly Account* 48, IMA, p24
148 For guidance on drawing up financial statements if the client is a member of a couple, see P Madge, 'A Single Statement', *Adviser* 147 updated by L Charlton and republished in *Adviser* online, 8 January 2020
149 See R Curry and S Wilcox, 'Debt Relief Orders – approaching the grey areas', *Quarterly Account* 52. In the article, the DRO team is quoted as saying such expenditure would be allowed in 'exceptional circumstances' but this may be challengeable under the Insolvency Rules.
150 See P Madge, 'Property in Debt Relief Orders', *Adviser* 161

151 See Insolvency Service, 'Personal Injury
Compensation', *DRO A-Z*
152 See A Cumming, 'DRO 2', *Quarterly
Account* 43, IMA
153 r9.22 I(E&W) Rules 2016
154 Where the client moved due to a risk of
violence during the moratorium period,
s/he would need to obtain a PARV order
for the new address so this could be
withheld from the Individual Insolvency
Register.
155 However, a 'transitional payment' of UC
where the client was previously in
receipt of the severe disability premium
could be disregarded. See Shelter
Specialist Advice Service, 'Enquiry of the
month', December 2019 available in the
Resources Directory of the NISP section
of the IMA website.
156 See L Charlton, 'Something to report –
Parts 1 & 2', *Adviser* 187 and 189
157 s13 and Sch 4 para 17 Mental Capacity
Act 2005
158 For the meaning of fraud in this context,
see *Ivey v Genting Casinos t/a Crockfords*
[2017] UKSC 67 (*Adviser* 183 abstracts)
159 *SSWP v Payne and Cooper* [2011] UKSC
60 (*Adviser* 149 abstracts)
160 DWP, *Benefit overpayment recovery
guide*, December 2018, paras 6.10-6.12
and 6.16-6.17
161 The current version is v16, although for
advice on technical issues the DRO
Team suggests advisers refer to v14.
Both are available in the DRO toolkit.
Version 17 is expected to be available
shortly.
162 See L Oliver, 'Consultancy corner:
challenging the OR's decision to revoke
a DRO', *Adviser* 185. Fee 3.12 is now
£95.

Chapter 16

. . . .

Business debts

This chapter covers:
1. Introduction (below)
2. Types of small business (below)
3. Stages of debt advice (p522)

1. Introduction

This chapter covers certain types of debt that arise during or after running a business. It also looks at the ways in which the debts or strategies covered elsewhere in this *Handbook* need different consideration when advising someone who is, or has been, running a small business.

This chapter must be used in conjunction with the rest of the *Handbook*. Provided you are familiar with the processes of debt advice outlined throughout, this chapter will often be a starting point when dealing with someone who has recently run, or is running, a business.

This chapter is not a guide to business credit or business viability, which are both specialist areas in their own right.

Debt advisers often declare themselves unable to deal with a person's debts while s/he is still running a business, and it may be necessary to refer people to other professional specialists – eg, tax or business advisers. Business Debtline, a free telephone helpline for self-employed people and small businesses, can advise clients who are still trading (tel: 0800 197 6026). However, this chapter assumes that some limited involvement with the debts of a trading businessperson is possible. In addition, many ancillary debts (particularly after a person has ceased trading) can be handled by a debt adviser.

2. Types of small business

It is important to understand the type of business a client has because this determines her/his liability.

Sole trader

A person who is self-employed without business partners is described as a sole trader. Typical sole traders might include joiners, electricians and taxi drivers, and also sales people who work on a purely self-employed basis. Sole traders can work either in their own name or using a business name.

Sole traders are legally responsible for their business debts in exactly the same way as they are responsible for their personal debts.

Partnership

A partnership is the relationship that exists when two or more people carry out a business together in order to make a profit. A partnership can be informal – eg, if musicians perform together and share their expenses and payments. No formal written agreement is required for a partnership to exist, but this is useful if disputes or problems arise. Partnership agreements should cover how any profits are to be distributed (which will be equal unless stated otherwise) and how the partnership can be dissolved. In the absence of a partnership agreement, the Partnership Act 1890 applies. Partnerships may trade under a particular business name or the names of the partners.

A partnership is considered a single legal entity. Unless the partnership rules state otherwise, contracts can be entered into by any one of the partners and all partners are jointly and severally liable. There is one exception to this rule: each partner always has sole liability for her/his own income tax.

A partner is normally only responsible for debts accrued during the period in which s/he was a member of the partnership (although sometimes new partners agree to take responsibility for any partnership debts accrued by their predecessors). Partners continue to be responsible for debts accrued during their partnership, unless they all formally agree otherwise and their creditors agree to transfer their liability – eg, to the remaining partners. However, it is rare for creditors to agree to this. Partners may even be held liable for debts incurred by the partnership after they have left, unless notice was given to the creditors. Outgoing partners should ideally get legal advice when leaving a partnership to ensure they take all necessary action to avoid this happening.

Limited company

A limited company is a separate legal body that is established to trade and make a profit. It is distinctly separate to its directors, shareholders and managers. In most cases, losses usually fall to the company rather than the individuals who have set it up, but there are exceptions and you should obtain specialist advice.

A limited company can be public (ie, where the shares can be bought or sold on the stock market) or private (where shares are owned and transferred among a limited number of people allowed by the company's rules). Companies are owned by their shareholders. They are run by their directors who may also be shareholders (in most small companies this tends to be the case), but they need not be. Directors are elected by shareholders and are employees of the company.

Companies are governed by legislation, much of which is administered by Companies House, where records of the company, its directors and accounts are kept. Company legislation is intended to encourage entrepreneurship by protecting unsuccessful businesspeople from the individual consequences of corporate debts. Company law is complex and outside the scope of this *Handbook* – it is vital to advise clients to get specialist advice where appropriate.

Unlike in a partnership, the directors are not personally responsible for the debts of a company unless:
- they have agreed to act as guarantor for some, or all, of the company's debts. This is often the case with bank loans to small companies; *or*
- they have acted fraudulently and the company has been liquidated; *or*
- they have continued to trade while the company was insolvent and the company subsequently goes into insolvent liquidation.

The above list is not exhaustive and there are other reasons for a director being held personally liable for a company debt. If liability is not clear, you should always refer a client for specialist advice.

Co-operatives and franchises

These are rare and specialist advice should be sought if liability is in doubt.

Limited liability partnership

Limited liability partnerships have some of the characteristics of a partnership and some of a company. The liability of the 'members' (not partners) to contribute to the debts of the partnership is limited to its assets. There is no recourse to personal assets unless a member has been personally negligent.

You should refer queries about debts of a limited liability partnership to a legal specialist or an accountant with expertise in this area.

3. Stages of debt advice

This section highlights the factors to be taken into account in the debt advice process, as outlined in Chapter 3, when advising someone who either runs, or has run, her/his own business, whether as a sole trader, a partner or a company director.

Create trust

People who have run their own business may pose particular challenges to your trust-building skills. Being self-employed requires independence and self-confidence ence, which may make it difficult for a person to ask for help. If an employee becomes unable to pay her/his debts after being made redundant, at least s/he can see that the causes are beyond her/his control. However, someone whose indebtedness arises after the collapse of her/his own business may have to face feelings of personal failure in addition to the usual problems associated with serious debt. S/he may also have to consider the position of her/his employees.

You should also ensure that as much responsibility as possible for undertaking the tasks necessary to sort things out is carried by the businessperson. If s/he has already run a business (often for many years), s/he may feel both deskilled and disempowered if you take over simply because the business is no longer successful.

List creditors and minimise debts

Minimise debts by ceasing to trade

Note: you should not attempt to advise a company on ceasing to trade. This is an area that requires specialist advice.

If a client is still running a business but is seriously in debt, s/he should consider whether or not to continue trading. There is no point in doing so if this is just increasing indebtedness and the situation is unlikely to change. In some cases, continuing to trade in this situation could become an offence at a later stage if the business is a limited company. This is a highly complex area and specialist help should be sought from a small business adviser – eg, via Business Debtline or the business's own accountants. The process may be helped by drawing up a business financial statement. It is usually recommended that this should be for a period of no longer than three months, unless the business is a seasonal one.

Do not attempt a business income and expenditure list for a limited company. In this case, the director of the limited company should obtain monthly drawings figures from the company's accountant that can be used as income on a personal financial statement.

The business financial statement is similar to the personal financial statement drawn up for the client (see p55), except that it deals with the income and outgoings of the business.

- **All the business's assets.** This should include equipment or machinery with its approximate resale value. This will be different from amounts shown in professionally produced accounts, where the 'book value' is based on the original cost of an item and its theoretical life. The greatest asset of a business may be the work it has in hand and the debts owed to it. These are difficult to value. The likelihood of a debt owed to the business being paid must be assessed and the contractual status of work in hand measured. For instance, a painter and decorator may have agreed in the autumn to paint the exterior of an existing customer's house the following spring. If the customer loses her/his job during the winter, in the absence of any binding agreement the work may not materialise.

A realistic value for any premises or leases on premises that are owned should be estimated – eg, by a local estate agent. **Note:** valuations of business premises are not usually free of charge (as they are for domestic premises). The client's estimate of value may therefore have to be sufficient. Business premises are particularly susceptible to a fall in value caused by developments elsewhere in the locality. For instance, the opening of a new supermarket could possibly cause a collapse in the business of a corner shop and potentially a fall in the value of its premises. In this way, a reduction in the market which causes a business to flounder can also reduce the value of its assets, which would otherwise have been its major protection from financial problems. Valuing a lease is complex and can only be accurately assessed by a professional. Leased business premises are not valued in the same way as domestic premises. The shorter the period that the lease has left to run, the less likely it is to be of any value. **Note:** if there is no one prepared to take over the lease, this might represent a liability rather than an asset (because the client/tenant remains liable for the rent until the lease expires).

Items like cars should always be valued at the price likely to be obtained at auction rather than a price an optimist might expect to get from a private sale. There are various used car price guides available online and from newsagents that give a trade price for reasonably modern cars, and these can be used as a guide.

- **Likely income to the business.** If the client is using a business financial statement to help forecast the future viability of the business, it may help to draw up a list of payments that the business might expect to receive based on a conservative, but realistic, assessment. Note the dates when payments can be expected.

- **Expenditure by the business.** A similar, dated list of payments that the business is required to make must be drawn up next. This must include, for example, bank interest and charges, lease or rental charges for both property and equipment, regular bills for fuel and other services (eg, telephones and waste disposal), payments required by suppliers, VAT payments, wages to any staff, and estimated tax and national insurance (NI). Some expenditure can be split between business and personal use – eg, travel costs. You should have some knowledge of how to complete a business financial statement in order to do this – it may be appropriate to refer the client to a specialist adviser.

The excess income over expenditure gives a rough idea of how much is available for the businessperson to pay her/himself in 'drawings'. If there is no foreseeable likelihood of anything being available, this indicates that trading may need to come to an end. However, the client must obtain expert assistance before taking such a major step, because items like liability for tax or payments due under a lease, which can be very complex, could make the difference between viability and insolvency. A lay adviser is not generally qualified to make this decision.

If a client is trading as a partner, the decision to cease trading may not be hers/his alone. If one partner wants to cease trading but others do not, s/he should ensure that s/he has formally severed her/his partnership agreement in order to limit her/his liability to those debts that have accrued at that time. S/he should try to gain the agreement of creditors and ex-partners, preferably in writing, that s/he is not liable for any debts which subsequently come to light and which relate to the period of her/his membership of the partnership. If a partnership is informal and there is, therefore, no prescribed way of leaving it, legal advice should be sought so that an agreement can be drawn up to terminate it. If possible, this should include an agreement that those remaining in the business will 'indemnify' (ie, agree to pay instead of) those leaving against claims against them for past actions (or bills).

Sometimes, informal business partnerships exist between people who have personal relationships, such as married or cohabiting couples. It is often the custom that either party can enter into contracts on behalf of the partnership (for which both partners become jointly and severely liable). In such a case, it is important that suppliers are informed that the partnership no longer exists, if this is desired – eg, if a personal relationship ends and so a couple cease trading together.

Minimise other debts

Business borrowings are often secured by banks against a person's home.

Sometimes such security is not enforceable if the agreement was entered into as a result of undue influence or misrepresentation by the creditor or another client (see p151 and p152). This commonly occurs if a person who is not the borrower is required to agree to a charge being made on a property in which s/he is either a joint owner or has another interest (perhaps because s/he lives with the owner). In one case, it was decided that a charge was not enforceable where a client's wife had signed it but had not been recommended to take separate legal advice and had been told that her husband's business would be closed down by the bank if she did not do so.[1]

If undue influence or other wrongdoing occurred at the time the security was signed, specialist or legal advice should be obtained, as the law is complex in this area.

The debts owed by a person who has run a business may include tax debts. See below for ways in which these might be minimised.

List and maximise income

The scope for improving the income of a person running her/his own business is often greater than that of an employee. Specialist business advice can improve profitability, for instance, through better marketing, reducing production costs or overheads, or diversification. You should, therefore, refer the client to someone who can help with this.

In addition, there are many grants and other facilities (eg, cheap loans) available to small businesses, which should be investigated. Information can be obtained from gov.uk/business-finance-support. The payment of tax may use up a substantial proportion of income and, therefore, all the relevant individual tax allowances, reliefs and expenses that a business can offset against tax should be claimed. Consider asking the client to consult an accountant, as this can be a complex area.

Self-employed people may be able to claim universal credit (UC). The claim is assessed on a monthly period so there is no need for a projection apart from when the claimant is in her/his first assessed month. They may also be able to claim council tax reduction and disability benefits. If they do not come under the UC system, they may be able to claim housing benefit, income-based jobseeker's allowance or income support. If NI payments are up to date, it may be possible for a self-employed client to claim employment and support allowance if s/he is unable to work because of sickness.

List expenditure

When drawing up a financial statement for a businessperson, you need figures from the business financial statement.

The personal financial statement is a different document and should be kept separate. The expenditure required by the business (even of a sole trader) should be listed separately from personal or household expenses. Sometimes this is not easy, particularly with a sole trader – eg, a car might be needed for work and to provide family transport. Send the business financial statement along with a personal financial statement to creditors.

Be careful not to double count items shown as outgoings on the business financial statement (and, therefore, reduce the available income), but which may also be paid as part of the household outgoings. For example, if a car is used for both domestic and business purposes, it should be apportioned partly to the business account before the drawings from the business are shown, and then only the remaining (domestic) portion should be shown on the personal financial statement.

Deal with priority debts

Services

If a business has ceased trading and utility debts on commercial premises are outstanding, the gas and electricity bills may need to be treated as a priority. This is because energy suppliers can disconnect home premises for non-payment of commercial bills if the supplies are in the same name and provided by the same supplier.[2] If someone has been trading from home, therefore, gas and electricity arrears are priority debts. If s/he traded from part of the same building (eg, she ran a shop and lives in a flat above it), s/he should separate the supply to the two premises before arrears accrue to avoid the risk of disconnection of the domestic premises.

Water companies cannot disconnect the supply to residential premises and can only disconnect a supply to the premises to which the water was supplied.[3] It is not entirely clear how this affects mixed-use premises. Ofwat has issued guidance stating it believes the disconnection of mixed-use premises could be illegal and reminds customers of their right to take court action if this happens. In practice, companies rarely disconnect mixed-use premises.

Water companies can disconnect separate non-domestic premises. The environmental risk of a business being without water could lead to its closure.

Non-domestic rates

Non-domestic rates (business rates) are sometimes not charged on empty premises, but this may vary between local authorities, so you may wish to check local discounts. If the ratepayer has a lease on the premises, s/he is liable for the business rates for as long as her/his tenancy exists, even if the premises are empty.

Non-domestic rates are collected and enforced in the same way as council tax (see p95), except that, for instance, tools of the trade are not exempt. This means that bailiffs can take control of a ratepayer's property from anywhere (including her/his home address) once a liability order has been made. Another difference is that attachment of earnings orders and charging orders are not allowed for business rates, nor are deductions from benefits.

In practice, local authorities may remit, or write off, large amounts of unpaid non-domestic rates. They have the power to remit unpaid business rates if there is 'severe hardship' and if it is reasonable to do so. In practice, most local authorities use this power to write off unpaid rates if a business has ceased trading and those responsible for the rates depend on benefits, or if a business could close (with job losses) if rates were to be pursued. Local councillors should be approached to put pressure on officers if this is not done.[4]

Rent arrears

Recovery of commercial rent arrears is possible as soon as seven days' rent is overdue. No court order is necessary. If a client is continuing to trade, it is probably impossible to stop bailiffs (who act on behalf of the landlord) from making a peaceful entry to her/his premises (since they are likely to be open to the public). Some landlords regard taking control of the whole of a business's stock as the easiest way of recovering rent arrears, but this will usually force the client to cease trading. Priority must be given to securing an arrangement with a business's landlord if the client wishes to continue trading. The bailiff cannot take control of goods at the client's home address (unless s/he has taken goods there to avoid them being taken by the bailiffs).

See p413 for more information about bailiffs and commercial rent arrears.

Leased premises

Many businesses lease their work premises. In some cases, the unexpired part of a business lease can be a valuable asset that can be realised if the client decides to cease trading or trade from other premises. Professional advice should always be sought on the valuation of such leases. If a lease is to be 'assigned' to another person, legal advice should be sought. The permission of the landlord is required. In certain circumstances, if the new tenant fails to pay her/his rent, the earlier tenant can still be held responsible. In order to protect against this future liability, it is sometimes better to agree to surrender a lease, even if it may be sellable for a premium.

A landlord may be prepared to accept the surrender of a lease (which ends the tenant's contractual obligations, such as rent and therefore business rates) if it is clear that s/he is unlikely to get any more money from a particular tenant. If s/he wishes to sue for unpaid rent, a landlord must be able to show that s/he has mitigated the loss. If a client has ceased trading and is likely to remain unemployed for some time, and has responsibility for a lease, you could approach the landlord directly. Explain that the client is unlikely to meet her/his contractual obligations and, in some cases, landlords agree to a surrender. You should ensure that you are not dealing with a lease which is of value (perhaps because it forms a small part of a redevelopment site or because the rent has been fixed at a low rate for many future years) before the client gives it away. Specialist advice should be obtained.

Other leases

Many businesses have equipment like photocopiers, electronic scales or games machines which are held on a lease. First check whether or not the lease is a regulated agreement under the Consumer Credit Act 1974 (see p62). Many lease documents are complex and specialist help may be required.

A business lease runs for a number of years, during which time the owner of the goods (which may be a finance company) simply charges the rent to use them. At the end of the period, there is no automatic transfer of the goods to the lessee but, in practice, items are often not taken back by lessors. A lease usually contains provision for early settlement. However, in many cases, this figure is likely to be almost as high (usually 95 per cent) as continuing to pay rent until the end of the lease period.

Once a lessee is in arrears with the rent, however, the courts can intervene under common law and alter any clause designed to penalise a lessee who is in arrears. Because the courts have this power only when arrears arise, it may be useful to allow business leases to fall into arrears if a client has decided to cease trading.

Business leases are complex and, as the sums of money involved can be substantial, expert advice should always be obtained before reaching any agreement with a lessor about early settlement. Trading standards departments may be able to provide such advice.

In calculating the amount that should be paid by the client who is in arrears, the courts ensure that the lessor receives only the amount of money that it has lost as a result of the termination. This should include either the goods or their full value at the time of termination. In addition, lessors should receive the amount that would have been paid in interest less an amount (usually 5 per cent a year) in recognition of the fact that they are receiving this money early. If a lease contains service charges for the leased equipment, the courts may reduce the future service charges that will not be required after the goods are returned.

VAT debts

VAT is a tax on the increase in the value of most goods or services (some are exempt) between the time they are bought by a business and when they are sold. Businesses with a turnover of less than £85,000 a year (2019/20) do not have to register for VAT. All others have to submit returns at a frequency agreed with HM Revenue and Customs (HMRC) to show the difference between the VAT they pay to other suppliers (input tax) and the VAT they charge their customers (output tax). Most businesses are legally required to submit their VAT returns online and pay electronically. If they have collected more VAT than they have paid, they must enclose this with their return and submit it by a due date (usually a month after the end of the relevant quarter). If a return is late, the amount due is increased by an automatic penalty. If a return is not made, HMRC can estimate the amount due and issue its own assessment, which becomes payable immediately.

Local HMRC officers who collect VAT vary greatly in their approach to struggling or failed businesses. In general, they consider themselves to be collectors of a tax which has already been paid by a third party to the client and of which the client is only a custodian. While this may bear little relation to the realities of running a small business, this attitude means they are assertive and swift in their recovery process.

Once payment is outstanding, the HMRC officer at a local office usually uses the threat of bailiff action to take control of goods to force payment. This may initially consist of a visit, phone call or letter to state that bailiff action will be used. An enforcement notice giving seven clear days before action will then warn that immediate payment is required and bailiffs will be used in default.

A warrant to take control of goods is then signed by an HMRC officer. A court order is not needed.

The warrant is usually used by a firm of private bailiffs with an HMRC officer in attendance. HMRC can obtain a warrant to force initial entry, but this is very rare. However, most business premises are accessible to the public (including bailiffs) and therefore negotiation is essential. A client who is still trading should always try to give the bailiffs some money and treat this debt with utmost priority. Taking control of goods can provoke or escalate the collapse of a business, both by removing necessary stock or equipment and also by reducing confidence in it.

If you have a client with unpaid VAT, you should:

- contact HMRC, explain the position and request a short time to organise the client's affairs;
- get an accountant to check the amount claimed, particularly if it is an assessed amount;
- explain the seriousness to the client. Use a small business adviser if necessary to look at the viability of the business – eg, its credit control procedures.

See Chapter 14 for details of how to deal with bailiffs. Note the detailed list of exempt goods.

Where taking control of the client's goods is not appropriate, HMRC often uses bankruptcy as a means of collection (see Chapter 15).

Income tax debts

Self-employed people and businesses are responsible for making a return to HMRC, on which tax bills are based. Under the self-assessment system, taxpayers calculate their own tax and send a payment to accompany their return for a particular year. A small business should always get specialist help in claiming all the allowances against tax to which it may be entitled, and in treating its profits and losses in the most tax-efficient way. The tax bill is based on simple 'three-line accounts' for small businesses with a turnover of less than £85,000 a year. These are required to show:

- total turnover;
- total expenses and costs of purchases;
- net profit (gross profit, less all the business expenses).

In addition to the tax due on its profits, a business may also owe tax (and national insurance contributions) on wages paid to employees.

The assessment process is outside the scope of this *Handbook* and you should, if necessary, get specialist help to check the amount of tax demanded. TaxAid is a useful source of help (see Appendix 1).

If the client fails to file a tax return, HMRC makes its own 'determination' of how much tax is due and this is enforceable immediately. It can only be overturned by filing a return. HMRC can impose penalties for late filing of returns and/or non-payment of tax. If there is no tax to pay when the return is filed, the penalty is not reduced and is therefore still payable by the client. S/he can appeal the penalty on the grounds that s/he had a 'reasonable excuse' for the failure. It is still important to file returns, however late, as HMRC has a policy that payment arrangements are not accepted until returns are up to date.

If a tax bill is unpaid, HMRC may:

- use a debt collection agency;
- take control of goods – ie, use bailiff action without a court order (see Chapter 14);

- use the magistrates' court (see Chapter 13);
- use the county court and follow the judgment with a third-party debt order, attachment of earnings order, information order, charging order or instalment order (see Chapter 11);
- seek a bankruptcy order (see p464).

As with VAT, HMRC is likely to be particularly strict if the money owed includes tax already collected by a business from employees and not passed on to it. **Note:** it will still consider starting bankruptcy proceedings, even if this is unlikely to lead to a payment being made.

A summons to the magistrates' court is usually used to collect unpaid tax of up to £2,000 if the debt is less than 12 months old. The client is summonsed to appear at a hearing at which the magistrates make an order that s/he pay the tax. The client should attend the hearing with a financial statement and ask to pay the tax by instalments. The courts cannot consider arguments that the tax is not owed or the wrong amount is being claimed. If the client still does not pay, the magistrates may summons her/him to a committal hearing. At this, the client will need to show that s/he has not 'wilfully refused' or 'culpably neglected' to pay this tax (see p407). However, HMRC rarely uses this method of enforcement.

If the county court is used, the client can ask for an instalment order in the usual way.

If the client owes HMRC at least £1,000, it can ask her/his bank whether there is any money it can take to pay this debt. Usually, the first £5,000 in an account is protected. A client must be aware that if s/he has a lump sum of money to offer various creditors, HMRC could access this in her/his bank account and can do so without a court order.

HMRC is entitled to claim interest (3.25 per cent a year) on any unpaid tax until payment, and enforces this even after a county court judgment.[5] Once a judgment has been made, the possibility of an administration order exists if the debts are below £5,000 (see p445).

It is possible to negotiate with HMRC. Although it is generally easier to negotiate after the client has ceased trading, as with all negotiation, the outcome depends on the circumstances of each individual case. If the taxpayer has been caused problems by maladministration, the Parliamentary and Health Service Ombudsman can be contacted via her/his local MP. There is also an adjudicator at HMRC, who may intervene in cases of particular hardship or unreasonableness, and appeals can be made to HMRC in cases where the wrong amount of tax is being charged.

Draw up a personal financial statement

Creating a personal financial statement for a client who is running her/his own business is no different from that of an employed person, except that expenses may need apportioning and the amount of her/his income may be less predictable. Both these things should be made clear on the personal financial statement.

The figure for earnings ('drawings') net of tax and NI contributions should be taken from the business financial statement produced to help decide the viability of the business. It is important that the business budget is used to extract a figure for drawings, rather than asking a client how much s/he draws from the business. The client's drawings may well exceed profits. If this is the case, specialist advice should be obtained. If the client is a director of a limited company, the accountant should be approached to obtain a monthly drawings figure, which can be used as income on the personal financial statement.

Choose a strategy for non-priority debts

Bankruptcy and individual voluntary arrangements are discussed in Chapter 15. Bankruptcy may often be the most satisfactory way out of the large debts that can arise after the failure of a business. Bankruptcy, in itself, does not necessarily mean the business must cease trading, particularly if there are no assets of significant value. However, remember that although discharge from bankruptcy may occur after one year, a person's credit rating will be affected for considerably longer and, if s/he wishes to run a business that will require credit in the future, bankruptcy can be an obstacle to this. Someone with an otherwise viable business but serious debts may be better advised to consider an individual voluntary arrangement.

Notes

. . . .

3. **Stages of debt advice**
 1 *Royal Bank of Scotland v Etridge* [2001]
   UKHL 44; [2002] HLR 4
 2 Sch 6 para 1(6) EA 1989; Sch 2B para
   7(1) and (3) GA 1986
 3 s1 and Sch 1 Water Industry Act 1999
 4 s49 LGFA 1988
 5 TMA 1970

Chapter 17

Student debt

This chapter covers:
1. Financial support for students (below)
2. Stages of debt advice (p536)
3. Types of debt (p543)
4. Minimising debts (p556)
5. Maximising income (p556)
6. Dealing with priority debts (p572)

1. Financial support for students

The availability and rates of student loans have steadily increased since their introduction in 1990 to help pay for the living costs of full-time undergraduates and the substantial tuition fees of both full-time and part-time students. Consequently, the vast majority of students now graduate with some level of debt. In England, the average student loan debt is likely to exceed £50,000 by graduation. Many students, especially those from less wealthy backgrounds, also expect to accumulate some commerical debt during study, most commonly bank overdrafts.

The student finance system has become increasingly complex and has changed considerably since 1990. The current arrangements were introduced in 2016 in England and in 2018 in Wales, but students generally continue to study under the rules applicable when they started. While the last students funded under the 'mandatory grants' system available between 1962 and 1997 graduated in 2008, and those funded under the system of fixed fees available between 1998 and 2005 in 2015, advisers may encounter students funded under the various iterations of the systems introduced since, especially the post-2012 arrangements.

There are different arrangements in England and Wales (and also in Scotland and Northern Ireland). Both English and Welsh universities and colleges can charge new, full-time students up to £9,250 per year in 2019/20, but there are different rates of student loans and grants in each country. Pre-2018 Welsh-domiciled students can also receive a fee grant.

There are four types of student loans: 'mortgage-style loans' available to students receiving a mandatory grant, two income-contingent loan schemes for undergraduates and postgraduate teacher training students, the most recent of which became available to new students in 2012/13, and a further scheme for other postgraduates.

Undergraduate students can generally access a mixture of grants and loans to pay for the cost of tuition and maintenance. Entitlement depends on whether the student is domiciled in England or Wales, whether s/he studies full or part time, and the year of entry.

Welsh-domiciled students on certain healthcare-related courses, such as nursing, midwifery, occupational therapy, and English- and Welsh-domiciled students in the later years of medicine and dentistry courses, are funded by the NHS under a separate scheme. They do not pay tuition fees. English-domiciled students who started non-medicine and dentistry healthcare courses before 2017/18 are also funded under this system, but new students from 2017/18 are funded under the standard undergraduate rules, with some minor additional elements.

Postgraduate students on taught master's courses can get a student loan to help with the cost of their fees and/or maintenance. Separate funding arrangements exist for teacher training students on Postgraduate Certificate of Education courses and social work students on taught master's programmes. Doctoral degree students can access a student loan to help with the cost of their fees and/or maintenance, or may be able to access funding from research councils via their institution. Students who want to study for a second (or subsequent) undergraduate course will find their access to funding severely restricted, with two main exceptions: full- or part-time nursing, midwifery or other healthcare subjects, and some part-time courses in science, technology, engineering and maths.

Student loans are also available for certain further education courses in England, with the same repayments conditions as in higher education. Other funding for further education courses is limited.

English-domiciled students applying for student financial support must apply to Student Finance England, part of the Student Loans Company. Students in Wales apply to Student Finance Wales. Those funded under the separate healthcare-related system must usually apply for support from the NHS in England or Wales and also to Student Finance England and Student Finance Wales.

See CPAG's *Student Support and Benefits Handbook* for more information.

Advising students

When advising students and ex-students about debt, you may need to adopt some different strategies and should be aware that students expect to owe money both before and at the end of their studies. Most creditors (banks and the Student Loans

Company) have structured repayment programmes for 'normal' student debt once the student starts earning. Such indebtedness should not adversely affect the student's creditworthiness (eg, for obtaining a mortgage), although any repayments made (or due to be made) are listed as outgoings in affordability calculations in future credit applications.

Most of this chapter follows the structure of the rest of this *Handbook*. Issues are discussed only if the position of the students differs from that of other clients. If an issue is not covered in this section, refer to the main text.

The student finance rules discussed in this chapter are generally those available to new students in England or Wales in 2019/20, except where stated. For detailed information on previous iterations of the rules, see previous editions of this *Handbook* or see the Student Finance England or Student Finance Wales websites.

Definitions

Home student. This chapter covers only home students in higher education living in England and Wales. A 'home student' is defined as someone who is settled in the UK within the meaning of the Immigration Act 1971, and is ordinarily resident in England or Wales on the first day of the first academic year of the course, and has been ordinarily resident in the UK, the Channel Islands or the Isle of Man throughout the three-year period preceding the first day of the course.[1] The residence must not have been wholly or mainly for the purpose of receiving full-time education.

'Ordinary residence' was defined in the case of *Shah and Others v Barnet and Others* in 1982 as: 'habitual and normal residence in the United Kingdom from choice or settled purpose throughout the prescribed period apart from temporary or occasional absences'.[2]

In addition, a student may be regarded as a home student if s/he (or a certain member of her/his family):

– has refugee status;
– is a European Union (EU) citizen with right of permanent residence, and who has been resident in the UK for three years or more;
– is a European Economic Area (EEA) or Swiss national who has taken up employment in the UK and was ordinarily resident in the EEA or Switzerland for three years immediately before starting the course;
– is the child of a Turkish national who has taken up employment in the UK and was ordinarily resident in the EEA, Switzerland or Turkey for three years immediately before starting the course;
– has been granted humanitarian protection or, in Wales, discretionary leave to remain in the UK.

A student who comes into one of the above categories must still be ordinarily resident in England or Wales to be treated as a home student.

Note: residency rules are complex, and a student may be eligible for home student fee rates but still be ineligible for student support. The financial position of international students is not discussed in this chapter. You should contact UKCISA (see Appendix 1).

Changes to the residency rules following the UK's departure from the EU are likely, but details are unavailable at the time of writing. You should check the Student Finance England and Student Finance Wales websites for more information.

Full-time student. A student is eligible for support for a full-time course provided the course is 'designated'. It must be a full-time course, a sandwich course or a part-time course for the initial training of teachers, be at least one year in duration and be wholly provided by a publicly funded educational institution.

A 'designated course' includes:[3]

– a first degree;

– a higher education diploma;

– a Higher National Certificate or Higher National Diploma;

– initial teacher training;

– a course for the further training of teachers or youth and community workers;

– a course to prepare for certain professional examinations of a standard higher than A levels or Scottish Highers, or Higher National Certificate/Higher National Diploma, where a first degree is not required for entry;

– a course not higher than a first degree, but higher than those described in the above bullet point – eg, a foundation degree.

Part-time student. A student is a part-time student if the course has been designated as part time. There is not a more precise definition, and usually a course is deemed part time if it does not meet the criteria to be classed as full time.

2. **Stages of debt advice**

The stages of debt advice described in Chapter 3 must be applied when working with students, as with anyone else. There are, however, some additional issues to be considered. These are highlighted below.

Exploring the debt problem

Most higher and further education institutions and many students' unions offer money advice services. The majority of these are experienced in dealing with student debt and have student-specific information resources. Many students may, therefore, prefer to use this service. There can, however, be issues of impartiality, independence, confidentiality and trust arising when advisers work for the educational institution, particularly when the institution is the creditor (see p544). It may not always be appropriate or ethical for an adviser employed by the institution to assist a student in this position. Even when an adviser works for the students' union, the student may need reassurance that the service is confidential and/or impartial.

In order to create a position of trust with a student in need of debt advice, be aware of the different causes of student debt and do not make a judgement about the position in which a client finds her/himself. Very often, clients do not seek help for causes of problems, but their effects.

There are many reasons why a student may be in debt. In addition to those that apply to the general population, these can be as a result of:

- above-average course costs;
- Student Finance England or Student Finance Wales assessments not being a true reflection of parental disposable income;
- errors in student finance assessments that mean support has been 'overpaid' and must be repaid, or subsequent payments have been reduced;
- debts incurred before the client became a student;
- aggressive marketing towards the student group;
- tuition fees; *or*
- coping with an income paid in irregular instalments.

Some students can cope with increased levels of debt, accepting that a certain level of indebtedness is inevitable and part of the student experience. For others, it can have a more negative impact. You could be faced with a student who may be extremely anxious, ashamed, desperate, worried or confused. The stage at which the student presents may also have an effect on her/his emotional state, as many wait until the situation can no longer be dealt with without external assistance before seeking help. The impact can be that the student may be experiencing poor health, mental ill health, relationship difficulties and difficulties with her/his course – eg, low marks, missed deadlines and exam failures. Some students may feel forced to withdraw from their course completely.

List creditors and minimise debts

When noting the status of the debt on the creditor list, it is important to consider the sanctions connected with non-payment in order to determine whether the debt should be recorded as a priority or non-priority. In addition to the criteria referred to in Chapter 8 (if non-payment would give the creditor the right to deprive the client of her/his home, liberty, essential goods and services or place in the community, that debt has priority), you must consider the sanctions available to, and used by, the institution if it is the creditor. Outstanding tuition fees can be listed as a priority debt. For some ex-students, outstanding tuition fees can remain a priority debt as the majority of institutions withhold awards until the debt is cleared. Students entering some professions (eg, teaching) need their degree conferring or their degree certificate before they can take up employment. Prioritisation needs to be discussed with the client.

Be aware of the threats posed to the client by the recovery action, and whether they are appropriate. See p545 for details of what sanctions should be imposed on the different types of debt s/he may have with the institution. Also, be aware when negotiating with creditors that some types of student debt become repayable in the future, and any offers of repayment must reflect this.

List income

Student loans for living costs and some elements of grants are taken into account as income for benefit purposes. It is, therefore, important that loans are listed as such. Most creditors will otherwise suggest that they should be used to make repayments. If a loan is not listed, the financial statement is likely to show a hugely unrealistic deficit, so explain that the loan is used only for living expenses, that interest is accruing, and that repayment will be required at a future date.

Disabled students can receive non-means-tested additional allowances in their loan or grant. These are to help the student with the extra costs of studying; they are not to help with her/his living expenses. It is not necessary to include them as income, as they will have been already allocated.

Students with dependants may also be entitled to additional allowances. These should be included, but need to be balanced by the expenditure incurred – eg, childcare costs.

If a grant, bursary or any other additional allowance is paid, it must be listed as income.

Parental contributions, if paid regularly, should be listed as income. These are intended to make up for any shortfall in the grant or loan. **Note:** a student's support partially depends on a means test of her/his parents' income and financial statements from Student Finance England or Student Finance Wales may refer to a 'family contribution' payment (or similar). However, this cannot be enforced and, in reality, many students do not receive any parental contribution.

Period to be used

Students, institutions and advisers tend to think of students' income within the framework of the instalment periods for which it is paid – ie, termly, quarterly or annually. Creditors are more likely to understand income expressed in weekly or monthly periods. Breaking down income into these periods is also a helpful exercise for students, as the irregular payment periods often reduce their budgeting ability or financial control.

If a grant is paid to a client, establish the period it is meant to cover. If extra weeks' allowances are paid, the payment period should include the total number of weeks.

For final year students, this income ceases to be taken into account once the course has finished (usually at the start of the summer).

How income from a student loan is listed depends on the client's personal circumstances. It can be spread over 52 weeks if it is likely to be her/his main source of income over this period or, if s/he has an alternative income during the summer vacation, it can be listed as spread over the length of the course. Consider the financial benefit to the client when deciding how to show this income to creditors. The client should be made aware of the distinction between the income calculation for benefit purposes and that shown on a financial statement or part of a budget plan.

List expenditure

In addition to the items outlined in Chapter 3, students have additional expenditure, which must be included and which may be required by the course. At this stage, you can help the client identify areas where it may be possible to reduce expenditure – eg, by claiming help with health costs. This area is often where you can be of most use to a client, as some students may have little or no experience of budgeting and financial planning. This process should also highlight how debts have arisen and, therefore, help prevent further financial difficulty. You should also help the client deal with irregular income, and both regular and irregular expenditure.

Expenditure	Period to be attributed	Ways of reducing cost
Tuition fees: full-time undergraduate students	For most students, these do not need listing here, as repayment of fees is deferred through a loan. The loan for tuition fees is only available to pay a student's fees, not as general income. Otherwise, if a source of income is paid directly to the institution solely for tuition fees, it can be ignored in any financial statement (along with the corresponding tuition fee liability). If the income is paid to the student (and s/he then pays her/his own fees), apportion over the length of the course and include the corresponding amount of tuition fees.	Ensure that liability is correctly attributed. Ensure no (further) assistance is available. Students can usually apply for a loan to cover any fee liability. In Wales, eligible Welsh-domiciled students who started their courses before 1 September 2010 or after 1 September 2012 and before 1 September 2018 can apply for a non-means-tested grant to cover some of their fees, and the adviser should ensure they have done so.
Tuition fees: part-time undergraduate students	For part-time students studying at more than 25 per cent intensity (that is, no slower than	Ensure the client has applied for fee support from Student Finance England or Student

Expenditure	Period to be attributed	Ways of reducing cost
	four times the normal length of a full-time course), a loan is usually available, so again these do not need listing – though for Welsh-domiciled students studying in Wales, the fee may be higher than the loan available and thus the excess will require listing. If any other source of income is paid directly to the institution solely for tuition fees, it can be ignored in any financial statement (along with the corresponding tuition fee liability). If the income is paid to the student (and s/he then pays her/his own fees), apportion over the length of the course and include the corresponding amount of tuition fees.	Finance Wales. Check whether any extra help can be provided from university hardship funds or from an employer.
Tuition fees: postgraduate or second degree students	Postgraduate Certificate of Education (PGCE) students are treated as undergraduate students in the student finance system, as above. Otherwise, loans for both master's- and doctoral-level study are available, but may not cover the cost of the course. Excess fees should therefore be listed where a student's entitlement to a loan does not cover these costs. Second degree students cannot normally receive further support for tuition fees (with the exception of some part-time courses in science and technology) and so fees should be listed. If a source of income is paid directly to the institution solely for tuition fees, it can be	Ensure that the client has applied for any fee support from Student Finance England or Student Finance Wales. Check that liability is correctly attributed. Ensure the client has been categorised correctly by the university or college and that no further assistance is available.

Expenditure	Period to be attributed	Ways of reducing cost
	ignored in any financial statement (along with the corresponding tuition fee liability). If the income is paid to the student (and s/he then pays her/his own fees), apportion over the length of the course and include the corresponding amount of tuition fees.	
Books/reading packs	The period over which expenditure on books should be attributed should mirror the period of time over which the student loan or main source of income is attributed – ie, over the length of the course or year (43 weeks). Attribute a realistic figure for the particular course. if this cannot be determined, use the set figure for books included in the student loan.	Suggest: using the university library; sharing resources with students on the same course; second-hand book stalls or schemes; and local libraries. Students in the year above can advise on books that are absolutely necessary. Increasingly, core texts are available online.
Stationery	Attribute over the length of the course.	Printing facilities should be provided by the institution.
Materials – eg, fabrics, photographic equipment, costs related to field trips	Attribute over the length of the course.	As above. Bulk purchasing may reduce costs, if possible.
Transport Costs	Any transport costs the student has may vary depending on time of year, personal circumstances and whether s/he has any dependants. If these costs cannot be attributed, use the set figure for travel in the student loan, plus the cost of at least four journeys home per year.	Some students, usually those on professional courses related to health or social care, may be able to claim travel expenses related to placements, so check to ensure that they have done so. Season tickets are often available, as are discounted student travel cards.

Expenditure	Period to be attributed	Ways of reducing cost
	Some students on particular courses (eg, nursing and teacher training) may have higher travel costs than others, in which case this should be made clear.	
Room insurance	Attribute over the rental period, which can differ from the length of the course, or for the life of the policy or payment plan.	Check whether this is necessary, as some policies held by parents can cover items temporarily removed from the family home. The amount of cover can be too little or too much depending on the student's personal effects. Some institutions may have block insurance for their halls of residence and it may be worth checking what any such policies cover.
Telephone/ broadband	As above.	Almost all students own a mobile phone and have broadband in their homes. Some creditors may need convincing that these are a necessity rather than a luxury, although most now do not question this. However, the student may need guidance on how to ensure costs are kept to a minimum – eg, on the type of contract, comparison of the different packages provided by providers, and alternatives, such as using university-provided internet services.

Advisers often have local knowledge that may help students who are new to the area reduce their expenditure – eg, shops and services that offer National Union of Students (NUS) discounts. There is a free NUS discount card called 'TOTUM' which attracts nationally agreed discounts. For a payment of £14.99, it can incorporate other features such as the International Student Identity Card.

If you and the student decide to use a period of 43 weeks to list the main student income and expenditure, it is usually necessary to draw up a new financial statement showing revised figures for the remaining nine weeks, the long summer vacation. This statement does not need to include study-related costs and related funding.

3. **Types of debt**

This section lists some types of debt specific to students (and ex-students) and which are not included in Chapter 5.

Bank overdraft

For a definition and the legal position, see Chapter 5.

Special features

Student overdrafts have certain features that are different to other clients. Most high street banks offer full-time undergraduate students and some postgraduate students special interest-free overdrafts up to a set limit. However, these are usually subject to certain residency requirements and credit checks and, in most cases, banks do not allow a student to open a new account if one already exists with a competitor. Packages vary – eg, students in different academic years may have different overdraft limits. If the overdraft limit is exceeded, interest should be charged on the excess only. In these circumstances, inform the bank that the student is seeking assistance with her/his finances. Try to negotiate an increase in the limit at least to reflect the new overdrawn figure. If the bank refuses, challenge the basis on which it is unauthorised – ie, if cheques have been honoured or funds have been released, this would have been authorised. Some banks have specialised student account managers.

Chapter 5 outlines the strategy for opening a new account in order to prevent an existing bank overdraft swallowing income. In the short term, you could also advise on the use of 'first right of appropriation'. This is when the client states how a deposit made into an overdrawn account should be used. The student should inform the bank, preferably in writing, what specific amounts are to be paid and to whom. The bank must carry out these directions from her/him. However, the bank may still charge for the use of the overdraft. This facility should only be used on a short-term basis and you should discuss the overdraft with the client in terms of debt advice and maximising income.

Students may not be allowed an interest-free facility on a new account until they can show a closing balance on an existing account. If a student is unable to open an account (eg, because of low credit scoring), contact the Money and

Pensions Service for information about basic bank accounts where basic facilities are available, even if overdrafts are not.

Most banks allow a student terms that continue for a period after s/he has graduated. The length of time varies between banks and can often be extended by negotiation. This is preferable and you should negotiate this option rather than agreeing to overdrawn accounts being 'converted' into graduate loans, as it is more beneficial to the student. Most banks offer preferential graduate terms – eg, free currency exchange and lower mortgage rates for limited periods.

Debts to the educational institution

Students are often in debt to their institutions for a wide variety of items – eg, library fines, hardship loans made by the institution, rent, tuition fees and disciplinary fines. University regulations govern the circumstances in which fines may be imposed and fees are due. However, the introduction of the Tenant Fees Act 2019 and the Renting Homes (Fees etc.) (Wales) Act 2019 means that since June 2019 in England and September 2019 in Wales many fees and charges levied by university accommodatoin providers became unlawful. Check when the tenancy or licence started and challenge or appeal any charges if appropriate.

If you are an adviser directly employed by the institution, you need to be aware of the potential conflict of interest when advising a student with debts to the same institution.

The main sources of students' indebtedness to their institutions are discussed in this section.

Accommodation charges

Most institutions provide accommodation for their students. Charges are made for the rent and services provided. Services usually include items such as fuel and cleaning. These charges may be called 'residence' or 'accommodation' fees. You should check that any charges are allowable under the Tenant Fees Act 2019 in England or the Renting Homes (Fees etc.) (Wales) Act 2019 in Wales.

The legal position

Rent is payable under the tenancy agreement or licence. The terms of these agreements may be in a student's contract and/or in university regulations.

Special features

The accommodation provided directly by institutions to students varies. Some of this is in halls of residence, some in houses or flats in the locality owned by the university or leased to it by private landlords.

The length of tenancies may vary, but are rarely longer than 52 weeks, especially in halls of residence. Many tenancies are for the academic year only – excluding the summer vacation. Some tenancies exclude all vacations. The usual practice is to charge three instalments. There may be a financial penalty for late payment. A student in financial difficulties may be able to negotiate delayed payments or a more flexible instalment arrangement.

The accommodation charge due for a student's current home is a priority debt. While institutions are often reluctant to evict or take court action against their own students, they do try to enforce repayment using other means – eg, by refusing to allow the student to return to university-managed accommodation in subsequent years. In the past, debts were often enforced through refusing to allow the student to progress to the next year of study, or to graduate from the course. Following guidance from the former Office of Fair Trading in 2014, this practice should be challenged if encountered (see p546).

Fines and other charges

Certain costs incurred by students arise from fines or charges. If an appeal procedure exists to resolve disputes about liability or amounts, a client should be encouraged to use it. You may be able to assist by providing supporting information or representation. In some cases, institutions take into account extenuating circumstances and may waive or reduce certain fines or charges.

The consequences of non-payment differ between institutions and according to the student's circumstances. For instance, if a debt for tuition fees could legally prevent the student from graduating, it could also prevent her/him from progressing to a course of further study or employment and, therefore, needs to be treated as a priority debt. However, if withholding qualifications would not impede the student's progress, the debt could be treated as non-priority. A student may consider any outstanding debts to an institution to be a priority if s/he wants to continue studying. Discuss this carefully with the client, especially if s/he has mistaken notions of the consequences of non-payment.

Tuition fees

Almost all students are liable for tuition fees. Full-time home undergraduates and, in England, part-time home undergraduates, have legal caps on the fees they can be charged. Other students are not subject to such caps. With certain eligibility conditions, student loans are available to pay the fees charged to home students, both undergraduate and postgraduate (see p572).

This means that for undergraduate students, the amount of the maximum loan should be equal to the fees for which a student is liable (except, potentially, for part-time students in Wales). Postgraduate students may be charged a higher fee than the loan available. Certain others, primarily those on second degree courses or part-time students studying at 'low intensity' (ie, at a pace which means they would take longer than four times the length of a standard course to achieve their qualification) may not be able to get a loan for their fees. Students who begin their studies and then subsequently leave may be given a date by which they can do so without having to pay anything towards their fees. This date is fixed by the university.

For full-time undergrauate students in Wales, the loan matches the full cost of the fee the university or college charges for a whole year, although there is some scope for negotiation to allow the fee to be divided over the academic year minus holidays, with the student only paying for the period s/he has actually attended. If a student has to pay fees after transferring from one university to another, the two institutions must negotiate with each other about the transfer of the payment. In theory, both could charge for a full year. However, government guidance advises institutions not to charge these students fees outside their range of support. Although this is not binding, it is normally adhered to.

For full-time undergraduate students in England, support for fees is staggered over the year, in a ratio of 25:25:50. So, in term one the student can draw 25 per cent of her/his fee loan, a further 25 per cent in term two and the remaining 50 per cent in term three.

Although universities and colleges can charge a full year's fees for only partial study, the Department for Education strongly encourages the higher education sector only to charge fees for which a student can access the requisite loan to cover.

Recovery of debts to the institution

Methods of recovery vary between institutions. Many do not allow a student to continue into the next year of study if debts are outstanding. If the debt is for tuition fees, this procedure is probably legitimate, although any such action should be proportionate to the debt outstanding and a blanket policy that does not take the student's personal circumstances into account may not be legal.

In the past, some institutions did not permit a student to continue if other charges (eg, accommodation fees and library fines) were outstanding. Similarly, if debts remained at the end of the student's course, most institutions refused to give the student a certificate of qualification or to allow her/him to collect her/his results. The Office of Fair Trading (now the Competition and Markets Authority) investigated the terms and conditions of universities and made it clear in a 2014 report that these practices are highly likely to be unfair. Its view is that institutions cannot threaten, or carry out, sanctions against students by withholding services provided in another, different contract. Nor can they take action that is disproportionate to the debt outstanding or that is applied in blanket fashion and regardless of the student's individual circumstances. This means that universities cannot withhold academic services (eg, tuition, use of library facilities and publication of results) if debts remain outstanding for accommodation services, or if other breaches have occurred. Library fines may or may not be regarded as academic debts, but it is unlikely that withholding progression or graduation is a proportionate means to recover the relatively small debts involved, especially where students may have paid £27,000 or more for the course.

Universities may make use of other, standard debt recovery procedures as with any creditor, including court action, but should be encouraged wherever possible to come to a negotiated repayment plan.

Institutions now offer a wide range of financial incentives to students, including bursaries and scholarships. These are only significant as debts if it is claimed that they have been awarded in error. If the client has provided incorrect information, it is possible the bursary may be recoverable and you should prioritise accordingly. In all other cases, advisers should argue that the bursary awarded to the student informed her/his choice of institution, repayment could cause hardship and, if applicable, that repayment would not be possible for at least the remaining length of the course.

If a student is awarded a bursary and s/he has outstanding debts to the institution, the institution may choose to use the bursary to pay all or part of the debt rather than pay this money to the student. You should argue that other bursaries should be paid in such a way that the student can use them for their specified purpose, rather than simply paying off debts to the institution.

Some institutions may continue to make threats of action that are illegal in order to ensure payment. These practices put students under considerable pressure to pay outstanding charges and may constitute harassment (see p29). While most students are anxious not to jeopardise their future and are reluctant to take any action other than to clear their debts in full, the Office of Fair Trading guidance should be highlighted and, if necessary, a complaint raised with the local trading standards office.

Graduate loan

Some banks offer personal loans to students at or just after graduation to help cover costs related to graduation and starting work (eg, clothing, relocation costs), and/or to consolidate other (commercial) student debts. They are only usually authorised if the bank has evidence that the student has secured employment.

The legal position

Graduate loans are regulated credit agreements (see Chapter 4).

Special features

Graduate loans attract a preferential interest rate. Some banks offer a deferred period of repayment.

Income-contingent student loan

Income-contingent loans have been available since 1998 to help higher education students meet their living costs and, since 2006, tuition fees.

'Scheme one' loans were available to undergraduate students who started their course between 1 September 1998 and 31 August 2012 (see p548). 'Scheme two' loans have been available for new, full-time undergraduate students since 1 September 2012 and for part-time undergraduates in England since 1 September

2018 (see p549). There are different repayment and interest arrangements for each scheme.

Advanced learner loans for students in further education are repaid on the same basis as scheme two loans.

Postgraduate loans for master's degrees or doctoral study have similar repayment rules to scheme two loans, but with slightly different rules on repayment thresholds and interest (see p550).

Scheme one loans

The Department for Education or, in Wales, the Welsh government sets the rates of loans for living costs. The amount depends on the year of study, type of course, where the student lives and household income. It may also depend on the amount of any maintenance grant received. Subject to the maximum rate set (see below), the student decides what level of loan s/he needs and applies to Student Finance England or Student Finance Wales.

The tuition fee set by the institution for the student's course determines the maximum rate of the loan. Under current arrangements, this is not more than £3,465 in the 2019/20 academic year, but may increase by inflation in later years. Note that only a small number of current students now remain funded under scheme one loans, although advisers may work with graduates or those who otherwise left their course and who took these loans out in previous years.

The legal position

The Secretary of State for Education or, in Wales, the Welsh government is the creditor; the Student Loans Company is the agent and repayments are made through HM Revenue and Customs (HMRC). The loan is exempt from the Consumer Credit Act 1974,[4] although in practice it is treated as a 'low-cost loan' under the Act's provisions.

Special features

Interest is normally at the rate of inflation. However, as with low-cost loans, interest cannot be applied at a rate higher than 1 per cent above the highest base rate of any one of several nominated banks.

Repayment is made at 9 per cent of earnings over the threshold amount (in the 2020/21 tax year this is £19,390 a year, and due to rise by the Retail Price Index (RPI) each subsequent year).

Repayment does not begin until the April after the student finishes or otherwise leaves the course. Clients paying tax through the pay as you earn (PAYE) system have their repayments deducted by their employer. As these are calculated over income payment periods, not on yearly income, some clients can overpay if their earnings are erratic. If this is the case at the end of the year, the client can obtain a refund. Self-employed clients have their repayments calculated through the self-assessment system.

Tax credits do not count as income for calculations. Extra repayments can be made, but it is unlikely that a client in debt should consider this.

If a client started her/his course before September 2006, any outstanding income-contingent loan is cancelled when s/he reaches 65. If s/he started the course on or after 1 September 2006, any outstanding loan is 'written off' after 25 years (35 years for clients funded by the Student Awards Agency for Scotland). An income-contingent loan is also cancelled if the client dies or is permanently incapacitated from work through disability (see below).

If the client does not repay the loan or fails to update the Student Loans Company about changes, a penalty charge can be added to the outstanding loan amount.

A client living overseas must contact the Student Loans Company to arrange repayment. Living overseas does not cancel liability for student loan repayment any sooner than living in the UK. Repayment calculations may use a different threshold amount, depending on the cost of living in that country. The Student Loans Company can advise on this. Details of each country's threshold are available at gov.uk/repaying-your-student-loan.

The interest rate can triple if the client goes overseas and fails to inform the Student Loans Company that s/he is no longer in the UK tax system, or if s/he fails to provide information about living overseas.

Since 2004 it has not been possible to include income-contingent student loans in a bankruptcy petition, and since 2009 they cannot be included in an individual voluntary arrangement (IVA).

Disabled clients

Any disability benefits received by the client do not count towards the threshold income (even if they are taxable). If an ex-student is permanently unfit for work because of her/his disability and s/he is receiving a disability-related benefit, her/his liability for the loan is cancelled. There is no guidance on how this is done and no definition of 'permanently unfit for work'. If the client passes the test used for benefit purposes, you can use this when negotiating to have the debt cancelled. See CPAG's *Welfare Benefits and Tax Credits Handbook* for further information.

Checklist for action

- Check the client's income, taking into account the fact that repayments are being deducted by the employer or through self-assessment.
- Note on the financial statement that repayments will automatically be deducted and will, therefore, not be available income from the date repayments start.

Scheme two loans

The Department for Education or, in Wales, the Welsh government sets the rates of loans for living costs for undergraduate students who start their course on or after 1 September 2012 in the same way as for scheme one loans.

The tuition fee set by the institution for the student's course determines the maximum rate of a loan for fees. Under current arrangements, this does not, in any case, exceed £9,250 in the 2019/20 academic year for full-time study. Within this limit, the student decides what level of loan is needed and applies to Student Finance England or Student Finance Wales.

Postgraduate loans for master's degrees or doctoral study and advanced learner loans for students in further education have different eligibility criteria, depending on the different levels of study they fund, and are paid at different amounts. However as with loans for undergraduates, the student applies to Student Finance England or Student Finance Wales for a loan up to the given limit. The repayment rules are similar, but with some important differences for postgraduate loans as set out below.

The legal position

The Secretary of State for Education or, in Wales, the Welsh government is the creditor. The Student Loans Company is the agent and repayments are made through HM Revenue and Customs. The loan is exempt from the Consumer Credit Act 1974.[5]

Special features

Interest on scheme two loans is variable. For full-time undergraduate students, interest is charged at the rate of inflation (as measured by the RPI) plus 3 per cent. From the April following graduation or the student otherwise leaving the course, the interest rate varies. If the student's annual income in the 2020/21 tax year is:

- below £26,575, the interest rate is set at the RPI;
- above £47,835, the interest rate is set at the RPI plus 3 per cent;
- between £26,575 and £47,835, the interest rate is set on a sliding scale between RPI and RPI plus 3 per cent.

Note: the above thresholds increase by average earnings each year.

For part-time undergraduate students, repayment starts either from the April following graduation, or from the date the student leaves the course, or after her/his fourth year of study, whichever comes first and regardless of how many years of study remain. Interest rates then vary according to income, as for full-time students.

Repayment is made at 9 per cent of earnings over the threshold amount (currently £26,575) and increasing in line with average earnings each year thereafter.

Interest on postgraduate loans for master's degrees are fixed at RPI plus 3 per cent regardless of income. They are repaid at 6 per cent of earnings over the threshold amount, and are paid concurrently with undergraduate loans (either scheme one or two). The repayment threshold is also lower than for scheme two loans, at £21,000 a year, and there are no current plans to increase this in future years.

Clients paying tax through the PAYE system have repayments deducted by their employers. As they are calculated over income payment periods, not on yearly income, some clients can overpay if their earnings are erratic. If this is the case at the end of the year, the client can obtain a refund. Self-employed clients have their repayment calculated through the self-assessment system.

A client living overseas must contact the Student Loans Company to arrange repayment. Living overseas does not cancel liability for student loan repayment any sooner than living in the UK. Repayment calculations may use a different threshold amount, depending on the cost of living in that country. The Student Loans Company can advise on this. Details of each country's threshold are available at studentloanrepayment.co.uk.

The interest rate can triple if the client goes overseas and fails to inform the Student Loans Company that s/he is no longer in the UK tax system, or if s/he fails to provide information about living overseas.

Tax credits do not count as income for calculations. Extra repayments can be made, but it is unlikely that a client in debt will be able to consider this.

Outstanding income-contingent loans are 'written off' after 30 years. They are also cancelled if the client dies or is permanently incapacitated from work through disability (see p549).

Failure to repay or update the Student Loans Company about changes can result in penalty charges being added to the outstanding loan amount.

Since 2004, it has not been possible to include income-contingent student loans in a bankruptcy petition, and since 2009 they cannot be included in an IVA.

Checklist for action

- Check the client's income, taking into account the fact that repayments are being deducted by her/his employer or through self-assessment.
- Note on the financial statement that repayments will automatically be deducted and will, therefore, not be available income from the date repayments start.

Mortgage-style or fixed-term student loan

Full-time students who began their course between September 1990 and September 1998 (or who were treated as a continuing student when they began their course in the 1998/99 academic year) were eligible for 'mortgage-style' or fixed-term loans.

Mortgage-style or fixed-term loans are repaid over five or seven years, depending on how many loans were taken out.

Since 2014, all the outstanding loans have been sold to one of three private investors. This does not affect the terms and conditions of repayment, but it means that clients are repaying loans to an agent, rather than the Student Loans Company. The three agents involved are:

- Honours Student Loans (see hsloans.co.uk);
- Thesis Servicing (see thesis-servicing.co.uk);
- Erudio Student Loans (see erudiostudentloans.co.uk).

It is possible that an individual borrower's loans have been sold to more than one investor, requiring them to deal with more than one agent.

Repayment can be deferred if the client's gross income is below 85 per cent of the national average earnings. Only income is taken into account in this calculation; no account is taken of the client's expenditure and financial commitments. An application for deferral should be made when repayment is due to start and applications for deferral must be made each year. Deferments are not automatic, and proof of income should be submitted with the annual application. Usually, payslips for the preceding three months or a letter from an employer is sufficient. Interest continues to be charged during any period of deferment.

It is important that the relevant agent is aware of any changes of address to prevent default action. Many of the remaining borrowers of these loans are in default, having lost contact with the Student Loans Company or the new agent over the years and consequently not having made repayments or maintained annual deferments. Even if a borrower's annual income would have allowed deferment, s/he can only apply for three months' retrospective deferment. Failing to actively defer, and therefore defaulting on the loan agreement, usually means such borrowers are no longer able to defer under the standard rules. In these cases, you may need to negotiate with the agent for a reasonable repayment plan.

Mortgage-style loans cannot be included in a bankruptcy petition or as part of an IVA.

The legal position

Agreements are regulated credit agreements (see p62).

Special features

Interest is at the rate of inflation. Repayments are monthly and are usually by direct debit from the client's bank account. The student will have signed an agreement to repay by direct debit at the time of borrowing.

Unless they are deferred, repayments are expected to be made over five years (seven years for those who borrowed for five years or more). If more than one loan is outstanding, they are repaid concurrently. The amount owed (including interest) is totalled and divided by the number of months (either 60 or 84) to arrive at monthly repayment. This is reviewed annually.

Provided repayments are not in arrears, any amount still due is cancelled after 25 years, or when the client reaches the age of 50 (whichever is earlier). If s/he last borrowed at the age of 40 or over, the outstanding amount is cancelled when s/he reaches 60. It is also cancelled if the client dies, or is permanently incapacitated from work through disability.

As with other agreements regulated under the Consumer Credit Act, repayment of student mortgage-style loans is enforceable through the county court and the owners of the loan can be expected to take court action against anyone in default. Problems may arise if a student has closed the bank account from which the agent expects direct debit repayments and has not made alternative arrangements, or if the account is so overdrawn that the bank will not honour the direct debit arrangement.

Although information about student loan repayments is not passed to credit reference agencies, the government makes an exception for a small number of 'serial defaulters' of mortgage-style loans where other means of debt recovery have been unsuccessful. Details of arrears may, therefore, appear on a client's credit record.

Checklist for action

- Check the client's gross income (and help her/him to apply for deferment where appropriate).
- Prioritise the debt accordingly.

Overpaid grant for living costs

Students are required to repay some, or all, of their grant for living costs if it has either been overpaid (that is, they have received more than they are entitled to under the student support regulations) or if they leave their course (both temporarily or permanently) during a period for which a grant instalment has been paid in advance. In the latter case, the amount of grant for the weeks after the student has left her/his course is calculated and repayment of only this amount is required.

The legal position

Student Finance England and Student Finance Wales have a statutory duty to recover overpaid grants and must do so during the period of the award where possible – ie, before the student completes her/his course. This includes situations where the overpayment has arisen because of an error on the part of Student Finance England or Student Finance Wales rather than any action of the student's. If a student receives more than one type of grant, an overpayment of one grant can be recovered from ongoing payments of any other grant. They have the discretion not to pursue recovery – the circumstances in which they would use this discretion are not defined.

Special features

Approaches may vary depending on individual circumstances, but normally the relevant authority attempts to recover the amount in full by deducting it from the next instalment.

You should negotiate with Student Finance England or Student Finance Wales in the usual way to arrive at an affordable level of repayment. However, if a student continues to receive a grant, Student Finance England or Student Finance Wales is in a powerful position, as it holds the instrument of recovery in its own hands – the next instalment. Be aware that while Student Finance England or Student Finance Wales has a statutory duty to recover during the period of the award, reductions of each future grant instalment are also permissible. If it remains unwilling to extend the repayment period, evidence of hardship should be presented to higher levels of management. Regulations state that the recovery action to be taken should be appropriate to the circumstances and so ensure that Student Finance England or Student Finance Wales is fully aware of the student's situation.

Overpaid income-contingent student loan

As with overpaid grants, Student Finance England and Student Finance Wales have a statutory duty to recover overpaid income-contigent student loans and must do so during the period of the award where possible – ie, before the student completes her/his course. This includes situations where the overpayment has arisen because of an error on the part of Student Finance England or Student Finance Wales rather than any action of the student's.

See pp547–548 for further details of the definition and legal position.

Special features

This type of student loan is not regulated by the Consumer Credit Act 1974. If the loan has been made properly (ie, the student is eligible but the amount is classed as an overpayment), it can be recovered from the amount of loan for which the student is eligible for the following academic year. If the student has completed her/his studies, recovery may be through the normal repayment process, although advisers may need to negotiate with the Student Loans Company for this to happen. In recent years, the Student Loans Company (especially Student Finance England) has required overpaid borrowers to repay more swiftly, even where the Student Loans Company itself made the error giving rise to the overpayment.

Where Student Finance England or Student Finance Wales insists on more immediate repayment, advisers should negotiate in the usual way to arrive at an affordable level. However, if a student continues to receive a loan, Student Finance England or Student Finance Wales is in a powerful position, as it holds the instrument of recovery in its own hands – the next instalment. Evidence of hardship should be presented if required. Regulations state that the recovery action to be taken should be appropriate to the circumstances and so ensure that Student Finance England or Student Finance Wales is fully aware of the student's situation.

Professional and career development loan

Professional and career development loans are similar to professional studies loans, with the added feature of having some government backing. For the legal position and definition, see the section on personal loans on p125. This loan scheme closed to new applicants in January 2019, but advisers may still encounter borrowers who took loans out prior to this date.

Special features

Repayment is deferred during the course and for up to one month afterwards. During the deferment period, the Education and Skills Funding Agency (an executive agency of the Department for Education) pays the interest on the loan. There may be circumstances in which the period of deferment can be extended when the loan becomes payable – eg, if the client is receiving an out-of-work benefit. The terms and conditions of the loan should be checked.

Professional studies loan

Professional studies loans are personal loans offered by certain high street banks or specialist lenders (such as Future Finance) to students undertaking certain professional qualifications, usually at a postgraduate level or for a second undergraduate degree. As with all other personal loans, they are offered at a fixed or variable rate of interest. In some cases, a guarantor may be required. Student clients should be advised to consider such loans carefully and to check on their entitlement to standard student loans from Student Finance England or Student Finance Wales, as these are almost invariably cheaper forms of borrowing with more generous repayment terms. Referrals to hardship funds or other sources of support may also be appropriate.

The legal position

Like other personal loans, professional studies loans are regulated credit agreements (see Chapter 4).

Special features

The terms of these loans vary between the different banks and according to the type and duration of the student's course. The most significant common feature of these loans is deferred repayment. Interest usually accrues during this period. Some loans allow a student to defer repayment until after the course has ended. In other cases, repayment begins part way through the course. Interest rates can vary, depending on the perceived creditworthiness of the student and whether or not s/he has a guarantor.

4. **Minimising debts**

See also Chapter 6.

Reducing council tax bills

Check the client's liability for council tax. Any dwelling solely occupied by full-time students is exempt for council tax purposes.

A student is not jointly liable to pay council tax if s/he lives in a property in which s/he has an equal legal interest with others. If there are non-students or part-time students who are liable, the bill may be reduced because a full-time student attracts a 'status discount'. So, if there is only one non-student or part-time student living in the property with one or more full-time students, a 25 per cent discount should be awarded.

Educational institutions may provide local authorities with lists of full-time students attending courses and, if requested, they must issue a letter to a student establishing her/his status. Some institutions have been known to charge for this letter and you should argue that this is not appropriate. Students should inform council tax offices of their status in order to obtain exemption from, or reduction of, council tax.

See CPAG's *Council Tax Handbook* for more information.

5. **Maximising income**

Information on financial support for students is widely available online or in CPAG's *Student Support and Benefits Handbook*.

There have been a number of changes to student funding arrangements (see p533) and the information required to maximise income and check eligibility is complex. What follows is a guide to the likely sources of income for students in higher education, and who are new students in 2019/20. Those who commenced courses prior to this date may have different rules which apply. **Note:** the legislation for support and fees is different in England, Scotland, Wales and Northern Ireland.

Students seeking debt advice may be doing so as a result of not being able to manage irregular payments effectively when they have regular expenditure. Therefore, care must be taken to establish future budgeting and financial management to prevent the situation worsening in future payment periods.

It may be appropriate for you to deal directly with some creditors and, in certain circumstances, to request that they overpay to assist the client with budgeting. Creditors need a detailed explanation of the student's funding situation to appreciate fully the request being made and to dispel some myths or misinformation they may have about money available to students.

Income could be maximised by the client or adviser contacting Student Finance England or Student Finance Wales and detailing her/his particular circumstances.

If the available help is means tested, the test is normally carried out using the student's parents' income, unless the student has independent status. A student has independent status if:

- s/he is aged 25 or over at the start of the academic year for which s/he is applying; *or*
- s/he married or entered a civil partnership before the start of the academic year for which s/he is applying; *or*
- s/he has supported her/himself for at least three years before the start of the first year of the course; *or*
- s/he has no living parents; *or*
- s/he has care of at least one child on the first day of the academic year for which s/he is applying; *or*
- s/he is a part-time student.

If a student has independent status, her/his parents' (or step-parents') income is not taken into account when Student Finance England or Student Finance Wales assesses her/his entitlement to means-tested support.

If none of the above applies, the student could still be treated as an independent student, if:

- her/his parents cannot be traced; *or*
- her/his parents live abroad and trying to trace them may put them in danger; *or*
- s/he is permanently estranged from her/his parents; *or*
- s/he is in the care of a local authority or voluntary organisation under a custodianship order on her/his 18th birthday, or immediately before the course, if s/he was not 18 when it began.

If a student is married or in a civil partnership, and is not separated, her/his spouse's or civil partner's income is included in the means test. Students aged 25 or over and who are living with a cohabiting partner of the opposite or same sex also have their partner's income included.

In general, student support is available for the ordinary length of the course, plus a year, less any years of previously supported higher education study. Additional years of support may be available if there are compelling personal reasons why the student did not complete a year or previous course. You should outline the reasons in the application and their detrimental impact on the client's studies.

With the exception of supplementary grants (see p570), further support is not generally available for students who have used up their entitlement to funding. However, income-contingent loans for maintenance continue to be available to students who do not already have an honours degree and to graduate students on courses leading to a professional qualification, such as a medical doctor, veterinary doctor, dentist or architect.

Loans for fees and maintenance may also be available to full-time students domiciled in England who already hold a degree but wish to take a second or subsequent course in one of the allied health professions (such as nursing or midwifery). In Wales, students can apply for further funding for healthcare courses from NHS Wales. Loans for fees may also be available to part-time students domiciled in England or Wales who already hold a degree but wish to take a second or subsequent course in science, technology, engineering or maths.

Given the potential impact on future funding, these rules on previous study should be highlighted to students thinking of withdrawing or transferring their course.

Bank loans

Banks may offer loans to students at competitive rates. A client should be advised, however, that the interest rates on loans from Student Finance England or Student Finance Wales make these a cheaper form of long-term borrowing.

A bank loan is usually offered towards the end of the student's course. If overdraft facilities appear no longer appropriate, the bank may offer to convert the overdraft to a loan. This offers the advantages of a lower interest rate than the excess overdraft and allows the student access to additional funds. However, unless the loan has a deferred repayment arrangement, the repayments are usually too high to be met from the student's income and may create an overdraft in her/his current account, resulting in her/him paying interest on two accounts. In this way, it can become a very expensive, usually unmanageable, option. Be aware that most banks now allow student terms on their overdraft to extend to graduation and beyond (in some cases for a number of years) and this may be a cheaper option.

Students often feel pressured into accepting loan arrangements, as the banks present them as a positive alternative and are reluctant to allow further borrowing on any other terms. A client will often be better off by ceasing to use the existing bank account and using an ordinary building society savings account. You can then negotiate with the bank as with any other creditor. However, this strategy results in the loss of the interest-free overdraft facility.

See also p569 for information on professional studies loans.

Bank overdrafts

Most of the major banks and some building societies offer interest-free overdraft facilities on students' current accounts, up to a set limit. These limits change each year and vary between banks. This special facility is essential to most students in maximising income, both to cover temporary periods of cash-flow shortage (eg, between payments of funding instalments) and for long-term financial management.

Clients who are prospective students with existing bank accounts should change to a student account with either their own or a different bank in order to benefit from the facilities offered. When choosing a bank, students should consider the following factors, rather than any 'free gifts' on offer:

- which bank offers the largest interest-free overdraft, and the period for which it is offered – generally these extend beyond the end of the course, but can vary;
- the proximity of the bank to where the student lives or studies;
- the availability and quality of service provided by telephone, smartphone app and internet banking;
- the interest rates and charges imposed for exceeding the interest-free facility;
- the attitude of campus bank managers or student advisers in local banks – debt advisers in institutions or students' unions can be consulted on these matters.

Managers of campus banks are usually more familiar with student finance issues and are therefore more sympathetic and realistic when difficulties arise, though as with bank branches more generally, such outlets are becoming less common over time.

A student's credit rating is checked when s/he opens a new account. S/he may be refused the usual student deal if there is a recorded history of credit problems. A student requires an account that can accept direct credits in order to receive her/his student loan. If a student has no bank account and is refused one because of her/his credit rating, the money adviser in the institution or students' union may be able to negotiate with the bank.

Benefits

This section is intended as a general guide to eligibility. You should refer to CPAG's *Welfare Benefits and Tax Credits Handbook* or *Student Support and Benefits Handbook* for full details. Most full-time students cannot claim social security benefits. However, there are a few groups of students who can receive status benefits or who are not excluded from universal credit (UC) – or in some legacy cases, the means-tested benefits system – including:

- lone parents, including lone foster parents (if the child is under 16 years old);
- one of two full-time students with responsibility for a child under 16 years old (or under 20 if still in full-time non-advanced education);
- disabled students who satisfy certain conditions;
- pensioners;
- in certain circumstances, refugees who are learning English;
- students waiting to return to their course after taking time out because of illness or caring responsibilities.

Make sure you highlight the rules on entitlement to benefit, and advise students not to accept automatically Department for Work and Pensions (DWP) or local authority statements that students cannot claim benefits.

The DWP and local authorities find the calculation of students' entitlement highly complex and, in many offices, it is rare for the first decision to be correct. Clients must be advised to have their claims checked by an expert in the institution, students' union or local advice centre.

Check that decision makers do not include the student loan as a client's income if s/he is not eligible for a student loan. You should also inform a client who is entitled to a maintenance loan, but reluctant to take one out (or take out the full amount), that the full loan is taken into account as income, whether or not it is received by the client.

In general, grants or loans paid specifically for tuition fees or course costs are disregarded as income. If a student receives allowances towards extra expenses because of a disability (see p570), these are disregarded in full when calculating her/his benefit entitlement. The childcare grant and parents' learning grant are also disregarded.

The postgraduate loan for master's and doctoral degrees is paid for both tuition and maintenance costs. For this reason, 30 per cent of the maximum loan entitlement (whether the student borrows the full amount or not) is taken into account for benefit purposes, with the remainder of it being ignored.

Universal credit

Check whether s/he is in one of the groups of students who can claim UC. Rules on work-related requirements and sanctions should be carefully explained, as certain groups of students, particularly postgraduates without access to loans, may be at greater risk of incurring these. For more information, see CPAG's *Student Support and Benefits Handbook*.

Child tax credit

Students can receive child tax credit (though most new claimaints will be required to apply for UC instead – see above). Those getting the maximum amount (and no working tax credit) are entitled to free school lunches for their child(ren). Help is means tested and paid by HM Revenue and Customs, which has a calculator facility on its website to help work out eligibility and the amount available (see gov.uk/tax-credits-calculator).

Health benefits

Students under 19 and those on income support (IS), income-based jobseeker's allowance (JSA) and some tax credit claimants, qualify for health benefits, as well as those getting UC with income below a certain level. Otherwise, students must apply for assistance on the grounds of low income using Form HC1. These forms are often held by student services departments in institutions, students' unions/ guilds/associations or health centres.

Housing benefit

Check whether the client is in one of the groups of students who can claim housing benefit (HB), or whether s/he has a partner who can claim on her/his behalf. Most new clients will need to apply for UC instead (see p560).

Income support

Check whether the client is in one of the groups of students who can claim IS, or whether s/he has a partner who can claim on her/his behalf. Most new clients will need to apply for UC instead (see p560).

Income-based jobseeker's allowance

If the student has a partner who is able to claim income-based JSA, s/he should be aware that working in the vacations may result in a loss of benefit. Most new clients will need to apply for UC instead (see p560).

Students taking time out from their studies

Some students (sometimes known as 'intercalating students') need to leave their course temporarily – eg, because of ill health, exam failure, or family or personal problems. Benefit regulations exclude most full-time students from claiming UC (or, in a small number of legacy cases, IS, HB, or income-based JSA) for the whole duration of their period of study. For precise definitions of this period for each benefit, see CPAG's *Welfare Benefits and Tax Credits Handbook*. Students who are eligible to claim benefits are entitled during a period of temporary absence from their course.

Students cannot get UC (or legacy benefits) if they take time out from their course because they are ill or have caring responsibilities (unless they are classed as a disabled student), but they can claim these benefits once the illness or caring responsibilities have come to an end. They can claim from this point until they restart the course or up to the day before they start the new academic year. They can only qualify if they are not eligible for student support during this period.

If a student takes time out for any other reason, s/he is treated as though s/he were on a full-time course and therefore not entitled to UC (or legacy benefits). Students in this situation should obtain advice from their students' union or institution on alternative means of support.

Bursaries

A student may be eligible for a bursary or scholarship from her/his university or college.

Bursaries are paid separately from the standard student finance package.

There is no set upper limit, and institutions can decide on the amounts they offer. Some are several thousand pounds or more, although high rates are rare. Many bursaries are paid in cash, but can be paid by other means – eg, by providing accommodation or course-related equipment. The criteria vary: some bursaries and scholarships are awarded on the basis of income or geographical location only; others have an application process; and some are awarded on the basis of, for example, academic or sporting achievement or potential. All institutions should publicise their bursaries or scholarships on their websites, and the Universities and Colleges Admissions Service (UCAS) website has a section on each institution's funding opportunities.

If a bursary is paid for course costs, it should not be treated as income for benefit purposes, and institutions are encouraged to be clear about the purposes of the support. The institution should provide the student with a letter confirming that her/his bursary is for course-related costs.

Students on health-related courses may be eligible for a bursary from the NHS (see p566). However, new healthcare students in England starting courses on or after 1 August 2017 must apply for the standard package of student loans from Student Finance England. The NHS continues to offer some limited additional finance for healthcare student parents, in respect of travel and accommodation on placement and in cases of hardship, as well as bursaries to medical and dental students in the final years of their course.

Charities

See also p199.

Many charities provide assistance to students. However, support is usually in the form of small grants and it is highly unusual for a student to be able to access full funding through charitable routes. Many charities also experience high demand for their funds.

Applications are more likely to succeed if the student is close to completing her/his course, and/or where funding arrangements have broken down. There are a number of fund-finding websites and publications specialising in helping students access money from trusts and charities.

Employment

Traditionally, undergraduate students have worked during their vacation periods; many now also work part time through the term time. Income from part-time or casual work is disregarded for the purposes of assessing student support. You should warn clients of the uncertainties of relying on vacation work to supplement their mainstream income, especially given the increasing number of zero-hour contracts and 'gig economy' roles students may have to accept. Annual budgeting based on the expectation of an income from vacation work will falter if a job fails to materialise or is offered for fewer hours or weeks than anticipated.

Increasingly, institutions and students' unions provide information on jobs available to students. The institution may have regulations restricting the number of hours students are allowed to work. You can help clients to balance their time between employment and study, and you should check that the student is profiting financially from the work after travel and other expenses are taken into account. You should also check the student is receiving the correct rate of minimum wage, as there is a comparatively high rate of non-compliance with minumum wage rules in the sectors in which students often find work.

Tax refunds

A student who has been working before starting her/his course, or for part of the year, may overpay tax. If so, s/he should be advised to claim a refund of income tax when the employment ceases by completing Form P50 (usually available from students' unions or tax offices). The form should be submitted to the tax office of her/his last employer, along with the student's P45.

Grants

Maintenance grant in England

A maintenance grant is available to undergraduate students who started their course before 1 September 2016. It has been abolished for students who started their course on or after this date. For details, see CPAG's *Student Support and Benefits Handbook*.

Welsh government learning grant

Eligble students who normally live in Wales may be entitled to significant grant support from from the Welsh government to help meet general living costs.

In 2019/20, full-time students who began their course in 2018/19 or later receive at least £1,000 as a non-repayable grant regardless of household income. In addition, all students are entitled to a set package depending on their residence and place of study, and household income then dictates the proportion of this paid in grant or loan. For example, students living away from home and studying outside London receive the maximum grant of £8,100 if their household income is £18,730 or less, and an additional student loan of £1,125. A student with a household income of £59,200 or more will receive the minimum £1,000 in grant and can take out up to £8,225 as a student loan. Full rates are available on the Student Finance Wales website.

The grant is paid in three instalments, one at the start of each term.

Those who can receive means-tested benefits should apply for an additional student support element which increases the level of student loan available regardless of income.

For students who started in earlier years, grants are also available but lower in value. See CPAG's *Student Support and Benefits Handbook*.

Travel allowances

Students who attend an institution outside the UK for at least eight weeks (whether obligatory or optional) and have taken out medical insurance, and those who must attend a placement in the UK away from their main college as part of a medical or dental course, can get help with their travelling expenses above the normal allowance paid in their loan. Healthcare students in England who start their courses after 1 September 2017 and who no longer qualify for NHS bursaries can also claim this help. Students studying abroad can also claim help to cover the cost of medical insurance. The travel grant does not cover the first £303 of the expenses.

Disabled students may also qualify for help with travel in the disabled students' allowance (see p570).

Care leavers

Care leavers in England who enter higher education are entitled to a one-off £2,000 bursary from their local authority.[6] Otherwise, local authorities remain responsible for providing support in all vacations to their care leavers. Check to ensure all support is being provided.

In addition, many higher education institutions now offer extra bursaries for care leavers, and therefore should be approached to check what funding is available.

Social work courses

Bursaries are available for undergraduate students on social work degree or diploma courses in England, paid by the NHS Business Services Authority. Students must meet the residency eligibility criteria, and must be on an approved course, must not already hold a higher education social work qualification and must not be receiving support from a social care employer. First-year students do not receive a bursary, and not all students in later years receive support, with places allocated according to local criteria. Check with the university.

The bursaries are non-means tested and paid in three instalments. Students can also access the standard student support package from Student Finance England.

Undergraduate students who normally live in Wales and who are studying for a social work degree are entitled to similar support from Social Care Wales. First-year students in Wales can also receive a bursary.

Full-time eligible postgraduates living in England receive a non-means-tested basic bursary from the NHS Business Services Authority, and can also apply for an additional mean-tested bursary. However, as with undergraduates, not all applicants are successful.

Successful applicants also receive help with tuition fees, paid directly to the institution, and a contribution to practice learning (placement) opportunity expenses.

A childcare grant, adult dependants' allowance and parents' learning allowance are also available, paid on the same basis as for undergraduates (see pp570–571).

Eligible postgraduate students in Wales can apply to Social Care Wales for a similar package of support.

Hardship funds

Most universities and colleges have discretionary hardship funds to assist students in financial difficulties.

Provision varies and students should approach the institution for details of the fund it operates, if any, and its eligibility criteria. It is likely that such funds will prioritise certain vulnerable groups for help – eg, students with children, disabled students and care leavers. Help may be in the form of short-term loans rather than grants, especially if the issue is immediate cashflow – eg, caused by delays in processing a student finance application. If payments remain unpaid, such loans can be classed as a debt to the institution (see p544).

You can help a student make a successful application by identifying the criteria and priorities of a particular institution's funds, and providing evidence or a supporting letter to show how s/he meets them.

For the purpose of means-tested benefits, payments from discretionary hardship funds are usually treated as capital if paid as a lump sum or taken into account as income if paid regularly (subject to some disregards). See CPAG's *Welfare Benefits and Tax Credits Handbook* for more information.

Loans for living costs

In order to support themselves while studying, undergraduate students can get loans, grants (for certain groups of students), bursaries and help from hardship funds. For English-domiciled students, the vast majority of support comes through loans, in contrast to the much more generous grant funding available to Welsh-domiciled students. A student must meet the personal eligibility requirements – ie, the rules on where s/he lives, previous attendance, funding and age.[7] For postgraduate student loans, see p568.

Income-contingent student loans

Full-time students, sandwich students and part-time students in England (part-time initial teacher training students only in Wales) are eligible for a student loan for their maintenance. In Wales, loans for living costs are not available to those aged 60 or over, and in England those aged 60 or over can only access limited loan funding. Previous study affects eligibility and students who already hold an honours degree are not eligible unless their course is exempt.

The Department for Education or, in Wales, the Welsh government sets the maximum loan available. The amount a student can borrow varies enormously and depends on the calendar year the student commenced the course, the year of study, type of course, where the student lives, whether the student is entitled to claim certain benefits, and household income. Within the overall limits, the student decides what level of loan is needed and applies to Student Finance England or Student Finance Wales. The amount can be changed later, up to the maximum – a student applies for this on a loan adjustment form.

In England, the loan is partially means tested on household income – ie, the student's income and that of her/his parents or spouse or partner, as appropriate.

In Wales, students are entitled to a set amount of support, and household income affects the proportion of this support that is provided via a loan as opposed to a grant.

Part-time students in England access a lower amount of loan than full-time students, with the exact amount proportional on the intensity of study.

Students domiciled in England who are entitled to claim certain social security benefits are entitled to a higher rate of loan (the additional amount is known as 'the special support loan'). In Wales, a similar additional entitlement to further loan funding exists, though most such students will also recieve the maximum grant. In both cases, check that this is included in their entitlement.

Long courses loan

A student can apply for a set amount for each additional week s/he has to attend the course on top of the basic academic year. The amount of the long courses loan depends on whether the student is living in her/his parental home, away from home, or in London. Loans are made in addition to the student loan for maintenance and may be means tested. They must be repaid in the same way.

Studying abroad

Additional support is available to students who spend time studying abroad for at least eight weeks as part of a UK-based course (the period abroad does not have to be a compulsory part of the course). Students studying abroad for at least eight consecutive weeks who must take out medical insurance also get help to cover these costs. Help is means tested and paid by Student Finance England or Student Finance Wales. Insurance grants are equal to the cost of the policy. Travel costs are only paid if they are reasonable and, in any case, the first £303 of any claim is not paid.

Change in circumstances

If a student has a change in circumstances during the year, s/he should inform Student Finance England or Student Finance Wales in order to have the level of loan s/he can take out reassessed.

NHS bursaries

NHS bursaries are available for full-time or part-time pre-registration courses in Wales, and in England if the student started her/his course before 1 August 2017.

New bursaries for living costs have been announced for healthcare students in England, due to be available from September 2020. For a list of prescribed courses and up-to-date information, see nhsbsa.nhs.uk/student-services or nwssp.wales.nhs.uk/student-awards. Applicants must meet certain residence conditions. The bursaries are non-taxable and are paid in monthly instalments.

In all cases, the NHS pays the tuition fees.

NHS-funded degree and postgraduate diploma-level students can get a £1,000 non-means-tested bursary and an additional means-tested amount, depending on family income. Degree students can also apply for a reduced-rate student loan through Student Finance England or Student Finance Wales. Postgraduate diploma NHS students are not eligible for student loans.

Additional allowances may also be payable for:
- disabled students;
- practice placement costs;
- students entering training from care;
- extra weeks' attendance;
- childcare;
- adults and children who are financially dependent on the student.

There are also maternity, paternity and adoption allowances.

Undergraduate medical and dental students living in England and Wales on standard five- or six-year courses in any UK country are eligible for NHS bursaries and help with their tuition fees in their fifth and sixth year of study. This includes English-domiciled students starting courses after 1 August 2017. Those students in England and Wales on the four-year graduate-entry medical programmes are also eligible for NHS bursaries and help with tuition fees, although some upfront contributions to fees are required. Medical and dental students can also apply for NHS hardship funds through NHS Student Bursaries. You should help clients to present their case, as there is no prescribed form or process. It is, therefore, advisable to add a covering letter explaining the circumstances and the nature of the application.

Other healthcare students in England who start their courses on or after 1 August 2017 should apply for the standard undergraduate funding package. Some additional support is available for these students if they have a dependent child, placement expenses or in cases of hardship – it is claimed through NHS Student Bursaries. The government has announced additional bursary support for healthcare students in England will be introduced from September 2020. Details are limited at the time of writing but NHS Student Bursaries will have further information later in 2020.

Part-time support

Part-time students in England who start their course on or after 1 September 2012, and part-time students in Wales who start on or after 1 September 2014, can apply for a loan to cover the cost of fees in the same way as full-time students (see p572). Courses must be at least 25 per cent the intensity of an equivalent full-time course, and support can be provided for up to 16 years.

In England, part-time students can apply for additional loans for living costs if they started their course on or after 1 September 2018. No support for course or maintenance costs is available if they started before this date.

In Wales, students who started their courses on or after 1 September 2018 and are studying at least at 25 per cent intensity are entitled to a set package of support, the proportion of which is grant or loan varying by household income. If the student started before this date and is studying at least at 50 per cent intensity, a course costs grant is available, depending on income. In both cases, students in Wales may be entitled to additional grants for dependants.

Applications are assessed by Student Finance England or Student Finance Wales, and support is available for a maximum of 16 years.

Postgraduate support

Income-contingent student loans are available for taught postgraduate master's and doctoral courses from Student Finance England and Student Finance Wales.

For master's courses, a maximum loan of £10,906 in England and £17,000 in Wales is available in 2019/20. It can be paid for one year's full-time study, or two years' part-time study at master's level, where other state funding is not available – eg, if the student is receiving a social work bursary. Students must be aged under 60 on the first day of study, but in Wales some limited bursary funding may be available for older students.

For doctoral courses, a maximum loan of £25,700 for a full-time or part-time doctoral course is available in both England and Wales in 2019/20. If the course is part-time, it must take no longer than eight years to complete. You cannot receive more than £10,906 of your entitlement in any one year. You cannot access a loan if you receive other state funding such as a research council studentship. You must be aged under 60 on the first day of the course.

In both cases, applicants must meet residency and course requirements, and must not already have a master's level or doctoral qualification as appropriate. The loan can be used to cover tuition fees, living costs or both, and is partially taken into account when calculating means-tested benefits. It is paid in three instalments over the year, directly to the student.

Postgraduate research students studying at doctoral level can apply for studentships from research councils instead (see p569). Competition for these is usually strong, and students must usually have at least a 2:1 degree at undergraduate level. They are normally paid in the form of non-repayable grants.

Disabled postgraduate students are eligible for a disabled students' allowance (see p570) from either a research council (see p569), Student Finance England or Student Finance Wales if they must pay extra costs in their postgraduate study as a result of their disability. Details of the levels and type of support available, and information on how to apply, are on each research council's website, or from Student Finance England or Student Finance Wales.

A client can obtain appropriate information and assistance from the department in which s/he intends to study and the university careers service. Clients should begin their enquiries well in advance of the start of their course – applications may need to be made at the start of the academic year before the year in which they intend to study.

There are also organisations which offer awards for vocational courses, and a limited number of companies offer assistance to postgraduates. Sponsorship is usually linked to particular courses and institutions, rather than individual students. Clients should be advised to contact the appropriate careers/advice centres at the relevant institution.

Professional studies loans

Professional studies loans are now rare, but some of the major banks or specialist lenders make personal loans available to postgraduate (and sometimes also 'second degree') students to cover their course fees and living costs. The loans usually offer deferred repayments, which begin only after the course has finished, although this is not always the case. Such loans are often only available for specific courses, especially those leading to professional qualifications. Different interest rates may apply, depending on the student's credit record and whether or not s/he has a guarantor. The terms and amounts of loans vary between different lenders, and a client should check which is most suitable for her/him and how the terms offered compare with those available from a professional and career development loan, if s/he is pursuing a course for which either might be payable. S/he also needs to consider whether s/he can afford the amount of indebtedness involved.

Research councils

There are seven research councils that fund postgraduate study via non-repayable studentships, though the numbers are relatively small and competition high:
- Biotechnology and Biological Sciences Research Council (bbsrc.ac.uk);
- Engineering and Physical Sciences Research Council (epsrc.ac.uk);
- Economic and Social Research Council (esrc.ac.uk);
- Medical Research Council (mrc.ac.uk);
- Natural Environment Research Council (nerc.ac.uk);
- Science and Technology Facilities Council (stfc.ac.uk);
- Arts and Humanities Research Council (ahrc.ac.uk).

Supplementary grants

Certain 'supplementary' grants are available for full-time students with additional support requirements. Most are not available to part-time students in England, except the disabled students' allowance. All these grants are available to part-time Welsh-domiciled students, on a pro rata basis, assuming their course takes no longer than twice the time of the equivalent full-time course to complete.

Except for disabled students' allowance, supplementary grants are also means tested, both as part of the main means test for support and on the income of any dependants the student has.

Disabled students' allowance

Part-time students, full-time students, distance learners (including Open University students), postgraduate students and undergraduate students who have a disability which makes it more expensive for them to take their courses may be entitled to a number of extra allowances for equipment, non-medical personal support, miscellaneous expenses and travel.

Part-time students must complete the course in no more than four times the time it takes to complete a full-time equivalent course.

Postgraduate students in receipt of an award from a research council (see p569) and those getting an NHS bursary (see p566) are not eligible for a disabled students' allowance from Student Finance England or Student Finance Wales, but receive very similar grants from those funders.

The allowance is a non-repayable grant. It is not affected by any rules on previous study and is not means tested. It is usually paid directly to any provider of approved specialist equipment or personal support.

In England, if a student is given support towards IT equipment, s/he is normally expected to contribute the first £200 of the cost. If a client is unable to do so, s/he could contact the hardship fund at the university or college.

Adult dependants' grant

Full-time students who have a spouse, partner or adult member of the family who is financially dependent on them may be eligible for a means-tested, non-repayable adult dependants' grant. It is paid by Student Finance England or Student Finance Wales in three instalments with the maintenance loan.

Childcare grant

Full-time students with independent status and with dependent children in registered, approved childcare can get a childcare grant of up to 85 per cent of the actual costs. The maximum limit depends on whether the student has one child or two or more. This grant is non-repayable and it is not taken into account when calculating entitlement to means-tested benefits and tax credits.

Students cannot get a childcare grant if they (or their partner) receive the childcare element of universal credit or working tax credit or claim the equivalent allowance in an NHS bursary.

Note: in England, a new system introduced from 2019/20 means payments are made directly to childcare providers. Students are given a budget based on their entitlement for the year, but if they draw this down in the earlier stages, it may mean they have limited funds for childcare towards the end of the year.

In Wales, the childcare grant is calculated using estimates of childcare costs and paid directly to the student. This can often result in overpayments, as the student may not inform Student Finance Wales that s/he is using less childcare than expected. Overpayments are usually reclaimed in the same way as other overpaid grants (see p553). The student may need to negotiate with Student Finance Wales if the overpayment will cause hardship if taken in one lump sum from future payments.

Parents' learning allowance

Means-tested help with course-related costs can be paid to students with dependent children.

The grant is paid by Student Finance England or Student Finance Wales in three instalments and is non-repayable. This grant is not taken into account when calculating entitlement to means-tested benefits and tax credits.

Teacher training incentives

In England, there are teacher training bursaries of up to £28,000, depending on the subject the student is studying to teach and the undergraduate degree mark s/he holds – the higher priority the subject and the higher the degree mark, the more money is available. Some students are not entitled to any bursary.

The qualifying subjects and the amounts of the bursaries available are on the Get into Teaching website at getintoteaching.education.gov.uk/funding-my-teacher-training/bursaries-and-scholarships-for-teacher-trainings.

The bursaries are generally paid monthly over nine months and are available for home students undertaking postgraduate courses that lead to qualified teacher status at colleges in England (Postgraduate Certificate in Education (PGCE) or Postgraduate Diploma in Education (PGDE) courses), but who are not currently employed as teachers. Some of the larger bursaries may have elements paid on the completion of certain stages of the course.

PGCE and PGDE students in England can also apply for the full undergraduate package of support. Teacher training students on graduate-entry programmes funded via schools receive a salary instead.

In Wales, home students on postgraduate courses leading to qualified teacher status at institutions in Wales (except those already qualified as teachers or employed as teachers) receive a training grant of up to £20,000 on a similar banding structure to English students. Teacher Training and Education in Wales lists which subjects qualify for which levels of funding at discoverteaching.wales/teacher-training-incentives.

Some students studying in the Welsh language can apply for Welsh medium incentive supplements. Applications should be made to the institution.

Help with tuition fees

Eligible, full-time undergraduate students in England and Wales can apply for a loan to cover the cost of their tuition fees.

Full-time Welsh-domiciled students may also be entitled to a grant, which significantly reduces their total fee liability, though these are not available to new students who started on or after 1 September 2018. Student Finance Wales should consider these as part of the standard application process – if this does not appear to be the case, contact Student Finance Wales. Loans are available for any remaining liability.

Part-time, English-domiciled students who started their course before 1 September 2012 and Welsh-domiciled part-time students who started their courses before 1 September 2014 may be eligible for a means-tested grant to cover all, or part, of their fees.

Part-time English-domiciled students who start their course on or after 1 September 2012, or Welsh-domiciled students who start their course on or after 1 September 2014, can apply for a student loan to cover the cost of their fees in the same way as full-time students (although in Wales this may not cover the whole cost). The course must be at least 25 per cent intensity of an equivalent full-time course – ie, the course must take no longer than four times the length of the full-time course.

There are no age limits for help with tuition fees or for tuition fee loans. Payment is made directly to the institution by Student Finance England or Student Finance Wales.

Additional funds to assist students

Many institutions and some students' unions and religious groups have a number of small funds available to meet specific circumstances, as well as general hardship funds. Some funds make grants, others offer interest-free loans. Students should consult the student services department or students' union at their own institution for advice.

---

6. **Dealing with priority debts**

Certain debts to the educational institution may need to be treated as priorities because of the consequences of non-payment. Wherever non-payment carries a legitimate threat of loss of accommodation, the debt should be treated as a priority (as outlined in Chapter 8). However, in addition, there are some cases where the threat of not being able to continue with study or not being allowed to graduate leads to prioritisation. See p544 for those debts that could lead to this.

See Chapter 8 for more information on dealing with priority debts.

Notes

1. **Financial support for students**
   1 Sch 1 E(SS) Regs; Sch 1 E(SS)(W) Regs
   2 For the extract of the judgment, see notes for guidance in Sch 1 E(SS) Regs or Sch1 E(SS)(W) Regs.
   3 Sch 2 E(SS) Regs

3. **Types of debt**
   4 s8 SSLA 2008
   5 s8 SSLA 2008

5. **Maximising income**
   6 Children Act 1989 (Higher Education Bursary) (England) Regulations 2009, No.2274
   7 E(SS) Regs; E(SS)(W) Regs

Appendices

Appendix 1

Useful organisations

Trade bodies

Association of British Insurers
Tel: 020 7600 3333
info@abi.org.uk
abi.org.uk

Association of Chartered Certified Accountants
Tel: 0141 582 2000
info@accaglobal.com
accaglobal.com

British Insurance Brokers' Association
Tel: 0344 770 0266
Consumer helpline: 0370 950 1790
enquiries@biba.org.uk
biba.org.uk

Civil Enforcement Association (CIVEA)
Tel: 0844 893 3922
admin@civea.co.uk
civea.co.uk

Consumer Credit Association
Tel: 01244 394 760
cca@ccauk.org
ccauk.org

Consumer Credit Trade Association
Tel: 01274 714 959
info@ccta.co.uk
ccta.co.uk

Consumer Finance Association
Tel: 020 3553 3668
enquiries@cfa-uk.co.uk
cfa-uk.co.uk

Credit Services Association
Tel: 0191 217 0775
info@csa-uk.com
csa-uk.com

Finance and Leasing Association
Tel: 020 7836 6511
info@fla.org.uk
fla.org.uk

High Court Enforcement Officers Association
Tel: 0844 824 4575
hceoa.org.uk

Insolvency Practitioners Association
Tel: 020 7623 5108
secretariat@ipa.uk.com
insolvency-practitioners.org.uk

Institute of Chartered Accountants in England and Wales
Tel: 01908 248 250
contactus@icaew.com
icaew.com

Lending Standards Board
Tel: 020 7012 0085
info@lstdb.co.uk
lendingstandardsboard.org.uk

R3 (Association of Business Recovery Professionals)
Tel: 020 7566 4200
association@r3.org.uk
r3.org.uk

UK Finance
Tel: 020 7706 3333
ukfinance.org.uk

UK Payments Administration
Tel: 020 3217 8200
enquiries@ukpayments.org.uk
ukpayments.org.uk

Ombudsmen and regulatory bodies

The Adjudicator's Office
PO Box 10280
Nottingham NG2 9PF
Tel: 0300 057 1111
adjudicatorsoffice.gov.uk

Department for Business, Energy and Industrial Strategy
1 Victoria Street
London SW1H 0ET
Tel: 020 7215 5000
enquiries@beis.gov.uk
gov.uk/government/organisations/
department-for-business-energy-
and-industrial-strategy

Department for Education
Piccadilly Gate
Store Street
Manchester M1 2WD
Tel: 0370 000 2288
gov.uk/government/organisations/
department-for-education

Department for Education and Skills Wales
Tel: 0300 060 4400
gov.wales/education-skills

Financial Conduct Authority
12 Endeavour Square
London E20 1JN
Tel: 020 7066 1000
Consumer helpline: 0800 111 6768/
0300 500 8082
Firms helpline: 0300 500 0597
consumer.queries@fca.org.uk
fca.org.uk

Financial Ombudsman Service
Exchange Tower
Harbour Exchange
London E14 9SR
Tel: 0800 023 4567/0300 123 9123
financial-ombudsman.org.uk

Information Commissioner's Office
Wycliffe House, Water Lane
Wilmslow SK9 5AF
Tel: 0303 123 1113
ico.org.uk
(for complaints concerning out-of-
date or inaccurate personal information)

The Insolvency Service
16th Floor, 1 Westfield Avenue
London E20 1HZ
Tel: 020 7637 1110/0300 678 0015
gov.uk/insolvency-service

The Law Society (England and Wales)
113 Chancery Lane
London WC2A 1PL
Tel: 020 7242 1222
lawsociety.org.uk

Legal Ombudsman (England and Wales)

PO Box 6806
Wolverhampton WV1 9WJ
Tel: 0300 555 0333
enquiries@legalombudsman.org.uk
legalombudsman.org.uk

Local Government and Social Care Ombudsman

PO Box 4771
Coventry CV4 0EH
Tel: 0300 061 0614
lgo.org.uk

Ministry of Housing, Communities and Local Government

2 Marsham Street
London SW1P 4DF
Tel: 0303 444 0000
gov.uk/government/organisations/
ministry-of-housing-communities-
and-local-government

Ofcom (Communications Regulator)

PO Box 1285
Warrington WA1 9GL
Tel: 020 7981 3000/0300 123 3000
Advice/complaints: 0300 123 3333/
020 7981 3040
ofcom.org.uk

Ofgem (Office of Gas and Electricity Markets)

10 South Colonnade
London E14 4PU
Tel: 020 7901 7000
ofgem.gov.uk

Ofwat (Water Sector Economic Regulator)

Centre City Tower
7 Hill Street
Birmingham B5 4UA
Tel: 0121 644 7500
Enquiries/complaints: 0300 034 2222
(England)
or 0300 034 3333 (Wales)
mailbox@ofwat.gov.uk
ofwat.gov.uk

Ombudsman Services: Energy

PO Box 966
Warrington WA4 9DF
Tel: 0330 440 1624
enquiry@ombudsman-services.org
ombudsman-services.org/sectors/
energy

Parliamentary and Health Service Ombudsman (England)

Millbank Tower
30 Millbank
London SW1P 4QP
Tel: 0345 015 4033
ombudsman.org.uk

The Pensions Ombudsman

10 South Colonnade
London E14 4PU
Tel: 0800 917 4487
enquiries@pensions-ombudsman.
org.uk
pensions-ombudsman.org.uk

Public Services Ombudsman for Wales

1 Ffordd yr Hen Gae
Pencoed CF35 5LJ
Tel: 0300 790 0203
ask@ombudsman.wales
ombudsman-wales

Welsh government
Cathays Park
Cardiff CF10 3NQ
Tel: 0300 060 4400
customerhelp@gov.wales
gov.wales

Organisations giving advice or representing advice networks

AdviceUK
101E Universal House
88–94 Wentworth Street
London E1 7SA
Tel: 0300 777 0107/0300 777 0108
mail@adviceuk.org.uk
adviceuk.org.uk

Association of British Credit Unions
Holyoake House
Hannover Street
Manchester M60 0AS
Tel: 0161 832 3694
info@abcul.org
abcul.org

Business Debtline
Tel: 0800 197 6026
businessdebtline.org

Citizens Advice
3rd Floor North
200 Aldersgate Street
London EC1A 4HD
Tel: 0300 023 1231
Advice: 0344 411 1444 (England) or
0344 477 2020 (Wales)
citizensadvice.org.uk

Institute of Money Advisers
4 Park Court
Park Cross Street
Leeds LS1 2QH
Tel: 0113 242 0048
office@i-m-a.org.uk
i-m-a.org.uk

Law Centres Network
Floor 1
Tavis House
1–6 Tavistock Square
London WC1H 9NA
Tel: 020 3637 1330
lawcentres.org.uk

Money Advice Service
Holborn Centre
120 Holborn
London EC1N 2TD
Tel: 020 7943 0500
Advice line: 0800 138 7777
or 0800 138 0555 (Welsh)
enquiries@maps.org.uk
moneyadviceservice.org.uk

Money Advice Trust
21 Garlick Hill
London EC4V 2AU
Tel: 020 7489 7796
info@moneyadvicetrust.org
moneyadvicetrust.org

National Debtline
Tel: 0808 808 4000
nationaldebtline.org

National Union of Students
Tel: 0300 303 8602
nus.org.uk

Shelter's Specialist Debt Advice Team

Tel (advisers only, Mon–Fri
9am–5pm): 0330 058 0404
Online enquiry service:
shelter.org.uk/debtadviceservice

TaxAid

Tel (advisers only, Mon–Fri
10am–12pm and 2pm–4pm):
0300 330 5477
Helpline (clients, Mon–Fri
10am–4pm): 0345 120 3779
taxaid.org.uk

UCAS (Universities and Colleges Admissions Service)

Tel: 0371 468 0468 (undergraduate)
0371 468 0470 (conservatoires)
0371 468 0469 (teacher training)
0371 334 4447 (postgraduate)
ucas.com

UKCISA: UK Council for International Student Affairs

Tel: 020 7288 4330
International students advice line
(Mon–Fri 1pm–4pm):
020 7788 9214
ukcisa.org.uk

Appendix 2

* *

Useful publications

A debt adviser should have access to the latest edition of most of the following publications.

Debt

Cheshire, Fifoot and Furmston's Law of Contract, M P Furmston, Oxford University Press, 2017

Woodroffe and Lowe's Consumer Law and Practice, G Woodroffe and others, Sweet and Maxwell, 2016

Consumer Credit Law and Practice: a guide, D Rosenthal, Bloomsbury Professional, 2018

Debt Relief Order Toolkit, Citizens Advice, available at citizensadvice.org.uk to subscribers to AdviserNet or at wiseradviser.org for registered users

Fisher and Lightwood's Law of Mortgage, W Clarke and P Morgan, LexisNexis, 2019

Tolley's Tax Guide 2019–20, C Hayes and R Newman (authors); A Hubbard (ed), LexisNexis, 2019

Council Tax Handbook, CPAG, £31 (13th edition, late 2020)*

Fuel Rights Handbook, CPAG, £29 (19th edition, 2019)*

Manual of Housing Law, A Arden and A Dymond, Legal Action Group, 2017

Schaw Miller and Bailey: Personal Insolvency – law and practice, Mohyuddin QC and others, LexisNexis, 2017

Increasing resources

Welfare Benefits and Tax Credits Handbook, CPAG, £65 (2020/21, April 2020)*

Child Support Handbook, CPAG, £40 (28th edition, summer 2020)*

Disability Rights Handbook, Disability Rights UK, £36 (May 2020)*

A Guide to Grants for Individuals in Need, I Pembridge, Directory of Social Change, 2020*

* * * *

Voluntary Agencies Directory, NCVO, 2017

Charities Digest, Wilmington, 2018

Employment Law: an adviser's handbook, T Lewis, Legal Action Group, 2019

Courts and the law
Anthony and Berryman's Magistrates' Court Guide, A Turner, LexisNexis, 2019

The Civil Court Practice (The Green Book), LexisNexis, 2019

Black's Law Dictionary, B Garner, Thomson West, Thomson Reuters, 2019

Defending Possession Proceedings, J Luba and others, Legal Action Group, 2016

Sealy & Milman: Annotated Guide to the Insolvency Legislation, D Milman and P Bailey, Sweet and Maxwell, 2019

Muir Hunter on Personal Insolvency, J Briggs and J Tribe (eds), Sweet and Maxwell

Practical Banking and Building Society Law, A Arora, Blackstone Press, 1997

The Law and Practice of Charging Orders on Land, Falcon Chambers (ed), Wildy, Simmonds and Hill Publishing, 2013

Taking Control of Goods: Bailiffs' Powers after the Tribunals, Courts and Enforcement Act 2007, J Kruse, XPL Publishing, 2014

Skills
Client Care for Lawyers, A Sherr, Sweet and Maxwell, 1998

Periodicals and ebulletins
Adviser, Citizens Advice, available at https://medium.com/adviser/debt

Spotlight articles and ebulletin, Shelter Specialist Debt Advice Service, sign up at shelter.org.uk/debtadviceservice

Quarterly Account, Institute of Money Advisers, i-m-a.org.uk

Welfare Rights Bulletin, CPAG, cpag.org.uk*

* Indicates that books are available from CPAG. For a full publications list and order form, see cpag.org.uk/shop; write to CPAG, 30 Micawber Street, London N1 7TB; email bookorders@cpag.org.uk or call 020 7837 7979.

Appendix 3

Abbreviations used in the notes

AC	Appeal Cases
Admin	Administrative Court
All ER	All England Reports
Art(s)	Article(s)
BPIR	Bankruptcy and Personal Insolvency Reports
CA	Court of Appeal
CCR	County Court Rules
CCLR	Consumer Credit Law Reports
Ch	Chancery Division
ChD	Chancery Division
Civ Comm	Civil Division Commercial Court
CPR	Civil Procedure Rules
ChD	Chancery Division
Cr App R	Criminal Appeal Reports
EG	Estates Gazette
EWCA	England and Wales Court of Appeal
EWHC	England and Wales High Court
FCA	Financial Conduct Authority
FLR	Family Law Reports
FOS	Financial Ombudsman Service
HC	High Court
HL	House of Lords
HLR	Housing Law Reports
IMA	Institute of Money Advisers
IP-PD	Insolvency Proceedings Practice Direction
JP	Justice of the Peace
KB	King's Bench Reports
para(s)	paragraph(s)
PD	Practice Direction
QB	Queen's Bench Reports
QBD	Queen's Bench Division

r(r)	rule(s)
reg(s)	regulation(s)
s(s)	section(s)
SC	sheriff court
Sch(s)	Schedule(s)
UKHL	United Kingdom House of Lords
UKSC	United Kingdom Supreme Court
WLR	Weekly Law Reports
WLR(D)	Weekly Law Reports Daily

Acts of Parliament

AEA 1971	Attachment of Earnings Act 1971
AJA 1970	Administration of Justice Act 1970
AJA 1973	Administration of Justice Act 1973
CA 2003	Courts Act 2003
CAA 1995	Criminal Appeal Act 1995
CCA 1974	Consumer Credit Act 1974
CCA 2006	Consumer Credit Act 2006
CCA 1984	County Courts Act 1984
CJA 1982	Criminal Justice Act 1982
CLSA 1990	Courts and Legal Services Act 1990
COA 1979	Charging Orders Act 1979
EA 1989	Electricity Act 1989
EA 2002	Enterprise Act 2002
FSMA 2000	Financial Services and Markets Act 2000
GA 1986	Gas Act 1986
IA 1986	Insolvency Act 1986
JA 1838	Judgments Act 1838
LA 1980	Limitation Act 1980
LGFA 1988	Local Government Finance Act 1988
LGFA 1992	Local Government Finance Act 1992
LPA 1925	Law of Property Act 1925
MCA 1980	Magistrates' Courts Act 1980
MOA 1958	Maintenance Orders Act 1958
RA 1977	Rent Act 1977
SCA 1981	Senior Courts Act 1981
SGA 1979	Sale of Goods Act 1979
SGSA 1982	Supply of Goods and Services Act 1982
SSAA 1992	Social Security Administration Act 1992
SSCBA 1992	Social Security Contributions and Benefits Act 1992
SSLA 2008	Sale of Student Loans Act 2008

TCA 2002	Tax Credits Act 2002
TCEA 2007	Tribunals, Courts and Enforcement Act 2007
TLATA 1996	Trusts of Land and Appointment of Trustees Act 1996
TMA 1970	Taxes Management Act 1970
UA 2000	Utilities Act 2000

Regulations and other statutory instruments

Each set of regulations or order has a statutory instrument (SI) number and a date. Ask for them by giving that date and number.

CC(AE) Regs	The Community Charges (Administration and Enforcement) Regulations 1989 No.438
CC(DI) Regs	The Consumer Credit (Disclosure of Information) Regulations 2010 No.1013
CC(IJD)O	The County Courts (Interest on Judgment Debts) Order 1991 No.1184
CC(IR) Regs	The Consumer Credit (Information Requirements and Duration of Licences and Charges) Regulations 2007 No.1167
CT(AE) Regs	The Council Tax (Administration and Enforcement) Regulations 1992 No.613
CT(AE)(A) Regs	The Council Tax (Administration and Enforcement) (Amendment) Regulations 1992 No.3008
E(SS) Regs	The Education (Student Support) Regulations 2008 No.529
E(SS)(W) Regs	The Education (Student Support) (Wales) Regulations 2013 No.3177
FS(DM) Regs	The Financial Services (Distance Marketing) Regulations 2004 No.2095
HCCCJO 1991	The High Court and County Courts Jurisdiction Order 1991 No.724
I(E&W)R 2016	The Insolvency (England and Wales) Rules 2016 No.1024
MCDO	Mortgage Credit Directive Order 2015 No.910
RAO	The Financial Services and Markets Act 2000 (Regulated Activities) (Amendment) (No.2) Order 2013 No.1881
SS(C&P) Regs	The Social Security (Claims and Payments) Regulations 1987 No.1968
TC(PC) Regs	The Tax Credits (Payments by the Board) Regulations 2002 No.2173
TCG Regs	The Taking Control of Goods Regulations 2013 No.1894
TCG(F) Regs	The Taking Control of Goods (Fees) Regulations 2014 No.1
UC,PIP,JSA& ESA(C&P) Regs	The Universal Credit, Personal Independence Payment, Jobseeker's Allowance and Employment and Support Allowance (Claims and Payments) Regulations 2013 No.380

Other information

CONC	*Consumer Credit Sourcebook*
DISP	*Dispute Resolution: Complaints*
PERG	*Perimeter Guidance Manual*
PD	Practice Direction
MCOB	*Mortgages and Home Finance: conduct of business sourcebook*
TM	*Technical Manual*

Index

. . . .

How to use this Index

Entries against the bold headings direct you to the general information on the subject, or where the subject is covered most fully. Sub-entries are listed alphabetically and direct you to specific aspects of the subject.